RICHARD McNEMAR

RICHARD McNEMAR

―⁓―

FRONTIER HERETIC AND SHAKER APOSTLE

CHRISTIAN GOODWILLIE

INDIANA UNIVERSITY PRESS

This book is a publication of

Indiana University Press
Office of Scholarly Publishing
Herman B Wells Library 350
1320 East 10th Street
Bloomington, Indiana 47405 USA

iupress.org

© 2023 by Christian Goodwillie

All rights reserved
No part of this book may be reproduced or utilized in any form or by any means, electronic or mechanical, including photocopying and recording, or by any information storage and retrieval system, without permission in writing from the publisher. The paper used in this publication meets the minimum requirements of the American National Standard for Information Sciences—Permanence of Paper for Printed Library Materials, ANSI Z39.48-1992.

Manufactured in the United States of America
First printing 2023

Cataloging information is available from the Library of Congress.

ISBN 978-0-253-06504-9 (hardback)
ISBN 978-0-253-06505-6 (paperback)
ISBN 978-0-253-06506-3 (ebook)

Dedicated to Gretchen and Douglas Goodwillie
(Mom and Dad)
with love and gratitude

CONTENTS

Acknowledgments   ix

Maps   xiii

Introduction   1

PART I: *Presbyterian and Schismatic*

1. Youth   9
2. Westward Migration and Education   16
3. Ordination   27
4. Revival   37
5. Rebellion   59

PART II: *Shaker*

6. Rebirth   71
7. The New and Living Way   85
8. Community Foundations   100
9. Shakers and the Shawnee Prophet   120
10. Shaker Publications and the Expansion of Missionary Efforts   127
11. Gospel Order in the West, James Smith, and the Ohio Mob   140
12. War Comes to the Wabash   159
13. Perfidy, Pilgrims, Prosecution, Progress, and Pestilence   176
14. The End of the Beginning   186
15. "There's Something Dead upon This Ground," or, "The Buzzards and the Flesh"   203
16. The Struggle with Abijah Alley and Aquila Bolton   222

17. Eleazar Goes East   *237*

18. Eleazar and the Covenant   *247*

19. *Custos Sacrorum*   *268*

20. The Great Snake and the Patriarchal Skeleton   *280*

21. Unrest in the West   *305*

22. Freegift to the West   *313*

23. "The Name or Memory of Mr. McNamar"   *326*

24. The New Era   *341*

25. War in Heaven   *356*

26. A Wandering Star   *375*

27. Look Homeward, Angel   *384*

28. Aftermath and Legacy   *393*

Appendix 1: Richard McNemar, "A general outline of the past Journal of my life"   *403*

Appendix 2: Richard McNemar, "Testimony of E[leazar] Wright"   *407*

Appendix 3: Richard McNemar, "My years on earth have been but few"   *413*

Appendix 4: [Archibald McCorkle?], "A few mourning thoughts on McNemar's fall," and Richard McNemar, "An Answer to the Mourning Thoughts on McNemar's Fall"   *417*

Appendix 5: The Expulsion of Richard McNemar   *425*

Appendix 6: [The Redemption of Richard McNemar]   *431*

Notes   *435*

Bibliography   *489*

Index   *503*

ACKNOWLEDGMENTS

THIS BIOGRAPHY HAS BEEN TEN years in the making, although it was conceived in 2001, when I began what was supposed to be a temporary job as interim curator of collections at Hancock Shaker Village in Pittsfield, Massachusetts. My interests in music, Shakerism, and early United States history converged in the person of Richard McNemar. Many projects served as preparatory work for the writing of the biography, including critical editions of two Shaker-published hymnals, one that contained seventy of McNemar's hymns, and the other originally published by him. *Millennial Praises: A Shaker Hymnal* was published in 2009 by University of Massachusetts Press. My coauthor on that project was Jane F. Crosthwaite, who has also been a great mentor to me in all things Shaker. *Richard McNemar, Music, and the Western Shaker Communities: Branches of One Living Tree* was published in 2013 by Kent State University Press. My coauthor on that project was Carol Medlicott, and I can truly say that she, more than anyone else, has pushed me to dig deep into the history of the Shaker West. Carol's scholarship, attention to detail, and critical thinking all inspired me as I began work on this biography in earnest in 2011.

This work would not have been possible without the support of the Faith Andrews Fellowships for the Study of Shaker Life and Material Culture at the Winterthur Library and the Shaker Village of Pleasant Hill Research Fellowship. The research resources and seclusion of these institutions afforded me two incredibly productive periods of writing.

My journey through Shaker scholarship has been long, and I have been blessed by the friendship and support of many people along the way through many different projects: books, articles, exhibitions, and conferences. I have many people to thank for their assistance in researching and writing this biography. At my alma mater Hancock Shaker Village, these include my wonderful first boss Larry Yerdon, Mary Rentz, esteemed librarian Magda-Gabor Hotchkiss, Sharon Koomler, and Lesley Herzberg. At South Union Shaker Village, director Tommy Hines has always been an inspiration, truly one of the most dedicated museum professionals I have ever known and a great friend. I have very fond memories of reading McNemar's *Kentucky Revival* while staying in the Shaker Tavern there during the autumn of 2000. At the Shaker Village of Pleasant Hill, former curator Larrie Curry was unfailingly encouraging of this project and generously shared her own transcriptions of some of McNemar's letters. Likewise, former curator Aaron Genton and current vice president Billy Rankin provided key support and friendly hospitality that allowed me to write in a place where McNemar had a long tenure. At Winterthur Library, E. Richard McKinstry, Jeanne Solensky, Emily Guthrie, and Laura Parrish were great hosts and provided first-class research assistance (especially you, Jeanne!). At the Western Reserve Historical Society, Ann Sindelar has been a great help for many years in providing access to the marvelous Shaker manuscript collection as well as providing images for this book. At the Library of Congress, Eric Frazier was a great host and subsequently supplied me with images of McNemar imprints in their collection. The staff in the Library of Congress's manuscript division were similarly accommodating, although I did not get to know any of them personally. At the Shaker Museum, Chatham, New York, Jerry Grant was helpful in providing access to key materials and images. At Canterbury Shaker Village, Renee Fox has been a wonderful host on research visits and supplied an image for the book. At the Shaker Library in Sabbathday Lake, Maine, I am grateful for the help of Michael Graham, Chuck Rand, and, of course, Brother Arnold Hadd, who encouraged my interest in the Shakers and their history beginning very early on in my career. At Fruitlands, and now the Trustees of Reservations, Roben Campbell, Michael Volmar, Shana Dumont Garr, Sarah Hayes, and Alison Basset have all been incredibly helpful over the years. At the beautiful Enfield Shaker Museum, I have been assisted by Mary Ann Haagen, Galen Beale, and Michael O'Connor. Thanks to Michael Coyan, John Zimkus, Mary Allen, and Pat Allen at the Warren County Historical Society, who cheerfully provided encouragement and images for the book. Rich Roth's digital version of the Cathcart Index of Shaker names from the Western Reserve Historical Society was very useful and convenient as I traced the stories of so many people. University archivist Lois Hamill at Northern Kentucky University helpfully shared an image of James Smith's portrait for the book. Nancy Richey at the Kentucky Library, Western Kentucky University, and staff at the Presbyterian Historical Society helped me to obtain images for this book, for which I thank them. Finally, I would be remiss in not mentioning M.

Stephen Miller, the late Mario S. De Pillis, Scott DeWolfe, Elizabeth DeWolfe, Peter Hoehnle, Kathleen Fernandez, John H. Ott, Lili R. Ott, Rob Emlen, Walter A. Brumm, Marc Rhorer, Darryl Thompson, Jeff Bach, Don Pitzer, Don Janzen, and Martha Boice, all of whom have been great friends, collaborators, and supporters over the years.

A few individuals in particular have gone above and beyond in assisting me as I worked on this project. The noted historian John Putnam Demos offered me much encouragement in my decision to undertake this project. His confidence in my ability to do the work meant more to me than he could ever have known, and I thank him for it. The late renowned scholar of American religious history Stephen J. Stein encouraged Indiana University Press to consider my manuscript. I am deeply grateful to him for his help in finding a home for this book. David Newell and Jane F. Crosthwaite, my great friends and mentors in all things Shaker, provided valuable comments and criticism on the first half of the book. Etta Madden, whose wide-ranging interests have taken her work far beyond the bounds of communal studies, very generously shared her discovery of a cache of letters relating to McNemar's final days, for which I owe her a huge debt of gratitude. Glendyne R. Wergland, my coauthor on previous projects and one of the foremost scholars of Shakerism, provided unfailingly generous help as I researched McNemar's life. The outstanding work of independent scholar Sandra A. Soule has given me many hours of enjoyment, and her book on Aquila Bolton was very helpful to me as I worked on that section of the biography. The inestimable scholars of Shakerism, my friends Stephen J. Paterwic and Carol Medlicott, read the entire manuscript and offered tremendous insights that helped to bring it over the finish line. Joscelyn Godwin, one of my scholarly heroes and someone I am lucky to call my good friend, also read the completed manuscript and offered feedback. Matthew J. Grow, managing director of the Church History Department of the Church of Jesus Christ of Latter-day Saints, offered excellent advice to me when I was seeking a publisher. Thomas Sakmyster and Douglas Winiarski each passed along valuable pieces of information that helped me flesh out McNemar's story, for which I am very grateful.

Hamilton College has been my home since 2009. At Hamilton, I have been extremely lucky to have the active support and encouragement of many people in my scholarly work. Randall Ericson, the former Couper librarian, has been a great friend and indefatigable researcher of Shaker publications. Randy made it possible for me to be in the situation that allowed me to write this book. He has my eternal gratitude. His successor, vice president Dave Smallen, likewise supported my scholarship, allowing me to travel on research fellowships. Finally, Joe Shelley, the current vice president for libraries and information technology services, has been a great boss, friend, and advocate for everything I do at

Hamilton. Joe also secured subvention funds that helped underwrite the production costs of this volume for which I extend my sincere thanks. Professors Robert Paquette, Douglas Ambrose, Jesse Weiner, and Carl Rubino have all provided valuable encouragement and help with Greek and Latin translations, for which I thank them. Most important at Hamilton has been the assistance of my friend Mark Tillson, who cheerfully transcribed many pages of McNemar's dense writing that made it much easier for me to digest the unbelievably large body of manuscripts he left behind. Similarly, Antonia Ambrose and Avery Cook were both brilliant student workers who helped with transcription, and in Antonia's case, some Latin translation.

I wish to thank Gary Dunham, Ashante Thomas, Anna C. Francis, Lesley Bolton, and Pete Feely at Indiana University Press, for working with me to bring Richard McNemar's story to the reading public.

Finally, and most important of all, I must thank my mother and father: Gretchen and Douglas Goodwillie. This book is dedicated to them. They have supported my (sometimes bizarre) interests and aspirations unfailingly throughout my life. This book literally would not exist were it not for them. My wife, Erika Sanchez Goodwillie, has likewise been a steadfast supporter of this effort, patiently shepherding our beloved children, Douglas, Sabine, and Miles, during times when I was absorbed in this work. Again, without her help and care, this book would not exist. Thank you!

Christian Goodwillie
August 2021
Clinton, New York

MAPS

Map 0.1. John Filson's map shows northern Kentucky as McNemar would have found it. Limestone (today's Maysville) was at the head of Limestone Creek. McNemar eventually preached at Cabin Creek just to the east. The initial meetings that exploded into the Kentucky Revival took place in south-central Kentucky near Muddy Creek, Gasper River, and the Barrens region. In 1805, Shaker missionaries entered Kentucky through the Cumberland Gap (*lower right*). They traveled northwest, finding willing hearers for their message at Matthew Houston's Presbyterian congregation in Paint Lick, Kentucky. John Filson, *A Map of Kentucky*. London: J. Stockdale, 1793. Library of Congress Geography and Map Division Washington, DC.

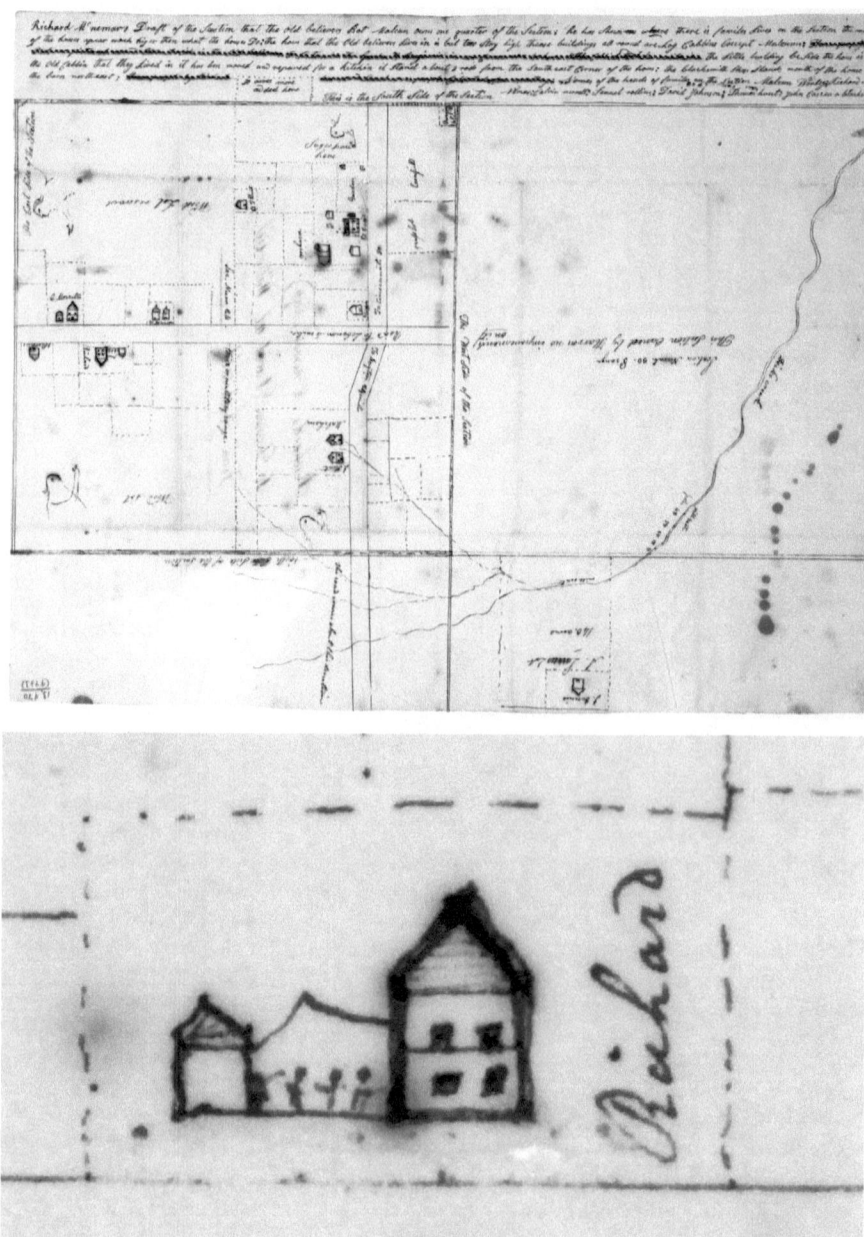

Map 0.2. "Richard McNemar's Draft of the Section that the old believers Bot," Turtle Creek, Ohio, 1807. McNemar depicted Shakers going forth in the dance on a covered platform attached to his house (*see detail*). The houses of Shaker converts Samuel Rollins and Calvin Morrell are to the left of McNemar's; David Johnson's is just to the right; Malcham Worley's and Joseph Stout's are just below the center of the map along the road to Dayton. Shaker Museum, Chatham, NY.

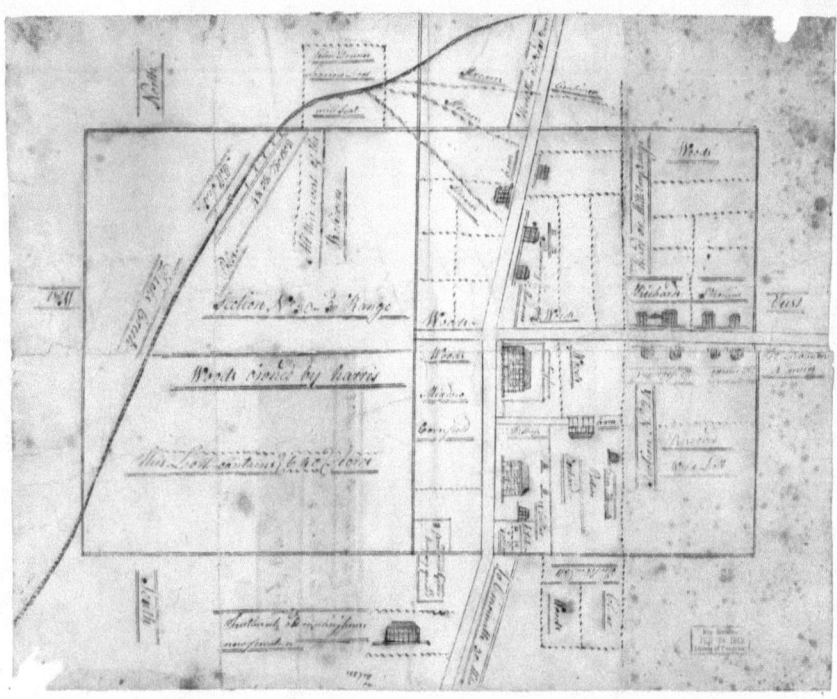

Map 0.3. "A plan of the section of land on which the Believers live in the state of Ohio, Nov. 7th, 1807." The original Turtle Creek meetinghouse where McNemar preached is shown at bottom center, labeled, "Turtle creek old meetinghouse now forsaken." G4084.O825 1807 .P6, Library of Congress Geography and Map Division Washington, DC.

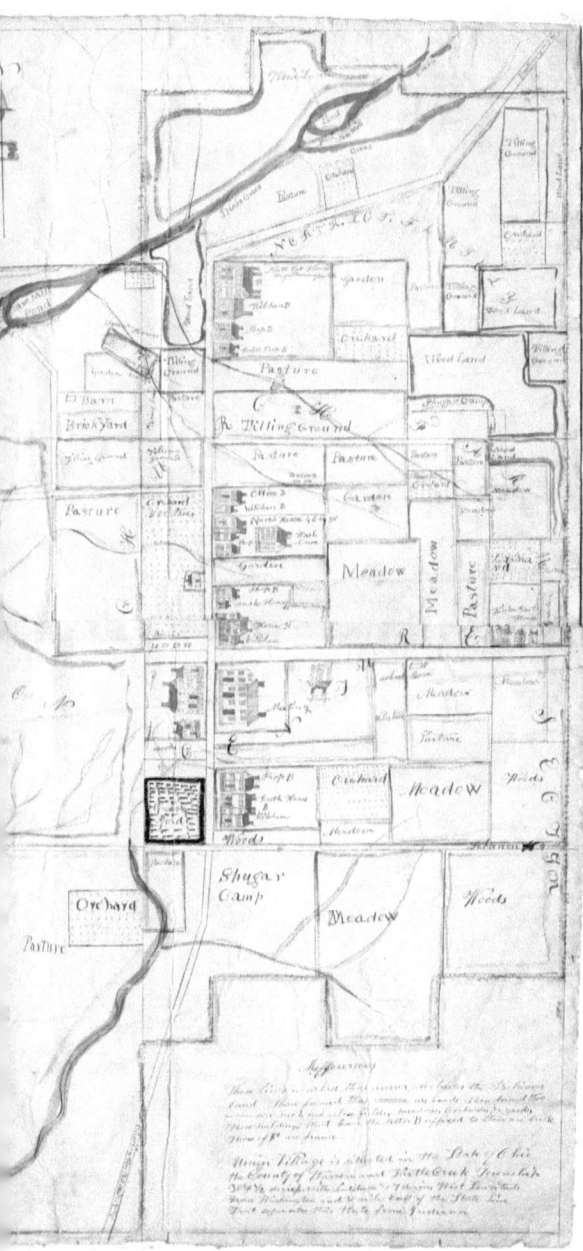

Map 0.4. "Plan of Union Village in 1829." This monumental map, measuring nearly two by three feet, depicts the Union Village, Ohio, Shaker community at its peak. Richard McNemar lived in many families here over the years. His original property comprised the East Family. He was appointed elder of the West Lot, also known as the Brick House Family, on December 13, 1825. Following his travels defending the Shakers in court and at state legislatures, the peripatetic McNemar returned to live in the attic of the North House, Centre Family, in January 1831. McNemar's final resting place was in the Shaker graveyard (*lower left*) south of the Centre Family Dwelling. In time, the individual grave markers were removed, and today a single monument memorializes the Union Village Shakers interred there. Collection of the Western Reserve Historical Society.

RICHARD McNEMAR

INTRODUCTION

ON THE MUGGY NIGHT OF July 27, 1903, Sister Susannah Cole Liddell tossed and turned in her bed at the Union Village Shaker community. Located in southwestern Ohio, it was geographically and culturally poised at the upper edge of the American South, a product of the intense religious revivalism that pervaded the region beginning at the end of the eighteenth century. Sister Susannah, now seventy-nine, was a rare living eyewitness of the leading characters of that distant time and place. Toward the middle of the night, unable to sleep, she heard a rustling near her door. To her amazement, a male figure entered. He had "an opened pamphlet held in his hand intently reviewing, it seemed, as some precious thing." The nearly six-foot-tall man was square-shouldered and clad in antiquated Shaker apparel. His homemade straw hat was broad-rimmed, and a smoothly combed wealth of thick black hair draped his clean white collar. The man was dressed for a Sunday church meeting. His suit, made "from the sheep's fleece backs that whitened the meadow," evidenced the hands of a skilled tailor. The man and his clothing impressed Sister Susannah as being "clean as the snow."[1] His face, until now shaded by the brim of his hat, was suddenly revealed as if lit from within to be that of Richard McNemar—who died in 1839.

Suddenly aware that he was visible, McNemar muttered inaudibly to Sister Susannah. Then, taking control of her inner sight, he revealed his thoughts to her, mentally leading her to records of personal historical importance. The pamphlet he held in his ghostly hand was the text of a speech given by Robert Wickliffe before the Kentucky Senate when McNemar worked side by side with him, defending the Shakers' legal rights in 1831. McNemar then showed her the

Figure Intro.1. Sister Susannah Cole Liddell of Union Village, Ohio.

contents of an ancient desk, particularly a small, carefully wrapped package of writings. McNemar warned Sister Susannah not to share them with "those who know not the people." Finally, he revealed to her a record of his own life experience, "incidents there, still precious to him." His faith confidently placed in her, McNemar's "spirit looked pleased," and disappeared "in gladdening light."[2]

Richard McNemar had reason to be pleased. Sister Susannah's vision was consistent with hundreds of other affirmative supernatural experiences experienced by her fellow Shakers since the mid-eighteenth century. McNemar's appearance to her validated her interest in and efforts toward preserving the heritage of the Union Village Shakers. As a young woman, she was mentored by Sister Abigail Clark, who was born in 1792 and joined the community at its inception in 1805. Throughout her life, Clark salvaged manuscripts and printed records of the community. For thirty years, she had charge of the "rag room," where paper was gathered for reduction into fibers. Clark vigilantly plucked treasures from the rag bags, secreting them away in a chest in her retiring room. In 1876, on her deathbed, Clark passed the contents of this chest to Sister Susannah, imploring her to "have them printed, if possible, [for] coming generations as matters of history."[3]

Beginning in 1879, Sister Susannah spent considerable time examining the contents of Clark's chest, immersing herself further in her community's past, which was also her own. Her childhood memories of Richard McNemar were particularly captivating. She recalled his "manly and winning address" as he rose at meetings, often ending his speech with poetry, then "striking up some favorite song and starting the march up and down the church aisle his hands and his feet timing his voice. . . . And singing his song all alone." She also recalled McNemar's disgraceful end as a physically broken man who was brought down by the very community he helped to found, on the very land he had consecrated to the faith. Sister Susannah's personal interest in Shaker history was validated and encouraged by the attentions of Universalist minister and historian John Patterson MacLean, who began visiting the community in the late 1890s. MacLean published many works on the Shakers, including the first bibliography of works printed by and about the Shakers. MacLean considered Richard McNemar the "father of Shaker literature" and published the first biography of him in 1905.[4]

MacLean was not far off in his assessment of McNemar's importance, nor was Sister Susannah in her admiration of his many talents. Although largely forgotten today, McNemar's life encompassed the full sweep of the early American republic. He was a crucial force during the expansion of Christianity in the trans-Appalachian West and in fomenting the Kentucky Revival. Many histories of the revival focus on the better-known Barton Stone, a founder of the Disciples of Christ. However, McNemar's embrace of Arminian, or freewill, tenets preceded Stone's move into the same theological realm. Having left the Presbyterian Church, the two worked together in forming the Springfield Presbytery. In his conversion to Shakerism, however, McNemar went further than Stone was prepared to go in living a life dedicated to Christ. The reverberations of McNemar's free-will preaching are still felt today throughout the so-called Bible Belt.[5] At the time of these events, McNemar was thirty-five with a wife and seven children, but his second life had just begun.

In March 1805, three Shaker missionaries completed their arduous journey to southwestern Ohio from the Shaker community at New Lebanon, New York. They were seeking subjects of the revival to reveal to them a deeper commitment that offered salvation in the here and now. These missionaries knew of McNemar by reputation and found him at his house in Turtle Creek, Ohio. The missionaries told McNemar that although he had great light and understanding, there was a further cross to bear—he must make a full confession of all the sins he had ever committed, forsake his personal property, remain celibate in his marriage, and embrace his blood relatives as brothers and sisters in Christ, ceding his role as a parent and husband. He must also acknowledge that the Christ spirit had returned to Earth, choosing as its vessel a young woman from Manchester, England: Mother Ann Lee. After a long spiritual struggle, McNemar acknowledged the greater light of the Shaker missionaries and threw his all into their cause.

McNemar became an apostle of Shakerism, traveling all over Ohio, Kentucky, and Indiana to successfully preach the Shaker gospel of confession of sins, celibacy, communal property, and pacifism among the hearty inhabitants of the frontier—all of this achieved through the saving grace of Mother Ann Lee. During these travels, he had meaningful interactions with Native American leaders, most especially the Shawnee prophet Tenskwatawa. McNemar's role in defending Shakerism placed him squarely at the center of public debates about familial relationships, religious liberty, and communal ownership of property. While pursuing all these important activities he also found time to be a prolific writer of polemical and theological tracts and hymns, and a printer and furniture maker.

However, when the Shaker community at Union Village, Ohio, formally executed their legal covenant, McNemar was intentionally left off the membership rolls. This strategic decision, made by his spiritual superiors, left McNemar a disinterested witness to Shakerism. He was free to travel among the communities as a problem-solver for the ministry and also to represent the sect before courts of law and legislatures, and was referred to as a "minute man" for the gospel. This independence, while perfectly suited to a man of McNemar's intelligence and enthusiasm, was fundamentally antithetical to the theocratic and hierarchical principles on which Shakerism rests. McNemar's importance to the Shakers, his public notoriety, and his ego swelled with the advancing years. Tragically, at the end of his life, Richard McNemar was forcibly separated from his friends, blood relations, and the very land he had given to build the Shaker community of Union Village. His independence was no longer of value to the ministry, but he found himself unable to relinquish the role he had played as a "wandering star" and assume his place among the humble ranks of Believers.[6] This fact, combined with spiritual tumult caused by the Shaker religious revival known as the Era of Manifestations, led to his downfall. In an episode reminiscent of the Salem witch trials, McNemar was expelled from the community based on the revelations of a twenty-two-year-old woman, freshly arrived from Ireland, who spoke for the spirit of Mother Ann Lee. Her unchallenged authority outweighed the overwhelming evidence of McNemar's faith, a faith demonstrated in his lifelong commitment to promote and defend Shakerism.

This biography provides the fullest exploration yet of McNemar's life and work. It presents the man in full, gathering all available evidence of his character and actions—both positive and negative. It is the result of ten years of research and the examination of more than ten thousand pages of manuscripts and printed sources. Richard McNemar was a genius and a polymath. He left a monumental written record. This biography seeks to restore Richard McNemar to his rightful place in the pantheon of religious figures of the early American republic, and also to unfold the tale of his brilliant life and tragic end, a life lived against the colorful backdrop of the American frontier.

PART I

PRESBYTERIAN AND SCHISMATIC

ONE

YOUTH

THE DETAILS OF RICHARD MCNEMAR's childhood and adolescence are mostly lost to time. McNemar himself sketched out the few remaining facts in the last decades of his life. In June 1828, he wrote a testimony of his faith in Shakerism, prefacing it with a brief autobiography.[1] Subsequently, he recorded substantially more information in "A general outline of the past Journal of my life," likely penned in the early 1830s when he was nearing sixty.[2] These sources can be used to reconstruct a sense of the people and environment that surrounded McNemar as he found his callings in vocation, matrimony, and faith. The backdrop to his childhood and adolescence was the Revolutionary War and its attendant frontier struggle with Native Americans. The McNemar family moved often, perhaps sowing in Richard the restlessness that permeated his life. Despite the upheaval, he farmed, learned skilled trades, and experienced religious conversion.

Richard McNemar was born on November 20, 1770, in the Tuscarora Valley of central Pennsylvania's Cumberland County. His father was named Morris McNemar; all that is known of his mother is that her last name was Knox.[3] Morris "McNamara" is found on the 1773 tax list for Dublin township as an inmate, meaning a tenant or renter with enough personal property to warrant taxation. He was assessed a £1 tax.[4] Richard stated that his "parents belonged to the church of England, & in that order I was baptized & taught the general doctrines of the Christian religion."[5] A separate source confirms that he "was born and raised in a Christian manner brought up and educated according to the strictest rules and manner of the high church of England."[6] McNemar's ethnic heritage is somewhat murky. His early biographer John MacLean lumps the McNemar family in as part of the "great Scotch-Irish migration that swept over and populated the western half of Pennsylvania."[7] This population mostly comprised Presbyterians, a faith McNemar didn't embrace until later. Therefore, it is likely that the McNemar family was Irish.

The McNemar surname has its origin in County Clare on Ireland's west coast. McNemar is believed to be a variant of "McNamara," an anglicized form of the Gaelic "Mac Conmara," derived from *cù* (hound) and *muir* (sea), meaning "son of the hound of the sea."[8] McNemar was unaware of this meaning and later in life asserted that his name meant "son of no mother."[9] The surname is spelled countless ways in manuscripts and printed records by members of the McNemar family and others. Variants include McNemar, McNamer, McNamar, McNemer, M'Nemar, M'Namar, McNemarre, and so on. The question of how Richard McNemar pronounced his name has not been answered. If he was Irish, then the Gaelic pronunciation would sound something like "Mac-Nuh-Mar." Conversely, twenty-first-century inhabitants of Ohio and Kentucky with this surname pronounce it "Mic-Nee-Mer." Richard McNemar's poetry offers conflicting evidence, and he seems to have made his surname rhyme in various ways according to his poetic needs. The meter of the poems also affects which syllable is stressed in pronunciation, yielding different results. Ultimately, I have chosen to pronounce the name "Mac-Nuh-Mar."[10]

As Church of England members, McNemar's family would have been an anomaly. Most of his Scotch-Irish neighbors likely belonged to one of the nine Presbyterian churches formed in Pennsylvania's Cumberland or Franklin Counties by 1745.[11] It was in the First Presbyterian Church at Carlisle on July 12, 1774, that backcountry settlers agreed on seven resolutions to support the cessation of trade with England. The Scotch-Irish of central Pennsylvania were signaling their support of the beleaguered people of Boston to conservative and pacifist elites in Philadelphia. Aside from patriotic sentiments in McNemar's later poetry, we know nothing of his family's political stance as the colonies slipped into rebellion.[12] His neighbors, for the most part, would have been rebels, particularly the Presbyterians, who were wary of the establishment of a Church of England Episcopacy over the state and taxation toward its maintenance.[13] The few loyalists in central Pennsylvania tended to be Anglican; the McNemars' position is unknown.

In 1775 or 1776, when McNemar was six, his parents moved north to the frontier community of Hart's Log (now Alexandria), Pennsylvania, located on the Frankstown branch of the Juniata River. Founded by German trader John Hart before 1750, the name came from a hollowed-out log Hart had placed conveniently by the road to feed hungry horses.[14] Historians have written, "For the first quarter-century of settlement, those who inhabited the

Juniata Valley lived beyond the reach of sovereign authority, but ever since they have lived beyond the limits of historical scholarship."[15] This observation certainly applies to young Richard McNemar and his family. Finding details about their lives, or even their presence, in the area at that time has proven difficult. When they arrived in the Juniata Valley, it was populated by English, Scotch-Irish, and German settlers. These settlers supported the effort for independence, but they were mainly concerned with defending their settlements from the renewed threat of attack by Native Americans. Delawares and Shawnee to the west of the valley were a constant worry to the scattered families protected by a string of forts throughout the region. Fort Hartslog, or Lytle's Fort, was the nearest fortification to the McNemars' home. It was "built of heavy logs, and was provided with a number of loopholes."[16] Although the fort was never attacked, its presence must have given local families some peace of mind.

Presbyterian minister Philip Fithian of New Jersey traversed Huntingdon County, Pennsylvania, in August 1775. His diary provides a colorful account of the frontier environment Richard McNemar grew up in. As he approached the town of Huntingdon, he met "two men on horseback. As they neared me I smelled their breaths; it was strong of whiskey.... There was a drum beating, several antic loud singers, every now and then a most vociferous laugh, and candles thinly scattered, shining here and there from the houses. I expected to find a few of our American bedlams. These small towns, especially when they are growing fast, and a new thing, go before every other place in most sort of vice, but especially drinking and a few of its nearest allied attendants."[17]

Around 1780, the McNemars pulled up stakes again, moving ten miles northeast to Shaver's Creek, a settlement begun around 1750 by Peter Shaver. In 1778, Anderson's Fort was constructed in the vicinity for the protection of local families. This did not, however, prevent the abduction and murder of a young mother and her two children by Native Americans in August 1781.[18] Perhaps this persistent danger prompted the McNemars to move twenty miles farther east to the Kishacoquillas Valley in the fall of 1783, when Richard McNemar was thirteen. It was around this time that he became affiliated with the Presbyterian Church. McNemar later wrote, "At twelve years old I began to think seriously about a future state, to reflect on my past life, to feel compunction for sin, to retire occasionally in secret & pray to God for pardon & forgiveness, from which period I was greatly protected from actual sin, as far as my light & knowledge extended, & was taken under the care of the Presbyterian church as a minor according to the general rules of which, I ever after felt conscientious to keep my justification."[19]

McNemar had two brothers (that are known), Garner (born 1766) and John (birthdate unknown), and two sisters, Betsy (birthdate unknown) and Cassie (born 1768). Richard recalled that as the youngest he was "more easily spared from manual labor I was early put to school & contracted a taste for learning."[20] He respected and loved his parents, writing later in life that he relied on their "counsel & good-will."[21] In the summers, he farmed with his family; in the winter, he attended school until he "became master of the english language in its several branches including Arithmetic." In 1786, he "was called to take charge of a school in the standing stone valley, & taught with acceptance for one year which commenced April 1, 1786, & terminated Apr. 1787."[22] The Standing Stone Creek is a tributary of the Juniata River in Huntingdon and Centre Counties, Pennsylvania, located west of McNemar's Kishacoquillas Valley home. After spending the summer of 1787 recovering from a serious foot injury, McNemar and his brother Garner embarked in the fall for southwestern Pennsylvania's Redstone Country. The region got its name from the ferrous sandstone that lines the Redstone Creek, a tributary of the Monongahela River. The first settlement, known as Redstone Old Fort, was built in 1754 as a supply house.[23] By the end of the 1770s, it became an important embarkation point for settlers traveling on the Ohio River to Kentucky.

Over the winter of 1787–1788, McNemar found employment as a weaver and singing master. Weaving cloth and teaching music (presumably from written notation) were skilled trades—remarkable accomplishments for a seventeen-year-old raised on a war-torn frontier. Unfortunately, McNemar makes no mention of where he learned either trade or if he served any kind of apprenticeship to learn weaving. With the importation of English cloth curtailed by war, Americans were forced to weave their own. Weavers were usually men, who traveled the area working finite jobs. It was a perfect trade for a man with McNemar's budding wanderlust.

Music remained a chief love of McNemar's throughout his life. Newspapers mention a few musicians as far west as Carlisle, Pennsylvania, beginning in 1790, but McNemar never mentioned a singing master or tunebook by name in any of his reminiscences.[24] In March 1788, he returned to Kishacoquillas and worked on his family's farm. That fall, he taught school for three months before experiencing a pivotal life event.[25]

On Christmas night, 1788, Richard McNemar "was cured of frolicking & thrown into a state of trouble from which no human power [could] release me." He wrote of this experience, "In the 18th year of my age my troubles of mind increased to such a degree, that I took to travelling to see whether I could not get releasment & recover my early relish for the g[ood?] pleasures of the world.

I visited kentucky which was then a new country & afforded many objects for amusement."²⁶ McNemar's troubles of mind may have been typical growing pains of late adolescence, combined with a deep and dreadful insecurity about his prospects for salvation. Alternatively, he may have experienced his first epileptic seizure, a malady he later references in his autobiographical sketch. In the spring of 1789, McNemar began the year as the teacher at a large school in the Jacob's Creek settlement, just east of Washington, Pennsylvania, on the Youghiogheny River. However, after only three days of teaching, he was overcome by what he described as a "rambling fit." He left the school and took a boat from Sewickley on the Ohio River to Limestone, Kentucky (today's Maysville). McNemar's sudden desertion of his teaching job is evidence of his emotional turmoil and anxiety.

McNemar traveled through Kentucky as far as Lexington, staying for a while at McClelland's Station, near the Royal Spring in modern-day Georgetown. Here he found employment weaving in order to raise the money to return home. In June, he ascended the Ohio, stopping in Marietta to meet with his brother John.²⁷ He continued by land to Wheeling and was back at Jacob's Creek in time to help with the harvest. Through the remaining fall and winter, he worked as a journeyman weaver in Mount Pleasant Township with a forty-year-old Irish Presbyterian weaver named Robert Newell.²⁸ He also worked as a farm laborer to one Samuel Boyd.

Convinced that his travels during 1789 had been "to no purpose, & [I] rather growing worse I returned to my occupation of school keeping in the western part of Pennsylvania,"²⁹ McNemar engaged to teach a school in the Ligonier Valley for one year beginning January 1, 1790. That spring he returned to Kishacoquillas. This may have been the last time he saw his father, Morris. By that time, tax records list Morris and a female (presumably Richard's mother) settled on a fifty-acre tract in Mifflin County, Armagh Township, with one horse and one cow.³⁰ While on this visit home, Richard McNemar "got a remedy" for epilepsy. He elaborates no further on what this remedy was or on the severity and frequency of his seizures. In fact, not a single additional reference to his disease was found among the thousands of pages of his manuscripts examined for this biography. A tantalizing reference was recorded, however, in the diary of Shaker Benjamin Seth Youngs, who would be key in McNemar's conversion to that faith in 1805. Youngs wrote that during an enthusiastic meeting on June 2, 1805, McNemar told the assembly, "14 years ago in a ball room [I] was struck on the floor with a convulsive fit & that at that time [I] vowed to dedicate [my] whole soul & body to the Lord."³¹ In the eighteenth century, epilepsy was known as the "falling sickness," because sufferers often dropped to the ground. It was also known by the Latin *morbus herculeus*, owing to the "difficulty of cure," as well as the "strength displayed by the miserable patient in a paroxysm of this disease." A Philadelphia physician noted in a treatise on the disease in 1796 that it was also called *morbus sacer*, "from the supposition that the gods punished men with this disease, as a particular mark of their displeasure." He observed that a person, in perfect health, falling down in violent agony for no apparent reason would, indeed, "induce the ignorant to ascribe it to some supernatural agent." It is no wonder that McNemar was shaken to his core by the experience.[32] As will be discussed later, it seems that at least one of his children eventually suffered from the same malady. It is quite extraordinary that the symptoms of this illness—including falling down with jerks of the body—are so similar to the physical manifestations for which the Kentucky Revival became famous. The traumatic convulsive fit McNemar suffered in the ballroom threw him into great anxiety for assurance of his salvation.

McNemar left his horse at Kishacoquillas and returned on foot to his school in the Ligonier Valley. That summer, he attended the ordination of the Reverend John McPherrin of the Redstone Presbytery.[33] The thirty-four-year-old Pennsylvanian was installed as minister for the Salem and Unity churches in Westmoreland County, Pennsylvania. That fall, as McNemar was returning west from another trip, he had a chance encounter with McPherrin on the Conemaugh Road in southwestern Pennsylvania. McPherrin invited McNemar to come and live with him in Salem (near modern-day Derry), and he gladly accepted. After completing his duties as a schoolmaster, McNemar departed for Salem to live with McPherrin and teach school locally. On February 7, 1791, McNemar had his first meeting with the noted preacher Elisha Macurdy.[34] Joseph Smith, historian of the Redstone Presbytery, described Macurdy as someone who "had more of the spirit and fire of the early preachers than any of his contemporaries, was once a *road*wagoner, and always spoke of himself as such."[35] Macurdy made his first profession of faith to McPherrin at Salem during a religious revival. The meeting was "distinguished by the accession of an unusually large number of men.... These were John, Abraham, James, and Benjamin Boyd (brothers), William Morehead, John Thompson, and Richard M'Nemar, all of whom subsequently became ministers of the gospel."[36]

This revival was likely the one McNemar recalled later as the first "society meeting" of the Presbyterian Church he ever attended. It was held on March 13, 1791, at John Boyd's house in Salem, Pennsylvania. Boyd, an Irish immigrant, was a ruling elder in the local Presbyterian congregation.[37] A society meeting, as historian George P. Hutchinson explains, functioned as follows: "As the Covenanters [Presbyterians] came to America, they organized themselves into Praying Societies with periodic General Meetings of a representative nature. They were, at first and often, without ordained ministers or elders and thus without formal preaching and the administration of the sacraments. Yet they were orderly, closely-knit groups—their leaders dealing with problems of doctrine, membership, discipline, and finances as they arose."[38] McNemar wrote of his experience, "A revival of religion broke out of which I became a subject," and "the power of God was manifested in a manner that no one present had ever before witnessed."[39] He recalled that his conversion "was deemed rather singular; such as in that day was common among the Methodists. From that period I became what was called zealous in religion devoting all my leisure time to prayer, meditation, reading, & pious conversation, from which I never after deviated."[40] Indeed, much later in his life, McNemar said this event "shaped my course for time & eternity."[41] In remarking that his peers deemed his conversion "singular" and comparing himself to contemporary Methodists, McNemar invokes the public religious enthusiasm and visionary experiences displayed by early American Methodists.[42] He thereby was prominent in his first public religious experience, setting a precedent for his behavior in those arenas that he followed throughout his life.

After a six-month sojourn in Salem, McNemar traveled to Virginia with Reverend Carey Allen in August. Allen was a rising star in the Presbyterian Church, described as "a mirthful, fun-loving, pleasant companion, and a great wit and satirist. Sanguine and impulsive, his sallies partook occasionally of no little eccentricity; yet he would say the oddest things and take the boldest flights with such an easy and natural air, that no one felt his sense of propriety shocked."[43] Allen loomed large in Presbyterian circles during McNemar's early days in Kentucky. In September 1791, McNemar attended a sacramental meeting of the Presbyterian Church at George's Creek (modern-day New Geneva), Pennsylvania. At this meeting, McNemar partook of bread and wine symbolically representing the body and blood of Christ, called "The Lord's Supper" by Presbyterians. Later that month, McNemar left Pennsylvania for good, setting out for Kentucky and a future he could scarcely have imagined.[44]

TWO

WESTWARD MIGRATION AND EDUCATION

RICHARD MCNEMAR EMBARKED FROM PENNSYLVANIA for Kentucky in September 1791. He arrived at Limestone (renamed Maysville in 1799) "2 days after St. Clair's defeat." This reference point dates his arrival in Kentucky to November 6, 1791, although in another account he states it was November 8. General Arthur St. Clair and his army suffered a disastrous defeat at the Battle of the Wabash on November 4, 1791, near present-day Fort Recovery on the central-western Ohio border. St. Clair lost nearly one thousand men—in what remains the worst defeat of US military forces at the hands of Native Americans—to an army led by the Shawnee chiefs Blue Jacket and Little Turtle.[1] Sixteen years later, the paths of McNemar and Blue Jacket would cross in a most interesting way.[2]

Incredibly, an account of McNemar's journey to Kentucky survives. He joined a group of settlers and missionaries traveling in a flatboat convoy for safety. Robert W. Finley, who later became a mentor to McNemar, led the party. James B. Finley, Robert's son, described the journey in his autobiography. His poignant account conveys the dreadful anxiety of travelers taking leave of civilization and entering an alien environment. Depending on water levels, the trip from western Pennsylvania to the major portage at the Falls of the Ohio (opposite modern-day Louisville) could take anywhere from ten days to a month—and prolonged travel often meant the difference between life and death.[3] Finley's party embarked from George's Creek in today's New Geneva, Pennsylvania, and floated down the Monongahela River toward Pittsburgh, where they entered the Ohio River.

> I shall never forget the deeply-thrilling and interesting scene which occurred at parting. Ministers and people were collected together, and after an

exhortation and the singing of a hymn, they all fell upon their knees, and engaged in ardent supplication to God, that the emigrants might be protected amid the perils of the wilderness. I felt as though we were taking leave of the world. After mingling together our tears and prayers, the boats were loosed, and we floated out into the waters of the beautiful Ohio.

The day on which the emigrants started was pleasant, and all nature seemed to smile upon the pioneer band. They had made every preparation they deemed necessary to defend themselves from the attack of their wily foes. The boat which led the way as a pilot was well manned and armed, on which sentinels, relieved by turns, kept watch day and night. Then followed two other boats at a convenient distance. While floating down the river we frequently saw Indians on the banks, watching for an opportunity to make an attack.

Just below the mouth of the Great Scioto, where the town of Portsmouth now stands, a long and desperate effort was made to get some of the boats to land by a white man, who feigned to be in great distress; but the fate of William Orr and his family was too fresh in the minds of the adventurers to be thus decoyed. A few months previous to the time of which I am writing, this gentleman and his whole family were murdered, being lured to shore by a similar stratagem. But a few weeks before we passed, the Indians attacked three boats, two of which were taken, and all the passengers destroyed.... Being too well posted in Indian strategy to be decoyed, we pursued our journey unmolested....

In company with my father, and in his boat, there were two missionaries—the Revs. Carey Allen and Robert Marshall—and also Mr. James Walsh and Mr. Richard M'Nemar, both of whom afterward became ministers in the Presbyterian Church.[4]

In an earlier version of this narrative, Finley elaborated tellingly on McNemar, writing: "The notorious Richard M'Nemer, of Shaker memory, was then a boy, and under my father's care. You will say this boat had its share of divinity, and these men were for the weal or woe of many."[5]

Limestone (Maysville) was the primary landing for Ohio River boats not bound for Louisville. It sat at the head of the Maysville Road, an ancient buffalo trace used by Native American hunting parties. During the 1780s, this sixty-five-mile-long conduit linked a chain of white settlements—fortified blockhouses and stations—extending from the Ohio River south to Lexington. Natives used the road to wage guerilla war against the settlers. By 1784, however, Simon Kenton had built a blockhouse on the site of Limestone, and the Natives had largely retreated north of the Ohio River. Soon after, noted frontiersman Daniel Boone also established a tavern and trading post there.

The 1790 Federal Census recorded 24,055 whites, 32 free blacks, and 4,889 slaves living in the counties through which the Maysville Road passed.[6]

McNemar traveled southwest on the Maysville Road and lodged with Joseph Caldwell, who likely lived at Cane Ridge or Paris, Kentucky. Caldwell was another transplanted Presbyterian from Westmoreland County, Pennsylvania.[7] He served his congregation as a ruling elder and was a suitable host for the zealous young convert.[8] Over the winter, McNemar engaged in the study of Latin with fellow Presbyterian and church elder Malcham Worley, who operated a grammar school. Twenty-nine-year-old Worley was one of fifteen children born to Caleb Worley and Rebecca Allen from Botetourt County, Virginia, along the James River. Malcham (born on July 19, 1762) and his brother Nathan would both figure into the Shaker story.[9] Caleb joined the Presbyterian Church in Virginia and, according to his son Malcham, "raised his family in that order."[10] Caleb was granted four hundred acres for his service in the French and Indian War along the Salt Fork branch of the Sandy River in Fayette County, Kentucky (he also assisted the patriot cause in the Revolutionary War by supplying beef and wheat to the army). The land was surveyed in 1785, and according to Malcham's later account the family relocated there that year. Malcham was selected by his father to receive a classical education in preparation for the ministry. He graduated from Liberty Hall Academy (now Washington and Lee University) in Lexington, Virginia, around 1788. This education prepared him to teach school on his arrival in Kentucky. Over time, he became one of Richard McNemar's closest associates, and the two men's fates were intertwined from this moment on. Intriguingly (in light of later events), since early childhood, Malcham Worley was "subject to convulsion fits which so affected his nerves that he was in a certain degree an invalid all his life." Although Worley's affliction sounds more severe, he and McNemar shared this physically—and spiritually—vexing condition, possibly epilepsy.[11]

In March of 1792, McNemar traveled farther down the Ohio River, making his first visits to Cincinnati and settlements at Columbia and Round Bottom, Ohio.[12] Cincinnati was then in its infancy. Its strategic location opposite the mouth of the Licking River and near the Great and Little Miami Rivers made it a key location in the Ohio Valley. Permanent white settlement of the area began in 1788. When McNemar visited Cincinnati, its center was Fort Washington, erected in 1789. Years later, he recalled a shocking incident he witnessed walking along the banks of the Ohio, probably near the fort.

> Years ago when God had brought me as a wanderer & as a pilgrim through the wilderness & to Cincinnati in the time of Genl Waynes Campain as I was walking on the banks of the Ohio at Cincinnatti behind the logs & under the

banks (I hope I shall not intrude upon female modesty) there, there, I saw them scattered in open view in their brutal acts of abomination like the very brutes of the field. I remember that there my very bowels were in pain—I leaned over a stump and made a covenant with God that I would ever give my soul & body unto him!—I wanted then to go into Waynes garrison (but was not permitted) & ring damnation over their heads![13]

McNemar's physical revulsion at seeing—presumably—wanton public sexual intercourse demonstrates that he already had an aversion to the sins of the flesh. In June, he returned to Kentucky and boarded at Malcham Worley's schoolhouse until December. McNemar next moved to Cane Ridge and lived with the settlement's Presbyterian minister, Robert W. Finley, in whose flatboat convoy he had traveled.[14]

In his bare-bones "general outline of the past Journal of my life," McNemar prosaically wrote: "April 1793 I went to live at John Luckies."[15] He made no mention that he married John's daughter Jane, or "Jennie," Luckey on April 8, 1793, at Cane Ridge, Bourbon County, Kentucky. The original marriage license survives but is damaged, and the name of the officiant is not preserved. Likely, it was Robert W. Finley.[16] McNemar's in-laws, the Luckey family, originated in Scotland and fled to Ireland to avoid religious persecution. Patriarch Robert immigrated to Lancaster, Pennsylvania, where he died in 1757. His son John was born in 1735 and eventually settled in Rowan County, North Carolina.[17] John and his wife, Mary "Anna" (Patterson), had nine children. Their daughter Jennie was born on March 9, 1766. The family moved to Cane Ridge in 1790, where John became a ruling elder in the Presbyterian congregation.[18] McNemar was fortunate to marry into an established local family, rooted in the Presbyterian Church and rich in material goods. Given that McNemar wrote his "general outline" toward the end of his life, more than forty years since his marriage and thirty since he had eschewed marital relations forever and embraced celibacy, it is understandable that he made no mention of the event in his narrative. His writings—from both before and after his conversion to Shakerism—rarely mention his blood relatives, other than recording births and deaths. This attitude toward his natural relations was in keeping with Shaker practices, which demanded suppression of any special feelings for one's own flesh and blood above any other fellow Believer.

The Luckeys were a prosperous family, as evidenced by John Luckey's will, made on December 28, 1793. On his death, in either late 1793 or early 1794, he made a generous provision for newly married Jennie: "Item. I give and bequeath to my well beloved daughter Jinney one bed and furniture, one chest, one mare and saddle and seven head of cattle, one negroe wench named Seely, and their living till God in his providence lays out a way for them to remove." We can only speculate as to how McNemar felt about taking ownership of the child slave Seely (Celia Anderson), born (ironically) on July 4, 1789. Most of his fellow Presbyterians were opposed to slavery in principle, if not always in practice. John's wife and other children received a variety of other goods, including land in North Carolina, furniture, eleven horses, more than twenty head of cattle, and five other slaves: Tab, Lucy, Tilly, and the father-son pair of Pompy and Jake.[19]

McNemar's whereabouts during 1794 are unrecorded, though he likely lived on the Luckey's farm in Cane Ridge. His first child, a son named Benjamin, was born on February 9.[20] It may have been during this year that McNemar attended Robert W. Finley's Bourbon Academy. Although McNemar makes no mention of it, James B. Finley wrote that McNemar studied in a school administered by his Princeton-educated father. Finley described the curriculum, which was probably far more rigorous than the simple primary schools that McNemar had attended and taught in.

> In my father's academy I enjoyed the advantages of a thorough drilling in Latin and Greek, and even now I can repeat whole books of the Aeneid of Virgil and the Iliad of Homer. I could scan Latin or Greek verse with as much fluency as I can now sing a Methodist hymn; and I could find the square root of a given number with as much precision as in my youthful days I could drive a center with my rifle.
>
> In my father's academy, it being the first institution of learning in which the classics were taught in the western country, were many students who came from a distance; and among the number were the Howes, Robinsons, and M'Nemar, Dunlevy, Welsh, Steele, and Thompson, all of whom became Presbyterian preachers. Judges Trimble and Mills were educated here, and several students who afterward became doctors of medicine. Here my brother John and myself studied the Greek and Latin languages, and mathematics.[21]

A memoir of the aforementioned Judge Robert Trimble mentions that he enrolled in the "Bourbon Academy" in Cane Ridge, Kentucky, in 1795. This was likely the name by which Finley's school was known and was described as "the most flourishing institution of the kind in Kentucky."[22] In light of later events, McNemar did not have much reason to reminisce about his time with Finley, although the knowledge of Latin and Greek he acquired there served him throughout his life.

The education of clergy and settlers was a growing concern in Kentucky. As historian Stephen Aron observed, "Across the Kentucky countryside, clergymen bemoaned the sunken state of religious affairs." Deism and so-called nothingarianism (a lack of religious affiliation) were common among Kentucky settlers, who also lacked trained clergy to serve them. As Aron notes, by 1793, the Kentucky legislature had even dispensed with the traditional services of a chaplain.[23] On April 25, 1794, the Transylvania Presbytery met at Minister Samuel Shannon's house near Versailles. A Princeton graduate, Shannon was a giant of a man. Presbyterian historian Robert Davidson wrote a wonderful description of him: "His fist was like a sledge-hammer, and he was said to have lopped off a stout bough at a single stroke of his sword, when charging through the woods. Notwithstanding his strength, he was one of the best-natured men in the world, and nothing could provoke or ruffle him. He had also a mechanical turn, and invented a piece of apparatus called The Whirling Table; but he was out of his place in the pulpit. To a rough, awkward, slovenly appearance, which might, however, have been overlooked, was added a slow and stammering utterance."[24] It is ironic, then, that Shannon's house was chosen for this particular meeting, since its purpose was to found a school for training ministers in Kentucky. To counter the "general causes of the prevailing declension of religion," a number of men agreed to fund a public seminary with a combination of cash, live cattle, pork, flour, and hemp.[25] Among these men was Col. James Smith, who had moved to Cane Ridge with his family in 1788.[26] His presence loomed large over the settlement of Cane Ridge, and of Bourbon County in general. Smith and McNemar were well acquainted, and many years later their strong personalities clashed in an epic battle over religion and family.

Col. James Smith was born in Franklin County, Pennsylvania, in 1737. In 1755, he was taken captive by a mixed band of Native Americans near Bedford, Pennsylvania. He remained in captivity until 1759 and published a narrative of his captivity in 1799.[27] In 1765, five years before Richard McNemar's birth, Smith led a group of white settlers called the Black Boys in the destruction of a pack train carrying trade goods, liquor, and weapons to the Natives. The government of Pennsylvania responded by capturing and imprisoning seven of the Black Boys, which led to Smith and a group of three hundred men investing Fort Loudon in what was arguably the first act of armed rebellion carried out against the British army in North America. Over the late spring of 1765, Smith and his men harassed the fort's commander, Lieutenant Charles Grant, surrounding the fort two more times and disrupting further trade with the Natives. As a result, Grant branded Smith a rebel. In early June, however, Governor John Penn decided that the Black Boys were justified in their actions, and charges against Smith were dropped. In return, Smith ceased his depredation of pack trains.[28] At the outbreak of the Revolutionary War, Smith was chosen to represent Westmoreland County, Pennsylvania, in the 1776 General Assembly in Philadelphia. In 1777, he saw action in New Jersey at Rocky Hill. For the duration of the war, Smith defended the Pennsylvania frontier against Native attacks. In 1788, following his immigration to Bourbon County, Kentucky, he was appointed to represent the settlers at Danville, where the separation of the state of Kentucky from Virginia was being negotiated. Smith represented Bourbon County in the Kentucky legislature through 1799.[29]

On October 10, 1794, the Transylvania Presbytery met at Paint Lick, southeast of Lexington, Kentucky. To counter maverick preaching and ensure orthodoxy, it was decided that no congregation could invite an unknown minister to serve them without the approval of the presbytery or a sanctioned local committee. Serving on the committee for northern Kentucky were Robert W. Finley and Malcham Worley (whose surname is ironically misspelled in the original as "Worldly").[30] On October 13, the presbytery decided that all slaveholders under their care should teach slaves less than fifteen years old to read the Bible and encourage them to attend worship.[31]

In the spring of 1795, perhaps in part due to simmering troubles with Robert W. Finley, McNemar moved to Paint Lick, Kentucky, to teach school for the year.[32] McNemar's friend Carey Allen ministered to the Presbyterian congregation at Paint Lick. Sadly, the much-beloved Allen died of tuberculosis that same year on August 5, at only twenty-eight.[33] The Transylvania Presbytery convened at Ash Ridge Church near Lexington beginning on February 17, 1795. On the second day of the meeting, McNemar's mentor Robert W. Finley was called to respond to charges of public drunkenness. Finley countered efforts to hold a trial by petitioning that a session from churches adjacent to his own at Cane Ridge be gathered to hear his defense. Additionally, he requested a counteraction for scandal against his accusers—Richard McNemar, Peter Houston, and his son John Houston. Born in North Carolina in 1761, Peter Houston immigrated to Kentucky in 1779 with Daniel Boone. Houston and Boone fought with Native Americans and established Fort Houston on the site of present-day Paris, Kentucky. In 1787, Houston married Sarah Jane Luckey, the sister of McNemar's wife, Jennie, and settled at Cane Ridge.[34] The presbytery denied Finley's requests, prompting his resignation from the Presbyterian Church. The presbytery's minutes record the reasons why Finley's requests were denied, chief among them was that "Reports of this nature respecting Mr. Finley have circulated in this country for some years past & appear now to have become recently flagrant." The presbytery accepted Finley's resignation and barred him from ever again preaching in the name of the Presbyterian Church.[35]

Finley, however, wormed his way back into the presbytery later that year at its meeting held at Cane Ridge on April 15, 1795. He agreed to a trial to determine whether accusations of public drunkenness were true. The trial was scheduled for July 30 at Cane Ridge, Finley's home congregation.[36] On April

18, at Cane Ridge, following the debate over Finley's fate, a young man applied to the presbytery as a candidate for the ministry. His name was John Dunlavy, and, like Malcham Worley, his life became inextricably linked to that of Richard McNemar. Dunlavy was born in Virginia on March 27, 1769. He and his brother Francis attended Presbyterian minister John McMillan's Canonsburg Academy (later Washington & Jefferson College) in Canonsburg, Pennsylvania, one of the earliest academies for the study of English, Latin, and mathematics west of the Appalachians. Dunlavy had also attended Finley's academy (as noted above). Now twenty-six, he stood six feet tall and weighed two hundred pounds. He had "wiry black hair," blue-gray eyes with brown spots in them, and a strikingly large head—"the first thing a stranger would notice." In time, Dunlavy was known as the "Demosthenes of the western world" for his ability to sway audiences with his preaching.[37]

Ultimately, Robert W. Finley's trial never happened. He refused to appear and instead leveled a series of charges against the presbytery. Finley submitted his resignation to the presbytery for a second time at their meeting at Cane Ridge on August 3, 1795.[38] In light of his behavior, on August 4, the presbytery concluded that there was no evidence to support Finley's long-standing countercharges against McNemar and the Houstons, and "therefore said charge against Richard M'Namar John Huston & Peter Huston ceases in the same manner as if it had not been brought against them."[39]

A key moment in Richard McNemar's life happened the same day: he was received on a trial basis toward becoming a minister in the Presbyterian Church. The presbytery's minutes record: "Mr Richard M'Namar having applied to this Pby as a candidate of the gospel ministry and having received sufficient testimonials in favour of his moral and religious character, of his being in the communion of the church and being satisfied that he has gone through a regular course of literature, having examined him on his repentance & the views that influence him to seek the sacred office of the gospel ministry—and receive him on trial."[40] In response, McNemar read a discourse he had prepared on the Epistle of Paul to the Romans, 5:1, for the approval of the presbytery. "Therefore being justified by faith, we have peace with God, through our Lord Jesus Christ." This statement was accepted, and he was assigned to give a lecture on Jude 6:13 for the next part of his trial toward becoming a licentiate.[41] Intriguingly, this passage of scripture serves as a General Epistle to Christians against fornication and corruption in doing "what they know naturally, as brute beasts." Jude compares these sinners to "trees whose fruit withereth, without fruit, twice dead... wandering stars to whom is reserved the blackness of darkness forever." Certainly, McNemar had read Jude before this assignment, but one wonders if his fellow ministers later recalled their choice for his trial lecture when, ten years later, he embraced the celibate religion of Shakerism. Perhaps McNemar drew on the disturbing scenes he had witnessed in Cincinnati for his lecture. Additionally, and for far different reasons, McNemar himself would be called a wandering star near the end of his life.

McNemar's examination by the presbytery continued through the fall. On October 7, 1795, at Pisgah Church, near Versailles, Kentucky, he and his young colleague John Dunlavy successfully passed an examination for proficiency in Latin and Greek. The following day, each was assigned a passage of scripture to lecture on at the next meeting of the presbytery. McNemar was assigned Acts 8:37: "And Philip said, If thou believest with all thine heart, thou mayest. And he answered and said, I believe that Jesus Christ is the Son of God." On October 9, McNemar and Dunlavy were granted liberty to preach publicly, provided they do so no more often than once in two weeks, "not without first carefully digesting the matter of their exhortations," and for no longer than forty-five minutes.[42] These limitations evidence the concern Presbyterians had with the preaching of orthodox theology delivered by doctrinally sound, well-educated clergy. To the great concern of the presbytery, Robert W. Finley was still preaching in the area, despite his suspension.

Richard McNemar's second child, a son named James, was born on February 22, 1796.[43] It is not known exactly where McNemar's family was based at this time, but it was likely at his father-in-law John Luckey's farm in Cane Ridge, which was still in the possession of his widow. On April 15, at the meeting of the presbytery at Cane Run Church in Harrodsburg, McNemar delivered his sermon on Acts 8:37. His effort was approved, and he was assigned a further discourse on Matthew 16:16: "And Simon Peter answered and said, Thou art the Christ, the Son of the living God." Although Dunlavy's sermon is not mentioned in the minutes of the meeting, it must have passed muster, since he was assigned to deliver another on Ephesians 2:10.[44]

The presbytery convened again at Paris on October 4. Matthew Houston, a candidate for the ministry from Lexington Presbytery (Virginia) presented his credentials to the presbytery. Like McNemar's friend Malcham Worley, Houston was educated at Liberty Hall Academy in Lexington, Virginia, where he graduated around 1785.[45] Houston was admitted as a probationer in the Transylvania Presbytery. With Houston's arrival, three men who figured prominently in Richard McNemar's future had all come into his orbit: Malcham Worley, John Dunlavy, and Matthew Houston. On October 6, the presbytery examined McNemar and Dunlavy on science and deemed their knowledge satisfactory, bringing them one step closer to ordination. The presbytery decided to hold a special session early the next year and assigned Dunlavy to discourse on Revelation 3:11, and McNemar on John 7:48: "Have any of the rulers or of the Pharisees believed on him?"[46] For the remainder of the year, McNemar continued his peregrinations, moving back to Cane Ridge from Paint Lick in the autumn of 1796.[47]

The year 1797 began auspiciously for McNemar and Dunlavy. At the special session of the presbytery held on January 3–4 at Paris, Kentucky, they delivered their discourses. Both men also passed a final examination on divinity. These steps, combined with prior examinations, positive testimonials from others, evidence of good moral character, and adoption of the Confession of Faith, secured for them license "to preach the gospel of Christ as probationers for the holy ministry within the bounds of this Pby. or wherever they shall be orderly called." McNemar and Dunlavy were now officially eligible as supply ministers for frontier settlements requesting preaching or to fill in for absent ministers in established congregations. McNemar received his first official preaching engagements to supply one Sabbath each at Millersborough, Big Spring, Pleasant Point, Manchester, and Bracken. Dunlavy likewise was assigned to preach one Sabbath at Three Islands, Manchester, Green Creek, Pleasant Point, and two at Bracken. Both men were accepted as orthodox standard-bearers for the expanding Presbyterian Church in the West. At this same meeting, a young man from North Carolina presented his credentials and asked permission to preach within the bounds of the presbytery. This was granted to twenty-five-year-old Barton Stone, setting in motion a series of events that led to the Kentucky Revival and an epochal personal struggle over theology between Stone and McNemar.[48]

The presbytery tended to four more business matters that year, which had long-term consequences for the Kentucky Revival and the eventual rise of Shakerism in the West. On March 7, 1797, they met in southwestern Kentucky's Logan County with another transplanted North Carolinian, James McGready. McGready applied for membership in the presbytery for himself and his congregation at Muddy River, or Salem Church, and was accepted. Also present at the meeting was Minister William McGee.[49] Together, McGready and McGee led the Gasper River, Muddy River, and Red River congregations into the first wave of revivalism in Kentucky. These far-flung frontier congregations were on the edge of the administrative and spiritual powers of the Presbyterian Church. In light of this, it is not surprising that they were among the first to descend into the throes of revivalism.

On April 13, Matthew Houston preached a trial sermon from Acts 10:35. His effort was accepted, and by affirmation and laying-on of hands he was ordained minister of the congregations of Paint Lick and Silver Creek, Kentucky.[50] Less than eight years later, Houston was among the first clergymen in central Kentucky to encounter three curiously attired men who came through the Cumberland Gap preaching a strange new interpretation of the gospel—the first Shaker missionaries. On October 4, the presbytery received verbal supplication for preaching in the frontier Turtle Creek settlement north of the Ohio River, a first contact that yielded serious unforeseen consequences.[51] Also that day, John Dunlavy received a call from the Ohio River congregations of Lee's Creek, Big Bracken, and North Bracken, Kentucky, to become their minister. He was formally ordained at a special meeting of the presbytery on November 8, 1797.[52]

On April 10, 1798, the presbytery assented to a call from Robert W. Finley's former congregation at Cane Ridge, and another at Concord, for the appointment of Barton Stone as their preacher, although he had not yet been formally ordained. The congregation at Cabin Creek, on the Ohio River, called for Richard McNemar to preach there for two-thirds of his time.[53] McNemar readily agreed to this request, as he had moved to Cabin Creek with his pregnant wife, Jennie, two sons, and child slave Seely in September 1797.[54] The settlement at Cabin Creek lay only four miles upstream from the town of Limestone (Maysville) where McNemar had arrived in Kentucky ten years earlier. Historically, Cabin Creek was a crossing point for Native American war parties taking one of two trails that led there from the Upper Blue Lick spring and salt deposit on the Licking River.[55] Captain John Wilson first settled there in 1795 and called for Presbyterian preachers to minister to the families then gathering. Among the itinerants who preached at the settlement were John Dunlavy and Matthew Houston.[56] It was there that the McNemars welcomed their third child, a daughter named Vincy, into the world on October 21, 1797.[57]

The meeting of the presbytery at New Providence (southwest of Lexington, Kentucky) in April 1798 proved fateful. On April 11, the first steps were taken toward subdividing Transylvania Presbytery into three new presbyteries based on geographic boundaries. Initially, these were called Union (east side of the main Licking River and northwest of the Ohio River), Providence (west side of the main Licking and north of the Kentucky River), and Cumberland (south side of the Kentucky and the Cumberland area). John Dunlavy was assigned as a minister in the newly formed Union Presbytery, and Matthew Houston was assigned to the Cumberland. Richard McNemar had not yet been formally ordained. Geographically, he would have been part of the Union Presbytery, since his congregation at Cabin Creek was located on the Ohio River.[58] This plan was submitted to the Synod of Virginia for its approval. At the close of the meeting, plans were made for an intermediate session of presbytery for the ordination of Richard McNemar.[59]

THREE

ORDINATION

ON AUGUST 1, 1798, THE Transylvania Presbytery held a special session at Cabin Creek for the ordination of Richard McNemar. Captain John Wilson and other settlers had encouraged McNemar to make a permanent home among them. They listened as he delivered a final trial sermon, on Genesis 3:6: "And when the woman saw that the tree *was* good for food, and that it *was* pleasant to the eyes, and a tree to be desired to make *one* wise, she took of the fruit thereof, and did eat, and gave also unto her husband with her; and he did eat." Unfortunately, the discourses given at meetings were not recorded in the presbytery's minutes, and no manuscript texts from McNemar's pre–New Light and Shaker period survive. One would love to know the substance of his remarks on this crucial passage of scripture in light of his future conversion to Shakerism, which attempts to restore man and womankind to their prelapsarian (pre-fall) relationship through celibacy.[1]

The next day, August 2, fellow Pennsylvanian Reverend William Robinson preached a sermon based on Hebrews 13:7, whose text begins "Remember them which have the rule over you." This was a fitting admonition to a new minister in the extremely bureaucratic and hierarchical Presbyterian Church. The theme proved highly ironic in light of later events in McNemar's life, when he alternately embraced and struggled against his Shaker superiors. John P. Campbell spoke next, trying to impress on the gathered crowd the solemnity of the occasion. He then turned to McNemar and asked the questions confirming his orthodox views on divinity and church government. Did he believe the Old and New Testaments to be the word of God? Did he adopt the Presbyterian Confession of Faith? Did he approve of the government of the church, and would he subject himself to his brethren? Were his motives for joining the ministry from a love of God and desire to zealously promote the truth of the gospel? And, finally, would he be faithful and diligent in his public and private duties to the Cabin Creek congregation?[2] McNemar answered each one in the affirmative. McNemar's congregation was then solicited for their approval of his ordination, which they gave. Following this, the ministers of the presbytery sealed his ordination through prayer and the laying on of hands—each one giving McNemar the right hand of fellowship.[3]

The business of organizing the Cabin Creek church was quickly tended to, and McNemar met with the ruling elders of the congregation: Robert Robb, Robert Robinson, and Andrew Henderson, to agree on governing rules for the congregation. These men constituted a "session," or ruling body, of a Presbyterian congregation. McNemar presented the elders with rules he had drawn up, including one requiring that people who wanted to join the congregation provide testimonials of their orderly standing in another Presbyterian body and submit to an examination on experimental religion: a measure of how deeply they had probed the nature of faith through the scriptures, thereby inviting the presence of the Holy Spirit. Finally, applicants had to prove they were in a state of grace—that their faith had brought the favor of the Holy Spirit on them. The elders were uncomfortable with their own qualifications to judge applicants to their congregation but were persuaded by McNemar to accept his proposals. However, under pressure, McNemar agreed to rescind them before the end of the year. Joseph Darlinton joined the session as a ruling elder in December of 1798 and soon became one of McNemar's most vociferous opponents.[4]

Just two months after his ordination, McNemar sat on a committee at Cane Ridge on October 2, 1798, to examine Barton Stone on languages, sciences, church history, and church government. Stone delivered a sermon on Romans 8:15, passed his examinations, and was ordained two days later.[5] In his autobiography, written many years later, Stone reflected on this moment as "almost the beginning of sorrows." In his heart he knew that he did not agree with the Presbyterian Confession of Faith or the doctrines of election, reprobation, or predestination. Just before his ordination ceremony, he took presiding ministers Robert Marshall and James Blythe aside and revealed his doubts pertaining to church doctrine. According to Stone, Marshall and Blythe prevailed on him to agree to receive the Confession of Faith, to which Stone assented, but only "as far as I see it consistent with the word of God." Stone repeated this sentiment before the assembled public when asked the same question during the ceremony.[6] The dangerous seeds of doctrinal and scriptural interpretation had been planted at Stone's ordination. One wonders how much of Stone's

Figure 3.1. Barton Warren Stone as he appeared later in life.

sentiment Richard McNemar privately shared at the time. Unbeknownst to all, Stone's ordination was to be the last meeting of the Transylvania Presbytery in its original form.

Back at Cabin Creek, tensions continued to mount within McNemar's own congregation. Captain Wilson, an early proponent of McNemar, soon found that he took issue with ideas coming from the pulpit. Early on, McNemar's variance from orthodoxy was subtle enough to preclude public charges of heresy. Nonetheless, Wilson met privately with ruling elder Robert Robb and urged him to caution McNemar. McNemar reportedly "acknowledged his imperfections and Errors, but pleaded in excuse, that they were Errors in Language, and not of the head nor heart, That he believed firmly in the Doctrines of the Presbyterian Church, and did not deign to advance any other—However as he frequently repeated these blunders (as he called them) Jealousys were frequently aroused in the breasts of the above mentioned Persons." Prophetically, Wilson told others that he believed that McNemar would one day "rend the congregation." Wilson's death on September 23, 1800, saved him from witnessing the fulfillment of his fears.[7]

In 1799, the Virginia Synod agreed to the Transylvania Presbytery's request to be subdivided. In Lexington, Kentucky, on March 27, the synod was divided into three smaller presbyteries to more efficiently meet the demands of Kentucky's growing population. The names originally proposed to the synod of Virginia were not used. Instead, the new entities were established as follows: the Transylvania Presbytery, which encompassed central Kentucky west of the Kentucky River and south to the Cumberland River; the West Lexington Presbytery, whose territory lay east of the Kentucky River; and the Washington Presbytery, organized to minister north and east of the Licking River and across the Ohio River into south-central and western Ohio.[8] All three presbyteries were still under the auspices of the synod of Virginia. Richard McNemar found himself a member of the new Washington Presbytery.

The newly formed Washington Presbytery first met at Johnston's Fork Meetinghouse on the main fork of the Licking River, about four miles south of May's Lick, Kentucky, on April 9, 1799. Ministers present at the meeting were McNemar, John Dunlavy, John P. Campbell, and John E. Finley. On the second day of the meeting, McNemar presented a request from the Eagle Creek, Ohio, congregation to be taken under the care of the Washington Presbytery and supplied with preaching. John Dunlavy also secured dismissal from his care of the congregation at Lee's Creek near Washington, Kentucky. The third day of the meeting was momentous for McNemar. He was chosen by his colleagues to represent them the following month at the General Assembly of the Presbyterian Church at Winchester, Virginia. McNemar's selection for this prestigious task shows that he was clearly esteemed and trusted by his fellow ministers. McNemar was charged with the important and sensitive job of requesting that the three new presbyteries—Transylvania, West Lexington, and Washington—be organized into their own synod. The ministers of the Washington Presbytery felt "well convinced that in our remote situation & embarrassed circumstances a proper & uniform attention to order cannot otherwise be preserved." In light of subsequent events, it is ironic that this request for relative independence from the church hierarchy was prompted by a concern for maintaining order. The meeting closed with McNemar being assigned to preach at the Union congregation one-third of his time, and Dunlavy one Sabbath at Springfield (now Springdale), Ohio, and one at Cabin Creek, Kentucky. While McNemar was away in Winchester, his congregation received preaching from Campbell and Finley.[9]

Richard McNemar made his way to Winchester for the General Assembly of the Presbyterian Church. He probably traveled north from Maysville to Wheeling on Zane's Trace and then proceeded south over western Pennsylvania's old Braddock Road leading to Cumberland, Maryland, on his way to Winchester. The General Assembly convened on Thursday, May 16, likely meeting in the town's stone church built in 1788—which is still standing today. Here, McNemar found himself in company with highly educated clergymen from congregations scattered from Albany south to Baltimore, Connecticut west through Pennsylvania, and out to the newly formed presbyteries of the Kentucky and Ohio frontier. Among the business McNemar overheard was a request to the General Assembly that his wife's cousin, the Reverend George Luckey, be joined to New Castle Presbytery. A brief report was given concerning the state of missions on the frontier of western New York. Another speaker made the general observation about the frontier that "there are many thousands of people settled in that extensive tract of country, who are anxious to have the gospel and its ordinances dispensed among them."[10] Throughout the recorded minutes of the meeting, there are no specific mentions of problems on the Kentucky and Ohio frontier.

After a brief recounting of the modest advances of religion on the frontier, ministers were encouraged to continue collecting funds for the furtherance of missionary efforts. Notably, later in the meeting when the general state of the Presbyterian Church was the topic, a call was made for renewed efforts to ensure the "qualifications of candidates for the gospel ministry, with regard both to sincere piety, and to solid and extensive learning." Little did the General Assembly know that among them was a man hugely possessed of both qualities, but who would lead the way in subverting their church in Kentucky and Ohio. Congregations were again encouraged to provide financial support for their ministers so that the clergy could withdraw as much as possible from worldly matters and focus on their ministry. It was even suggested that ministers engage their congregations in formal contracts that could be examined by their respective presbyteries. All of these issues pertinent to the expansion of the Presbyterian Church on the frontier figured in the development of Richard McNemar's life and career during the next six years. The minutes, however, do not record whether or not McNemar carried out his primary duty of lobbying for the creation of an independent synod in Kentucky.[11]

Richard McNemar's fourth child, a son named Elisha, was born at Cabin Creek on September 29, 1799.[12] The Washington Presbytery next convened at Washington, Kentucky, four miles south of Limestone, on October 24, 1799. McNemar reported on his mission to the General Assembly, and the presbytery "expressed their approbation of his faithfulness as commissioner." The body agreed to comply with the General Assembly's request that "members be particular in their attention to Lecturing, Catechizing the vacancies and instituting societies for religious conversation, reading and Prayer." McNemar, Dunlavy, and Elder Edward Harris were appointed as a committee to draft a pastoral letter to congregations lacking a minister, asking them to contribute toward the support of a supply minister.[13]

The Washington Presbytery met again that fall at Orangedale (in Lemon Township, near Lebanon, Ohio), beginning on November 15. Their purpose was to ordain Archibald Steele as a minister for Orangedale's congregation. McNemar presided over the ceremony, and John Dunlavy was to give the ordination sermon. McNemar was pleased to find "a large and respectable congregation." He also met with Presbyterian minister James Kemper at the house of Jonathan Tichner—both men would figure prominently in McNemar's future. The presbytery was less than impressed with Steele's sermon that day, and members of the Orangedale congregation stated that they were unwilling to receive Steele as their minister. Accordingly, his ordination was postponed.[14]

McNemar returned to Cabin Creek, and later described the winter of 1799–1800 as a "trying time." In 1800, he built a new house, planted corn, and emancipated his slave Seely (who he calls Celia), who was eleven.[15] He wrote nothing else about this decision, but it was in keeping with the antislavery views of the Presbyterians.[16] Despite being willed to Jenny Luckey McNemar in her father's estate, Seely was said to have been raised in John Dunlavy's family, where her mother was enslaved. She remained with the McNemar family following her emancipation.[17] Her youth, social connections to the Luckey and McNemar families, and the limited prospects for free black females made this a logical step. The Washington Presbytery next met at Cabin Creek beginning on April 8, and McNemar was chosen as moderator. A call came in from the congregation at Eagle Creek, Ohio, for Dunlavy to come and minister to them. After two days of consideration, Dunlavy accepted the call on April 10. Richard McNemar was appointed to administer the "Lord's Supper," or sacrament of communion, to the congregation at Washington, Kentucky, with John P. Campbell on June 29.[18]

The Washington Presbytery met on October 7, 1800, at the Presbyterian Meetinghouse in Cincinnati. Richard McNemar was absent from the meeting, perhaps due to the impending arrival of his daughter Nancy, born on October 12.[19] At the meeting, a request for preaching was received from "the people on the heads of Turtle Creek and the Little Miami to be known by the name of Bethany," located just west of Lebanon, Ohio.[20] Additionally, the Orangedale settlement sent John Kitchell to renew their request for preaching, Archibald Steele having been refused. Both of these frontier outposts were pivotal to McNemar in years to come.

On October 9, the Presbytery reviewed the request of the Springfield, Ohio, congregation for John W. Brown (also spelled Browne) to remain as their preacher. Brown would become a key figure in McNemar's life. For the moment, the presbytery found

> insuperable objections to taking Mr. Brown under probation for the Gospel Ministry, or even permitting him to exercise the function of a public teacher in their bounds—The Law of the General Assembly designed to regulate their Presbyteries in receiving foreign Clergymen, requiring certain literary accomplishments is indispensable, which Mr. Brown does not possess; and the unfavourable reports, too extensively prevalent, relative to his moral character, leave Presbytery no alternative but to refuse him their countenance,—And while They are disposed to hope the best, as to his personal piety, and willing as they are, to trial him with all possible tenderness, yet finding him destitute of very important qualifications, and that general good report so necessary in an evangelical teacher, think themselves not at liberty to recommend him to the Congregation of Springfield

Brown rebounded from this rather harsh dismissal and started one of the first printing operations in Cincinnati and worked closely with McNemar in the future. Before the meeting adjourned on October 10, John Dunlavy and John P. Campbell were appointed to represent the presbytery at the 1801 General Assembly.[21]

The winter of 1800–1801 saw the advent of religious revival in northern Kentucky at Richard McNemar's Cabin Creek congregation. McNemar used the religious ferment to take bolder public steps against key Calvinist tenets of the Presbyterian Church. In a history of this time written by Cabin Creek Presbyterians in 1810, it was recalled that McNemar stated, "Religion would never flourish till Creeds and Confessions were done away, for he believed that they were detrimental to the life of Religion." Once again, Robert Robb was called on to reason with McNemar and bring him back to orthodoxy. This time, however, McNemar could not be dissuaded from his new insights and beliefs. He shared with Robb that "he believed that before the Millenium would commence, that there would be a new Revelation and addition to the Bible; That the present one was too mysterious and imperfect." This statement would have been utterly shocking to any orthodox Christian of the day, and we must bear in mind that it was attributed to McNemar by embittered former congregants nearly ten years later and after his conversion to Shakerism. In his enthusiasm, however, McNemar probably said something to that effect. Robb issued him "some very solemn warnings and Cautions about his wild notions." The revival at Cabin Creek eventually cooled, and the relationship, however uneasy, between minister and congregation carried on through 1801.[22]

Shortly after this, on March 22, 1801, McNemar wrote to an unidentified fellow minister at Washington, Kentucky. The text of the letter powerfully conveys the scenes of revival at Cabin Creek. Although a sizable amount of Richard McNemar's pre-Shaker writing found its way into print, there are no known surviving letters by him from before mid-1805—this being the sole exception.

> Dear Friend and Brother,
>
> I send this hasty information, that you may early share in the feelings of my heart. The master is come indeed, to our almost hopeless gospel-trodden congregation; to relate the particular operations of his hand at this early stage of the business, I cannot fully. On last Thursday, he singled out a poor youth, in whom he fixed the arrows of conviction with peculiar sharpness.—There was evidently, a breathing of the blessed spirit, and a shaking among the dry bones, with many tears. We met again at candle light; and through the exercises of society, the same hopeful appearances continued: Yesterday we met for sermon, and the Lord was among us, of a truth; my feelings I dare not describe, for fear of the rising idol, self. O! to lose sight of every thing but Jesus Christ, and him crucified! O to arrive at the full assurance of understanding of the mysteries of God, and the Father, and of Christ! of sinners brought back to the favor and love of God; made heirs of God, and joint heirs with Christ; not by works of righteousness, but by the renewing of the holy ghost, and the sprinkling of the blood once shed for sins. O the blindness of men! to make that way crooked, which is strait, and the way to heaven hard; because it is easy. Lift up your hands which hang down, let your fearful heart be strong; cry aloud and spare not, the Lord is at hand, and verily he is a God that heareth prayer. Tell our dear friends in Washington, to arise, and trim their lamps. Behold the bridegroom cometh! My love be with you, and all that love our blessed Lord Jesus, in sincerity. I conclude with the apostle's request—brethren pray for us.[23]

McNemar referenced this important period in a poem he later wrote titled "John the Baptist." The first lines are "The twenty-first of the third month, in eighteen hundred one, the word of God came unto me, that word which came to John."[24]

McNemar's letter was published in William W. Woodward's *Increase of Piety, or the Revival of Religion in the United States of America*. This collection, printed in Philadelphia and Newburyport, Massachusetts, gathered thrilling and detailed reports of revivals from throughout the country. Newspapers and religious magazines were also publishing reports of the revival all along the East Coast. McNemar was featured prominently in an article printed in the *Hartford*

Courant that described the events unfolding in Kentucky. The Shakers likely learned of the religious awakening west of the Appalachians through one of these publications.[25]

The Washington Presbytery's last meeting before all of Kentucky and the Ohio frontier were launched into revival took place at Red Oak (near modern-day Ripley), along the Ohio River on April 14, 1801. McNemar opened the meeting with a sermon from I Timothy 6:12: "Fight the good fight of faith, lay hold on eternal life, whereunto thou art also called, and hast professed a good profession before many witnesses." The next day the presbytery met at the house of John Dunlavy, who by this time was married to Richard McNemar's sister Cassie.[26] Presbyterian historian Robert Davidson has left us this description of Dunlavy, which, despite its clear bias, is worth quoting in full:

> He was the exact opposite of Mr. McNemar, by whose influence, however, he was led astray. He was one of the most gloomy, reserved, and saturnine men that ever lived; his soul seemed to be in harmony with no one lively or social feeling, and the groans which he continually uttered drove away all pleasure in his company. He was above the middle stature, and well proportioned, but of swarthy complexion and dark, forbidding countenance. His manners were coarse, rough, and repulsive. His talents were not above mediocrity; his knowledge was superficial; he was never regarded as a leading or influential man, nor was he a popular preacher. His favorite topics were those of terror, not consolation.[27]

At Dunlavy's house on April 15, the presbytery granted requests from the Springfield and Orangedale, Ohio, congregations for the shared services of Minister John Thompson. Thompson had been a member of the West Lexington Presbytery, but he transferred to the Washington Presbytery at this meeting. As the Kentucky Revival unfolded, he found himself allied with McNemar and Dunlavy in the New Light movement.

The thorny issue of congregations being able to support the living and expenses of their ministers surfaced again—this time between McNemar and his Cabin Creek congregation. Undoubtedly, some in McNemar's congregation were reluctant to support a man whose preaching they considered heretical. The minutes record: "Mr. McNemar requested Presbytery to dissolve the pastoral connexion between him and the Congregation of Cabbin-creek, Mr. Darlinton a Commissioner from the said Congregation represented that on account of their inablity to comply with the Terms of Mr. McNemars settlement they agree to a dissolution of their connexion with their Parson, provided he be continued half his time. Whereupon Presbytery direct that Mr. McNemar employ only half his time in that Congregation, and that they pay him proportionally according to the terms of his settlement." By this time, McNemar had five children and a wife to support. He traveled frequently to supply preaching to congregations lacking ministers and also to attend presbytery meetings. These demands surely made it impossible for McNemar to maintain a farm or pursue a trade to supply income; therefore, his congregation's support was crucial. In light of this, the presbytery ordered members to "be careful to collect mony in their respective Congregations."[28]

Before the meeting closed, the presbytery appointed John P. Campbell, Dunlavy, and McNemar to a committee for the examination of candidates put forth by congregations to be taken on trial for the ministry. The committee would judge if the candidates were "possess'd of sufficient talents, piety, knowledge and prudence."[29] Within a short time, the idea that McNemar and Dunlavy could be judges of orthodoxy was unthinkable. Finally, the presbytery came to the painful decision that Archibald Steele was unsuited for ordination. He was asked to return his license and find another vocation. The immediate effect of rejecting Steele's services was to put further stress on the rest of the presbytery's ministers to supply preaching to congregations on the north side of the Ohio River. The long-term consequence was the weakening of orthodoxy among these congregations, leaving them extremely vulnerable to revivalism—and then Shakerism.

FOUR

REVIVAL

THE FIRST INSTANCES OF THE type of revival meetings that came to characterize the Kentucky Revival occurred in modern-day Logan County in 1797. Minister James McGready took charge of congregations at Red River, Muddy River, and Gasper River in January 1797. He found that a "universal deadness and stupidity" prevailed in these congregations until May of 1797, when "the Lord visited Gasper river congregation with an out-pouring of his spirit," awakening the congregation to a "deep and solemn sense of their sin and danger."[1] Similar scenes unfolded throughout 1798 and 1799, particularly in the Gasper River congregation, now under the care of John Rankin. There, beginning on July 25, 1800, the first large-scale outdoor camp meeting was held. Rankin, McGready, and also the brothers McGee—William, a Presbyterian, and John, a Methodist—were among the preachers who held sway.[2] John Rankin described the scene:

> On Friday morning at an early hour, the people began to assemble in large numbers from every quarter, &, by the usual hour for preaching to commence, there was a multitude collected, unprecedented in this, or any other new country of so sparse a population. The rising ground to the west & south of the meeting house, was literally lined with covered wagons & other appendages—each one furnished with provisions & accommodations, suitable to make them comfortable on the ground during the solemnity. When I came in view of this vast assemblage, with their new and singular preparations which they had made to qualify them to attend & sustain the meeting without interruption to themselves or others, I was astonished!

The meeting raged on for three days, and by Monday evening, worshippers

> began to fall prostrate on all sides, & their cries became piercing & incessant—Heavy groans were heard, and trembling & shaking began to appear throughout the House ... cries of penitential & confessional prayer sounded thro' the assembly—Toward the approach of night, the floor of the Meeting house was literally covered with the prostrate bodies of penitents so that it became necessary to carry a number out of doors & lay them on the grass or garments, if they had them. The night was beautiful; heaven & the elements seemed to smile on the occasion.—Some found peace through the night—others continued tribulation.—All set out for home Tuesday morning.[3]

Richard McNemar's involvement with the revival beyond Cabin Creek began on April 26, 1801, at a sacramental meeting near Flemingsburg, Kentucky, about seventeen miles south of Limestone. In his history, *The Kentucky Revival*, he recalled the striking scene of two nine-year-old girls crying and praying for mercy. Finally, one turned to the other and exclaimed, "O! you little sinner, come to Christ! ... You are not a greater sinner than me! You need not wait another moment."[4] The interaction between these two young girls perfectly encapsulates the revolutionary nature of the revival. What the girls had manifested toward each other was what McNemar identified as the key tenet of the revivalists who became known as New Lights: "That the will of God was made manifest to each individual who honestly sought after it, by an inward light, which shone in the heart. Hence they received the name of *New Lights*."[5] By their actions, these two little girls effectively rejected the Calvinist doctrines of total depravity, unconditional election, and limited atonement as well as the need for a formal written creed or clergy.

These doctrines are worth examining, as their rejection represented a seismic religious and cultural shift, the magnitude of which is hard to fathom in the twenty-first century. Total Depravity was the belief that because of Adam and Eve's fall, all human beings are incapable of choosing to follow God, since they are by nature trapped in sinful self-interest. Unconditional Election meant that God had chosen those who would be saved before the beginning of time. These people were predestined for salvation through Christ, and they could not avert that fate, any more than someone who was not predestined could avoid eternal damnation. Finally, Limited Atonement meant that Christ's crucifixion atoned for only the sins of those already among God's elect and did not have the potential to offer salvation to humanity in general. These doctrines were foundational principles of the Westminster Confession of Faith, which was theological orthodoxy for the Presbyterian Church in America. When McNemar, Dunlavy, and Houston accepted ordination, they explicitly agreed to uphold the Westminster Confession. However, as Barton Stone wrote, "In truth, that book had been gathering dust from the commencement of the excitement."[6] People swept up in the revival were seeking assurance of their salvation—knowledge that the ambiguous doctrines of Calvinist Presbyterianism could not provide.

On May 3, the epicenter of the nascent revival moved to McNemar's Cabin Creek congregation. According to McNemar, it was again a young girl—this time twelve years old—who first cried out in lamentation of her lost state. From there

> a new scene was opened, while some trembled like one in a fit of the ague; wept or cried out, lamenting their distance from God . . . others were employed in praying with them, encouraging them to believe on the Son of God—to venture upon his promise—give up their wicked rebellious heart, just as it was; for God to take it away, and give them a heart of flesh;—singing hymns, and giving thanks to God, for the display of his power, without any regard to former rules of order. At this, some were offended and withdrew from the assembly, determined to oppose it, as a work of the wicked one.

The spiritually hungry people of Cabin Creek held another meeting a few nights later, where they spent the whole night singing, praying, and encouraging each other. Novel physical aspects of the revival were also manifested, such as when one man was "struck down," lying in a seemingly lifeless state for more than an hour. The all-night character of these meetings resulted in the practical expediency of camping on the ground. Thus, at least in northern Kentucky, the camp meeting was born.[7]

The General Assembly met on May 21, 1801, in Philadelphia, unaware of the tumultuous events unfolding at that very moment at Cabin Creek. Despite Dunlavy and Campbell's appointment to represent the Washington Presbytery, their presence is not recorded. Additionally, the minutes fail to mention either the Washington Presbytery or its members. Clearly, however, some information about the first stages of the revival in Logan County had reached the General Assembly. Their *Acts and Proceedings* reflect a cautious embrace of these developments, expressed with full awareness that events were far beyond their control. "From the west the Assembly have received intelligence of the most interesting nature. On the borders of Kentucky and Tennessee, the influences of the Spirit of God seem to have been manifested in a very extraordinary manner. Many circumstances attending this work are unusual: And though it is probable that some irregularities may have taken place; yet, from the information which the Assembly have received, they cannot but exceedingly rejoice in

Figure 4.1. A. Rider, *Camp-meeting*, Kennedy & Lucas Lithography, c1829. A later image of a frontier camp meeting. Library of Congress Prints and Photographs Division, Washington, DC.

the abundant evidence given them that God has visited that people, and poured out his spirit remarkably upon them."[8]

The first camp meeting in northern Kentucky was held at Cabin Creek beginning on May 22. It lasted four days and three nights. Worshippers gathered from Cane Ridge and Concord, Kentucky (Barton Stone's congregations), and Eagle Creek, Ohio (John Dunlavy's congregation). Of course, those among Richard McNemar's followers sympathetic to the revival also attended. On the third night, a remarkable phenomenon occurred: so many people were spiritually struck down that "to prevent their being trodden under foot by the multitude, they were collected together and laid out in order, on two squares of the meeting-house; which, like so many dead corpses, covered a considerable part of the floor." Another five-day camp meeting was held at the end of May at Stone's Concord church. McNemar estimated nearly four thousand people attended from all classes, sexes, and races. The following week, events moved across the Ohio River to Dunlavy's Eagle Creek church for four more days of powerful preaching and worship.[9] Practically every week, another revival meeting was held in northern and central Kentucky.

Figure 4.2. The Cane Ridge Meeting House, photographed in 1934 before its enclosure in a larger protective structure. Historic American Buildings Survey, HABS KY,9-CANRI,1—2, Library of Congress Prints and Photographs Division, Washington, DC.

In Lexington, on June 28–29, 1801, the Reverend John Lyle attended the camp meeting and witnessed Malcham Worley and many others falling to the ground in agony for sinners.[10] Virginia-born Lyle kept a diary from 1801 through 1803; it is one of the most important contemporary sources about the Kentucky Revival. It offers candid portraits of many of the camp meetings, ministers, and all the extravagances associated with the revival. Lyle witnessed Richard McNemar preach on multiple occasions and also had the opportunity to confront him personally about some of his perceived excesses.

The Washington Presbytery had appointed Richard McNemar to preach on August 9, 1801, at a Mr. Horn's on Brush Creek (probably in modern-day Green County, Kentucky).[11] He did not fulfill this assignment. Instead, he joined Matthew Houston, Barton Stone, and a host of other ministers at the epochal camp meeting at Cane Ridge, which began on August 6. Stone later wrote, "The roads were literally crowded with wagons, carriages, horsemen, and footmen, moving to the solemn camp. The sight was affecting. It was judged, by military men on the ground, that there were between twenty and thirty thousand collected." This meeting was unique, not just for the numbers gathered but also for the seven days of continuous, simultaneous preaching from Presbyterians, Methodists, and Baptists. For a glorious moment, it seemed that doctrinal hairsplitting was transcended and humankind could together enjoy salvation through Jesus Christ. The meeting was attended with a tremendous variety of physical exercises, descriptions of which thrilled newspaper and magazine readers throughout the country. As previously, many individuals were struck down, but added to this were physical manifestations of the spirit, including the jerks, the barking exercise, the dancing exercise, the laughing exercise, the running exercise, and the singing exercise.[12]

John Lyle, not entirely sympathetic to the revival, witnessed McNemar preach on Saturday, August 8. In his diary he commented:

> In the afternoon Mr. McNamar preached on Rom. I am not ashamed of the gospel of Christ &c. He preached us a discourse unintelligible to myself & others with whom I conversed about it but it contain'd the substance of what Mr. Stone & he call the true new gospel which (say they) none preach but ourselves. He spoke of the gospel bringing a pardon with it & talks the design of it is to bring persons to self despair at once.... Mr. McNamara is a weak man but lively in desultory exhortation & speaks & sings with all his powers & in address much like a Methodist. He sometimes rises to ecstatic joy, it smiles through his face. His people, numbers of them, have fallen out with him because of his new gospel & its effects.... Saturday evening the people crowded the meeting house. Some fell down. There was the greatest sense of confusion I ever saw in such a place & the air very warm indeed. I went twice to talk to the distress'd but it was so hot I could do nothing. I saw McNama here praying when the womans voice for whom he pray'd appear'd to be the highest & many others singing praying and groaning all around some rejoicing and some crying for mercy.

It should be noted that Lyle compared McNemar to a Methodist in his enthusiasm.

Prophetically, Lyle commented about this scene: "I expect the conduct of these hot headed men & the effect of their doctrine will separate the Church of Christ & quench the revival."[13] The gospel that Lyle accused McNemar and Stone of preaching was epitomized eloquently by Stone, who wrote that during the revival "the people appeared as just awakened from the sleep of ages—they seemed to see for the first time that they were responsible beings, and that a refusal to use the means appointed, was a damning sin." This individual responsibility for one's own salvation, or free will, found its ultimate expression in Shakerism for McNemar, Dunlavy, and many other participants in the revival.[14]

Lyle wandered the campground for the rest of the evening, speaking with Matthew Houston and others. He finally ran into McNemar, who told Lyle that "he was tired of the way matters were going on &c. & readily agreed to have a meeting at the tent (it was sometime after dark) Mr. Houston, myself & McNamara each deliver'd a discourse. Houston on the easy yoke &c. I on mans depravity & recovery by the spirit applying the benefits of Christ's redemption. McNamara exhorted but had near forgot his new gospel." Lyle left the scene and found a place to take a nap. He woke before dawn to find Houston still preaching and McNemar exhorting the people "not to oppose but to come & taste the love of God."[15]

Writing many years later, McNemar reflected on the excitement of these times as a beginning, but by no means an end. "In the early stage of that work I received a renewed manifestation of the power of God similar to what I had felt in my first conversion, & altho I had never for one moment doubted the truth of revelation or the quality of my experience from the period of my first light yet I found to my great sorrow that as yet I remained far short of salvation which I now set out to pursue at the risk of every thing dear on earth."[16] Simultaneous to events at Cane Ridge, the Washington Presbytery held a special meeting at Bethany, near Lebanon in Ohio, on August 5. Richard McNemar was, of course, absent. Providentially, the meeting opened with a sermon by John Thompson on Revelation 3:20: "Behold, I stand at the door, and knock: if any man hear my voice, and open the door, I will come in to him, and will sup with him, and he with me."[17]

Two weeks later, Lyle traveled to Paris, Kentucky, where Minister Samuel Rannels was holding a sacramental meeting. There, on Saturday afternoon, August 22, Lyle again witnessed McNemar's preaching. He described it as "a strange contradictory jumble of a discourse with a number of good expressions here & there in it. Some people were attentive and seem'd pleas'd but others inattentive & some displeas'd." The preaching continued all afternoon and into the evening. McNemar delivered the last sermon of the night, which shocked Lyle. "He stamp't & roar'd Hell & Damnation loudly but still no crying out or falling that I knew of. I talk'd to Mr. McNamara about these violences I do not know what effect it will have. He acknowledg'd that stamping slaping &c. were no gospel institution & as we had no promise of a blessing to attend them & as they were a cause of offense & stumbling to many we had better let them alone." Lyle also witnessed the underbelly of these frontier gatherings, including "six men and one strumpet under the [preaching] stand" and "a man & a woman in the cornfield in the act of adultery."[18]

The mix of humanity and spectrum of behaviors unleashed by the revival was truly astonishing. The revival afforded all comers unprecedented liberty of expression. McNemar saw children "eight or ten years old, raised upon the shoulders or held up in the arms of some one, in the midst of vast multitudes, [who] would speak in a manner so marvellous and astonishing, that persons of the most rugged passions would dissolve into tears." He wrote of seeing "a bold Kentuckian (undaunted by the horrors of war) turn pale and tremble at the reproof of a weak woman, a little boy, or a mean African." The revival was a great leveling work among Christians of different races, genders, and classes in Kentucky. As historian Sam Haselby has observed, men such as the Methodist Francis Asbury and McNemar "never indicated that class, nationality or colour prescribed any religious obligation to subservience or rule, obedience or command. For them, Christianity was a greater and more radical force than the revolutionary republicanism of secular intellectuals."[19] McNemar believed New Lights—as some revivalists came to be known—"intended to tear down and remove the rubbish of old systems, and therefore the subjects of it, had practically and experimentally, to handle and prove the corrupt materials of the whole fabric." Quite simply, salvation was freely available henceforth to all who would believe in Christ.[20]

McNemar "set out for redbanks" later that August.[21] Red Banks was the original name for modern Henderson, Kentucky. As early as January 1801, a correspondent writing from Cane Ridge noted that the revival that had begun in Logan County had reached the settlement.[22] McNemar probably traveled there to participate in revival meetings and meet like-minded ministers. The Washington Presbytery met on October 9 at Eagle Creek, Ohio. McNemar was still absent, but Ohio congregations eagerly called for preaching from him and John Thompson. The Springfield congregation called for two-thirds of Thompson's time, while the Hamilton congregation called for the other third. The desperate congregation at Turtle Creek asked for preaching from whoever was available, and warned that if the Washington Presbytery could not meet their needs, they would seek permission to apply to another presbytery. Acknowledging their lack of preachers, the presbytery granted permission for Turtle Creek to look elsewhere. Tellingly, the Bethany congregation, near Turtle Creek, called "for as much of Mr. M'Nemar's time as can be granted."[23]

David Spinning, a transplanted New Jerseyan living near Lebanon, Ohio, later recorded his memories of the start of the revival in Ohio. Spinning learned Latin and Greek from Minister John Thompson and Francis Dunlavy (John Dunlavy's brother). In mid-1801, he accompanied Thompson to a large revival meeting at Blue Springs, Kentucky. Greatly affected, he carried the revival spirit back to Ohio, stoking its flames among his neighbors, who then held meetings without a preacher. These people eagerly called for Richard McNemar, who first visited them late in the fall of 1801. Toward the end of McNemar's first visit, after several days of preaching with no visible effect, a final meeting was held at Francis Bedle's on the eve of McNemar's departure.

> After we had sung and prayed for some time, Richard proposed to pray & dropped on his knees & many others done the same. He prayed very earnestly & while thus engaged the first movement of extraordinary exercise began in the state of Ohio. Aged Polly Bedele was the first that fell under the stroke of power. Some were panic struck and strove to get out of the house, but the room was so full it was difficult for them to make their escape. Some were praying, some exhorting, some had lost the use of themselves, & the meeting continued till a late hour. Some went home, joyfully praising God, while some were sober & others vexed. Richard went home and we had no preacher.[24]

McNemar's personal charisma sparked the same chain reaction of revivalism—manifested physically—at Turtle Creek that it had at Cabin Creek. He left in his wake a hopeful, optimistic multitude yearning for more of these experiences. He also left bitter resentment among those opposed to the revival. Some even accused McNemar of using magical powders to bewitch the people. Opposing views existed within families and between husbands and wives. The people of Turtle Creek did not know it, but they were beginning a long journey that would culminate in life decisions few of them could imagine.[25]

During the fall of 1801, McNemar led the people of Cabin Creek further into revival. According to the "History of Cabin Creek Church," written in 1810, it was at this time that he began to depart unabashedly from Calvinist ideas and "to reprobate them with a great deal of virulence." McNemar asserted that "a sinner could believe in Christ as Easy as disbelieve in him, without any influence of the Spirit of God disposing him thereto." He believed that faith came through acceptance of the spirit of Christ but was not given or withheld by God. He proclaimed "faith consisted in the sinner persuading himself assuredly that Christ died for him in particular . . . and that the moment that a Sinner Believes assuredly that his sins are pardoned that very moment they are pardoned." Most shockingly, he divined the will of God by claiming, "God had done all that he could or would do for the Sinner untill he believed. That the Doctrine of Election was a damnable doctrine hatched in hell!"[26]

Robert Robb again convened the elders to remonstrate with McNemar, but McNemar had converted Elder Andrew Henderson to his ideas. McNemar also had a sizeable band of adherents within the congregation. From this position of strength, he treated the ecclesiastical session with "ridicule and contempt."

Simultaneously, he began to preach with a "great deal of zeal, animation, vociferation and such gestures of Body as were calculated to inflame the passions of the hearers; The minds of the People got adjitated and a bodily exercise Commenced among them." Even the Cabin Creek elders saw some positive and faith-affirming qualities in the physical manifestations stoked by McNemar—provided the ecstatic worship affirmed Calvinist dogma. At this point, the congregation split into three factions: revivalist followers of McNemar and his ideas, revivalists who wanted to reconcile with Calvinism, and orthodox Calvinists who categorically rejected any enthusiasm or physical manifestations in worship. The effect was that even revivalists who were inclined toward Calvinism were pushed into McNemar's camp by the conservative faction's intolerance. Thus, McNemar's party grew into the majority, and the elders were powerless to counteract it.[27]

Exercising his power, McNemar called for the election of new ruling elders. His faction voted in three new candidates, and a day was set for their ordination. In the end, however, Robb, Robinson, and Darlinton were able to hold on to their authority and steadily consolidated an opposition party. They consulted Rev. John P. Campbell (who had presided over McNemar's ordination only three years prior), for advice on how to resolve the conflict. Campbell labored unsuccessfully with McNemar to moderate his views. Finally, the elders called for a weekday meeting of the congregation at which McNemar's conduct and theology were denounced and following which they "vindicated the Calvinistick scheme." This public shaming temporarily checked McNemar's progress.[28] A last attempt was made, with the help of John Dunlavy and two of his elders, to get McNemar to agree to uphold the Westminster Confession and Presbyterian Church principles. McNemar defiantly said he "would be bound by no system, but the Bible; and that he believed that systems were detrimental to the life and power or religion."[29] Faced with this rebellion, the only step available to the elders was to formally complain about McNemar to the Washington Presbytery.

On November 11, 1801, the Washington Presbytery convened at Springfield, Ohio. McNemar attended for the first time since April 1801, when the Cabin Creek congregation's inability to provide him financial support was exposed. This time, the presbytery was presented with a letter from Cabin Creek elders "containing certain charges respecting doctrines against the Revd. R. M Nemar."[30] The Cabin Creek congregation's complaint survives, in part, because McNemar himself later published it. Elders Joseph Darlinton, Robert Robb, and Robert Robinson informed the presbytery of their "unhappy situation" with McNemar and sought "counsel and interference." They recounted the past year's trials with McNemar, including attempts at reconciliation, mediation, and their ultimate decision to denounce McNemar in a special meeting of the congregation.[31]

The Cabin Creek elders also submitted to the presbytery a document explicating six points on which McNemar deviated from orthodoxy. These provide a direct insight into the theological smelting furnace that was the revival.

1. He reprobated the idea of sinners attempting to pray, or being exhorted thereto, before they were believers in Christ.
2. He has condemned those, who urge, that convictions are necessary, or that prayer is proper in the sinner.
3. He has expressly declared, at several times, that Christ has purchased salvation for all the human race, without distinction.
4. He has expressly declared, that a sinner has power to believe in Christ at any time.
5. That a sinner has as much power to act faith, as to act unbelief; and reprobated every idea, in contradiction thereto, held by persons of a contrary opinion.
6. He has expressly said, that faith consisted in the creature's persuading himself assuredly, that Christ died for him in particular: that doubting and examining into evidences of faith, were inconsistent with, and contrary to the nature of Faith: and in order to establish these sentiments, he explained away these words, *Faith is the Gift of God*, by saying it was Christ Jesus, the object of faith was there meant, and not faith itself; and also these words, *No man can come unto me, except the Father who hath sent me, draw him*, by saying that the drawing there meant, was Christ offered in the Gospel; and that the Father knew no other drawing, or higher power, than holding up his Son in the Gospel.[32]

John Dunlavy arrived the next morning to deliver an ordination sermon for John Thompson. The theme suited the times, being derived from 2 Peter 1:19: "We have also a more sure word of prophecy; whereunto ye do well that ye take heed, as unto a light that shineth in a dark place, until the day dawn, and the day star arise in your hearts." Fortunately for McNemar, the presbytery decided to table the complaint from Cabin Creek since no one from the congregation was present to substantiate the charges.[33] Finding himself in the clear, at least for the moment, McNemar asked for liberty to comment on the charges made against him. He acceded to the first charge, citing Romans 10:14: "How then shall they call on him in whom they have not believed?" To the second, he answered that no more conviction was needed than that which was presented in the word of God. He acknowledged the third charge of regarding Christ as a universal savior. He also affirmed his belief (reflected in the fourth charge) that a sinner could hear the word of God at any time, citing Romans 10:17: "So then faith cometh by hearing, and hearing by the word of God." On the fifth charge, he defended each individual's capacity to believe or disbelieve based on the evidence. In support of this, he cited 1 John 5:9: "If we receive the witness of men, the witness of God is greater: for this is the witness of God which he hath testified of his Son." The only portion of the Cabin Creek charges he flatly refuted was the first part of the sixth charge, wherein faith was attained by self-persuasion that Christ had died for him in particular. On the second part of charge six, McNemar strongly disavowed the idea of doubting God and looking inwardly for the foundation of faith. He observed that self-examination should reveal the fruits of faith, not the foundation. Finally, with a touch of bravado, in response to the final charge of his "explaining away" (reinterpreting) scripture, he said, "If that was explaining them away, he had done it."[34] By the close of the meeting, McNemar had dodged his first brush with charges of heresy. He had addressed his congregation's charges with intelligence, flair, and even humor, and got off without even a warning. These charges, however, were the first hint of serious troubles awaiting McNemar, and other New Light ministers, at the hands of orthodox congregants and Presbyterian Church authorities.

McNemar returned to his wife and family at Cabin Creek for the winter of 1801–1802, during which time revivalism continued to flourish in the congregation. Perhaps chastened by his narrow escape, McNemar extended an olive branch to the Cabin Creek elders. He proposed a special session to examine the controversy. Accordingly, Robert E. Finley and an elder named Sebastian Shrofe met with the parties. McNemar claimed the elders had "misunderstood him and that he never had Reached the Doctrines that they had charged him with." However, the elders were not persuaded of this disingenuous argument. McNemar earnestly declared his belief in the principles of the Westminster Confession, and the elders, eager for resolution and reconciliation, agreed to retain his ministerial services. A certificate to that effect was signed on March 6, 1802, by McNemar and Elders Darlinton, Robb, and Robinson. "Whereas a difference has Existed for some time between the Reverend Richard McNemar of the one part and Joseph Darlinton, Robert Robb, and Robert Robinson, ruling Elders of the congregation of Cabin Creek of the other part upon certain points of doctrine which has threatened much Evil to that branch of the Church, We having met and Entered into a free and full conversation on the subjects in controversy do now mutually agree to pass over all past altercations, and cordially unite in Communion for the future." This optimistic proclamation was read to the congregation the following Sunday. The very next week, however, Richard McNemar and his family removed to Ohio in a "very precipitant manner."[35]

It was fortunate for all parties that McNemar was called to relocate and take charge of the congregation at Turtle Creek, Ohio.[36] At the meeting of the Washington Presbytery at Washington, Kentucky, beginning on April 13, McNemar was appointed to supply half of his time to Turtle Creek and one-quarter to Bethany, both congregations near Lebanon, Ohio. At this same meeting, the presbytery also received momentous news that the Virginia Synod had approved the union of the West Lexington, Transylvania, and Washington Presbyteries into one synod. This merger eased bureaucratic logistics and put this group of ministers—who entered the throes of revivalism together—locally in charge of deciding theological controversies and resolving difficulties between ministers and congregations.

McNemar described the central role that the Turtle Creek church played in the religious life of New Lights in southwestern Ohio.

> A call was presented to M'Namar for the whole of his time signed by 60 responsible and calculating an equal number of women the whole number of members composing the church at [that] time was equal to the number of the disciples at Jerusalem by which the first gospel church was founded, but taking the whole number of adults and minors who were united under one Ministry they must have amounted to several hundreds as there were four respectable societies united of which Turtle Creek was the center, to wit on the East Bethany two miles above Lebanon, Salem, West about two miles from Monroe and Orangedale about 9 miles N.W. and Beula 20 miles N. East from the center. Here were five presbyterian societies combined Each having a meeting to which we might add Clear Creek congregation about six miles north all of whom held relation to Turtle Creek as the foundation and where they semiannually had a general convention and solemn communion.[37]

It is worth examining the frontier settlement of Turtle Creek in some detail, as it was the scene of McNemar's final separation from his fellow Presbyterian and New Light ministers and conversion to Shakerism. Turtle Creek, the watercourse, originates in the center of Warren County. It flows through the town of Lebanon and continues southeasterly until meeting the Little Miami River. John Dunlavy's brother Francis opened a school on the north bank of the creek, just west of Lebanon, in 1798. In 1799, one Henry Taylor built a mill along the creek.[38]

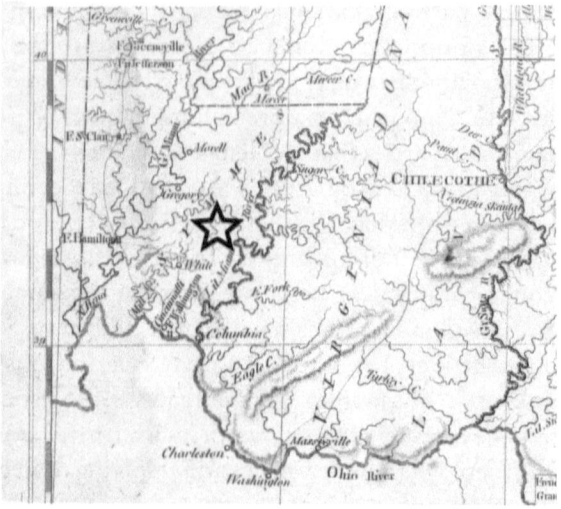

Figure 4.3. Southwestern Ohio, where Bedle's Station was established near Turtle Creek in 1795 (indicated by the black star). Arrowsmith and Lewis, *Ohio*, (detail) [Boston: Thomas & Andrews, 1805]. Library of Congress Geography and Map Division, Washington, DC.

Five miles west of Lebanon and two miles south of where Shakers eventually settled Union Village was Bedle's Station. Settled by New Jerseyan William Bedle (also spelled Beedle and Beadle) in 1795, it was probably the county's first permanent white settlement. Bedle purchased section 28, comprising 640 acres of land, in township four of the third (or military) range, for $250. He moved there with his wife, Esther, son James, and daughters Susanna, Lydia, Phebe, and Mary. All the Bedle children were married, and there were numerous grandchildren at the settlement. According to early Ohio historian Henry Howe, Bedle "built a block-house as a protection against the Indians.... Here several families lived in much simplicity, the clothing of the children being made chiefly out of dressed deerskin, some of the larger girls being clad in buckskin petticoats and short gowns."[39] All were members of the Turtle Creek Presbyterian congregation, which first requested preaching from Transylvania Presbytery in 1797.[40] Their church was erected in 1789 and stood just north of Bedle's Station in section 29. James Kemper served as its first minister.[41]

As a child, Anthony H. Dunlevy (son of Francis and nephew of John) heard Richard McNemar preach many times. He recalled winter meetings of the

Turtle Creek congregation where overflow attendees were forced to stand outside around log fires to stay warm. Dunlevy described McNemar as "a man of singular talent and as a preacher had great power over his congregation. At the old meeting house, in summer, meetings were usually held in a grove and on sacramental occasions I have seen congregations of two thousand... gathered around the stand. McNemar would command the closest attention of the whole mass of people, often swaying the multitude as if by magic."[42]

Turtle Creek congregation was generally pleased with McNemar's preaching, New Light tenets and all. However, some objected to his unorthodox teachings, particularly Jonathan Tichner. The trouble with Tichner began in October 1802, when, without warning, he complained about McNemar to fellow worshippers at a service. Others prevailed on Tichner to stop his divisive talk and bring specific doctrinal objections to the attention of the Washington Presbytery. Seemingly mollified, Tichner disavowed any intention of going to the presbytery.[43]

Richard McNemar was a hot topic at the October 6, 1802, meeting of the Washington Presbytery at Cincinnati. Elder Francis Bedle renewed the Turtle Creek congregation's call for half of McNemar's ministerial labors.[44] The following day, McNemar's Cabin Creek adherents presented a statement of their beliefs to the presbytery and demanded redress for grievances. After McNemar departed for Ohio, the Reverend Stephen Bovel was sent to Cabin Creek. However, McNemar's followers refused to attend unless Bovel preached ideas they wanted to hear. Consequently, Bovel's tenure was short. Elder Robert Robb then took it on himself to vociferously and proactively defend the Westminster Confession, further alienating what was now known as the "newlight" party. In response, the New Lights prepared a detailed statement of their beliefs and boldly presented it to the Washington Presbytery on October 7.

The Cabin Creek New Lights affirmed their belief in one eternal God: a triune Godhead comprising Father, Son, and Holy Ghost; that God created all things (except sin), and that man was created in his image. They asserted Adam fell by his own free will and deserved eternal fire, but God in his mercy allowed him to populate the earth. God then sent his son Jesus Christ, who "compleatly satisfy'd the law and Justice of God for Mankind." As creatures of free will (like Adam), they radically proclaimed they could either believe—or disbelieve—the above, provocatively stating, "We believe that there is no necessity of any new faculty of Soul in order to our believing what Christ Jesus the Lord has done for us Rebels, for with the heart man believeth unto Righteousness and with the mouth Confession is made unto Salvation: He that believeth on the son hath life." The thirty-seven signatories to this document (who apparently included some minors) accused Elder Robert Robb of "raising cavils against

Richard McNemar" and stated, "there are more Errors in the [Cabin Creek] church then in the Church of Rome." Finally, they accused Robb of having McNemar sent away.[45] Unfortunately, these well-intentioned efforts backfired on McNemar, as, unbeknownst to him, additional accusations of heresy were forthcoming.

McNemar later claimed that on the last day of the meeting, Sunday, October 10, his colleagues used a procedural trick to facilitate the sentry of a formal admonition against him into the minutes. That day, either Moses Miller or Joseph Reeder (elders in James Kemper's Cincinnati congregation) accused McNemar (by hearsay) of propagating false doctrine. Tichner was present, perhaps by design, and Miller or Reeder named him as an eyewitness to such proceedings. McNemar verbally objected to this ambush, insisting charges should be presented to the presbytery in writing. In light of what happened, McNemar came to believe that Kemper, the first minister at Turtle Creek and McNemar's colleague in the Washington Presbytery, had poisoned Tichner's mind against the revival.[46] Minister Matthew Wallace's absence due to illness meant the assembly lacked a voting quorum. Kemper called for the body to adjourn and reconvene at Wallace's house to ensure a quorum. McNemar was asked to leave Wallace's house while the presbytery deliberated a written censure of him, authored by Kemper. Ironically, despite the circumstances, McNemar was sent to preach in the Cincinnati meetinghouse that afternoon.

After deliberation, the written indictment of McNemar was entered into the minutes. His fellow ministers' findings show how serious the situation had become.

> Whereas it has been reported for more than a year past that the Revd. Richard McNemar held tenets hostile to the standards of the Presbyterian Church and subversive of the Fundamental doctrines contained in the sacred scriptures and whereas these reports have daily become more clamorous notwithstanding Mr. McNemar has from time to time been warned of these things both privately and more publickly both by private persons and the members of Presbytery separately and jointly, Therefore the Presbytery have thought it necessary to enter into a more particular and close examination of Mr. McNemar on the doctrines of particular election, human depravity the atonement and the nature of faith upon which examination had it is the Opinion of this Presbytery that Mr. McNemar holds these doctrines in a sense specifically and essentially different from that sense in which Calvinists generally believe them and that his ideas on these subjects are strictly Arminian tho' clothed in such expressions and handed out in such a manner as to keep the Body of the people in the dark and lead them

insensibly into arminian principles which are dangerous to the souls of men and hostile to the interests of all true religion.

Ordered that a copy of this minute be forwarded by the stated Clerk as early as may be to the churches under our care.

McNemar returned from preaching about sunset to find he had been tried in absentia. Questioning the legality of the proceedings, he insisted that the text inaccurately reflected his beliefs. He requested that the case be referred to the Kentucky Synod for review. In response, the ministers backpedaled, assuring him that he was not under formal censure, even though they had ordered the indictment to be distributed throughout the Washington Presbytery. McNemar hesitated to bring the matter to the synod's attention himself, as it required him to attack his own presbytery. Thus, matters were left at a very uneasy standstill.[47]

Incredibly, following McNemar's censure, he was given further preaching assignments, spending "one half of his time at Turtle Creek . . . two sabbaths at Orange dale two at clear creek two at Beulah and one at the forks of Mad River the rest at discretion." This strange decision indicates how much the Turtle Creek congregation approved of McNemar and his beliefs. It also, however, demonstrates how desperate the Washington Presbytery was for clergy. Despite more than a year's worth of complaints, McNemar was still sent to preach—even after his fellow ministers declared him "hostile to the interests of all true religion."[48]

The Kentucky Synod met for the first time at Lexington the next week, on October 14. McNemar, Kemper, and John Thompson attended as representatives of the Washington Presbytery. Others present were Matthew Houston of the Transylvania Presbytery and Elder Malcham Worley of the West Lexington Presbytery. McNemar waited uneasily to see if the charges against him would be raised. To his relief, they were not, but this was only delaying the inevitable.[49]

The term "Arminian" was increasingly used to describe McNemar's theological deviations, as perceived by the Presbyterian Church. Theologian Jacobus Arminius first posited these notions, stressing free will contrary to Calvinism, around 1600. His followers were called Arminians (as opposed to Calvinists, who stressed predestination) and were deemed heretics. Arminians believed Christ's death offered atonement to all people, provided they sought salvation through faith. Additionally, they believed humans have free will to voluntarily embrace faith in Jesus and that by that faith, salvation is ensured. The idea that a believer could find assurance of their salvation through faith threatened to undermine the hierarchy of any organized church. Orthodox Presbyterian clergy considered these beliefs extremely dangerous; to their horror, McNemar, Stone, Houston, Thompson, and other ministers throughout Kentucky and Ohio openly promulgated them.

By the spring of 1803, the controversy surrounding Richard McNemar came to a head. When the Washington Presbytery convened on April 6 at Springfield, Ohio, the session opened with a renewed call by the Turtle Creek congregation for McNemar's services. The next day, Robert Robb, representing the orthodox faction of the Cabin Creek congregation, asked again for the services of Rev. Bovel, who wisely refused. Cabin Creek further asked the presbytery to send a special delegation to "assist in further satisfying the minds of the people with regard to any difficulties which may exist as to the members of Session or any of them." Troubles in McNemar's old congregation had not abated with his departure. Fittingly, the next item of business was the presentation of a petition from congregations at Beulah, Turtle Creek, Clear Creek, Bethany, Hopewell, Duck Creek, and Cincinnati, requesting that McNemar and John Thompson be reexamined "on the fundamental doctrines of religion or on what the Petitioners call Free will or Armenian doctrines." Signed by fourteen members of the various congregations, including Jonathan Tichner, it was the second instance in three years that members of McNemar's own congregation lodged an official complaint with the presbytery. The first signatory was William Lamme, and the presbytery and the Kentucky Synod came to refer to the document as "Lamme's Petition." A majority of ministers present were sympathetic to McNemar and voted to ignore the petition, writing that it was "improper to go into the examination of Mr McNamar and Mr Thompson on the prayer of said peti[ti]oners, as being out of order." They later defended this position by saying that it would have required them to examine themselves with respect to doctrine. For McNemar and his cohorts, the powerful events attending the Lord's Supper (communion) administered at the presbytery's meeting were "sufficient evidence that our ministrations in the gospel were not injurious to the souls of men; and we still hoped that those of the contrary part would desist, lest haply they should be found *fighting against God*."⁵⁰

On the last day of the meeting, April 11, the presbytery granted Turtle Creek's call for McNemar's preaching and also assigned him to supply congregations at Clear Creek and Forks of Mad River and to hold a sacramental meeting with John Thompson at Orangedale on June 12. To end the meeting, the orthodox faction, by then a minority consisting of Kemper, Wallace, and elders Joseph Reeder and Stephen Wheeler, recorded a formal protest in the minutes about the handling of Lamme's Petition. Their congregants, they claimed, "cannot be deprived of the right of proposing to Presby for discussion such difficulties respecting the doctrines taught them . . . Mr. McNamar's principles in particular now stand condemned by the last meeting of Presby as Armenian." Logically, this contingent also protested against giving McNemar further preaching assignments, particularly his continuance at Turtle Creek. They asserted that the presbytery "refuses to pay any attention to Mr. McNamar's principles or doctrines," despite repeated cause for concern. With that, the meeting closed. McNemar later asserted that his colleagues generally avoided him in a passive-aggressive way and tried to use bureaucratic methods to silence him (such as the censure given while he was absent in Cincinnati). McNemar boldly opined that such measures were "better adapted to affright the dupe of a civil establishment, than to fix a mind at liberty to think for itself."[51]

Secure in his acceptance at Turtle Creek, McNemar purchased a homestead on June 1, 1803, from Jonathan Dayton, one of a consortium of land speculators who purchased "Miami Lands" from John Cleves Symmes (who would later lobby Congress to fund an expedition to journey to the center of the earth). McNemar paid $400 for 160 acres: one-quarter of section twenty-four of the fourth township of the third (or military) range. Located northeast of the Turtle Creek meetinghouse, and thirty miles north of Cincinnati along a main north-south road, this site ideally suited McNemar's ministerial duties and travels. By the summer of 1803, McNemar's family comprised his wife, Jennie, and six children: Benjamin, James, Vincy, Elisha, Nancy, and the newest addition, Betsy, who was born on February 27 of that year. The McNemars' emancipated slave Seely (or Celia) was still living with the family. Shortly after taking possession of the acreage, McNemar probably began construction of his home, appearing on early maps as a double pen, or "dogtrot" style, log house. This was a common form developed in Georgia, North Carolina, and Tennessee. Settlers brought it into Kentucky and Ohio after the Revolutionary War. The form was developed due to the size limitations of available logs. Joining, or splicing, two logs together made long walls unstable. Instead, two complete log boxes, or pens, were built and connected by a long roof covering the open space between them. One pen was typically used for a kitchen and living room, while the other served as a bedroom. The logs were notched and joined at the corners and chinked with mud. The interiors were sometimes plastered with clay and lime. These structures were usually one-and-a-half stories high, with the second-story ceiling being the roof. Insects and rodents inevitably cohabited with humans in these structures, and livestock rambled through the covered passage. An 1820 Ohio account of this type of house noted that the passage was used for "the swill barrel, tubs, pots, kettles, etc. Here the hogs almost every night dance a hornpipe to a swinish tune." The passage at Richard McNemar's would also eventually be used for dancing—but of an entirely different kind.[52]

On the theological front, matters rested quietly for Richard McNemar from April until the Kentucky Synod met at Lexington on September 6, 1803. This meeting—only the newly formed synod's second—would see its fracture, with consequences that reverberate across the religious landscape of America to this day. Present from the Washington Presbytery were James Kemper, John P. Campbell, Matthew Wallace, John Thompson, John Dunlavy, and Richard McNemar. Among the elders present for Washington was James Ewing, who had signed Lamme's Petition. Of members from the Transylvania and West Lexington Presbyteries, it is worth noting the presence of ministers Matthew Houston, Robert Marshall, John Lyle, and Barton W. Stone, and elders Malcham Worley and David Purviance. David Rice, the Kentucky Synod's unofficial patriarch, opened the meeting with a sermon addressing the complexities of the revival. Born in 1733, the seventy-year-old minister was the first Presbyterian clergyman permanently assigned to Kentucky in 1783. Widely respected, Rice had the difficult task of praising the revival's positive qualities while also chastening those who had gone too far in unorthodox enthusiasms. McNemar must have squirmed when Rice spoke of exposing enthusiasm that arose

> from a mistake about the operations of the divine spirit.... Being mistaken here, men think some strong impulses or impressions on their minds, caused perhaps by the heat and strength of their imaginations, or a tumultuous motion of various passions, are a kind of revelation from heaven.... Under the influence of these enthusiastic mistakes men may positively conclude this or that doctrine to be true or false, not because they find or do not find it in the holy scriptures; but because they felt so and so, when praying, thinking or speaking about it.... This is in effect making the exercises of their mind, or their religious feelings, a new or an additional revelation from heaven.[53]

Rice's words did not bode well for men like McNemar. Before the end of the first day, a committee was formed to review petitions and supplications from the synod's congregations—McNemar's stalwart opponent James Kemper was the first minister assigned to it.[54]

On the second day of the meeting, committees examined the minutes of other presbyteries to ensure proper record-keeping and adherence to church polity. Houston, Lyle, and Robert Stuart were appointed to examine the Washington Presbytery's minutes. Their report brought to the synod's attention the past year's reports and petitions regarding Richard McNemar. It was agreed that a serious review of these documents was in order. Later that day, the synod resolved to recommend that congregations "procure as early, & as generally as possible the Confession of faith of this Church." It was now clear how deeply the beliefs of the revivalist ministers had penetrated and subverted congregations in the newer settlements of southern Ohio.[55]

On Thursday, September 8, the committee that examined the Washington Presbytery's minutes made their report. It was not good. At the presbytery's meeting of April 6, 1803, they had

> acted contrary to the Constitution of our Church, & the interests of religion in casting the petition of Lamme & others under the table & taking no further notice of it Seeing the said petition implicated a charge of a most serious nature.
>
> If the charge were false, Prby. ought to have investigated and found it so, & have dealt with the Complainants according to the Calumny, or imprudence of their conduct.
>
> This appears to us, to have been necessary, in order to have complied with the book of discipline & also clear Messrs. McNemar & Thompson from the odium cast on their characters.
>
> But on the other hand as it appeared from a previous orderly examination, of Mr. McNemar, that he held Arminian tenets, the Pby. ought as guardians of the Churches under their care; to have entered on an enquiry into those important matters laid before them. Your Committee also reports that we think it was improper & irregular in Said Pby. to present a Call to Mr. McNemar whose religious opinions stood condemned on their minutes.[56]

This report brought matters to a head. McNemar's colleagues could no longer ignore his transgressions, nor could they ignore the petitions of their orthodox congregants. The situation would have to be dealt with. The question was put to the synod: would they approve the portion of the Washington Presbytery's minutes censuring McNemar in absentia and calling him "hostile to the interests of all true religion"? Seventeen voted in approval (including Matthew Houston), and six in disapproval. These six were Robert Marshall, James Welsh, Barton W. Stone, William Robertson, David Purviance, and Malcham Worley. Battle lines were clearly drawn. The day closed with another vote on the propriety of the Washington Presbytery notifying their congregations of McNemar's dangerous views, which motion was carried. The net effect left McNemar marginalized and cornered, still a member of the synod but clearly regarded as a threat to be officially controlled.[57]

The next day, the synod took up the question of the Washington Presbytery assigning McNemar further ministerial duties after his official censure. Although the vote was closer—seven yeas to ten nays—it was decided McNemar should not have been allowed to continue preaching in southern Ohio. Additionally, the synod decided overwhelmingly that the Washington Presbytery were derelict in not addressing Lamme's Petition. Shortly after this, a frustrated minority comprising Robert Marshall, Barton W. Stone, and Malcham Worley absented themselves from proceedings.[58]

The Kentucky Synod began its meeting on Saturday morning, September 10, with five members absent: Robert Marshall, Barton W. Stone, John Dunlavy, John Thompson, and Richard McNemar. As Stone later wrote, "The other four of us well knew what would be our fate, by the decision in McNemar's case; for it was plainly hinted to us, that we would not be forgotten by Synod." This group of five men met in a private garden, prayed, conversed, and drew up a written protest against the synod's treatment of McNemar. This document also declared independence for these men from the jurisdiction of the Kentucky Synod—a total rejection of church hierarchy and authority. Meanwhile, oblivious to events unfolding in the garden, the synod examined the beliefs of McNemar and Thompson, as Lamme's Petition had requested. Again, McNemar was tried in absentia. Dramatically, and without warning, the five dissenters entered the room. Marshall stepped forward and presented their declaration to the moderator. Stone recalled that this "was altogether unexpected by them, and produced very unpleasant feelings; and a profound silence for a few minutes ensued."[59]

The declaration was read aloud to the synod. It bridled against the synod's approval of the Washington Presbytery's censure of McNemar, calling it a "distorted and false representation" of his sentiments. The five ministers claimed the privilege of interpreting scripture, citing "no other but the Holy Spirit speaking in the scriptures" as the "Supreme Judge" of all religious controversy. Finally, they openly dissented from the doctrine of grace as defined in the Westminster Confession of Faith, saying that it "strengthened sinners in their unbelief, and [subjected] many of the pious to a spirit of bondage." Conversely, the idea that anyone had free will to accept Christ and achieve salvation through faith—something completely at odds with the Confession of Faith—was a key teaching of the revivalists. This rejection of a core Calvinist tenet was the final breaking point between these five ministers and the Kentucky Synod, whose authority they declared they could not "in conscience acknowledge." In closing, the five dissenters stated that they still viewed their former colleagues as brethren in the Lord and would not exclude them from their communion, but they must "bid you adieu, until . . . it seem good to your rev. body to adopt a more liberal plan, respecting human creeds and confessions." McNemar, Dunlavy, Stone, Marshall, and Thompson exited the meetinghouse immediately after their declaration was read.[60]

FIVE

REBELLION

THE MEMBERS OF THE KENTUCKY Synod sat stunned in Lexington's First Presbyterian meetinghouse. Five of their ministers had just departed en masse after presenting a written statement of theological disagreement and effectively declaring their independence from the synod. Bureaucrats to the core, the synod's first reaction was to appoint a new clerk (Robert Marshall having vacated the position) and then organize a committee to respond to Lamme's petitioners and assure them their concerns were being addressed. The synod then began trying to repair the damage to their own body. David Rice, James Welsh, and Matthew Houston convened a committee to reason with the dissenters. They were dispatched "seriously & affectionately to converse with Messrs. Marshall, Stone, McNemar, Thompson & Dunlavy. To labour to bring them back to the standard doctrines of the church."[1]

Matthew Houston would become increasingly prominent in Richard McNemar's life. Presbyterian historian Robert Davidson wrote an amusing and evocative, but probably biased, description of Houston.

> He was not a man of talents, nor a close reasoner. He seldom meddled with doctrinal points, but indulged in a style of inflammatory declamation. He was a fleshy man, of plethoric habit, florid complexion, reddish hair, and sanguine temperament. He was utterly destitute of solemnity, always joking and keeping everybody round him in a roar, and was never known to be serious except when praying or preaching. He was a very Boanerges, having a strong clear voice that could be heard at a camp-meeting to the distance of a mile. He was animated in his action, and labored in preaching till the perspiration oozed through his coat.[2]

Despite Houston's vote to approve the Washington Presbytery's censure of McNemar, his attendance at many large revival meetings in 1801 and 1802 shows where his sympathies lay.

After the committee's appointment, in an almost comic effort to stem the tide of heresy, the synod hurriedly commissioned the printing of one thousand copies of the Confession of Faith for use in Kentucky. On Sunday, September 11, 1803, the synod's special committee met the five dissenters at a private house in Lexington. Stone recalled the meeting:

> We had with them a very friendly conversation, the result of which was, that one of the committee, Matthew Houston, became convinced that the doctrine we preached was true, and soon after united with us. Another of the committee, old father David Rice, of precious memory, on whose influence the Synod chiefly depended to reclaim us, urged one argument worthy of record, it was this—that every, departure from Calvinism was an advance to atheism. The grades named by him were, from Calvinism to Arminianism—from Arminianism to Pelagianism—from Pelagianism to deism—from deism to atheism. This was his principal argument, which could have no effect on minds ardent in the search of truth.[3]

The committee reported back to the synod on Monday morning, acknowledging their initial failure but reporting that the dissenters had agreed to discuss doctrine in a written exchange with the synod—a proposal soundly defeated by a vote. Houston was open to the idea, but Kemper and eleven others ruled it out. In a last, almost futile gesture, the synod appointed Kemper, Houston, and Samuel Rannels to meet with the dissenters and hear their specific objections to the Confession of Faith.[4]

Time for reconciliation was running out, particularly since McNemar, Dunlavy, Stone, Thompson, and Marshall had boldly constituted themselves as an independent body—the Springfield Presbytery. They appointed a moderator and a clerk and opened their first official meeting by drafting a letter to sympathetic brethren in churches under their care. They did not wish to withdraw from the Presbyterian Church and still considered themselves members. However, as long as their "liberty of reading, studying, and explaining the word of God" was infringed on, they had no choice. Regarding the Westminster Confession's authority, they provocatively cited the confession itself: "The infallible rule of interpreting Scripture, is not the Confession of Faith, nor any human writings whatever, but the Scripture itself."[5] In standing on their principles, these ministers were risking their livelihoods and ability to care for their families in what was still a frontier region. Their zealous faith, however, and the unwavering support of many of their followers, confirmed their decision to separate themselves from the church that had ordained them.

Kemper, Houston, and Rannels tendered the synod's last olive branch. The dissenters refused it, as they were not willing to write their objections to the Westminster Confession. By way of cold comfort, they assured their former colleagues that they were in their "hearts, to live and die with you; our hearts are bound to you in love." On Tuesday, September 13, the synod officially accepted their resignations from the Presbyterian Church. According to the *Apology* (the Springfield Presbytery's 1804 account of the proceedings), the synod acted before even receiving the last communication from the dissenters.[6] The synod's minutes record that the five persisted "in their scismatic disposition, Therefore resolved that synod do & they hereby do solemnly suspend Messrs Marshal Dunlevy McNemar Stone & Thompson, from the exercise of all the functions of the gospel ministry, until sorrow and repentance for the above schism be manifested." To cement this act, the synod ordered the drafting of a circular letter explicating the substance of the schism forwarded to churches under their care. Additionally, ministers were sent to the dissenters' congregations to inform them of what had transpired and attempt to bring them back to orthodoxy. William Robinson was sent to Springfield and Turtle Creek, Ohio—formerly McNemar's posts.[7]

The synod's *Circular Letter* expressed their sadness that "some who once were under great awakenings, and appeared fair to bid for the kingdom of heaven, have since turned aside to the paths of the destroyer; and are now following the devices of the wicked one." The minutes of their last meeting were included in an effort to demonstrate fairness. The synod claimed that due to Lamme's Petition (which they claimed more than eighty people signed) and the reports that their churches "were embracing a most dangerous system of doctrines, &c. &c. first propogated in Ohio, by mr. M'Nemar, and then by mr. Thompson," they had no choice but to examine McNemar and Thompson. They approved of the Washington Presbytery's decision to warn their churches about McNemar's opinions but claimed that the precipitous defection of McNemar and his cohorts prevented them from a similar examination. The synod declared they would not meet with the five defectors again, as the dissenters would only negotiate with the synod as a separate body—a heretical entity that could not be validated by recognition. The synod instructed adherents not to listen to the dissenter's preaching, as that would only encourage their declinature (the renunciation of the jurisdiction of the church) and schism. Instead, they should pray fervently for them. Finally, the synod designated McNemar, Stone, Dunlavy, Marshall, and Thompson, as schismatics—"men . . . who have broken off from the church, and formed themselves into a separate body, and seem intent to draw away disciples after them."[8]

Retrospectively, McNemar argued that the Springfield Presbytery was never intended as a permanent body but rather a *"pro tempore* . . . asylum for those who were cast out." Many revivalists flocked to its banner, and new churches formed under its ministerial care. On April 20, 1804, the newly organized ecclesiastical session of schismatics from the Turtle Creek congregation declared "the holy scriptures as the only rule of faith and practice, the only standard of doctrine and discipline." Espousing liberty and egalitarianism, they declared church elders to be no better than ordinary members and decided session meetings would be public. A four-point document comprising these sentiments was read to members and approved by seventy-four of them. Among the signatories were "William Bedel, Malcham Worley, Matthias Spinning, Aaron Tullis, Samuel Sering, Francis Bedel, [and] Richard M'Nemar."[9]

Malcham Worley, the ardent Presbyterian revivalist, antislavery campaigner, and McNemar's old schoolmaster from 1791, moved to Ohio in late 1803. On December 12, Worley purchased a 160-acre tract of land from David Bradbury for $1,045.00.[10] Worley paid nearly three times as much as McNemar did for the same number of acres only six months later, which indicates either that it was much better land or that prices were rising with the influx of settlers. The forty-one-year-old Worley settled his wife and six children near Bedle's Station and the Turtle Creek church. Worley's land abutted McNemar's, and their houses were literally around the corner from each other.[11] Worley's home was a one-story wood-frame house, measuring eighteen by twenty feet. Attached to it was an eight-by-twenty foot "lean to" with a fireplace.[12] Anthony H. Dunlevy (John Dunlavy's nephew) described Worley years later: "He was a man singularly excitable and was so entirely carried away by the great Kentucky revival that for three or four years he thought of nothing else. Yet he had some earthly tendencies. He lost his first wife in 1804, a most excellent woman; and at her funeral, it was said that he prophesied that she would rise from the dead on the eighth day. But she didn't, and in about three months he married again, and in about three months more he and his new wife became Shakers. But Malcham Worley was a most conscientious man."[13] Minister David Purviance said of Worley, "His mind [was] somewhat unstable, and some of his friends believe he was insane, (or partially so)."[14] Sane or not, Worley was known to all as a zealously religious man. In March 1804, exercising their new authority, the Springfield Presbytery recommended Worley as a preacher to churches under their care. Barton Stone, in his clerical capacity, signed the recommendation certificate—he later regretted giving Worley such license. The presbytery also authorized the preaching of David Spinning, one of McNemar's earliest Ohio followers.[15]

Following the publication of the Kentucky Synod's *Circular Letter*, a print war began between them and the Springfield Presbytery. In January 1804, the Springfield Presbytery published *An Apology for Renouncing the Jurisdiction of the Synod of Kentucky*. The first half was written and compiled by Robert Marshall, the Kentucky Synod's clerk before the schism. The *Apology* justifies the Springfield Presbytery's withdrawal from the synod's jurisdiction using extensive documentary evidence from both the synod and the Washington Presbytery. The second half is titled "A Compendious View of the Gospel." Barton Stone claimed authorship of this distillation of schismatic theology in his *Biography*.[16] The work posits the idea that all men are dead in sin and "death consists in being carnally minded: for to be carnally minded is death. This carnal mind is enmity against God: for it is not subject to the law of God, and neither can it be." This is a striking instance of how schismatics came unwittingly close to Shaker ideas of rejecting the flesh. The idea that someone could receive grace before having faith was rejected as absurd: "For receiving is a fruit of faith, and cannot come before." The final section contains the Springfield Presbytery's "Remarks on the Confession of Faith"—solicited by the synod the previous September. John Thompson is credited with writing this portion; however, the ideas of all five men are expressed throughout the book. Thompson declared that the Springfield Presbytery "believes God has an *elect*, a chosen people on earth . . . we find they are the same with *believers*, who have the spirit of Christ." This radical departure from the Calvinist concept of an exclusive elect threw open the door of salvation to anyone who believed. Creeds and confessions were totally renounced, since "God has not recommended any *help* to understand the scripture, but his spirit of wisdom." The Springfield Presbytery asserted, "Confessions of faith keep the soul away from the word of God. These things we know by experience. That book [the Westminster Confession] never helped, but hindered our faith."[17]

The *Apology* was answered by a rival minister's pamphlet, *Two Letters Written by a Gentleman to His Friend in Kentucky*. Although the work is anonymous, the letters are signed "I. A." Internal evidence suggests that the writer may have been a Presbyterian minister from Pennsylvania. Besides attempting to scripturally disprove theology posited in the *Apology*, the author specifically took exception to the Springfield Presbytery's licensing of Malcham Worley to preach and giving David Purviance a trial for the ministry. I. A. states that no Presbyterian body would have licensed either of these men due to their unorthodox beliefs and lack of qualifications; by doing so, the Springfield Presbytery had "fully manifested a party spirit." This accusation of "party spirit" belied what McNemar sought to avoid in his separation from the Kentucky Synod. It may have planted the seed that shortly thereafter resulted in the official dissolution of the Springfield Presbytery.[18]

The most controversial schismatic position concerning the nature of atonement was later attributed by McNemar to Malcham Worley. Stone explicated it in his *Atonement: The Substance of Two Letters Written to a Friend*—the friend, in this case, was sympathizer Matthew Houston. The first letter is a careful deconstruction of Calvinist principles constituting Presbyterian core beliefs as expressed in the Westminster Confession. Stone made his case successfully, for Houston replied he was "convinced that Calvinism has no foundation in truth," leading him to ask, "What is truth? For what purpose did Jesus Christ come into the world, live and die?"[19]

Stone's second letter addressed Houston's concerns. Crucially, Christ's death, or blood, was the price paid by God to the Devil for man's redemption. Specifically, and very controversially, schismatics believed that God gave Christ to the Devil in order to destroy the Devil, which in turn destroys the Devil in man—sin. As Stone wrote, "It may now be asked if Christ, or God in Christ, redeems from the devil and sin, and if he gave his blood as the ransom or price, Who got the price? The apostle to the Hebrews, 2.14 answers: 'Forasmuch as the children were partakers of flesh and blood, he also himself likewise took part of the same; that through death he might destroy him that had the power of death, that is the devil.' Here we see that the devil had the power of death, and he got the price, which was the death of Christ."[20] Stone's and McNemar's former Presbyterian colleague John P. Campbell was highly offended by the concept of "the devil getting the price." In time, Stone agreed "to eat those dreadful words." However, this protoperfectionist sentiment jibed well with ideas that would soon be espoused by Shaker missionaries.[21]

John Thompson later claimed it was McNemar who conceived the schismatics' unique ideas on atonement. Whether Thompson, who wrote in 1811, merely wanted to distance himself from ideas he had since rejected by scapegoating McNemar (by then a Shaker and well beyond redemption) or McNemar had conceived of the schismatics' theology on atonement cannot be known. Religious historians have always credited them to Stone, perhaps logically, since he brought them into print. Although central to Stone's theology, McNemar's and Worley's ideas typically go unmentioned in histories of the Stone–Campbell movement. Thompson wrote,

> I believe I was the first of the preachers to whom Richard M'Nemar communicated the first principles of that System on Atonement which is

contained in Stone's letters. His statement was plausible, suited to the times, and seemed to be agreeable to the spirit of the gospel, and the glorious Revival. I thought it was true. This took place in the first winter after we separated from Synod. In the March following the Springfield Presbytery met at my house. Then Richard M'Nemar imparted his theory to the rest of the brethren. They all had considerable objections against the plan, at first; and, even when they returned to Kentucky, scarcely any of them appeared to have fully embraced it. But when I saw them in June, at Caneridge, they were generally established.[22]

In *The Kentucky Revival*, written after his conversion to Shakerism, McNemar provides insight into key New Light tenets—tenets that accorded well with fundamental Shaker ideas, then unknown to the schismatics. Building on Stone's ideas, McNemar wrote that reconciliation, or atonement, meant to be at one. Since God is one with Christ, Christ is one with God. But since God is without sin, he cannot be at one with fallen man, unless man is at one with Christ. Hence, for a man who accepts Christ, Christ is the mediator, the vehicle for atonement. McNemar rejected the idea of vicarious atonement, arguing that it would be "unreasonable and unlawful to hang a civil honest man in room and stead of a murderer, that the latter might be delivered out of the hands of justice and set free." McNemar viewed it as each individual's choice to be reconciled with God through Christ. Further, he declared that schismatics believed true followers of Christ still suffered for Christ and that it was *Christ* within them that actually suffered. This suffering brought about union with Christ and, by extension, God.[23]

McNemar also epitomized the New Light belief that mankind's alienation from God had caused mankind to forget God's true loving nature and instead caused man to fear God. Therefore, Christ's life, ministry, and execution served not to atone for mankind's sins but to make an end of sin in the world. Malcham Worley was particularly strident in spreading this idea as a schismatic preacher. In June 1804, he wrote down a list of principles that even McNemar conceded were viewed by some as "ascribed to a disorder in the brain." Worley believed two opposite natures battled within each person, the "seed of the woman" (good) and "the seed of the serpent" (bad). Thus, since Adam, all human beings were "double minded." Jesus's human aspect was imbued with the same conflicted natures, and the evil one had died on the cross. This left the immortal spirit, imbued with the "woman's seed," to ascend to heaven. Thus, Worley argued, a redeemed "second man" was born, first child of the "woman's seed." Jesus opened the way for the advance of the "woman's seed" in all mankind, culminating in its redemption and rebirth. These ideas proved very popular with many of the schismatics—and again, remarkably in accordance with those of Shakers, whose salvation was premised on the return of the Christ spirit to Earth through the agency of Mother Ann Lee.[24]

In June 1804, the Springfield Presbytery met at Cane Ridge. True to the *Apology*'s rejection of creeds and confessions, they went one step further. Concern had grown among the six (now including David Purviance) that the print war was forcing the Springfield Presbytery to adopt fixed theological positions, thus defining them, much to their disgust, as a sect or party. According to Marshall and Thompson, Richard McNemar "prepared a piece at home, and brought it to the last meeting of our Presbytery . . . entitled, The Last Will & Testament of Springfield Presbytery. None of us had the least thought of such a thing when we came to that meeting; and when it was proposed, we had many objections against dissolving our Presbytery. But, after being together several days, those enthusiastic fancies so far gained the ascendancy over our judgment, that we consented to subscribe the obnoxious instrument. In this we dissolved all formal connexion between the ministers, and all good order in the churches."[25]

The *Last Will and Testament* is a remarkably concise document. It existed only in manuscript form until it was eventually printed in 1807 as a three-page appendix to McNemar's *Kentucky Revival*. Historian John B. Boles, who judged McNemar to be "a very impressionable man," argues that the *Last Will* is largely a restatement of many points in Rice Haggard's pamphlet *An Address to the Different Religious Societies on the Sacred Import of the Christian Name*. Haggard, who associated with the schismatics in 1804, emphasized the centrality of a simple Christian identity to their movement and urged the final overthrow of all creeds, including that of the Springfield Presbytery.[26] Indeed, the *Last Will* announces the death of the presbytery, the disuse of ministerial honorifics, the end of ecclesiastical government, and the end of the formal licensing of preachers. Instead, congregations were instructed to choose their own preacher and support them by free will offerings, and to consider the Bible as the only guide for preachers and congregations. The six signatories advised their "weak brethren, who may have been wishing to make the Presbytery of Springfield their king [to] . . . follow Jesus for the future." Finally, in a jab at the Kentucky Synod, they proposed an examination of "every member, who may be *suspected* of having departed from the Confession of Faith, and [to] suspend every such suspected heretic immediately; in order that the oppressed may go free, and taste the sweets of Gospel liberty."[27]

In retrospect, Marshall and Thompson—who were left hanging when Dunlavy and McNemar became Shakers and Stone founded his own movement—regretted abandoning the Presbyterian Church government. In their

1811 apologetic *A Brief Historical Account of... the Newlight Church*, they blamed McNemar for leading them astray and credited him, not Haggard, with the decision to dissolve the Springfield Presbytery.

> Richard M'Nemar, that excentric genius, who was then believed by most of us to possess a high degree of piety, power, and great light in religion, took it into his head, that our existence in a formal body, as a Presbytery, was contrary to scripture—that our bond of union was a carnal bond—that we ought to be united by no bond but christian love—and that this delegated body stood full in the way of Christ, and the progress of the revival; which revival would run like fire in dry stubble, if our Presbytery was out of the way.

Marshall and Thompson repentantly called *The Last Will and Testament* "a burlesque," and its employment of scripture "profane. It evidenced a high degree of fanaticism, and resembled more the production of maniacs than of ministers of the meek and lowly Jesus." They were "heartily ashamed to look back at the career we have run."[28]

The deed, however, was done—the Springfield Presbytery was dissolved, and all hierarchy abandoned. The resultant separate churches were distilled through the anarchic leveling tendencies of the revival. A remarkable social revolution occurred in the wake of the Turtle Creek congregation's embrace of these new religious principles. According to McNemar, men confessed their sins publicly to the whole congregation who embodied Christ, as Christ was within every one of them. Therefore, confessing to the whole Church was confessing to God—since Church, Christ, and God were now unified. McNemar wrote that egalitarian, or "republican," church government gave the congregation a sense of being "filed off in a separate capacity, and the surrounding multitude were considered as belonging to a different family." By 1804, a protocommunal ethos had crept in among the people of Turtle Creek. Along with radical theology that spoke of a life free from sin, their new identity as a separate people prepared the congregation for the message of Shaker missionaries.[29]

A third schismatic characteristic most outwardly resembled the Shakers—shaking and dancing in worship. McNemar wrote that members gave each other the right hand of fellowship while singing hymns. In time, members "would shake not only their hands, but their whole bodies, like one churning, with such violence that the place would seem to quiver under them." The difference between these movements and the jerks (and similar movements) exhibited earlier in the revival is that these were deliberately undertaken by the worshipper, whereas the jerks were supposedly involuntary outbursts of the spirit. Soon, the schismatics also leaped, skipped, and danced in a bold public display of their faith. In the spring of 1804, at a sacramental meeting at Turtle Creek, John Thompson danced for an hour around the preaching stand "all the while repeating in a low tone of voice—'This is the Holy Ghost—Glory!'"[30]

Schismatics also experienced wild involuntary movements in worship. McNemar cataloged these broadly: (1) the rolling exercise, wherein a person would roll like a hoop—head touching toes—or like a log, sometimes through the mud; (2) the jerks, like someone being goaded "alternately on every side, with a piece of red hot iron," "female jerkers" often cut their hair short since at the first jerk their kerchiefs would fly off and their hair was tossed "in the utmost confusion"; (3) the barks, where a person would assume "the position of a canine beast, move about on all fours, growl, snap the teeth, and bark." For many, the only escape from these exercises was to dance voluntarily. These unpleasant manifestations were proof to the schismatics that they, and Christ within them, must suffer "before they could reign with him."[31]

Schismatics expected the imminent advent of the Millennium, Christ's earthly reign with the faithful. They experienced spiritual visions of all sorts, and some claimed to leave their bodies, enjoying the delights of a world only they could see. In the summer of 1804, a shower of what was believed to be blood fell from the sky seven miles from the Turtle Creek meetinghouse. Schismatics seized on these visions and signs as harbingers of a time when those in the Christ spirit would come together as one body, irrespective of sects or parties. By the close of 1804, clusters of schismatics gathered in Ohio at Turtle Creek, Eagle Creek, Springfield, Orangedale, Salem, Beaver Creek, and Clear Creek, and in Kentucky at Cabin Creek, Flemingsburg, Concord, Cane Ridge, Indian Creek, Bethel, Paint Lick, and Shawnee Run.[32]

As winter set in, plummeting temperatures in no way chilled the heat of the revival. In fact, dancing took hold more than ever before. McNemar later wrote, "*Schismatics* began to encourage one another *to praise God in the dance* and unite in that exercise; just believing that it was their privilege to rejoice before the Lord, and *go forth in the dances of them that make merry.*"[33] Many who danced that winter never knew it, but their dancing prepared them for a deeper commitment to salvation than they had ever conceived of—a faith whose messengers were already wending their way toward them across the frozen landscape.

PART II

SHAKER

SIX

REBIRTH

THREE STRANGERS EMERGED FROM THE woods into the clearing surrounding Matthew Houston's farm. "Their appearance was prepossessing—their dress plan and neat—they were grave and unassuming at first in their manners—very intelligent and ready in the scriptures, and of great boldness in their faith."[1] It was Monday, March 4, 1805. Houston had invited these men to his house after encountering them the previous night at a religious meeting. That day, the missionaries explained their faith to Houston and his family, who received it with "deep consideration at least they appeard conscientious not to speak evil of it but to lay it to heart."[2] After a grueling wintertime journey of slightly more than two months, the missionaries found an open mind and heart, which began a chain of events that further rent the churches of Kentucky and Ohio.

Benjamin Seth Youngs, John Meacham, and Issachar Bates left the Shaker community of New Lebanon, New York, at 3:15 a.m. on January 1, 1805.[3] They traveled by sleigh down the Hudson Valley to New York City and crossed into New Jersey. The winter was so cold that year that travelers "crossed the R[iver] on the ice, the first instance perhaps since the year 1780 of peoples crossing from the York to the Jersey shore." At Trenton, they crossed the Delaware River into Pennsylvania, reaching the outskirts of Philadelphia in a hailstorm on January 10. There, Youngs and Meacham each bought pocket Bibles. Continuing on through Wilmington, Delaware, they traveled southwest of Baltimore, reaching Washington, DC, on January 19. They crossed the Potomac at Georgetown, stopping for the night in Virginia. Over the next month, they coursed steadily southwest through the Shenandoah Valley. At Leesburg, they stayed in a tavern owned by a Methodist woman who told them that in Greenville—140 miles farther ahead—"there is a people exercised with opperations called the jerks."⁴ On January 25, in Middletown, a young man asked Issachar Bates, "What denomination are you of?" Bates answered, "We are of no denomination." The man inquired further, "What do you call yourselves?" Bates replied, "We call our selves believers: we are not of any denomination or name, but we expect a name better than of sons & of daughters." To this the young man replied, "There are many of such people in Kentucky who will be called by no name but Christians & many have left the Pres & Methodists & gone to them."⁵ Bates, Youngs, and Meacham were encountering the outermost ripples of the revival and were beginning to find the people they were seeking.

Five days later they met a minister from Tennessee who had witnessed physical manifestations, including "jumping, shouting, laughing, Singing, dancing, Jerking, running, &c." On January 31, Youngs and Bates decided to meet with "jerkers" just outside Greenville. They lodged with Presbyterian elder Robert Tate and his family and heard their experiences with the spiritual and physical aspects of the revival. Youngs recorded their comments in his journal, then asked them if "through the power of God, & of Jesus Christ, there might be even a probability of a way to live free from all sin?" Stunned, the Tates affirmed their belief in "Calvinistic doctrine." However, Youngs was encouraged to hear that the revival had given local young people an aversion to marriage. During the two-hour conversation, three people arrived and were taken with the jerks. Youngs described that "while sitting on the chair their bodies would instantly appear stiff, the hands locked, the eyes closed, & the head jerked backwards over the chair—all as quick as lightning—they would remain thus from 2 to 5 seconds, & then moderately bring their heads forward again." Youngs and Bates saw the power of God in these movements. Meacham wrote the Shaker Ministry at New Lebanon that in Virginia they witnessed merely "the utmost twigs of a tree, or as the distant rays of the Sun, in comparison to a greater & deeper work of God, in the States of Kentucky & Tennessee."⁶

The travelers moved onward, crossing into Tennessee on February 17, where they heard more reports of jerkers in the vicinity. On February 21, they lodged overnight near Knoxville at the house of a Presbyterian named Dobson. At a church meeting the next day, they witnessed the most spectacular physical worship yet.

> About dark 40 people assembled young & old—some were professors & some were not—soon after candle light the meeting began & was op[ened] by singing—previous to which a young woman was taken with the Jerks & as they were all preparing to sing she arose from her seat went out doors & in 4 or 5 minutes returned & sat down again—but continued jerking so

violently that her hat flew off—& she was jerked from her seat & on the floor & from this it increased to swift walking across the floor with a distressed & quick bucking which coincided with the steps—In the meantime a young man was violently exercised by Jerking & he was sitting on the seat & singing this increased to a loud & quick barking like a dog, together with the Jerks—which in the time of barking would twitch the head up & down, partly between the knees, & this increased to such violent jerking that he was taken from the seat, onto the floor & jerked as if every joint must part asunder—& from this to shacking, trembling, leaping, & dancing—the person who led the meeting while sitting in a chair & singing was also taken with the barking nearly the same time—soon after these were taken 3 young women more were taken with the Jerks which increased to swift walking, sometimes partly running—claping hands, running[?] & instantly jumping without the least fear of danger—sometimes immediately against the walls or door,—& sometimes fall all along on the floor flat on their backs as far from any shame, & as regardless of any honour or persons, as if they were dead & would lay motionless—whenever any one fell down they would be taken up by some one, or 2 & held till they came to again—& as soon as they came to they would begin to walk back & forth—& every little while a very sudden start, give a sharp screech, & a jerk & fall down again . . . what appear'd very striking was their swiftly walking from one part of the room to the other with their eyes fast closed, would turn punctual, & regular whenever they came near the wall, or near any person, & even when they had walked across the whole length of the room 20 or 30 times without cessation—if the way happened to be blocked up or obstructed by persons steping in their way or the like—they would turn just as regular, & as swift before they touched the person or as they did before & as well as if their closed eyes were open. . . .

Nowithstanding these powerful operations—the people are yet lost in sin & joined with the world in most of their pursuits—& many even who are powerfully wrought upon by outward operations, when ever these are off remain the same carnal creatures in all their conversation & conduct!

After the meeting, 883 miles into their trip, the Shaker missionaries preached for the first time since leaving New Lebanon. Youngs wrote, "We spoke but a very few words, & that in a manner sublimely—they however found themselves more lacking than they were apprised of—& were evidently sensible that they were comprehended." In other words, the congregation—though deep in the throes of the revival—was not prepared for the self-examination demanded by the missionaries' sharp testimony.[7]

After journeying north for nine days and traversing the Cumberland Gap, the missionaries entered Kentucky on Friday, March 1, 1805. They learned a

Sunday meeting was scheduled for March 3 at Paint Lick, Matthew Houston's congregation. That afternoon and evening they witnessed more extreme physical agitations and were invited to Houston's house the next day. That day, they revealed their faith to him, and he received it with an open mind—the first man to do so on their three-month journey of more than one thousand miles.[8]

On Thursday, March 7, Houston conducted the missionaries to the Paint Lick meetinghouse to read a letter from New Lebanon addressed to revivalists in Kentucky and Ohio. This was the first reading of the epistle west of the Appalachians, and only the second public opening of Shaker testimony. Youngs mounted the pulpit but then, in a calculated gesture, descended and spoke directly to the 150 hearers as equals. He told the story of a revival that took place twenty-five years earlier, during which Mother Ann Lee and her English followers—the witnesses—unveiled their radical message of the true path to salvation.[9]

> The Church of Christ Sendeth unto a People in Kentucky and the Adjacent States, &c. We have heard of a Work of God among you; which Works in Divers opperations of his power; for which we feel thankful.... The time being nearly finished; that Antichrist Should Reign; (Which is according to the Scriptures) and time fully come, for Christ to make his Second appearance; God ... Raised himself up Witnesses and gave unto them all those Gifts of the Holy Ghost that were Given to the apostles in the Day of Christ's first appearance.... Although We had Been a People greatly wrought upon By the Spirit of God; and were looking for the Coming of Christ; yet the Light manifested in the Witnesses Showed us that we were unspeakably Short of Salvation, and had never Traviled one Step in the work of Regeneration towards the New Birth; for it Shewed us that it was Imposable for them that Lived in the works of the flesh, to travil in the Great Work of Regeneration and the new Birth; and as these Witnesses had Received the Revelation of Christ in this New and Last Dispensation of the Display of the Grace of God to a Lost World; they taught and Opened unto us the Way of God which is a way out of all Sin in the manner following; firstly, to Believe in the Manifestation of Christ and in the mesengers he had Sent; Secondly to Confess and forsake all our Sins; thurdly to take up our Cross against the flesh, the world, and all Evil; Which We by Receiving and Obeying from the hart have Received the Gift of God which hath Seperated us from the Course of this world and all Sin in our knowledge for twenty years past and upwards....
>
> We therefore as Servants of Christ and Children of the Resurrection; Testify to all People that Christ hath made his Second appearance here upon Earth; and the Poor Lost Children of men knoweth it not.... We have had

a great Desire that Som of you might have visited us Before now; as we have Been waiting for Sometime to know the mind of God In Relation to you; we now out of Duty to God and our fellow Creatures, have sent three of our Brethren unto you ... Whom We trust Will Be able to Declare these things more perticular and open the way of Eternal life unto you Which is out of all Sin. ... Receive them therefore as messengers of Christ And friends to your Salvation.[10]

This message shook the people to their core, bringing many to tears. The missionaries were invited to elaborate further at private homes. They spoke unopposed at William Provine's house to a grateful audience. Youngs wrote, "These things are all new—it never so much has entered into their minds to confess their sins or take up such a cross."[11]

The missionaries left Houston's the next day. He had been greatly affected by their visit and accompanied them through the woods as they left Paint Lick, telling them, "I believe without a doubt you are men of god, & I have no doubt of the testimony of your origin—& further I can say—We never have taken up a full cross."[12] The ideas fermented in Houston's brain until one month later, on April 10, he notified the Transylvania Presbytery that he was separating from them. The presbytery noted Houston "had relinquished the faith of our church & declined the authority of our judicatories." In a futile gesture of revenge, they suspended his ministerial privileges.[13] It had taken two years, but Matthew Houston, who had been sympathetic to the schismatic ministers since their break with the Kentucky Synod, followed them out of the Presbyterian Church.

The missionaries traveled on, through Lexington then northeast from Bryan's Station, arriving at Cane Ridge on Wednesday, March 13. Youngs observed the "remains of the encampings of the great camp meetings." Here they met Barton Stone for the first time. Stone acted "very free" with the missionaries and invited them to his house.[14] The Shakers told him, "They had heard of [the revivalists] in the East, and greatly rejoiced in the work of God amongst us—that as far as we had gone we were right; but we had not gone far enough into the work—that they were sent by their brethren to teach the way of God more perfectly, by obedience to which we should be led into perfect holiness."[15]

That evening they spoke to one hundred people but were not well received. Returning to Stone's house the next morning, they spent the afternoon in conversation about sectarian strife and the revival. That evening, the missionaries told Stone their beliefs plainly and read him the letter from New Lebanon. Youngs was disappointed, that although Stone "felt broke off from tradition &c

& were in trouble & appeared seeking after the truth, yet upon having the cross presented to view, it seemed as if they immediately were for finding weapons & would almost openly reject their own testimony." On the morning of March 15, they conversed once more with their hosts, who "appeard more calm & seemed to have a fear that these things should prove to be truth." Leaving confusion and anxiety in their wake, the missionaries set out for the Ohio River.[16]

After a tortuous four-day journey, they reached the Ohio River at the mouth of the Licking River in the afternoon on Tuesday, March 19. They crossed, lodging overnight in Cincinnati. The next morning, they set out for Springfield, seeking John Thompson. Thompson was convinced they were Quakers until dissuaded otherwise. Luckily, he had a magazine in his house giving an account of Shakers, and the missionaries used it to enlighten him about themselves and their beliefs. Youngs wrote, "It appeard some prejudices had been imbibed—but we spake our faith to him with a measure of plainness out of duty, though he felt very whole & against the cross." That evening, the Shakers witnessed a meeting of about one hundred schismatics with the usual manifestations—pointedly, they were not given a chance to speak.[17]

The Shakers set out the next morning after an unfruitful discussion with Thompson. It frustrated Youngs that although the revivalists spoke ardently against the flesh, "not one of them has ever had a single thought on the true sense of it"—in other words, proceeding to confess their sins, becoming celibate, and separating from the world. They set out at 11 a.m. with directions to Richard McNemar's house. Around dusk, they reached Malcham Worley's house and spent the evening in conversation. Youngs considered that Worley's "light was great & singular from other people—though also much lost—believing that the fulness of the Godhead dwells in him." Youngs's first impression of Worley jibes with that of others who thought Worley verged on insanity. The next morning, Worley's pregnant wife, Peggy, endured an episode of the jerks in her bed. At 8 a.m., the three walked a half-mile east to McNemar's—a household consisting of McNemar, six children, the freed slave Seely, and Jennie McNemar, herself eight months pregnant. This fateful meeting would change thousands of lives.[18]

Youngs carefully noted his first impressions of Richard McNemar: "A maried man of abt 35 who was brought from the back parts of Pensylvania about 14 years ago by Marshall . . . this McN at his first awakenings in Pensylvania was greatly convicted of the flesh & became a powerful preacher but he soon lost his power & got maried—In the course of the day we conversed with him but not with much freedom—as he felt in a manner determin to still build on something of his own—or to have God manifest himself by some mighty power &c."¹⁹ The stage was set for a gentle, yet determined, contest of wills between the fervent and headstrong McNemar and the quiet and thoughtful Youngs. At thirty-one, Youngs was a few years McNemar's junior. Physically small, he was nicknamed "Little Benjamin" by his fellow Believers. He was, however, was an intellectual whose knowledge of scripture, theology, and classical languages matched McNemar's. During the following month, Youngs labored with McNemar, proceeding steadily through a series of theological arguments in an effort to win the most radical of the western revivalists to the Shaker faith. For his part, McNemar wrote that meeting Youngs, Bates, and Meacham "was the first means by which I knew that a church or people by such a name or description existed on earth."²⁰

The missionaries lodged with McNemar that night and resumed the conversation the next morning, with John Meacham taking the lead. McNemar admitted that times had been difficult since late 1804, as demand for his preaching had forced him to neglect his material circumstances. Despite this, the Shakers were relieved when McNemar told them his house and possessions were "ours as well as his & that we might stay as long as we pleased." That afternoon, they accompanied Worley to the Turtle Creek meetinghouse and heard him preach "very promptly against the flesh." Bates and Youngs also spoke, reading the letter from New Lebanon. Many among the 250 hearers were reduced to tears, while others jerked violently. The Shakers returned to Worley's that evening and conversed, finding that their ideas about rejecting the flesh were quite similar. Worley told them of his first wife's death the previous year and that his second marriage was by the Lord's direction. Worley married Miriam "Peggy" Montfort/Monfort on October 8, 1804, at a service officiated by Richard McNemar. Peggy was twenty-eight-years-old—fourteen years Malcham's junior. He told the missionaries, however, that following his second marriage, his material wealth and spiritual power had waned. He added ominously that for the previous six weeks he had "been expecting something to come & take the earth." These words were welcome to the Shaker missionaries, as they sought nothing less than the transformation of Worley's life.²¹

Returning to McNemar's house the next day, they found that his mood had greatly changed. In a late-night conversation dominated by McNemar, "he showed a bitter spirit, bringing bitter & philosophical invectives against any & every sort of order which might be in the church &c. his spirit was dark & distressing." Ever rebellious, McNemar struggled against Shaker ideas, which promised salvation and freedom, but only through total subjugation of self. McNemar's mind was still shut to the Shakers the next morning. Youngs wrote, "Every thing appeard very dark just as if the gospel never could find its way among men"—particularly McNemar. Meacham made a last appeal to McNemar, which proved futile. Finding themselves at an impasse, the missionaries returned to Worley's, whence Bates set out for Cane Ridge the next day, hoping to arrive before the Sabbath.[22]

On Wednesday, March 27, the Shakers made their first western converts. At 11 a.m., Malcham and Peggy Worley confessed their sins to Youngs and Meacham. The Shakers called this "opening the mind." Youngs labored through the afternoon for confessions from Worley's fifteen-year-old daughter Rebecca and former slave Anna Middleton. McNemar was "staggered" by Worley's conversion. Over the next four days, the missionaries spoke to many individuals and families around Turtle Creek. Four members of the Campbell family opened their minds on March 31, and Anna Middleton did the same on April 1. The Shakers gently explained such practices as kneeling silently in prayer and not lying with your spouse. McNemar, heretofore the people's acknowledged spiritual leader, was confounded by the situation unfolding around him. His brethren and sisters were moving beyond him into a realm where spiritual perfection seemed possible.[23]

Youngs and Meacham next met with McNemar on the afternoon of April 1. The conversation lasted an hour, ending in agreement and mutual good feeling. McNemar was warming to their teachings. A busy week of proselytizing excited more interest, culminating in a crucial meeting with the Bedle family, founders of the settlement, on April 5. Francis Bedle and his wife offered "no opposition at all . . . but rather the contrary—having faith to believe that the flesh must be done away with." The next day, McNemar showed the men his manuscript of the Springfield Presbytery's *Observations on Church Government*, conceived of at their final meeting in June 1804. It was not designed as a formal creed but instead to describe "that church which is governed by an internal law, without any written form of words, and thereby direct the enquiring mind to the true foundation of God when it should appear."[24] The document impressed the missionaries. They noted similarities to Shaker internal governance, which in 1805 had not yet been published for non-Shakers. McNemar also produced drafts of his sermons and the *Last Will and Testament of Springfield Presbytery*, which Youngs called "remarkably striking." Although McNemar reported that people complained to him about the Shakers and faulted him personally for allowing them to spread their doctrine, he admitted to being increasingly drawn to their ideas. Encouraged, Youngs wrote that McNemar was "very open appears to see clearer & clearer & from his heart wishes the work to go on."[25]

Issachar Bates returned from Cane Ridge, where he had attended a religious meeting with preaching by Barton Stone, Robert Marshall, and Matthew

Houston. He reported that although Stone was initially hospitable, when the time came for Bates to address the meeting, he was not allowed to speak. However, sixty people ardently desired to hear him, so he preached to them from the end of a log, and they "were sensibly struck & appeard very solemn." Houston had last seen Bates three weeks before and implored Bates to return to his house as soon as possible. Before Bates left Cane Ridge, Stone apologized for not letting him speak. This was a defensive measure on Stone's part, as the foundation of his congregation had been undermined, and they were now among a number of religious bodies thrown into confused self-examination by the Shakers.[26]

A letter from Stone to McNemar expressed this sense of foreboding. Delivered by Bates, the letter was dated Cane Ridge, April 2. It opened with an expression of fraternal love from Stone to McNemar: "My dear brother Richard, I never longed to see any person so much—If I was not confined in this clay tabernacle, I should be in your embrace in less than an hour." After recounting the revival in Kentucky, including Matthew Houston's advances in spirituality, it transitioned into a section written in Latin, presumably to keep Bates and others from reading it. Stone's use of Latin underscores his anxiety about the Shaker missionaries as much as the words he wrote. "What shall I say? I know not: my heart grieves within me. Certain men from afar whom you know, inject terror and doubt into many; and now religion begins to lament in the dust among us. Some as I suppose will cast away the ordinance of Baptism, the Lord's Supper, &c. but not many as yet. Most dear Brother; inform me what you think of these men among us and you."[27] From this point forward, things were never the same between McNemar and Stone. The Shaker message resonated deeply in many who parted ways with the nascent Christian Church to travel the demanding path of Shakerism.

Nearly three hundred worshippers from a ten-mile radius gathered at the Turtle Creek meetinghouse on Sunday, April 7. In the cool afternoon, Richard McNemar preached a sermon carefully tailored to the occasion, based on Second Corinthians 5:17–18: "Therefore if any man be in Christ, he is a new creature: old things are passed away; behold, all things are become new. And all things are of God, who hath reconciled us to himself by Jesus Christ, and hath given to us the ministry of reconciliation." This message of reconciliation through Christ was familiar to the hearers, but the sentiment of old things passing away and the advent of a new age jibed with the Shaker message. Youngs spoke, urging the people to a deeper understanding of God's work than could be gained merely by reading the Bible. He argued subtly that God spoke directly through those with an indwelling Christ spirit; in other words, the Shakers. This accorded with the reconciliation of man and God preached by the schismatics. Next, Youngs attacked marriage as a cloak under which "the propensity of a nature which ever was contrary to God is mysteriously indulged." Sexual relations were part of the "mystery of iniquity" that must be revealed and destroyed. Finally, Youngs appealed for the open confession of sins to God, a practice already known among the Turtle Creek schismatics.[28]

Next, in one of the most crucial moments in the lives of everyone present, Richard McNemar addressed the multitude, preaching from his heart and with full ministerial authority.

> I confess I feel my self in a critical situation, I have stood as a watchman & have endeavourd to warn the people of approaching dangers—for if the watchman see the sword coming & warn not the people ... I would not have the people surprised, for evry dispensation has ever appeard to turn things upside down—I would recommend to the reading of all who desire it the writings of Soame Jenyns, who states that the doctrines of Christianity go directly to contradict the whole System of the government of this world & therefore ... opposers cannot be of God.

Hearing these words, Youngs realized that McNemar had come over to the side of the missionaries. He now preached in support of the Shaker idea that full separation from the world was the only way to salvation. Many were shocked by what they heard, as they had hoped McNemar would stem the creeping Shaker influence. Instead, their preacher was on the cusp of conversion.[29]

During the next week, the missionaries met with David Spinning, who was open to their message, but his wife and parents were very opposed. In general, however, the Shakers were succeeding in the vicinity of Turtle Creek. McNemar's neighbors Samuel Rollins, Daniel Doty, Jonathan Davis, Revolutionary War veteran Joseph Stout, and the Bedles were far along the road to conversion. On Friday, April 12, Jennie McNemar gave birth to a son—Richard McNemar Jr. Perhaps sensing that this would be her last child, after the birth she "broke out in shouting & crying God has delivered me & now thanks to his name the way has been opend that we shall no more live after the flesh!" McNemar himself cried out with tears, shouting, "Amen!" His last child and namesake bitterly disappointed him in years to come, but his arrival was cause for joy, particularly for Jennie McNemar, now freed from the physical toll and dangers of pregnancy and childbirth.[30]

On Sunday, April 14, McNemar preached from a wagon to a crowd of nearly five hundred people outside Calvin Morrell's house. A physician by trade, Morrell was another New Jerseyan. His home was ten miles northwest of Turtle Creek near the Orangedale congregation. McNemar's discourse was even more pivotal than the previous week's. The crowd was larger and agitated due to the Shakers' progress. McNemar based his remarks on Matthew 11, in which disciples sent by John the Baptist ask Jesus, "Art thou he that should come, or do we look for another?" The implications were tremendous, casting McNemar as John the Baptist investigating if the Shaker missionaries represented the return of Christ. McNemar cataloged previous Christian reformations, dismissing each one as "the old beast with 7 heads & 10 horns conceived & brought forth its own likeness which again was a monster if not the same beast, it would be an image like unto the beast—commited fornication again with its mother & begot again & again its own likeness." Then, perhaps turning to the missionaries, he asked, "Art thou he that should come or look we for another!"[31]

That evening, a large crowd remained at Morrell's house jerking, whooping, and dancing. Addressing them, McNemar publicly affirmed his belief in the teachings of the Shakers.

> I call God to witness before you all that I have heard many of you cry to God in the Sincerity of your Souls that God would open a way to Save you & deliver you from all Sin—& that if it should come even to the laying down of your lives he would send by whom he would send—is it reasonable to think that any of you if your children were hungry & should ask bread would thrust down their throats a Serpent or a Scorpion? can you reconcile this to yourselves how much more shall not then God send faithful labourers to us according to our earnest requests? & how can we reconcile it with a faithful God that he could send delusion instead of truth? we can not do it. If God Sends us food by ravens let us not refuse it—If God has raised up faithful witnesses to whom he has committed the Gospel of Salvation, & has Sent them all the way from N York—let us my brethren take care! for my part I confess before God & you all, that if any creature stands in need of Salvation, he who now speaks to you does—I have again & again Sinned against the light which God has given me & have from time to time gone to the flesh pots of Egypt! I think not that Richard is beside himself—if he is it is unto God—if he is sober it is for your cause—it is not a new fancy—it has been shewed me for years that the works of the flesh shall have an end & now the time is come.[32]

McNemar then recounted the lurid anecdote from his youth regarding the public fornication he had witnessed outside the walls of Fort Washington in 1791. Continuing, he admitted:

> I have fallen into the flesh many a time & again & again grieved the holy spirit of God! but I have always been faithful to you, you have been near to me as

my own life—If ever I have heard faithful prayers to God for deliverance from Sin it has been in Orangedale congregation—now my brethren who knows but the time is come—let us not be afraid of delusion & let us stand upon our watch tower—it is reported as though a doctrine that goes about goes to part man & wife! but I Say it is a lie!—it goes one to destroy the works of the flesh which must have an end I have Seen it for years—but those who are determin to live after the flesh—or walk in the pleasing gratification of the flesh—let them go & die, till they go to hell! there they will have wine & concubines enough—do not think that R[ichard] is mad, bear with my brethren a little in my follow—I desire to use plainness—I have led you as far as I can in the flesh—& those who mean to live in the flesh—I must now leave behind & those who are determined to forsake all for Christs Sake I am still willing to take you in my arms & help you along—if not I must bid you a final Adieu!

Following McNemar's stunning remarks, through which he had thrown down the gauntlet to his loyal followers, Youngs read the letter from New Lebanon. McNemar then resumed preaching "with double zeal & astonishing plainness against the flesh."[33] The die was now cast, and Richard McNemar had publicly committed himself to the Shakers and their radical faith. However, he had not yet confessed his sins or, as the Shakers called it, "opened his mind" to the missionaries.

Following the meeting, the missionaries conversed with McNemar and Morrell for four hours while people danced and jerked around them. McNemar, having publicly said his piece, opened up to the missionaries, unburdening himself of former doubts and candidly sharing his initial impressions of the men.

When you first came to my house I thought you were very bold, to come & tell us that we had never had the gospel—but strangely by some of my notes I recollected that last Summer I told J Thompson that we had not the gospel—our feet were only shod with the preparation of it!—I also thought that you were 3 stupid sort of Quakers who once had had light & had got into Some form upon which you placed your confidence & were come over to Prosylite us! but that it might now be that through Some providential hand you was brought here to have your life renewed, receive Spiritual things & it might be that we might receive Some of your carnal things! assuredly gathering that you did not know what the nature & power of the work was which was among us! &c. &c. &c.—But I Soon found that you had verily Supplanted me & I had nothing to stand on—& the building which we were trying to erect you had already erected & therefore you must increase but I must decrease.[34]

With these words, McNemar humbled himself to the greater spiritual gifts of the Shakers. This must have been incredibly difficult for him, given his rebellious nature and prominent leadership in the revival. However, he was convinced his salvation was at stake as well as, equally important, the salvation of his family and followers.

McNemar addressed the very name Shaker and his conflicted road to embracing it. Some of his disappointed former followers asked him, "How can it be that you should be carried away with Such delusion: Why, them men are Shakers!" To which McNemar responded, "I traced the Scriptures I will Shake terribly the earth: Who? why God! therefore He is a Shaker!—And father of Shaking. & again, I will Shake all nations—who? why God: therefore God is a Shaker!—And if I am Shaken, or are made to Shake others, Surely then I Shall be a Shaker—thus I Soon found that the horrid tang of Shaker was lost!"[35] News of McNemar's stunning conversion traveled quickly throughout southern Ohio. During the next week, he was visited by outraged colleagues, some willing to listen to his pro-Shaker arguments, others bitterly opposed to his endorsement of their pernicious doctrine. The missionaries visited McNemar on Thursday, April 18. Youngs observed that McNemar "seemed much down when we first came in." McNemar told Youngs that one angry man "gave me no room to Say any thing—& blasted away upon me without reserve—I said nothing—& his words had no more effect to turn me aside than trying to throw a feather through a stone wall—notwithstanding he brought a dark spirit upon me." McNemar showed them a letter he had drafted to John Thompson explaining his acceptance of Shakerism. He was eager that it should properly reflect the sentiments of the Shaker missionaries. By this act, McNemar became an apostle for Shakerism, embarking on the path that engaged him for the second half of his life.[36]

On Friday, April 19, McNemar found the Shakers at Worley's house and told Youngs and Bates he wanted to open his mind. Having not yet confessed his sins, he told them he was "sensible that he cannot abide in that Situation long he wants ground to stand upon & to feel his union to something." The next morning, Bates and Youngs went to McNemar's house at 8 a.m. They heard Richard's confession first and then his wife Jennie's. Youngs recorded their ages in his diary—thirty-four and thirty-eight, respectively—and simply remarked, "Here were 2 faithful openings."[37]

On a rainy Sunday afternoon on April 21, Richard McNemar mounted the pulpit at the Turtle Creek meetinghouse and preached his last sermon to a faithful congregation. He confessed that he was caught up in the things of this world, particularly "a morsel" of meat—his wife. Shakerism, however, had shown him a way out of this fallen creation. He assured his congregation that he would not abandon them but instead they would all advance together into the New Jerusalem.

> The words which at present impress my mind are these, Hereafter I will not talk much with you, for the prince of this world cometh & hath nothing in me It has been reported as from me that there would be no communion next Sabbath but I have intimated no Such thing to any one & I expect that those whose concern it is to See to the affairs of the church will make provisions necesary for Such an ocaision—but it has long been my mind that those things would have an end, & not only So—but it is very evident that none of us have had any authority in a line of Succession from the Apostles to stand as the viceregents of Xt [Christ] on earth—from whence could Luther get his authority, but from the church of Rome? And did he get it from the church of Rome? no, he did not for he was excommunicated & his authority taken from him. & thus it has continued to the present day—throughout all the reformation—even to the very last limb of the beast—the Presbytery of Springfield—The church of Rome having lost its pure authority, & all the Separates pretending to a Succession of authority through that poluted church evidently prove the whole invalid—So that it is also evident that no manifestation can be made under any pretence of Succession whatever—but only by immediate revelation! These things are not new to me—I have plainly Seen that there must be an entire change of circumstances before we could get any further but in what way it would be brought about I could not tell—This I was more Sensibly struck with last fall at the time when I had the fever & ague—I saw that my treasures were things of time & Sence—take away my hymns, my few outward tears & what have I more?—take away but every thing that is outward & what have I more? I plainly Saw that things of time had my effections—& by closer & closer examination I found that I was the most inveloped with a morsel of meet: a wife!—think not that I am going to leave you but things that we have been looking for are come: here behind this window have been Seen in visions of God what he was about to accomplish on this ground And I do believe that the new Jerusalem is coming down from God out of heaven that we may step into it![38]

SEVEN

THE NEW AND LIVING WAY

ON APRIL 27, 1805, JOHN Meacham wrote a letter to the Shaker Ministry at New Lebanon, New York—only the second communication sent by missionaries since January 1. After recounting their travel from Virginia to Ohio, Meacham penned a lengthy section describing their most important convert to date: Richard McNemar.

> At first he opposed us with hard judgings, but being a man of Sincerity, & great penetration, he observed with diligence the effect it had, both on himself & us, & found something in the testimony which he never had met with before—So that 4 weeks after our first interview with him he opened his mind—He is a Metaphorical preacher, was born in the Pennsylvania (an Apollos indeed) mighty in the Scriptures, has had true light respecting the works of the flesh—& has truly been an instrument in the hands of God of doing much good, especially in this revival—he was the first & principal breaker in all this Seperation which has taken place in Kentucky & Ohio Since the Summer of 1801.

Meacham's comparison of McNemar with first-century Christian disciple Apollonius was extremely insightful. According to Acts 18:25, Apollonius was an Alexandrian Jew, who "spake and taught diligently the things of the Lord, knowing only the baptism of John." Christians Priscilla and Aquila heard his preaching and taught him about Jesus Christ, rendering him an erudite and powerful preacher of the gospel. Likewise, Meacham realized the tremendous value McNemar's intellectual oratorical gifts added to the missionaries' cause. Meacham reported that thirty people had opened their minds at Turtle Creek in the last month. Sharing news of ongoing revivals in North Carolina and

Tennessee, even among Native Americans, he requested more missionaries, despairing, "How shall three weak children be able to secure all this that nothing be lost?"[1]

Meacham composed his letter amid the tumult of a sacramental meeting of schismatics at the Turtle Creek meetinghouse. Several hundred people gathered on the cold Friday evening of April 26. Those who opposed the Shakers, and were afraid McNemar might deny them communion or baptism, showed up in force and shouted the Shakers down when they tried to speak. John Thompson preached on Saturday with many from his Springfield congregation present. He denied the Shakers were "he that should come," as McNemar had preached two weeks prior. In fact, Thompson declared, the three men came five hundred miles to go "about breaking up familys... they are deceivers—they are liars! they are liars!" This invective resonated with anti-Shakers, who shouted, "Away with them, away with them! go home you deceivers!" McNemar attempted three times to respond but was not allowed. When he finally mounted the outdoor preaching stand, he addressed the crowd tenderly, in stark contrast to Thompson's fiery rhetoric. McNemar said, "I am a Watchman, God has Sat me on the wall as a watchman. I have made no noise, but I have been Sitting & watching, God has Set me as a watchman, & I will blow the trumpet of the Gospel as long as he shall give me strength!"[2]

On Sunday, April 28, two hundred people received sacraments inside the meetinghouse. McNemar, however, sang and preached that worldly rudiments, including the sacraments, were ending and urged everyone to embrace a greater work of salvation. Thompson preached again, with less anger than before. The meetinghouse doors were kept shut all day to prevent the Shakers from preaching, greatly disappointing travelers who had come thirty miles to hear them. The meeting moved outdoors and lasted into the night. Issachar Bates was assaulted by two men while returning home around one in the morning. Local people were still quite frightened of the Shakers as rumors abounded of their destructive effect on families and churches. On Monday, a deranged young man with a Bible entered the meetinghouse, pronouncing judgment against the Shakers as "false prophets."[3]

That evening, those who believed the Shaker message gathered at McNemar's house with Bates and Youngs. There, McNemar related a dream he had had shortly after the missionaries' arrival.

> I Dreampt that you came to me & pretended to have a parcel of Silver dollars in your hands & kept them back & concealed & would not let me have them unless I would put out my hand to receive them—which I finally did & took them all in my hand—& found them to be nothing but a parcel

of metal buttons without eyes! by this it appeard plain to me what you were—but afterwards I still saw Something plainer—I Saw that while I was in opposition in the day time & pleading for the flesh—the devil was able to furnish me with Suitable materials to continue that opposition through the day—I plainly Saw it was from the devil![4]

The next morning, Youngs spoke to McNemar's six eldest children, who he described as "very feeling." Youngs left no description of what exactly he told the children: Benjamin, eleven; James, eight; Vincy, seven; Elisha, five; Nancy, four; and Betsy, two (and newborn Richard Jr.). However, having grown up in the McNemar household the children were surely well versed in religion and must have sensed the momentous change these strangers had effected in their mother and father. The same morning, Bates heard the confession of the McNemars' emancipated slave Seely, now sixteen. By now, McNemar felt comfortable enough to show the missionaries Stone's letter with its warning about the Shakers encoded in Latin. The Shakers must have been astonished to see the tumult they had caused among the formerly united ministers of the Springfield Presbytery.[5]

This was in full evidence at the Salem meetinghouse on Saturday, May 11. Before three hundred onlookers, John Thompson read letters from Robert Marshall and Barton Stone denouncing the Shakers. McNemar rebutted him by reading a letter from his brother-in-law John Dunlavy in support of the Shakers. Dunlavy was only the second Presbyterian minister in the state of Ohio to speak in support of the Shakers, but he was by no means a believer yet. A letter he sent to McNemar in 1804, however, expresses exactly the sort of spiritual yearning that eventually brought him into the Shaker fold. Dunlavy told McNemar that he "would be willing to travel with you to heaven" and would "strip off everything but Christ and his holy spirit, to enter the narrow gate." Dunlavy lamented his "poor congregations" and saw "but little prospect of encouragement," but he still hoped "to see Jesus King in Zion." The next day, McNemar preached but was soon drowned out by the singing of opposers. Meanwhile, Bates spoke privately to people in the meetinghouse, while Youngs met with inquirers on the edge of the woods.[6]

The following Monday, May 13, John Thompson unleashed his harshest attack yet on the Shakers, claiming that "the intrigues of Satan had [been] used by 3 men to destroy the church of Christ." He systematically refuted the Shakers' assertion that by living in Christ they were living in the resurrection; mocked their practice of confessing sins; assailed their denial of marriage, procreation, and the sacraments; and scorned their claim that the scriptures were incomplete without a final revelation. Erroneously, Thompson (an ardent religious dancer) thought that the Shakers did not dance and demanded, "Did not David rejoice at the return of the Ark of God?—did he not leap & dance with all his might? Yes, & it was not a figure! it was positively so!" He was also incredulous of the Shakers' communal ownership of property, stating, "These men also pretend that the people to which they belong have all things in common, but in what manner?—Why they have a treasury into which they cast all their interest, & each one as he needs it, draws out of his own Interest!" Thompson finished by protesting that he had not been rash in judging the Shakers but rather had suspended his judgment as long as possible. Thompson sought to undermine the still-fragile faith of many Believers in attendance. Ruefully, Meacham commented that "a more refined, a more polished, and a more blinding discourse perhaps never proseded out a man's mouth." In his diary, Youngs wrote, "A Day of power for the enemy was this."[7] The Shakers were not allowed to respond. An astonished Meacham noted that even "Richard McNemar who through all the revival in Kentucky, and more especially in renouncing the Calvinistick principles has been foremost among them all, and to whome all the other preachers of this class, both in Kentucky and here have looked up to for counsel and instruction, as children look to parents, was at this time prohibited from speaking."[8]

McNemar responded to Thompson's assault as he typically had, and continued to do, throughout his life—by picking up his pen. When Bates and Youngs returned to McNemar's house late on May 15, they found him "writing his views of prevalent reports [about the Shakers], Thompson's testimony, &c." The next morning, McNemar "manifested a desire to proceed in the worship of God," specifically in the manner of the Shakers—to dance. Though his request heartened the missionaries, they put it off until they could properly instruct a group of converts. Youngs and Bates set out for Calvin Morrell's house, while McNemar remained at Turtle Creek, sensing that it was a critical time for his flock. As he feared, the meeting at Turtle Creek over the weekend of May 18 was again highly contentious. Although many opposed him, McNemar preached and read his written remarks in answer to Thompson's attack of the week before. D[avid?] Cory vociferously opposed McNemar, prompting him to pen another remonstrance. Other threatened clergymen also increased their vitriol against the Shakers. Three Presbyterian ministers named Stockwell [probably John], Kilpatrick, and McClung even traveled from Kentucky to itinerate through southern Ohio and preach against the Shaker missionaries. Stockwell and Kilpatrick lodged with their former colleague McNemar the night of May 21. Issachar Bates also lodged there that night—a situation that must have been very awkward for all concerned.[9]

On Thursday, May 23, at David Hill's farm near Turtle Creek, McNemar's wish to go forth in Shaker dance was realized. The missionaries led the first Shaker meeting west of the Appalachians. Forty people who had confessed their sins, along with a handful who indicated some measure of belief, heard preaching from Youngs, Bates, and Meacham. The converted were assured that Shakerism would "bring about the destruction of all antichristian forms" and restore the "true worship of God by ... dancing." A hymn was then struck up, beginning, "With him in praises we'll advance, and join the virgins in the dance." Jennie McNemar, Richard's wife—only six weeks postpartum—continued dancing long after the hymn ended. Bates sang a laboring song to impress on the gathering the mortification of the flesh sought by the Shakers. Youngs and Meacham demonstrated this deliberately slow and physically demanding form of Shaker dance. Richard McNemar and Calvin Morrell began to dance as well and were "soon clasped together & rolled on the floor." The missionaries were gratified when Polly Kimball, a twenty-seven-year-old woman who had not yet converted, exhibited a remarkable gift of turning, something they had not witnessed since leaving New Lebanon. Many more danced before the invigorating and spiritually affirming meeting concluded. The missionaries warned the multitude not to invite persecution by assertively promoting their newfound faith among non-Believers. Instead, they must be like Christ and his followers, who were "inoffensive, harmless, separate from sinners, & never persecuted any, neither good nor bad."[10]

During this meeting, McNemar shared a poignant personal testimony to further confirm that Youngs, Bates, and Meacham, were messengers of God:

> Soon after the brethren came, one night after my family were all gone to bed I was sitting up late, & just as I was thinking whether these were the true messengers whom God had sent, or no, one of my children lying up stairs was taken with a fit to which he had been subject. In consequence that they were [true messengers] I bid the unclean spirit in the name of Jesus Xt be gone out of the child—Jane hearing the child in distress desired me to go up to the child & speak to him—I answered Jesus Xt has spoke to him—& immediately the child was at peace & has not been troubled since. many are saying shew us a sign? well here now is a sign![11]

If McNemar indeed suffered from epilepsy, as he wrote, it appears that at least one of his children inherited the condition.

On the next Sabbath, May 26, McNemar preached at Turtle Creek to nearly one hundred hearers. His theme was Revelation 21, describing the walls of the New Jerusalem. One vocal opposer challenged the Shakers' doctrine of celibacy. Another, James Miller, threatened McNemar with his gun—which had fortunately been left outside the meetinghouse. Bates and David Spinning also preached, and the meeting closed peacefully with a hymn.[12] The following Tuesday, May 28, Youngs and Bates set out to visit converts at Beaver Creek, also known as Beulah, the settlement eventually organized as the Watervliet, Ohio, Shaker community. While lodging with William Stewart that Saturday, they met a twenty-year-old woman named Jane who had witnessed some of the most remarkable events during the Kentucky Revival. To a rapt audience she recounted the story of Jennie McNemar's sister Esther (whose married name was Knox), who had "a gift of songs within her breast which would be distinctly heard across the room, & that she would beat the notes with her fingers on her breasts as upon an organ, & dance after it!" A sight considered by Jane to have been more "solemn & striking than any thing she ever saw or heard." Following their return to Malcham Worley's house the next day, the missionaries again held a Shaker meeting. McNemar and his wife were enthusiastic participants, and Youngs noted that Richard sang two songs, marking the beginning of his pivotal involvement in Shaker music and hymnody.[13]

In a letter to the ministry at New Lebanon, the missionaries reported their successes in the neighborhood of Turtle Creek. They also described their two most prominent converts' material situations, especially McNemar's straitened finances:

> Malcom Worley & Richard McNemar both live on one half Section which is very good land & a beautiful place—Malcoms quarter is free from all incumbrance & is brought into midling good order—Richard has paid for his but one fourth part—& as he is unable to pay for the remainder he wishes to have it taken off his hands—Abt 300 Dollars is yet behind, all to be paid within two years from this time—he feels loth that it should fall into the hands of the world, because when he settled upon it which was last summer he believes that he had a special gift of feeling that God would begin to set up his Church on this spot of ground—but in what manner he could not tell—Malcom also has had the same feeling.

The letter provided further information about McNemar's background, especially his involvement in the renunciation of Calvinism, his separation from the Synod of Kentucky, and his eventual renunciation of all creeds.[14]

The missionaries, judging McNemar's conversion stable and genuine, discussed the idea of his accompanying them to Kentucky to visit the subjects of the revival. They likewise approached David Spinning, and it was agreed that the journey should be made soon. Distressingly, while these conversations were ongoing, Calvin Morrell renounced his new faith, according to Youngs, "by reasons of books &c."[15] It is documented that some anti-Shaker literature was circulating in the area. In a letter to New Lebanon written on June 1, the missionaries requested a copy of Shaker Reuben Rathbun's denunciation of his father Valentine Rathbun, who published much against the Shakers in the early 1780s.[16] Although he was a steadfast Believer through the 1780s and 1790s, Reuben eventually also apostatized and left his position of church family elder at the Hancock, Massachusetts, community. In 1800, he published a pamphlet, *Reasons Offered for Leaving the Shakers*, which had made its way west.[17] The missionaries wanted Reuben's earlier defense of the Shakers to counter the impact that his scandalous, and sexually charged, pamphlet could have on young western Believers. Additionally, at Danville, Kentucky, a 1795 article about the Shakers titled "An account of the people, known by the name of Shakers" was reprinted as an appendix to a popular play. Unfortunately, the only known extant copy of the work is fragmentary and lacks its terminal leaves. Thus, it is unknown whether the printer added contemporary, presumably negative information about the Shakers to the already unflattering account.[18] Indeed, Youngs specifically mentioned it in the preface to the *Testimony of Christ's Second Appearing*, published at Lebanon, Ohio, in 1808, so it must have had a deleterious effect on the Shaker mission.[19]

A Sabbath meeting was held at the Turtle Creek meetinghouse on June 2. Meacham, McNemar, Bates, and Youngs took turns preaching that day. Before the beginning of worship in the dance, McNemar recounted the story of his conversion fourteen years before, when he was "struck on the floor with a convulsive fit" in a ballroom. From that moment on, he had "vowed to dedicate his whole soul & body to the Lord." Richard then bade the Believers to go forth in worship. A laboring song was performed by some of the faithful, while thirty more of their number encouraged them with praise, clapping, and shouting. Bates and McNemar took turns singing. Samuel Sering, under inspiration, broke through the crowd and cried, "Farewell world!" and joined in the worship. Non-believing observers ringed the faithful, "Some crying, some screaming, some threatening, some laughing & some were solemn."[20]

On Monday, June 3, thirty-five Believers assembled at McNemar's house. He told them he was leaving for Kentucky the next day and read them "Observations on Church Government," written by the Springfield Presbytery the previous year, before its dissolution. While McNemar was reading, a mob entered his house armed with clubs and hickory staves. The Believers responded by singing hymns, "jerking," dancing, and then kneeling on the floor. The intruders leveled many accusations against McNemar, most shockingly that he had beaten and abused his mother—who happened to be right outside his house! McNemar called her in and asked, "Mother, did I ever lay hands on you or beat you?" To which she replied, "No, my son you never did." The unexpected presence of McNemar's mother diffused the tension, and the mob dispersed in consternation. This brief mention of McNemar's mother in Youngs's diary is one of only two known references to her. McNemar never mentioned her again in any of his extant writings. Her name, and ultimate fate, are thus far unknown. Through his conversion to Shakerism, McNemar attached himself to a new mother, Lucy Wright of New Lebanon, and was bound to sever prior fleshly relations. His omission of any information about his biological mother is poignant, as McNemar believed, erroneously, that the literal translation of his name meant "son of no mother."[21]

That evening, Youngs transcribed a copy of the original letter from the ministry at New Lebanon to the subjects of the revival for Richard to take with him to Kentucky. He set out at nine the next morning, June 4, with David Spinning. Bates gave the cash-strapped McNemar $4 to cover expenses.[22] Meanwhile, worship continued at McNemar's house in his absence. At dusk, Chloe McDonald was taken with a fit of barking. Youngs wrote that those present interpreted her utterances of "Bow, Bow" to mean, "Every knee shall bow." Chloe focused her spiritual fervor on the McNemar's former slave Seely, who had confessed her sins to Issachar Bates in late April. Chloe chased her around the house, outside, and through the fields in the darkness.[23]

On Wednesday, June 12, thirty Believers and about fifteen spectators held an epic evening meeting at James Bedle's. There was singing throughout, including many of what Youngs termed "wordly songs." He was concerned that opposers might conclude that the meeting was "like the carnal Dances of the world." To his relief, Jennie McNemar pitched up a song in a more "solemn style," similar to the wordless Shaker songs from New Lebanon. The meeting's intensity increased, drawing people both voluntarily—and involuntarily—into dancing, jerking, bowing, and running. The group dispersed at midnight, but Youngs was delighted to hear the spirit once again alight on a group traveling home through a copse of trees just south of Bedle's. Chloe McDonald's barking echoed through the forest night. Polly Kimball threw her shoes aside and danced round in a large circle, crying, "This is holy ground. The Lord has made it holy with his presence!" Her body then flew "round like a top" as she implored, "Shout all ye trees of the woods!" Observing at a distance, Youngs declared the whole scene "truly solemn—it being Moon light." The twelve worshippers continued their sylvan meeting for more than two hours before returning to the house, where a number of them danced a further two hours, not finishing until nearly four in the morning.[24]

A more restrained meeting took place that Sunday, June 16, when more than two hundred people gathered at Turtle Creek to hear Youngs preach in place of the absent McNemar. Over three hours, Youngs "opened the gospel" to Believers through a series of key scriptural passages to undergird their faith. He began with 1 John 1: "We . . . shew unto you that eternal life, which was with the Father, and was manifested unto us; That which we have seen and heard declare we unto you, that ye also may have fellowship with us"; then Ezekiel 43, on the restoration of God's glory and the altar in the temple at Jerusalem; Zechariah 12, on the destruction of the enemies of Jerusalem; and, finally, 1 Thessalonians 4, "This is the will of God, even your sanctification, that ye should abstain from fornication: That every one of you should know how to possess his vessel in sanctification and honour." United in their new faith through Youngs's preaching, they slowly coalesced, consciously separating further from the world. Youngs wrote approvingly that "people through the whole of the meeting were truly solemn & attentive . . . the work of conviction and faith, appears evidently increasing in the minds of many." Despite this large-scale public affirmation of the Shakers' message, Youngs was dismayed the next day to meet anti-Shaker men he perceived as "really dangerous." These men directly and explicitly threatened Richard McNemar.[25]

McNemar returned from his journey on Tuesday, June 18, having visited his former home and congregation at Cabin Creek. Youngs wrote that it was there, on June 1, 1801, that the New Light doctrine, which some called "Cabin Creek Religion," first began. McNemar had attended a sacramental meeting on June 9 at Cabin Creek presided over by his brother-in-law John Dunlavy. Men from Cane Ridge opposed Dunlavy's message, which aimed at "perfection—& destruction to shadows & formalities." Although McNemar did not preach, he visited and spoke with thirteen families in the region who had converted to Shakerism. Dunlavy had not yet opened his mind to the missionaries. McNemar stayed with Dunlavy at his Eagle Creek home and visited his sister Cassie (Dunlavy's wife) and sister-in-law Esther, wife of John Knox. Dunlavy also held at least one slave, a girl named Lucy.[26]

Meanwhile, the New Lebanon Ministry wrote their first letter to the missionaries on June 19. They expressed approval and joy at the success of the mission, despite their "long and wearysome journeys." They also acknowledged the missionaries' request for more assistance and said, "Perhaps we shall send our next letter by some of our brethren though we shall be more satisfyed when we have received another letter from you."[27]

The first meeting following McNemar's return was held on Thursday, June 20, at James Bedle's house. The missionaries appealed to those still bound to the things of this world, be they husbands, wives, children, friends, or farms. The converted, but not fully committed, were encouraged to come out of the world through hymn singing and dancing. Youngs noted the sweltering heat, "So that many were as wet as water." The next day Youngs, McNemar, and Worley were sent to the Beulah settlement on Beaver Creek where Robert Marshall, McNemar's former colleague, was holding a sacrament on Sunday. That morning, four hundred people assembled around the preaching stand in the woods to hear Marshall preach. One hundred and fifty of these took communion. Youngs called the proceedings "very dead & formal."[28] In direct opposition to the Shakers, Marshall declared that the kingdom of Christ had not yet come.

Following the sacrament, a meeting was held at William Stewart's house, where the Shaker missionaries lodged. In attendance were people both sympathetic and opposed to the Shakers. Nathan Worley, Malcham's brother, demonstrated particularly remarkable gifts of the spirit through his prayer and singing. As the worship reached a fever pitch, some began to ridicule the Shakers for "pretending to be in the kingdom." At this, according to Youngs, the spirit immediately withdrew, opening the way for him to preach to the group. During this time, McNemar met with Marshall and John Thompson in the nearby woods. No record exists of their presumably heated discussion. The next morning, Marshall resumed preaching from the stand, cautioning his listeners against the Shakers. Youngs and Malcham Worley worked unsuccessfully to convert Nathan Worley. When Marshall finished, McNemar asked for the privilege to preach to the people but was denied. The missionaries left an estimated eight or ten Believers at Beulah and returned to Malcham Worley's at Turtle Creek that evening.[29]

The next day, the missionaries decided to build an outdoor stand of their own at Turtle Creek for public meetings. They justified the need to the ministry at New Lebanon: "The cause of this place being built was that the weather through the summer season was very hot & su[l]tery & the houses being all smal & pent & we being also greatly throng by spectators we were pressed upon beyond measure so that many times it was dificult especialy for women to keep their breath, several times we were obliged to hold meeting out of doors in the open air."[30] McNemar, Worley, and the missionaries selected a suitable spot adjacent to the settlement "in the woods—shaded by large Oaks & White Walnut—it is a beautiful level spot with a small descent towards the North about 100 E yds f[ro]m the great road that leads f[ro]m Cincinnati to Marion by way of Beaver creek—it is on the quarter Section belonging to Malcom & joins upon Richards on the East—& it is about 300 yds S[outh] of Malcoms house."[31]

The stand was elevated two feet above the ground. The floor measured eighteen by twenty-five feet and was made of split puncheons (logs split in half with a smooth upper face) nine feet in length and laid end to end. It was enclosed by "banisters or poles in places to keep the people from falling off.... Severall feet above the Lower banisters was another tear [tier] of poles with pegs in them for the convenence of hanging away our hats—we had also placed seats round about the stand on the ground for the acomodation of strangers, for they were not alowed to come within." The spectators' seats were made of logs. The fact that the Shakers chose to re-create the peg rail so ubiquitous to their eastern meetinghouses and other buildings for this wilderness stand is a powerful testament to the communal order gradually being instilled in new converts.[32]

As the weather warmed, the eastern missionaries found that their winter clothing was ill suited for the humid climate of southern Ohio. Jennie McNemar and Peggy Worley led the effort to make a new coat, jacket, and trousers for Youngs, who departed with David Spinning on Thursday, June 27, for a mission to Kentucky. Along the way, they visited Richard McNemar's brother Garner, who lived near a saltworks on Eagle Creek. They arrived the next day at the homes of McNemar's brothers-in-law, John Knox and John Dunlavy, and lodged with Knox. They delivered a letter from McNemar to Dunlavy, who in turn shocked them with a letter from Barton Stone of Cane Ridge, Kentucky, dated the previous Monday, June 24. Stone exulted that five people had "come out of the delusion" of Shakerism, which he had also referred to as "Worleyism," on Sunday, June 23. Stone's letter accused Worley of having left the Shakers to establish a "community of wives & community of goods." To steady his faith, Youngs talked at length with Dunlavy that day, writing in his diary that Dunlavy "felt very near & appears to be after the truth."[33]

On the Sabbath, June 30, sixty people gathered at the Eagle Creek meetinghouse to hear Baptist preacher Hampton Pangburn, whose sermon, according to Youngs, left the people "lifeless." Surprisingly, he invited Youngs to mount the pulpit and address the gathering. Youngs's address was unopposed but met with mixed results. Youngs accompanied Cassie Dunlavy (McNemar's sister) home and preached at John Knox's until late in the evening, successfully reaching those he judged as "the most sensible men." After more preaching engagements in the vicinity, Youngs and Spinning returned to Turtle Creek on Tuesday, July 2. They had met no serious opposition among the people of Eagle Creek and were invited to make a return visit. Ominously, on the way home, they discovered handbills posted along the road, claiming the Shaker missionaries had come west to castrate children.[34]

Back at New Lebanon, the missionaries' encouraging reports prompted the ministry to send more Shakers west. David Darrow, on whose land the church family at New Lebanon was gathered, headed the group. Darrow was fifty-five and served as first elder of the First Order of the Church Family. Dispatching him was a tremendous sacrifice by his home community and demonstrates how committed the Shakers were to consolidating gains made in Ohio. Daniel Moseley, specifically requested by the missionaries as a man whose "gifts and faculties are so calculated as to be very useful to the people here," was also sent.[35] Solomon King rounded out the trio. His mother was Ruth Meacham, sister of the first American Shaker leader Father Joseph Meacham. Ruth had married Gideon King, but he had not followed his wife into Shakerism. Their son Solomon, along with Darrow, represented the founding families of Shakerism converted by Mother Ann Lee. The three men left New Lebanon in a covered wagon loaded with clothing on July 1, 1805, exactly six months after the initial mission.[36]

Youngs itinerated throughout southern Ohio and Kentucky during July, spending significant time with John Dunlavy, Barton Stone, Matthew Houston, and Peter Houston. Dunlavy and Matthew Houston inched closer toward conversion, but Stone was perhaps their most ardent enemy. Despite this, and rather incredibly, Stone hosted Youngs at his house. On Sunday, July 21, Youngs arrived at Cane Ridge to find Richard McNemar waiting for him at Peter Houston's house. Houston was another of McNemar's brothers-in-law, whose houses seemed to serve as way stations for the missionaries. Houston was married to Sarah Jane Luckey, sister of McNemar's wife, Jennie. However, whereas Jennie had enthusiastically embraced Shakerism, Sarah Jane forced McNemar out of her house the night of Friday, July 19, and he slept in the nearby woods. David Purviance, McNemar's former Springfield Presbytery colleague, was also present, and he stoked Sarah Jane Houston's anger. Issachar Bates was also in the vicinity, having accompanied McNemar to Cane Ridge.[37]

On Monday, July 22, Peter Houston walked with McNemar to the edge of the woods near his house and opened his mind. This critical moment was interrupted when Houston was called away, presumably to derail his conversion. McNemar and Youngs then left Cane Ridge and found Bates eight miles away. He had just visited James Smith Jr., who had opened his mind. Unbeknownst to them, Smith Jr.'s conversion eventually led to great difficulties for the Ohio Shakers. His father, Col. James Smith, whom Youngs described as a "sensible man," also met with the Shakers that day, and McNemar lodged overnight at Smith Jr.'s. Youngs, Spinning, and possibly Bates joined him there the next day. They had come from Stone's house after collecting their coats and saddlebags, which had been stored there since March. Youngs appraised Smith Jr. as an "honest upright man & his f[ai]th appears to be well grounded," as it indeed turned out to be in the strife of years to come.[38]

On Saturday, July 27, the missionaries returned to Eagle Creek, where John Dunlavy preached at a sacramental meeting the next day. Purviance and another preacher named Gill traveled from Kentucky to oppose the Shakers. Conscious of physical peril, McNemar and Dunlavy had agreed that as long as the Kentuckians were at Eagle Creek, McNemar would lodge with Dunlavy, likely for mutual protection. Sunday's meeting was intense. Again, the Shakers were denied the chance to speak. They withdrew and preached separately to interested hearers. The meeting continued Monday, and anti-Shaker worshippers drowned out the Shakers' attempted preaching with loud singing and shouting. The county judge finally intervened, allowing them the chance to speak. On Tuesday, July 30, Youngs sensed Dunlavy was close to conversion, and at 10 a.m., Youngs and Bates heard his confession. With his accession to their cause, the Shakers were now allied with two of the six most prominent schismatic ex-Presbyterian ministers. Meanwhile, Richard labored with his sister Cassie, Dunlavy's wife, who confessed her sins the next day. As he left Dunlavy's, Youngs was satisfied that the family was "very strong in faith."[39]

The party arrived back at Turtle Creek on Friday, August 2. To their delight, they found the New Lebanon Shakers waiting for them. Darrow, Moseley, and King had traveled by wagon, passing through Pittsburgh and Chillicothe on their journey. They arrived at Turtle Creek on July 29, having made the trip in twenty-eight days. Youngs wrote, "By [their] coming our spirits are greatly refreshed." That evening, the reunited brethren held a meeting of "power and gladness of heart" at Worley's house. The next morning, clothing sent from New Lebanon was distributed as a blessing to the faithful.[40] Darrow wrote the New Lebanon Ministry that he "found as much faith as I Expected, but Not So large a number." He also informed them of the great need for female Shakers to guide the newly converted women. He recognized that his greatest challenge would be to shore up the converted without appearing to usurp the original missionaries. This task would have to be accomplished before any further outreach was made to the world.[41]

Sunday, August 4, was a momentous day for the Turtle Creek Shakers. A public meeting was held at the newly completed outdoor stand for the first time, and fifty worshippers assembled there at eleven o'clock. The two hundred spectators were warned that the stand was consecrated to serve "the living God," and that only faithful Believers were welcome on it. McNemar opened by preaching for more than an hour, before singing a hymn he had written just for the day. The Believers knelt in prayer and then went forth in the first large-scale public Shaker meeting west of the Appalachians. The newly arrived Solomon King sang for the dancers. Meacham, Bates, and Youngs also preached. In the afternoon, McNemar's sister-in-law Esther Knox exhibited her singular gift of "singing from the breast." On hearing it, Youngs was astounded to recognize the tune as "a propper Solemn song as is sung in the Church!" Knox manifested a broad range of enthusiastic movements in worship. Youngs described "her hands & fingers playing on her breast as on an organ shewing they shall come with the voice of doves labring on their breasts it was the most striking & solemn sight of all the exercises we had yet seen." Knox formally opened her mind to Bates the next day, although she had been "convicted of the works of the flesh" since before the Shakers arrived in the West. Now McNemar's wife, sister, and sister-in-law had joined him in Shakerism.[42]

During the week following the first meeting at the stand, many Believers in the vicinity chose to move closer to it, as it represented the visible center of Shaker union. Youngs wrote that many people in the region were focused on Turtle Creek "as though something very extraordinary was there—either of the work of God or of great delusion." The Believers met again at the stand on Monday afternoon. During this meeting, McNemar sang the first Shaker solemn song in a public meeting in the West, followed by several hymns. In the coming years, McNemar distinguished himself as one of the foremost Shaker hymnodists.[43]

On Thursday, August 8, Youngs, McNemar, and Nathan and Malcham Worley set out to attend a camp meeting at Concord in Bourbon County, Kentucky. McNemar later claimed that Stone sent them a written invitation to attend. They arrived late on Saturday night, at the end of the second day of the meeting. On Sunday morning, with James Smith Jr., they approached the campground. To their surprise, they were quickly accosted by Robert Marshall and Stone and asked to refrain from preaching. The reason given was that Stone and Marshall had been appointed to preach. The Shakers agreed not to disturb the proceedings, and Youngs told Stone, "I am sorry to see you abusing your own light."[44] Despite this, the Shakers were continuously pulled aside by individuals who wanted to hear their message. That evening, Youngs and Malcham Worley preached at a private gathering of fifty willing hearers.

Undeterred, the Shakers returned to the camp meeting on Monday, August 12. They were again forbidden to speak and were forced to listen to preaching by John Thompson, Marshall, Stone, John Stockwell, Matthew Houston, Purviance, and A. Brannon that rebuked the Shakers and their message. McNemar later wrote bitterly of this incident, recalling that individual Shakers were "named out, pronounced liars, [and] defamed by many slanderous reports which they could have proved false, had they been allowed to speak." The solidarity that had bound these men together in withdrawing from the

Kentucky Synod only two years before was now forever lost. The crowd was moved against the Shakers, and Youngs was dismayed to find that even James Smith Jr., who had accompanied them to the meeting the day before, dared not offer them lodging at his home. McNemar stayed with his brother-in-law Joseph Luckey that night.[45]

Following the camp meeting's conclusion, the missionaries planned further itinerations in north-central Kentucky. The next day, Youngs visited James Smith Jr. and his father, Col. James Smith, and left feeling "measurably satisfied." On Wednesday the 14, the party rode through Paris, Kentucky, and were hailed by a group of deists, some of whom had been pupils of Malcham Worley. They treated the Shakers to breakfast at the tavern, heard them out, and invited them to visit again. Youngs wrote that "so much more do the nonprofessors shew a xtn [Christian] spirit towards us than the professor." Malcham Worley visited his mother and some of his siblings, but their feelings were "intolerable to the gospel." During the next two weeks, the missionaries visited Shawnee Run, where the Shaker community of Pleasant Hill was eventually established. They also called on, and heard confessions from, members of the Banta family, some of whom had made earnest inquiries of the Shakers at the Concord camp meeting.[46]

Youngs continued to itinerate in Kentucky, visiting Peter Houston, Joseph Luckey, and James Smith Jr. By coincidence, Colonel Smith arrived there at the same time, having returned from a five-day visit to the Shakers at Turtle Creek. Colonel Smith now manifested negative feelings toward the Shakers, which Youngs felt he was able to somewhat mollify. During a visit to John Dunlavy's, Youngs's horse wandered away (or was maliciously set loose or stolen). Determined to return to Turtle Creek, he set out on foot on September 17 with Dunlavy; his wife, Cassie; and two other Believers, walking twenty-five miles to New Market, Ohio. The next day he continued alone. Failing to find a place to stay after walking all day, he spent the night on the ground. He reached Turtle Creek at four o'clock in the afternoon on the nineteenth after an absence of six weeks preaching the gospel throughout southern Ohio and north-central Kentucky. With satisfaction, he noted in his journal, "20 have op[ene]d their m[in]ds in Miami & 24 in Kentucky and Eagle Creek. The whole number is now 126 in Ohio & Kentucky of grown persons."[47]

EIGHT

COMMUNITY FOUNDATIONS

IN THE LATE SUMMER OF 1805, Richard McNemar received a troubling letter from Jonathan Dayton of New Jersey. Dayton was a prominent Federalist politician, a revolutionary war veteran, Speaker of the House of Representatives from 1795 to 1799, and a sitting US senator when he penned his letter to Richard McNemar on August 15, 1805. Dayton owned vast tracts of land in southwestern Ohio, including the plot on which McNemar's house was located. He had repeatedly tried to collect the balance of $225 McNemar owed him. Dayton warned McNemar that he would retain an attorney to sue him unless he settled his debt by September 6—just three weeks away. Finding himself in an impossible situation, McNemar was more than willing to accept $225 from the Shaker missionaries in exchange for the title to his lands. In a letter to New Lebanon Shaker deacon David Meacham, David Darrow justified the purchase, writing, "This we did because [McNemar] is a forward & helpful man, & one that feels wholly willing to devote & give up both himself & all that he has to the use of the gospel, & was in a straight for the money to pay for the land he now lives on & had no way to get it." Thus, the Shakers made the first concrete step to establish a firm foothold at Turtle Creek. Fittingly, McNemar's house and land became the center for the first Shaker community west of the Appalachians. It was considered the best tableland in the vicinity on which to establish a community and farm.[1]

On Saturday, September 21, the brethren worked to erect a dwelling for Samuel Rollins. It was built right on the property line of McNemar's section. The next day, the worship meeting was again held at the stand. Issachar Bates and McNemar preached, followed by the newly converted John Dunlavy, who bore an emotional testimony. Dunlavy poignantly said that twenty-five years earlier he had had a vision that the latter day would be "directly contrary to the whole system of a carnal nature." Dunlavy had attended the Concord camp meeting, at which the Shakers had been forbidden to speak. Reflecting on that experience, he told the assembly that at Concord "he was neither able to stand for nor against the testimony" and that the anti-Shaker "preachers beat him so that when he got away he could just make out to breathe." After that experience, Dunlavy was determined to follow the Shakers and never look back. Around this same time, Dunlavy's brother Francis, who was the local circuit judge, heard a case about the Shakers' right to worship as they pleased. Francis Dunlavy upheld the Shakers' religious liberty in accordance with federal and state laws. Three of the Shakers attended the trial and reported that Dunlavy spoke affirmatively of liberty of conscience for "half an hour in a very solemn manner."[2]

David Darrow decided that Issachar Bates should return to the ministry in New Lebanon to report in person about the missionary efforts in Ohio and Kentucky. Shortly before Bates's departure, some of the brethren began felling timber to prepare for the construction of a proper meetinghouse to serve the growing body of Believers at Turtle Creek. Richard McNemar and his wife each wrote a letter for Bates to deliver to the ministry.[3]

McNemar's letter is worth quoting in full. It is the distillation of a lifelong journey of faith, written by one who has finally found a spiritual home among a people previously unknown to him but whose "understanding of the things of God" was strikingly similar to his own.

Turtle Creek, Septr 25th 1805.

Dearly Beloveds,

   A Copy of your letter dated Decr. 26th 1804, is now before me, to which I feel impressed to send you a short answer. The contents of it by the mercy of God have found an entrance into my heart, and however unfruitful the soil, I am constrained to send you a little usuary, if nothing more than my unfeigned thanks for your diligence and care in sending us the genuine Gospel. For upward of fifteen years my soul has been on the wheel forming into union with professed followers of the Lamb, but never did I find my mate till I found the spirit from New Lebanon.

   Now I can say with the prophet "This is my God, I have waited for him; this is my saviour, I will rejoice in his name." Deliverance from sin sounds sweeter in my ear than all the music that is employed around the golden image, and a furnace seven times hotter than Nubuchadnezzars I should prefer to an antichristian bed of lust. Salvation from all sin! how strangely have we overlooked this costly Jewel, this pearl of great price, this little stone, but

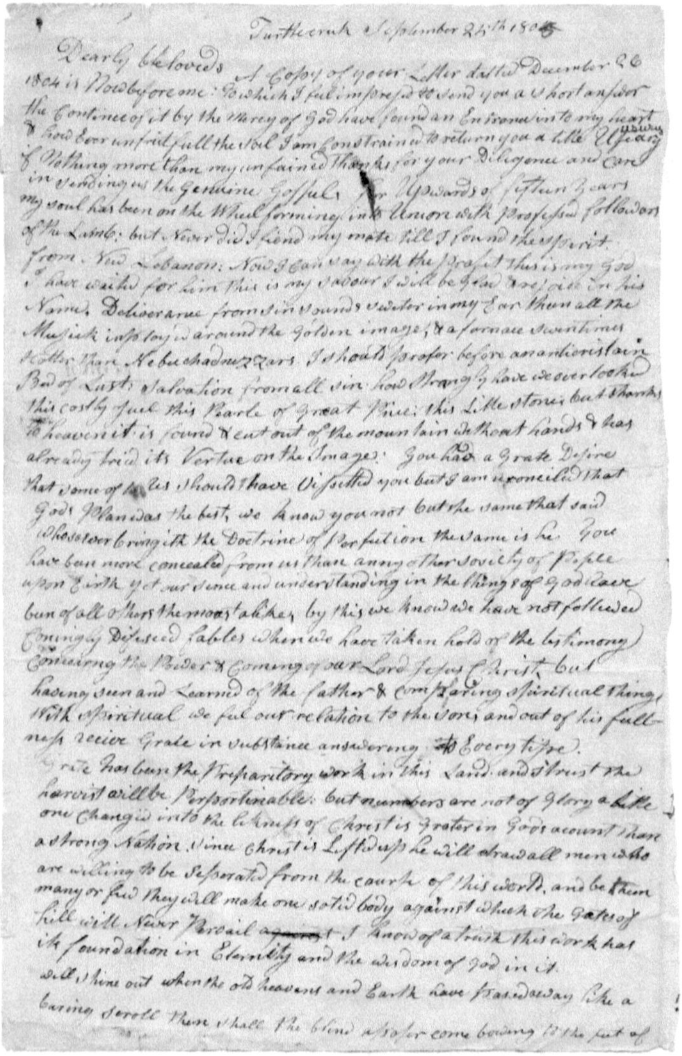

Figures 8.1a and 8.1b. Richard McNemar's first letter to the Shaker Ministry at New Lebanon, New York, dated September 25, 1805. Collection of the Western Reserve Historical Society.

thanks to heaven it is found and cut out of the mountain without hands and has already tried its virtue on the image.

You had a great desire that some of us should have visited you, but I am reconciled that God's plan was the best, we knew you not but the same that said whosoever bringeth the doctrine of perfection, the same is he. You have been more concealed from us than any other society of people upon earth, of those whom he hath ∫ufered and acknowledge them the only favourites of Heaven, I do not feel to inlarge at pre∫ant on any subject nor do I Desire to introduce my∫elf to you as a creature of note, if you can take knowledge of one that I have been with Je∫us it will afore you all the sati∫faction that I wish you to feel on my acount. I know I have many ∫teps to tracil through the garden of morfication before my fellowship with you can be compleat, but since the way is open I tru∫t I shall never Loose sight of you: you will Ruive ex∫en∫iv∫ull information from the bearer respecting the afairs of Zion in this quarter I tru∫t amongst other plea∫ing burtens he will Deliver my love to the Brethren warmer than I can possibly convey on paper.

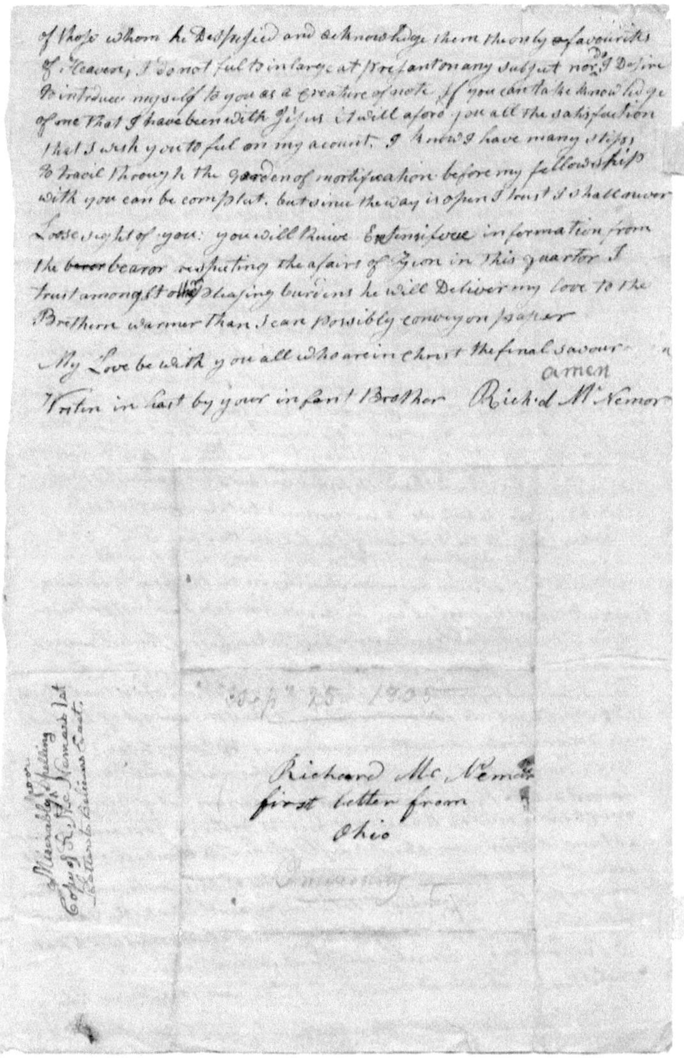

My Love be with you all who are in christ the final savour
amen
Written in ha∫t by your infant Brother Rich'd McNemar

Richard McNemar
first letter from
Ohio

Figures 8.1a and 8.1b. (*Continued*).

and yet our sense and understanding in the things of God have been of others the most alike. By this we know that we have not followed cunningly devised fables when we have taken hold of the testimony concerning the power and coming of our Lord Jesus Christ but having seen and heard of the Father, and comparing spiritual things with spiritual, we feel our relation to the son, and out of his fulness receive grace, in substance answering to every type. Great has been the preparitory work in this land and I trust the harvest will be proportionable; but numbers are not our glory, a little one changed into the likeness of Christ is greater in God's account than a strong nation. Since Christ is lifted up, he will draw all men who are willing to be separated from the course of this world, and be them many or few, they will make one solid body against which the gates of hell will never prevail. I know of a truth this work has its foundation in eternity, and the wisdom of God in it will hold out when the old heaven and earth have passed away like a scroll—then shall the blind opposer come bowing to the feet of those whom he dispised and acknowledge them the only favorites of heaven. I do not feel to enlarge at present on any subject, nor do I desire to introduce myself to you as a creature of note. If you can take knowledge of me that I have been with Jesus, it will afford you all the satisfaction that I wish you to feel on my account.

    I know I have many steps to travel thro the garden of mortification before my fellowship with you can be complete, but since the way is open I trust I shall never lose sight of you.

    You will receive extensive information from the bearer respecting the affairs of Zion in this quarter, and I trust among other pleasing burdens, he will deliver my love to the Brethren, warmer than I can possibly convey it on paper.

    My love be with you all who are in Christ *the final Saviour*, Amen.
    Written in haste by your infant Brother
    Rich'd M'Nemar[4]

It is telling that McNemar disavows his "desire to introduce myself to you as a creature of note," and that he acknowledges that he must undergo further spiritual mortification to travel further into the annihilation of will and ego required by Shakerism. In this, his very first letter to his elders, McNemar partially foresaw the causes of his eventual fall from grace.

Jennie McNemar's letter was addressed to the sisters at New Lebanon. She told them, "We have witnessed a Great work of God in this land and many of us thought we had almost attained the End of our calling." She was grateful to learn that celibacy, or "crucifying" the flesh, was the final step toward salvation, writing, "I cannot Say my flesh is all Destroyed—or that I am allready perfect—but this one thing I can Say that to be redeemed and purified from all

Iniquity is my Daily Labour." Acknowledging her cheerful spiritual submission to these strangers in the East, she closed: "I hope you will remember us as Little babes Just begining to learn of Christ—this much we have allready learned as little children to Love one another—and I no that Nothing but Love could have Induced me to write to those I Never Saw. Jenny Luckee McNemer."[5] Issachar Bates set out for New Lebanon on September 26, 1805, bearing these missives, along with letters from Darrow and the original missionaries. In one of them, Darrow described the Little Miami River area as "a beautiful country of good land ... so it is that our lot is fallen in its centre." He called Turtle Creek "the Seat & foundation of the Gospel in this part of the world."[6]

The night of Bates's departure, local anti-Shaker forces mobilized and set the worship stand on fire around midnight. They had piled the spectators' seats on the stand to form a pyre. Since the wood was green, the stand burned slowly. One of the Worley family realized it was ablaze around two in the morning and raised the alarm, but the Shakers dared not approach for fear of violence and leaving their own dwellings unattended. In a letter to New Lebanon describing the incident, David Darrow wrote that they had decided to leave the charred remnant of the stand for a "moniment to remind these ungodly persicutors of their dark & wicked works & as this place has a very disolate & malincoly appearance if they could but consider their End is to be according to their works it might be a strikeing leson to teach them somthing what their end must be."[7]

Despite the omnipresent threat of destruction, the Believers continued building. One of these ongoing projects was a new house for Richard McNemar. Given the lateness of the season, it was decided that the house would double as a meetinghouse during the coming winter. McNemar, Darrow, and Moseley worked at building in late September and through October. At a meeting of Believers only, held at McNemar's house on October 2, those couples who claimed to have taken a full cross of celibacy, yet "still lay together," were encouraged not to be overcome by their own weaknesses. That tenet of Shaker life was proving to be a challenge for some of the converts at Turtle Creek.[8]

STRIFE AT CANE RIDGE, UNION AT EAGLE CREEK

At Cane Ridge, the strange new faith continued to stir up strife among families and the wider community. Peter Houston wrote a letter to his brother-in-law John Dunlavy, begging him to come and preach at his house on October 1. Houston warned Dunlavy that "the spirit of persecution is much increased since I wrote last, I am like to be beat down in the mi[ddle] of the streets. I send to you to come & help me." Dunlavy and his wife, Cassie, heeded his request.

Youngs arrived at Dunlavy's on October 18, Dunlavy having returned the day before. Dunlavy reported the harrowing scene he had witnessed at Peter Houston's. Houston, who as a younger man had been the warrior companion of Daniel Boone, was confined to his bed, physically ill from the stress of community opposition to his conversion to Shakerism. His wife, Sarah Jane (Sally) Luckey (sister of Jenny Luckey, McNemar's wife), was bitterly opposed to his choice. She had given her husband until the next evening to decide if he would remain a Shaker. On Dunlavy's arrival, however, she issued an ultimatum to Houston to decide there and then. Houston decided that he must "follow the Lord," at which Sarah Jane took her child and left the house, abandoning her husband.[9]

Meanwhile, at New Lebanon, Deacon David Meacham penned a reply to the letters Bates carried back to the East. The ministry agreed that the missionaries should "have a habitation of your own not only for your own comfort or [word missing] but for the real good and protection of others," and permission was granted to engage for the purchase of lands in Turtle Creek. The ministry also acknowledged receipt of the letters from McNemar and his wife, deeming them "kindly received and acceptable to us, altho we do not feel a gift to answer them by letter at this time." The ministry's lack of response reflected the function of the Shaker hierarchy. To respond directly to new converts would have been a violation of carefully established protocols designed to keep the ministry at a remove from the rank-and-file membership.[10]

Youngs traveled on, ceaselessly proselytizing in central Kentucky. On November 11, he stayed at Samuel Banta's near Harrodsburg. After a pleasant day spent husking corn with the family, Youngs and John Meacham were awakened around midnight by two men lurking outside. Suddenly, a two-pound rock crashed through the window, knocking a candle and hat off the windowsill and landing on a bed. Fortunately, the rock missed the Shakers, though the sound of a gunshot in the vicinity further intimidated them. In the morning, it was discovered that their horses had been mutilated. Meacham's horse had its ears, mane, and tail cut off, and the tail and neck were deeply gashed. Youngs's horse had its right ear cut off, tail and mane cropped painfully close, and the tail was similarly cut and gashed.[11]

Youngs and Meacham reached the house of James Smith Jr. at Cane Ridge on Sunday, November 24. They dared not visit Peter Houston but sent him a note making their presence known. They were gratified to learn that he remained firm in his faith. The next day, Youngs and Meacham called on Barton Warren Stone. Stone's wife let Youngs into the house. On seeing Youngs, Stone's "countenance turned pale as a corpse & his spirit & limbs trembling such was the agitation of his mind." Stone plainly told Youngs, "I believe you to be antixt [antichrist]." By an amazing coincidence, Stone was reading Shaker apostate Daniel Rathbun's lengthy 1785 *Letter* when the men arrived, and he literally held it in his hand as he chastised them. Youngs confronted Stone about his recently published *Reply to John P. Campbell's Strictures on Atonement*, in which he lamented the conversion of McNemar and Dunlavy to the "wild enthusiasm" of Shakerism. In acidulous tones, Stone wrote to Campbell: "You have heard, no doubt, before this time, of the lamentable departure of two of our preachers, and a few of their hearers, from the true gospel into wild enthusiasm, or shakerism. They have made shipwreck of faith, and turned aside to an old woman's fables." Of the Shaker missionaries, he wrote, "These wolves, in sheep's clothing, have smelt us from far, and have come to tear, rend and devour." It is not surprising that Stone warned Youngs off and angrily noted that his own influence on his congregation "was much lost on account of receving [the Shakers] ... so he wanted none of our conversation or company." As they left, Stone warned the men to repent.[12] In a subsequent letter to Mother Lucy Wright, Ohio Shaker leaders described Stone's published attack as "the venomous Spitings forth of the cruel poison of Dragons; in which our principles & practice are Set forth in the most dispicable light, & painted in the most false colours which the Father of lies was able to invent."[13]

Youngs and Meacham left Stone and proceeded to Peter Houston's. Stone had shown Rathbun's *Letter* to Houston, and it had seriously damaged his faith. On seeing the missionaries arrive, Houston's wife (who had returned) grabbed a shovel and barred the door. Houston sat alone in a corner behind her. She warned the men to leave the property and never return. The missionaries quickly went to warn the Smith family about Rathbun's scurrilous account. Youngs felt defeated, writing, "It appears almost as impossible to get a believer out of Cane R. as to get light out of darkness." To his relief, Smith Jr. remained firm in his faith.[14]

Youngs and Meacham returned to more hospitable environs at Eagle Creek, arriving at John Dunlavy's home on Sunday, December 1. After Dunlavy preached, Meacham took him aside, and the two conversed earnestly for two hours. Meacham affirmed Dunlavy's gift "to labour in the Gospel," and assured Dunlavy that the Shakers would support his temporal needs so that he could continue to follow his call to preach. In the dancing that followed the sermon, Esther Knox again distinguished herself "in complete dancing as ever was danced after a violin." The song she hummed while dancing was a new composition of Richard McNemar's and was brought to Eagle Creek from Turtle Creek. Youngs wrote, "That song which Rd composed on the dispensations, &

dancing, was particularly striking." The hymn, "Typical Dancing," was printed in the Shakers' first hymnal eight years later.[15]

Youngs and Meacham returned to Turtle Creek on December 5. They had been away for eight weeks and two days. On the final leg of their trip, they passed Native American ruins, which Youngs described as "the remains of either a fortification, or place of worship—which plainly shews that this country was once inhabited by a people (who now are not)." The missionaries paused long enough for Youngs to make a detailed inspection and description of the site in his journal. At Turtle Creek, Youngs was heartened to learn that Issachar Bates had arrived at New Lebanon on October 17, making the journey in a remarkable twenty-two days. Richard McNemar had preached to the Believers at Turtle Creek in the absence of Youngs, Meacham, and Bates. It is a testament to David Darrow's confidence in McNemar's understanding, and embrace of, Shaker doctrine that he was entrusted with the spiritual guidance of the young Believers. To further cement McNemar's importance to the faith, the Shakers met for the first time to worship at McNemar's new house on Sunday, December 1. Remarkably, a surviving illustration of the structure—made by McNemar—shows an open dancing platform bridging the gap between his new house and either a shed or his original house (see map 0.2). The house was made from hewn logs and was two stories high. Youngs noted that there was little room to meet in it, especially when spectators were present. However, during that first meeting, "the visible power or opperations were great & extraordinary."[16]

VIOLENT OPPOSITION ERUPTS

Violence against the Shakers increased as they visibly established themselves by erecting structures and consolidating the newly converted around a central place of worship. A number of men, led by William Green, physically disrupted a meeting at McNemar's house on Sunday, December 8. They attempted to join in the dance and abused the Believers with blasphemous and "filthy" language. One man stripped off his coat to fight and threatened Worley that "he would mark him to his grave." Another man named Eaton opened his mind to Youngs—but not before telling him that he had come that day armed with a knife to kill him if he had become subject to physical operations of the spirit before his confession. On Wednesday, December 11, Youngs and a number of believing families with children were lodging at Malcham Worley's house. Just before eleven o'clock, ruffians smashed two windows with clubs, and it was thought a gunshot was heard.[17]

In the morning, Youngs discovered that the same ruffians used stones and clubs to vandalize windows at the homes of McNemar, James Bedle, Elijah Davis, and David Hill. A dreadful and palpable "spirit of wickedness" and "bloodshed" permeated the settlement that day. At candlelight, the Believers gathered for worship at James Bedle's house, although some left to guard their own homes and families. Ultimately, the threat failed to emerge, and the meeting was unusually powerful, with some jerking "like a great wheel or roller—swiftly going in all directions of the house." Daniel Moseley declared war against the spirit of evil, and some of the worshippers spoke in tongues, the first time this gift had been seen by the missionaries in the West. The meeting continued until midnight and later moved into the nearby woods. Youngs wrote that so many were exercised in gifts of dancing, singing, and speaking that it was "difficult to get out a full sentence." The spirit of light had prevailed over the spirit of darkness, and the church embodied this victory through its extraordinarily powerful meeting.[18]

McNemar hosted a contingent of Believers from Eagle Creek and his old congregation of Cabin Creek during the weekend of December 14. On Sunday morning, a number of McNemar's guests "freed their minds," confessing their sins to Youngs, David Spinning, and Issachar Bates, who arrived back at Turtle Creek on Tuesday, December 10, having made the journey of 774 miles in twenty-three days. Green and the ruffians again disrupted the meeting in the afternoon with the "spirit of hell." Polly Kimball bore a "strong agonizing testimony" against them, all the while "darting her fists at them." The ruffians baited her to strike them, but she refused, saying, "I do not want to strike; God bless your souls—I love your souls . . . but I hate your sins as God hates them."[19]

Throughout the month, the burgeoning community worked at finishing the chimney on McNemar's house and erecting buildings for Spinning. David Darrow and Daniel Moseley hewed shingles, and Solomon King made shoes. The eastern Believers demonstrated the core Shaker belief that all must labor with their hands, no matter their spiritual rank. On Christmas day, an initially lifeless meeting suddenly became the arena for prophecy, as Believers started "signing out the spreading of the gospel . . . toward the South & SWest & some towards the N & NE." The following day, for safety, Moseley and Worley rode into Lebanon together to mail lengthy letters from the missionaries back to New Lebanon. The letters gave detailed accounts of the persecution lately endured by Believers. A request for additional help from the East—especially for sisters to work with newly converted women—was tempered with the statement "It is by no means our wish to frighten any of those, who may be in an expectation of coming to this country; if any will be disheartened at these trifles, they may as well stay at home; for we look upon these things as only a small begining of what will be; and none but Good Solgers [soldiers] will answer the purpose here." In a separate missive, Youngs wrote directly to Elder Ebenezer Cooley of New Lebanon's North Family, which was the gathering order for newly converted Believers. Cooley performed many missionary journeys in the early days of Mother Ann Lee and had probably mentored Youngs in that capacity. Youngs expressed his joy at Bates's return, calling him "my brother, my right hand." Beyond himself and Bates, he told Cooley that "Rd McNamer & Jn Dunlavy both preachers are the next & the only ones who stand as immediate & propper helps towards the world—these are worthy men both in nature & in faith."[20]

On Monday, December 30, Youngs, Bates, and McNemar set out for Kentucky, planning to stop first at Eagle Creek. They reached John Knox's house at eight o'clock in the evening on New Year's Eve. As they sat by the warmth of Knox's hearth, Youngs and Bates could reflect on what must have been one of the most important years of their lives. They had each traveled thousands of miles—Bates having made three trips between New York and Ohio. They had converted hundreds of souls to Shakerism, despite overwhelming, and sometimes violent, opposition. And finally, they had laid a foundation at Turtle Creek from which Shakerism could grow west of the Appalachians. Richard McNemar, who sat with them, had also lived the most important year of his life and was instrumental to their success. McNemar embraced Shakerism after great spiritual travail, but once he did, he opened his home to the missionaries, preached on their behalf, and ultimately sold them his land to use as the base for their mission and the center of their community. Additionally, the homes of McNemar's extended family throughout southern Ohio and north-central Kentucky had served as way stations for the missionaries, and those families had also yielded many converts. McNemar was thirty-five years old, and his new life was just beginning.[21]

BUILDING AND CONSOLIDATING COMMUNITY

As 1806 dawned, Youngs, Bates, and McNemar journeyed through Kentucky shoring up the faith of recent converts and doubtless preaching the gospel wherever they found willing hearers. Darrow reported to New Lebanon: "Those From whome we feel the Greatest help at Preasant are Richard M Nemar & John Dunlavy."[22] Youngs's diary during this period is lacking, and no correspondence exists to fill in the details of this mission. However, journals compiled retrospectively at the South Union, Kentucky, community from Youngs's (now lost) originals provide some information. On Sunday, January 5, the Believers met at Eagle Creek for the first time in public worship. After preaching by their former minister John Dunlavy, as well as McNemar, Bates, and Youngs, the Shakers went forth in worship, some falling, some shaking and jerking. The fervor was enough to draw Anthony Dunlavy (probably John's brother, although his father was also named Anthony), who had not been physically active in worship before, into the whirlwind of devotion.[23]

McNemar visited his brother Garner before the missionaries traveled on to his old congregation at Cabin Creek, where he arrived on January 17. Unsurprisingly, they were not allowed to speak at the regular Presbyterian meeting. After adding a couple more converts, they moved on to Cane Ridge, arriving at James Smith Jr.'s house on January 23. They attended a Methodist meeting, after which they were invited to preach in a private home. Youngs and McNemar were gratified to have one hundred interested hearers there. By January 30, they reached the vicinity of Shawnee Run and Paint Lick, communities roughly forty miles apart, where there were pockets of Believers. They met with members of the Banta family as well as Matthew Houston for the next ten days, preaching wherever an opportunity was available. Momentously, on January 11, Matthew Houston confessed his sins to Youngs, officially embracing Shakerism. Confessing along with Houston was his slave Isaac Newton, described by Youngs as "Bright mulatto, part Indian."[24]

After nearly two months spent shoring up converts in central Kentucky, the missionaries returned to Bourbon County, where they unnerved Barton W. Stone by attending his preaching at Cabin Creek on February 28. Youngs wrote, "Paleness & death sat on his countenance—no appearance of life in meeting nor people!" On Sunday, March 1, Garner McNemar's wife, Betsy, confessed her sins to Youngs at Eagle Creek. The party returned to Turtle Creek, reaching Malcham Worley's on March 11, after almost ten weeks of itinerant preaching in midwinter. In the wake of their successful efforts, they spent March preparing for an influx of Believers and considered the placement of buildings, organization of communal families, and harvesting timber suitable for building. They planned to construct a thirty-by-forty-foot frame house, the first purpose-built Shaker dwelling west of the Appalachians.[25]

The fervor of the new converts was expressed in a bizarre Sabbath meeting at McNemar's house on March 23, where "6 or 8 [Shakers] at once putting their heads together about a foot from the floor chattering as with unknown tongues, while their fingers were engaged drawing figures on the floor . . . others wrestling (chasing) with their utmost strength! In one meeting they all sat in a circle & played Button." The month closed with McNemar and Youngs spending a week at Beaver Creek, where they arrived on March 26. They returned to Turtle Creek on April 1, having converted ten more, including Peggy Buchanan, whose husband told her, "She should never enter his house again if she joined the Shakers"; he "said not a word when she informed him of the fact."[26]

At the beginning of February, the ministry at New Lebanon wrote a letter to David Darrow approving his plans to send a mission to Tennessee that year. The ministry desired "that there mite no Loss come through neglect in any of those neighbouring places." Additionally, they forwarded the reassuring news that the missionaries' request for more help was going to be fulfilled that year, writing, "It is expected that there will one Brother and six Sisters set out for the State of Ohio in the spring (viz) Peter Peas Ruth Farrington Molly Goodrich and Ruth Darrow: whom we expect will remain there." A second letter from New Lebanon's deacon David Meacham sent on February 4 promised that the incoming western party would also bring furniture, bedding, and house and tableware, which the frugal deacon expected could be procured much more cheaply back East.[27]

Benjamin Seth Youngs's copious correspondence is one of the main sources of information during this period. Despite his heroic missionary efforts, it is clear from one of his letters to Ebenezer Cooley at New Lebanon that he was having second thoughts about remaining in the West for the rest of his life. Buried within a long letter to Cooley about accepting his duty and performing it faithfully, Youngs subtly dropped hints about returning east, writing, "I have had a great desire to see N Lebanon once more." Although Youngs was resigned for his life to "be laid down in this 'dark and bloody land,'" he still asked if he could "leave this country so soon as next fall it would be my desire as my feelings are—but if it should prove to be inconsistant my faith teaches me to be reconciled."[28]

Youngs's moment of doubt must have passed rather quickly though, as he penned an ebullient report of the state of Shakerism in the West in a subsequent letter to Cooley on March 20, 1806.

Believers in Miami—grown persons	94
70 miles E by S from thence to Eagle Creek Ad. co	66
14 m. S from thence, near Washington (Ken)	6
15 m E to Cabbin Creek, Mason County	12
50 m S.W. to Cane ridge, Bourbon co.	3
73 m S. by W. to Paint lick, Garrad co.	8

23 m N.W. thence near Danville, Mercer co	21
55 m. NW to Shelby co. 20 m. W. by S of Frankfort	10
	220[29]

In light of these numbers, David Darrow and John Meacham wrote David Meacham at New Lebanon to justify their decision to build a two-story frame house, thirty by forty feet, with a gable roof and two chimneys. Up to this date, the missionaries had lodged mainly with Worley, the result being that his one-story house and lean-to typically housed fifteen, with more people continually visiting. Darrow needed to plan for the ingathering of more converts and the accommodation of visitors to the settlement. The Believers prepared their own shingles, clapboards of white oak, and timber for framing. They had spent considerable money on land, cows, wheat, corn, pork, beef, feathers, cloth, saddles, axes and tools, and traveling expenses for missionaries—$2,525 in total, all of which they accounted for in their letter to Deacon Meacham. They had only $303 remaining and were in urgent need of hiring carpenters and buying plank and brick. They did not yet feel comfortable asking the new converts to contribute money, but they asked for more funds from New Lebanon to shore up the settlement. Additionally, Darrow requested a copy of the manuscript history of the Shaker church written by Deacon Daniel Goodrich of the Hancock, Massachusetts, community. This document would help anchor the faith of new Believers in the West and counter the efforts of those circulating the publications of apostate and anti-Shaker writers.[30]

Darrow's desire for more housing surely reflected the impending departure of the company from New Lebanon. The ministry wrote to Darrow on April 18 that Samuel Turner had been added to the group. They were concerned that since Peter Pease was to have been the only brother in the company that "the gift of singing would be stronger with the sisters than with the Brethren there fore we thought it wisdom to labour for another singer to go." The ministry also replied directly to Youngs that if Darrow approved, Youngs could return to New Lebanon that fall.[31] Cooley later responded personally to Youngs and urged him to be reconciled to his duty in the West, but he added that if Youngs were to come back, he would "have nothing against it."[32] Privately, however, the ministry urged Darrow to speak candidly with Youngs about his dissatisfaction, cautioning Darrow, "You must consider the Elder must open for the younger, the younger cannot for the Elder."[33]

The newly emerging hierarchy among the western Shakers posed challenges not just for the eastern Believers but also for the western converts, who had to learn their place in union with their elders. Some of these converts, like

McNemar and Calvin Morrell, had been men of influence and enjoyed, in McNemar's case, fame greater than anything the eastern Believers had experienced. Accordingly, a special "humbling" was arranged for McNemar and Morrell at the evening meeting on Saturday, April 5. The ritual is worth recounting in full, as it illuminates the requirement of Shakerism to subjugate one's ego and will, something that proved particularly difficult for McNemar.

> In the evening meeting Dr. Calvin Morrell & Rev. R. McNemar underwent the following: The Dr was first laid on the floor & made to lick the dust & lie as one dead—putting dust on him thus settling the Doctor—They, the chief actors, David Corey & Saml Rollins, next went mockingly to R. McNemar saying: How do you do Rev. Sir? This is the great Rev. McNemar, your vain philosophy and systems of divinity shall be brot down into the dust—they then brot him down and put his head with the Doctors & both their faces in the dust; then dragged him over the floor—rolled him over & over—S. Rollins kicked the dust over him—danced round him putting his foot on his head—D. Corey also put dust on him, in a sign of burying the Dr. & Divine—after this scene of mortification—The Rev. began to use scripture in his defence—They silenced him saying, "Not a word out of your mouth—you have explained away the sense of scripture long enough—your head knowledge shall have an end—Not a sentence out of your mouth," & took him down and humbled him a second time—After this, the Sigh of Esau & Jacob closed the scene.[34]

Despite the reconciliation alluded to in the end, McNemar must have been deeply affected by this ritual. Putting an end to his "head knowledge," the source of his greatest power, represented a form of ego death. His attempted defense of himself while undergoing this humbling does not appear to have been part of the script. It is highly emblematic of the character he retained throughout his Shaker life, where he tried to maintain a separate identity within the sect, a stance that ultimately led to tragedy.[35]

A conflicted Youngs and a newly humbled McNemar set out for Kentucky on May 7. Their destination was the home of McNemar's former colleague Matthew Houston at Paint Lick. Houston had accommodated the missionaries on their initial arrival in Kentucky, and it was hoped that more of his congregation could be converted. At Turtle Creek, preparation continued on the new dwelling house, as the new eastern Believers were daily expected. Bates, Worley, and Calvin Morrell took a wagon and met them at Chillicothe on Tuesday, May 27. Their journey had been relatively easy, and the travelers were met with unexpected hospitality throughout the trip. They arrived at Turtle Creek on Saturday, May 31. The group of ten, of whom nine would remain, made the journey in forty-one days, traversing the Alleghany Mountains.[36] The very next day, they attended their first meeting in the West at McNemar's house (although he was still in Kentucky). The women among the new converts in the West "were very deeply affected being greatly filled with joy and wonder" at the first eastern Shaker sisters they had ever seen. David Darrow wrote, "Some fell flat on the floor—others shouted or cryed out and the greatest Part were immediately in tears." Two hundred spectators assembled to see this momentous meeting, and, according to Darrow, some of the bitterest opposers were also brought to tears at the solemnity of the proceedings.[37]

McNemar returned to Turtle Creek on June 4 and rejoiced in meeting the newly arrived easterners. Of this group, Ruth Farrington would serve as "Mother," the spiritual counterpart and balance of David Darrow's "Father." On June 5, Darrow and some of the other easterners moved into the newly completed dwelling. The Worley family was quite upset about losing their holy lodgers. McNemar never remained in one place very long, and during the summer of 1806, he made two more missionary journeys. The first took him, Bates, and Daniel Moseley to Beaver Creek, where they arrived on July 8, returning to Turtle Creek on July 14. On July 30, McNemar set out with Bates for Eagle Creek. Their horses disappeared during the night but were later recovered. Their mission to Eagle Creek was especially important, as the faith of the converted was flagging. Youngs noted they would "unwisely run wild" at their meetings and were in dire need of guidance from their spiritual elders. Bates and McNemar returned to Turtle Creek on August 7. During late August, McNemar worked with Worley and Peter Pease to stake out a new road running from his house to the main road. He also went on another mission to Beaver Creek with Bates and William Davis.[38]

REVEALING *THE TESTIMONY OF CHRIST'S SECOND APPEARING* TO THE WORLD

On August 19, one of the three original eastern missionaries, John Meacham, began a journey back to New Lebanon. He carried important correspondence with him, including a letter from David Darrow to the ministry, wherein Darrow confided, "We are sensible that not all, if any of us have fully got rid of that soft, delicate & retired manner . . . that neet, compleet & orderly way and feeling, in which we have lived in the Church. So that the ways & methods of the people in the wilderness appear the more raw & uncultivated . . . we have not yet become fully seasoned to hardships."[39] Despite their physical discomfort, their letter noted that the most violent and bitter opposition had largely abated in fortunate coincidence with the arrival of the party from New Lebanon. Darrow noted that there were 260 Believers over fifteen years old now in the West, this despite the presence of anti-Shaker literature in the region, which Darrow reported to his elders. "Many of the accusations that were Spread in the First opening of the gospel have been brought to this country—& they are surculated in adition to a very numerous multitude of fresh ones that have been raised against the worck of God here, one of the rathbun books has also been Brought—& they have made great use of it, carying it & Reading it from place to place."[40]

John Meacham also carried an early manuscript of *The Testimony of Christ's Second Appearing* to the ministry at New Lebanon.[41] Youngs began writing the work on July 7 in an attic room of the new dwelling.[42] Darrow wrote a letter accompanying it that declared, "We have for some time past from prevailing circumstances been greatly pressed in our minds to publish our faith to the world by letter." He lamented that those who might be sympathetic to Shakerism lacked a source of good information and were being exposed to works like Rathbun's. He queried, "Is it not high time that the world knew that God has a foundation now on the earth?" Darrow proposed publishing it under the names of Worley, McNemar, Dunlavy, and Houston, whom he described as "men of good & simple faith, as well as men of learning, who will be able to see that the work is finished according to good sense, & the perfect order of the letter." Darrow also beseeched the ministry to open to the world "the first Foundation & Pillar of the present appearing of Christ"; in other words, Mother Ann Lee. He implored, "Must it be hid from the world till the eye Witnesses of Her power & Majesty are all gone?" Darrow was troubled that, at least in the West, the Shaker gospel was portrayed as the product of a "drunken old woman."[43]

John Dunlavy took the opportunity to send along his own testimony with Meacham. In it, he credited his conversion to his "dearly beloved & Ever faithful brother Richard MacNemer." Addressing the New Lebanon Ministry, Dunlavy wrote, "I began greatly through [McNemar] as the instrument to learn that salvation is brought to men in the gospel of Christ in a much more liberal and equitable measure than I had heretofore understood."[44] As with the McNemar's letters, Dunlavy received no direct reply from the ministry.

Meacham arrived at New Lebanon on September 16, 1806.[45] He shared Youngs's writing with the ministry, eliciting a positive response that entrusted the entire publishing project to the Believers in the West. Mother Lucy Wright wrote that she was "satisfied that what you have written is the Gift of God, that you have received by your faith & obedience to the true & genuine Gospel.—I have felt & experienced considerable with Father Joseph in relation to writing, & making more fully known to the world the foundation of our Faith—We always felt the time was not come—But now I feel satisfied that time is come, & the gift is in you, & with you to accomplish this work." Wright gave Darrow complete editorial oversight, foregoing any further inspection or approval of the text. However, she did warn him not to "get anything printed out but what you are willing to live by & die by."[46] Wright also sent with Meacham some writings of Father Joseph Meacham, saying, "I think they may be of great service to those that is called to write our faith."[47]

David Darrow reported to Deacon David Meacham on November 2, 1806, that the Believers at Turtle Creek had moved into a new house and relocated the cabin to function as a kitchen. The Shakers held meetings in their own house for the first time on September 3, 1806, moving the scene of worship from McNemar's house.[48] Relieved, Darrow wrote that they were "more comfortable than we have been sence we came from the church." He also reported the return of Youngs and Bates from Kentucky, where they had been since August 28, leaving one hundred grown converts in their wake.[49]

John Meacham returned to Cincinnati on November 25, 1806, where Peter Pease, Matthew Houston, and twelve young Believers from Kentucky met him.[50] He left New Lebanon on October 13, and his return trip was smooth. Meacham reported that although he was treated very kindly by the "commander & boatsmen" on the Ohio River, "their vain and profain cursing & Swearing, & their quarriling & fighting among themselves was a continual vexation to [my] Spirit."[51] He delivered his valuable cargo to Turtle Creek two days later, where western Believers were overjoyed to receive clothing, bedding, leather, cheese, dried apples, and much more that was contributed by the Shaker communities in New York and western Massachusetts.[52]

On Sunday, December 7, around one hundred Shakers held a meeting at the stand at Richard McNemar's house. There, for the first time in Ohio, the role of Ann Lee as the "second part of the man Jesus" was preached to the public. A drunkard heckled the Shakers, and as the weather turned, the Believers moved the meeting inside. The drunkard hurled his body against the door, attempting to break it down. The Shakers judged him to be the "seed of the serpent," railing against the opening of the gospel. Youngs and McNemar preached on the theme, and the meeting closed with a song on the theme of redemption.[53] This was probably "The Day of Redemption," which speaks of the serpent deceiving Adam and Eve and his wounding at the opening of man's path to salvation.[54] That evening, a smaller group met at Calvin Morrell's, where Youngs elaborated further on Mother Ann Lee. With relief, he noted in his journal that "all things are well received appearantly among all."[55] Thus, the boldest theological tenet of Shakerism was fully proclaimed, leaving the Shakers open to ridicule and the prospect of violence.

A company of Turtle Creek Believers, including Malcham and Peggy Worley and Jenny McNemar, had visited the Believers at Eagle Creek in October, thereby strengthening their faith. The Eagle Creek converts greatly desired to meet the eastern Shakers. On December 9, David Darrow responded to their entreaties and traveled via Limestone to Eagle Creek to visit them, accompanied by Richard McNemar, Solomon King, and Issachar Bates. At a Sabbath meeting there, on December 14, McNemar proclaimed for the first time to those at Eagle Creek that Christ "made his second appearance in the woman, even in her that is called Ann Lee." To their relief, this potentially controversial message found willing hearers. Darrow, King, and Bates returned to Turtle Creek on Christmas Day, having gained six new converts.[56] Meanwhile, McNemar and John Dunlavy left Eagle Creek on December 18 to journey farther into Kentucky to visit Believers and preach at the request of another interested group of people. They traveled first to Indian Creek, fifty miles south of Eagle Creek, a community greatly affected by the revival. There, they hoped to find open ears among those who had participated in "one of the most powerful camp-meetings in all the western country." McNemar and Dunlavy held several public meetings there, which were well attended.[57] A handful of new converts were made, and the previously converted were left "stedfast in the faith."[58]

At Turtle Creek, communal bonds were greatly strengthened by a special meeting held on Thursday, January 1, 1807, at Malcham Worley's suggestion. On the previous Sabbath, Worley interrupted the meeting to request a respectful commemoration of "the day of the year in which the three first brethren Set out from N.L. to this country." At the meeting, Worley addressed the new converts first, admonishing them to be grateful for the opportunity they now had for salvation. Then he spoke to the easterners "from the inermost feelings of his Soul," individually thanking John Meacham, Issachar Bates, and Benjamin Seth Youngs, and the later eastern arrivals, for leaving the comforts of New Lebanon and making the arduous journey to bring the gift of salvation to the people in the West.[59]

On January 12, 1807, Darrow reported to Mother Lucy that Prudence Farrington and Molly Goodrich, whose "sence was to high and some times would rise against their elder," were slowly reconciling themselves to the strong leadership of Mother Ruth Farrington. Darrow hoped that in time they would become "more simple." The eastern women were all recovering their physical strength. John Meacham was more fully reconciled to his new home in the West following his return, feeling more "union & freedom in the family." Darrow also noted that the eastern Shakers' songs were "great conviction & strength to the people." Richard McNemar's first efforts at hymn writing from the Shaker theological standpoint surely complemented these. Darrow described

McNemar as "full of faith light Life & power." Darrow also revealed "our first Mother is publickly preached in her order & Lot. So plain as to say her name was Anne Lees, & proved in the most clear manner by the scriptures of truth, that Christs Second appearing was to be in the woman." Finally, following the practice of the Shaker Ministry in the East, Darrow had begun to withdraw himself from direct contact with most other Believers. He affirmed to Mother Lucy: "Since I have been able to Separate more from the people & Shut them more off, I feel stronger in body & spirit."[60]

In a separate letter to Deacon David Meacham written on January 15, Darrow reported on the ongoing process of purchasing adjacent tracts of land to consolidate a single, large holding at Turtle Creek. Darrow confided to Meacham, "Richard McNemar has for a long time expressed a great desire to be free from the burden of his land." The eastern Believers had already advanced McNemar money in September 1805 when he was being pressed by Jonathan Dayton's attorney for past-due payments. Since then, McNemar had received an additional $182 and had fully transferred his property to the Shakers.[61] McNemar's commitment to the faith was complete. On January 19, he returned to Turtle Creek with John Dunlavy following an arduous forty-day mission to Kentucky in midwinter. Although he was technically a young Believer, Youngs held McNemar's theological and spiritual judgment in such high esteem that he submitted his writing on the primitive church to McNemar "for inspection." He also collaborated with McNemar on writing about the reign of the Antichrist for the "public writings"—almost certainly the initial stages of what would become *The Testimony of Christ's Second Appearing*.[62]

McNemar proposed to write on behalf of the Shakers for the first time in February 1807. His "Messenger Dove" was approved by Darrow, Meacham, Youngs, and Bates and was completed on February 3.[63] Although this writing is not known to have survived, its existence confirms that McNemar was viewed as a near equal by his eastern spiritual elders. Just as he had emerged as a leader during the Kentucky Revival, he was rising to a uniquely powerful position in the nascent western Shaker hierarchy. His talents made him invaluable for the work of spreading the gospel, and he was constantly used in that capacity. In a way, he became the indispensable man of the western Shaker expansion. However, his peripatetic nature and ambition—couched as it was in Shaker humility—set a dangerous precedent. McNemar was embarking on a road that would ultimately leave him without a firm place in the hierarchy that he worked so hard to establish, thereby setting the stage for his downfall.

NINE

SHAKERS AND THE SHAWNEE PROPHET

THE SHAKERS AT TURTLE CREEK became aware of an ongoing spiritual revival among the Shawnee, who were known to be relatively close to their location. During Richard McNemar's travels in Kentucky the previous winter, he was told of the Shawnee prophet Tenskwatawa, who had dreamed that "the old God that had governed the world had got so old that he was not able to govern it any longer—& his son A new God was a going to govern it now & he was to come in the spring & deliver them." As early as February 12, 1807, Benjamin Seth Youngs broached the topic of visiting the prophet. On March 17, David Darrow, McNemar, and Youngs set out to locate the Shawnee band, which they did, eighty miles northwest of Lebanon, Ohio. Darrow explained his rationale for the mission to Mother Lucy Wright, that it "would often strike my mind—that the time was not far distant when God would fulfill his promise—to give the heathen to his Son for an inheritance &c—and that God would be exalted among the heathen & he would be exalted in the Earth." Darrow was compelled to offer the gospel to the Native Americans. One wonders if McNemar, who grew up amid the frontier violence of Revolutionary western Pennsylvania, which often involved Native Americans, felt any trepidation in embarking on this mission. Indeed, the Shawnee band visited by the Shakers had moved inside the boundary line claimed by the US government and were seen as a potentially hostile force by nearby settlers.[1]

On March 23, the Shakers arrived at the Shawnee village and were amazed to find a large frame building "about 150 by 34 feet in size, surrounded with 50 or 60 smoking cottages." They discovered that this large building was a sort of church used by the Shawnee to worship the Great Spirit. Seeking the chiefs, they were told that Tecumseh and his brother Lal-lu-e-tsee-ka (Tenskwatawa, the prophet) were off at a sugar camp. They journeyed there and found Tenskwatawa sick in his tent. George Blue Jacket, son of the war chief Blue Jacket, who served as an interpreter, informed the Shakers that the prophet would not see white ministers, as they ridiculed his spirituality. The Shakers assured Blue Jacket that they were different from other whites. He asked them, "Do you believe a person can have true knowledge of the great spirit, in the heart, without going to school and learning to read?" They replied that that was "the best kind of knowledge."[2]

Eventually, the prophet emerged from his tent and addressed a group of people seated around a fire. Blue Jacket was unable to translate the prophet's words for the Shakers, but they were struck by his solemnity and heartfelt eloquence. During their visit, they gleaned that the prophet was formerly a doctor, and a wicked man, who lived on the White River in Indiana. During a time of great sickness, he had a vision that a forked road was presented to him. One fork was for those who abandoned wickedness, while the other led deeper into sinfulness, though it initially offered opportunities to cross back to the good fork. Drunkards, in particular, were drawn along the bad fork, until they were irredeemably lost. When the prophet shared this vision with the Shawnee, it divided them. Those who believed followed Tenskwatawa and his brother Tecumseh to Greenville, Ohio, where they established a camp.[3] (See Figure 4.3.)

The Shakers discerned that the Shawnee viewed humankind as fallen and that they were interested in learning about Christ. They also eschewed witchcraft, poison, fighting, murder, whiskey, wife-beating, and fornication, and they confessed their sins to the prophet and their chiefs. The Shakers were struck by the poverty and scarcity of provisions at the camp and witnessed forty people sharing a single turkey for a meal. The missionaries witnessed impressive preaching that evening and again in the morning. They felt that "surely the Lord is in this place!" and that they were among the "tribes of Israel, on their march to Canaan." They saw in the Shawnee a simplicity that accorded with their own notions of religious communal life. As they left to return to Turtle Creek, they were sure that "God, in very deed, was mightily at work" among the Shawnee. They arrived home on March 26.[4]

Epidemic illness struck Union Village beginning in February 1807 and tragically evicted a particularly beloved young eastern sister from her "house of clay." Alarmingly, John Meacham was severely ill from mid-February until mid-March. His prognosis was uncertain, and "the picture of death was so far formed in his countenance" that his fellow Shakers were "ready to give him over to the grave." Luckily, he recovered, but the malady lingered within the community. On April 1, the Believers gathered to hear David Darrow, Benjamin

Seth Youngs, and Richard McNemar tell of their mission to the Shawnee. During the meeting, Prudence Farrington suddenly became violently ill and left in haste. She was afflicted with a high fever and intense pain throughout her body. As the illness worsened, she vomited uncontrollably, and her internal organs swelled. She was given paregoric (an opiate) and spirits of nitre (an antispasmodic), which "threw her into a violent extacy." Following this, live chickens were cut open and applied to her feet in an attempt to bring down her fever. Shaker physician John Wallace, or possibly John Dunlavy (who had some medical training), may have initiated these treatments in an attempt to stay the sickness, but they ultimately gave her up as lost.[5]

On the day she died, she gathered the Believers to her bedside and addressed them on the subject of love, saying, "I feel to sing a song of love." Samuel Turner and Molly Goodrich sat at her bedside and sang a new laboring song. Prudence "united with her lips & with her hands & feet, But her voice could not be heard for want of strength." After singing, she felt a gift that they should all drink milk together in remembrance of love and of the day. The young Believers visited her bedside throughout the day. When Richard McNemar came, she asked if he would "be so kind as to strengthen his Brethren?" He answered, "Yea, I will. I leave my love with you," to which she replied, "Take mine & keep it." Prudence finally passed at four o'clock the next morning, on April 11. She had arrived in Ohio less than a year before, on May 1, 1806, and was only thirty years old. In his harrowing account of the episode, Youngs wrote that Prudence left "a beutiful & smiling corpse."[6]

Prudence Farrington's death was a great tragedy for the Ohio Believers, but it greatly cemented their bonds of love and union. The day following her death was the Sabbath, and the public meeting was held as usual. A funeral song was sung, and Youngs preached at length on the meaning of her death. McNemar then read a new hymn of his own composition, which was then "very feeling sung & suited to the case."[7] The first verse read:

> Farewell loving Sister, farewell in the lord
>
> Now called to receive your, immortal reward
>
> We shall not forget the[e], thou vessel of grace
>
> Nor that blessed day, that we first saw thy face

Subsequent verses celebrated Prudence as a "virgin," a "soul undefil'd," and a "dove." McNemar had penned a powerful memorial to his elder sister from the East. His powers of oratory were well known, and now his talent for poetry and music made him one of the foremost hymn writers among the Shakers, east or west. Meacham included this hymn in his letter to Lucy Wright, along with others McNemar had recently composed. Aware of the potential spiritual pitfalls of having a young Believer compose theological hymnody, Meacham explained, "We do not send [the hymns] Because we Suppose the light & understanding by which they were composed is perfect but that their faith concerning us may appear." Thus, he affirmed the role of McNemar's verse in the developing culture of the western Shaker communities.[8] While Prudence Farrington's life slipped away, a new spiritual energy gripped the community stemming from the report of the missionaries to the Shawnee. Sisters Polly Kimball and Nancy Duncan began to speak in Indian tongues. In Youngs's opinion, Kimball was able to "stammer in the very tone of the Shawneese."[9]

Meanwhile, at Eagle Creek, the faith of some of the new converts was slipping, and some had "gone into the flesh," and others back to the world. McNemar and Bates were dispatched there on April 30 to shore up the Believers. In the vicinity of Turtle Creek, the threat of physical violence had become a reality. On April 11, Cornelius Campbell and a Believer named Elisha were beaten, knocked down, and kicked as they lay on the ground. On the morning of May 7, the day McNemar and Bates returned home, anti-Shaker agitator Robert Gray repeatedly whipped John Stewart with a hickory stick.[10]

The Shaker mission to the Shawnee continued with the dispatch of John Patterson, John Stewart, and James Patterson to Greenville, Ohio, on May 25. When they arrived, the Shawnee were in a religious meeting overseen by Tenskwatawa, who was arrayed in "costly apparel & abundance of silver." At a break in the meeting, the chiefs greeted the Shakers warmly and shook their hands. Through the interpreter Peter Cornstalk it was established that the three newly arrived men were of the same faith as Darrow, Youngs, and McNemar and that they "had the good spirit." They were given a tent to lodge in and watched in amazement as nearly five hundred Indians from a variety of tribes visited the encampment to see the prophet.[11]

Heartened by the Shakers' visit and grateful for a gift of salt, a party of Shawnee set out for Union Village on May 28. Stewart and James Patterson left the day before and waited in Dayton to guide the Shawnee to Union Village. It happened to be a training day for the militia in Dayton. The citizens there were outraged at the Shakers for visiting the Shawnee and threatened to imprison them. The Shakers were forced to leave town, but serendipitously a non-Shaker guided the Shawnee to Union Village, where they arrived at four o'clock on May 30. They camped in the woods with thirty-six horses they had brought.

Prominent among the band were four Shawnee chiefs, including Tecumseh and George Blue Jacket, and two Wyandot chiefs. The arrival of Peter Cornstalk the next day completed the group of twenty-five Indians.[12]

On Sunday, May 31, Darrow, Youngs, and McNemar conversed with the Indians through interpreter Peter Coon, who had been captured as a child and raised among the Shawnee. The Shawnee told them that they were sent to Turtle Creek by Tenskwatawa, who had previously been there "himself in spirit and had seen us." They discussed the work of the Great Spirit and the number of horses laden with provisions desired by the Indians, and they made plans for a return visit. At noon, perhaps the most remarkable Shaker meeting ever held began at the outdoor stand. Nearly three hundred spectators watched the Shakers lead their guests onto the platform "with their Silver ornaments and paints & tomahawks." Darrow, Youngs, and McNemar all preached. Non-Shaker observers were greatly alarmed at the scene, which united two sources of local terror—Shakers and Indians—into one bizarre spectacle. Meetings continued intermittently into the evening. Youngs wrote that the "Indian Chiefs & the principal body of the Indians were there & appeared very solemnly struck & under the deepest exercise of mind." Youngs interpreted their silence as an acknowledgment that the Shakers' religious work was "before theirs & that there was something here which they could not comprehend."[13]

The Shaker leaders had met with interpreters Cornstalk and Coon and "opened to them the nature of the present worship of God" in the hopes that the interpreters could accurately explain it to the Indians, who believed that "dancing was wicked." The next day, Youngs and McNemar conducted the chiefs Tecumseh and Blue Jacket, and the Wyandot Squahghkewelenoh to the burned remnant of their original outdoor worship stand. While surveying the ruin, the group had a long talk, during which the Indians revealed that the Prophet Tenskwatawa had requested that the Shakers return to Greenville as soon as possible for a great meeting. The Shakers agreed to this, and the chiefs immediately dispatched a rider to bring the news to Tenskwatawa. That same day, Peter Pease and McNemar accompanied them into Lebanon to sell furs, a public display of the connection between the two peoples.[14]

On June 2, Youngs and McNemar again conversed with Tecumseh and Blue Jacket and tried to give the Indians advice on how to secure their land from unscrupulous speculators. That evening, the Shakers and Indians joined in a singing meeting, with the Indians arranged Shaker-style in two ranks. Youngs was gratified that two Native women took Shaker sisters' caps as gifts. Blue Jacket, who was eighty-two, spoke for an hour longer back at the Indians' camp. The next morning, Youngs composed a letter for the chiefs to carry back to their people. It was read to them through the interpreter Coon. McNemar also presented them with "a hyreogliphic of the work of God." The appearance of this remarkable symbol remains a mystery. The Indians loaded their horses with provisions supplied by Believers, including wheat, corn, cured hams, bacon, salt, gunpowder, shot, and more—twenty-seven loads in all. They departed for Greenville on June 4, "fully & remarkably satisfied & very thankful."[15]

Youngs's letter appealed to the Indians on a religious basis and his perceived notion that they worshipped the same God. "Our fathers & your fathers were once united in one good spirit, & when they did what the great spirit told them by the prophets then there was peace & love—But when they would not obey the prophets and chiefs who could speak to them by the good spirit, then the bad spirit separated them, & led them into wicked ways, & made them get drunk with spirituous liquors, & hate one another, & abuse their women, & fight and kill one another, & corrupt themselves worse than the wild Beasts." The Shakers proclaimed love for them in the name of the good spirit, which they believed both groups followed. They also expressed sympathy for the ridicule experienced by the Shawnee revivalists, assuring them that those who could not understand the gifts of the spirit subjected Shakers to the same treatment. Crucially, the Shakers stated that they believed the Shawnee did not want to make war on the frontier settlements, saying, "We know you want to be good."[16]

The New Lebanon Ministry, however, were concerned that the westerners were expending too much effort and incurring too much risk regarding the Shawnee. In a private letter to Darrow, Mother Lucy wrote that she had "heard of your going after the Indians I have felt some tribulation on that account . . . whether it would not been better to have sent some of the young believers than to have gone your self I leave you to judge . . . the increasing weight of years that you must feel would admonish you that a careful consideration of the above lines would be a means of prolonging your gift in your present lot in that country."[17]

Although the ministry acknowledged the legitimacy of the work of Tenskwatawa, based on reports they had received, they were doubtful about the prospects of saving Indians on the same basis as white people. They advocated sending some young Believers from Turtle Creek who had received basic instruction in Shaker tenets to the Indians, "for they are indians & will remain so, therefore cannot be brought into the order of white people, but must be Saved in their own order & Nation." The ministry believed "that God is able to rais up them of their own Nation that will be able to lead & protect them, by receiving Some council from [young Believers], therefore we believe it to be wisdom not to meddle much with them, but own them in there own order & measure that they are able to travel in."[18]

Youngs spent the whole month of July ministering to converts at Paint Lick and Shawnee Run. He returned to Turtle Creek on July 31, having traveled a total of 558 miles throughout central Kentucky.[19] That summer, another small party of Shakers left New Lebanon to travel to Turtle Creek. Brother Archibald Meacham accompanied three sisters, Rachel Johnson, Susanna (Anna) Cole, and Lucy Bacon; they arrived on August 15.[20]

On August 10, McNemar and Bates set out for Greenville to meet with the Shawnee and their prophet Tenskwatawa.[21] McNemar wrote of their impressive preaching and singing in *The Kentucky Revival*, stating that "they needed no invitation to pay another visit to Turtle-Creek."[22] A party of fifty Indians returned to Union Village on August 28, led by Chief Tecumseh. Local militia officer Samuel Trousdale threatened to put the Shakers to the "sword's point" for their interaction with the Shawnee. The Natives left on September 3, carrying with them a grindstone for sharpening axes and hoes, wheat, rye, and meat. Youngs, Bates, and McNemar also drafted a letter to be carried by Tecumseh to his brother, the Prophet Tenskwatawa. The letter reaffirmed the Shakers friendship with the Shawnee and expressed their satisfaction that the tribe were pursuing the path of peace. They extended a rather tepid invitation to the Indians to visit again, but qualified it by saying, "We will love to talk with you again, but we think it not best for too many to come."[23] This sentiment was bolstered by McNemar's backhanded affirmation of the Shawnee's spiritual revival, of which "the believers at Turtle creek are not ashamed; yet they are far from wishing [the Shawnee] to turn to the right hand or to the left, to form an external union with them, or any other people."[24] David Darrow's dream of converting the Indians ultimately remained just that—a dream.

TEN

SHAKER PUBLICATIONS AND THE EXPANSION OF MISSIONARY EFFORTS

INCREDIBLY, WHILE UNDERTAKING SO MANY missionary journeys, Richard McNemar completed the manuscript for his history of the Kentucky Revival. As a leading participant, McNemar was uniquely situated to recount the dramatic spread of the work throughout Kentucky and Ohio. Because of his conversion, however, he recast the entire revival as a preparatory work to the rise of Shakerism in the West. Up to this date, the Shakers had only published the *Concise Statement*, a brief theological treatise issued in 1790. Otherwise, they had avoided putting any of their beliefs down in writing.[1] The fact that Darrow and Youngs sanctioned McNemar undertaking and publishing such a work as a Shaker evidences his importance to the movement. McNemar traveled to Cincinnati on June 10 and gave the manuscript to John W. Browne. Browne was an old acquaintance of McNemar's. He had been a failed candidate for the Presbyterian Ministry, but he now operated the Liberty Hall press, named, perhaps, for the famous Presbyterian academy in Virginia where Malcham Worley and Matthew Houston were educated. McNemar rode back and forth to Cincinnati correcting his work at the press. On June 19, he returned to Turtle Creek with the first proof of his *Observations on Church Government*.[2] The work was printed in its entirety by early September. The total cost for printing 150 copies of *The Kentucky Revival* was $154.[3]

On September 13, 1807, McNemar wrote a covering letter to be sent with a copy of *The Kentucky Revival* to the ministry at New Lebanon. Acknowledging the uniqueness of having lived through the revival, he enumerated four points in his letter to help provide context for the easterners, should any "think this little history worth perusal." First, he explained that he wrote it for people personally affected by the revival, giving them "great diversity of

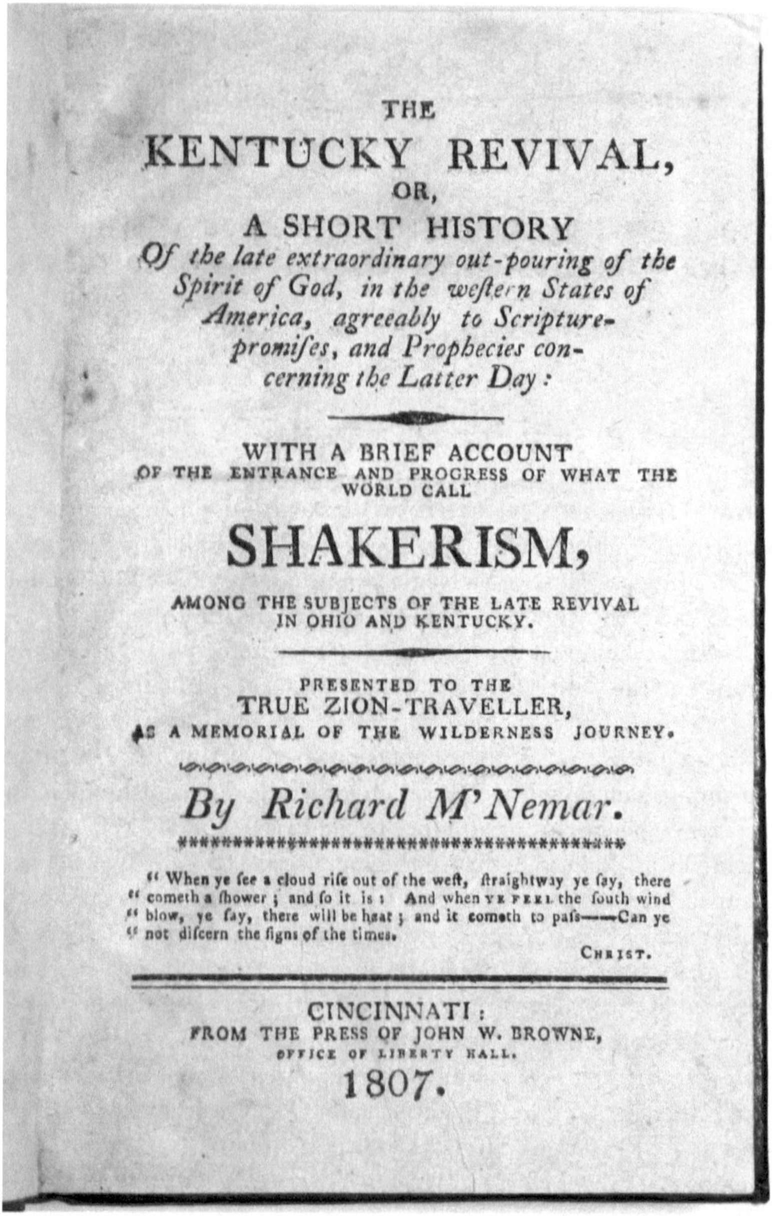

THE
KENTUCKY REVIVAL,
OR,
A SHORT HISTORY
*Of the late extraordinary out-pouring of the
Spirit of God, in the weſtern States of
America, agreeably to Scripture-
promiſes, and Prophecies con-
cerning the Latter Day:*

WITH A BRIEF ACCOUNT
OF THE ENTRANCE AND PROGRESS OF WHAT THE
WORLD CALL

SHAKERISM,

AMONG THE SUBJECTS OF THE LATE REVIVAL
IN OHIO AND KENTUCKY.

PRESENTED TO THE
TRUE ZION-TRAVELLER,
AS A MEMORIAL OF THE WILDERNESS JOURNEY.

By Richard M'Nemar.

" When ye fee a cloud rife out of the weſt, ſtraightway ye ſay, there
" cometh a ſhower; and ſo it is: And when YE FEEL the ſouth wind
" blow, ye ſay, there will be heat; and it cometh to paſs——Can ye
" not diſcern the ſigns of the times.
CHRIST.

CINCINNATI:
FROM THE PRESS OF JOHN W. BROWNE,
OFFICE OF LIBERTY HALL.
1807.

Figure 10.1. Richard McNemar's *Kentucky Revival*, printed in Cincinnati in 1807. Shaker Museum, Chatham, NY.

Sentiment . . . and such different degrees of light." Secondly, he lamented that many subjects of the revival, through the subtlety of Satan, "declined any further Search for the Kingdom & Set to building themselves up on on what they had Received." In doing this, they had "shut their eyes against the pure Light of the Gospel," as opened through Shakerism. Thirdly, McNemar apologized for having to explain "debates about doctrins bodily Excercises Gifts of the Spirit Signs & which are so fresh on the Memmory of the generality in this Country"[4] but that could have little meaning to those who were not eyewitnesses. Finally, he regretted having to cite printed polemical works published at that time, which he assumed were not available to eastern Shakers. McNemar hoped that his work would prompt those not yet willing to join him in Shakerism to consider their salvation. He wrote:

> It appears remarkable that if any thing can benifit those who have pitched their tent Short of mount Zion it must be a faithfull account of their former Journey by one who Who traveld with them Step by Step & plain investigation of the paths into which they were finily led by the adversary of all righteousness
>
> When things are Stated just as they took place from the first Rays of light that Stired up the people to See the blackness of antichrists Kingdom untill the true Gospel & Church of Christ was revealed it then remaines for Each to judge for him Self whether he has got possession of that which cannot be Shaken But Should these things remain forever obscure to the cittizens of Mount Zion who have never groaned under the babylonish captivity it can be to them no meterial Disadvantage[5]

The eastern Believers already knew of McNemar's talents as a poet, as previous letters contained hymn texts of his authorship. In this letter, only the second personally written by him to the Shaker leadership, he chose to summarize his religious experience in an autobiographical poem. He metaphorically compared himself and his fellow revivalists to moles blindly burrowing through a dirt hill, carving their own paths, incapable of seeing the sunlight of salvation until the advent of Shakerism among them.

> 1 The moles little path ways are far out of Sight
> from the lofty Eagle that flies in the Light
> Nor can She be charmed with his wonderful Skill
> in piling up Dirt for his little mole hil
>
> 2 Ten thousand reformers like So many moles
> have plowed all the Bible & cut it in holes
> and each has his Church at the end of his trace
> Built up as he thinks of the Subjects of Grace

3 Through all their dark mole paths for more than ten years
I Saught for Salvation with groaning and tears
their courses of Duty did faithfully run
But never could come to the light of the Sun

4 At length I grew weary of Such fruitless toil
and prayed for an Earthquake to Shake off the Soil
and God in his mercy did answer my prayer
And let in more light than my vessel could bear

5 I lookd towards heaven, and raised the Shout
and all that could hear it began to dig out
The new light was precious & each that came in
cried Glory to God their's Salvation from Sin

6 The flaming Schismatics a while did unite
to tear down the mole hills and let in the light
for this is the work of the light loving Soul
So long as its bound to Earth diging mole

7 At length comes the Shakers to teach the new birth
how Souls might git loose from the mole of the Earth
they looked like the eagles that fly in the air
and O how my Spirit did long to be there

8 The last little mole hill that mortals have pland
Is built of new Christians but this cannot Stand
the name will not answer in this mighty Shake
nor Christ Spare the Sinner just for his name Sake

9 I know all the Systems in antichrist's plot
and what the Schismatics & Christians have got
Been Born & converted & true to the cause
was never accused for breach of their laws

10 I've heard & believed what the Gospel declares
and Strictly obey'd it for more than tw[o] years
and yet you may See after all that is done
My name is McNemar or nobodys Son[6]

The poem closes with a line based on the meaning of his surname as he understood it. To ensure the meaning was clear, he included a postscript: "Litterly Son of no Mother."[7] His decision to close the poem and letter, which he knew would likely be read by Mother Lucy Wright, with this complex declaration is puzzling. He had embraced Shakerism body and soul, and central to that was his union to Mother Lucy as the head of the church, founded by *Mother* Ann Lee. However, there is no clear sentiment expressed indicating that he had now *found* a Mother in the Shakers.

An alternative, though unlikely, reading of this line suggests that he was staking out a degree of independence within the Shaker faith. Although his commitment was total, his life as a Shaker was far more autonomous than almost any other prominent Believer of the period. This led to trouble for McNemar many years in the future, but at this time, he seems to have rather ambiguously situated himself as a singularly unique champion for his new faith. Whatever his true intentions were, he must have been gratified to receive enthusiastic thanks from Mother Lucy for his efforts. On October 22, she wrote, "Mother thanks Brother Richard McNemar very kindly for the little Book he sent her as a present, Entitled the Kentucky Revival—A Mothers Love is with her thanks." The other ministry members also thanked him, writing that his book had given them a clearer understanding of the preparatory work of the revival. Crucially, they wrote, "We believe that this little History may answer a good purpose to those that are waiting for Salvation in Christ, while groaning under the bondage of Sin & Antichristian tyrany—And we believe it will answer the purpose intended, & that it is very Suitable to go before the public."[8] McNemar's first publication on behalf of the Shakers was a resounding success.

MISSION TO GASPER

The epochal events of the Kentucky Revival originated in Logan County, Kentucky, in 1798. Unsurprisingly, less than ten years later, a remnant people there were still seeking a deeper religious commitment. Issachar Bates and Richard McNemar set out for Gasper, Kentucky, (which eventually became the Shaker community of South Union) on September 22, 1807.[9] They traveled with Matthew Houston until they parted ways with him and set their course southwest toward a region of plains scattered with timberlands called "the Barrens." They arrived there on October 17, finding a people "who were prepared for the Gospel."[10] Chief among these was Presbyterian minister John Rankin, who confessed his sins and embraced Shakerism on October 28.[11] McNemar referred to Rankin in the *Kentucky Revival* (though he did not explicitly name him) as the agent for bringing the revival from Cane Ridge to North Carolina.[12] By the time the second edition of *The Kentucky Revival* was printed in 1808, McNemar added a footnote: "One person in particular here alluded to, who went on this important mission, was John Rankin, Minister of the Presbyterian church at Gasper, Logan county; the first who received the spirit of the revival in that place, and under whose ministry the extraordinary work began. Since that time he has escaped from the old house of antichrist, divided against itself, and with the major part of his Gasper congregation, embraced the Gospel of Christ's second appearing."[13] David Darrow reported to Mother Lucy Wright that the new Believers in "Warren and Logan Counties are able and in good circumstances as to temporal things as the Believers in Kentucky generally are." He rejoiced in the expansion of the gospel to the southwest and held out hopes that further openings would be made in the Cumberland region of Kentucky as well as the Carolinas.[14] Rankin was the type of convert McNemar yearned for—one who had been through the revival but thus far had pitched his tent just short of Mount Zion.

At the Gasper meetinghouse on Sunday, November 8, Rankin preached a last warning to his former congregation, urging them to confess their sins and join the Shakers. Some families among the converts were slave owners, and the Shakers heard the confessions of both slave and slave owner alike. Among these unique pairings were Frances Whyte and his slave Neptune, and Charles Eades and his "yellow woman" Eunice Freeheart. This was not unprecedented, as McNemar's freed slave Seely, as well as Matthew Houston's slave Isaac Newton, had joined the Shakers. When Bates and McNemar departed the Barrens on November 20, they left twenty-five converts in their wake.[15] On December 4, newly arriving eastern Believer Joseph Allen met McNemar and Bates in Cincinnati on their way back from Gasper.[16] They conducted Allen to Union Village, arriving on December 7.[17] Allen's eyes were quickly opened to the dangers of his new environment when anti-Shaker arsonists burned a barn full of provisions on December 12. Nearly the whole season's harvest was lost. Fortunately, the seven horses in the stable were saved; their halters were cut at the last moment.[18]

Samuel Turner, who arrived at Turtle Creek in May 1806, penned a letter to Calvin Green, a Shaker friend back at New Lebanon on February 28, 1808. Turner enclosed a new hymn, writing, "I have a feeling to make the[e] a little present of a hymn; Composed by Richard M Nemar to the Tune that was formerly cauld Black Joke."[19] This hymn was later titled "The Seasons." Historian Jane Crosthwaite points out that the text illustrates McNemar's "knowledge of the history of fringe Christian sects, particularly dualist ones." Dualism is presented "as a seed that has been cared for and passed down from antiquity." McNemar references Quaker founder George Fox, as well as the French Prophets, who appear in the poem as precursors to the flowering of the seed in the form of Shakerism on "fair Columbia's shore."[20] The final four verses honored David Darrow, Ruth Farrington, and deacons Peter Pease and Joseph Allen. McNemar's choice of "The Black Joke" as the tune is ironic, as it was one of the most vulgar songs of the Revolutionary era. The title is a slang reference to female genitalia.[21]

On March 4, the publication of *The Testimony of Christ's Second Appearing* was announced in the *Western Star* newspaper of Lebanon, Ohio. *Star* printer John M'Clean also printed *The Testimony*. Youngs finished writing the text on April 10, nine months after he began it on July 7, 1806. Printing began on June 15 and continued through the year.[22] The volume was completed by New Year's Eve, and it comprised 603 densely written pages. Youngs returned to Turtle Creek that day from Cincinnati bearing freshly bound copies.[23] The last two pages contained a poem written by Richard McNemar—offered as a "short abridgment" of the entire text! McNemar's poetic genius was up to the task, however, and the eighteen stanzas concisely distill the core elements of Shaker theology, as presented by Youngs. This poem was republished in 1813 as the first text in the first Shaker hymnal *Millennial Praises* with a new title: "The Testimony of Eternal Truth."[24]

Union Village leaders continued to use McNemar's missionary talents. He and Malcham Worley were sent to Eagle Creek on February 4 and returned on the twentieth. Just a few weeks later, on March 7, McNemar, Worley, Solomon King, and recent eastern arrival Archibald Meacham left Turtle Creek to visit the Shawnee at Greenville.[25] Meanwhile, unbeknownst to McNemar, the New Lebanon Ministry reprinted *The Kentucky Revival* for the benefit of those in the East. The firm of E. and E. Hosford of Albany printed an edition in April 1808. However, due to economic troubles caused by Thomas Jefferson's Embargo Act, there was little market for these publications. The ministry informed Darrow, "The Deacons have been to the expense of getting 1600 copies of the Kentucky Revival printed and now cannot scarcely sell one of them—the world's people say money is not to be had, it is all shut up; but we are not shut up from the privilege of giving them away."[26]

Three years had passed since the arrival of Shaker missionaries in Kentucky and Ohio. Hundreds of converts were now scattered throughout the two states. Shaker leadership began taking steps to consolidate their gains and organize converts into communal families according to eastern Shaker models. The Believers at Union Village began to frame a new meetinghouse on March 22.[27] This permanent structure replaced the outdoor stands and cramped private homes. An enclosed meetinghouse would make it more difficult for anti-Shaker agitators to disrupt worship. Communal families for young Believers were organized in May at the behest of Matthew Houston and Amos Valentine. Richard McNemar's original homestead became the East Family, henceforth a gathering order where incoming members could try Shaker life without making a full commitment.[28] On May 23, McNemar, David Spinning, and Samuel

Rollins left again for Eagle Creek and Cabin Creek, where they converted eight souls. Easterners Samuel Turner, Lucy Smith, Anna Cole, and original missionary John Meacham were dispatched on October 26 to reside permanently with the young Believers at Shawnee Run as their ministers. In the gently rolling hills of the Bluegrass region, they created the beautiful community that became known as Pleasant Hill.[29]

JOURNEY TO THE WABASH

For the Shakers at Turtle Creek, 1809 dawned with a mixture of hope and anxiety. On New Year's Day, Deacon Peter Pease penned a rather dire report to Deacon Richard Spier at New Lebanon. Spier was the western Shakers' lifeline in terms of money and material supplies. Pease recounted the grim close of 1808, colored as it was by ill health, widespread flooding, scarce money and clothing, and multiple failed attempts to erect a dam for a badly needed sawmill. Pease hoped that a fulling mill could be built at Turtle Creek, enabling the Believers to enter the clothing business and earn some badly needed cash. Much of the money sent from the East had gone to cover the cost of printing *The Testimony of Christ's Second Appearing*. By the time the last pages were printed in December, $965.86 was spent, a considerable sum.[30]

On the bright side, Constant Moseley departed for New Lebanon on January 3, carrying with him eighteen copies of the completed *Testimony*.[31] In a covering letter, Darrow confided to Mother Lucy that publishing the work had been "an almost insupportable burthen." Darrow acknowledged that the early Believers eschewed writing their faith, as "they saw at once that the work of salvation was not in the letter but in the spirit and therefore wisely let go the letter which killeth for the spirit which giveth life." In light of this, he asked for "carefulness & moderation" from the easterners as they examined what was only the second published work of Shaker theology.[32] Also, the new meetinghouse was completed, except for some interior finish carpentry. The building's footprint was forty by fifty feet. It had two stories and a "strate roof," as opposed to the gambrel roofs typical in eastern Shaker meetinghouses.[33] The first meeting was held there on Sunday, January 8, 1809. Darrow and Youngs presided over the joyous occasion, attended by two hundred Believers, including John Rankin from Gasper.[34]

One of the most picaresque episodes in all of Shaker history began on January 16, 1809, as Youngs, Bates, and McNemar set out for the Wabash country, a journey later immortalized in Shaker lore. In 1808, Bates, Worley, Dunlavy, and Houston had visited the area as well as Gasper and Red Banks in Kentucky. They returned to Turtle Creek on July 17 after more than three months of itinerant preaching. Darrow reported to Mother Lucy that they had brought the "gospel to the lost world of whom about 80 grown people were added to the faith; about 70 opened their minds at one place."[35] He wanted to ensure the retention of this new group of converts. As Carol Medlicott points out, Darrow was worried about the efforts of Methodist evangelist Peter Cartwright, who was determined to thwart the Shakers.[36] Accordingly, Darrow dispatched his three strongest missionaries to traverse the watery country of southern Indiana, which had experienced the same flooding as Union Village. Youngs's journal of the trip provides the harrowing details.

They traveled the first thirty-five miles to White Water, on the Ohio border with Indiana, on horseback. From there, the flooded and frozen landscape precluded further use of their mounts, and they proceeded cautiously on the "cracked ice." They crossed some creeks on the fractured ice, were forced to wade through the frigid waters of others, and even poled themselves along others astride floating logs. Eventually, they found the head of a new road through the wilderness near Locry [Laughery Creek], Indiana, which would take them to Vincennes, which lay thirteen miles south of Busro, where the converts lived. That night they "cut timber & split some boards for our bed & under a large fallen Beach tree spent the night—a good fire at our feet."[37]

The next day, they traveled thirty-seven miles and reached the Muscatatuck River, which they waded at twilight. On the western bank, they made a fire and slept on blankets over brush while it rained through the night. On Sunday, January 22, they passed two Indian camps, and the rain turned to snow as evening fell. The men erected a structure made from poles and covered in poplar boards. Inside, they kindled a fire to dry their soaked clothing and shoes. On Monday, they reached a broad floodplain of the Muscatatuck, which Bates tried to cross by tying poles to his feet. He turned back after falling through the ice. With their food running low, the men were forced to camp for two days, hoping the river would freeze. While exploring the vicinity, they found a turkey carcass left by a fox from which they salvaged a leg and breast. Finally, on the morning of the twenty-fifth, they built a raft and crossed safely. That night they built a fire and drank melted snow before settling down on bushes laid over the snow.

Their feet became swollen and blistered as they trudged onward; eventually, they were shod only in tattered stockings. When they reached a higher landscape of "knobs," or hills, they "were overjoyed & sang & danced on the first Knob." They traveled another sixty miles over three days, reaching the East Fork of White River on January 29. Flummoxed by this vast and impenetrable barrier, they considered their options. First, they tried talking to an Indian they had encountered, but they had no success. Eventually, they found a settler's cabin and were "answered by the bark of a dog which truly was a pleasant sound at this distressing period." The settler, one McCoun, welcomed the men, and his wife cooked them a breakfast of bear meat, venison, corn bread, and coffee. McCoun then gave them passage over the icy waters in his canoe. After another twenty miles, they found lodging with a man named Palmer.[38] But when they reached the West Fork of White River, no friendly stranger was there to assist them. Issachar Bates later wrote an epic ballad recounting the harrowing trip. Of this portion, he wrote:

> There 20 furlongs of ice and water
> Were mingling in one great uproar
> But being set across the current
> We forced our passage to the shore[39]

After drying their clothes at a camp of Miami Indians, they lodged overnight with a man named Booth. The next day, January 31, they at last reached the home of Believer Robert Gill, having traveled 235 miles. Bates's and McNemar's frozen feet had to be poulticed, but Youngs was overjoyed to find that Gill had retained his "steadfast faith in the gospel."[40]

While at Busro, the missionaries each had a pair of moccasins made for themselves. This region was truly the frontier, and during their visit, the Shakers met with a band of Creek Indians on their way to meet the Shawnee prophet, to "find out if he was of God." They also visited the home of Harry Price, who they deemed a "sensible black man." The meetings they held were well attended by both Believers and a virulently anti-Shaker public who labored "under great death and stupidity." Visitors traveled to meet the Shakers from the Red Banks settlement along the Ohio River in Kentucky (present-day Henderson). Among these was John Slover, who was captured at New River, Virginia, as a child of eight by the Miami Indians in 1763. He was sold to a Delaware and then lived with the Shawnee until he was claimed by relatives. He reluctantly left the Indians following Lord Dunmore's War in 1774. Slover enlisted in the Continental Army during the Revolutionary War and was again captured by Indians during Crawford's expedition in the Ohio country in 1782. He was to be burned to death, but he managed to escape, covering more than a hundred miles in one day to elude his captors.[41]

On February 23, McNemar left Busro to visit the Believers in Red Banks accompanied by Slover. There, he met former Presbyterian exhorter and fellow revivalist Lawrence Roelosson. Roelosson was active with revivalist James McGready in the vicinity of the Muddy, Red, and Gasper River Congregations in southern Kentucky. Despite this, he seems to have taken umbrage at the extreme tenets of Shakerism. He and McNemar locked horns during the latter's stay at Red Banks. A letter written to Roelosson by McNemar on March 3, 1809, defends Shakerism, likely in response to an attack (now unlocated) written by Roelosson. In the letter, McNemar sympathizes with Roelosson as a fellow revivalist and former mainline Presbyterian, but he also states he is "sorry that your lamp should go out & your soul be eventually numbered with the foolish virgins" for not accepting the further light of the Shaker gospel. In closing, McNemar attempted to relight the revival fire in Roelosson, writing, "I know your soul has once been sick of sin & of that confused Babylon where it is covered with a sanctified profession: and if you sincerely continue to walk by the same rule, I can say to you as the angel said to the beloved disciple, Come up hither & I will shew thee the Bride the Lambs wife, & you shall see that holy city the new Jerusalem."[42]

Ultimately, the mission was a success. Over the next six weeks in Indiana, Youngs, Bates, and McNemar traversed 186 miles, preaching, attending meetings, and hearing confessions. They concluded their trip with a meeting of 110 Believers at Robert Houston's house. Many new converts were left firmer in their faith, and the groundwork was laid for the eventual organization of a Shaker community at Busro. The missionaries departed on March 18, and returned to Turtle Creek on the twenty-ninth.[43]

While they were gone, a letter from the New Lebanon Ministry arrived expressing their satisfaction with *The Testimony of Christ's Second Appearing*. They wrote, "We have received by the hand of Brother Constant the product of your long (and without doubt) wearisome & painful labours, and we have read it with the greatest satisfaction—We feel sensible that you have had a special gift and inspiration of God—we view it as the most consistent, beautiful & enlightening publication ever exhibited." After more compliments, the ministry acknowledged that in such a large undertaking there were some points of doctrine that they wished to see explicated in a clearer or different way. After expounding on some of these, they reaffirmed their approval of the work, writing, "We expect the Book will be reprinted in these parts as soon as convenient—if you should think best to make any amendments or alterations, or add any notes, we desire to be informed as soon as convenient."[44] With great relief, Darrow wrote to New Lebanon, "The approbation with which the Ministry together with our Elders and Brethren have received the work was far beyond our expectation."[45]

That spring, Bates and McNemar continued their missionary activities. On April 11, they left for Beaver Creek, Mad River, and Pickaway (the region just south of present-day Columbus).[46] While pockets of converts were coalescing throughout the Ohio River Valley and into Kentucky, not all were able to break away from their families or congregations and make the leap into Shakerism. Tragically, during the winter of 1808, a man "that had faith, but his old light connections would not let him obey—while his family was at dinner he went into his barn & first castrated himself, & then cut his throat & expired."[47] Such setbacks as these, particularly when combined with castration, fueled anti-Shaker sentiments in the region. John Davis caused a commotion at the dancing platform on May 1 in an attempt to reclaim his wife, Elizabeth. On May 3, he succeeded in wresting her from the nascent communal household of his father, Jonathan Davis, and "by violence carried her off."[48] Davis remained a bitter enemy of the Shakers for years to come.

On May 26, 1809, Comstock Betts, Hortence Goodrich, Hopewell Curtis, and Mercy Pickett arrived at Turtle Creek from New Lebanon. Rejoicing in their safe arrival, the Union Village Ministry wrote to the New Lebanon Ministry, "We are all fully satisfied & pleased with each other who have come to this country, & with the gift of God by which we believe we were all sent." They also recognized that they had been a financial burden to the eastern communities, but assured the ministry of the worthiness of their cause, writing, "The nature & extent of the work, & ourselves having no perminent abode, & in a strange country, unavoidably required that we should lay some foundation for the establishment of the gospel in this land, at our own expence.—And, although lands, tools, materials for building, & almost every unavoidable & necessary article in the course of our duty, were extremely high, yet the desired foundation is laid, & we have reason to believe forever established."[49]

In the nascent community at Turtle Creek, the young Believers expressed concern that their children were not being educated, and Darrow was concerned that "a great part of them would be lost" if a school was not established. This was soon accomplished under the supervision of Malcham Worley. One hundred and ten students enrolled; Malinda Watts taught the girls, and John Woods taught the boys. To attend, the students had to confess their sins to their teachers. However, corporal punishment, common in schools at the time, was banned.[50]

In July, the New Lebanon Ministry requested that Youngs return east to help with editing the second edition of *The Testimony*. Darrow politely objected, saying that Youngs had been "so long in that work that he has not yet gained the gift he had before—he has been two long journeys since he left writing—But I find his gift is but small to what it was before he began to write—his public gift in particular is much needed in this land." A remarkably detailed and lengthy correspondence ensued between the East and the West that dealt with areas of theological dispute. These letters contain important insights into the development of Shaker theology, as fomented by the western expansion. As if to highlight the constant efforts of the missionaries, Darrow noted that "Issachar and Richard are here, only long enough to get strength & then they have to go again."[51] The duo had traveled to Pickaway on June 12. After a brief respite, they left on another journey to Mad River, Beaver Creek, and Pickaway, on July 25, 1809. They tarried there a week, returning on August 1.[52]

The threat of violence, ever present, manifested itself late on the evening of August 12, 1809. Fifteen to twenty thieves entered the dwelling at Union Village where the Shaker leaders resided. They "entered the upper floor rooms & presented their pistols to those in bed—forbid their moving on pain of death." For a half hour, they rummaged through chests and drawers, pocketing six dollars. As they descended the stairs, Jethro Dennis, described as a "strong and robust fellow," threw a chair down on their heads, and they fled, dropping their booty.[53] The next day, Richard McNemar composed a poem about the event titled "Robbery." He may, in fact, have thought it up during the robbery, since it was ready for him to sing at the meeting on Sunday morning. Its opening line, "Will a man rob God?" echoes Malachi 3:8.

> The Church was beset by a black painted band,
> With their candles and clubs and their pistols in hand:
> Twelve strokes of the clock told the dark silent hour
> when those wretches came rushing like wolves to devour[54]

The thieves were eventually caught. Youngs happily reported on September 30, "Bob Cain ironed & put in prison—the leader of the gang Kent, shot through the sholder in the prison at Xenia. Aaron Richard & 3 more brot from Cincinnati & incarcerated in the prison at Lebanon on the 10th of Oct.—The way of transgressors is hard."[55]

On October 24, 1809, James Smith Jr. and his children arrived at Turtle Creek to live. Smith had visited the Shakers with his wife the year before, on September 7, 1808.[56] When Smith joined his estranged wife, Polly Smith did accompany him, but she eventually joined him—only to leave four months later.[57] The Smiths had been part of Barton W. Stone's congregation at Cane Ridge, Kentucky, which was torn asunder by the Shaker missionaries.[58] The Smith family had known McNemar since the 1790s, when he lived and studied at Cane Ridge. Smith's arrival at Union Village occurred without comment at the time, but it soon became the flashpoint for the Shakers' first major conflict in the West.

ELEVEN

GOSPEL ORDER IN THE WEST, JAMES SMITH, AND THE OHIO MOB

NEARLY FIVE YEARS HAD PASSED since the Shaker missionaries arrived at Turtle Creek. In the spring of 1810, David Darrow made a detailed report to the New Lebanon Ministry, asking when he might formally establish eastern-style gospel order among the new Believers in the West. Darrow noted that he had not been hasty in bringing people out of "fleshly relation—for their outward circumstances would not admit of it." For the past eighteen months, however, western Shaker leaders had "begun to break up their old flesh nests—& to call the prisoners from their prisons." Four communal families had been gathered. One was near the meetinghouse, and another was at Richard McNemar's original property to the East. Fifty grown Believers lived at these locations, along with a number of promising children and teenagers. Two other families, comprising forty Believers, were less than two miles away. Darrow explained, "All these families have put their properties together to support a Joint interest in family relation."[1] Additionally, they had voluntarily separated from their children, who were under the care of Shaker deacons.

The two families that lived near the meetinghouse had begun to build a large dwelling house, fifty by forty feet and two stories high. Darrow knew that once this was completed, he would have to introduce a more formalized eastern-style Shaker order, complete with a legal covenant that would protect both the members and the larger society. He requested guidance from his spiritual lead at New Lebanon. Darrow was also faced with making choices about which of the easterners to send to preside over, or assist with, the work at other nascent Shaker communities. Busro on the Wabash River in Indiana was particularly challenging, as it was the most difficult location to reach. He was certain, however, of whom he could not spare for such dedicated duty. In his letter to Mother Lucy, he acknowledged that "Benjamin Issachar Richard, & such ones as have a gift in word & doctrine to the world—must not be bound to any people steady—but must be ready to go when ever the gift comes."[2] Indeed, McNemar spent parts of January and March at Mad River, ministering to converts there.[3]

Just seventeen days after McNemar's return to Turtle Creek, Darrow sent him and newly arrived easterner Archibald Meacham to Busro on March 27, 1810.[4] Archibald was John Meacham's cousin, who was one of the original Shaker missionaries to the West. Darrow considered Archibald Meacham to have "the greatest fore sight & best judgment of any of the brethren."[5] Darrow had visited Busro in September 1809 to "fix A Seat or Senter for the Society—& the place to Build their meetinghouse, & other buildings when they get able." He counted 224 Believers there, 116 of them older than fifteen. He was quite taken with the site, calling it "the beautifullest Country That my eyes ever beheld—they are Settled on the north end & west side of a large dry prairie—Containing upwards of 30000 acres of land & so level that we Could See their Cabbins for five or six miles before we got to them."[6] Darrow's efforts were followed up quickly by a company led by Issachar Bates that left on December 14, 1809, and stayed through January 1810.[7] From the start, Busro was a precarious location for a community, despite its beauty. Sickness had plagued the people there the previous autumn, and anti-Shaker sentiment was high in the area. Darrow sent Meacham in hopes that he could rely on him, along with Ruth Darrow, to remain at Busro and oversee the converts there. Meacham and McNemar returned temporarily to Turtle Creek on May 1, accompanied by John Slover from Red Banks.[8]

That summer, the western Shaker settlements were graced with a visit from William Deming, from the Hancock, Massachusetts, community. He kept a detailed record of what he saw and heard. William was the son of John Deming, who Mother Ann Lee had once advised to "put your hands to work and your heart to God," and he had lived among Shakers virtually since birth.[9] Deming heard McNemar preach numerous times during his visit and made note of his poetic and musical gifts. At the June 21 meeting, Darrow shared love sent from the East for all the western Believers, and a "hymn was sung which Richard had composed on the occasion of our coming & which he afterwards sent to Mother." In his journal, Deming recorded the vigorous activity at Turtle Creek, where a community was steadily coalescing. Buildings were being framed, stone quarried, grain harvested, looms built, and trees planted. On July 5, Deming walked to Lebanon with Benjamin Youngs to the *Western Star* newspaper office, where *The Testimony* was printed. Youngs made a special point of showing him "the log on which Richard tried to kill the little quail & about which he made the little hymn" (about which, more below). Deming also saw "the place where the robbers cut their clubs & hitched their horses."[10] Juxtaposed against the recent robbery, Deming's reference to McNemar's hymn about the quail is especially poignant. Unbeknownst to him, the Turtle Creek community was about to face a raging mob.

It is worth examining "The Little Quail," as it reveals McNemar's sense of the Shakers' security by the summer of 1810. He wrote, "How much progress we can make, since our lives are not at stake." He had made an impulsive, failed attempt to kill a peaceful quail with a stick. Shocked at his thoughtless actions, he transformed the incident into a revelation wherein God's will toward the Shakers is manifested. Just as McNemar, the persecutor of the quail, had failed, so would the persecutors of the Shakers. McNemar took this to mean that "persecution's at an end," but in this, he was quite mistaken.[11]

> Traveling once along the way,
> Thinking of this latter day
> How much progress we can make,
> Since our lives are not at stake.
> Ancient saints could little gain,
> Still by persecutors slain;
> Now protected from the foe,
> Saints can have full time to grow.
>
> Next I thought, If sinners knew
> That we thus our safety view,
> Would they not yet try to kill?
> Could they not our vitals spill?
> Through my mind this thought I cast,
> While a log I closely passed,
> Where a little quail did sit
> Fair and easy to be hit.
>
> Instantly I made a stand,
> With a stick I raised my hand;
> Thrice I struck with all my skill,
> But no vitals did I spill.
> Once my stick just grazed his tail,
> But the well-protected quail,
> Sound and nimble took its flight
> Through the forest, out of sight.

Instantly the spirit spoke,
"As this quail escaped thy stroke,
So the wicked strike in vain
In the great Messiah's reign."
O, what wonders I did view
As the little creature flew!
Every flutter of its wing
Seemed to cry, *"The Lord is King."*

Had I then an army seen,
Full of rage and cruel spleen,
I should felt no more surprise
Than amidst a host of flies.
While the cross of Christ I bear,
Under his protecting care,
Every danger I shall shun,
Till my work is fully done.

He who gave this striking sign
Has stretch'd out his meas'ring line:
Persecution's at an end;
Now we may with Christ ascend.
Blessed day how bright and clear!
O what fruits the saints can bear!
Righteousness through every stage,
Now can grace this Golden Age.[12]

JAMES SMITH AND THE OHIO MOB

The spring of 1810 saw the Believers at Turtle Creek embroiled in a series of difficulties with apostates and disgruntled relatives of those living among the Shakers. On February 18, a group of men came to the meetinghouse to drag away Margaret Marshall, whose parents left the Shakers the week prior. On the twenty-sixth, they returned with the constable and a search warrant. That evening, they assaulted John Wallace's house and tried to carry away a child from the Bedle family, beating the brethren and sisters there with sticks.[13]

Between these violent episodes, on February 24, Polly Smith, the wife of James Smith Jr., left Turtle Creek with her sister Peggy. They were helped to leave by Smith's own brother. On March 5, they came back to Turtle Creek, "perplexing" James Smith Jr. and trying to recover the children—only this time, they had James Smith Sr. with them.[14] James Smith Jr.'s move to Turtle

Figure 11.1. "Portrait of Col. James Smith," artist unknown, c. 1800–1810. Photo courtesy of MS-018 Warren J. Shonert Americana Collection, Eva G. Farris Special Collections. W. Frank Steely Library, Northern Kentucky University.

Creek had massive, unintended consequences for his nuclear family as well as his new Shaker community. His conversion to Shakerism left his father, James Smith Sr., sad, bewildered, and adrift in his old age. At the age of seventy-three, he lived with and greatly depended on his son and namesake. In fact, Smith assigned the copyright for his 1799 autobiography, *An Account of the Remarkable Occurrences in the Life and Travels of Col. James Smith* to his son and had also given him twenty acres of land with the understanding that "James Smith junr. agreed to decently support his father Col. James Smith, his life time." But after his conversion to Shakerism, Smith Jr. sold his Kentucky property and failed to honor his agreement with his father. At the end of Smith's long life, this betrayal by his son, paired with what Smith perceived as an existential threat to the country whose liberty he helped to secure, drove him to suggest a military solution to the Shaker problem.[15]

Smith, a seasoned polemicist, launched an anti-Shaker campaign in the public press throughout Ohio and Kentucky, creating a publicity nightmare for the burgeoning Shaker movement. His status as a former Indian captive, Indian fighter, Revolutionary patriot, and frontiersman made him a formidable enemy for the Shakers. He had lived with the sect for about a week before rejecting Shaker life. Based on this limited experience, he wrote an article titled "An Attempt to Develope Shakerism." Published in regional newspapers in July 1810, it offered a thumbnail sketch of the devastating impact of Shakerism on his family.[16] Smith compared the Shakers with the Roman Catholic Church, accused David Darrow of licentious sex (specifically of hosting bacchanals with groups of women), and child abuse. His "Attempt" made for a dense and shocking indictment of the Shakers in the public press.

A recurring theme in Smith's writing—and one that Richard McNemar would later twist to attack Smith—was Smith's service to the colonies in the French and Indian War and the American Revolution. Smith writes as an authentic, battle-hardened protector of American civil and religious liberties. Shakerism represented to him a hierarchical, authoritarian system very similar to that of the English government he fought to eliminate. Of the Shakers, he wrote, "Principles of servile subjection are so ingrafted in them, that they may be wretched dupes, tories, and pests to society. And under the pretence of worshiping God, the root of civil and religious liberty is deeply wounded. It has been said, if those under the Shakers are in bondage, they are *voluntary slaves* ... when I see a snake in the grass, or a poisonous worm gnawing at the root of the TREE OF LIBERTY, shall I not at least cry out 'TAKE CARE.'"[17]

At the end of his "Attempt" Smith stated, "I intend, soon to publish a pamphlet, wherein Shakerism will be more fully stated." *Remarkable Occurences, Lately Discovered Among the People Called SHAKERS; of a Treasonous and Barbarous Nature, or SHAKERISM DEVELOPED* was the realization of Smith's intentions. It was published in Paris, Kentucky, just ten miles from Cane Ridge.[18]

Remarkable Occurrences begins with a scurrilous eleven-point explication of the Shakers' faith. Smith reiterated the same allegations of physical violence, child abuse, licentious sex, alcohol abuse, and servile obedience leveled at the Shakers in the "Attempt" article. Added to these is a greatly expanded account of his attempt to recover his grandchildren from the Shakers. To stoke the flames of public outrage regarding the Shakers' treatment of families and children, Smith accused them of abortion and infanticide, saying that if the Shakers "beget children, they put them out of the way." Smith labeled Shakers enemies of Christianity, the US government, and the Constitution, writing, "Let Shakerism predominate, and it will extirpate Christianity, destroy marriage and also

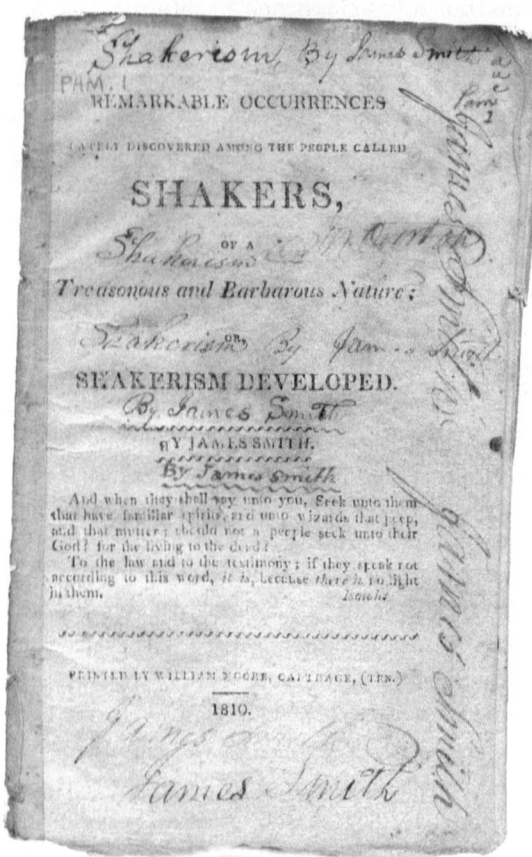

Figure 11.2. James Smith Sr.'s anti-Shaker pamphlet *Remarkable Occurrences, Lately Discovered Among the People Called Shakers* (Carthage, TN: Printed by William Moore, 1810). Courtesy of Library Special Collections, Western Kentucky University.

our present free government, and finally depopulate America. According to their scheme, civil and ecclesiastical government are blendid together, theirs is a despotic monarchy." Smith claimed that Shakerism was just a money-making scheme designed "to collect a fund in order to raise and pay an army of Tories whenever an opportunity offers." In a frontier society threatened on its western border by hostile Indians supported by the British Empire, this was no light accusation. In summation, Smith declared Shakerism to be "a political evil, under the pretext of divine worship."[19]

Another anti-Shaker writing was published anonymously in a number of newspapers in August. The article, provocatively titled "Who are the Shakers?" added further charges against the sect to those leveled by Smith. Robert Gill, a prominent convert at Busro, situated along the tense frontier border, was quoted as saying, "The Shakers would ultimately prevail in the United States, and in the event, as the Shakers would not fight, the British would again be masters of the country." And, in a blatant and false attempt at scaremongering, Aaron Burr was alleged to have visited the Shakers during his doomed attempt to treasonously separate the western territories from the United States. The author asked what "could have induced *Aaron Burr* to honour the Shakers ... with his attention and presence, at their places of worship and elsewhere, whilst he was recruiting in this country?"[20]

The popular outrage resulting from the publications of James Smith Sr. and others culminated in a mob action against the Shakers at Turtle Creek on Monday, August 27, 1810. Since July, the Shakers were aware that a "subscription paper" was circulating, enlisting members for such a mob. The sheriff had served James Smith Jr. with a writ on July 18 on Polly Smith's complaint.[21] The Shakers were warned that James Smith Sr. intended to take his grandchildren and also to "tar and feather R. McNemar, drive the old Shakers out of the country, and restore the rest to their former faith and manner of living." Fearing the potential onslaught, James Smith Jr. traveled to Lebanon with his children on Friday, August 24, placing himself in the custody of the sheriff, who confined them to the debtor's cell. On Sunday, August 26, Captain John Robinson came to a Shaker meeting to explicitly threaten that a violent mob would come the next day. In defiance, Youngs, Matthew Houston, and McNemar preached about "the spirit of injustice against the gospel, & on the nature of the gospel in opposition to the spirit of the world."[22] Meanwhile, legal authorities attempted to talk the mob out of their plan, to no avail.[23]

On Monday morning, five hundred men assembled three miles from the Shakers with the expressed goal of taking the Smith children from their father. The mob comprised local militia units and their officers, including the Springfield Light Horse, Presbyterian minister Matthew G. Wallace, and many agitated citizens. First Circuit judge Francis Dunlavy, John's brother, arrived at Turtle Creek ahead of the mob to observe and try to stop any illegal actions. The mob, with soldiers in the vanguard, arrived at one in the afternoon and halted in front of the meetinghouse. Benjamin Seth Youngs described the scene:

> The whole body of people now collected on the ground consisted of about fifteen hundred—some supposed upwards of two thousand. Besides the five hundred troops in military order, many scattering ones, who came with the multitude, were also armed, but undisciplined persons; old gray-headed men, boys and others, who exhibited a very mean and mob-like appearance. Some of the undisciplined multitude were armed with guns—some with poles, or sticks, on which were fixed bayonets; and others with staves, and hatchets, and knives and clubs. The exhibition presented a scene of horror, the intention of which was covered with duplicity.[24]

Youngs concluded that the show of force was merely a gambit to force the Shakers into a dialogue with a committee appointed to parlay with them. The committee called for the original three missionaries, Bates, Youngs, and Meacham, whom the community held responsible for introducing the plague of Shakerism into their midst. Youngs was the only one present; he walked out to meet the committee of twelve. The chief speaker was Reverend Wallace. His animus toward Richard McNemar was of long standing. He was on the committee of the Washington Presbytery that had censured McNemar for his preaching in 1802. The committee demanded that two more Shakers meet with them in addition to Youngs. Matthew Houston and Peter Pease joined him, and the committee insisted that they meet in the woods half a mile from the meetinghouse. The Shakers had no choice but to agree.[25]

The committee blamed the Shakers for causing "great disturbances in the minds of the people, and led to the extinction of civil and religious society ... and led mankind into bondage and oppression." They warned the Shakers that violence would ensue unless they complied with a series of demands. The first three of these dealt with restoring children of converts to their non-Shaker relatives, including the Smith children. Youngs pointed out that the Smith children were with their father, and that a lawsuit was ongoing regarding their custody. The committee accepted this explanation, and this demand was tabled for the moment. The committee's main demand was that the Shakers "cease publicly to inculcate our principles, and that we cease our practice; that we cease to dance on the Sabbath-days and on the week-days." If they could not meet these demands, they were warned to leave Ohio by December 3, 1810. The Shakers were given one hour to respond.[26]

Judge Dunlavy warned a member of the committee of the illegality of what was transpiring, but they refused to drop their demands. The two parties met again in the woods, where the Shakers gave their response. They explained that they held their faith "dearer than our lives, and therefore meant to maintain it, whatever we might suffer as the consequence." Further, the Shakers refused to leave their private property, which they had purchased and owned outright. They invoked the right of conscience and reaffirmed their peaceful intentions. Astonished, Wallace asked the Shakers how they could "withstand a thousand men?" At this, the Shakers walked away.[27]

Outraged, Wallace stood in front of the meetinghouse and declared that any who had charges to level against the Shakers should step forward. Two apostates, John and Robert Wilson, charged Believer Amos Valentine with whipping to death a young boy who was subject to fits. The Shakers promptly produced the boy and disproved the charge. Judge Dunlavy again attempted, without success, to disperse the mob. Major William Robinson led the soldiers in front of the recently constructed elders' dwelling, where the eastern Shakers lived. He loudly demanded to know if the Shakers would comply with the committee's demands—but he received no response. He then commanded the Believers to come out of the house and form a circle in front of him—but none moved. Robinson goaded the crowd into "a general loud and hideous yell" that it was their will that the Shakers leave the country. The doors of the dwelling were then forced open.[28]

A committee mainly consisting of military officers systematically searched the building to see if any were held there against their will. They specifically questioned the sisters, including Jenny McNemar, and none of them wished to leave. Captain Cornelius Thomas was apparently satisfied and, after drinking some cold coffee, declared he "saw a decent house, and decent people in it." They then conducted the same examinations at the young Believers' order and the school with the same results. In his account of events, written just days later, Youngs was proud that "no disturbance of confusion appeared among Believers through the whole occasion. The generality kept busy at their usual employments—took dinner in their usual manner, and entertained such as they could with convenience. They answered those mildly who spoke to them, whether peaceably or in a taunt." The committee and mob, somewhat embarrassed, left Turtle Creek soon thereafter.[29]

News of the mob action was reported in newspapers throughout the United States.[30] And, following his usual custom, Richard McNemar wrote a fifteen-stanza poem recounting the event.[31] Incredibly, Polly Smith returned to Turtle Creek on October 1, confessed her sins, abandoned her lawsuit against her husband, and took up residence with the Shakers. Darrow wrote that James Smith Sr. was "terrible mad about it—and he threatens to take away all the children from both their parents."[32] He redoubled his efforts to attack the Shakers in print, conducting a war of words with McNemar in the pages of Lebanon's *Western Star*. Due to the sporadic survival of issues of the *Western Star* from 1810, most of these writings have been lost.[33] The culmination of Smith's anti-Shaker publishing was his magnum opus, *Shakerism Detected*, which was copyrighted on November 21, 1810, less than three months after the mobbing of Turtle Creek.[34]

Shakerism Detected offered an innovation in anti-Shaker writing through the use of affidavits by former Shakers and non-Shaker witnesses. Although, as McNemar pointed out in his response to *Shakerism Detected* (titled *"Shakerism Detected &c." Examined & Refuted, in Five Propositions*), six of Smith's ten witnesses were his relatives. These included Smith's son, three stepsons, his daughter-in-law, and her brother.[35] Nevertheless, from then on, affidavits were routinely used in anti-Shaker publications. In his preface, Smith refers to a "long publication" by McNemar denying one of Smith's chief claims—the infallibility of Shaker leaders. In that publication McNemar also apparently challenged Smith's actions in the 1765 "Black Boys" uprising, thereby striking at the core of Smith's public persona as a revolutionary patriot. Unfortunately, this writing by McNemar, likely published in the *Western Star*, is presumably lost.[36]

Smith took the bait offered by McNemar's criticism of his heroic past. Consequently, a large portion of *Shakerism Detected* is an autobiographical defense by Smith of happenings forty-five years before. Smith even penned a specimen of doggerel verse about the heroism of the "Black Boys"—written, ironically, to the popular and vulgar "The Black Joke" tune also used by the Shakers. In rising to defend himself and his past, Smith allowed McNemar to divert him from the main thrust of his ire, the Shakers. Smith maintained that McNemar's criticism of his actions against the British in 1765 was evidence of sympathy for them in 1810, a serious accusation on the eve of the War of 1812. He taunted that when McNemar's "beloved toryism was plainly struck at, you kicked and pranced like a horse when his sore back has received a heavy stroke."[37]

Smith continued his allegations that the Shakers were secretly colluding with the Shawnee Indians in advance of a British attack on the frontier. He used an affidavit from Stephen Ruddle, a Baptist preacher who had lived among the Shawnee and spoke their language, to illustrate the (alleged) shocking discourse between the Shakers and the Shawnee at Greenville, Ohio, in 1807:

> What is the reason that the white people are always cheating red people out of their country and land: Now said they, if white people would give us back our country, then we would believe them. But yet, they said, they believed that there were still some good white people that loved red people. Now said they, there are our friends, the shakers; they are honest; for, said they Richard M'Namar told us that the white people had cheated us out of our

land ... he told them to continue their own worship, and not to mind the white people when they come to you with their book which they call the word of God, as that book is good for nothing now—it was once good, but bad men had changed it and made it bad.—But the Great Spirit had now revealed to Indians the same that he had to the shakers; and now they were brothers.[38]

Although some of this affidavit rings true to what Shaker missionaries had told the Shawnee, McNemar was able to rebut Ruddle's claims in his reply to Smith. He found an affidavit from Ruddle dated September 22, 1807, that was published in the *Scioto Gazette* and offered Ruddle's affirmation, as an interpreter, of the peaceful intentions of the Shawnee.[39]

McNemar challenged Smith's authority to write anything about Shaker life or theology, and Smith was forced in *Shakerism Detected* to respond specifically about how long he lived with the Shakers: "I was with the shakers about a week, and went with them night and day to your places of worship, and where they were preaching or making proselytes; insomuch that some supposed that I had really fallen in with, & joined the shakers, I stayed with them until I was tired of them, and I believe that they were heartily tired of me."[40] McNemar also infuriated Smith by questioning the authorship of his first anti-Shaker article "An Attempt to Develope Shakerism," proposing that it was actually written by David Purviance, a former colleague of McNemar's in the Springfield Presbytery. This charge hit a nerve with Smith, who felt compelled to produce affidavits that he had actually written the work.

Smith was still driven by his quest to retrieve his grandchildren from the Shakers, and more information is presented about that sad story in *Shakerism Detected*. Smith's stepson William Irvin traveled to Turtle Creek with Polly Smith so she could see her children. He alleged that John Woods (who later apostatized and published his own anti-Shaker narrative), who had care of the Smith children, told him to "go home, & quit my whoring, meaning for me to quit my wife." Polly Smith gave Irvin some sugar to give to her children, "but they refused that; she then rode off weeping."[41] Smith closed his pamphlet with a powerful appeal for justice in light of his service in the cause of American liberty: "I suffered much in procuring the happy liberty that we now possess, I lost my old Brother in the contest ... and I myself was nigh unto death (while in the army) with the camp fever; I also lost almost all that I possessed by the depreciated money. After all this can I bear to see my grand-children raised up traitors to the free government that protects them, to be pests of society and slaves to pope David?" This Smith could not countenance. Instead, he proposed that the militia be excused if, owing to the civil government's failure to address the problem, "they send the shakers off to live with their beloved Shawanoe prophet and his brother." The onset of the War of 1812 gave Smith an outlet for his anger. Deserted by his son but still fired by his patriotism, he returned to what he knew and loved best—warfare. On September 12, 1812, the *Reporter* of Lexington, Kentucky, noted, "Col. James Smith, of Indian memory... who is nearly 80 years of age, has gone to join our army."[42] Shortly following his brief and remarkable return to the battlefield, Smith passed away on April 11, 1813.[43]

McNemar surely exulted in the death of this enemy of Shakerism, although there is no evidence of this. The mob of August 1810, and the protracted print war with Smith, was the first major public battle with apostates the Shakers had engaged in since 1800, when Reuben Rathbone left the Hancock Shakers and published a damning narrative of his life there.[44] The conflict with Smith allowed McNemar's talents as a writer and rhetorician, already displayed in the *Kentucky Revival*, to again shine brightly in defense of his faith. Throughout the rest of his life, McNemar filled this role repeatedly, especially for the western Shaker communities, thereby increasing his public profile in a decidedly non-Shaker way. Like much else in his life, this probably engendered internal conflict between his need to adhere to Shaker tenets of humility and his deep-seated desire (perhaps unconscious) for recognition and notoriety.

The Shakers waited with anxiety for December 3—the mob's deadline for their departure—a day that thankfully came and went without incident. However, the threat was modified, and New Year's Day was designated the day of vengeance. It was proclaimed that on that day, Shaker leaders would be whipped, tarred, and feathered, and the rank and file would be forced to renounce their faith at sword point. The persecutors threatened to bring a barrel of whiskey and make themselves so drunk that their violence would be uninhibited. They also promised to make the Shakers drink with them and to pour it down their throats if they refused. The eastern Shakers hid their possessions and papers in the homes of the young Believers, as the mob had promised not to harm their former friends and neighbors, except for Richard McNemar. The young Believers tried to persuade the easterners to leave and let them defend their liberty of conscience for themselves. Ultimately, the easterners chose caution and spent New Year's Eve at the home of Ichabod Corwin in Lebanon. Fortunately, none of the threats was carried out.[45]

News of the "Ohio Mob," as it came to be known in Shaker lore, was published all over the United States. In Marshfield, Massachusetts, Proctor Sampson, a former sailor and follower of Freewill Baptist preachers Benjamin Randall and John Buzzell, had read Richard McNemar's *Kentucky Revival*. He resolved to contact the Shakers but, feeling he "had been unfaithful to the light" given him, doubted his worthiness.[46] In a later memoir, he wrote that reading about the Ohio Mob in a newspaper had prompted him to write to McNemar in the autumn of 1810 requesting information. On January 5, 1811, McNemar sent Sampson a pointed, and poignant, response that both resonated with him and satisfied his mind, prompting him to join the Shakers. McNemar wrote:

> The Presbyterians, Seceders and New lights are generally united against this way, for two special reasons: 1st because it doctrinally exposes the absurdity of their false cloak of imputed righteousness, and demonstrates the necessity of being Christ-like, and doung right, in order to be esteemed righteous in the discerning eye of God;—and 2nd. because it practically reproves their vicious lives by openly shewing how the true followers of the Lamb do, in reality, live. When the Angel (or Messenger of God) stands in the sun of righteousness, and reveals the wrath of God against all unrighteousness, men are scorched with a great heat. They could bear to hear a great deal said against sin, and for holiness; but when we come to pluck out the right eye, and cast off every weight, and the sin that doth so easily beset us, and enter upon a life of positive obedience to God, and stand in it, this touches their plagues and sores to the quick, and sets them to blaspheming to some purpose. But the more they blaspheme, and vent their persecuting venom against this strait and narrow way of self denial, the more it turns to use for a testimony that it is the only way of God. I am truly pleased with thy honesty, in stating they experience and opening thy case, and tho I wish thee in a better condition, yet I know how to sympathize with one in thy situation, as many years of painful experience have taught me the hopes and fears, the longing desires, the vigorous exertions, and various exercises of a miserable sinner, struggling with the body of this death. I should be glad to communicate many things to thee on this subject, which I cannot in the compass of a short letter. This however I would observe: that it is hard to be obliged to sail on dry land, to keep in a way where there is no track, or to follow where none go before. When the denominations around us testify that it is their faith to commit sin daily, in thought, word, and deed, we do not dispute it; and we think we are equally entitled to credit, when we say, that it [is] our faith to "be blameless and harmless, the sons of God without rebuke": and it must reasonably be granted that they, and we respectively, live up to our profession, unless the contrary is proved out by our actions. I mention this, that thou mayest be guarded against the false insinuations, and slanderous aspersions that might be cast into thy way, to prevent thee from inquiring into the real character of this people.[47]

Sampson was a wealthy man. He became a truly dedicated Believer and was instrumental in the Shakers' eventual expansion into the Great Lakes region.

THE OHIO LEGISLATURE

When the threat of mob violence against the Shakers failed to achieve the desired ends of the anti-Shaker portion of the public, they resorted to legislative remedies. McNemar wrote to eastern Shaker Proctor Sampson, saying that the mob "either becoming ashamed or affraid to make an open attack and the more honorable part of the club have resorted to other measures and have petitioned for a law against the Shakers, which petition is before the legislature." McNemar included some poignant observations on his former coreligionists in his letter: "The Presbyterians, Seceders and Newlights are generally united against this way, for two special reasons; 1st because it doctrinally exposes the absurdity of their false cloak of imputed righteousness and demonstrates the necessity of being Christ-like in doing right in order to be esteemed righteous in the deserning eye of God, and 2nd because it practically reproves their vicious lives by openly showing how the true followers of the Lamb, do, in reality live."[48]

The Ohio General Assembly checked the "followers of the lamb" on January 11, 1811, by the passage of an "Act providing for the relief and support of women who may be abandoned by their husbands." The law was specifically directed at the Shakers and initiated by David Purviance, McNemar's former colleague in the Springfield Presbytery. Purviance, now serving as a state senator, presented two anti-Shaker memorials to the senate on December 18, 1810.[49] Wives abandoned by their husbands could file a complaint requiring their spouses to appear in court. If the marriage was deemed legitimate, and spousal abandonment established, it was at the court's discretion to award the woman a portion of her husband's property and real estate. Crucially, the act also stated that a husband who had joined the Shakers had effectively "renounced and divested himself of all the authority he could have otherwise exercised over his children . . . and such child or children shall be and remain under the care and direction of the mother." To circumvent a husband's legal consecration of property to the Shakers, without his wife's consent, the act rendered such gifts "utterly void; and all money or property so given, granted or devised, may be recovered at the suit of the party injured." Finally, any person who would "entice or persuade such person to join any sect" where the marriage covenant was renounced would be liable to a fine of $500.[50]

Persecution continued at the local level too. In a letter to New Lebanon, the transplanted eastern Shakers lamented that anti-Shakers "published the most scandalous & blasphemous things about us they could—and offered to swear to it untill the printers would not insert no more of their stuff."[51] In the fall of 1810, lawyer Thomas Freeman of Lebanon published a five-part series titled "A Retrospective View of Shakerism" in the *Western Star*.[52] In fact, Darrow blamed him for instigating the anti-Shaker legislation that Purviance shepherded through the General Assembly. Darrow wrote, "To reward him for his kindness, we have taken his father and his mother, and have got his oldest brother and wife into the dance with us, and expect to get some more of his connexions, and poor Thomas feels very slim about it—So we think we have paid him very well for his trouble in slandering us."[53] Apostate Robert Wilson, who lived at Turtle Creek with his natural brother John Wilson for a little over a year, sued David Darrow. The judgment went against Darrow, who was liable for $287. The Shakers appealed the case to the Ohio Supreme Court, which reversed the verdict in September.[54]

Despite the legal troubles, the faithful Believers at Eagle Creek gathered at Busro and Turtle Creek in the spring of 1811. Eighty were sent to Busro, and seventy went to Turtle Creek—including Richard's brother Garner McNemar, who arrived on April 1 with his wife, Betsey, and their four children.[55] Richard McNemar spent the early summer of 1811 in Kentucky traveling between Shawnee Run and Gasper, ministering to converts with Youngs. They left Turtle Creek on April 8 and were on the road until they returned home on August 2. They were present at Shawnee Run on Sunday, May 28, when the converts there agreed to rename their settlement Pleasant Hill. It would be the last time the two men traveled together for a significant time as missionaries. On September 25, Benjamin Seth Youngs moved permanently to Gasper (shortly to be renamed South Union) to reside there as first elder.[56] Youngs and McNemar had been nearly constant companions for the past six years. Youngs had educated McNemar in the principles of Shakerism, and McNemar had confessed his sins to Youngs and Bates. Additionally, Youngs was likely the only person with whom McNemar could discuss sophisticated theological matters, and each man valued the other's opinion of his writings. Youngs's relocation must have been difficult for McNemar, although, as a good Believer, he seems to have made no objections. The two men would reconnect late in life under highly stressful circumstances.

The day before Youngs's departure for South Union, he, McNemar, Matthew Houston, and Calvin Morrell had presented a declaration to the General Assembly of Ohio. Dated September 24 at Warren County, the declaration remonstrated further against the act passed on January 11, 1811. The men questioned the constitutionality of passing a law against an entire religious body based only on the petitions of their enemies and without giving the accused any chance to defend themselves. They confirmed the Shakers' requirement that any male member of their society with a wife or children must "provide honestly and liberally for their support." They invoked the honor of the state, asking, "Must the youngest Sister State in the Union and the west, gloried in for her freedom and liberties, be the first to set the example of religious intolerance?" The Shakers affirmed their loyalty to the government and the Federal Constitution, requesting only that the law written specifically against them be reevaluated in the context of their guaranteed rights as American citizens.[57]

When the Ohio General Assembly reconvened in December 1811, Shakers Ashbel Kitchell and John Wallace presented a remonstrance asserting that the act was unconstitutional at both the state and federal levels.[58] According to Darrow, when the remonstrance was read, "it struck the whole house with consternation and threw them into confusion." Anti-Shaker activists then presented the assembly with a petition signed by more than four hundred people requesting that a law be made allowing for the removal of children from the Shakers. Incredibly, while these events were transpiring, a massive tremor struck. "The house where they were sitting was shaken, and the doors and windows and seats to that degree that the men were struck with paleness, and some fled out for safety." With particular satisfaction, Darrow wrote, "David Purviance, the Newlight preacher, was so frightened that he ran clear across the street and took hold of a man for protection." Kitchell and Wallace were in the chamber when the earthquake struck. Afterward, they spoke individually with a number of the legislators, who assured them that they opposed the anti-Shaker legislation, although the law remained on the books for years to come.[59]

The New Madrid Earthquakes of 1811–1812 attracted much attention from the Shakers. Daniel Moseley, an easterner, even composed a hymn inspired by the huge temblor, which was estimated to have measured over 8.0 on the Richter scale and was clearly felt at Turtle Creek, Ohio. Moseley interpreted the earthquake to be the work of God, proving his power even to the "stupid soul" and the "deaf and dumb." In contrast with the terror experienced by the unredeemed, the Shakers reveled in this natural marvel. In his hymn, Moseley described "fields and forests fall to dancing, / Dwelling houses crack for joy."[60] Solomon King even credited the earthquakes with lessening the ardor of Shaker persecutors. He wrote New Lebanon Shaker Rufus Bishop that "many of our inemis have been very much alermed by reason of the Repeted Shaking of the earth . . . many have appeared to been very much surprised & ceased [seized] with a fearful looking for of Judgment."[61]

THE COVENANT OF 1812

In January 1812, David Darrow penned an unusually lengthy letter to Deacon Richard Spier at New Lebanon. Darrow shared his hopes for Turtle Creek, which was renamed Union Village around November 1811, almost certainly in light of the pending implementation of a joint economic interest among the converts.[62] Darrow, however, was also candid about the unpleasant realities of Shaker life on the frontier with the new converts.

> We have gathered upwards of 200 people, old and young, on your land here, to support a joint interest, that we call Believers—and they have cleared a heap of land last year, and got in a fine chance of wheat for another crop—and they have raised a fine chance of corn to make much [mush] and pawn [pone] of plentifully—likewise they have got plenty of pork to make bacon, all which the people here are very fond of—indeed they begin to work middling well, only some of our woods boys are a little too fond of hunting yet—but I expect we shall by and by persuade them to lay down their arms and stick to their business....
>
> But O brother Richard—to give a true statement of the people's faith here according to my sense and understanding, is this—We have a goodly number of good believers whose faith and obedience is as firm as a rock, and who have remained steadfast and unshaken through all the persecutions and false accusations that the wicked have brought against us, and I have no doubt but they would freely lay down their lives for us if required; for which we love them dearly—But I expect if thee was here, they would feel very dirty and nasty to thee—But O consider the state they were in when we found them, and how we had to go down to the bottom of misery and take them by the hand and lead them out.[63]

To separate themselves from the body of the community, David Darrow and Ruth Farrington moved into the newly built meetinghouse on January 14, 1812, following the precedent set by the eastern Shaker Ministry. The next day, 156 members—65 males and 91 females—signed the church covenant. This was the first legally binding instrument of its kind employed by the Shakers west of the Alleghenies. Jenny McNemar's signature appears first in the sisters' column, and fifteen-year-old Vincy McNemar's appears on the last page. On the brothers' side, sixteen-year-old James McNemar's signature appears toward the end. Richard McNemar's signature, however, is nowhere to be found on this crucial document. Turtle Creek leadership had decided that McNemar should be "reserved from signing the ch[urc]h cov[enan]t in order that [he] might at

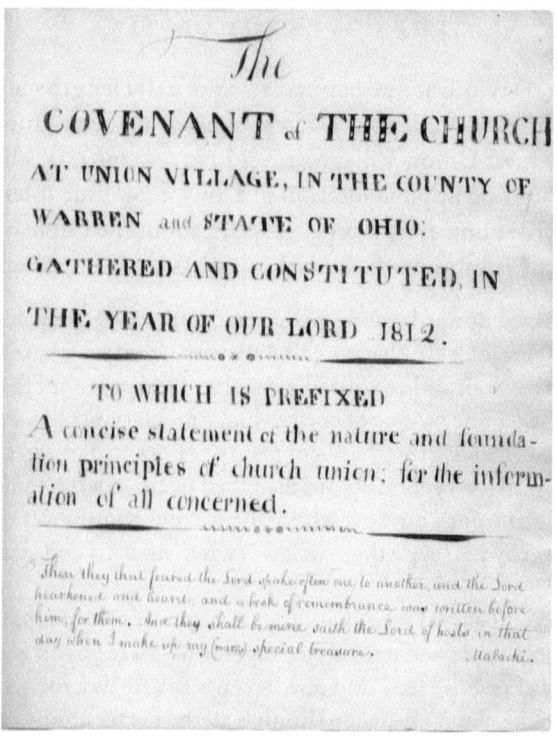

Figure 11.3. The covenant signed by Shakers at Union Village, Ohio, in 1812. Collection of the Western Reserve Historical Society.

any time appear as a faithful & disinterested witness to that sacred instrument." This was in keeping with Mother Lucy's instruction that McNemar "must not be bound to any people steady." McNemar was happy to assume this role for the cause of Shakerism, but he could not foresee the dire future repercussions of not signing the covenant.[64]

On January 16, a number of the covenanted members moved into the newly constructed dwelling house. Eldress Ruth Farrington and Elder David Darrow were given the titles of Mother and Father, respectively. This was a nod to earlier, eastern Shaker tradition and also an acknowledgment of their crucial role as spiritual parents to the converts in the West. Shaker hierarchies were now implemented, and offices of elders and deacons were set up among the nascent families at Union Village. After seven years of hard labor on the western frontier, order was beginning to emerge from the chaos.[65]

TWELVE

WAR COMES TO THE WABASH

THE BELIEVERS AT BUSRO FOUND themselves on the front lines of the War of 1812. The Battle of Tippecanoe, fought on November 22, 1811, pitted the forces of Indiana's Territorial Governor William Henry Harrison against the Shakers' friend Tenskwatawa and a Native American alliance forged by Tecumseh (who was not present at the battle). Archibald Meacham, now the presiding elder at Busro, described the dread that hung over the Shakers in a letter to David Darrow, dated April 20, 1812: "The Battle of Tippecanoe and succeeding circumstances have so forcibly opporated on their imaginations—that they have become the wretched pray of tormenting fear and restless anxiety—since that engagement their spirits have sunk—and the courage of their hearts failed them." Darrow gathered the Believers at Turtle Creek, and Richard McNemar read the letter aloud to them, at which "they appeared generally to be deeply affected." Non-Shaker families in the vicinity of Busro were murdered or had their houses burned, while American military officers were insistent on either drafting Believers or receiving payment instead. The Shakers' hostile neighbors threatened that if "the Indians do not kill us they will."[1]

Darrow and the Union Village leadership asked McNemar to draft the reply to beleaguered Busro, as he had performed more spiritual labor among them than any of the other missionaries presently at Turtle Creek. McNemar responded frankly, "That your faith will be tried to the utmost appears altogether likely." He assured them that those at Turtle Creek were praying for them, but "it remains for you to stand your own trial, & to prove your own faith." McNemar cited their holy calling and mission as the reason they must stand their ground, for if "your temporal safety & happiness was the uppermost object, your plans would be easily concerted." In other words, the Busro Believers

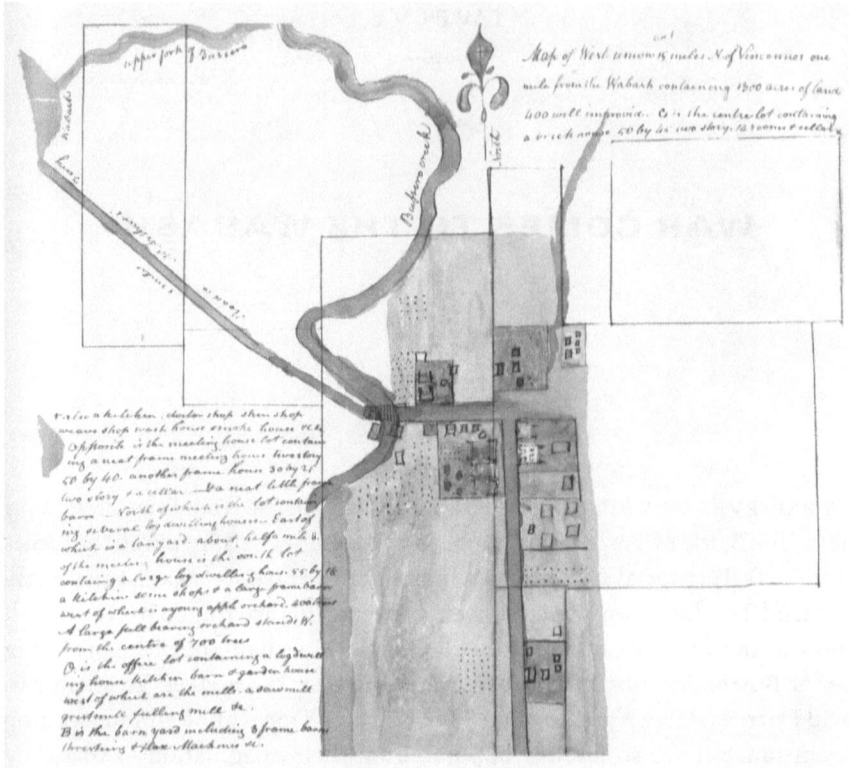

Figure 12.1. A map of the Busro, or West Union, Indiana, Shaker community drawn by Richard McNemar. Collection of the Western Reserve Historical Society.

must not retreat and should be prepared for martyrdom. Finding themselves "between you[r] fellow citizens and the savages," they should stand as witnesses to "see & judge, & more over to give an example to both parties." Practically, McNemar advised them not to "straggle about much alone, either in the forest or on the farm." In closing, he reassured them, "Fear not little flock, there is a better country than the Wabash a more enduring substance than the soil of the great praira, and property that robbers cannot break through upon; an inheritance that is incorrupted undefiled & reserved in the heavens for every faithful soul."[2] Such sentiments must have been cold comfort to people facing frontier warfare.

Two days later, after further consideration, McNemar offered the Busro Believers a softened stance, telling them, "We cannot bind you to anything beyond your own understanding & choice." He advised them that although they were "harmless as doves you may be as wise as serpents, and you may actually do many things toward your own safety & protection which may be productive of much good & no evil." He opened the possibility that women and children could evacuate to Union Village; however, Shaker leaders were not "certain that it is the call of God yet for any to leave the ground [since] the gospel was planted at Busro under the special providence of God." With the unemotional detachment of a true Believer, McNemar wrote, "It doubtless feels weighty to you to be upbraided with keeping the people there till they are all butchered... & if any do stay & are killed it must be, absolutely without compulsion or even persuasion."[3]

McNemar compared the Busro Believers to Jesus, who allowed the Jews and Romans to kill him, though he could have escaped. Rather callously, he wrote that if they "had to pay 500 dollars for your delinquency in fighting the Indians last fall, & should let the savages have a little of your blood this summer perhaps both parties will be satisfied you are enemies to neither," framing it as an opportunity to "honor the gospel." The Union Village Shakers expressed their desire to send help but pleaded that their "wing feathers are plucked quite bare." McNemar personally assured them, "Gladly Poor Richard would be among you to take share of the cup, but it seems necessary that he should remain with the stuff at present." Offering a more realistic approach to their situation, he advised gathering the families together behind a defensive wall, posting watchmen with trumpets to sound the alarm, and even discharging weapons into the air to influence "the brutal spirit of a savage to drive him from his prey." The letter was signed by McNemar and ten other Believers, and, for good measure, it conveyed the love of Darrow and Ruth Farrington.[4]

That spring of 1812, McNemar was busy, traveling extensively to minister to new converts. He visited Preble County (west of Dayton) and Beaver Creek with Matthew Houston in February. At home, the Union Village Shakers dealt with myriad troubles. McNemar and Samuel Rollins journeyed to Dayton on June 2 to meet with Governor Return Meigs Jr., probably to seek military exemptions for the Shakers. Sadly, on June 10, while McNemar was away, his nine-year-old daughter, Betsy, died at Union Village. No cause of death is recorded in the Shaker records nor any reaction from her blood relatives, who by this time would have likely eschewed any display of grief for a flesh-relation. Following his return from Dayton, McNemar was off again to Beaver Creek with John Rankin from the Gasper community (which became South Union).[5]

Meanwhile, the fate of Busro was unknown. As the Wabash frontier smoldered during the summer of 1812, sickness plagued the community, claiming the lives of four brethren. Finally, at midnight on Saturday, September 19, Issachar Bates and John Lockwood arrived at Union Village to let the ministry know that Busro had been evacuated. The Busro Shakers traveled to Red Banks on the Kentucky shore of the Ohio River and camped there until arrangements could be made to bring them to Union Village. By November 10, they were safely ensconced there, some in hastily built accommodations quickly erected for the refugees.[6] To add to this tension, on October 8, Nancy Dunn lodged a complaint with Warren County justice of the peace Enos Williams that a month earlier, Richard McNemar and two other Shakers "came to [her] house, and took away [her] daughter." Dunn charged that her daughter Sarah Naylor was "unlawfully deprived of her liberty and . . . at present imprisoned or detained by the said Richard."[7]

Four days later, a writ of habeas corpus was served on McNemar, demanding that he produce Sarah Naylor by nine o'clock in the morning on October 14 at the courthouse in Lebanon. The writ was requested by attorney Thomas Freeman, McNemar's old nemesis who published the scathing "Retrospective View of Shakerism" in 1810. McNemar returned the writ, writing on the back: "That it cannot be said that Magy (otherwise Sarah Naylor) is by me detained in any other sense than from her attachment to the religious society of which I am a member & the principles which I as a public preacher inculcate—that seven years ago this fall she became a member of said society, & as far as I know has ever since been at full liberty to chuse & act for herself without control from any." McNemar further informed the court that Naylor had gone to Kentucky and that any questions about her status could be answered in court.[8]

On the fourteenth, McNemar appeared in court with Union Village Shakers John Wallace, David Spinning, Elizabeth Sharp, and Sarah Naylor's husband, John. Attorney Freeman attempted unsuccessfully to cross-examine all of them. His efforts were severely damaged by Nancy Dunn's ranting; she was "railing in such a manner that the judges had her stopped & set down." John Naylor affirmed that his wife had gone to Gasper in Kentucky of her own free will and that he expected her to come back when she chose. At that, all were acquitted, the judge dismissed the case, and the matter was ended.[9]

The year 1812 was a tough year for the Union Village Shakers. In a letter to Richard Spier, David Darrow summarized McNemar's legal difficulties. He also detailed a lawsuit brought against himself in the state supreme court by apostate Robert Wilson for $250 in damages. Happily, he reported that the suit was settled "honourably on the side of truth." Darrow wrote that in both cases, "it was Evident to the court their witnesses were false—so in every public attack the wicked have made upon us—they have failed of getting their Invious minds answered."[10] In addition to the legal troubles, community resources were further stretched by the refugees arriving from West Union on November 12, 1812. Darrow again lamented to Spier, "It is terrible times here on this part of the globe—the world & earth is very much convulsed—both by wars & Earthquakes." Adding to their difficulties, the state legislature passed a new law levying a fine of twenty dollars per month on each Believer who refused militia duty as a conscientious objector. Union Village brethren had already accrued $920 in fines, and the sheriff was now threatening to confiscate property instead of payment. Eight more brethren were drafted for a term of six months, leaving the Shakers liable for a further $960.[11]

As if all of this were not enough, the late winter and early spring of 1813 saw a deadly epidemic sweep through Union Village. Darrow stated that the refugees from Busro brought it to the community, although pestilence was sweeping the entire western theater of the War of 1812.[12] Since December 10, 1812, at least 160 were ill at Union Village. The sickness peaked in March and hit young adults particularly hard. Wistfully, Darrow remarked that they were "as good believers as we could wish for." One such, Jethro Dennis, who had thrown the chair down on the heads of the robbers, was described as the "first that gave himself up to the gospel in all this Country." He had sung for a meeting on March 21, 1813. He fell ill shortly thereafter and was so sick that it took "the flesh nearly of[f] [his] bones." On March 29, he died. In the days that followed, up to twenty-seven Believers at a time lay ill, a "number of them looked like corpses."[13] Richard McNemar and Matthew Houston had been sent to the Beulah settlement (now renamed Watervliet) of Believers on March 1, where McNemar fell ill. Nathan Sharp was dispatched to bring him back to Union Village on March 15. At that time, thirteen sisters and six brothers were seriously ill in the Centre Family alone. In all, seventeen Shakers succumbed to the sickness between October 1812 and May 1813.[14]

The Union Village community was spared direct involvement in the War of 1812, except for the housing refugees from Busro. On September 7, 1813, however, the realities of the conflict hit home when seven of the brethren were drafted for service in the Army of the Northwest, a new unit tasked with control of the state of Ohio and the Indiana, Michigan, and Illinois Territories. That month, they were taken under guard to Dayton for refusing to fight. They escaped from Dayton when their unit marched on and no one was left to guard them. Ultimately, they were summoned again for service on October 1. Before leaving Union Village, they were issued instructions by a committee consisting of David Darrow, Solomon King, Richard McNemar, and Matthew Houston enjoining them to "strictly regard their sacred profession and in no case to violate their vows, and obligations to God." For maximum impact, the instructions were read aloud to them in front of Colonel Daniel Reeder, the leader of their militia unit, who had come to muster them in.[15] The men were asked to minister the gospel to their fellow soldiers not through "public harangues" but by setting an example. The committee officially ordained them as ministers of the gospel, basically in the capacity of preachers. The committee gave the seven the "right hand of fellowship to take part of this ministry with [them] therefore by good Soldiers of Jesus Christ."[16] The committee described themselves as "Elders of the Church at Union Village," indicating that by this time, McNemar was just below Darrow and King in the church hierarchy. The drafted brethren, armed only with their instructions, were marched to Lebanon and charged with desertion for having failed to report for duty.[17]

MILLENNIAL PRAISES

During the tumultuous year from 1811 to 1813, Richard McNemar's attention was pulled in many different directions. But his love of writing hymns and poetry did not abate in the face of the many difficulties confronting the Shakers. Back East, a project was underway to compile the first printed collection of Shaker hymns. On August 6, 1811, Jethro Turner and Seth Youngs Wells, members of the Watervliet, New York, Shaker community, wrote to the New Lebanon Ministry officially proposing the project.[18] The hymn as a song form was a very recent innovation among the Shakers, who initially eschewed songs with English-language lyrics. However, beginning around 1804, Shaker poets and musicians began writing songs structured ABB, with multiple verses and texts on theological, doctrinal, or historical themes. Turner and Wells set out to collect hymn texts from Believers in the East and the West.[19]

On November 21, 1811, the New Lebanon Ministry wrote to David Darrow specifically requesting hymn texts from Richard McNemar for the book. The active participation of the ministry in collecting, and commissioning, hymn texts for the project demonstrates its importance.

> We have a small request to make, which, if agreeable to thy feelings, we wish may be answered as soon as convenient—It is to have thee send us a few hymns, which have been composed by Brother Richard, or others who have a gift in that line, such as may be judged by thee to be suitable for the Believers in these parts—
>
> We have also a desire (if agreeable to thy feelings) to have Brother Richard compose three Hymns, one to be on the subject of faith—another to be entitled The carnal Resurrection—and the last to be entitled the Spiritual

Relation substanually shewing the nature and unreasonableness of a carnal Resurrection, and the nature and reasonableness of the Spiritual Resurrection, elucidated in such a manner as to carry conviction to rational people of the world & be suitable to sing in our public meetings. We have no choice in the measure, but are willing it should be such as Brother Richard may think best adapted to the subject."[20]

This letter demonstrates that the ministry continued to have a high level of confidence in McNemar's capability to explicate Shaker theology, particularly on such important matters as the nature of the resurrection. The effect of this confidence on McNemar and other western Shaker hymnodists is apparent in the large number of hymns attributed to them in the finished hymnal, *Millennial Praises*, published in 1813. Of the 140 hymn texts in that volume, at least seventy are attributed to McNemar and another six variously to him or other composers.

David Darrow and Ruth Farrington responded in the affirmative, stating, "We shall send such Hymns as we may think suitable—& then submit them to the ministry for Examination—whether they are fit to publish or not."[21] Eastern transplant Daniel Moseley forwarded another hymn by McNemar in a letter to Deacon Richard Spier at New Lebanon, writing, "As my sheet is not full yet, I send a hymn that was composed to follow an anthem on the 6th Chap. of the Revelations. Composed by Richard."[22] The hymn, titled "The Day of Retribution," framed the struggle of Believers to slay their carnal natures in the context of the final battle of Armageddon, as described in Revelation.

In December 1813, real battles were taking place at Union Village. Apostate James Bedle, who had indentured his children to Trustee Peter Pease, came to the Centre Family on December 16 to recover his four children by force. The mob used a battering ram to break down the door of the Centre Family house, where they committed "considerable violence and abuse; but failed in getting the children." On December 29, another mob was assembled, and under threat, Pease decided to release the children from their indentures. Their father took them on December 30, according to the Shakers "much against their wills. They went off screaming and hallowing. The Mother and the 2 Oldest children have fled to some other quarter to avoid violence & enjoy their own faith."[23] Unfortunately, mob attacks like this plagued Union Village for the rest of the decade.

In August 1814, Richard McNemar's original homestead, referred to as the East House, was repurposed as a Young Believer's Order, or Gathering Order. The buildings had housed the Busro refugees, but they returned to Indiana on August 4. On August 11, Matthew Houston was installed as elder of this new

East House family, with Malinda Watts as his counterpart.[24] As for McNemar himself, little record of his activities for late 1814 survives. A Union Village account book contains many entries for chairs made by McNemar throughout 1813 and 1814, so he may have contented himself with hand labor, an integral part of Shaker life for members of every level.[25] He did travel to Watervliet, Ohio, in early September to attend the funeral of Polly Woodruff.[26]

As 1815 dawned, Darrow and Farrington worked to refine and unify their converts by formally declaring war against the flesh and the devil. The effect was to spur an internal revival yielding powerful bodily exercise and gifts of the spirit—surely a refreshment following three years of sickness and tribulation. Darrow described the events as "such as we never witnessed before . . . great numbers speaking with tongues at once—turning stamping with their feet throw down and tossed about . . . with such indignation against the beast & whore—warring and roaring against the flesh."[27] By now, the communal families at Union Village were largely gathered into order. The New Lebanon Ministry wrote the Union Village Ministry, inquiring, "We have heard of the Church at Union Village—but we do not hear who is the Elder Brother—nor who is the Elder Sister in the Church &c[?]" In response, Darrow and Farrington wrote, "Currently we have to confess that Elder timber is very scarce among us."[28] They did, however, provide the names of six out-families—the South, North (Children's Order), Youth's Order, Mill Family, East Family, and West Section—along with their elders and eldresses.

As for the Church Family, they replied in a tongue-in-cheek manner that all were housed in a "big yellow house opposite the Meetinghouse they are a most all Elders and some are midling good too—but to be honest in the matter—we have never told them yet who was their Elder Brother or Elder Sister—we had rather keep them in the fire a year or two longer—untill the flesh is burnt to a crisp—then to give it any power to do mischief." The New Lebanon Ministry also inquired about Richard McNemar, whom they called "an Apollo indeed."[29] Darrow wrote, "Richard is live & full of the spirit & doing well a part of his gift is to Believers & a part to the World to help Brother Matthew."[30] This is probably a reference to McNemar filling a public preaching role at the East House and working with new converts living there under Houston's care.

Daniel Drake, a prolific writer, physician, and polymath, published a complimentary report about the Union Village Shakers in his 1815 book, *Natural and Statistical View, or Picture of Cincinnati and the Miami Country.*

Union or Shakertown. This is situated on an elevated fertile ridge, four miles west of Lebanon. It is exclusively inhabited by a religious association, denominated Shakers. They occupy a number of large handsome wooden houses, and have several capacious shops, where trades and manufactures are prosecuted. Their gardens and fields are extensive, neat, productive, and cultivated in common. The whole village is, indeed, held in joint tenancy, and the products of its soil and shops are thrown into a common stock, in the use and enjoyment of which all are said equally to participate. By these and corresponding moral and political regulations, they have been enabled, in a manner to insulate themselves, in the midst of that society of which they were once members. This seclusion and monastic contempt of the prevalent social enjoyments, have brought upon them the obloquy of many. Without enquiring to what extent this is just, it may be briefly stated, that they are temperate, cleanly, frugal, peaceable, and honest in pecuniary dealings; that their new motives produce more industry than the old, but that their religious creed contains principles which mankind in general will not soon adopt, while their organization of secular affairs, on a large scale, would be wholly impracticable. They are not likely, therefore, to become either very numerous or powerful.[31]

Drake closed his report by noting the passage of the 1811 anti-Shaker law by the Ohio legislature.

Despite positive reports such as Drake's, relations between the Shakers and the surrounding community were still fraught, and the threat of violence was ever present. Darrow and Farrington lamented that local anti-Shakers were working with apostates and "printing and publishing all the slander and false swearing reports they can get hold of . . . and sending out their depositions in their public papers thro the world in order to stir up the envy of mankind against us."[32] In defense of their burgeoning commerce, trustees John Wallace and Nathan Sharp published a notice in the *Western Star* dated February 13, 1815, that the Shakers reserved the right not to do business with those who "trampled on our rights and privileges, especially those who came last winter in a riotous manner, and abused our persons and property." They requested that such people not "come into our shops or mills, nor do we wish to have any thing to do with them, in the line of common dealing, until they manifest a willingness to treat us with that degree of respect that the laws of our land secure to all civil citizens."[33]

The institution of Shaker order at Union Village had come very far since 1805, but David Darrow still worried about the soundness of the Shakers' legal title to their lands, particularly as they were deeded to individual trustees in the name of the church. He wrote Deacon Richard Spier at New Lebanon requesting copies of all deeds to western lands that had been consecrated in advance of the creation of Shaker trustees in Ohio. Darrow confessed that even while he lived at New Lebanon, he "often felt trouble on account of the titles of land—that was given up for use of the gospel—for fear that one day or other—it would fail—but I hope it is now secure." Darrow assured Spier that all deeds to land in Union Village had been "given for the full value received—to them in hand paid—this was thought by a number of brethren here—to be the most safe." For years, Spier had been Darrow's closest confidant, correspondent, and advisor. He pointed out to Darrow that a clause in the fourth article of the Union Village covenant could potentially be exploited by dishonest trustees who might appropriate community assets for personal gain. Accordingly, Darrow consulted with Richard McNemar and redrafted the section, changing the language in the hopes of preventing such financial malfeasance.[34] Sadly, their hopes on this front would be entirely dashed, as future events proved.

The autumn of 1815 saw yet another round of sickness sweep through the village. Nancy McNemar, daughter of Garner McNemar (Richard's brother), succumbed to the "ague and fever" illness on October 2; she was only fourteen. Her death was little noticed at the time, but it laid the groundwork in years to come for one of the most severe trials ever faced by the McNemar family and Union Village. Sadly for Garner, on December 28, his wife, Betsey, died at fifty-one. Her fellow Believers remembered her as "one of the most worthy & highly esteemed sisters in Union Village."[35] No writings of Garner's are known to have survived from this period, so we cannot know how he reacted to these losses in his natural family.

On April 14, 1816, Malcham Worley, Richard McNemar, Francis Bedle, Joseph Stout, Calvin Morrell, Samuel Rollins, and Ashbel Kitchell—all early western converts—were granted the privilege of writing to Mother Lucy Wright, first eldress of the New Lebanon Ministry.[36] Eleven years after their conversion, having clearly proved their dedication to the faith, they were allowed direct contact with the spiritual fountainhead of the entire Shaker movement. David Darrow and Ruth Farrington sent a covering letter stating, "A number of the believers here that have often felt very desirous to communicate . . . their faith and love, & thankfulness to thee—for the blessings of the gospel which thou hast sent them." They informed Mother Lucy that they had not told the believers what to write and had given them "liberty" to "write nothing but the truth." In closing, they absolved Mother Lucy from answering the letter, stating that the writers would not expect it.[37]

The lengthy epistle written by the seven fills four sides of two large sheets of paper. A tone of absolute veneration and supplication is maintained throughout. Mother Lucy is thanked for the "unspeakable mercies" she has afforded them. The men assured her of their "determination to be subject and obedient to that gift and order which thou hast set four our protection & salvation." Describing their state when the Shaker missionaries arrived in 1805, they wrote, "We were a mixed multitude, endowed with different talents and different degrees of light which principally consisted in visions and the opening of prophecies. It was then our general faith that the kingdom of heaven was at hand." They acknowledged the work of the missionaries, travailing in the mud, combating opposers, and defending their charges, and credited their perseverance to Mother Lucy's spirit. Affirming their loyalty to the Union Village Ministry, they wrote, "The revelation of Christ in our immediate parents and elders we never can dispute."[38]

Despite this, they were honest about the difficulties of uniting in communal order. Coming off the high of their conversion, they were eager to enter "into the order and relationship of a church, without duly considering what it was that must join and unite us together in that relation." However, when that was instituted, they found that "the old evil root was not yet destroyed, but could work and shew itself in many ways, in direct opposition to the spirit & nature of the work into which we were then called." In time, they realized that it was only love that could unite them, one to another, and in subjection to their elders.[39] Thus, they cautiously hoped that through the past eleven years of labor on the part of Darrow, Farrington, and their charges, they had matured into a community that could be compared with those back East.

TROUBLE WITH THE DAVIS FAMILY

The year 1817 was to be an eventful one for the Union Village Shakers. Scribes noted the death on February 28 of Seely, the slave formerly owned by the McNemars. The notice of her death is the only written source that also supplies her last name: Anderson. Seely was only twenty-seven and had lived as a Shaker since confessing her sins to Issachar Bates in 1805.[40] We have no reaction to her death from any of the McNemar family, a circumstance not uncommon among the Shakers. In all of his vast writings, McNemar rarely addressed the issue of slavery. His sentiments about it, however, are expressed quite clearly in an 1832 letter sent to a correspondent in Virginia, where slavery was being debated in the legislature. McNemar wrote,

Is it a forward march of intellect to base their municipal & moral laws on the mere color of the skin, & that the very surface? Instead, he stated forcefully that until Virginia "shall base her laws impartially on moral principle, & establish her rights of freedom & her rules of bondage on the wholesome doctrine of free agency she may then begin to feel proud of her Washingtons, Jeffersons &c. but till they fearlessly come forth & show as much economy in preserving a good breed of negroes as of breeding mares & turf horses, I shall consider their legislative harangues no better than tinkling brass & a sounding cymbal. Either emancipate their black people & treat them as human beings or exercise the same authority over them that they do over their horse, mare, & gelding & other animals held and treated as their property.[41]

Enemies of the Shakers perceived that their own kin were held by Shaker leadership in a form of bondage every bit as evil as African American slavery. The early summer of 1817 saw the culmination of more than a decade of turmoil between the Union Village Shakers and the extended Davis family. The Davis brothers, Jonathan and Elijah, were original settlers at Bedle's Station, purchased by William Bedle in 1795. Bedle's daughter Susanna married Jonathan, and another daughter, Lydia, married Elijah. Jonathan and Susanna joined the Shakers in 1805 with their sons William and John and daughter Hulda. Elijah and Lydia also joined with their daughter Esther and sons William and Daniel. By 1807, they all lived in a communal family gathered on Jonathan's farm. According to his later affidavit, Jonathan consecrated 250 acres to the Union Village community.[42]

John Davis married Elizabeth Sering in June 1805. They had a child and lived with John's father, Jonathan Davis. By 1807, Jonathan had been made elder of the family, Susanna eldress, and son William a deacon. John and Elizabeth Davis's lives were in turmoil, with each alternately vacillating between leaving the Shakers or committing and taking up their cross. John finally left in 1808. On May 3 of that year, he obtained a writ and led a civil officer and ten men to his father's to take back his wife. From then on, John lived in Lebanon and was a committed enemy of the Shakers. He was a leading participant in the mob of 1810.[43]

William Bedle wrote his will on March 9, 1812. He had never forgiven his daughters, the Davis wives, for joining the Shakers. A non-Shaker daughter, Mary Hole, was given 272 acres of land. To his Shaker daughters, Susanna and Lydia, he left five dollars each. To his grandson, bitter apostate John Davis, he willed one hundred acres of land, the very land that "his father, Jonathan Davis had formerly lived on." To add insult to injury, he also gave John an additional hundred acres where his uncle, Shaker Elijah Davis, once lived.[44]

John's mother, Susanna, was increasingly unhappy with her Shaker life. Union Village leaders decided to send her to live at Busro. Upon learning this, John attempted to help her leave but was unsuccessful. Susanna returned to Union Village with the Busro evacuees in November 1812. She left the Shakers soon after. Her husband, Jonathan, followed two months later, and he wrested their daughter Hulda away shortly after.[45] His brother Elijah and his family remained committed Believers for the moment.

Jonathan Davis sought relief in the courts for his property loss in 1816. David Darrow reported to Richard Spier, "The suit old Jonathan Davis commenced against the brethren . . . that he appealed to the Supreme Court—is settled—when the court came to examine the case—they told him he had no witness in his favor—no foundation to act upon—so they threw it out of court—that has settled it once for all." Darrow noted, "The world here at present appear to be quiet & peaceable towards believers and it is the wisest thing they can do."[46] Sadly, this brief lull in hostilities between the Shakers and their anti-Shaker neighbors evaporated by the summer of 1817.

Sixteen-year-old Jonathan Davis ran away from the society on December 29, 1816, but he was quickly recovered.[47] Sometime during the summer of 1817, he absconded again, leaving his parents, Elijah and Lydia, and seeking refuge with his cousin John Davis in Lebanon. On July 31, Jonathan's brother William and Union Village trustee John Wallace (who was also the brother-in-law of apostate John Davis) tried to get him back. They found Jonathan "at work with John Davis only in a certain spot of woods . . . early in the morning and come upon them unaware, took the boy and brought him home."[48] William Davis claimed that his cousin John threatened him with a large knife during the affray. Later that day, in retaliation, John Davis once again raised a mob to attack the Believers at Union Village.[49]

As David Darrow related, "Wicked John was so angry that he soon made an alarm, and by 2 Oclock P.M. a large mob came on of about 50 men in a dreadful rage, with pistols, clubs &c. and threatening to kill all the Shakers, and burn their village." John Davis attempted to ascend to the upper part of the kitchen, claiming that he wanted to see his sister Polly, who was a Shaker. Richard McNemar and Samuel Rollins intervened physically, "ordered him out, and shut the door against him." The brethren who had returned Jonathan to Union Village were forced to Lebanon by a mob of up to forty men, where they were bound over at the court of common pleas for trial on the charge of "unlawfully assembling and putting John Davis in fear." The rest of the mob stayed until night but caused no harm to people or property. Jonathan Davis remained with his father, Elijah.[50]

John Davis filed a complaint of assault and battery against McNemar and Rollins, for which they were indicted at Lebanon on September 5. John Wallace, Nathan Sharp, Thomas Hunt, Lewis Wait, and William Davis were also indicted on what the Shakers deemed John Davis's "false oath."[51] The case was continued; Rollins pleaded not guilty and gave $100 bond for his appearance at a future court session.[52] At this time, Lebanon's *Western Star* newspaper had come under the control of a new anti-Shaker editor, Abram Van Vleet. Van Vleet was a member of the Presbyterian Church in Lebanon and a justice of the peace for Warren County.

In his capacity as justice of the peace, Van Vleet took affidavits from Jonathan and Susanna Davis and many others. He printed these, as well as other anti-Shaker writings, in the *Western Star* from August through November of 1817. Van Vleet prefaced the series by lambasting the "noxious conduct" of the Shakers and accusing them of seeking "wealth and power" and holding "young, innocent, *free born* citizens in bondage." In his affidavit, Jonathan Davis specifically named Richard McNemar as having come to him "with a Gift, that the family should be broken up—that [Davis] should go and reside in one family and his wife in another, which were about four miles apart."[53]

In 1817, the eastern Shaker communities became embroiled in a public controversy with apostate Eunice Chapman. The troubles—between Chapman and her believing husband James—centered on the custody of their children. The print media in New York covered the quarrel as it escalated from a pamphlet war to the state legislature. Abram Van Vleet acquired a copy of Eunice Chapman's pamphlet *An Account of the Conduct of the Shakers, in the Case of Eunice Chapman and Her Children*.[54] In a letter to the New Lebanon Ministry, Darrow warned that Van Vleet, "a bitter enemy to the Gospel," had announced in his newspaper that he was preparing a full-length book against the Shakers. Darrow requested a copy of Chapman's pamphlet and information on other eastern apostates, so the Ohio Shakers could "head them when they do come."[55]

Union Village leaders discovered that citizens from Warren and Butler Counties had prepared a petition for presentation to the Ohio state legislature. It accused the Shakers of fraudulent land dealing, child abuse, and a host of other crimes.[56] On December 2, 1817, McNemar and Calvin Morrell were dispatched to Columbus, Ohio, where they planned to present a remonstrance to the state legislature against Van Vleet and others in Lebanon, who persecuted them both physically and in print.[57] The Shakers were fearful that anti-Shaker agitators were trying to get a law passed against the Shakers to "deprive us of our civil privileges." They determined it was time for their "civil rulers to know that this is the very Christ And be no longer imposed upon buy the tounge of common fame & slander."⁵⁸ McNemar and Morrell arrived after traveling three days through the bitter cold. They were gratified that their county representatives met them "with expressions of real friendship" and introduced them to influential fellow legislators. Most important, they offered to present "any thing which we wished to lay before the assembly." McNemar and Morrell waited five days for a petition allowing them to present their remonstrance. They were dismayed to find in the meantime that Van Vleet's anti-Shaker writings had circulated freely among the legislature. Their remonstrance was finally printed in the *Columbus Gazette* on December 11 as a countercheck, affixed with the signatures of 123 adult male members of the Union Village. Additionally, McNemar and Morrell composed a memorial on the subject of exemption from militia duty for the Shakers, which was presented to both the house and senate.⁵⁹

McNemar and Morrell entertained many questions from legislators about Shakerism in the privacy of their lodgings. Finally, they were invited to address the legislature by candlelight in an evening session. McNemar wrote that the "sacred weight and importance of this arrangement is beyond the power of language to express." The men rose to the challenge of addressing this diverse body of "free Masons, Methodists, Baptists, Newlights Presbyterians, seceders Friend Quakers, Deists, Militia officers, Bankers, Merchants, Doctors Lawyers & preachers not a few." They framed their address on Shaker doctrine in the manner credited to Father James Whittaker: "Speak the truth, and spare the truth."⁶⁰ Hoping to excite curiosity among potential converts, they "introduced the most important points of the gospel and treated them plainly to the understanding of all at the same time reserving the divine secrecy and more accurate knowledge for such as were excited to make a more particular enquiry." Their text was from Acts 17 and 19, in which Paul and Silas boldly preached the resurrection in the synagogues of Thessalonica, Berea, Athens, and Ephesus. They likened their sermon to that of Paul's given at the Areopagus in Athens before an audience—that, like Paul's—McNemar deemed "respectable characters . . . wishing to hear the new doctrine fairly stated." Their discourse covered Shaker ideas such as spiritual resurrection, confession of sins, celibacy, and communal property. The audience "behaved with the most perfect decorum, & retired with silence & perfect civility."⁶¹ Follow-up inquiries came mostly from Freemasons, Methodist preachers, and militia officers, who asked specific questions about Shaker pacifism and the Shakers' sufferings at the hands of mobs.

McNemar particularly enjoyed his conversations with the Freemasons, during which "the light of the gospel shone with some degree of freedom." The Shakers acknowledged that some of their members were Freemasons, but McNemar and Morrell "did not immediately say any thing about ourselves"—possibly indicating that both men were initiated into Freemasonry. A Methodist preacher solicited McNemar's opinion of the brotherhood:

> I informed him that my first acquaintance had been with a clandestine set who were a dishonour to any society professing morality, that since I had learned the orders of a regular lodge my sentiments were altered I admitted that in many respects it had been a useful institution in preserving the monuments of science & the signs of invisible realities that the utility of the institution depended on the objects to which it was applied—that in point of charity & many social virtues it was not inferior to many one side of the real gospel that in matters moral & political it had contributed to the overturning of false fabrications but in relation to the final order of the building of God the real work of salvation they had that yet to learn and sooner or later would have to become debtors to the Shakers for the proper use of the compass & square.

McNemar argued that Freemasonry, as guided by the Shakers, would result in a cleansing of the inner court of the temple, rendering it suitable for dedication "as the habitation of the shechinah and that new thing in the earth a woman shall COMPASS a man." His reference to the feminine aspect of divinity must have shocked the company, but his Masonic pun, quoting Jeremiah 31:22, "How long wilt thou go about, O thou backsliding daughter? for the LORD hath created a new thing in the earth, A woman shall compass a man," was surely appreciated by the Masons, even though they may not have understood its whole import when spoken by a Shaker devoted to the divine feminine. McNemar claimed to his auditors that the Masonic Lodge in Lebanon, Ohio, played a central role in the mob attack of July 1817. John Davis, the ardent apostate who led the mob, was a member there. So was Eli Fruit, who McNemar claimed gave young Reuben Morris a sword with which to fight his believing Shaker parents. The Freemasons McNemar conversed with denied that the lodge had any involvement in the July mobbing of Union Village.[62]

McNemar reported to Matthew Houston that the mission to Columbus was a success and that he felt "like lying down in the dust before God with a humble sense of gratitude that I have lived to see a nation & people, rulers & ruled who can peaceably hear those sacred innocent & lovely truths of the gospel for which the blood of millions has been immolated at the altar of brutal tyranny & diabolical priestcraft." He and Morrell returned to Union Village on December 24, 1817.⁶³

Manuscript journals from late 1817 show that Richard McNemar apparently was given, or adopted, a new name: Eleazar Wright. The reasons for this or any underlying meaning to the name remain unknown. In later years, he referred to Richard as his "primitive name" and Eleazar as his "Chh [church] name."⁶⁴ Eleazar may have been a reference to the Old Testament high priest of the same name. Eleazar was the son of Aaron and nephew of Moses. If, as subsequent references will show, the Ohio Shakers considered David Darrow a sort of Moses, then McNemar's standing as a nephew in relation to him makes sense. As the Israelites moved through the wilderness in Exodus, Eleazar carried the oil for the lamp, the incense, and the offerings of grain and anointing oil; and he oversaw the carriage for the Ark of the Covenant, the altar, the table for showbread, and other fittings of the tabernacle. These duties made a fitting metaphor for the multifaceted role played by McNemar in spreading the light of the Shaker gospel through the wilderness of the Ohio River Valley, Kentucky, and Indiana. The surname Wright is likely an acknowledgment of his filial regard for Shaker Ministry Eldress Mother Lucy Wright, who lived at New Lebanon, New York. Intriguingly, her husband—who had converted to Shakerism before her—was named Elizur Goodrich. McNemar likely knew this fact, and one has to wonder at its relevance to his new name, which became his primary cognomen among the Shakers for the rest of his life.⁶⁵

THIRTEEN

PERFIDY, PILGRIMS, PROSECUTION, PROGRESS, AND PESTILENCE

THE YEAR 1818 OPENED IN a harsh way for the Union Village Shakers. Trustee John Wallace, who had so valiantly defended his brethren during the troubles with the Davis family the year before, left for Columbus on February 14, ostensibly on community business. Wallace was married to Samuel Sering's daughter Sarah. The large Sering family had been members of Richard McNemar's Turtle Creek congregation; they were associates of long standing. Wallace and much of his extended family became Shakers in 1805.[1] It was especially painful, then, when Wallace traveled to Cincinnati and borrowed $3,000 from the United States Bank for a term of sixty days in the name of the Shakers—and never returned, leaving the community liable for the debt.[2] Rather than bring a lawsuit, Union Village leaders opted to repay the loan.[3] This type of personal fraud, committed by a single trustee but leaving the whole community on the hook, was exactly what David Darrow feared could happen with the land deeds.

On February 19, with Wallace's perfidy as yet unknown, Richard McNemar—now known as Eleazar Wright—traveled with Calvin Morrell to meet a "strange traveling people at Xenia who call themselves Pilgrims."[4] The founder of the sect, Isaac Bullard, was called "Prophet Elijah" by his followers. He was described as being of "diminutive stature, with a club foot." His earliest documented whereabouts are at Ascot, Quebec, about twenty miles north of the Vermont border. He claimed that he had suffered a severe illness, after which he fasted for forty days. After his sudden recovery, he developed the capacity for prophecy and vision and "declared that he was commanded to plant the church of the redeemer in the wilderness."[5]

Bullard and around forty followers left Woodstock, Vermont, in July 1817.[6] On August 25, they arrived at the Shaker community of New Lebanon, where they stayed for two days. A Shaker scribe, probably Isaac Newton Youngs, wrote a detailed description of their visit:

> A man by the name of Isaac Bullard was their leader, and was by them styled The Prophet, to whom they all seemed to yield implicit obedience, not even daring to eat or drink, or to wash their dirty clothes with out his permission: and it was found that some of the company, particularly the females were, by travelling & fasting, reduced to great weakness. The men wore their beards, and the whole company were very dirty & filthy; and by travelling in this manner they became very lousy. It was said that some part of the company had been people of respectability and property in the world; but had left it all for the sake of their religious zeal & their resolution to follow their prophet on pilgrimage. It was difficult to find what their religious principles were; but in their devotion they had strange motions & gestures, and used very incoherent language, often repeating the same expressions many times over with a very rapid utterance; such for instance as the following; "My God my God my God my God my God, what wouldst thou have me to do?—Mummy jum, mummy jum, mummy jum, mummy jum, mummy jum." By the frequent repetition of this last expression they got the name of The Mummyjums. Some part of them were married people, and had their families with them; others were unmarried, young people and children who had followed their parents. Bullard the prophet had his wife along with him, with an infant child, which they affirmed to be a holy child, and called his name Christ, or the Second Christ. They walked back & forth through our street most of the day, with a very short staff in each hand; so that they were obliged to walk with their bodies bent in a horizontal position, which with their long beards, odd grimaces, incoherent language, and singular manouvres, gave them a very ludicrous appearance. They were very severe in their censures against our Society, prophesied judgments upon us, and uttered many curses against us.[7]

It is not known if the Union Village Shakers were aware of the Pilgrims. Possibly, the New Lebanon Ministry wrote to David Darrow to warn him of their approach, but such a letter has not been located. However, the bizarre sect's progress was widely reported in newspapers all over the country, so it seems likely the Union Village Shakers were watching for their arrival.

McNemar's surviving journals and other sources of the period lack any account of the visit he and Morrell made to the sect at Xenia in February 1818. The Pilgrims arrived in Lebanon, Ohio, where they preached on March 6. They reached Union Village on March 10, twenty days after the Shakers visited them. The Pilgrim band was by this time fifty-five in number. On Wednesday, March 11, five Pilgrims were allowed to preach in the Shaker meetinghouse, three men and two women. Following their harangue, they quickly withdrew, as the Shakers thought, "probably to avoid hearing any reply." Another Shaker journalist noted, "They are a poor blind set of beaings, they pretend to marry a woman in God & by so dooing sanctify the flesh—after they ware done preaching they imediately left the house for feare some of the brethren or sisters would preach to them." This reference to marrying a woman "in God" implies that the Shakers believed the Pilgrims were engaging in sexual relations outside the bounds of standard Christian matrimony. The Shakers kindly lodged the Pilgrims in a brick shop and "returned the compliment" by preaching to their now-captive audience, "which made them verry mad." Ominously, it was noted that the Pilgrims were infected with smallpox. Despite the presence of this virulent disease, the Pilgrims and their animals were fed free of charge. Notwithstanding the typically kind treatment afforded the Pilgrims by the Shakers, they promptly left the next morning, chastising the Shakers for not receiving their message and asserting "that every word [the Shakers] spoke was of the Devil."[8]

In the three-day whirlwind visit to Union Village, the Pilgrims did not make a favorable impression on the Shakers. One of the Pilgrim band, however, was very taken with what she had seen among the Shakers. Fanny Ball, whose husband, Peter, "was an eloquent preacher among [the Pilgrims], received a strong impression that Believers were the people of God, but did not break her connection with the Pilgrims."[9] She ultimately regretted not following her impulse to stay with the Shakers. One of her compatriots, William Jaycock, was sought out by Union Village Shaker Ashbell Kitchell; he returned to Union Village on April 6 and became a Shaker.[10] Fanny Ball, however, continued with the Pilgrims south to Cincinnati, where they arrived on April 11, to the disgust of the city. The mayor requested that they camp in the woods a mile from town due to the highly infectious smallpox they carried. The *Western Spy* reported that throughout the following week, "hundreds every day, and thousands on some days, have been flocking to their encampment to gaze at this unparalleled specimen of filth, rags, wretchedness, and disease." A local citizen warned the populace against visiting the Pilgrims, lest they carry smallpox into the city proper. The *Western Spy* published with relief that the sect would "take water passage here, and it is very probably we see them no more; a source of no regret."[11] After selling their wagons and horses, the Pilgrims bought a boat and embarked on the Ohio River in Cincinnati, heading downriver to the confluence of the Ohio and Mississippi Rivers. Throughout that summer, many of the sect died of starvation and disease, until some finally abandoned Bullard. Some of these survivors, notably the members of the Ball family and Samuel

Tuttle (sometimes rendered "Tuthill"), returned to Union Village and became Shakers.[12]

Deacon Peter Pease wrote an account of the Ball family's internal struggle regarding Shakerism in the wake of the Pilgrim catastrophe.

> Now I reckon you would like to hear something about Peter Ball the pilgrim that I spake of when I was with you he returned to the miami country about the month of July, found fanny his wife and three sons among Believers which he did not quite so well like, so he took them away all exept the oldest which is man grown the two youngest sons one about 12 the other 17 years of age, but so it was, that after keeping them a while they proved too strong for him and they have all returned. Peter himself has set out to be a Believer So there is now, of that pilgrim collection among Believers ten persons tho three of them are small children.[13]

In the end, the Balls lived out their days as good Believers, as did Samuel Tuttle.

The trial of Samuel Rollins and Richard McNemar for the assault and battery of John Davis was finally held on March 24, 1818. Surprisingly, lawyer Thomas Freeman, who in 1810 wrote the extensive anti-Shaker piece "A Retrospective View of Shakerism," represented them in court. Why he had changed his opinion of the Shakers is a mystery. Rollins and McNemar pleaded not guilty, but the jury returned a guilty verdict for both men. Freeman asked for a retrial since neither he nor the defendants were present when the state deposed the witnesses against the Shakers, so Freeman had been unable to cross-examine them. A new trial was granted, and Rollins and McNemar each deposited a $50 bond for their future appearance. The retrial of the Davis case was held on August 11, 1818. Rollins was found guilty and ordered to pay a $5 fine and $35.26 in court costs. McNemar was found not guilty.[14] In the end, the Davis case was more of a nuisance to both men than a real threat, consuming time and financial resources and keeping them embroiled in a bitter public relations battle that was not yet over.

Barely a month after their encounter with the Pilgrims, McNemar and Calvin Morrell left Union Village to visit the Harmony Society on April 25, 1818.[15] They were following up on an earlier visit by a group that included David Darrow. In a July 1817 letter to Issachar Bates, Seth Youngs Wells mentioned that news had reached Watervliet, New York, of "a society of Germans called Harmonians; that they lived not far from you, and had formed some acquaintance with you—that they supported a joint interest and took up a cross against the flesh—but whether they confessed their sins we did not hear—I have often thought of these people and should be glad to hear more particularly about them. From what part of Germany did they emigrate? What is their foundation? And how long has been their standing?"[16] During a visit to Busro (now renamed West Union), in July 1817, David Darrow, Ruth Farrington, Solomon King, Hortency Goodrich, and some West Union Shakers took the opportunity to visit New Harmony, seventy miles south on the Wabash. Darrow reported that on their arrival the Harmonists "gathered round us much, both men and women, they appeared very glad to see us ... they appeared to be under real mortification, like faithful believers." Darrow was impressed that the celibate Harmonists had taken up a cross against the "flesh," were pacifists, and also confessed their sins. The Shakers struggled to communicate fine points of theology with the German-speaking Harmonists, and Darrow was disappointed to find that although they had a Father in George Rapp, they had no Mother among them. He viewed this as evidence of the Harmonists' incomplete understanding of the nature of Christ's second appearing.[17] Unfortunately, neither Shaker nor Harmonist sources reveal what transpired during McNemar and Morrell's visit, from which they returned on May 13, 1818. McNemar would visit the Harmonists once more during his life but under far different circumstances.[18]

Later that summer, McNemar's thirteen-year-old son, Benjamin, who had been ill for months, died on July 22. McNemar's itinerant travels and involvement in affairs beyond the sphere of Union Village, as well as the fact that Benjamin was living in a children's order apart from his father, makes it likely that he saw little of his son throughout his illness and demise. Additionally, Shaker beliefs would have supported sympathy for the sufferer as a fellow Believer, but not as a natural child, since the emphasis on these fleshly ties was discouraged. Ultimately, as with the passing of McNemar's daughter Betsy in 1812, none of his extant writings reveal any reaction to this event.[19]

On October 12, 1818, David Darrow wrote a detailed report on the material state of the Shaker West for Deacons Richard Spier and Stephen Munson at New Lebanon. Among the accomplishments he highlighted was the construction of a new meetinghouse to replace the one built in 1808, which he described as "a cold shell of a thing." The new building was sixty by forty-four feet, solidly framed, and finished with oiled cherry wood inside. Other structures, including a garden house for Calvin Morrell, were also completed. Soberly, Darrow reported the defection of Trustee John Wallace. One consequence of Wallace's action was the signing of a new covenant at the Union Village community and a printed warning to the non-Shaker public "not to trust any member of the Society on the credit of the joint interest without a written certificate well authenticated from the body." Sadly, this would not be the last time that Union Village was defrauded by a trustee. Darrow also noted the precarious finances of the western Shaker communities, who were all (except for West Union) heavily indebted to non-Shaker creditors. Pleasant Hill and South Union each owed many thousands of dollars and were struggling to repay their loans. He ended his letter on a positive note, saying, "The world has been peaceable toward us for a long time—& we have been peaceable towards them—& I am willing it should remain so."[20]

As Darrow wrote his favorable report, news began to trickle into Union Village of a serious outbreak of fever at the West Union, Indiana, community. The epidemic began in August 1818. Issachar Bates described the horror: "They were seized with such violence that in a few hours their breath would be stoped—and no medicine would have any effect." Shakers well enough to worship gathered at the meetinghouse to labor for the relief of their brethren and sisters. Darrow dispatched Dr. Calvin Morrell from Union Village to supervise medical care at the embattled outpost. Elder Archibald Meacham lay near the point of death for seventeen days; Bates observed that "he was the sickest person in the society"—but he survived. Although more than one hundred Believers were sick at a given time, in the end, Bates rejoiced that "the destroyer got nothing but one wicked little boy." Bates and Morrell returned to Union Village on January 8, 1819. In his letter recounting these sad events to the New Lebanon Ministry, Bates lamented that he had to further burden his "friends in the east with our calamitys either by the distresses of war—or sickness—or some other work of the devil." The devil's work, however, was not yet done at West Union.[21]

THE OTHER SIDE OF THE QUESTION

Abram Van Vleet's compendium of anti-Shaker writing appeared in the late spring of 1819.[22] David Darrow informed the New Lebanon Ministry that "since Eunice Chapman's & Mary Dyer's false publications & false witnesses, have been reprinted at Lebanon here and circulated through the whole country—the world has waked up to some purpose."[23] Van Vleet's work comprised a reprint of Chapman's *Account*, apostate Thomas Brown's *Refutation*, and apostate Mary Dyer's *Deposition*. Of most concern to the Ohio Shakers, 27 of the work's 105 pages were an "Appendix" of fresh testimony and accusations of physical abuse against members at Union Village, in which Richard McNemar featured heavily. In his preface, Van Vleet (and associate editor William A. Camron) lambasted the "wild delusions" of the Shakers, accusing them of tearing "tender offspring from the disconsolate mother" and depriving their members of the "right of conscience ... and violating the Constitution of the U. States." His purpose was "laying before the unwary, the melancholy example of those who have been ruined by Shaker cunning and duplicity; that they may thus avoid the rock on which so many of our fellow citizens have split."[24]

Van Vleet rehashed the accusations leveled by Colonel James Smith in his pamphlets of 1810 and 1811, which had long since been dealt with by McNemar. However, McNemar was freshly targeted with sensational accusations of child abuse. An affidavit from Henry Baily claimed that at a Shaker meeting around Christmas 1816,

> there were two lads about 15 years old, James Irwin and Samuel Hill, who did not engage in the dance, but stood by the fire. After a few minutes, Richard M'Nemar, who had the command of the dance that day, came forward and took hold of one of the lads by the arm with the one hand and by the throat with the other, and pushed him backwards over a seat on the floor, where he, maintaining his hold, got on the boy with both his knees, and pressed him against the floor with all his strength—after which he caught the other lad and served him in the same way. Then the said M'Nemar went back to his former stand, and after a short space of time returned to the boys and repeated the abuse rather more severely—for he appeared to be in a great rage, while he said *The devil is in you, and I will beat him out of you!!* The boys standing by the fire bemoaning themselves as if they were much hurt, he made an attempt to approach them a third time, but was stopped by a young member of the said society, which excited a warm dispute between them.[25]

This likely referred to the evening meeting on Wednesday, December 25, at which McNemar preached.[26] Shaker journals for that day fail to record the violence that Baily describes, but that is unsurprising, if it actually occurred.

Van Vleet's publication spurred more mob actions against Union Village—despite McNemar's hope that "the shameful and iniquitous practice of mobbing was at an end; that those scenes of riot, which had so often disgraced the character of Warren [County] . . . would never be repeated." On Saturday, August 7, forty mounted men, attendees from a nearby camp meeting that had begun seven days earlier, worked themselves into a frenzy and mobbed the South Family. They were seeking a young woman named Phoebe Johnson, whose father had left her in the Shakers' care. Only sisters were present, and they barricaded themselves in the dwelling. Soon some brethren arrived and dealt with the men, who left after several hours, vowing to return with a larger force. The next Monday morning, "a very black, wicked cloud came from the North, of more than 200 horse men & foot men . . . & rushed on to the South house, with more fury of hell then has scarcely been known before—it appeared they would kill & devour all before them." They were armed with "fists and clubs and loaded whips," and they rushed past the Shaker deacon, who appealed to them on the basis of law. Remarkably, David Johnson, Phoebe's non-Shaker father, appeared and tried to dissuade the mob from violence, but to no avail. The brethren kept them out of the house, but some were grievously injured, including Calvin Morrell, who was badly beaten. Eventually, Shaker sisters dispersed the mob by removing the top rails of wooden fences and throwing them into the enclosure where the mob had tethered their horses. The horses became frightened, and many started to bolt, forcing their owners to abandon the attack to recover their mounts. As they did, they "cursed the sisters for a parcel of impudent women [and] knocked one down but did not hurt her much."[27]

That autumn, the Union Village Shakers responded to Van Vleet and his anti-Shaker partisans. David Darrow explained to the New Lebanon Ministry that the Union Village Shakers had waited to answer Van Vleet until they could "see what effect their slanders & lies would have on mankind."[28] It was now abundantly clear that the Shakers needed to defend themselves in print. They published a book of their own, *The Other Side of the Question*, which was primarily written by Richard McNemar. This was, however, obscured by the fact that he signed his new name "Eleazar Wright" at the end of the preface.

Richard McNemar sent a covering letter and copies of *The Other Side* to noted journalist William Leete Stone in Albany.[29] His refutations of Eunice Chapman and her supporters, including apostates Josiah Terry and Thomas Brown, culminate in the observation that all Chapman's efforts are those of a woman trying to "tear down a society, which a woman was instrumental in building up.—That against that holy and *Motherly Spirit*, first manifested in Ann Lee, and afterwards in Lucy Wright." McNemar then produced his own tranche of affidavits to prove that the Shaker elders were "not wine bibbers, whoremongers, nor gluttons, neither promoters of riot disorder, or disobedience." The testimonies, all collected from western converts—some relatives of anti-Shaker agitators—uniformly lauded the conduct of the eastern Shakers and specifically addressed the treatment and education of children at Union Village. The work concludes with a supplement signed by ninety-five young women residents at Union Village attesting to the fact that the Shakers did not hold women in bondage, compel them to work, or prevent them from reading the scriptures. Among the signatories were two Davis girls, Phoebe Johnson (the focus of the August 1819 riot), and Richard McNemar's two surviving daughters, Vincy and Nancy.[30]

While *The Other Side of the Question* was being written, Daniel Doty, one of a group self-styled the Rational Brethren of the West attacked the Shakers from another front. Doty was born on March 23, 1765, in New Jersey. He lived for a time in Cincinnati beginning in 1790. In 1796, he returned to New Jersey and married his second wife, Elizabeth Crane. They immigrated to Ohio, initially settling in Warren County. According to one source, Doty "lived out-doors for more than two weeks, cooking and sleeping in the open air while his cabin was going up."[31] Doty and his wife eventually settled near modern-day Middletown.[32] A number of other New Jersey families moved to Ohio after the Dotys, including Calvin Morrell and his family. Doty and Morrell were close associates in the New Light, or schismatic, movement during the Kentucky Revival. Doty had also been a friend of McNemar's. Although he associated with the Shakers during the excitement surrounding their arrival, he was heartily disappointed when many of his friends and neighbors dissolved their families and embraced the celibate Shaker life.

Doty and his associate William Ludlow were key members of the Rational Brethren, a quasireligious/scientific association. In their 1819 publication *Belief of the Rational Brethren of the West*, they stated, "Some have endeavored to excite a prejudice in the minds of the people, by declaring us Shakers. Although the Shakers, in some respects, are an example to a legal-thieving world, yet we believe, that they are guilty of opposing the providence of God, in his wise order of creation."[33] The Rational Brethren concluded that if Shakerism prevailed, the world would shortly be depopulated—an outcome not intended by God. McNemar railed against the anti-Shaker statements of the Rational Brethren in his *Other Side of the Question*.[34]

Daniel Doty's house had served as a safe harbor for boys running away from Union Village, a fact that did not endear him to the Shakers. Doty was surprised and apparently caught off guard by McNemar's attack in *Other Side*. Counting on his former friendship with McNemar, Doty went to Union Village on two separate Sundays to talk with him about the controversy. It was at one of those meetings that Doty claimed McNemar called him "a hardened wretch [who] ought to be hung by the neck."[35] This incident laid the groundwork for Doty's 1820 publication *An Address to the People at Union Village, and a Solemn Warning to the Whole Human Family against Shakerism and Delusion*. Doty and his coauthor William Ludlow (who eventually associated with the Owenites at New Harmony) found a most willing printer in Abram Van Vleet. Doty's narrative is a lengthy remonstrance of the Shakers that plays on the well-worn themes of popery and financial chicanery associated with them. What makes this work unique is the bitterness with which Doty recalls his former friends McNemar and Morrell. According to Doty, McNemar told him that through Shakerism he "had learnt more of God in five minutes, than [he] ever learnt in all [his] life before; and that at *that time* [his] senses were entirely *null*." Doty also suggests that he had been a spiritual mentor to Morrell and McNemar, claiming, "I am the same man, Richard, that I was when you said that I was far before yourself in the light of the gospel. That was before you lost your senses; & my friend Calvin Morrell acknowledged to us after he had unfortunately joined the Shaker society, that he well knew I had more of the light of God than all the people for ten miles round, when we were sitting together in the *prairaie*."[36] Doty chose to believe that McNemar had willfully blinded himself to the folly of Shakerism, and he lamented, "It is truly a grief to me when I see you fixed just like a stool pigeon, with the eye of your understanding closed, and trying to deceive all that pass by. There you have to flutter, dance, and to use your tongue in uttering falsehoods to try to bring other poor undiscerning souls to do sacrifice to that shameful thing."[37] Doty concluded that if Ann Lee had been as void of sense as McNemar was, the Shakers "ought to be dealt with according to the act made for *insane* persons."[38]

As for Calvin Morrell, Doty reminded him of a dream he had shared "of How you was pursued by Richard, and David Spinning, to castrate you." He implored Morrell to go back to his wife, Rhoda, and live by God's commandment as husband and wife.[39] Doty's coauthor and Rational Brethren member William Ludlow taunted Morrell, questioning his intelligence: "Now Calvin, ... I believe you are a mere follower of your leaders, from a personal knowledge that I have of your mental faculties." Ludlow believed that while Morrell was an innocent dupe, McNemar was "more like the wolf dressed in wool, than that of the lamb, in innocence."[40] A lengthy poem by Ludlow concludes the *Address*. It contains one couplet that is tragically prescient in the case of Richard McNemar:

> For reason's power, will the world protect,
> From all deceivers, fools and visionists.[41]

The conflict between McNemar and Doty seems to have tapered off after this, although McNemar dealt with many more apostates in the remaining nineteen years of his life. Doty lived until May 8, 1848. He is remembered as an axe-in-hand, Indian-fighting settler and founder of Middletown, Ohio. A history of the town published in 1908 dedicated three pages to Doty—the "first white man"—and noted his anti-Shaker activities thusly: "In the latter years of his life he wrote a pamphlet on Shakerism, many copies of which are still in existence. He did not like the fundamentals of the Shakers and he did not mince his words about saying so."[42]

FOURTEEN

THE END OF THE BEGINNING

THE YEAR 1820 PASSED RATHER unremarkably for the Shakers of Union Village, which must have been a relief. Letters between their ministry and the New Lebanon Ministry acknowledged the lack of newsworthy topics and consequent slackening of correspondence. The New Lebanon Ministry, concerned for David Darrow's health and his suddenly infrequent letters, reached out to him in a humorously chiding letter, asking, "Has he got something against us?"[1] Darrow responded that such a thought "cannot exist a moment in his mind—& will not till time shall be no more." He admitted that there wasn't much to write about and that life at Union Village was "sometimes joyous & sometimes grievous." He painted an honest picture of the rabble gathered around him: "Indeed we think we have already a few out of almost all nations gathered—English, Irish, Scotch, Dutch, French, Germans, Prussians, and I hardly know what not—so we have a mixed multitude to take care of—like Moses of old—without mentioning their poverty—and if ye should come here one of these days ye would find that ye could not understand some of their talk no better than you could geese—how ever by some interpreters & other means they make out to confess their sins after a sort—so as to get joined."[2]

The rabble was about to expand when the Shakers came into contact with a group of New Englanders who settled at Darby Plains, just west of Columbus, in Union County, Ohio. They were adherents of the Christian Connexion sect, a movement that sprang up independently in Virginia and New England during the 1790s and 1800s. Abner Jones and Elias Smith led the New England contingent. Their followers rejected Calvinism and believed in free will salvation and a separation from the organized churches. Minister Douglas Farnum was the leader of the group that settled at Darby Plains. He was renowned as a magnetic preacher and said to have "a musical voice, a fluent delivery, somewhat of a 'holy' or singing tone. He spoke with mouth, hands, feet, and, in fact, with the entire body." Farnum was born in Vermont and mentored by Christian ministers John Rand, Elias Cobb, and Uriah Smith (brother of Elias). He gained prominence in Coventry, Rhode Island, in 1813, when he preached at a gambling den and converted noted gambler Sam Rice and his associates, described as a "wild set of men." Farnum's followers, dubbed "Farnumites," donned sackcloth and ashes before baptism and performed other acts of contrition.[3]

Following dissension in his church in the spring of 1815, Farnum sent his loyal follower Rice to Darby Plains, ostensibly to locate a new home for the group. In June 1817, eighteen wagons of Farnumites moved there. Preacher Nathan Burlingame, described as a "man of good talent, great mind, and a powerful orator," accompanied Farnum. Together, they baptized over one hundred converts that summer. On a trip back to Connecticut that fall, Farnum was accused of being a religious impostor and keeping three wives. An ecclesiastical body in Hartford, Connecticut, wanted to try him, but he denied their authority and weathered the controversy. Isaac Bullard's Pilgrims also visited the Farnumites, probably in January 1818, shortly before Richard McNemar and Calvin Morell saw them at Xenia. In the fall of 1818, Farnum relocated to Darby Plains permanently.[4]

Journalist William Henry Smith described the Farnumites for an early history of Union County:

> Our county was not free from eccentric people, but their eccentricity took on the character of religious fanaticism. These were the Farnhamites (also called "The Creepers"), followers of Douglas Farnham.... The leaders taught the birth to sin, and salvation only through public confession and walking humbly and contritely before the world. The fanaticism consisted in the absurd acts which were inspired and performed. Sackcloth and ashes and creeping in the dirt were not the most objectionable. An estimable young lady was converted, and told that it was necessary to display the corrupt nature of her heart. She conceived this novel plan. One night she rode several miles to the farm of a well-known citizen, visited his corn-crib, filled a bag with corn, which she carried home. The next day, in the light of the sun, this bag of corn was placed upon the back of a horse, and upon that the young lady rode to the farmer's, to whom she confessed the theft in contrite words and with many tears. This fanaticism soon disappeared and left no evil effects, as it touched only a handful in the community.[5]

It is unclear how or when the Shakers first came into contact with the Farnumites. Historian Carol Medlicott has speculated that the Farnumites may have come to the attention of the Watervliet, Ohio, Shakers, whose village was only fifty-eight miles to the southwest. Historian John Patterson MacLean cites a now-lost manuscript of Shaker elder Charles Sturr from White Water, Ohio, that claims Richard McNemar and Calvin Morrell visited the Farnumites in June 1820.[6] I have not located any extant manuscript source for this visit. A Union Village journal records that on June 7, 1820, "2 men stays here last night of the Christian Society." This is a possible reference to Farnumites, who referred to themselves merely as Christians. On August 5, Douglas Farnum and two followers arrived at Union Village, where Farnum preached at the Sabbath meeting the next day. As the Shakers and Farnumites realized their basic affinities, it was decided to send McNemar and Morrell as missionaries to Darby Plains on October 23. They returned on November 1, but the details of their trip are unknown. The visit, however, began a multiyear process that led to the dissolution of the Farnumites and the conversion of many at Darby Plains to Shakerism.[7]

During the nineteenth meeting of the Ohio General Assembly, convened on December 7, 1820, the Shakers finally won exemption from paying fines instead of their militia service. General William Henry Harrison, who had interacted with the West Union Shakers during the tumultuous War of 1812, had moved to Ohio and become a state senator. According to Solomon King, Harrison "took a very active part in the legislator, on our behalf, he made four very able speeches to shew the propriety & justice of the Shakers, being exempt from military fines." King noted that there were a good many "Yankeys, or new england people" in the legislature who agreed with Harrison. To their relief, rather than pay a fine or report for duty, the Shakers were allowed to work on the highway each muster day, which was only three days a year. With this decision, one of the Ohio Shakers' most vexing problems was finally resolved.[8]

The Union Village Shakers received crushing news from New Lebanon in a February 14, 1821, letter. It was addressed to them as "Sympathising friends; you will weep with us when we tell you that God has called home his Anointed—that our Ever Blessed Mother is no more!" Mother Lucy Wright died at Watervliet, New York, on February 7, 1821.[9] She was only sixty-one, and her passing left a void among Shakers everywhere, as she had effectively been the head and fount of Shakerism since the death of Father Joseph Meacham in 1796. It was to Mother Lucy that all Shakers—east and west—looked for guidance in spiritual and temporal matters. Shaker culture stabilized and coalesced into its classical form during her tenure. The tenets she inculcated, following the examples of Mother Ann Lee, Father James Whittaker, and Meacham, were adopted as regulations of the societies (albeit against her wishes) soon after her death.

Despite the loss of their spiritual mother, Shaker missionary work continued. On April 21, 1821, Richard McNemar and Calvin Morrell set out for Darby Plains. In his journal, McNemar recalled, "During their united gift & labors... a considerable number had opened their minds as early as the year 21." Further details of their visit are unrecorded, but they strengthened the bonds that would bring many from Darby Plains into Shaker ranks in the coming years. Late that summer, at Union Village, Garner McNemar's daughter Martha died of tuberculosis, at twenty-five, on August 13, 1821. Slightly more than two months later, Union Village suffered the devastating loss of their Mother. Ruth Farrington died on October 25 around midnight, "haveing been chiefly confined to her room & bed for 12 Months & 4 days, and her sufferings & afflictions have been such, that since the first of April, she has not been out of her room but a few times." Mother Ruth had been sensible until ten minutes before she passed. The day before, she exhorted and encouraged those around her "in a very comforting manner."[10] With the loss of Mother Lucy Wright in the East and Mother Ruth Farrington in the West, the Shaker world saw the passing of two strong female leaders at the highest levels.

The Shakers continued to find more openings for their gospel. During 1822, multiple missions were sent to Warrensville, Ohio, on the shores of Lake Erie. There, Ralph Russell's extended family had enthusiastically embraced Shakerism and were busily gathering communal families into order. Russell had encountered Shakers Matthew Houston and Richard Pelham by chance while they were visiting David Darrow's relatives in Stow, Ohio. This seems to have occurred in early June of 1820.[11] According to Pelham's account, Russell was visiting his relatives nearby when he had to seek lodging overnight at James Darrow's house. It was there that he serendipitously heard the Shaker missionaries.[12]

Russell visited Union Village in October 1821 and requested to move his family there the following spring. When spring came, David Darrow prevailed on him to stay at his fine farmstead and establish a community there.[13] To support him in these efforts, Darrow dispatched James Hodge and Pelham on two missions in March and June. On September 9, 1822, Richard McNemar joined Hodge and Pelham, along with sisters Anna Boyd and Betsey Dunlavy, to minister to four nuclear families who had confessed their sins. McNemar remained there until November 13. Early in 1823, he made two more missionary trips. The first was to Darby Plains with Issachar Bates on January 8. They returned to Union Village on February 24. After only two days' rest, McNemar was off again, this time to Warrensville—soon renamed North Union—with Charles Hampton. By the end of that trip, around eight more people had confessed their sins. It also became apparent to McNemar that "a better foundation for the gathering [of Believers] than ... Darby" must be found. The climate there was judged to be unhealthy and similar to that of West Union. Also, the lands were part of an old military tract, and the settlers' title to them was questionable. Soon after his return to Union Village on April 2, McNemar, now fifty-three, was relieved of his traveling duties to take on a much more important job for the rest of 1823.[14]

REPRINTING *THE TESTIMONY OF CHRIST'S SECOND APPEARING*

David Darrow wrote the ministry at New Lebanon on December 8, 1821, requesting permission to undertake the most ambitious Shaker printing and publishing project to date: a third edition of *The Testimony of Christ's Second Appearing*. First printed at Lebanon, Ohio, in 1808, and then at Albany in 1810, the work was now in short supply in the West. In his letter, Darrow wrote,

> The Brethren here have a strong mind to print a new edition ... if they can have your approbation & union in it—they feel fully able & willing to undertake the work—as there is a considerable call for them books—often men of good understanding from a distance wants them books—& the believers here have spared so many—that perhaps they are not now half supplied themselves—we intend to copy after the second edition printed at Albany—without adding—except a few notes at the bottom of the pages—but keep the body of the work entire for we do not believe we can better it by altering it—the brethren intend to do the work among themselves, and not trust it in the hands of the world—the number of copies is not fixed yet—perhaps—2 or 3000—they intend to accomplish it—in the course of next year—but we shall wait to know your minds—before we make much preparations &c.

In a troubling aside, Darrow confessed that he often felt that his "days are drawing to a close—that works me up a little bit—to see that I finish my work in righteousness so as to go in justification."[15] For Darrow, shepherding this important work through successful revision and publication would go a long way toward the justification he was seeking.

The New Lebanon Ministry approved the project. Before her death, Mother Lucy Wright had proposed a new edition and specifically called for more content about the life and teachings of Mother Ann Lee. The ministry appointed Seth Youngs Wells, whom they called "a useful man in such labours," to propose a few minor changes to the work.[16] Wells wrote the Union Village Ministry on

April 25, 1822, enclosing a sheet of alterations that he said were "as few & as short as possible." This sheet has long since been separated from the letter and is now lost. It may never have reached its intended destination.[17]

David Darrow held a meeting to discuss the reprinting of *The Testimony* on January 28, 1823. Present were Solomon King, Issachar Bates, Matthew Houston, Richard McNemar, and possibly Malcham Worley. Darrow expressed his concern about "the enemy creeping in slyly through the young order, by means of some new doctrine contrary to the Testimony." He rehashed examples of problematic doctrines that had appeared at Union Village in recent years, "all which speculative notions he rejected, as having a tendency to lead the mind off from the gospel." Darrow called for the banning of all books except for the Bible, based on his concern that non-Shaker theological works were used to undergird arguments against Shaker beliefs. Malcham Worley was singled out as an excellent example for all, in that he had left behind all non-Shaker teachings and focused on "labouring for the Spirit." The meeting garnered unanimous support for the considerable undertaking of reprinting *The Testimony*.[18]

Later in his life, McNemar reflected on this time, recalling that Darrow "manifested what is called a superstitious regard for sertain parts of the testimony," which Matthew Houston and others wanted to revise. Darrow asserted his ministerial privilege, to which the elders yielded, giving "implicit respect to Fathers dictation in order that the work might go forward, for Father expressly forbade them to go on with the printing unless they abandoned such innovations." Key issues were the origin of evil and the immaculate conception of Jesus. The substance of changes desired by Houston and others is unknown, and a scholarly textual comparison of the four editions of *The Testimony* has not yet been undertaken. McNemar noted this period as a turning point; the first direct challenge to Darrow's spiritual authority. He wrote,

> The spirit of investigation proceeded from thing to thing until the infallibility or absolute authority of Father himself became a subject of altercation; and unhappily stood on docket undecided at Father's decease. The doctrine of absolute perfection so strenuously maintained by some in the beginning had lost some credit so that it was not deemed very heretical to suppose that Father David & his Mother and his grand Mother might all have come short of infinite wisdom and that the church in her forward travel might find it necessary not only to correct some points of doctrine, & to alter & amend some rules & orders.[19]

This was nothing short of a revolution in a theocracy such as Shakerism, whose entire order relied on the willing subjection of members at all levels to their spiritual superiors. Darrow's foreboding about the influence of novel doctrines on the Union Village community proved quite prescient, though he did not live to see the havoc they wreaked.

Some changes, however, were made to the text of *The Testimony*, but at Darrow's discretion. An undated letter, likely from early 1823, written by Matthew Houston at North Union to Solomon King (second elder in the ministry at Union Village), expresses Houston's approval of revisions to *The Testimony* by Darrow and McNemar. Houston had read manuscripts of changes proposed by McNemar and declared himself "well pleased with them." He affirmed Darrow's "right to amend the Testimony Book as seemeth to him good—and I do confidently know that in many things Father's light extends farr a head of many things herein stated—and therefore I judge that Father ought to have the honour and privilege of correcting it himself." Houston judged that McNemar "may well be intrusted with the editing buisness under Father—for I do verrily believe that he will steer along a middle & safe way that will give as little offence & alarm as possible and at the same time."[20]

In recognition of McNemar's deference to his spiritual superiors, Houston commented, "Depend on it Eleazer is determined to keep his fingers out of the fire unless some one in authority giveth him the command." Therefore, he submitted two pages of theological critique, "in hopes that they may be commited to Eleazer to be made use of as Father may direct." Despite the great care obviously taken by Shaker leadership and theologians in the preparation of this new edition, Houston stated that in his "judgment the main part of the intended alterations will never be noticed at all by 9 tenths of the Believers." While he was composing this letter, his fellow missionary Richard Pelham lay gravely ill by his side. Houston closed by noting "scarcely could I write this being interrupted 6 or 8 times & poor Richard Pelham is in the room with me being sick—I am affraid he will not live long. he hath puked blood plentifully & yet spits it."[21]

Preparations for printing *The Testimony* began in May. On the twenty-first, Shaker printer Andrew Burnett arrived at Union Village from Pleasant Hill. The next day, a new printing press and fonts of type arrived from Cincinnati.[22] Printing began on the "2d of June, and finished on the 4th of [October], to the amount of 3000 copies." In a letter to the East, McNemar proudly stated that all costs for press, type, paper, ink, and wages had been fully paid and that the book was the church's property, free and clear. This was an important consideration, as most of the western Shaker communities had been in debt to the world or relied heavily on financial support from the eastern Shaker communities. McNemar exulted in the success of the enterprise, stating, "We were peculiarly favoured and greatly prospered from first to last." A worldly printer, Brownlow Fisher, was hired to supervise the job and "conducted so well as to leave no room to wish for a better." He was assisted by Shakers Joshua Worley, who managed the press, and Andrew Burnett and Andrew Houston, who were principal compositors. Issachar Bates and Malcham Worley worked with McNemar in binding and folding and cutting signatures. McNemar noted wistfully that the only thing they lacked were Seth Youngs Wells's suggested amendments, a second copy of which finally arrived at Union Village ten days after the job was finished. In summation, McNemar declared that the new edition of *The Testimony* "came out entirely to the satisfaction of good Father David and all concerned."[23]

DEARLY AND WELL-BELOVED BROTHER SETH

As he was supervising the reprinting of *The Testimony*, Richard McNemar also began the most important epistolary friendship of his life. In Seth Youngs Wells, McNemar found his perfect match for erudition in matters pertaining to theology, politics, legal matters, poetry, and, of course, Shaker life and communal governance. Wells was born at Southold, Long Island, New York, in 1767. He worked as a schoolteacher and principal in Albany and taught at Hudson Academy, in Hudson, New York. He converted to Shakerism in 1798, joining the Watervliet, New York, community. Wells quickly converted his mother, father, and nine of his thirteen siblings—including his youngest brother, Freegift Wells, who loomed large in McNemar's later life. His uncles were Benjamin Seth Youngs, one of the first three Shaker missionaries to Ohio, and Isaac Newton Youngs, a talented Shaker polymath.[24] Seth Youngs Wells's intelligence and talent for writing quickly brought him to the attention of the New Lebanon Ministry. In time, he became their amanuensis and a key advisor on matters pertaining to law, politics, education, and theology. He also preached at public meetings, employing the rhetorical skills he developed for the classroom to advocate for Shaker beliefs. Wells authored and/or edited many Shaker books, including *Millennial Praises* (1813), the hymnal to which McNemar had contributed at least half of its 140 poems; *A Summary View of the Millennial Church* (1823), a primer on Shakerism for non-Shakers; and *Testimonies Concerning the Character and Ministry of Mother Ann Lee* (1827), the first major public statement by the Shakers about their founder, which was published to counter the works of apostates Eunice Chapman and Mary Dyer.

McNemar and Wells exchanged nearly fifty letters between 1823 and McNemar's death in 1839. McNemar's wit often comes out in his lengthy letters to Wells, whose dry and intellectually dense responses evidence his pre-Shaker life as a schoolteacher. The men confided in each other and often switched to Greek, Latin, and even Hebrew to conceal content others might have judged as too critical of their Shaker brothers and sisters. On February 10, 1824, Wells acknowledged receipt of a signature of the new *Testimony*, which he complimented as being "well executed, as to paper & printing, and is, I think, honorable to the Society, & to the brethren who bore the burden & performed the work."[25]

Unbeknownst to Wells, McNemar had already been sent on another missionary journey, traveling to visit members of the Halcyon sect at Straight Creek (today's Georgetown), Ohio, on January 21 with Charles Hampton. The sect was organized by the Reverend Abel Morgan Sargent, who supposedly began his religious career as a Baptist before embracing his own modified version of Universalism. According to McNemar, Halcyon believers professed "total releasement of all Adam's posterity from the miserable effects of their fall." Over two weeks, McNemar convinced at least two Halcyon followers to come to Union Village, but, as he reported to Wells, "I could not but pity these subjects of boasted light exulting in a universal redemption & restoration while one soul of them could not say that he was redeemed from all iniquity or even willing, in present tense to be redeemed." In effect, they rejected the immediate assurance of salvation offered them by McNemar in the form of Shakerism. Theologically, McNemar faulted the absolute logic of universal redemption, writing Wells, "If there be no everlasting punishment how could any one go away into it? or if there be no eternal damnation how could any one be in danger of it? & if the words everlasting & eternal do not imply duration beyond any fixed period, what security do we have that eternal life & the everlasting gospel will not come to a close." Finding themselves at an impasse, McNemar and Hampton returned to Union Village on February 4.[26]

McNemar's missionary efforts on behalf of the Shakers were now entering their nineteenth year. He proudly reported to Wells on March 22, 1824, that "there hath been a gift for the believers at the plains of Derby to move and gather with those on Whitewater, which gathering, in a few weeks, hath amounted to the number of 78 souls, besides 17 who are not yet moved from the plains."[27] Indeed, on February 9 and 22, a group of Darby Plains converts traveled to White Water, forming two communal families of young believers as the core of a new Shaker community in the West.[28] McNemar's letter was penned on the nineteenth anniversary of the eastern Shaker missionaries' arrival in the West. He described for Wells in great detail a commemoration of that event, during which Issachar Bates (the only one of the three then at Union Village) was honored with an exuberant display of singing and dancing. As Carol Medlicott noted in her biography of Bates, "The celebration may have been staged as a surprise for Issachar and Malcham [Worley] . . . honored as the missionaries' first convert." McNemar brought the scene alive for Wells and included the text of a commemorative hymn, probably of his own composition:

> Six o'clock P.M. the different families met at the brick house and after opening the meeting & singing & laboring awhile, Elder brother Malcham was placed on a chair & taken up by Ashbel & Caleb Pegg, the company then moved with Elder brother in front across the yard & lane into the public yard front of the Elder's shop, where they were intercepted by Elder Issachar, who was brought out of his lodging on a chair by two brethren & so the march continued with singing leaping and shouting into the meetinghouse. The Elder and Elder brother being placed on their chairs in the centre and surrounded by brethren & sisters, senior and junior, the following verses were sung.

> Our good first Elders from the east
> This day we call to mind
> Twill furnish us a little feast
> Of precious good old wine.
> To think that after all their search
> The different states around
> The 22d day of March
> A resting place they found.

> One soul convicted of his loss
> Did freely take them in
> And did set out to bear his cross
> And put away all sin.
> Thus by the righteousness of one
> Rejecting ev'ry lust
> The work hath long been going on
> Till many are made just.

> There is no period on record
> That can more thanks demand
> Than that in which the living word
> Was opend in this land.
> Then brethren let us all rejoice
> And sisters all be free
> Ye sweet musicians raise your voice
> And strike a higher key.

The Elder now is on the ground
Who gave the first pure Gospel sound
Which hath been spreading all around
To fill the land with Shakers.
The Elder brother too is here
Who first set out his cross to bear
And did the way of God prepare
That we might be partakers.

Our well beloved Father too
And ministry are all in view
Our love to them we must renew
In this commemoration.
They left their kindred in the east
And brought to us this precious feast
And, nineteen years, have never ceas'd
To minister salvation.

Come! come young elders lead the way
And on this memorable day
Let's have a little children's play
And all contention bury.
While each can say the gospel's mine
All gather'd to the chosen vine
We'll eat the grapes & drink the wine
And all be wise & merry.

Come loving sisters if ye will
Tune up your voice with heav'nly skill
Our water pots we all may fill
From Mother's flowing river.
And when we draw the liquor out
'Twill be new wine beyond a doubt
So we will sing and dance & shout
And praise the Lord forever.

When the song was over, the Believers danced with joy, including a novel form of circular dance surrounding Bates and Worley. McNemar compared this to the Jewish Hag and wrote Wells that "it felt both awful & glorious, to see such a vast body of well trained believers in a solid body of brethren and sisters alternately move round like the rushing of a mighty wind, while the elder & elder brother sustained the mortification of marking the centre of their circular procession." He closed his letter with heartfelt thanks to all of the gifts sent to

Figure 14.1. Shakers at Watervliet, New York, worshipping in a circular dance in 1870, as illustrated in *Frank Leslie's Illustrated Newspaper*, November 1, 1873, based on Joseph Becker's sketch. Communal Societies Collection, Hamilton College.

western Believers by those in the East. With great emotion, he confessed to Wells, "This heartmelting theme hath extracted such a flow from my two little water-pots that the paper was in danger of being spoiled."[29]

Wells gratefully acknowledged McNemar's letter, thanking him for his "pleasing information concerning the celebration of the 22d of March, and also for the hymn sung on the occasion—they were both agreeable & entertaining to us all." He had also finally received a complete copy of *The Testimony*. McNemar must have been extremely gratified by the praise he received from his eastern spiritual superior. Wells liked it better than the edition printed at Albany in 1810, the production of which he was most certainly involved in. He complimented McNemar on the additional footnotes, deeming them "very useful" and also noted "improvements upon several passages with which I am well pleased." In summary, Wells judged that "the substance of it is essentially improved."[30]

The revision and republication of *The Testimony* marked the high point of David Darrow's leadership. Although no one knew it at that time, 1824 was one of the last, best years for the western Shaker communities. McNemar renewed his correspondence with Proctor Sampson, whom he had helped convert to

Shakerism in 1811. In a letter to Sampson, he painted a detailed and glowing picture of the communities in Ohio, writing, "Without hesitation we can say that at present there is more real good in this place than hath ever been at any past period, I do not mean more good books or other good property, but more peace, more love, more joy, more zeal, more union, more obedience, more faith and faithfulness in every respect." McNemar's letter proceeded to describe the communities under ministerial care of Union Village. There was Watervliet, Ohio, where McNemar had recently preached twice at public meetings. He visited the families there and found them "under a special blessing both in things spiritual and temporal," and proudly reported that twenty new members had joined. He described North Union as "handsomely situated within about 4 miles of the nearest part of the lake [Erie], and the believers own a respectable mill-stream, on which a sawmill and small gristmill are already in operation." Thanks to additions from Darby Plains, the burgeoning community at White Water now numbered eighty. Farnumite preacher Nathan Burlingame held sway there, assisted by local magistrate and convert Brant Agnew. And finally, McNemar reported that the crowd in the meetinghouse at Union Village that very day—July 4, 1824—was the largest ever seen. He marveled, "What is remarkable they could for near the space of two hours endure sound doctrine & behave civilly & disperse without the least disorder." Times had certainly changed for the western Shaker communities. Although the threat of violence still existed, it had diminished considerably, and that provided the stability for that last great phase of growth in the Shaker West. Lastly, McNemar informed Sampson on David Darrow's behalf that Darrow was "yet alive in the gospel—that hitherto he hath kept Mother's faith & is determined to keep it to the end of his days." Darrow's leadership and the extreme veneration he quietly elicited from his followers had borne good fruit. Sadly, that was all about to change.[31]

As 1824 ended, the communal families at Union Village still included McNemar's five surviving children and his wife, Jennie. There is no evidence of his interaction with any of them in his extant papers. His brother Garner and nephews Levi and Richard G. were also present, but the nature of any relationship they had with Richard McNemar cannot be established for lack of evidence. It is perhaps unsurprising, given that their interactions happened in person, that no letters survive between these people. However, the absence of any mention of his family in McNemar's correspondence indicates a total embrace of core Shaker principles that eschewed fleshly ties of natural kin. Union Village journals reveal that James McNemar, Richard's second child—now twenty-eight—traveled to Indiana, Darby Plains, and North Union on preaching trips with Samuel Sering, Calvin Morrell, and Issachar Bates, beginning in 1823. He must have shown promise as a preacher and modeled a worthy example of a young Shaker male. As the years passed, some of Richard McNemar's children rose to prominence among the Believers, while other relatives would cause great tribulation.[32]

One of the few insights we have into Garner McNemar comes from a letter he wrote on December 7, 1824, to David Thomson, an old neighbor from Cane Run, Kentucky. Garner's friendly missive briefly described his fourteen years with the Shakers, the whereabouts of his kin, and accompanied a copy of the newly printed *Testimony*. In closing, he requested "a few lines in friendship from thee" and stated that he remained Thomson's "friend and well wisher."[33]

The reply Thomson penned nearly a year later on November 15, 1825, could not have been more scathing. Thomson began by fondly recalling the "many social hours which we had passed together," Garner's purchase of land in Ohio from Thomson, and "the agreeable time we had together at your house after you had improved the place." Then his tone shifted. Thomson wrote,

> The recollection of these events must give you pain because they have passed away not to return. They were the golden days of your existence. The voice of reason was then the man of your counsel. You were the kind and obliging husband, the affectionate father, the friendly neighbor and the worthy citizen. But alas, how is it now? In place of reason you have superstition, blindly submitting to priestcraft. In place of being a kind and obliging husband, you have without cause dissolved the sacred ties of matrimony, falsified your vow made on the altar in the presence of God. You have discarded the wife of your bosom, the mother of your children, dissolving the tie of blood and kindred, and the decree of heaven which gave woman to man as a helpmate, you have set at naught. In place of being an affectionate father, the tender offspring is abandoned, or, what is worse driven by a parental authority beyond the confines of reason and prosperity into a state of mental slavery and brutal drudgery totally subversive of human character.

Thomson continued in the same vein, charging Garner with voluntarily descending from the station God had created for him as a rational being and embracing Shaker life, which rendered him "like the other beasts of the field . . . well qualified for your master's use." He considered Garner "beyond the reach of friendship's warning voice" and instead offered him brutal honesty regarding both his decision to live as a Shaker and the contents of *The Testimony of Christ's Second Appearing*.[34]

Father David Darrow, the spiritual bulwark of all Shakers west of the Appalachian Mountains, grew progressively weaker in the spring of 1825. He was seventy-five and had lived amongst his western brethren and sisters for twenty of those years. From March 20 onward, he was confined to his room in the meetinghouse. Richard McNemar was called on to watch him at night beginning on March 22. After May first, he ate very little and vomited up much of what he did eat.[35] A letter from Matthew Houston to John Dunlavy written in early June noted that he had "eaten almost nothing at all for many weeks, ... he grows weaker and weaker daily—of course we cannot calculate upon his long stay with us." Houston knew the turmoil that this would unleash in the community and added, "Then the vital strength of the faith & subjection of many will be tryed—I for my part shall as well because I shall be obedient to God's Joshua."[36] This allusion is telling, in that it seems to place Darrow in the role of Moses and reveals Houston's determination to place his loyalty with Solomon King, second elder in the Union Village Ministry. Joshua was the assistant of Moses in the books of Exodus, Numbers, and Joshua and assumed leadership of the Israelites on his death. Carol Medlicott has noted that the allusion to Joshua may equally refer to Issachar Bates, who had been a close companion of Darrow's for more than twenty years and was also arguably a more popular choice as his successor.[37]

Richard McNemar recorded the substance of Darrow's last address in his diary. Its date is unknown, but its content is revealing and somewhat tragic. Darrow spoke on the subject of church order. He shared with the Believers the substance of the many emergent "orders," or rules and accepted behaviors, by which the New Lebanon Shakers lived. He admitted that despite his efforts to instill such order at Union Village, "he had strove to have it gained but had utterly failed." McNemar, writing retrospectively, believed that many, in fact, were "waiting & hoping for a relaxation of order at his death." Many of the orders Darrow had taught were abandoned soon after his death. McNemar saw this sad fact reflected in the chaos that enveloped the community during the second half of the 1820s. McNemar himself yearned for the enforcement of order, a stance he regretted in later years.[38]

During the final phase of his illness, Darrow reported that "he had been with Mother & the Elders, with Father Joseph & Mother Lucy, & others that are gone hence." From his sickbed, he exhorted his charges to keep the way of God. David Darrow died around 4:40 a.m. on the morning of June 27, 1825. As with Mother Ruth Farrington, he was conscious and communicative until shortly before his decease.[39] His death deprived the western Shakers, particularly the families at Union Village, of the founding leader who had unified them, ministered to their spiritual needs, and presided over the growth of Shakerism in the West. Darrow had achieved the stature of something like a living God. Only the first parents, Mother Ann Lee, Father William Lee, and Father James Whittaker, and the recently deceased Mother Lucy Wright, rivaled his status. His passing left a void in spiritual leadership that was quickly filled with a clamor of discordant voices undermining Shaker order with the novel theological ideas Darrow feared, ideas that were, at their core, antithetical to Shakerism.

The Union Village Ministry informed the New Lebanon Ministry of Darrow's passing in a letter, writing, "Such has been the love & universal esteem of the believers in the western country for Father, that it could not other wis be expected but what this great eventful change, must give a heavy shock to the feelings of the people generall." They described Darrow as a "faithful planter, supporter, & defender of Mothers gospel in this western country from the beginning, of which there are many living witnesses." His funeral was held on June 28 at 2:00 p.m., with as many as five hundred Believers in attendance.[40]

Richard McNemar preached the opening sermon of the funeral. Over an hour, McNemar preached from Psalm 58: "Verily there is a reward for the righteous: verily he is a God that judgeth in the earth" and from Proverbs 11:18: "The wicked worketh a deceitful work: but to him that soweth righteousness shall be a sure reward." McNemar framed Darrow's reward as a victory over the flesh and a permanent possession of "the lot & standing for which we labor"; in other words, salvation. He quoted Isaiah 9:6, "For unto us a child is born, unto us a son is given: and the government shall be upon his shoulder: and his name shall be called Wonderful, Counseller, The mighty God, The everlasting Father, The Prince of Peace,"—clearly conflating Darrow's spiritual authority in this day of Christ's second appearing with that of Jesus himself.[41]

McNemar asserted that Darrow's reward was "spiritual & eternal, to be owned forever as the spiritual Father of all who received the gospel thro him." Then he put the question to his audience: would they be willing to be judged by the standard he had set, and live according to the order that they had all created? McNemar warned his hearers "not to think that Father's gift was at an end" and that his spirit was not remote but instead that it was still among them. Issachar Bates preached next and was followed by Solomon King, Darrow's presumed successor. King echoed McNemar in testifying that "Father was not gone but would be able to be of more help to this body of people than what he had been while under weakness." King's belief proved sadly mistaken as disagreements over Darrow's spiritual authority, successfully tamped down during his life, boiled over in the years following his death.[42]

Following the sermons, the Believers lined up on the street running through the village, forty preceding the corpse, borne by four pallbearers. The ministry walked alongside Darrow's body, followed by the elders and the remaining community members. The solemn procession marched in an orderly manner to the grave. Darrow's body was said to have an "uncommon pleasant appearance," and he looked no older than forty. Most important, and giving him an air of purity approaching sainthood, "it was remarked that there was not the least smell of a corps about perceived from the time he breathed his last till it was put into the ground."[43]

Darrow's body was not yet cold when intrigues began about who would succeed him. McNemar lamented the "party zeal" regarding "who was next to feed the sheep?" He claimed that the privilege of appointing a successor was Darrow's, but many questioned this supposed purview of the Shaker hierarchy. In a sense, McNemar felt that Darrow had "died intestate, that he made no explicit will [and] named no legitimate heir." As a result of this confused state, McNemar was soon horrified to discover "pieces that were written & dropped about to stir up contention & a party spirit." In his view, this strife left no room for the "gift of God to open."[44] He was correct. No clear gift of God was forthcoming, and the resultant problems figured large in his eventual fate.

FIFTEEN

"THERE'S SOMETHING DEAD UPON THIS GROUND," OR, "THE BUZZARDS AND THE FLESH"

FATHER DAVID DARROW'S DEATH THRUST the western Shakers into uncharted territory. The New Lebanon Ministry was mindful of the difficulties that could lay ahead. They wrote Archibald Meacham at West Union, informing him of their advice to the Union Village Ministry: "We hope the believers, throughout, in the West, will be so wise as to gain and not lose by Father David's sufferings. And we hope you have an understanding that the removal of the most important pillar does not alter the order of God, nor take away the birthright of a society." They hoped, perhaps naively, that western Believers would "gather closer to the standard [and] strengthen your union by meekness & simplicity."[1] Slowly but surely, the opposite happened.

Richard McNemar reflected on this troubled time in his diary. He wrote that for some time before Darrow's death, a "spirit of anxiety began to prevail, to know how matters were to be adjusted subsequent to that event, in relation to the powers of government." The root of the conflict lay in the relationship between the spiritual authority (ministry and elders) and the temporal authority (trustees). At issue was whether the trustees should be united under the leadership of the ministry or maintain separate realms of authority. Shaker leaders were concerned that trustees were exercising too much independent decision making on behalf of the community as a whole. These individual trustees held titles to real estate and were empowered to borrow money and manage assets for the community. The possibilities for malfeasance were ripe, as the prior defalcation of John Wallace had shown.[2]

As Darrow lay dying, the elders debated the fine points of the covenant, since they would shortly have to rely on it, rather than on Darrow's divinely inspired edicts. These issues were perhaps the ones that Darrow lamented he had never resolved. McNemar acknowledged that there "was a lack in the level of the Church not having come up to the full measure of that order which father David expected to establish in his stay," and these were problems Darrow "never could fully settle in his best days, [and] excited much tribulation & suffering in the Ministry & no little animosity in the body." Shortly before his death, Darrow had a final spiritual revelation, which he shared with ministry sisters Rachel Johnson and Eunice Sering and also with Malcham Worley and McNemar. Lying in his sickbed at night, "under an extreme burden from difficulties among the leads which he said he had no gift to settle," he heard a voice from heaven declare: "There is no judgment." Quite simply, this gave Darrow the freedom to abdicate any responsibility to mediate between competing factions of the ministry and the elders. Darrow declared that his job was to set up the commonwealth and establish the laws of Zion, which contained no controversies or disputes. Therefore, he had no gift to settle such conflicts and would side with no party. His loyal followers were astonished, but they yielded to his divine will. Despite this, McNemar wrote that "some hung on to the last . . . as long as they could get a whisper from him on any subject," hoping he would take their side.[3]

Solomon King, Darrow's loyal second since their arrival at Turtle Creek on July 29, 1805, now found himself in the eye of the storm. King was born in New Lebanon, on July 9, 1775. He was fifty and had lived among the Shakers since childhood. His mother, Ruth Meacham, was Father Joseph Meacham's sister. He was a cousin to Shaker missionary John Meacham, who led the Pleasant Hill community until his return to New Lebanon in 1818, and also to Elder Archibald Meacham, who was then overseeing West Union. King's twenty-year apprenticeship to the godlike Darrow had left him ill prepared for the problems now facing him.[4]

Joining King in the new Union Village Ministry were Rachel Johnson and Eunice Sering. For the moment, no second elder was appointed. As Carol Medlicott has observed, despite Issachar Bates's popularity, and arguable claim to the role, King appointed him instead to oversee the community at Watervliet, Ohio. Apparently, no one else was considered for the second elder's position. King averred that "as Father gave us no advice with regard to gathering any body more into the meeting house, we have not felt to be over anxious about it as yet." Absent Bates's strong leadership, the main challenge for the new ministry was fostering union among their increasingly disgruntled followers. The family elders could not agree in what manner they were subject to the new ministry. This fact, combined with pretensions of leadership on the part of the Centre Family, sowed further seeds of discord among the body of Believers at large. Many refused to acknowledge the new ministry, and, as McNemar observed, this "gave latitude to a disorderly sense & led to a kind of conspiracy to make light of the authority of the Eldership altogether, & to set up for a revolution that would place them in a situation more to their mind." For better or worse, the ministry's response to this threat to their authority was to reduce "the gift of government . . . to greater mildness" in the attempt to stave off dissent and apostasy.[5]

On July 24, 1825, the Centre Family convened at the meetinghouse for Sabbath services. Poignantly, the ministry advised them of the "necessity of puting away every thing, that was an obstruction, or hindrance to there travil, and increase in the gospel." The ministry acknowledged that there had been complaints by some members "of a lack of confidence in their Elders." As a result, all were invited to speak freely and openly about their concerns, among themselves or to their elders and the ministry. The ministry promised to "give them an attentive hearing, and labour to do justice to all as far as we were able." This was quite a remarkable development in the theocratic hierarchy of Shakerism. Although the intentions of the ministry were surely good, this episode more than likely exposed their weakness in the face of Darrow's death. King reported to the New Lebanon Ministry that this effort was a success and that visits were made to each family to hear their grievances and rectify difficulties. Sadly, his optimism proved shortsighted.[6]

The unsettled state of leadership among the Ohio Shaker communities required Richard McNemar to be sent to assist Bates in managing the Believers at Watervliet. He left Union Village on July 2, just a week after Darrow's death. McNemar did not remain there for long, as, on December 13, he was appointed elder at the West Brick Family, called the "Brick House," one of the four families that made up the Centre Family of Union Village.[7] He replaced Malcham Worley, who was thrown into an emotional tailspin by David Darrow's death. It is worth mentioning here that McNemar still had not signed the Shaker covenant of any community or family. Apparently, this was not an obstacle to holding the office of elder.

Slightly more than a year after Darrow's death, on July 3, 1826, a group of thirty-two Union Village Believers, male and female, wrote an optimistic letter to the New Lebanon Ministry. Although they acknowledged that "the loss of our immediate parentage has been a grievous dispensation," they asserted, "The gift of God, in this place, has not even slept, tho it has been changed from one instrument to another." They declared the chief goal of the Union Village leadership was to promote reconciliation. Prematurely, they claimed that the "point has been so effectually gained that not a dog can move his tongue against the order established by Father and Mother and now firmly supported by their successors."⁸

Malcham Worley did not agree. That same month, as previously mentioned, he was removed from his position as elder, which he had occupied since March 7, 1821. The Union Village Ministry justified the decision to the New Lebanon Ministry as a "consequence of heavy afflictions that he has laboured under of a long time, which rendered him intirely incapable of dischargeing the duties of an Elder in a family." Despite this, Worley was honored as a "very worthy brother, haveing been a real pillar in the work of God her[e] from the beginning." As noted above, Richard McNemar was asked to take his place. Solomon King opined, "Eleazar . . . executes the office of an Elder well, but he is not exempt from preaching to the world occationally when he is wanted."⁹ McNemar did not get the chance to execute the office for very long, as less than two months later he departed for West Union. Worley's mental breakdown was symptomatic of the type of spiritual upheaval David Darrow fought to stave off, particularly regarding the introduction of new doctrines among Believers. His efforts, however, were in vain—a fact he was painfully aware of as he lay dying.

RECKONING AT WEST UNION

The West Union community had bravely met many challenges since their return to Indiana in August 1814. Under the leadership of Archibald Meacham and Issachar Bates, the community constructed a commodious brick dwelling, which they moved into in 1822, the same year they began building a frame meetinghouse (finished in 1824). Cotton and flax production were solid enterprises, and the episodic malaria that had plagued the community, and continued to hamper Meacham, seemed to diminish in frequency and severity. As Carol Medlicott notes, by 1822, the "Busro Believers were on a roll." Despite all of this, the community's future was in doubt. By 1826, the decision was made to close West Union. In her analysis of West Union's closure, Medlicott states that the reasons were complex, but chief among them were continuing illness, the deaths of solid Shakers, the lack of commitment to the faith on the part of their children (who were now young adults), and Indiana's draconian militia law that imposed military service or heavy exemption taxes on the Shakers.¹⁰

Archibald Meacham and Andrew Houston left Union Village on July 4, 1826, for New Lebanon, where they would meet with the ministry regarding West Union's fate. They carried a damning letter from the Union Village Ministry lamenting that the Believers at West Union were becoming "more & more reduced in numbers & strength, it appears that dissatisfaction; & discouragements are becoming more & more prevalent among the remaining few, that instead of there being able to increase and honoring the gospel in that place, that they will gradually waist away." Crucially, there was "scarcely one remaining among the brethren that is really capable of filling the lot of an Elder."[11]

In Meacham's absence, John Dunlavy, who lived at Pleasant Hill, was temporarily appointed to lead West Union. He arrived there on June 3. Sadly, while there, he unexpectedly took ill and died. This was a crushing blow to western Shakerism, as Dunlavy was one of the most important early converts. He had been McNemar's colleague in the Springfield Presbytery, as well as his brother-in-law and one of Shakerism's foremost theologians. Dunlavy's death on September 16 punctuated a period of renewed illness at West Union. The ministry relieved McNemar of his eldership at the Brick House on September 23 and dispatched him to West Union by way of Pleasant Hill. He was given the doleful task of replacing Dunlavy as the temporary elder at West Union.[12] Additionally, McNemar confronted a body of Believers who had lost confidence in their ministry and still claimed the property vested in the authority of the trustees by virtue of the covenant. McNemar had to convince them that their rebellious course left all of their property vulnerable to revert to the state of Indiana by escheat. This fear fostered a temporary reconciliation in the body, allowing time to plan an orderly dispersal of the Believers and property composing West Union.[13]

Meacham and Houston returned to Union Village on October 7, 1826.[14] They brought advice regarding West Union from the New Lebanon Ministry. Based on their report and the general sentiments of Shaker leadership in Ohio and Kentucky, the Union Village Ministry penned a circular to the West Union Believers on October 16. After reviewing all of the assistance provided to the community since its inception, the ministry reluctantly concluded that "all these things it appears have not nor cannot remove the serious dificulties, and imbarrisments comon, or natural to that country." Noting that dissatisfaction among Believers there had reached a peak, the ministry advised, "It will be more for your future increase & prosperity for you all to evacuate that unhealthy countrey." Individuals who wished to remain Shakers were advised to return as individuals to the communities where they sought refuge during the War of 1812: Union Village, Pleasant Hill, or South Union. Those who had joined since that time were free to choose from among these as well as Watervliet and White Water, Ohio. All were advised to wait until the spring of 1827 to relocate.[15]

On November 19, 1826, Richard McNemar—once again the ministry's roving problem solver—gathered the West Union Believers together. He had the unenviable task of reading them a letter from Archibald Meacham that summarized the recommendations of the New Lebanon Ministry. The upshot, as recorded in the journal of longtime West Union Shaker Samuel Swan McClelland, was that "it was universally thought and felt best for all the people to rise once more and move away from Busro, and so abandon the place forever!" People began to trickle away almost immediately, some to Union Village, others to Pleasant Hill. McNemar accompanied some visitors from South Union as far as New Harmony, Indiana, where the nascent Owenite community was itself only a few months from failure. As winter set in, others who remained at West Union succumbed to illness. The settlement had not yet claimed its last victims.[16]

Richard McNemar convened the remaining Shakers in the brick house on New Year's Day, 1827. Three days before, trustee Nathan Sharp had arrived at West Union from Union Village. He brought a legal document that McNemar now presented to the gathering. All adults were required to sign this instrument, which conveyed all property to trustees Sharp and Francis Voris of Pleasant Hill, who were tasked with liquidating the site and its assets. Although many West Union Shakers remained committed to the faith and went on to live at other Shaker communities, this must have been a bitter moment, as they signed away everything they had struggled for through twenty years of war and disease.[17]

Archibald Meacham returned to West Union for the last time on January 25, 1827. On March 10, four wagons with twenty-eight Shakers left for their new home at South Union. Three more parties, one each for Union Village, South Union, and Pleasant Hill, loaded their belongings into the steamboat *Lawrence*. McNemar traveled overland with one of the companies bound for South Union. On March 20, at 5:35 p.m., the boat pushed off from McCartye's landing. Of this scene, McClelland wrote, "[We] bid a final adieu to all our hard-earned and dear-bought possessions on Busro Prairy. The pen—even of the learned—would fail, should it undertake to describe the feelings of this unfortunate people. Comment would therefore be useless, as everyone concerned can think or forget it for themselves, just as you please."[18]

Elder Archibald Meacham landed at Lawrenceburg, Indiana, on March 28. From there, he journeyed to the newly gathered community at White Water, Ohio, where he resumed his leadership role. That same day, the company bound for Pleasant Hill left the Ohio River and entered the Kentucky River. Poles and oars were substituted for the steam engine on their boat. They arrived safely on April 9, after a journey of twenty days.[19] In the end, forty-five West Union Shakers moved to Union Village, forty-three to Pleasant Hill (many of whom were more advanced in the faith), twenty-six to South Union, twenty to White Water, and two to Watervliet, Ohio.[20]

Richard McNemar, who traveled on to Pleasant Hill from South Union, left no record of his feelings at the end of this ordeal. He must have been relieved to have safely overseen the exodus of so many of his fellow Believers. But surely he was also bitter about the fate of West Union. McNemar included a hymn titled "The buzzards and the flesh. W.U. 1827" in his 1833 *Selection of Hymns and Poems for the Use of Believers*. The first stanza employs the imagery of death and decay but rebuts such scenes with the words of a committed Believer, who will rise above the situation.

> There's something dead upon this ground
> I see the buzzard's hov'ring round,
> The stink begins to take the air,
> The horrid smell I cannot bear!
> Ye honest souls who really mean
> To keep the gospel and be clean,
> Be on your guard and come not near
> Where those flesh-hunting fowls appear.[21]

McNemar returned to Union Village on May 4 but was back at Pleasant Hill just twenty days later. With the tribulations of West Union still fresh on his mind, he was off to face a whole new set of challenges in the Bluegrass region of Kentucky.

UNPLEASANT TIMES AT PLEASANT HILL

While the events surrounding West Union's closure unfolded during 1826 and 1827, an equally disturbing series of events was underway at Pleasant Hill, and, just as at West Union, Richard McNemar would play a central role. Father John Meacham, one of the original three missionaries of 1805, was recalled to New Lebanon in 1818. Since that time, leadership there had fallen solely, in a practical sense, to Mother Lucy Smith. Many Believers at Pleasant Hill considered her "as a being superior to all other beings now on earth." The lion's share of spiritual and temporal concerns was committed to her care, a concentration of powers that the Union Village Shakers were aware was potentially problematic. To make matters worse, her male counterpart at the Pleasant Hill ministry, Elder Samuel Turner, was viewed by some as unfairly marginalized, even regarding affairs he was better qualified to handle. This situation led to the formation of factions within the community and provided inroads for "infidel philosophy" of the type that so troubled David Darrow.[22]

The philosophy of Robert Owen and his New Harmony community formed a backdrop to this unrest. Shortly before Darrow's death, the Union Village Ministry, possibly still with Darrow's input, remarked in a letter to the New Lebanon Ministry that they knew of Owen, writing, "We understand that a good many people are pleased with his Cystem, others seam rather disposed to pick it to pieces."[23] Seven months later, on December 30, 1825, Robert Owen visited Union Village.[24] The Welsh social reformer's teachings and reputation preceded him. His landmark tract *A New View of Society* (1813) elaborated on the system he put into practice at his textile mill in New Lanark, Scotland.[25] Owen believed that inculcating children with carefully managed physical, moral, and social influences would result in gradual social reform, ultimately bringing about a "New Moral World." This, combined with his ideas on labor and the treatment of the working class in a rapidly industrializing world, made his ideas very attractive to reformers on both sides of the Atlantic. Eventually, Owen conceived of a model for a communitarian system that he hoped to implement in North America. In October 1824, he arrived in the United States with his son William, and the next January he purchased the Harmonist settlement at New Harmony, Indiana, from Father George Rapp and his followers. The Shaker settlement at West Union was only ninety miles up the Wabash River, and the Shakers had already visited New Harmony many times during the Harmonists' tenure. The press publicized Owen's communal venture far and wide, and his ideas permeated Shaker communities in a way that David Darrow would surely have disapproved of.[26]

One Owenite follower, John Whitbey, set in motion a series of events at Pleasant Hill that spawned years of trouble for the community. Whitbey and the problems he left in his wake consumed Richard McNemar's attention into the early 1830s. Whitbey was a square peg in a round hole if there ever was one, and his cool rationalism nearly destroyed Pleasant Hill. Benjamin Seth Youngs described him thus: "In his outward appearance & manners, he was very mild, prudent, and exemplary—but at the same time very sly, undermining, cunning & deceitful—at heart a perfect infidel—secretly & assiduously, under a most pious cloak, insinuating ideas & inculcating principles of the most dangerous & infernal kind.—Infidelity, pride, presumption, disorder & confession, grew into a contagion—the contagion spread & grew into a plague."[27]

The remarkably intelligent Whitbey penned an apostate narrative, *Beauties of Priestcraft, or, A Short Account of Shakerism*, that is among the most effective ever written in demonstrating the effects of Shaker theocracy on those subject to it.[28] Whitbey was fixated on something that had troubled McNemar's old archrival, Colonel James Smith: the notion that the elders were infallible. Although such infallibility is not doctrine among Shakers, the leadership at Pleasant Hill—after enough calm probing by Whitbey—exploded at him in a blind authoritarian rage indeed suggestive of infallible self-righteousness. Whitbey's exposition of the "hierarchical monarchy" by which the community was led shed unfavorable light on the elders.[29]

Raised a Methodist, Whitbey joined the Gathering Order at Pleasant Hill in the spring of 1818. His elders were John Dunlavy and his counterpart, Betsy McCarver. Whitbey naturally had an inquiring, highly rational turn of mind. By the autumn of 1822, his questioning came to the attention of the Shaker leadership, and his faith was examined. Although he saw among the Shakers a degree of love and union "exceeded by no society on earth," he could not accept the divine inspiration of the elders. He "considered them to be nothing more than good conscientious men, anxiously employed in the use of such means as they thought were best calculated to bring us into a state of proper feelings and good order." Personally, Whitbey wished to make decisions for himself—a stance opposed to Shaker order. In exploring these impulses, Whitbey happened on Owen's *New View of Society*. The new elders of the Gathering Order, James Rankin and George Runyon, appointed in 1825, tried hard to suppress Whitbey's influence in spreading his excitement over Owen's philosophy, even going so far as to forbid family members from reading *The New Harmony Gazette*.[30]

The influence of Owen's ideas, in combination with preexisting factional strife, affected nearly every member of the society, leaving them "contaminated, or as they now call it, 'smoak'd.'" Benjamin Seth Youngs described their sentiments as, "Away with Ministry, Elders, and Deacons, but such as are of the PEOPLES own choosing," something instilled as much as possible in the young Believers. "Down with the priestcraft . . . Let the PEOPLE be liberated from bondage, & be free to judge, & to act for themselves."[31] These ideas were clearly not in keeping with Shaker theocratic hierarchy, but the ministry and elders failed to respond effectively to these sentiments.

Whitbey wrote a letter to Robert Owen requesting further information, for he "had long entertained a desire to see what could be done on the free principles of reason, unfettered by tradition and superstition." Surprisingly, the elders approved the letter and gave it to another Shaker to deliver. On that Shaker's return, Whitbey found that the letter had not been delivered. The brother who had taken it revealed that the elders had strongly hinted that he should "forget" to deliver it. Whitbey then realized the extent of the oppression he suffered. He found the Shakers hypocritical in opposing the persecution of fringe sects such as themselves, yet persecuting their own membership.[32] To make matters worse, Shaker authority was attacked from the outside on June 6, 1825, when a mob of around forty men assaulted Pleasant Hill. They were seeking Lucy Bryant, James Bryant's daughter. He had apostatized with his wife, and they had previously recovered their other children. The mob entered the Centre Family dwelling with clubs, dirks, and pistols, but the Shakers managed to turn them away. On June 12, however, an even larger mob of two hundred people led by the girl's mother returned and successfully retrieved her.[33]

By November 1825, the community had reached a boiling point, and John Dunlavy was called on to enforce orthodoxy and obedience to the ministry. At a meeting, he publicly called out Whitbey, labeling him an "abominable heretic." Accordingly, John Whitbey and his brother Richardson left Pleasant Hill on November 21, 1825, traveling to New Harmony. Whitbey was happy—for the moment—with what he found, writing that "the flame of truth shines brighter and brighter, enlightening the understanding, refining the feelings, and warming the affections of our most intelligent citizens;—many of whom have assembled together at New-Harmony."[34]

The net effect of his tenure among the Shakers was to destabilize the leadership, sow seeds of doubt in the membership, and bring unfavorable public attention to bear. Benjamin Seth Youngs viewed Whitbey with utter contempt. In a letter to the New Lebanon Ministry, he excoriated John and Richardson Whitbey, calling them "puffed up with new discoveries of light and knowledge & full of ministrations & commissions from the high school of infidel philosophy & corruption at P[leasant] H[ill]. . . . It is not necessary to inform you of the particular effects from the visits of these vile men."[35]

Whitbey's *Beauties of Priestcraft* was published at New Harmony in 1826. Its effects reverberated throughout the Ohio Valley, especially among those who apostatized following the dissolution of West Union. A web of anti-Shaker correspondents comprising those who had left Pleasant Hill, as well as some disgruntled members still at Pleasant Hill and South Union, and ex-Shakers still squatting at the former community of West Union, agitated community life further. Whitbey even had the gall to visit South Union while ministry elder Benjamin Seth Youngs was absent on a visit to the eastern communities in the summer of 1827. Richard McNemar immediately apprehended the seriousness of the situation at Pleasant Hill on his arrival there with the West

Union refugees on April 9, 1827. On May 4, he arrived at Union Village with Elder Samuel Turner, first elder of the Pleasant Hill Ministry. They informed the Union Village Ministry of the dire circumstances there.[36]

Many Believers had signed the Pleasant Hill covenant but not made a full consecration of their property, holding some of it back for themselves or their heirs. When apprised of this situation, the New Lebanon Ministry was appalled. When church order was established, every covenanted member with children was required to prove they were free from debt and also to apportion off their property between themselves and their children. On reaching the age of majority, the children were free to either sign the covenant and remain a Shaker or take their share of the property and leave.

In the case of founding Pleasant Hill member Samuel Banta, the ministry inquired, "Did not the leaders at Pleasant Hill break their own Covenant when they urged Saml Banta to sign it before he was clear of creditors & heirs? And how could he or his property be dedicated while he kept money of his own, had heirs without who were unsettled with, and went here and there at his own will?" The New Lebanon Ministry had little hope that the trustees at Pleasant Hill would prevail in a court case with apostates and urged them to settle out of court. Banta, seventy-five, left the community on April 24, 1827. McNemar called this circumstance "unhappy" and questioned "whether under the effects of dotage, the alarming appearance of things, or the insinuations of his children who were in the world, [Banta] got up the idea of recovering the interest which 13 years before he had dedicated to the use of the gospel, & with the advice & encouragement of an attorney left his comfortable home & best friends, to exhibit himself to a deceived world as an object of pity, poor & pennyless having been, as they pretended, striped by the Shakers of a good estate."[37]

The situation at Pleasant Hill had grown serious enough that, on May 24, 1827, Richard McNemar returned there with Elder Turner to assess matters and try to reinstate order.[38] There was much hostility directed at the Shakers in the region, as McNemar found out in Harrodsburg in late June, where he heard "heavy threats against Believers."[39] By mid-July, he suspected a conspiracy was developing among a party at Pleasant Hill who wanted to form "an article of agreement in & by which they might claim & secure the premises so as to be equal sharers in the interest whether they continued in the gospel or not." Mother Lucy Smith, the de facto leader at Pleasant Hill, was now sixty-two years old and had suffered from extremely poor health for nearly twenty years, including the expulsion of a twenty-foot-long tapeworm in 1817.[40] Now, under extreme duress and with her leadership under serious scrutiny, she asked McNemar to meet with the dissident faction. On Wednesday, July 18, nineteen male representatives from the Centre, East, West, and Mill Families, along with trustees, met with McNemar to talk through the current difficulties. All present alluded to "diss[atisfac]tion with the Ministry." The men desperately wanted the return of Father John Meacham, who had been recalled to New Lebanon in 1818. They were allowed to draft a letter and send it to the New Lebanon Ministry, "stating their grievances & petitioning for elder John to be sent as soon as possible as the last resource of relief." It was further agreed not to share the content of the letter with the Pleasant Hill Ministry and not to reveal the plan to the Believers at large until the Sabbath meeting on July 22. In the meantime, rumors of the plan, hatched by nineteen Shaker brethren, reached the sisters. They cornered McNemar, expressing their "jealous concern about Mother . . . they utterly discard the idea of her leaving the ground." They charged McNemar, now squarely at the center of the conflict, with defending her rights.[41]

McNemar perceived the chief issue at Pleasant Hill to be that the removal of the "Founders" explicitly named in the 1814 covenant—John Meacham and Lucy Smith—vacated the source of authority from which the elders and trustees of each family derived their own power. Only Meacham or Smith, in the view of many Believers, could transfer ministerial and temporal authority. Meacham was long gone, and Smith had lost the confidence of her followers. From a legal standpoint, McNemar judged that "the law in such cases pursues a regular chain in determining claims, & if a link be wanting the whole is without force," thus leaving the covenant void, and the consecrated interest of Pleasant Hill Believers at great risk.[42]

McNemar addressed the assembled Believers at the Sabbath meeting on July 22. The community's survival depended in large part on the remarks he prepared for this crucial gathering. He began his sermon with a challenge: "By the world you are called Shakers, by each other Believers implying, as your church covenant says, your faith in the testimony of Christ's second appearing. Will it do to be called Believers if we are not really such?" Each hearer was tasked with searching his or her heart to determine if Christ was there. McNemar reminded them that the church they were building was founded on the testimony of Christ, and not on a man nor any other incarnate human. He recalled that at his first meeting with John Meacham, Issachar Bates, and Benjamin Seth Youngs, he was told that they had come bearing a testimony for the "purpose of gathering [and] building up those materials in Chh order." McNemar had replied, "Amen to the proposition & surrendered myself to do with me as they chose." However, surveying the fractured group before him, he lamented that "much labor has been spent in dressing & polishing these materials & after all there appears to be danger that much loss & damage will yet come, from the unwise or improper choice of materials." He then demurred, stating that he had not been sent to Pleasant Hill as a building inspector. Instead, he broached the Believers' widely expressed dissatisfaction with the covenant, revealing that a letter had been drafted for submission to the New Lebanon Ministry, referring to them as "the skilful physician to prescribe the remedy, giving their judgment simply on that which the patient would be able to swallow." The community, therefore, had to wait for word from the East for a resolution to their difficulties.[43]

At the evening meeting on Wednesday, July 25, Believers gathered to hear the portion of the letter to New Lebanon dealing with Church order. Mother Lucy Smith opened the meeting with what McNemar described as "an affecting discourse all in the first person singular." The fact that he noted her use of the first-person singular is significant, as it perhaps demonstrates that she was focused too much on herself, to the detriment of the community. Mother Lucy recounted her labors during the nineteen years she had served western Believers. She finished by offering to "give the ground if they thought she stood in the way of their prosperity."[44]

That week, factions aligned themselves with either Mother Lucy or Elder Samuel Turner. McNemar received Turner in his room on July 26 and heard a letter Turner had written to the Union Village Ministry stating that "it had ever been his wish & labor to support [Mother Lucy's] gift & character that she might finish her work honorably & never quit the ground." After Turner left, Mother Lucy herself came to McNemar, telling him about a meeting she had with some prominent brethren who were "all anxious to have Elder Samuel go off the ground." These brethren had expressed their love for her and their desire that she remain at Pleasant Hill. One of them even offered to draft a petition for Turner's removal. Caught in the middle, McNemar could only sigh privately to his journal, quoting Cicero in lamentation, "O Tempora O Mores" [Oh the times! Oh the customs!].[45]

The brethren who drafted the letter to the New Lebanon Ministry included Rufus Bryant, who was second in the ministry to Samuel Turner. They claimed that for "six or seven years past [they] felt ourselves on the decline as it regards our prosperity as a society." Left without the ability to make decisions for themselves to alter this course, they had "been led irresistibly to the conclusion that there is something essentially wrong in the source of our ministration." Before Elder John Meacham's recall, they had been "a happy & prosperous people united at home & respected abroad" and obedient to the gospel. However, since that time, factions had developed in the church, fueled by perceptions of incompetence among ministers, elders, trustees, and deacons, and the leadership's unwillingness to address common concerns. Elder Samuel Turner, in particular, was thought to be of a "cramped mind and views," neglecting the fact "that all parts of the great family & system require their due proportion of attention and nourishment." He was accused of playing favorites. Mother Lucy was perceived as an overanxious woman, lacking in "sound firm judgment & sagacity which is necessary to the good conducting of so important a concern." She was consumed by conflict with Turner, and her age and weak physical state further undermined the members' confidence in her leadership. The disunion between the ministry eldress and elder was a "notorious, common & public matter to almost the youngest member of the society."[46] The letter closed with a plea for the removal of both Smith and Turner, and the return of Elder John Meacham so that Pleasant Hill could prosper once more.

In his diary, McNemar asked, "What can be done with such a people? but to let them work it out." On October 2, he described Pleasant Hill as follows: "The whole head is sick and the whole heart faint, wounds, bruises, putrifying sores. Not bound up not mollified with ointment, gone away backward." McNemar fervently believed that on the day of Christ's second appearing, "Judgment is committed . . . to the female sex; Female testimony will decide the matter with every soul of us." He reflected on the twenty years he had labored faithfully in support of Mother Ann's gospel, not under the control of a fellow mortal but of his own free will. For his part, McNemar was "unwilling that the female should be put down below her proper place & lot so long as she gives evidence of her chastity."[47] His sympathies were clearly with Mother Lucy Smith and what she represented as the embodiment of female Shakerism—the last to bear the title "Mother" in any of the western communities.

The New Lebanon Ministry found the situation extremely disturbing. They appealed to the Union Village Ministry to exercise some authority and guidance with respect to Pleasant Hill and especially in effecting a reconciliation between Mother Lucy and Elder Samuel Turner. Disapprovingly, they wrote, "To find that a large society were in such a state of anarchy and confusion that they had sought to be released from their Ministry, is truly shocking and lamentable." In response to the dissident Believers' request that John Meacham be returned to Pleasant Hill, the ministry replied, "We must say, we are sorry that he was asked for, as we consider him unable in body and mind to take that place again, therefore we are pretty confident that there can be no gift in his going there again." With regard to Mother Lucy and Elder Samuel, they directed that "the sooner they come away the better it will be, considering their present state and the feelings of the society there." Mother Lucy was free to live out her remaining years at Union Village or to return to New Lebanon, as she saw fit—but she must leave Pleasant Hill.[48] Accordingly, on November 19, 1827, Mother Lucy Smith ended her tenure at Pleasant Hill, returning to Union Village, where she had arrived with Samuel Turner on May 31, 1806. Turner remained at Pleasant Hill for the time being.

Regarding the body of Believers at Pleasant Hill, the New Lebanon Ministry charged, "They have been too big and too high." They had exalted their leaders beyond reason, and when the leadership "could not keep the gift of God," the people had torn them down. The ministry viewed this as the influence of "republican government," which was acceptable among Believers only for the civil and religious protection it afforded them, but it was of the world, not of the kingdom of Christ. The ministry asked, "If the people succeed in dismissing the Ministry at Pleasant Hill, the plague will not stop there . . . we consider it the most formidable attack which Satan has made against the work of God since the overthrow of the primitive christians."[49] Therefore, the Union Village Ministry—and, by extension, McNemar—were charged with helping the Believers at Pleasant Hill travel back down into the valley of humiliation and repentance, a daunting task, to say the least.

THE INVESTIGATOR: PLEASANT HILL DISSIDENTS APPEAL TO THE LAW

By this point in their history, the Shakers were less likely to face the threat of physical assault; however, their corporate and legal structure served as prime targets. Richard McNemar realized the double-edged sword that had resulted from publishing so much about their faith to the world. It had become necessary that all of the Shakers' "social contracts, rules, manners, laws or customs, . . . connected with our civil rights, should be explicitly known and understood." Popular ignorance of these provided an avenue of attack for apostates and anti-Shaker agitators, some of whom were members of government.[50] Eastern Shakers had already solicited McNemar's opinion on the legal power and authority of a trustee; specifically, in how those responsibilities concerning consecrated property functioned with regard to Shaker community members on the one hand and the civil and legal authorities on the other. This issue became the Shakers' most vexing problem in the late 1820s and through the 1830s—dealing with it consumed much of McNemar's attention for the next ten years of his life.

In answering these questions, McNemar first defined the Shaker Church—the highest covenanted order of Believers—as a company of free volunteers who had donated their property to the united interest, relinquished any right to it, and henceforth consecrated any profit from labor or other assets to the joint interest. Who, then, had legal claim to that property? McNemar argued that in the eyes of the law, this was the trustee, as he received all conveyances from incoming members of the church. Accordingly, the trustee had the power to convey and dispose of property, but under what restrictions? Just as the treasurer of a state, elected by the people, had no personal claim to state assets and could be removed by the people for malfeasance, a Shaker trustee, appointed by the ministry and implied consent of the church in accordance with Shaker hierarchy, could only dispose of assets at the ministry's direction, or be removed by them if necessary. Further, proceeds from any assets or property disposed of by the trustee must revert to the benefit of the whole Church and be equally distributed.

The Shaker covenant was most regularly attacked over a seceding member's right to sue the trustee to recover property consecrated to the Church—as was the case with Pleasant Hill apostate Samuel Banta. McNemar posited that no one could "recover from the trustee that which lawfully passed through his hands and perished with the using." The trustee could make no judgment about the donor's intentions, and the covenant was quite clear about the nature of consecrated property: once given, it could not be withdrawn. In fact, the June 1814 covenant signed at Pleasant Hill specifically stated, "Therefore, according to the faith, manner, rule, order and example of the Church, we do freely, and cordially, covenant, promise and agree together, each for ourselves, our heirs and assigns, that we shall never, hereafter, make any account of any property, labor, or service devoted by us to the purposes aforesaid, or bring any charge of debt or damage, or hold any demand whatever against the church or community or any member thereof, on account of either property or service given, rendered, or consecrated to the aforesaid sacred and charitable uses." In summary, McNemar urged that this bedrock principle of Shaker communalism be defended to the last; otherwise, "it would be better to divide the swarm than destroy the honey.... Why do not those who want private property put themselves in a situation to acquire it & cease to pester the church with their petty claims & vain proposals for a revolution."[51]

One such vain proposal came in the form of a petition submitted to the Kentucky General Assembly, or the legislature, by a group of ex- and anti-Shakers led by John Whitbey. Accusing the Shaker leaders at Pleasant Hill of "fraudulent conduct," they claimed they had been induced to join the group on the basis of their faith and that each individual had an equal right to property and no one could be expelled. They claimed that the Shaker leadership deviated from original principles and expelled the complainants based on personal, moral opinions, which are not explicitly named but seem to relate to Whitbey's claims of "despotic oppression." Following their expulsion, the seceders sought to sue the Shakers but were prohibited because the sect was not officially incorporated in Kentucky. Accordingly, they petitioned the legislature to pass an act allowing individuals to sue the Shakers. Eighteen men signed the petition, thirteen of whom had never been covenanted church members.[52]

The petitioners succeeded in their aim, and on February 11, 1828, "an act to regulate civil proceedings against certain communities having property in common" was passed by the General Assembly at Frankfort. The act allowed for anyone with a claim of more than fifty dollars on the community to sue the community collectively—without naming a single individual—by its common name; that is, "Pleasant Hill." Community trustees and other individual members could be made a party to suits. McNemar described the act in a letter to Seth Youngs Wells as "everything Satan could wish for," explaining that "if the society can be sued as a corporation by a public notice & made defendants . . . every member must appear in the eye of the law as interested & equally holding claim & consequently the plaintiff & defendent stand on equal ground as claimants."[53] The act erroneously stated that Shakers held all property in common. Actually, by the terms of the Shaker covenant, individual members held no property. Notifications of lawsuits against the community were to be fixed "to the door of the meeting-house" and read aloud at "one of the dwellings" with ten days' notice. Crucially, the act denied that it tendered seceding members, past or future, "any right . . . which he or she would not have had if this act had not passed."[54]

As the act stipulated, the Pleasant Hill Shakers learned of its passing when a copy was nailed to the door of the meetinghouse, "as if the house of God had become a den of thieves." In the wake of this rude violation of sacred space, Richard McNemar, as he had done many times before, took up his pen in defense of his faith. On Sunday, June 1, a meeting of ministry and elders at Pleasant Hill authorized the publication of McNemar's rebuttal to Whitbey, which also contained an appeal to the legislature and general public. Printing began in Lexington on June 9 and was finished by July 3. The next day, McNemar accidentally cut his leg while using a scythe, compelling evidence that this fifty-eight-year-old Believer was still performing manual labor in addition to his considerable mental exertions. McNemar folded and stitched the printed signatures himself, and in late July, *Investigator; or A Defence of the Order, Government & Economy of the United Society called Shakers, against Sundry Charges and Legislative Proceedings; Addressed to the Political World; By the Society of Believers at Pleasant Hill, KY* was released to the world.[55]

McNemar appealed to the public based on the First Amendment right to religious freedom, which no state legislature could abrogate. He stated, "As a community of Believers we disclaim the right or privilege of suing or being sued in a body." Members were accepted freely but were subject to the tenets of the faith, which, McNemar pointedly reminded Whitbey, would not be in sympathy with those who adopted "the opinions of Epicurus, Voltaire, or Robert Owen." Further, McNemar justified the society's right to police itself internally against those who usurped the authority of the ministry by distributing such ideas.[56]

To the General Assembly, he addressed a section titled "Objections to the Foregoing Act." He disputed the right for a suit to be served against the collective body by their common name, as each entity must have a legal name, not by "names and descriptions palmed upon us by the public," lest the legal process be undermined. He labeled the practice of affixing suits to the meetinghouse door as "incompatible with our religious rights." Finally, he strongly objected to the act's provision to name the defendant designated to represent the Shaker community, regardless of the community's official trustees or their own choice of agent. He charged this was "subversive of our common rights."[57] For justification of his positions, McNemar cited a similar case in the Pennsylvania legislature involving the Harmony Society.

McNemar's *Investigator* quotes Whitbey's *Beauties of Priestcraft* at length and even credits his accuracy in describing Shaker life. With great candor, McNemar acknowledged that Shakerism is "confessedly, a theocracy or divine government." Based on this fact, could anything be more "sacrilegious or dishonest" than for someone to consecrate their property freely to such a cause and then attempt to reclaim it? The covenant clearly disallowed the success of any such attempt. McNemar wrapped up his dense treatise by reassuring the Believers in Kentucky that the Shaker covenant had been challenged in many other states and had always withstood the test. He published specific examples from Massachusetts, Maine, and New Hampshire. McNemar called out Whitbey and Robert Owen, asking that they not mix their "water" with the Shakers' "wine," and averring that the Shakers were happy for the Owenites to "enjoy their *mental liberty*, only not try to force their sentiments or themselves into an unnatural association with our sentiments and our society." In a parting shot, he accused Owen of lifting many of his ideas from the Shakers' *Testimony of Christ's Second Appearing*.[58]

McNemar's work in Kentucky was done, for the moment. He left for Union Village on the wet morning of July 28. There, more trouble awaited him in the form of an egomaniacal and hypersexual prophet. Additionally, the novel doctrine of Swedenborgianism had made significant inroads during his absence, a circumstance that would have devastating personal effects.[59]

SIXTEEN

THE STRUGGLE WITH ABIJAH ALLEY AND AQUILA BOLTON

THE TROUBLES AT PLEASANT HILL were paralleled at Union Village, where agitation from rank-and-file Believers was also causing major disruption. A prominent ringleader in these disturbances was Abijah Alley, who joined in 1817. Alley showed promise as a young Believer, and in either 1822 or 1823, he was appointed elder of the North Lot Family, a gathering order of the church.[1] By 1825, however, he was removed from that position. His superior, East House elder David Spinning, concluded that Alley's "talents . . . were not competent to lead so large a family as that at the North but might be profitable in a smaller family."[2] In 1826, Alley was appointed second elder in the West Lot Family, a cluster of buildings that housed one of the smallest families at Union Village.[3] The timing of his demotion may have embittered Alley, especially if he was aware of John Whitbey's demands for reform at Pleasant Hill.[4]

On August 11, 1828, the elders initiated a major restructuring at Union Village, which Believers referred to as the "great move." They dissolved the South Family, created a new family at the West Branch, and removed the East House Family to the North Lot. Finally, they created an entirely new family at the old East House Family site. This new East Family was composed mainly of children, with a few older Believers placed in authority.[5] Abijah Alley was given a second chance and installed as first elder, with Samuel Parkhurst as his second. They were given the particularly sensitive job of ministering to young and impressionable members of the community, many of whom were entering adolescence.[6] Alley was thirty-six at the time of his appointment. It was around this time that he began to have visions and to share them without reservation with those under his spiritual care.

Beginning that autumn, Abijah Alley's years of frustration—sexual and hierarchical—erupted in dreams and what Alley, from his new position of authority, claimed were divine revelations. The extant records of his dreams and visions are some of the most explicitly sexual texts found among Shaker manuscript records. One such account, titled "A Vision or imagination of Ab Ally which he told to some of the sisters," relates:

> He was surrounded in his dream by a number of women (They seem to be church sisters) who got to picking & fingering about his posteriors as he supposed to execute the passions of nature but that he stood firm against all their excitements at length one of an enormous size (as big as a chimney and prodigiously swelled) approached him, & seemed to be intent on forcing him to violate his faith took him by the privates in the struggle to maintain his innocence he awoke... the monstrous woman was Elderess Malinda [Watts] swelled with the blood of the saints, that she appeared a dark yellowish colour & in her aspect resembled a huge serpent.[7]

Malinda Watts had been eldress of the former East House, the young Believers' order, where Alley probably lived during his first years at Union Village.

Brother Joseph Worley recorded another version of this dream, told in this instance to a young sister.

> I [Abijah] thought I was in heaven (it must have been a turkey buzzard heaven) and their was an host of women met me at the threshold of the door, and began to solicit me to join giblets with them or have to do with them in such a manner as would pregnate them with a SPIRITUAL CHILD, but I refused them then there was one presented her self before me as big [as] a chimney, and insisted on having the act performed I refused her, she acted like she was a going to commit rape on me when she reached out her hand and caught me by the PENIS, and was drawing me up to action, at this I awoke.[8]

Here, Eldress Malinda is not named, but the desire for procreation to bring forth a spiritual child is attributed to the sisterhood in general, when, in fact, it belonged entirely to Abijah Alley. His later justification for sharing these lewd dreams with his young Shaker family was that fellow elder James Smith taught him that if he was "defiled by filthy dreams or other involuntary attacks of the flesh to release himself by pouring it out on the family in meeting."[9] This was doubly damning in the eyes of the elders, who eventually investigated Alley, since he claimed that his behavior was the sanctioned practice of the church.

Alley's disturbing behavior came to the attention of the ministry and other elders, including Richard McNemar, at Union Village in mid-November of 1828.[10] It was then that they discovered that Alley was nursing a long list of grudges against the leadership. A trial was convened, and Alley enumerated accusations against fellow Believers, including blasphemy, tyranny, assault and battery, injustice, cruelty, robbery, and murder—the murder victim in question being Alley's soul. Alley claimed that before joining the Shakers, he "had acquired the keys of the kingdom of heaven ... was cleaned & purified from all lust—was perfectly dead to sin & alive to God conversed freely with angels, was commissioned by the Almighty to set up his kingdom on earth & had in his possession the foundation stone which he was instructed by an angel from heaven to lay among the Shakers as the ground work of the latter day temple."[11]

Alley also claimed that his former elder John Woods had abused him and filled him full of lust. This continued when he was subject to Elder David Spinning and Eldress Malinda Watts. After Spinning judged Alley incompetent by Spinning and moved him from the North Lot to the West Lot, Alley claimed Spinning and Watts metaphorically "cut his throat from ear to ear," resulting in the diminution of his spiritual powers. Shaker leaders, although astonished at these claims, agreed to arbitrate Alley's case on the condition that Alley would withdraw "the charge of murder exhibited against those persons as it lacked proof & forgiving all other offences on gospel principles." Alley declared that he held nothing personally against any of the Shakers, but he did begrudge "that spirit which had exercised all those reputed cruelties on him, & that he never would be satisfied or feel released till that spirit was put down."[12]

Alley's visions certainly cast doubt on his faith in the spiritual authority of the ministry and elders. In one of them, he saw western Shaker founder Father David Darrow "in hell, not eternal hell, but bound under torment for his cruelty and oppression." However, Alley asserted that "if Father David had been the means of souls perishing he would have to suffer for it until all such were raised again to life." Even when confronted by the ministry, Alley maintained his competing claim for spiritual primacy, contending that "the power of salvation was not with the Church but committed to him [Alley], & that the whole order had to come down & acknowledge his gift."[13] With these words, the trial recessed and the ministry convened a panel of seven members to reason with Alley and attempt to dissuade him of his convictions. Alley, however, refused to recant. Accordingly, the ministry relieved Alley of authority at the West Lot on November 27, 1828, and replaced him with someone who had "faith in subjection to a lead." The Shakers were charitable, allowing him to remain among them as a common member provided he stop disseminating his incendiary visions and revelations. Alley agreed, but shortly thereafter he was found to have returned to his unsanctioned preaching.[14]

Richard McNemar viewed Alley as someone who was always seeking popularity and a way to ingratiate himself with young members, especially the sisters. McNemar described him thus, "He laid himself open to the young people male & female to hear their secrets & their sentiments gathered their burdens on to him ... he opened in order those stirrings of nature that were excited by his freedoms among young females." The tumult caused by Alley's behavior is borne out by a staggering statistic. Between September 2, 1828, and April 2, 1829, when Alley finally left the Shakers, twenty-four Believers between the ages of seventeen and thirty-four left Union Village. This was a crippling loss of young members for the celibate community. Many of these apostates were the children of those who had been converted in 1805 and immediately thereafter. Among them were Archibald Houston and Patience Spinning, son and daughter, respectively, of leading western Shakers Matthew Houston and David Spinning. Most galling was the defection of McNemar's son and namesake, Richard McNemar Jr. on October 27, 1828.[15]

While still at Pleasant Hill, McNemar had written his twenty-three-year-old son Richard Jr. regarding his friend and fellow Shaker, Aquila Massie Bolton. Addressing his son as "Brother Richard," McNemar enclosed in his letter a long series of questions about Swedenborgianism directed to Bolton. Sandra Soule has shown in her biography of Bolton that he was a contentious, self-confident religious seeker who, like McNemar, had a penchant for expressing himself in poetic verse. If ever two men were destined to clash, it was McNemar and Bolton. Bolton, born in 1773, was three years younger than McNemar. He was raised a Quaker, but through the years he was also an atheist, a deist, an Owenite, and a Swedenborgian. He joined the Shakers at Union Village in the summer of 1826, fresh from the failure of the Robert Owen–inspired community at Yellow Springs, Ohio—a venture that included many Cincinnati Swedenborgians.[16]

Bolton was an enthusiastic convert to Shakerism and even published a lengthy pro-Shaker poem titled *The Whore of Babylon Unmasked*.[17] While McNemar appreciated Bolton's versifying and his ardent promotion of Shakerism, Bolton's belief that Swedenborgianism and Shakerism were compatible faiths caused McNemar serious concern. Bolton became a proponent of Swedish mystic Emanuel Swedenborg (1668–1772) while a Pittsburgh resident during the 1810s. Swedenborg, like the Shakers, believed that the second coming of Christ had occurred, not in person but through his word. He also believed that he had been chosen to reveal new doctrines to humankind that would lead to the establishment of the New Church, or New Jerusalem. Swedenborg professed to communicate with angels and wrote more than forty volumes of inspired teachings. Although Bolton saw many similarities between the two creeds, Shakerism would not and could not work in parallel with a competing faith. Here was another instance of the type of hybridization of Shakerism that Father David Darrow warned against.[18]

In his letter to his son, McNemar attacked Emanuel Swedenborg's pretensions of being a prophet, stating that the Bible was complete and no additional scripture was needed. McNemar asserted that people like George Fox, John Wesley, or James and Jane Wardley were prophets, not Swedenborg, who McNemar judged to have been "a delicate scribe snug'd up in his study room & with his pen investigating disputed points of theology & confirming his opinions by a kind of evidence that none could realize but himself!" Clearly threatened by his son's interest in Swedenborgianism, McNemar asked, "Did Mother, labor, suffer or run in partnership with Swedenburg?" The answer was no, therefore "both could not be equally authorised to open & teach the only way of God." Despite his concern about the infiltration of Swedenborg's doctrines, McNemar opined, "As the gospel has nothing to hope from the writings of Swedenburg so it has nothing to fear."[19] Little did he know that seven months after he penned that letter, his son and namesake would apostatize and become a "receiver of the doctrines" of the Swedenborgian church in nearby Urbana, Ohio. McNemar's initial tangle with Bolton in 1828 was only the beginning of their struggle.[20]

To make matters worse, Abijah Alley found a kindred spirit in Bolton. Bolton taught the evening school at Union Village, where he was able to share his religious ideas with many impressionable young people. Before long, Alley and Bolton were holding meetings where open rebellion against the ministry was discussed. Despite all the trouble Alley caused, his removal from eldership in November, and his return to disseminating his self-deifying doctrine, it appears that in December 1828, he was appointed to the eldership of the East House. This speaks to the disorganized leadership at Union Village and also to the probable lack of experienced men available to serve as elders.

At the East House, Alley met William Hewitt.[21] Alley was not the only Shaker beset by disturbing dreams. McNemar recorded that Hewitt had been "grevously troubled in his sleep with some invisible demon who would load him with distress & force him to vent the most alarming cries & vociferations on such subjects as suited the invisible genius. Which strange impulse got so habitual that they followed him into his wakeful hours & held him almost continually in distress."[22] Hewitt confided his visionary and spiritual torments to his elder—Abijah Alley—and, according to McNemar, the pair from then on "were mutually devoted to dreaming & construing & mounting figures & allegories to suit the times & in some way to bring about a revolution in which they would... stand as first pillars & bring the whole order of the church on to ground that suited their fancy."²³

McNemar and Matthew Houston questioned Hewitt on Monday, December 15, 1828, to discern whose visions came first, Hewitt's or Alley's. Hewitt claimed that he had been the first to pass into the spiritual world and converse with Father David Darrow. According to Hewitt, and echoing Alley's earlier dreams, since his decease Father David had been laboring unsuccessfully in the spirit world for the redemption of those who, through no fault of their own, had not been saved. Father David revealed to Hewitt that this was the reason for the absence of his spirit at Union Village. Hewitt further claimed that Father David had sent him to Union Village to open this work of salvation in the church, but that this calling had not been successful until Hewitt had opened the gift through Abijah Alley. Hewitt claimed, "After Alley had received the gift the angels flocked around him & surrounded him & if he was rejected the consequence would be dreadful."²⁴ McNemar and Houston confirmed to Hewitt that he was first in prophecy and asked him to commit to writing much of what he had told them, in a likely attempt to trick him into giving them written evidence of the pair's spiritual malfeasance. Instead of fulfilling this request, he consulted with Alley and delivered this devastating statement to a deacon that same afternoon.

> This is the will of god and unto me concirning the church that all rule and athority shall be committed unto the son. that god may be all in all concirning gifts this is what I feel that Father Richard should free himself of all burden and all rule and authority and lay it on Elder Solimon as a son for the redemption of the fathers and Father Mathew Houston in like manner to laydown all rule and authority and to release himself from all burdens through Father Richard Mcne[m]ar to E Solman And Elder David in like manner through Father Mathew and so one through the hole order By honestly opening acording to the above metioned order strictly the fathers shall be redeemed from all blame or fault This is the gift of god to me other wise judgment without marcy Wiliam Hewitt
> And if Elder Solimon finds himself unable to bare the in[i]quities of the fathers and the people let him aply to abijah Alley who holds the gift of a son Wiliam Hewitt²⁵

Alley and Hewitt were attempting to subvert the entire leadership structure of Union Village, living and dead, and were recommending Alley as a purgative to the "iniquities of the fathers."²⁶

Early the next morning, Alley came to McNemar's workshop and engaged him in a two-hour conversation about Hewitt's message, which was apparently in Alley's handwriting. Alley explained that he had taken it down verbatim as Hewitt spoke the words given by revelation, noting also that Samuel Parkhurst was present as a witness. Alley demanded that "the fathers were to come down to a level with the children & all rule & authority to cease for ever, to have no more preaching, but to let the spirit speak by the children that Elder Solomon must come down out of the meeting house & live in one of the families on a levil with the fathers & their bear the iniquities of all." He declared that he had no faith in the present salvation offered by Shakerism and that Elder Solomon was a "soul murderer." McNemar rebutted Alley's egalitarian notions and stated that if he continued in this line, "he would presently be raving thro the streets & round the buildings like W[illia]m Scales [a noted apostate and anti-Shaker activist of the late eighteenth century]."[27]

The next confrontation came on Friday, December 19, when the elders assembled and examined Alley, Hewitt, and Parkhurst. McNemar called them the "three disciples" in his journal. Their beliefs centered on their assertion that Solomon King was a soul murderer. Practically speaking, this "murder" was effected through the reawakening of lust within Abijah Alley—a lust he claimed to have laid to rest before becoming a Shaker. Alley's new revelations had once again freed him from lust, but only through his complete liberty of conscience to do and say as he pleased without subjection to any authority among the Shakers. Alley claimed, "that which was ordained to life [the spiritual rebirth of converting to Shakerism] I found to be unto death it deceived me & thereby slew me." McNemar wrote, "This slaying the silly creature calls murder & charges it to John Woods and others that had the rule over him."[28]

McNemar wrote to Alley on December 20 and tried to appeal to any lingering sense of loyalty he might have to the Shaker Church, telling him, "I never till quite lately doubted your having a lot of heirship in the gospel." However, it was now plain to McNemar that Alley was attempting to poison his fellow young Believers against the old Believers and to "flat the whole order, & yourself take the whole government on your shoulders."[29] As if to prove McNemar's point, on Sunday, December 21, William Hewitt revealed that he had "hardened his conscience against all reproof from the elders because the effect of reproof was to make him feel unhappy." Alley made an even more stunning claim that God had murdered Jesus Christ, was condemned for it and therefore gave up all power of judgment to his son, who bore God's iniquity and redeemed God. Alley believed that his situation was parallel with the Shaker hierarchy and that the Shaker fathers (McNemar, Houston, King) had murdered him and that he would now lead them to redemption. According to Alley, the Shakers could not achieve redemption until "all power was given [to Alley] & he was exalted as a prince & a savior." The previous day, Alley had heightened tensions with the Shakers by traveling into nearby Lebanon, Ohio, and meeting with five apostates bent on causing difficulties for Union Village.[30]

At some point on Sunday, December 21, Samuel Parkhurst delivered two private letters to Richard McNemar. These letters justified Parkhurst's allegiance to Alley and also expressed his disappointment in the leadership of McNemar and his cohorts. Parkhurst explained that a number of Believers at the East House (a family of which Alley was briefly elder) had received a new gift of salvation that had brought them back to "the Obedience of that Gospel taught by our first Parents" and gave them great "freedom of soul." They were upset that men such as McNemar, Houston, and King disapproved, stating it "seemed to us like a Dagger in our Bowels thrust in by the Draggon." They blamed the elders for "using their exersions to crush the work & Distroy the Manchild as soon as he is Born." Parkhurst then demurred, using the Shakers' own theology to justify the actions of Alley and company in rejecting the authority of the elders: "But shall I presume to Teach my Elders[?] nay I consider this quite unnessary for they have Taught us from the Beginning that the work of God is a Levveling work and that every knee shall bow to the God & Tongue Confess wherefore any Spirit that goes to Destroy this whether by word or Deed I can not acknowledge to be of God."[31]

An uneasy week passed at Union Village before Alley fulfilled the elders' request for a written statement of his charges against them. In a long and rambling discourse, filled with religious allegory, Alley presented himself as deluded and forsaken by the Shaker Church. Evoking Christian martyrs, he asserted that in response to his charges of injustice, the church had "set her great lions on me to tear me to pieces." Alley rejoiced in his subsequent escape from the spiritual subjection of the church and boasted, "I have shown both her & her priests their drunkenness, murder, & hardness & oppression." Alley compared himself to Balaam's ass, stating that the Shakers had "rode me these fifteen years"[32] and that despite their cruelties and abuse, he was now trying to open their eyes to their own madness—and to the new way of salvation he offered them. Most heinously, he charged that the elders had slain innocent souls and had become drunk with their blood.

Richard McNemar was once again at the center of conflict. It is clear from his journal that he believed it was his duty to "labor" with Alley, Hewitt, and Parkhurst and make every effort to turn them from error and thereby save their souls. This would in conjunction save the souls of the many young Believers under their influence. McNemar could only lament that his son and namesake was already lost.

Failing to persuade Alley to attend a face-to-face meeting, the elders responded in writing two days later. They acknowledged that Alley had been a promising young Believer, "though whimsical, self conceited, & stiff willed in your natural creation." His disappointment in being removed as elder of the large family at the North Lot was recognized, but the elders charged him with misleading young Believers, "ready to catch at occasions of trial against their leads—fond of novelty, thirsting for knowledge, gaiety, pleasure & every forbidden freedom suited to the passions of a youthful mind." The elders blamed the disarray at Union Village following the death of Father David Darrow in 1825 and the influx of West Union Believers for the lack of oversight that allowed Alley to remain as elder at the North Lot Family for so long. This leadership failure accounted for the "strange & almost unaccountable dispensation" that placed Alley once again as elder at the East House. It was at that point, they charged, that Alley knew that "now or never was your time to bring all your forces to bear on the church, to head a party, put down the whole order & place your petty self at the helm of affairs." The letter then repeated the multitude of Alley's offenses against the Church, including poisoning minds against the elders and meeting with apostates in Lebanon. Remarkably, it ended with an olive branch, a final offer to Alley that, should he repent and recant and cease his treasonous ministrations to the young, he could remain with the community. Additionally, he was required to attend public and family worship meetings, but as a silent observer only. He was not to participate until instructed to do so again by the elders. The letter closed, "If you comply with this reasonable request well & good, if not prepare for what follows."[33]

McNemar followed up with a personal letter, written in the legalistic style he favored in disputation. He posed six questions to Alley, one of which was "Who taught you to spend so much of your time in smoking and chating with sisters?" He also challenged Alley to prove his accusation that McNemar himself was personally culpable for the problems at Union Village. McNemar implored Alley to erase the seditious thoughts from his mind and learn the gifts of Father David Darrow, gifts he had obviously either forgotten or never learned in the first place. And so things stood as 1828 came to a close.[34]

The uneasy push and pull continued through January 1829 as the elders labored to save Alley and his followers. He refused to admit that his vision of a reformed Union Village with himself as its head would never be realized and that his life as a Shaker was at an end. After all, the "leveling" demanded by the "three disciples" was not a plan for equality. Alley himself claimed that Elder

David Darrow had communicated to him from the spirit world that Alley was to be the "lead."

During the Saturday evening meeting on January 10, 1829, it was announced that Alley would not be allowed to unite in the worship, as "it was generally known that he had separated himself and did not profess to hold and relation to the body." Alley reacted physically to this declaration, and "with a violent spring he reared & stomped with both feet," an act McNemar said "put it out of all reasonable dispute where the dragon spirit had its seat." Alley declared that he would worship God where he chose. Alley's follower Samuel Parkhurst declared that if Alley could not unite in worship, then neither would he. After the commotion subsided, one hymn was sung, and the meeting was quickly dismissed.[35]

The incident at the meeting prompted the elders to draft a statement of the charges against Alley to be read the following afternoon at the Sabbath meeting. In their view, the troubles following the dissolution of West Union, the restructuring of families at Union Village in August 1828, and the failure of Shaker leadership to address the concerns of young Believers led Alley to claim "special revelation & commission from God, and under this pretext to ingratiate himself into the confidence of a number of respectable characters even elders not excepted." The elders told the assembled multitude that Alley said "that he saw [Father David] in hell &c. suffering for his tyrannical government over the people: and saying moreover that the evil of so many going off was chargeable to the lead, & that the foundation was corrupt." The Believers were told that although Alley believed in spiritual resurrection through Christ and Mother Ann, he refused to recognize the gift of any subsequent Shaker leader, instead claiming that the pathway to salvation was reopened through him by the angels who ministered to him. Alley believed himself to be the first-born son of Mother Ann, and he denied the authority of any extant Shaker government. He demanded that founding western Shaker converts and elders Richard McNemar, Matthew Houston, and David Spinning renounce their authority and confess their iniquities to Elder Solomon King, who would then finally cede all spiritual authority to Alley.[36] (Unbeknownst to the gathered multitude, Malcham Worley, who had become a recluse since the death of Father David Darrow, secretly harbored similar theological sentiments.)

The members probably wondered why such behavior was tolerated for so long. The elders explained that they had labored with Alley in a spirit of charity and forbearance in case he could be brought back into gospel union. However, they had concluded that, since Alley himself maintained that he wanted no connection with the church as it existed, they would "take him at his word to seal his own deliberate choice—& loose him and let him go." Members were warned to avoid Alley, "lest by indulging either an undue sympathy for the man or a curiosity to hear his lectures you may lose your union bring yourselves into trouble & finally land in the same predicament." Alley, who was present at the reading, interrupted and attempted to contradict certain statements, but he was denied a chance to speak since he had voluntarily withdrawn from the society. And, if his behavior was not proof enough of his errors, the membership was invited to examine Alley's writings, a tactic that demonstrates some measure of renewed confidence among Shaker leaders.[37]

The next morning, Alley was relieved of work duties and asked to state in writing his objections to the previous day's statements by the elders. He refused and went to work in defiance of the Shaker leadership. On Tuesday, January 13, he informed the elders that he would appeal directly to the ministry at New Lebanon, New York, through a written memorial that Aquila Massie Bolton would prepare for him. Alley was told that this would have no effect, as the New Lebanon Ministry would not countenance such a memorial from a nonmember. McNemar went to the West Brick House that day and met with Bolton while Alley was present. Bolton sought their counsel about whether or not he should write Alley's requested memorial. He was told to use his own faith and judgment. Bolton decided to write for Alley.[38]

The pressure was becoming too much for Alley's accomplice, William Hewitt. On Sunday, January 18, Hewitt came to McNemar's room without an appointment and informed McNemar that he could no longer remain at Union Village or hold any union with Believers, and that he was leaving the next morning. Hewitt alluded to his continual physical and emotional problems, saying they had impaired his constitution and made him a burden to those around him. When McNemar offered him one last chance to save his soul, Hewitt replied that "he had not much soul any how and that of but little value, that his principle object at present was to get off from those spirits which continually tormented him." McNemar asked Hewitt if he thought Alley would leave with him. Hewitt said no, that Alley would remain. Hewitt "bitterly regretted that he had staid so long & involved himself in such difficulties," retracted his negative statements about the Shaker leadership, and lamented the fact that he was viewed as insane by the general membership due to his afflictions and vociferations. He did not recant any of the visionary messages that had been delivered to Abijah Alley through him and maintained that he had only opened his mind to Alley as his elder and communicated what came through. McNemar had to accept Hewitt's justification, as it validated the Shaker hierarchy. The men conversed for two more hours, during which time they explored the characteristics and judgments of individual Shaker leaders at Union Village. Throughout this time, McNemar read hymns to bring Hewitt's mind back into union with the Shakers, but his attempts were in vain. Hewitt departed quietly the next morning at nine, having requested that McNemar publish his confession.[39]

McNemar arose early on Friday morning, January 23, and by candlelight wrote in his journal, once again recapitulating Alley's actions and the subsequent justification for his removal from the Shakers. It seems the Shakers' tolerance for characters such as Alley had yet further limits, as McNemar allowed for a possible scenario whereby, with the approval of the deacon in Alley's family, Alley might stay and continue "the free exercise of his self created gifts & assumed authorities." However, should the deacon eventually find this inconvenient, Alley could then be farmed out, with the Shakers paying for his boarding, washing, and lodging. Alley was moved to the South House of the community, and in his journal, McNemar began referring to him as "Double Eyes," a theme he subsequently developed in a lengthy rhetorical poetic dialog between himself and Alley.[40]

On Friday, January 30, the community was addressed at the evening meeting concerning Abijah Alley—who had yet to leave Union Village. The Believers were told that Alley should settle his accounts at the office and move on, place himself under the care of the physician if he was insane, or remain among them as a lay member, but that he could not continue to attempt to unite in worship as a church member unless he opened his mind again and recanted. The question was posed, "How can we minister to such a character who ... declares that there is no salvation in the body but that we are goats, dragons, & every base character that the scriptures can furnish." Alley was warned that it was "insufferable to have him withdraw from his own sex with whom he ought to keep his union & cuddle about among the sisters."[41] This improper physical affection for the opposite sex remained a key aspect of Alley's conflict with Shaker leaders.

On Saturday morning, the church convened a committee of four brethren to examine Alley's case a final time. He demanded that two witnesses of his own choice be present. His request was denied, as the matter at hand was to simply establish whether Alley acknowledged the authority of the present Shaker elders. Alley refused to answer and retreated from the village into the nearby woods.[42]

On the Sabbath, February 1, William Hewitt's confession was read at the meeting. That night, Alley confided to Elder Matthew Houston that he wanted to open his mind, which he did the next morning. He claimed to feel like an idiot and asserted that young people had sought him out for his advice and that by challenging the elders, he was only trying to express the concerns of the young members and mollify them to prevent apostasy. He maintained that his true faith had always been with the elders and Church. In the afternoon, he confessed to Houston and McNemar that although he had gained some control of his lust, "he did not pretend to be clear of the flesh—that he was nothing but a man nor never expected to be any thing more in this life." Alley shared more of his dreams and visions and claimed he was induced to act by an "invisible agent" over which he had no control. As for the damage he had done to the church, Alley intimated that he did have the power to turn the people against the elders, but he felt he had caused no evil effect among the membership. He revealed to McNemar and Houston that he had made inquiries of S. M. (Samuel C. Manning) about purchasing a piece of land where he could resettle himself and his followers, which included a number of sisters. However, he maintained that he would bear his cross against the flesh forever, even if he left the Shakers. Alley closed by stating that he expected he and his followers would eventually leave unless his plan for a more "republican" form of government was adopted. He said that if a majority of elders and members asked him to go, he would. McNemar and Houston again asked Alley to respect the request not to unite in worship—which Alley refused, effectively ending the meeting.[43]

Things remained at a standstill through February. On March 20, Richard McNemar questioned Manning about Alley's plans, and Manning declared that he had spoken to some apostates in Lebanon about Alley's preaching and that they considered him "crazy." Manning himself stated that he thought Alley was "deranged" and that "he seemed to be greatly exercised in dreams & visions even surpassing Swedenburg." Alley had also shared with Manning his pretensions to being the third appearance of Christ.[44]

On March 28, 1829, Richard McNemar penned a final, rhetorical indictment of Alley in his journal. Although addressed to Alley, it is unclear if a copy was actually given to him. In it, McNemar gave Alley the benefit of the doubt about his professed good intentions for saving souls but required him to admit he was "actuated by a false spirit." McNemar bluntly asked him: "What moved you to reject the ministry the whole order of the church to denounce the whole order of Believers on earth to testify an entire falling away after the decease of first Mother, to traduce the church covenant as a yanky invention & trample any thing sacred underfoot to make way for a 3d appearing of Christ which was to be manifested in your own person?" McNemar charged Alley with wishing to lure good Believers away, consorting with apostates, and announcing his heaven-granted authority to "revive the long lost spirit of Jesus and Mother Ann" in order to "humble the Elders & purge out of them that spirit which you say murdered your soul." McNemar warned Alley that as long as evil remained in the church, there was a gift to search it out, and he compared the church to a lion, "mild to the faithful innocent Believer... but a fierce lion to tear in pieces the rebellious."[45]

McNemar's words seemed to resonate with Alley. On March 30, he wrote a letter to McNemar conceding that his "zeal was not according to knowledge" and that he would give McNemar his "word & honor that from henceforth I will do my endeavors to reconcile myself to the present order & administration as an example to others who may have been turned aside thro my influence." Alley begged a privilege to stay on the grounds of Union Village. The following day, he penned another letter to the elders offering to make a public recantation of all the sentiments he had preached about the Shaker Church and elders being the dragon's tail or the end—devoid of salvation. It does not seem that the elders responded to Alley's mea culpa. In a final note, Alley acknowledged the fairness of the elders in their dealings with him and the righteousness of their judgment. He gave up all hope of reconciliation or of another privilege at Union Village and closed his note by stating, "[I] know that I have no more place [on the] ground at present."[46] Following his journal entry recording these events, McNemar wrote the text of the hymn "The False Prophet," thus marking the end of the Alley controversy.[47]

After an agonizing period of nearly five months during which the patient Shaker leadership had been severely tested and their authority compromised in the eyes of many, Alley finally departed. On March 31, he walked to the Trustees' Office and announced his intention to withdraw from the Shaker society. He then visited the elders and told them of his decision, whereupon he was escorted back to the office to make his final settlement. He ultimately left Union Village on April 2, 1829.[48] At the Sunday, April 12, meeting, McNemar gave a sermon that attempted to put a period on the saga of Abijah Alley. He opened by comparing Alley to the Apostle Paul's companion Demas, who apostatized, "having loved this present world." McNemar then recounted the whole saga chronologically, beginning with the ministry's first knowledge of the "strange notions which it was said he recd in dreams and visions," beginning in November 1828.[49] He told of how Alley regarded the Shaker Church as being under the power of the dragon and that the brethren and sisters of the East House must rise up and reclaim it in the name of the Christ Spirit. Despite Alley's best efforts, the Shaker leadership ultimately prevailed, although the ordeal badly damaged the community.

Since the death of Father David Darrow, Richard McNemar's life had been consumed with tribulation and conflict. Following the death of his brother-in-law John Dunlavy, he had overseen the dissolution of the West Union community. Directly from there, he became embroiled with apostate John Whitbey, quelling rebellion, and managing legal troubles at Pleasant Hill. Then he confronted the same spirit of rebellion at Union Village, battling Abijah Alley and Aquila Massie Bolton but losing his son and namesake in the arduous process. If anyone needed a vacation, it was Richard McNemar. The New Lebanon Ministry had concluded that Mother Lucy Smith (formerly of Pleasant Hill) should leave her exile at Union Village and return to her original home community at New Lebanon. She wept when she received the news. Due to her "advanced age & rather feeble health," the Union Village Ministry assigned McNemar the task of accompanying the sixty-five-year-old matriarch on the journey. At fifty-nine, and after twenty-four years of devoted service to the cause of Shakerism, McNemar would finally get to see New Lebanon and the other eastern communities formed in the wake of Mother Ann's ministry. While the mission of bringing Mother Lucy away from the West was bittersweet, it afforded McNemar an opportunity for travel in the broader Shaker world that most Believers never got. In prior correspondence, he had alluded to his wish for a "privilege" to travel to the East and have "a personal interview with those whose names & characters have been very endearing." He received the news that he would travel on May 20, 1829. It certainly must have brightened his spirit after a very difficult three years. In his journal, he wrote in Latin, "Domine parato me pro tam magnum opus," which means "Lord, prepare me for such a great task!"[50]

SEVENTEEN

ELEAZAR GOES EAST

AT 5 A.M. ON TUESDAY, June 9, 1829, Richard McNemar left Union Village, embarking on one of the greatest adventures in his already adventure-filled life. He was accompanied by Mother Lucy Smith, Prudence Morrell (the daughter of his former missionary companion Calvin Morrell), and ministry eldress Rachel Johnson. Mother Lucy specifically requested Johnson for a traveling companion since she had nursed her through many health crises. Teamsters Hiram Kimball and William Runyon of Pleasant Hill were tasked with conveying the party to North Union. They traveled through Ohio by way of Greenfield, Chillicothe, Kingston, Lancaster, and Newark, where they boarded at "an elegant well furnished brick house." After resting a sick horse, they traveled on, heading north through Coshocton, where they were pestered by a sixty-seven-year-old "babbling drunkard."[1]

On Tuesday, June 16, they nearly met with disaster when their wagon overturned while ascending a rough road along a bluff above the nascent Ohio Canal. Only the weight of McNemar's "green box," packed with books to distribute to the eastern Believers, prevented the wagon from plunging into the ravine. A company of canal diggers helped right the wagon, and the party proceeded, arriving at Zoar that evening. The German Separatist community at Zoar was founded in 1817. They had interacted with the Shakers many times over the years, even nursing a convalescent Issachar Bates back to health for forty-seven excruciating days in 1824. McNemar and company were likewise "kindly received & hospitably treated." From there, they traveled along the construction zone of the canal bed and locks until they reached Cleveland by the weekend. Unfortunately, there is no information on the rest of their outbound journey in McNemar's extant journals.[2]

The route called for a stop at North Union on the shores of Lake Erie. From there, the Believers would either take a steamship from Cleveland to Buffalo or continue overland, depending on "the timidity of sister Lucy in going on the Lake."[3] They almost certainly took the Erie Canal starting at Buffalo and do not seem to have stopped at the recently gathered Shaker community at Sodus Bay. The party arrived at Watervliet, New York, on Friday, July 3, 1829, having disembarked at Schenectady at 1 a.m. that morning. McNemar went ahead to get wagons to bring the sisters and their baggage, and all arrived at the community's Trustees' Office at 6:30 a.m. The journey had taken twenty-five days. Freegift Wells, youngest brother of McNemar's correspondent Seth Youngs Wells, carried news of their arrival to the New Lebanon Ministry that same morning.[4]

Richard McNemar must have been extremely excited to find himself at Watervliet, the site of Mother Ann's original settlement and the location of her grave. He soon met—for the first time in the flesh—men who had succeeded the original Shaker missionaries as his theological mentors, such as Seth Youngs Wells and Calvin Green. A year before embarking on this journey, when the idea was only a fantasy, McNemar wrote to Green and Wells with self-deprecation, "I recollect that I was born & raised in the back woods & probably I had best keep somewhere on the frontier where I will pass for a midling good fellow, & not think of pushing myself into company where mortification would necessarily result from a display of my ignorance."[5] Now, however, he found himself in the spiritual heart of Shakerdom, and his tour of the East was just beginning.

McNemar preached at the public meeting in the Watervliet meetinghouse on July 5. This was likely his first public oration east of the Appalachians, though his fame as a preacher was known far and wide. The next day, he traveled with Brother David Hawkins to New Lebanon. As he approached the center of spiritual union for Shakers, McNemar must have thought of Mother Lucy Wright, who had died in 1821. He had never met her in person, but his pseudonym, Eleazar Wright, was taken partly in her honor. As Calvin Green and Seth Youngs Wells had written him, his new name was "received by becoming the son of a good and gracious Mother."[6] McNemar saw the 1824 Second Meetinghouse, surmounted by a marvelous curved roof that contained the largest Shaker worship space anywhere. He would have marveled at the capacious 1788 Church Family Dwelling, where more than one hundred faithful Believers of the highest spiritual rank lived. Apart from drinking in the architectural and technological wonders; wandering the well-tended fields, gardens, orchards, and farmyards; and sharing in the union of the brethren and sisters at New Lebanon, McNemar also had serious work to do.

During his stay at New Lebanon, he had a very important conference with the ministry, which then comprised elders Ebenezer Bishop and Rufus Bishop and eldresses Ruth Landon and Asenath Clark. They wanted McNemar's opinion on a number of pressing issues regarding the leadership, or the lack thereof, in the western communities. The difficulties following Father David Darrow's death were a particular point of concern. McNemar explained events in such a way as to "exculpate all concerned on the principle that all were conscientious & thought they were acting for the best." Despite this, the ministry did not like how the Union Village Ministry had subjected the elders there to criticism by the general membership, thus "flatting them in the esteem of the people." In his journal, McNemar admitted, "This was a knotty point on which I felt much on the reserve." The ministry closely questioned McNemar on the present state of the Union Village Ministry and their relationship with their followers. They were somewhat inclined to retain Eldress Rachel Johnson in the East, as they questioned her leadership abilities. They had heard from other sources that she could not delegate, thereby marginalizing other sisters, and that she was also too free with "the use of ardent spirits in the nursing line." McNemar strongly advised against removing Johnson, stating that if "such a change was made it must be gradual." The most important point to emerge from the conference was the need to renew the covenant at all of the Shaker communities. This was the first step "to lay a foundation for other regulations." This work of redrafting and renewing covenants throughout the western Shaker communities would become McNemar's primary task on his return to the West.[7]

On July 10, ministry elder Rufus Bishop accompanied McNemar on a tour to New Lebanon's East, or "Hill," Family, situated above the Church Family over the Massachusetts state line. The next day, they went to the Hancock, Massachusetts, community where McNemar likely met with natural brothers Elder Nathaniel Deming and William Deming. He had never met Nathaniel but had corresponded with him on important matters. McNemar had last seen William in Ohio in 1810; now he was in the throes of planning and building the Church Family Brick Dwelling, which was completed the next year. The famous Round Stone Barn, built just three years before in 1826, must have delighted McNemar's senses, as it far surpassed any Shaker agricultural structure in the western communities.[8] McNemar's journal for much of the trip, assuming he kept one, is presently unlocated, so much of his itinerary has to be reconstructed from the journals and letters of those he visited.

On Sunday, July 12, Richard McNemar penned a lengthy treatise for the benefit of the ministry on western Shaker perceptions of the covenant. This candid document, "Remarks on the Church Covenant of the United Society called Shakers," was surely prompted by the conference regarding issues in the western communities. It offers a concise overview of the westerners' views of the basis of the covenant and joint interest and how fundamental problems with it had been exposed by the turmoil at West Union, Pleasant Hill, and the poorly managed leadership transition at Union Village following David Darrow's death. McNemar admitted that "much was felt & but little said about renewing the covenant till I was sent to West Union." The problems he encountered there and later at Pleasant Hill brought the importance of revising and reconfirming the covenants at all of the western communities to the forefront of his attention.[9] McNemar gathered opinions about the covenant for the rest of his trip in preparation for the task of rewriting it. On Tuesday, July 14, McNemar left New Lebanon with his old friend Daniel Moseley, who had lived at Union Village from 1805 until 1812. They set out to visit the New England Shaker communities.[10] Twenty-four years after Youngs, Bates, and Meacham had converted him, McNemar had the honor of being the first western Shaker convert to see the communities east of New Lebanon.

McNemar and Moseley arrived at Canterbury, New Hampshire, on Tuesday, July 21. A special object of McNemar's visit there was to meet Father Job Bishop, the last living male Believer of that status in any community, east or west. Bishop was sixty-nine in 1829. He was originally from New Lebanon and had personally known Mother Ann Lee and the first parents. Bishop was sent as a Father to minister to converts at Canterbury and Enfield, New Hampshire, in 1792. Bishop was ill during McNemar's visit but met with him regardless. The two men spent the evening of Thursday, July 23, in deep conversation. The next day, McNemar recorded his impressions in his journal:

> The conversation last night with Father Job Bishop has turned the tide of my thoughts into the great deep of Chh government in a manner that induced a wish that my natural life might be taken away & my earthly tabernacle restored to the earth while under the care & protection of this venerable patriarch O Lord I have trouble & suffered affliction with thy people & gloried in it as a special privilege but in prospect of what may yet remain any soul recoils at the bitter draught & I am ready to cry out. Let this cup pass if possible. Nevertheless not my will but thine be done.[11]

Clearly, meeting Father Job was reaffirming and satisfying for McNemar, but his foreboding of the "great deep" that awaited him in renewing the western covenants was justified. The Canterbury Ministry hoped the conversation might "be a satisfaction to [McNemar] in future."[12] Nevertheless, McNemar understood the seriousness of the task before him.

McNemar was invited to speak at a meeting on Sunday, July 26, at Canterbury. He considerately wrote to the Canterbury Ministry, inquiring as to their customs when asking guests to preach, writing,

> it has been customary with me, whether at home or abroad, to receive some general instructions, at least, from the Ministry of the place, what to say & whereof to affirm. In fact, I have brought no doctrine or message from home to the people of this country, neither is it my feeling or wish to gratify the curiosity of the people who may wish to hear so remote a stranger or one who has made some noise among the orators of the day. Yet I am aware that it might be profitable on occasion of such visits for the stranger to say something in support of our faith & Testimony, for sake of union, & therefore some outline of the matter & manner of address from the angel of the church may be safe & profitable, at any rate, it would be very acceptable & alleviating to the feelings of—Eleazar[13]

Whether the ministry guided him or not is unknown, but on Sunday, July 26, McNemar "delivered a lengthy discourse upon the foundation principles of Shakerism." A large audience attended, excited by the novelty of hearing a western Shaker preach. He also sang a hymn for them:

> I never will leave the way of God
> While I have breath to breathe one word
> I never'll forsake the way of God
> The world I never will try it.
> I'll bear my cross I will be free
> Through time and in eternity
> For bound by death I never will be,
> There is power in Christ to defy it.
>
> This stanza we record as a key to the good brother's sincerity and devotion to the cause which he had espoused.[14]

The Canterbury Ministry reported to the New Lebanon Ministry that McNemar "seems to give great satisfaction to all to see and hear him speak." They also noted the gifts McNemar was given at Canterbury and Enfield for "union sake," including cloth, 120 dollars cash, a frock made especially for him, and gifts to pass along to Union Village Ministry members Solomon King and Rachel Johnson.[15] McNemar left Canterbury, traveling south with the Canterbury elders and Moseley to Harvard, Massachusetts, where he arrived on Tuesday, July 28. After stopping briefly for dinner, they left for Shirley, Harvard's sister community. They attended worship services there on Wednesday and toured the families, enduring heavy rain, thunder, and lightning, for the remainder of the week.[16]

McNemar and company returned to Harvard on July 31, and the bad weather continued. On Saturday, in the rain, they visited the stone marking the location where Father James Whittaker had been savagely whipped by an anti-Shaker mob on June 1, 1783. The next day, Sunday, August 2, McNemar preached at the Harvard meetinghouse. In his journal, Elder Joseph Hammond wrote, "A very Large number of spectators say between 4 + 5 hundred—+ a very full Assembly of Believers—Elder Eleazer has a very powerful Gift for the Spectators." Thirty-six Believers from Shirley were also in attendance. Following the meeting, everyone marched out of the meetinghouse and down the road to the Square House. The full text of McNemar's sermon survives, recorded by a listener.[17]

In his sermon, McNemar used the example of Jesus and his followers, despised by the Pharisees and great men in their day and therefore unworthy of serious consideration. He inquired rhetorically whether any of the great men of the present day had deigned to join the Shakers and then launched into a rather immodest answer using thinly veiled autobiography:

> You will understand by this time that I am a stranger in these parts—I belong in the State of Ohio. Well in that part of the country I am acquainted with a number of the rulers and the pharisees that have believed. There is one in particular with whom I have been acquainted according to the dispensation of Christianity was born and raised in a Christian manner brought up and educated according to the strictest rules and manner of the high church of England and when he arrived at the proper age chose a lot among the presbyterians and was a person qualified for usefulness in the church went through the degrees of literature necessary to introduce him a teacher in seminaries of education to train up pupils for the pulpit and also for the bar one that was believed to be a real convert a man who among all that was called Christianity was considered a true Christian and would pass muster among all the societies of religious people Congregationalists Baptists Quakers Methodists And I knew such a man who has admited the truth of this doctrine and openly acknowledged his belief that Christ has made his second appearing and that he has set up his kingdom among his people.
>
> But say you was he a ruler[?] I answer he was and had a seat in evry court belonging to the Jurisdiction from the common church session to the general assembly that was to make laws for the whole United States But say you I would see that man and hear him probably we would find him a fanatic surely he must be reft of his senses[?] What! a man that was reputed Christian! one

that was a teacher in the Seminaries of learning and a ruler among the people what could induce him [to] accept a religion such as this[?]

Well to release you a little I will just inform you that whoever has seen me has seen that man—And if you want to know what could induce him to lay off his clerical dignity and bow to such a testimony as this—renouncing the friendship of the world with all his wealth (be it much or little) if you want to know the reason of all this we shall be glad to take it out with you toe to toe out and out.[18]

McNemar then addressed the evidences of Christ's second appearing, noting that a chief objection to Shaker doctrine was Christ's failure to appear bodily, with demonstrable wounds and fanfares of trumpets. McNemar quoted Revelation 1:7, "Behold, he cometh with clouds." He asserted that the clouds in question were not atmospheric but rather clouds of witnesses, and he offered his personal testimony:

Have you heard of the extraordinary work of God in the western country called the Kentucky revival[?] perhaps some of you have read about it the subjects of that remarkable work were led to look for the second coming of Christ—who it was predicted should come in the clouds of heaven

How are clouds formed but by vapours that rise and collect to gather[?] just so the people in our part of the country were moved towards the latter end of the last century to come together as clouds hundreds and thousands Now if I should tell you that the voice that addresses you has been employed to address the multitudes as far as could be seen in every direction twenty or thirty thousand and a half a dozen orators to comfort the people a people all engaged for Christ to come come Lord Jesus come quickly you would think it looked like cloud sure enough hundreds and thousands flocking to the place of encampment carriages to be seen in almost every direction as far as the eye could extend.[19]

McNemar affirmed that the second coming of Christ was manifested in a female, Mother Ann Lee. Citing the literal Greek meaning of "Christ"—"anointed"—McNemar asserted that, although she was a woman, Mother Ann had received the same anointing as Jesus. And through her, the true cause of man's fall was revealed: sexual intercourse. According to McNemar, Mother Ann had "taken the fig covering from the very place for which it was first contrived so that mankind need be no longer in doubt as to what the act of transgression was." The only way to salvation, to restore humankind to their pre-fall Edenic state, was to take up the cross of celibacy. Finally, McNemar declared that to be a true Christian, one had to "forsake Father and Mother wife and children house and land and his own carnal life also."[20]

On Monday, August 3, McNemar and company spent much of the day at the Square House, where Mother Ann Lee had lived intermittently from 1781 to 1783. He must have been thrilled to see this legendary structure in person. In fact, a family at Union Village had been named in honor of this building where Mother Ann preached and oversaw tremendous growth among her followers. The party took leave of Harvard the next day, heading west toward New Lebanon. A letter from the Harvard Ministry to the New Lebanon Ministry called the visit "exceeding satisfactory" and complimented McNemar, saying that he had "been very persevereing and has acted the part of a good believer and we love him much."[21]

McNemar and Moseley returned to New Lebanon on August 6. On Saturday, August 15, McNemar and Rachel Johnson left for a tour of the Hancock Bishopric communities, visiting Hancock and Tyringham, Massachusetts, and Enfield, Connecticut. They returned to New Lebanon on August 26. To wrap up his momentous eastern tour, McNemar addressed up to seven hundred spectators at a public meeting at New Lebanon on August 30; unfortunately, the text of his remarks did not survive.

McNemar took leave of his brethren and sisters on September 5, traveling with Rachel Johnson to Watervliet, New York, to begin the journey home via the Erie Canal. They took the canal boat *St. Lawrence* at Schenectady and arrived the next day in Utica. The following day, they marveled at the salt works in Syracuse. On September 11, the party (including three Watervliet Shakers) left the canal at Lyons to visit the recently gathered community at Sodus Bay, where they tarried until resuming their travel on the fourteenth.[22]

Elder Matthew Houston had given McNemar advice about "bad manners" before his departure for the East. Perhaps disgust at traveling in such tight quarters with mostly non-Shakers aboard the *St. Lawrence* caused McNemar to reflect on his own personal habits. In a letter to Houston, penned aboard the canal boat, McNemar assured him that he had closely monitored his behavior. He admitted, however, that perhaps "a close observer of manners may on some occasion have detected me in the disagreeable practice of hocking. But I am not sensible of having indulged in that thing at any time in a manner calculated to disgust the most delicate feelings. It is true, in consequence of some slight colds, I have been troubled with Phlegm more or less, but when nature has solicited the necessary discharge I have usually retired from company to clear my pipes." On the positive side, McNemar had overcome his propensity for deep, gaping, sleepy yawns. He attributed this to the change of climate on his journey and boasted to Houston that he had "passed thro' every company that I have met with in perfect innocence."[23]

McNemar and Johnson reached Buffalo on Wednesday, September 16. The next morning, they shipped out for Cleveland on the steamboat *Niagara*. McNemar described his fellow travelers as "more than a hundred passengers of every description from gentlemen & ladies to beings nearly related to 4 footed grunters." McNemar helped Johnson get situated in a cabin, and since the weather was fair, opted for deck passage for himself. Shortly, however, a storm blew up, and large waves tossed the ship about, leaving ankle-deep water on the decks. McNemar and many other passengers began to get seasick, as he recounted colorfully to Seth Youngs Wells:

> But how about the sick stomach all this time? Dear O dear what shall I say! or how can I look back with composure at the ladies cabbin almost evacuated, & the bannisters round the deck receiving the impulse of their beating stomachs discharging over board what nature was found to exonerate, it was to be sure pitiful & distressing, but females, forsooth were not the only subjects of the epidemic, & as for myself no position that I could take, no excuse that I could adopt could possibly shield my pericranium from the effects of those agitations it is true I dismissed fear, tried to laugh & be cheerful but in the midst of all my exertions the involuntary hick up forced me to the bannister where a moderate emetic released me & I regained my usual health & composure.[24]

Thankfully, the storm passed, and the group arrived safely at Cleveland on Friday evening at nine o'clock.

A small lighter (a flat-bottomed barge used to load and unload ships at anchor) met the *Niagara* on the dark water. McNemar helped Johnson aboard and made sure her possessions were safely loaded. When his turn came, he noted that the lighter captain was a "furious being ... ripping and cursing like a privateer." He had misplaced the boat's rudder and was searching under all the baggage for it. He grabbed McNemar's precious box, containing his journals, papers, books, clothing, and treasures from his trip east. The captain would have dropped it overboard, had McNemar "not seized it at the same time & sternly ordered him to let that box alone that I had the command of it ... he saw I was in earnest & desisted another of the passengers united & we rebuked him so sharply that he grew mild professed his repentance."[25] After this unpleasantness passed, McNemar arrived at the Franklin House hotel where he was relieved to find Johnson safely ensconced.

The next morning, McNemar walked to North Union, where he breakfasted with Elder Ashbel Kitchell. Over the course of the next week, McNemar and Johnson worked their way back to Union Village, stopping at Watervliet, Ohio, along the way. They arrived home on Thursday, October 1.[26] The journey lasted 115 days and was surely one of the most memorable experiences of McNemar's life. In the East, he had met for the first time men he had corresponded with and admired for years. He was received with honor as a visiting dignitary and deemed worthy of preaching in the holy sanctuaries of the original eastern Shaker communities. In addition, he was sent back to the West with a crucial mission, to revise and implement new covenants in each of the communities. He carried with him the text of the new covenant and a circular epistle written by the New Lebanon Ministry. At fifty-nine, Richard McNemar had reached the peak of his importance and influence among his Shaker brethren and sisters. He could not know that during the next ten years, his health would fail and his influence wane, ultimately culminating in his tragic downfall.

EIGHTEEN

ELEAZAR AND THE COVENANT

IN THE AUTUMN OF 1829, Richard McNemar, who by this time was universally known by his pseudonym Eleazar Wright, settled back into life at Union Village. He was appointed as second elder in the Centre Family, occupying the office recently vacated by his son James McNemar, who'd had to leave the position due to ill health.[1] On October 8, McNemar visited Eldress Rachel Johnson in her quarters at the ministry's shop. He was startled when she related a bizarre dream to him that she'd had following discussions with her counterpart, Elder Solomon King, about whom they should appoint as junior elder and eldress in the ministry. In her dream, it was revealed to her that as "Malcham [Worley] & Eleazar were the first in the western country that had recd. the gospel & that the right of heirship properly belonged to their natural posterity, & that Joshua Worley & [Tirzah?], Nancy, or Vince McNemar... were the persons who were justly entitled to that lot & place."[2]

In his diary, McNemar admitted that he was caught completely off guard by Johnson's suggestion. She asked him how he felt about it, but he demurred, waiving "any conversation on the subject & withdrew intending to say nothing or to take any part in the decision of a case so delicate as it related to myself." Despite this, he still had to acknowledge her superiority as a member of the ministry and did not want to be seen as doubting the gift. Privately, however, he advocated the appointment of former Centre Family eldress Lucy Faith, writing, "My heart & soul were wrap'd up in Elderess Lucy." In his diary, he confided that he thought Johnson was threatened by Faith and wanted someone different as her second in the ministry. Mortified by the dilemma facing him, he wrote that he could "not make my self believe that it... was the spirit of Mother Ann that set up flesh kin for heirs & successors in the Ministry."[3]

Figure 18.1. Prominent Kentuckian and state senator Robert Wickliffe, aka "Old Duke," spoke in defense of the Shakers at the state legislature.

The issue of ministry appointments was left unresolved for the moment, and McNemar had to move on to the biggest task facing him, the revision of the covenant. He discussed the matter with Matthew Houston, explaining that "after the decease of the parentage [i.e., Father David Darrow and Mother Ruth Farrington] it became essentially necessary the order of the government should be changed to a constitutional form vesting the ruling authorities in a ministry Eldership trusteeship &c. without naming the persons." Houston reported these ideas to Elder Solomon King, who was not pleased with McNemar's plans. King summoned McNemar and "called me to an account & gave me a check that I could just bear without resentment."[4]

McNemar's horizons had been vastly expanded by his recent travels, and he felt that his relationship with King had been altered. He wrote, "The change of sense which I had almost imperceptibly undergone from my visit to the east rendered it extremely difficult for me to keep from giving occasion of offense." McNemar "felt fearful of losing what I had gained by my visit" or being "warped into a belief that they had gift enough here independent of New Lebanon." He now feared that at Union Village, they were entering on "a trial of spirits." Eldress Rachel Johnson had also been to the East and was instructed as to how to proceed with appointments to the Union Village Ministry—firsthand instruction that King lacked. Despite this, McNemar noted that while in the East he had heard "not a word nor a hint about natural kin to be promoted," which was Johnson's troubling proposition. Flummoxed and disheartened, he wrote, "this thing stuck to me all day, & without some special gift or light from source I saw no way that I was to get thro' it & be any how reconciled & comfortable."[5]

As it turned out, McNemar witnessed his second daughter Nancy's appointment on November 4 as second eldress in the Union Village Ministry. Additionally, Malcham Worley's son Joshua was appointed as second elder under Solomon King. In the end, Johnson's plan of natural heirship was implemented, which surely made McNemar uncomfortable. In fact, by the late 1820s, McNemar's surviving children, other than apostate Richard Jr., had all been appointed to leadership positions. One imagines McNemar must have taken some quiet pride in his faithful children, although no evidence exists to prove it.[6]

On November 8, 1829, the Union Village Believers gathered together to hear an important circular epistle from the New Lebanon Ministry. The letter encouraged the faithful, noting the growth of the gospel and the unity of Believers. It warned, however, that "there is no provision made for us to lay aside our watchfulness, take our ease, and imagine that all is safe and beyond the reach of danger." To foster union, the ministry advised that "Believers in all their labors for new improvements, whether in machinery, dress, manners or customs, should be careful to proceed in union, and by no means introduce new things into the Society without the consent & approbation of the Ministry." The Union Village Believers decided to use the circular as the introduction to the new church covenant, which Richard McNemar then read to the assembly.[7]

McNemar came to view the Shakers' church order and covenant in a providential light, part of a continuum of historical developments between the civil and ecclesiastical realms. He named George Washington as the "first patriarch . . . his word as head commander the law." From there, the states had evolved through the Articles of Confederation to the ratification of the Constitution. Similarly, to those who "enlisted under her banner," the word of Mother Ann Lee "was a law." As Shaker communities coalesced, they lived according to the "articles of agreement," that as the church matured were refined into the "general constitution" now being implemented throughout the societies.[8]

McNemar began drafting the new church covenant to be signed at Union Village on December 15. He also prepared a document of equal importance, to be signed before the covenant. This was an "Articles of Acquittance, or Mutual Release between Members of the United Society." It was read aloud to the membership on December 27. By signing it, each member abjured any right to claim any of the community's property or assets should they withdraw. This property was explicitly cited as "held in trust by the Deacons or Trustees of the Church." Finally, each signatory discharged the trustees and deacons of the community "from all charge of debt, damage, or blame," on account of any gift or labor consecrated to the society. Due to their legal troubles with apostates east and west, the Shakers were trying to put an ironclad foundation in place for the new covenant. In a letter to Seth Youngs Wells, McNemar described the document as "a prelude to the privilege of being enrolled in the general confederacy, and as a test of their plain & simple freedom with regard to a final sacrifice." He evidently believed this because he signed the document himself, unwittingly laying the groundwork for future troubles.[9]

On December 31, 1829, all Union Village Believers gathered in the meetinghouse to sign the Articles of Acquittance and the new covenant on December 31, 1829. After "another distinct reading" of the covenant, it was signed and executed. McNemar, Matthew Houston, and David Spinning legally witnessed the signatures of their brethren and sisters. McNemar's wife, Jenny, daughter Vincy, son James, brother Garner, and nephews Hugh and Richard G. (Garner's sons) all signed. His daughter Nancy was not required to sign, as she was now junior eldress in the ministry. His nephew Levi was a resident at the South House and thus did not sign the church covenant. Once again, McNemar had served as a witness, fulfilling the role Mother Lucy had assigned him many years earlier, yet the absence of his signature on the covenant would cause him great grief in years to come. Oblivious to these future developments, a satisfied McNemar wrote Seth Youngs Wells that the execution of the covenant "was effected with almost as little noise as the raising of Solomon's temple."[10] With this important piece of business done, the legally and spiritually strengthened community could enter a new year, and a new decade, with hopes that some of the turmoil of the past few years would be laid to rest.

ON THE ROAD AGAIN

With the new covenant in place at Union Village, Richard McNemar was free to resume his itinerant visits to the western Shaker communities. On January 13, 1830, he set out for Watervliet, Ohio, where he visited Issachar Bates, finding him "very agreeably [and] in good health." He returned to Union Village on January 23, only to leave for White Water on February 9, where he spent the remainder of the month. At White Water, he informed Elder Archibald Meacham of the new covenant and generally assisted "in regulating the affairs of that society." He also found time to finish "two chair frames," showing that he still labored with his hands, as every Shaker should. He left there on March 1, having instituted the covenant. According to Shaker folklore, no proper carriage was available to drive McNemar back to Union Village. Instead, an aged brother hitched the gardener's old horse to the vegetable peddling wagon and drove McNemar as far as the Great Miami River. McNemar disembarked there and walked the remaining twenty-five miles to Union Village, carrying his precious document trunk in his arms.[11]

While McNemar was away, his term as temporary elder at the Union Village Centre Family had ended. His son James McNemar was appointed second elder at the Brick House, putting another McNemar in a position of authority. James McNemar, thirty-four, was a carpenter by trade. He was of impressive physical appearance, described as "all of six feet tall, muscular, [and] alledged to be one of the strongest brethren in the village."[12]

On March 30, Richard McNemar left Union Village for an extended residence at Pleasant Hill, where once again he was tasked with instituting a new covenant.[13] He also found himself embroiled in the ongoing legal difficulties caused by apostates, which had not abated since his last tenure at the community in 1828. On his arrival at Pleasant Hill on April 4, the ministry there wrote to the New Lebanon Ministry, "Brother Eleazar arrived here with a new Covenant or Constitution, together with a Circular Epistle, all of which we felt happy to obtain, as we had been wishing for something of that kind for some years, and when it came, we were Glad to be sure."[14]

McNemar's presence was very welcome at Pleasant Hill during this crucial time. On April 7, he attended a court case brought against the community by apostate Charles Ballance. Once again, his legal knowledge of and expertise regarding the covenant were employed to protect his brethren and sisters. The ministry introduced McNemar at the Sabbath meeting on April 11 as "a regular messenger from the parent Church, with important communications." He spent the following week introducing Pleasant Hill's leadership to the new covenant.[15] On April 20, he read the covenant to the older members of the West Family, explaining that the changes and improvements to it were "found necessary from the increasing light of civil society & the growing state of the church—That the covenant itself was not written with paper & ink but with the spirit of God on the heart of every true Believer." Most important, the revisions were effected to safeguard junior members, as the "rising generation was to be considered as the ark of the covenant." The mass apostasies of young members from Pleasant Hill and Union Village were evidence enough of the Shakers' need to retrench their efforts to retain members. The next day, McNemar read the covenant and circular epistle to the "middle aged & junior Brethren & sisters assembled at the meeting house." He wrote with satisfaction in his journal, "All gave good attention and closed without a murmur."[16]

It wasn't long, however, until the membership at Pleasant Hill began to have concerns about the new covenant. At a meeting on Sunday, May 2, McNemar addressed the Pleasant Hill church members, which comprised the first order (the Centre and East Families) and the second order (the West Family). His topic was the rights and responsibilities of the highest order of Shaker membership. He then read the covenant and articles of acquittance and asked the members if they wished for any amendments or had any objections. Only one "respectable member" expressed concern that the old covenant considered "the property of the church as a joint interest." He had signed the old covenant with that understanding but admitted that he shared some of the same reservations about the new covenant as some "who had left the society." This was a troubling development.[17]

The next day, McNemar lamented in his journal that "spirits begin to stir & tongues also." He was dismayed that the members' concerns related to property and the power of the ministry and elders and not about the effect of the covenant on their salvation. Many were concerned that the implementation of the new covenant was a scheme to lay the foundation to dissolve the society, as had happened at West Union, and to distribute the assets and remaining members at other communities. Additionally, some did not like that this new covenant strongly affirmed the authority of the ministry and elders, thus checking the democratic impulses expressed by many at Pleasant Hill. McNemar continued to tinker with the text in consultation with Seth Youngs Wells and the New Lebanon Ministry. While dealing with these political matters, McNemar also kept himself busy with hand labor and recorded that he had finished making six chair frames in a week—this despite the fact that on May 1 he was "stationary with a lame back."[18]

McNemar worked throughout May with the ministry and elders on a document that clarified the rights and responsibilities of church members who signed the covenant. It was eventually published as *A Revision and Confirmation of the Social Compact of the United Society Called Shakers, at Pleasant Hill, Kentucky*.[19] This document explicitly stated the requirement that members unconditionally consecrate all of their property and assets, and waive any future claims on it or their service, should they leave the community. On May 20 and 21, all of the families at Pleasant Hill reviewed and affirmed the text, with 210 signatories.

McNemar's next task was the implementation of the new covenant. Benjamin Seth Youngs, one of the original missionaries sent to the West in 1805—and for many years the first elder at the South Union, Kentucky, Shaker community—arrived at Pleasant Hill on Wednesday, June 2. He agreed to assist McNemar and the Pleasant Hill Ministry in persuading the membership to support the new covenant. The formal signing of the instrument was carried out on June 10 and 11, 1830.[20] Pleasant Hill church records acknowledged the long-standing need for a new covenant: "The Church had passed through many trying scenes and gained much valuable experience and understanding in things both spiritual and temporal since the adoption of the Covenant of 1814; it was therefore considered important and necessary that we should renew our Covenant with God and each other conformable to the degree of increase attained."[21] McNemar's success at Pleasant Hill had not come easily, but the new covenant implemented there was instrumental in calming some of the ongoing tumult among that community.

McNemar continued his hand labor, finishing two armchairs, twelve side chairs, and twenty-four large spools by June 16. He surely enjoyed this physical work after completing such strenuous bureaucratic tasks. He did not get much time to rest his mind, however, as he was called to attend court in Harrodsburg from July 5 to July 9. Apostates Charles Ballance, James Gass, Samuel Banta, and Francis Sasseen had filed a suit against Pleasant Hill's trustees, seeking to recover the property they had consecrated to the church by the 1814 covenant. Now, finding himself embroiled in a lawsuit after all of his other efforts, McNemar confided to his journal on Friday, July 16, "I want to go home."[22]

On July 20, he found out that instead of going home, he was being sent to South Union to oversee the implementation of the new covenant there. Elder Benjamin Seth Youngs had told McNemar that he was willing to "stand out of the way" and acknowledge McNemar as the "plenipotentiary" sent from New Lebanon to accomplish the task. McNemar understood that Youngs was cleverly avoiding the probable controversy that would ensue. In the privacy of his journal, he wrote, "Deo juvante"—"God help me."[23]

On Monday, August 2, McNemar left the legal troubles surrounding Pleasant Hill behind him. He had been deposed in Harrodsburg on July 29, along with the Pleasant Hill trustees, in the suit brought by Ballance and his apostate accomplices. This was but one of nearly twenty lawsuits brought against the community as a result of the 1828 act of the Kentucky legislature. Nonetheless,

McNemar wrote Elder Nathaniel Deming at Hancock, Massachusetts, that "under all these trials Pleasant Hill stands as firm as the hardy bluffs of the Kentucky on which it is founded."[24] McNemar was sanguine that the community would prevail in all of their lawsuits.

Similar problems were plaguing South Union, where McNemar arrived on August 5. "Elder Eleazar Wright alias Richard McNemar arrived unexpectedly today—He came from Bowling Green, saddlebags on his arm," wrote the keeper of South Union's church journal. Notice of a suit against that community had been pinned to the door of their brick meetinghouse, just as had happened at Pleasant Hill. The plaintiff was tobacco merchant John Boon, who contracted with Brother Urban Johns at South Union for the construction of a flat-bottomed boat for use in transporting his crop to New Orleans. Boon claimed that when he paid Johns, he accidentally gave him a banknote for $1,000 rather than the agreed-on price of $100. The Shakers vehemently denied the charge but found themselves in court over the matter. Boon had secured the testimony of former members of South Union's East Family, now apostates, who were prepared to state that the Shakers had received $1,000. McNemar reviewed all of the documents pertaining to the case and attended court with Benjamin Seth Youngs and Johns at Russellville on August 9. Boon, however, failed to produce his witnesses and asked for a continuance, which was granted until the November term.[25]

McNemar left South Union for Union Village on August 25. The brethren and sisters gathered and sang him a special farewell song, newly composed for the occasion: "Kind Eleazar fare you well." Elder Francis Whyte, who was sixty-two and one of the founders of South Union, accompanied him. They stopped at Pleasant Hill along the way and were joined by Eldress Anna Cole, first in the ministry there, and Eldress Betsey McCarver, who had confessed her sins to Richard McNemar on May 27, 1806. The party arrived at Union Village on September 9. They left Union Village on September 22 to return to South Union.[26]

On Sunday, October 3, a special meeting was called, and the new covenant was read to 250 assembled members at South Union. Believers from the Centre and East Families signed it on October 12, 1830, and the North and West Families signed it on October 14. McNemar returned to South Union the next day with Francis Whyte, who preached a beautiful sermon at that Sunday's meeting and was stricken the following day with a "cramp colic." His one remaining wish was to sign the covenant, which he did, and "soon closed his eyes on all terrestrial things."[27]

The Boon lawsuit resumed at court in Russellville, Kentucky, on November 3. Court proceedings stretched on for seven days, with witnesses testifying for the plaintiffs for four days, before three days of legal dissection of the Act of 1828 by the Shakers' attorneys. The Shakers had a powerful legal defense team, including Lieutenant Governor John Breathitt and James Turner Morehead, a member of the Kentucky House of Representatives for Warren County. Both men won to the governorship of Kentucky in succession. McNemar described the scene in a letter to Seth Youngs Wells, "So the battle was pitched, & vollies of long argument such as Logan county never before witnessed.... Moorhead led the way with an astonishing discourse (he told us afterwards that he never had such feelings in his life that he felt as if he had a degree of inspiration)." Breathitt began his discourse on the third morning, but Judge Broadnax halted the proceedings and proclaimed that his mind was fully made up that there was no evidence sustaining the plaintiffs. The Shakers and their distinguished lawyers had carried the day. McNemar wrote that the company of ten brethren and four sisters from South Union returned home "glad and merry-hearted, yet cautioned by our lawyers to keep low and say little."[28]

The Shakers' legal triumph in the Boon suit laid the groundwork for their efforts to achieve a full repeal of the Act of 1828. This was to be McNemar's next task. On November 15, the grateful South Union Believers held a farewell meeting for McNemar. Sister Sally Eades praised him in verse,

> We'll keep the track, with Richard Mac
> Until we reach the tower,
> When clothed in white Elizar Wright
> Is clad in life & power.[29]

McNemar returned to Pleasant Hill, where he began efforts to repeal the Act of 1828, which left the Kentucky Shaker communities vulnerable to being sued collectively. He traveled to Harrodsburg on November 22 to print *A Memorial Remonstrating Against a Certain Act of the Legislature of Kentucky*, which was signed by John R. Bryant and Eli McLean, trustees of Pleasant Hill and South Union, respectively, but was probably authored by McNemar. In the *Memorial*, he took a parting shot at Robert Owen and the apostate Whitbey brothers, all of whom he held responsible for the troubles that had engulfed Pleasant Hill and led to the 1828 anti-Shaker act. McNemar folded and stitched the pamphlets himself, finishing on December 3. Next, he went to the state capitol at Frankfort, arriving on December 7. When the legislature adjourned for lunch, McNemar joined the members at their tavern, greeting friends such as the speaker of the senate. Member James Turner Morehead, the Shakers' defense attorney during the Boon suit, offered to present the Shakers' *Memorial* to the legislature the next day. On the morning of December 10, McNemar entered the legislative hall with a copy of the *Memorial* for each member, and Morehead publicly endorsed the document, which was referred to the judiciary committee.[30]

McNemar, Benjamin Seth Youngs, and Rufus Bryant returned to Frankfort through a blizzard of snow and hail on December 20 to see if their *Memorial* had its desired effect. By Wednesday, there had been no progress, but they tarried overnight, spending the evening getting acquainted with many of the legislators, including Robert Wickliffe, who would rise eloquently to the defense of the Shakers. Known to his constituents as the "Old Duke," Wickliffe was an attorney, one of Kentucky's largest slaveholders, and possibly its wealthiest citizen in the antebellum period. It is fascinating to imagine the conversation he and McNemar engaged in during their hour-long evening sojourn. Wickliffe, whom McNemar described as "an inveterate enemy of the famous act," brought a bill before the legislature seeking its repeal during the last week of the session, delivering a lengthy speech in defense of the Shakers. After a long debate, however, the bill was tabled and the session closed. McNemar and party left Frankfort the next morning, their goal of the act's repeal still unachieved. Wickliffe's advocacy was genuine, and McNemar was pleased to see that his speech was subsequently published in the newspaper *Kentucky Reporter* as "a battering ram against the brazen statute." The Shakers later reprinted it in multiple editions.[31]

After McNemar's return to Pleasant Hill, Elder Samuel Turner, with whom he hadn't spoken in more than a week, confronted McNemar about his wish to return to Union Village. McNemar was unhappy with his accommodations at Pleasant Hill, which were in a very public location, likely affording him little time for reading, writing, and correspondence. Despite the unpleasantness, McNemar preached the sermon that Christmas at Pleasant Hill, titled "To us a child is born to us a son is given." His wish to return home was finally granted. He boarded a steamboat and ascended the Kentucky River, meeting the Ohio and landing near the White Water Shaker village, which he visited. He finally arrived at Union Village on January 20, 1831, after an absence of nine months and twenty days. He made his home in the garret of the North House of the Centre Family.[32]

One of McNemar's first duties at Union Village was to address the Shakers at the January 29 meeting and tell of the successful implementation of the covenant at Pleasant Hill and South Union. He worked further on covenant and land title matters at Union Village throughout the spring. In an April letter to Seth Youngs Wells, he admitted, "If we have to show an unbroken chain of title to the whole consecrated interest, to prove the legality of titles their proper descent & present investiture we shall find it a pretty serious job." McNemar acknowledged that the way in which the Shakers had managed land titles could leave them open to legal claims by non-Shaker natural heirs of deceased Believers, who "may rise up & claim on the principle of escheat." McNemar recommended that all living Believers who had given their property before the implementation of the new covenant should renew their deeds and reaffirm their consecration to the community's trustees. On the legal front, he was glad to report, "For the present I feel sure that the horns of the wild bull (K. law of 1828) are broken off close to his head and left him a mere muly."[33]

In an interesting confluence of American religious history, on January 28 and 29, McNemar read the Book of Mormon. He learned from Elder Solomon King that Oliver Cowdery had recently visited the "North Lot" family of Shakers at Union Village, leaving a copy of the book. Cowdery was traveling west on the first mission to the Lamanites (Native Americans). McNemar wrote a lengthy appraisal of the newly revealed scripture in his journal; in fact, it was one of the first critical reviews of the work. He gave a relatively accurate summary of the Book of Mormon before ridiculing the process of translation and proclaiming it doctrinally inept. As a Shaker, he was particularly disturbed that the work contained "not a lick about the cross of the flesh." McNemar wrote, "It reminded me of the Persian tales which I used to read when a boy & with which I was much delighted. and excepting what this inspired writer & dictator took from the scriptures I supposed there was as much truth & reality in the one as the other." He was certain that "whatever benefit the Indians may derive from this book of Mormon certain it is we can derive none." McNemar warned, "To give heed to those cunningly devised fables [which?] minister strife rather than godly edifying may suit an apostate but not a settled believer[.] the law of Christ is not written on plates of brass or kept in boxes of stone but on fleshly tables of the heart & kept in the chh."[34] The Shakers and Mormons subsequently interacted at the North Union, Ohio, and Sodus Bay, New York, communities, but relatively few people left either sect for the other.[35]

In April, McNemar visited the community at Watervliet, Ohio, with Mathew Houston. On Sunday, May 1, Elder Issachar Bates introduced them to the assembled body of Believers as "messengers from the church capable of informing them of all matters necessary to be known in relation to the state of the different societies, the present gift & labor of the church." McNemar proceeded to explain the necessity of instituting a new covenant at the Watervliet community. His primary justification was that as the aged founders of Shakerism died, they wanted to make sure that "every thing was done necessary to leave matters in a safe condition for our successors." Therefore, the New Lebanon Ministry had directed that all societies "regulate all their temporal affairs, revise their important writings, [and] renew and confirm covenants." McNemar spoke for a half hour before the meeting closed with the circular march. The conversation, however, was just beginning.[36]

The next day, the ministry, elders, and deacons assembled to hear the covenant read. Questions and some objections arose immediately. Most pertained to an individual's quit claim to personal rights to property. This property was consecrated to the "joint interest" in the original covenant, language that was now amended to read "united interest." McNemar explained that the new word choice constituted no actual difference in practice but was instead a reaction to non-Shaker legal interpretations of the word "joint." In essence, the word "united" strengthened the covenant by showing that the community had a "common interest in the uses & benefits of the property while it was legally held & protected for that purpose by a trusteeship." Henry Miller questioned the legal accountability of the trustees to any members beyond the ministry and elders. McNemar and Bates assured him that a new Declaration of Trust would clarify and strengthen the trustees' role in managing communal assets and "exclude all pretext of personal right in the trustee or his heirs forever." Murmurs among the longtime members did not subside over the coming days, and Thomas Williams, Henry Miller, and John Martin were not shy about voicing their objections to the language of the new covenant. They specifically wanted to ensure that no real estate was ever sold by the trustees without the membership's consent. McNemar must have winced in recollection of his battles with the democratic spirit that had infected Pleasant Hill in the late 1820s.[37]

On May 5, the membership gathered to hear a reading of a revised covenant "suited to that society." Bates lamented that "a spirit of jealousy had got up among some that it was intended to insnare them, that such an idea was most unnatural & unreasonable considering that those things originated from our parentage who had sufficiently proved that their children were their only treasure & who would rather give us $10,000 for our help than take one dollar from us to our injury." McNemar reminded them that they were already united as a body under the old covenant and that they must proceed in union regarding decisions about the new covenant. Should any refuse to sign, that "did not release them from the obligations of that into which they had already entered." Pointedly, the names of all signatories of the existing church covenant were then read aloud. After more discussion of individual members' rights to property held by the trustees, the assembled Shakers heard the covenant read a final time. Unlike other communities, however, the noncommittal membership opted to defer to the ministry in scheduling a time to sign and implement the legally binding agreement—a deflating conclusion to the fraught proceedings. McNemar noted in his journal that the ministry was in fact present at that moment and had been put into a position tantamount to forcing the Watervliet members to comply. Instead, he remarked acidly, "The matter was referred . . . not to any ministers of God on earth or in heaven . . . but to the ministers of satan, and sure enough they have had the control of the business ever since." McNemar departed Watervliet for Union Village the next day, having failed to execute the covenant. All of this was a portent of greater tribulations ahead at Watervliet.[38]

During May, McNemar's time was consumed with difficulties relating to the White Water community—specifically Calvin Morrell, one of McNemar's earliest associates at Turtle Creek and the man with whom he had been ritually humbled at South Union in 1806. On May 3, Morrell had traveled from White Water to Union Village to ask to be released from his position as second elder. The ministry assented, and McNemar was sent to White Water twice during May to organize community records pertaining to land and financial matters. Morrell and McNemar had converted many of the White Water Believers during their missionary work in Darby Plains, Ohio. Morrell had served his community to the best of his ability until he was superseded by the appointment of Archibald Meacham as first elder following the closure of West Union in 1828.

Morrell and Meacham both had faults in the eyes of their followers. Virginian John Lin Carson, a hatter by trade, had confessed his sins to Morrell and was sorry to see him leave, telling McNemar that he believed he had entered into a personal covenant with Morrell. McNemar clarified to Carson that he had covenanted with the Christ spirit through Morrell. Carson confided in McNemar that although Morrell had "whipt & whack'd him back & sides face & eyes . . . he loves him the better for it & would prefer him to Elder A [Meacham] in a watermelon patch or garden but E[lder] A. [Meacham] is the man for building & mills & matters & things of general interest." In the privacy of his journal, McNemar wrote of his friend that, due to "growing infirmities of superannuation, Calvin came to feel as he did—that his gift was out and his labor finished."[39]

Part of McNemar's duties at White Water consisted of interviewing individual members to try to discern community sentiments regarding the new covenant, leadership change, and state affairs generally. What he found was not heartening. The members were very concerned that the new covenant placed ownership of their lands with trustees at Union Village. At a church meeting on Sunday, May 15, McNemar proposed an alteration to that clause, stipulating that the lands belonged to the trustees "in this place." This mollified the membership. More troubling, however, was the general feeling that the community's leadership were living in "luxury and idleness" off the labor of the rank and file. Following the meeting, Ezra Sherman Sr. confided to

McNemar that this was the reason for many recent apostasies. He complained, "Some are servants to others, separate tables & separate lodgings & every thing separate & the best of every thing that is going—the best of the apples garden sauce &c the best of the meat, flour &c. and the beer & other liquors must all be stoud [stowed] in the cellar & we know nothing of it, now this is the common complaint & it is even so & we cannot deny." Sherman averred that the community had "looked for examples of humility & self denial," but had not found them among the current leadership. Nonetheless, he was "prepared to standing anything" and declared, "I mean to live and die a Shaker." Further investigation by McNemar with the sisters showed that it was primarily the brethren who felt thus disaffected.[40]

Before leaving White Water, McNemar had a long talk with Samuel Rice Sr., the noted gambler and Farnumite that McNemar and Morrell had converted at Darby Plains. McNemar explained to Rice the paradoxical reasons why Shaker communities had a hierarchy when all were supposed to be equal. The trustees at Union Village, who had sent him to have care over the Believers at White Water, ostensibly supported Calvin Morrell; he was not obligated to "eat . . . and live like" his fellow brethren and sisters "on an equality in every way." If, on top of his commitment to caring for their souls, he chose to lower his own standard of living, it would have been a voluntary act of self-denial. McNemar told Rice that after all Morrell and company had done for the salvation of their souls, it would be "ungenerous in their disciples to begrudge them a little comfort beyond what they could furnish." McNemar asked Rice if Morrell, having "labored hard & watered the soil with his sweat" to establish a united interest at White Water, should return to Union Village to "live on pone & dodgers sopt in the oil of rusty bacon & drink spicewood tea without sugar & pick the bones after young believers[?]" Suitably chastened, Rice replied, "My soul! . . . what have we that is good that we have not received through our ministers, we owe our very lives to them."[41]

On Friday, May 27, Calvin Morrell made his final preparations to move back to Union Village. Following breakfast, when all was packed and the horses hitched to the wagons, Morrell approached McNemar and Meacham. He asked Meacham into the next room, where he "delivered his last will & testament recapitulating his labors & claim to the people & that notwithstanding he had formally resigned his charge & recommended them to the gift that remained for them." Morrell, however, was convinced "that he had been scrouged out of his place by a man that never could hold his own people together." This last comment was a cruel reference to the dissolution of the West Union, Indiana, community, which Meacham had led. Having vented his anger, Morrell hurried away from a surely stunned Meacham before the latter could reply. He then told McNemar, "If I have done any mischief... you must patch it up the best way you can: farewell." After recording this scene in his journal, an exasperated McNemar wrote: "So ends the dispensation at White Water village." A few years later, however, after Morrell's death, McNemar wrote of this time, "Union Village once more opened her arms & took into her bosom a worthy brother who had grown hoary headed and much impaired in his faculties, in his arduous labors to promote her interest."[42]

McNemar remained at White Water a few more days to patch things up. At the meeting on Sunday, May 29, he reminded the assembled Shakers that among them were many from Darby Plains and West Union and that although they had released his brother Calvin, "You have yet to release me." On the contrary, McNemar told them he had "an important gift that we have to settle." He reminded them that it was his job "to help souls thro the first stages of travel [and prepare them] for coming into church relation to constitute a body fitly joined & compacted as pillars to go no more out." McNemar assured them of his personal "faith & confidence" in the eastern ministry and let them know that until they were reconciled to Meacham as their new elder, he could not be released from his duty toward them. He vouched for Meacham, saying he had "no hesitation in commending him as a safe & substantial lead" and spoke in similarly glowing terms of the rest of the elders' order at White Water. The assembled Believers heard him out and assented to his release by professing their "willingness to gather to their present lead." The next day, new trustees—White Water residents—were appointed to hold the community's property in trust. His mission accomplished, a presumably physically and emotionally exhausted McNemar left White Water, returning to Union Village on May 30.[43]

Despite being consumed with the momentous task of managing the exit of an established leader from a community and learning the sobering state of affairs at White Water, McNemar still found time for other duties. He corresponded with Seth Youngs Wells on the proposed republication, in abridged form, of John Dunlavy's *Manifesto*, offering Wells a dense theological critique of sections of the volume authored by his deceased brother-in-law.[44] McNemar also oversaw the collection of declarations of faith by brethren and sisters at Union Village, some of which he recorded in his journal. He was not home long, however, as he departed on June 2 for Cincinnati, likely to seek legal advice regarding securing the titles to the Shakers' lands.[45]

After returning from Cincinnati, McNemar finally settled in at Union Village for the foreseeable future. Two excerpted stanzas from a poem he wrote

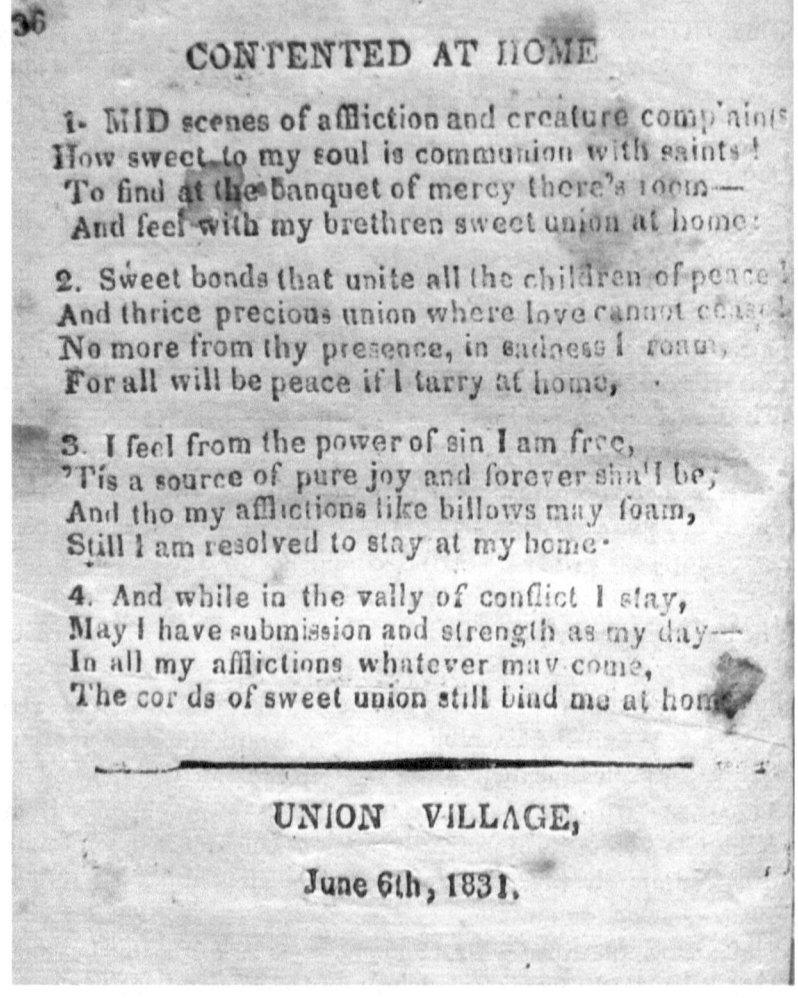

Figure 18.2. Richard McNemar's poem "Contented at Home," which he later printed, expressed his relief at finally returning home to Union Village after years of traveling to deal with contentious legal situations at the western Shaker communities. BX9786 .S5343 1830z no. 8, Rare Books Division, Library of Congress.

on June 6, 1831, titled "Contented at Home," evoke his joy at being back in residence there.

> Mid scenes of affliction and creature complaints
> How sweet to my soul is communion with saints!
> To find at the banquet of mercy there's room—
> And feel with my brethren sweet union at home:

Sweet bonds that unite all the children of peace!
And thrice precious union where love cannot cease!
No more from thy presence, in sadness I roam,
For all will be peace if I tarry at home.

McNemar suffered from a serious bout of colic that summer, which likely caused him intense pain in his intestines or urinary tract. He must have been thankful to be in his familiar home while enduring it, rather than perambulating through Kentucky. On September 27, 1831, he moved to the Brick House of the Centre Family with his old friend Ashbel Kitchell, who had just been released from his duties as elder at the North Union community. They moved into Matthew Houston's quarters, as Houston had been dispatched to North Union to replace Kitchell.[46]

That summer, McNemar wrote Seth Youngs Wells regarding the problematic issue of confirming land titles under the new covenant, which he called a "very important crisis to the Chh [Church] in the West." He and trustee Nathan Sharp sought expert legal opinions as to the validity of the original deed transfers executed. They visited lawyers Charles Hammond in Cincinnati and longtime community friends Thomas Corwin and Francis Dunlavy in Lebanon, Ohio. The three lawyers proffered the opinion that deeds executed by any combination of first trustee Peter Pease (who returned to New Lebanon in 1820 and died there in 1827), and/or trustee John Wallace (who apostatized in 1818), and/or current trustee Nathan Sharp were valid and legitimate. Further, Sharp was a legal party to them on behalf of the community and could buy or sell lands. However, they were certain that legal title to the lands would expire on Sharp's death, and they recommended that Sharp convey all deeds to two additional parties, thus reconstituting a triumvirate of trustees. McNemar sought Wells's affirmation that it was the right of the ministry, and not a trustee, to appoint cotrustees and successors. Further, he recommended that the western land deeds be tied to New Lebanon through the appointment of one person in trust at that community. He reasoned that, should a major conflict arise where non-Shaker heirs might claim land consecrated by a deceased relative, the case would at least have to go to federal court, since the legal title would be tied to two different states.[47]

McNemar next turned his attention to Union Village trustee Nathan Sharp. The two men exchanged letters giving their views of the land title controversy. McNemar opined that the ultimate right to the lands "remains in the east . . . and can never be lawfully alienated from the original claim & control of the parent institution." This gave the New Lebanon Ministry, through their trustees, final title to all the lands at Union Village. Sharp disagreed with McNemar's interpretation, stating that the New Lebanon trustees only held the land in trust temporarily and that "trust was conveyed to the trustees" at Union Village who were established by the membership on the institution of the 1812 covenant. Sharp also believed that Union Village trustees had made a contract with New Lebanon trustees for the land and held firm title. McNemar remained unconvinced, mainly because all of the initial land purchases made at Union Village were paid for with money from New Lebanon. Additionally, Peter Pease, the first trustee at Union Village, was a covenanted member at New Lebanon and never one at Union Village. In a privately written refutation of Sharp, McNemar called Sharp's title to the land "imaginary." He was appalled that Sharp was "so ignorant of the nature of a surrender of trust," and he found it "astonishing, that a man holding such a sense of independence should so long be suffered to hold peaceable possession of such an important office, and browbeat me & others on those matters (relative to the land titles) whenever they came in controversy between us." McNemar's suspicions about Sharp would eventually be confirmed.[48]

Following his exchange with Sharp, McNemar warned Elder Solomon King, first in the Union Village Ministry, that Sharp's independent claim as trustee to all land titles at Union Village, with no acknowledgment of rights on the part of New Lebanon, left the community very vulnerable. For instance, if Sharp was "permitted to trade and speculate and involve [himself] in debt to any amount, upon what ground is the interest secure to the use of the community? It requires but little foresight to discern the most threatening danger of a total shipwreck."[49]

Ultimately, the Union Village Ministry opted not to follow through with altering any of their land titles to include a trustee located at New Lebanon. McNemar reported to Seth Youngs Wells that a triumvirate of trustees was now in place, comprising Sharp, Henry Valentine, and Ithamar Johnson. Union Village leaders had "concluded that the chain of title had been brought along as safely, & was now as substantially settled as the nature of the case would admit." Ultimately, McNemar acknowledged the validity of Sharp's contention that Peter Pease and others in trust at New Lebanon had conveyed that trust to the Union Village trustees. There the matter rested, for the moment.[50]

McNemar's central place in the lengthy investigation of these legal matters, as well as the revision and institution of the covenants and legal battles in multiple states, kept his name (albeit as Eleazar Wright) on the tongue of every Shaker leader in the western communities and at New Lebanon. His tireless efforts in service to his brethren and sisters were well known and appreciated. Elder Samuel Turner of Pleasant Hill wrote to him to apprise him of positive legal news in the continuing battle with apostates in Kentucky. Separately, he told McNemar, "Good Brother you have many friends here, who think much of you, and often speak of you with feelings of love and esteem. Still bearing in mind your kind and faithful labors in this place, for all of which we feel much indebted."[51] In a letter to the Union Village Ministry, the New Lebanon Ministry similarly singled McNemar out, writing, "Give our best love & thanks to our good Brother Eleazar . . . for all his labors in defence of the testimony."[52] By this time in McNemar's life, many Shaker leaders considered him to be indispensable. Unfortunately, McNemar may have begun to regard himself in this way too, which was a problematic self-conception for a Shaker.

Richard McNemar traveled to Watervliet, Ohio, to spend Christmas with the community there, particularly his old friend Issachar Bates.[53] While there, on December 26, 1831, he had a remarkable dream that foreshadowed his chief pursuits during the last decade of his life—the preservation and printing of Shaker records, hymns, and poems from the western communities.

> On last monday night, at Watervliet, while in a deep sleep and in a very pleasant frame of mind I dreamed that I was in a dream at Union Village sitting at a writing table, Brother Matthew [Houston] lying on a bed and others of the aged Br[ethren] and sisters in the room. We seemed to be in a labor on the subject of recording the principal events that had occurred in the progress of the gospel in the west, and it seemed to devolve upon me to make out those records which I could not well do without the aid and concurrence of others who were equally interested. While I sat musing, Br Matthew spake out and said "You may truly use my name in any case that you may think proper" I instantly seized my pen & noted down his words—Next Jenny McNamar repeated the same words, which in a measure released me from any difficulty on the subject. Believing that a concise statement of all important facts would be acceptable & edifying to the church, and a benefit to our successors in the gospel.
>
> From this interview I was taken out into the open air near the centre of the village where I could view the heavens and the earth all around me, and while I stood in calm meditation it began to rain moderately & kept increasing until it came down in torrents that nothing could obstruct, in doors and out all was alike, it entered the buildings with as little interruption as it did the door yards, until it covered every place like a flood, but perfectly mild in its movements. In the meantime it raised every thing that would float. I observed the shops and where ever there was trash, that every light or dirty thing was on the surface of the water and beginning to move by a gradual descent—I thought with myself, this will make clean work, for I perceived that every thing that would float must go. I then maneuvered about to see what course the current would take and as I stood by the side of the street it came by me

pouring in from all sides considerably rapid. And I was ordered to strip & change my clothes, and while pulling on a clean shirt my vision terminated

A number being then in sight who were my first companions in the gospel particularly at Union Village & Pleasant Hill for it made no odds where they were, to me they appeared present and mutual partakers in the same interesting scene.[54]

McNemar considered this dream important enough to describe at length in his journal. Symbolically, it seems to represent McNemar's determination to cleanse, through documentation, the first twenty-seven years of western Shakerism. The cleansing waters lift and carry off the trash, and he receives fresh clothes. This is one of the last mentions I have located of McNemar's wife, Jenny, and it seems significant that her name appears as he prepared to summarize his history. Houston, along with all his other "first companions in the gospel," happily assented to his work in recording their history.

That February, in a remarkable echo of McNemar's dream, southwestern Ohio experienced the greatest flooding seen in years. On Sunday, February 12, a Union Village journalist recorded, "It is said, we have the greatest flood to day ever known in the country."[55] McNemar had departed Union Village two days before on his way to Watervliet. His mission was to organize the community's written records and to assess the general state of affairs, although his presence may not have been altogether welcome. On arrival, he planned to lodge in the upper level of the meetinghouse with the community's ministry, but he found it was perceived as "an incumbrance to the order." The next morning, he gained approval from Elder Issachar Bates to lodge in the trustees' office, also conveniently where the records were located.[56]

McNemar wrote that his "immediate concern is about the affairs of the office particularly the office books of account and of record." In a "commodious room" in the office, he was given the record books and began his examination. Ominously, shortly after he started perusing the records "thunder began to roar & the lightning to flash & the rain to pour down in such torrents as produced the greatest flood that has lately been seen. As the waters rose around him, in contrast to his dream, he was astonished that "among all the office Books I found no Book of records, & could not learn that any had been kept in the society except by Nathaniel while he lived at the West." After preaching at the Sabbath meeting the next morning, he asked the assembled membership to produce for him "any written memorandums of Events" that he could use to reconstruct the history of the community. Additionally, he discovered that the community's covenant was not even on site, having been taken to Union

Village for safekeeping. Finding himself at a standstill with regard to his organizational mission, he resolved to return to Union Village to collect whatever records he could, and he left Watervliet on February 14.[57]

The most difficult aspect of McNemar's visit to Watervliet that February was fully confronting the shortcomings of that community's leader, McNemar's old friend and mentor Elder Issachar Bates. It was Bates, after all (and Benjamin Seth Youngs), who heard McNemar's confession in 1805 when Shakerism began in the West. Bates's biographer Carol Medlicott has written, "The disarray at Watervliet was even worse than Richard had feared.... Issachar had pointedly put aside many aspects of normal Shaker order during his nearly eight years at Watervliet." Medlicott opines that Bates "was hoping to avoid accountability for the many thorny difficulties that had developed during his tenure."[58]

In his journal, McNemar wrote that the body of Believers at Watervliet were "sensible of lacks in the order of government for which they are not responsible & which it is out of their power to remedy." Bates led unilaterally, and his fellow elders and eldresses could hardly bear the burden of "the opposition that was generally felt to his ministrations." McNemar lamented that the community was "much lacking for talented members," but he was able to "sympathise with both sides believing that all were conscientious & sincere." The overarching sentiment, however, was that there was "an unsettled feeling in the Eldership as to the leading gift"—that is, Issachar Bates.[59]

The Union Village Ministry arrived at Watervliet on March 28. McNemar shared his findings with them. Consequently, an evening meeting was held on Sunday, April 1, 1832, at which it was decided to release Issachar Bates from his position as first elder at Watervliet and appoint Richard McNemar in his place. McNemar was appointed to lead meetings and to "go forward on all occasions as first in care of the society." He literally assumed Bates's "lot & place" in the meetinghouse garret, while Bates was relegated to the nurse room. McNemar wrote in his journal, "No dissenting voice has been heard." He soon found, however, that his optimism was premature.[60]

NINETEEN

CUSTOS SACRORUM

DURING RICHARD MCNEMAR'S TRAVELS TO the eastern Shaker communities in the summer of 1829, members there generously gave him money to defray his expenses. A letter from the Canterbury Ministry to the New Lebanon Ministry states, "We concluded it might be some satisfaction to the ministry to hear how much or how little the folks here have given to Brother Eleazer to help him on account of his expences back in his long journey, and soforth &c. At Enfield they gave him some cloth and some money for union sake—And here they mad[e] up with what he got there $120 dolars in Money and some other articles of clothing."[1]

In a letter to Elder Rufus Bishop, McNemar recounted how the germ of an idea to start a press of his own had formed on that trip: "When your benevolent order felt for me to accept of any donations that might be offered from the several societies for my use & benefit as a public servant I thought of neither meat drink or clothing, my special wants all centred in types & figures, and my calculation was, if possible, to start a printing establishment some where, and take the try out whether it could not be protected among Believers."[2] Accordingly, McNemar carefully set aside the money given to him by the eastern Believers.

Following his arduous 1830 sojourn attending to internal strife and legal matters at the Kentucky communities, McNemar prepared a memorandum of his experiences in Kentucky intended for the use of the New Lebanon Ministry. He appended a lengthy "Supplement" to this in which he persuasively made his case for why the Shakers should procure their own printing press. Ever mindful of union, he framed the need for a press in terms of its benefits for the society as a whole. His special personal interest in printing, however, comes through loud and clear. Much of his business in Kentucky had centered on printing jobs.

McNemar was forced to use his eastern money for associated travel expenses. Frustrated at having to expend his savings unnecessarily, McNemar redoubled his efforts to acquire a printing press.

In his private journal, McNemar wrote, "The principal object of Eleazars last trip to Kentucky [in 1830] was to assist in the line of printing." Type was supposed to have been procured in Cincinnati, but time had not allowed for that. Instead, when it came time to print the *Memorial Remonstrating* to the Kentucky legislature for the 1828 anti-Shaker Act, McNemar was peeved that the Shakers "became dependent on the world as usual for executing the job on hand, which gave occasion to what might be called some serious trials."[3] Reliance on non-Shaker printers forced the Shakers to plan strategically for printing sensitive publications, as timing with regard to the legislative calendar was crucial. If published too soon, it would give anti-Shaker factions time to react both in print and by lobbying legislators. McNemar, however, was in favor of an early printing so that he could circulate the text privately among the legislators, but the Pleasant Hill leadership opposed this plan. The *Memorial* was ultimately printed at Harrodsburg by a non-Shaker and predictably leaked to anti-Shaker factions, who, despite the limited time available, prepared counterarguments.

At South Union, Elder Benjamin Seth Youngs used a small hand press to accomplish the same purpose, a situation McNemar envied. While attending the legislature at Frankfort, McNemar and Youngs had "serious labor" about the subject of printing. McNemar lamented "the entire disgust which I had got at attending the worlds presses." The two men agreed that it would be "of great importance at this time to have a suitable press in some of our societies for the purpose of executing such jobs & for other purposes." They appealed to the ministry at New Lebanon for union to establish a press of their own.[4]

McNemar also discussed the possibility of acquiring a press with Elder Rufus Bryant of Pleasant Hill, opining, "Believers are likely to be put up to the necessity of using the press for the communication of light in the defense of the gospel beyond what has heretofore been deemed necessary." He pointed out that during the latest struggles with apostates, the eastern communities had published a "pamphlet illustrating & supporting those sacred principles which have long been recognized in the covenants & other writings of the church"—this was Calvin Green and Seth Youngs Wells's *Brief Exposition* (a work McNemar esteemed so highly that he reprinted it in 1832). Validating his own efforts, he also noted that the *Memorial* (which he called "our little blue books") he had seen through the press in Harrodsburg "did collect a surprising degree of light & energy." In the end, McNemar was allowed to spend $25 of the money he received in the East to travel to Cincinnati and purchase types.⁵

On April 2, 1831, McNemar went to Cincinnati "to the warehouse after four cases of types"—151 pounds worth—purchased "from S. Brown for 20 dollars."⁶ Samuel J. Brown was the son and business successor to McNemar's old friend John W. Brown, the printer of the *Kentucky Revival*, who died in 1813. McNemar spent April 14 and 15 making a composing stand on which to set his type. On Saturday, April 16, he recorded in his journal: "Print a hymn." Early the next week, he set the type for printing "Br. & Br's speeches," an imprint of uncertain identity (if any copies survive). On September 13, he returned to Cincinnati with Ashbel Kitchell and Rufus Bryant, lodging again with Brown. Kitchell purchased a font of "old great primer types." Meanwhile, McNemar visited the type foundry and "saw every part of the work." He purchased four pounds of scabbards (thin spacers), two pounds of "flowers" (printer's ornaments called fleurons), and one quire of blue paper, presumably to use as wraps for pamphlets.⁷ Having finally realized his longtime dream of outfitting his own printing press, McNemar began planning projects in earnest.

By April 1832, McNemar was ensconced at Watervliet, having been assigned to replace Issachar Bates as elder. Despite the challenges of this new position, McNemar made ample time to pursue printing, justifying his hobby as useful in the defense and promulgation of accurate information about the Shakers. His retrospective interest in western Shaker history came increasingly to the fore. He confided as much in an April 6 letter to Seth Youngs Wells, "For upwards of a year past I have been collecting and examining records relating to the several societies out of which I believe many things might be collected quite edifying to Believers & not injurious to the world if they should happen to fall into their hands."⁸ Wells responded to McNemar on April 17, writing, "I am glad to hear that you are collecting materials for perpetuating the remembrance of those interesting scenes which attended the opening the gospel in the western states."⁹ In a subsequent exchange, McNemar noted that although he had found few Shakers willing to put their reminiscences of the opening of the gospel in the West to paper, he had "carefully kept copies of most of our publications from the Apology (mentioned in the [*Kentucky Revival*]) on to the present date." Additionally, the "circumstances of my long visits in the several societies; regulating their journals & church records has furnished me with abundant matter of historical facts." Equipped with this array of sources, McNemar believed he had enough material to tell the story.¹⁰

Wells's own work as an oral historian and editor in compiling the 1827 publication *Testimonies Concerning the Character and Ministry of Mother Ann Lee*

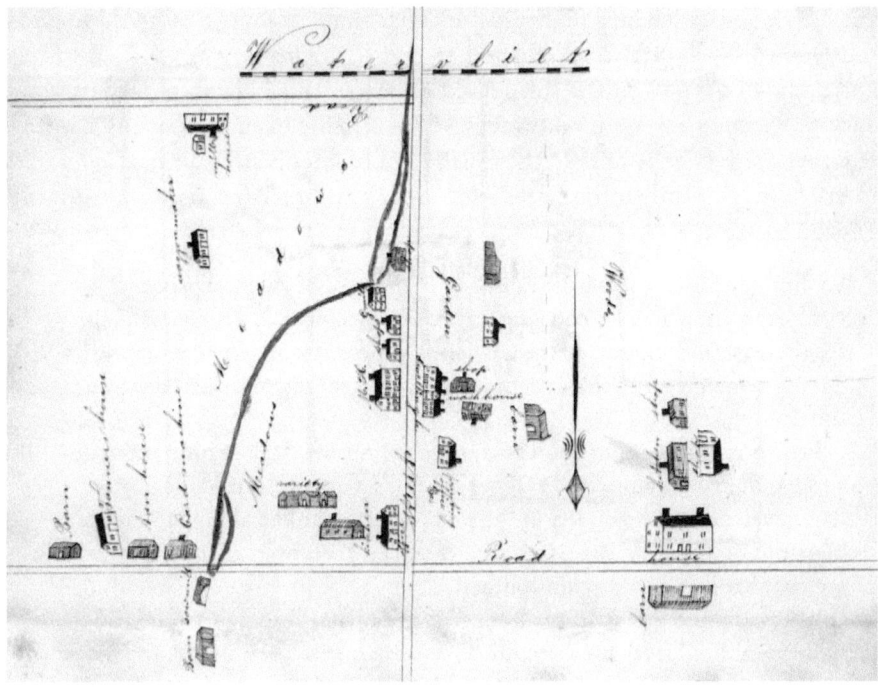

Figure 19.1. A map of the Watervliet, Ohio, Shaker community as delineated by Isaac Newton Youngs in 1834 and copied by George Kendall in 1835. Richard McNemar's "printing office" is depicted in the upper right of the crossroads. G1206. E423 Y6 1835, Library of Congress Geography and Map Division Washington, DC.

and the First Witnesses of the Gospel of Christ's Second Appearing served as a great inspiration for McNemar. In a reflective mood, McNemar wrote Wells, "I am getting considerably advanced in years, & begin to conclude that I have not much further to go, and that it may be about time for me to commence a retrospect of my past journey." He recalled "the important scenes that have been transacted west of the Alighany mountains, since the year 1790: at which period I left my kindred and my father's house & became a stranger in this western hemisphere: What I have seen & have felt & handled for the last 42 years of my life has been for some time past, more the subject matter of my thoughts, than any object future." The output of McNemar's press over the next five years mirrored these sentiments and reveals a man looking backward, although one who would be tragically swept forward by circumstances beyond his control.[11]

McNemar purchased yet more supplies in Cincinnati. On Monday, April 9, he visited a type foundry, acquiring an additional 115 pounds of type and a keg of ink, for which he paid the not inconsiderable sum of $46.75.[12] Momentously, on May 1, 1832, he published an *Epistle Dedicatory of the Union Press* and dedicated it to "To the Respected Ministry and Eldership of the *United Society*." Despite having already received permission to embark on his printing enterprise, McNemar offered the *Epistle* as a further justification. It is quoted in full here, as it fully illuminates McNemar's rationale for his all-consuming passion to print.

> We humbly present this brief *Epistle* as *Dedicatory* of the little printing establishment which we consider now and henceforth, at your service, for the increase and support of the gospel, by propagating and perpetuating its Divine principles, as held forth in the general Records, and Sacred writings of the Church.
>
> Printing, like all other good gifts, may be improved to the promotion of good, or it may be abused to evil purposes, as it doubtless is at the present day, nevertheless, the liberty of the press is justly ranked among the special blessings of this enlightened age, inasmuch as, thereby, truth and error, virtue and vice are brought fairly in contact.
>
> It is presumed that you are all sensible of the disadvantages under which we have labored, ever since recourse has been had to the press for the defence and propagation of our faith and testimony, having to depend entirely on the world to do our work; and after all, the work in many cases has failed of that accuracy which the honor of the Society, and the importance of the subject demanded; insomuch, that we have sometimes had to close with an humble confession, that "some errors had escaped inspection until too late to be corrected in the press;" or with half a page of Errata which, perhaps the reader would never notice.
>
> To remedy those inconveniences, we have long wished for a press of our own, independent, and entirely under our own control, so that every degree of satisfaction could be afforded to all concerned, as to the correctness of whatever might be printed, even to afford time for the most thorough examination before working it off, which in some cases would contribute much to union & a mutual good understanding.
>
> But these considerations belonging more immediately to the spiritual gift, we have patiently waited until in the course of events we could effect the object without troubling the deacons: And as it has been effected in that way, it is but fair and generous that those who have furnished the means should participate in the benefits.
>
> As to the choice and selection of matter, this will be left to the Ministry and Elders; our care will be to guard against disorder, and cheerfully devote our humble services to answer the regular calls and requirements of the Church.

Acknowledging our obligations to the contributors, and desiring the blessing of our good patrons, we remain their devoted helps in the present gospel.
The Editors.[13]

The language of the *Epistle* is careful, humble, and grateful, and it strives to emphasize that this incredible gift will be used in union with the wishes of the ministry. In practice, however, the ministry were not selecting the items McNemar chose to print. He was very much the editor-in-chief of the Union Press. Satisfied in this new role, he wrote in his journal on May 8 that he had "finished the first form having all things prepared for going into regular press work."[14]

In a letter to Rufus Bishop, McNemar referred to Watervliet, Ohio, and specifically to his printing office, as "Kirjathsepher," or a city of books. Quoting Joshua 15:15, he wrote, "This place has become the Kirjathsepher of the west the depository of almost every thing in the letter worthy to be preserved,—copies of covenants, deeds, forms of agreements Declarations of trust letters Hymns, journals, tracts & treatises Doctrinal & historical, with every thing necessary to exhibit to future ages, the faith light & experience of the Believers in the present day; together with the spirit of the world in their various persecutions & litigations. All these matters have providentially fallen into my hands." The information contained in these records provided McNemar with a tremendous amount of material for his press. In a subsequent letter to Bishop, McNemar referred to himself as "custos sacrorum," "keeper of the word"—as he translated it—but, more accurately, "keeper of the sacred."[15]

McNemar rather disingenuously wrote Bishop that assuming this role "was no trifling cross," but that he had done it in obedience to the gift. He lamented having "to get down from the high region of spiritual sensation in which I had soared, and dive again into the arcanum of the killing letter."[16] His concern for the preservation of the Shaker heritage—his heritage after all—is again reflected in a letter to Seth Youngs Wells, in which he remarked, "If all our Manuscript originals were absolutely secure from, thieves, robbers, & the destroying elements, less care might be required, but experience has proved the necessity of multiplying copies & records of such matters to a degree that time & chance cannot destroy their credibility not that we need to exhibit those sacred matters to the profane world or even to every department of the church, further than occasion may require."[17]

In a letter to Seth Youngs Wells that July, he described his rudimentary printing operation, which consisted of "an old paint stone, a wooden chase & a hand spike." The paint stone was probably used to mix ink, and the wooden

Figure 19.2. Richard McNemar's printing office still survives today, having been relocated to the Carillon Historical Park in Dayton, Ohio. Photo by Carol Medlicott; courtesy of Dayton History.

chase served as a frame for the type that McNemar set, possibly using his "hand spike," which may be a colloquial term for a composing stick. Matthew Houston gave him his first job, which was to record all the deaths in the community to the present date. Next, schoolteacher James Smith asked him to print an abridgement of Samuel Kirkham's popular grammar for his "boys to learn by memory." McNemar's love of music and poetry showed forth as "Various little hymns passed under the lever." He dismissed these crude early efforts at printing, however, and on sending some specimens to Wells advised him that they would "answer to wipe your razor on."[18]

Sometime in 1832, Richard McNemar conceived and undertook the largest printing job that would be issued from the Union Press. The book was published in 1834 (although the title page states 1833) under the title *A Selection of Hymns and Poems; For the Use of Believers*.[19] This ambitious work was the largest hymnal published by the Shakers since their first hymnal, *Millennial Praises*, published in 1813. McNemar had been a key participant in the production of that publication, supplying texts for more than half of its 140 hymns.[20] For the current project, McNemar adopted yet another pseudonym: *Philos Harmoniae*,

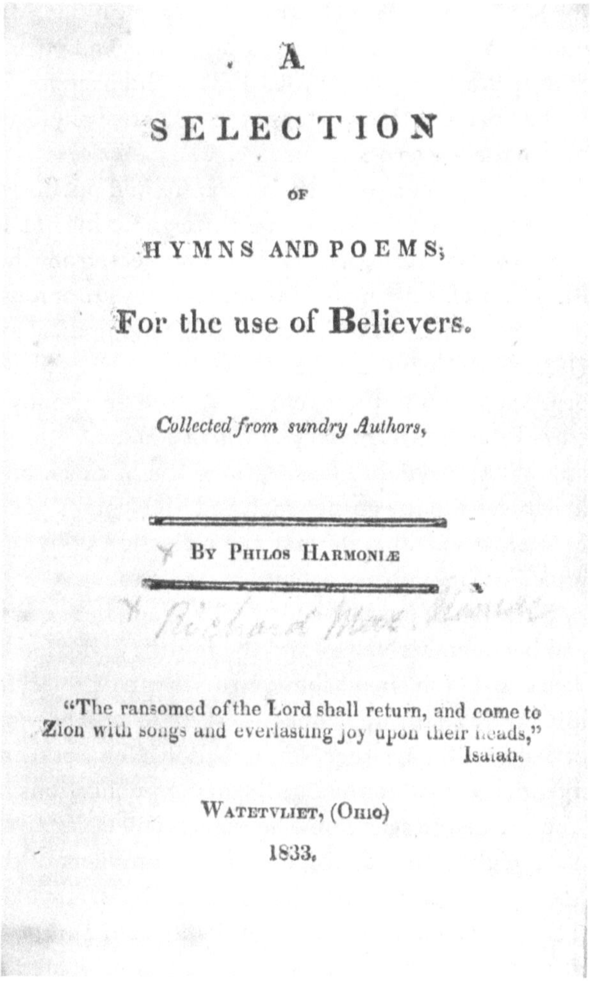
A

SELECTION

OF

HYMNS AND POEMS;

For the use of Believers.

Collected from sundry Authors,

By Philos Harmoniæ

"The ransomed of the Lord shall return, and come to Zion with songs and everlasting joy upon their heads," Isaiah.

Watetvliet, (Ohio)

1833.

Figure 19.3. The title page of Richard McNemar's *Selection of Hymns and Poems for the Use of Believers,* published in 1833 at Watervliet, Ohio, under the pseudonym of Philos Harmoniae (lover of harmony). Private Collection.

or "lover of harmony." He clearly outlined the work's purposes in its preface, "The object of this Selection is, in the first place, to preserve a variety of Hymns & Poems which have been composed by the Believers of different places." He then added, "Another object is—To promote general union among Believers, and perpetuate the various impressions attending those gifts in their first operations: For in singing a lively hymn, or perusing any striking piece of poetry, it is not uncommon to imbibe a degree of the spirit that dictated it."[21]

Union and preservation—these two concepts each played major parts in Richard McNemar's life. Union, the submission of personal will to the hierarchical authority of the Shaker church, had been the defining principle of his life since his conversion in 1805. Preservation, recognition of the value—both nostalgic and historical—of the "killing letter," had emerged more recently. McNemar's desire to preserve the Shaker heritage seems to have been stoked by the accumulation in his printing office of stacks of letters and manuscripts that told the life story not only of himself but of all those people dear to him in the Shaker faith. Fired by these twin aspirations, McNemar embarked on the process of collecting and printing hymns and poems illustrative of life in the Shaker West. It was a joyous and wistful exercise for the sixty-two-year-old. He had become the curator of the collective physical, spiritual, and emotional past of the western Shakers.

Verse as expressed in sacred hymns and poems was a favorite mode of creative expression for McNemar throughout his life. His pen was always at the ready to craft verse on almost any subject, from the spiritual yearning of "A Pure Church Anticipated," to the stoically humorous "Little Pin," to the mocking encouragement of "SLUG," to the methodical explication of "A Covenant Hymn." McNemar distilled the complexities of Shaker theology into eighteen brilliant verses in the poem titled "The Testimony of Eternal Truth," which closed the 1808 *Testimony of Christ's Second Appearing* and opened the 1813 hymnal *Millennial Praises*. Among the Shakers, only Issachar Bates, his fellow traveler in the gospel, matched McNemar's poetic gift. It was natural that McNemar would undertake the collection of hymns and poems as a special project, a labor of love for his Union Press.

But what of union—specifically union between the Shaker East and West and between McNemar and the ministry who led him? I have found no evidence that McNemar submitted his hymnal project for the consideration of the ministry, and the book does not seem to have been published by the direction of the ministry at either New Lebanon, New York, or Union Village, Ohio. The intent expressed in the *Epistle* that in publications issued by the Union Press "the choice and selection of matter . . . will be left to the Ministry and Elders"[22] was roughly adhered to, in that the compilers of the *Selection of Hymns and Poems*—Richard McNemar, Issachar Bates, and Salome Dennis—were technically elders in the Watervliet, Ohio, community. Richard McNemar seems to have assumed the prerogative by this time in his Shaker career to embark on an independent project like the *Selection of Hymns and Poems*. This was the sort of independent initiative, however well meaning, that would prove problematic in the final years of his life.

The other chief point justifying the Union Press made in the *Epistle* was that a Shaker-operated press would afford "every degree of satisfaction . . . to all concerned, as to the correctness of whatever might be printed, even to afford time for the most thorough examination before working it off."[23] Ironically, this was the farthest thing from the truth. McNemar's printing was notorious for its atrocious execution—a shortcoming that gave it a charm entirely its own. He even misspelled the *name* of his own community on the title page of the *Selection* as "Watetvliet," instead of "Watervliet." In the *Epistle*, he had noted that

> N. B From the embarrassments, under which this little work has been executed, sundry errata will be discovered in some copies, and more er less in all.
>
> The selection of the matter may be ascribed to a number; therefore. will better suit the various senses among Believers. What would be quite tasteless to one, may be very entertaining and edifying to another.
>
> Finally, Brethren & Sisters, If this selection should be deemed of any use as a kind of reservoir from which hereafter to select, it will fully answer the wishes and compensate the labors of----
>
> Your devoted Servant in the Gspel,
>
> ELEAZAR.

Figure 19.4. The errata note printed at the end of McNemar's *Selections* ranks as an unintentional classic of its genre. Communal Societies Collection, Hamilton College.

some commercially printed Shaker publications had been issued with errata sheets attached, much to the dismay of their Shaker publishers. This necessity was to be avoided by the advent of the Union Press. However, the errata note appended to the *Selection* ranks as a classic of the genre, reading in part: "N.B From the embarrassments, under which this little work has been executed, sundry errata will be discovered in some copies, and more er less in all."[24] Despite the unclear origins of the *Selection* and the accuracy of its contents, the project was planned with the best of intentions and with the best of spirits.

Although the majority of the hymn texts and poems in the *Selection* originated in the western communities, a letter dated November 20, 1832, from McNemar to Elder Rufus Bishop of the New Lebanon Ministry shows that contributions were solicited from the eastern Shakers. Sister Eunice Bedle was added to the informal editorial committee of McNemar, Bates, and Dennis—all of whom resided at Watervliet, Ohio, at that time. Hymn texts, and occasionally tunes, flowed between the East and the West, as evidenced by an April 6, 1833, letter sent from Wells to McNemar, in which he offered his "thanks for the Hymns, and by request I must include I.N.Y.s [Isaac Newton Youngs] thanks and love, and also the Elder sistership for those sent them, to be conveyed to Elder Issachar, Elderess Salome and Sister Eunice."[25] It is unclear whether this passage refers to initial printed signatures of the book that were sent east to Wells or to manuscript hymn texts that were commonly appended to Shaker correspondence.

It is not known when the actual printing of the book began, other than that it was in 1833. The *Selection of Hymns and Poems* was certainly finished by July of 1834. McNemar wrote to Wells on July 28 to arrange for shipping copies of the new hymnal. "The book is now finished containing 180 pages but how they are to go is not yet fully decided, as the visitors [visiting New Lebanon, New York, Shakers Rufus Bishop and Isaac Newton Youngs] could not be incumbered with them & no private conveyance to cleveland. We rather agreed to direct them to N. Union with a suitable number for that place, & thence to be sent on according to the directions."[26]

McNemar's journal shows that he had begun distributing the books to Believers in the West by August 24.[27] He continued to work at binding copies and wrote in his journal on September 16 that he had "finished in a superior manner 12 books."[28] On September 18, he noted the completion of eighty-five books. Twenty-two of these were "whole bound" books for notable Believers in the East. These are perhaps the handsome surviving copies bound in tree calf with red morocco binder's titles. Sixty-three copies were finished "half bound," meaning that they were backed with a calf spine but had paper-covered boards rather than a full-calf binding. Copies were also sent for general use to a number of communities: South Union, Kentucky, received three; Pleasant Hill, Kentucky, two; White Water, Ohio, two; and Watervliet, Ohio, four. McNemar dedicated forty-seven copies for use at Union Village, Ohio. In all, 151 copies of the book are accounted for in McNemar's journal, often with individual recipients named.[29] Today, only a fraction of that number is known to have survived.

The books were received in the East sometime in November. On December 1, Wells wrote McNemar on behalf of Rufus Bishop of the New Lebanon Ministry: "B. R. [Brother Rufus Bishop] wishes to return you his particular thanks for the liberal donation of Hymn Books, many of which are entirely new to us & very interesting."[30] In a separate, private letter dated the same day, Wells congratulated McNemar on his production. "The hymns, as far as I can learn, give general satisfaction ... are considered valuable & interesting as they afford a fair specimen of the good faith of the writers, and plainly show that they have a full understanding of the nature of the work of God and the requirements of the gospel." Since the original printed work contained only the texts and none of the tunes used to sing them, Brother Isaac Newton Youngs appended eastern Shaker tunes for the texts "Mother" and "The Precious Way of God" to Wells's letter in Shaker letteral musical notation.[31]

McNemar wrote Wells with great relief on December 22, secure in the knowledge that his precious cargo of hymnals had arrived safely in the East. He was also greatly pleased with the reception of his past year's efforts by his esteemed eastern colleagues: "No thing is more consoling to my feelings than to know that my little services in the gospel are acceptable to my superiors." McNemar's penchant for verse was not satisfied by issuing the *Selection,* and he couldn't resist filling the blank space at the end of his letter with a fresh effort, writing, "I hate to send you this whole leaf—I must put something on it. Will you please to accept of a little morning meditation on a certain occasion—a little offering to the muses who seem to have breathed into me at an early period, the art of rhyming."[32]

In fact, McNemar continued to print supplementary pages for the *Selection,* extending its total length to roughly 207 pages. Surviving copies have widely variant permutations of this content—erratic assemblies characteristic of McNemar's subsequent imprints. The *Selection* was just one of many publications McNemar issued from Union Press from 1832 to 1837. It is a culminating expression of the first generation of Shaker leadership in the West. McNemar and Issachar Bates died within the five years following its publication, and with them died the animating spirits of the western Shaker world and their impressions of its people, places, and things, save for the versified memories printed in the *Selection.* Richard McNemar must have known deep down that the word did not necessarily kill the spirit—that instead, it offered preservation, affording those of us in the present "a degree of the spirit that dictated it."[33]

TWENTY

THE GREAT SNAKE AND THE PATRIARCHAL SKELETON

RICHARD MCNEMAR'S PASSION FOR PRINTING may have served as a distraction from the intractable situation he found himself in at Watervliet, Ohio. Although his old friend and spiritual mentor Issachar Bates had been released from his eldership on April 1, 1832, he still lived at the community. Ideally, as a Shaker, Bates's loss of status and new role subservient to McNemar should not have been problematic, but unfortunately, it was. McNemar traced the problems back to his own visit in April 1831 when he failed to implement the covenant. The prospect of signing a new covenant had forced church members to acknowledge and confront the issues dividing them, and this fomented the formation of tacit parties with the "united" family. Following McNemar's appointment as first elder, these factions solidified, and Bates became the de facto head of the dissenters.

McNemar reckoned with this new state of affairs throughout the remainder of 1832. During July, Bates refused to hear the public reading of a letter from ministry elder Solomon King, sending word by a sister "that he don't like that road & intends to have no more to do with our order." McNemar smoothed things over with him, and Bates agreed to once again assume his place in worship. He now danced behind Robert Baxter, a ritual reflection of his lower status in the community's hierarchy.[1] Perhaps in an effort to pacify and distract Bates, McNemar requested that he write his autobiography. He reported the development in a letter to Seth Youngs Wells: "The only thing now presented here for the press, is a manuscript . . . *The Life & Experience of Issachar Bates*, written by himself. For my own part I consider it a well written affair, & worthy of all acceptation. Perhaps I feel some partiality towards it, as I was one among others who requested him to write it."² Although McNemar intended to print it, this never came to pass.

That summer, however, McNemar did print an expanded edition of Calvin Green and Seth Youngs Wells's *Brief Exposition*. It was one of the most handsome productions of his Union Press. He authored the supplementary content with David Spinning and explicated the process of joining a Shaker community and moving from a probationary membership to a fully covenanted church member. McNemar also published the covenant itself, in generic form, thus making it publicly available in an attempt to forestall the claims of anti-Shakers and apostates. When he finished the printing, McNemar excitedly wrote Wells, explaining that the covenant had been added "for the law hawks to pick the bones of."³

He inquired if Wells, the primary author of this now-revised text, would like a few advance copies sent before the bulk shipment—"a few drops before the shower." With the humility that he habitually adopted when writing his eastern superior, he demurred that Wells might not "be very thirsty, for the waters of the West; but your little cloud, having gone the rounds, & collected such a quantity of vapor, no doubt you will want to taste the contents of it, to know whether it is bettered or worsted by the increase." McNemar nervously feared Wells would judge the publication had become "so corrupted by his journey to the west that his lot will be in some back order till confession & purification entitle him to a readmittance into your fellowship."⁴

McNemar's epistolary friendship with Wells had grown considerably deeper by 1832. The highly educated Wells was the right-hand man and scribe of New Lebanon Ministry elder Rufus Bishop. Through him, McNemar had a direct line to the top of the Shaker hierarchy and a sounding board for controversial issues. Their correspondence is by turns erudite, humorous, gossipy, and, at least on McNemar's part, sycophantic. Wells very clearly admired McNemar's tremendous intellect and his undeniable commitment to and enthusiasm for Shakerism. His letters, however, convey an air of proper detachment, whereas McNemar's contain many playful allusions and reaffirmations of his subservient role in the relationship. For instance, he confided to Wells that he wanted to share his experiences at length, but then stated, "I feel cautious of grasping at any privilege there that would indicate that I felt any special claim to your notice or jurisdiction, one side of our common order."⁵

Despite this, because of their close work on legal matters, McNemar admitted, "I have almost imperceptibly contracted a feeling to open & detail matters & things to you, relating to my experience & views, with as much, (if not a little more) freedom, as I do at home, especially as I conceive that less mortification would result from a foreign gift than one that is set to check my excentric flights of fancy."[6] McNemar's "flights of fancy" did indeed become increasingly eccentric as the decade wore on, yet Wells remained a firmly committed correspondent who helped him to navigate the major changes that unfolded in the Shaker West. Dealing with such important issues over time, and at such a distance, was far from ideal, as Wells expressed to McNemar with humorous frustration:

> But if you would just step over the Allegany hills, or jump into a canal boat & come & sit down here in my room a few hours, we feel confident we could easily satisfy your mind in full—You might then step back again with some new ideas on the subject, which perhaps never before entered your heart. But I suppose you are so bound to your charge at Watervliet that you cannot get away; besides the hills are high, the canals are long & the lake is broad & deep, so I suppose what is done, must be done by scribbling, back & forth; unless you could send an ambassador to negotiate a treaty of general harmony of sentiment; and bring forth a new and more perfect covenant.[7]

McNemar was enveloped in legal matters throughout the summer and fall, requiring further travel. First, he was deposed at Harrodsburg for the lawsuit that Pleasant Hill apostates James Gass and Samuel Banta had brought against the community.[8] Next, he found himself deposing veterans of the Revolutionary War at Union Village. Following the passage of the Pension Act (4 Stat. 529) passed by Congress on June 7, 1832, Shakers were confronted with the awkward question of receiving monies for their services in war. Granted, the war was fought before the conversion of any of the men in question and was also viewed by the Shakers as providential, as it allowed for the establishment of freedom of religion in the new United States. Shakers, however, were committed pacifists and recoiled at the thought of receiving money for bloodshed. In fact, the year before, the sect published Seth Youngs Wells's vehemently anti-war book, *A Brief Illustration of the Principles of War and Peace*.

Despite this, a council of Union Village leadership decided on September 13 that it was acceptable for members to accept their pensions and contribute them to the united interest of the community. It was acknowledged that many of the "aged brethren are past maintaining themselves or fulfilling the common obligations of Chh members in supporting the interest by their actual services, it is highly proper that should be released from those obligations & enjoy the benifits of those provisions rightfully meritted from government in their younger days." Additionally, the Union Village Ministry decided that since Shaker communities paid taxes, thereby contributing "their equal part for the support of the government," receiving the pension monies was morally and ethically acceptable. Accordingly, McNemar sat with veterans Francis Bedle, Joseph Stout, John Houston, Abner Bonnel, Reuben Morris, Benjamin Howard, Abijah Pelham, and Benjamin Cox, carefully recording the details of their service for use in their pension applications.[9]

McNemar returned to Watervliet on September 17. Bates had also been away, and when he arrived home, tensions between the two ratcheted up again. As Bates's biographer Carol Medlicott notes, after he relinquished his eldership, Bates created "dynamics that were awkward at best and outright disruptive at worst."[10] Following the Sabbath meeting on December 9, McNemar wrote in his journal, "Heavy labors with E.[lder] I.[ssachar] His trials are heavy at the Eldership for acting in any matter without his knowing and judging of every thing that transpires." After three hours of reassurance, Bates was mollified, although McNemar knew his authority was tenuous at best. He despaired, "It is all a farce about his surrendering his gift & authority to Eleazar. There is nothing of it. His long labors among this people gives him a claim that he never means to relinquish."[11]

Clearly stung by Bates's intractable nature, the next morning McNemar recorded his thoughts on the surrender and transfer of power in his journal. Reviewing the full scope of spiritual authority from the time of the Kentucky Revival to the present, he wrote, "The gift has passed from one to another from the beginning." In his view, the three original Shaker missionaries to Ohio and Kentucky, Bates, Meacham, and Youngs, were given their license to preach from the ministry at New Lebanon. They were not, however, given the authority to gather the people into a community. That authority was given by the "existing order" of the "Turtle Creek session"; he used a Presbyterian term to mean the religious leadership of that nascent community. In McNemar's view, the spiritual "chain was never broken." When the missionaries arrived, they found that "all things were in perfect readiness & it remained for the workmen to go to work & do it according to the pattern already shown." Although the exact import of his comments is uncertain, McNemar clearly viewed himself as a qualified and sanctioned leader who had willingly submitted in 1805 to a higher spiritual authority. In 1832, he found that Bates, one his original mentors, was unwilling to surrender his "gift" under similar circumstances.[12]

McNemar was seized with a violent bout of dysentery in mid-December. The stressful situation he found himself in could not have helped his health. On December 18, a conference was held with regard to signing and implementing the covenant, a matter that had been delayed since McNemar introduced it at

Watervliet in April 1831. The purpose of the meeting was to explore the reasons why it had not been adopted and, more sensitively, to probe whether the eldership had worsened the situation "by unwise speeches." Bates quickly quashed that idea by stating, "I am not sorry for any thing I said nor ever shall be." More than ten other key members were still opposed, so the matter remained unresolved, to McNemar's great frustration.[13]

Covenant matters remained fraught as 1833 dawned. McNemar made some progress when, on January 15, fifty-two members signed a document called the General Rules (similar to the articles of acquittance signed at Union Village), which served as a mutual release regarding property held in common. This was a preparatory step to implementing the full covenant.[14] McNemar wrote to Wells of the continuing troubles at Watervliet and also ruminated on the local accommodations reflected in the language of the legal instruments signed at Pleasant Hill and elsewhere. He feared that these differences, "if they are finally suffered to pass, [would] ... veto the identity & unity of the instrument, and each Society remains as heretofore measurably independent of any general compact."[15]

This, he reminded Wells, was the "primary object" of implementing a new covenant: "To leave one Uniform and explicit covenant adapted to the general circumstances of each Society." McNemar also sought guidance about whether he and Bates should sign the Watervliet covenant and, if so, as subjects or merely witnesses. Bates had signed a covenant at Union Village in 1810, and McNemar had *witnessed* the new covenant at Union Village in 1829, but it was not a legal signatory. Although McNemar believed it would set a good example for reluctant Shakers at Watervliet to see these men submit to the instrument, he was uncertain of the propriety or legality of binding himself and Bates to the "united interest" of the community. McNemar was given latitude to seek the advice of the eastern ministry on this question by Union Village Ministry elder Solomon King.[16]

McNemar sent Wells a freshly printed version of the General Rules. Wells, greatly troubled by the document, wrote in a confidential postscript to McNemar, "Respecting the General Rules, I hardly know what to say." Wells considered that the first article—a statement guaranteeing individual religious freedom—was "calculated to nullify the intention of all the rest." He averred that Watervliet "would be in a safer situation without any Covenant at all" and judged the General Rules to be a "dangerous thing" as a legal instrument and wished that "every copy of it could be secured, original & all, and committed to the flames." Wells was careful to soften the blow by stating that he did not blame McNemar for this circumstance and was aware of the burdens he labored under.[17] In his reply, McNemar humorously wrote, "The sentence of ... consigning to the flames & setting fire to the office & taking the life of the Editor are expressions not very terrifying, yet softer terms from Brethren would better suit the delicate feelings of my little *domine*."[18]

Wells found the problems attendant to implementing the covenant at Watervliet appalling, writing, "I don't know what kind of Believers you have at Watervliet." He informed McNemar that the covenant had been instituted in the eastern communities with "no difficulty worth mentioning. If anyone did not chuse to sign, we did not chuse he should, because we want none but free volunteers, such as count it a privilege to be enrolled with their brethren & sisters in the bonds of gospel union." Wells wanted no "vacillating hesitating souls"; these "ought to go where more license and latitude can be indulged." In fact, Wells had traveled among the eastern communities during the winter of 1832/1833 and was "repeatedly told" that "they esteemed a privilege to receive any council or order, to adopt any instrument sent from, or recommended by, the church at New Lebanon." This was a harsh rebuke to many longtime western Shakers. As for McNemar and Bates signing, Wells explained that at New Lebanon the ministry and elders had signed on a blank page opposite, approving the covenant. Wells recommended that the same practice be employed in the western communities.[19]

In February 1833, however, the Shakers at Watervliet were still uncertain exactly who their elders and eldresses were! It finally fell to Issachar Bates to write the Union Village Ministry on February 4, stating that the people at Watervliet were ready to move forward but were waiting for "those who had been appointed as Elders" to be anointed. As long as they were mere candidates, the people were "suspicious of them." Bates recommended McNemar, Robert Baxter, Salome Dennis, and Eunice Bedle. Elder Solomon King wrote to the community in reply on February 8, confirming those four in their positions and stating that McNemar had been first elder at Watervliet for ten months already, a fact that many there had refused to acknowledge.[20] There could be no more definitive statement than this, yet matters still were not resolved.

Benjamin Seth Youngs visited Watervliet during May. Tensions there were greatly relieved when Bates departed with him on May 27 for a lengthy visit to Kentucky. McNemar accompanied them on their travels for the first fifteen days, suggesting a detente had been reached. After stops at Union Village and White Water, the party arrived in Cincinnati. There, Issachar Bates stopped at a pension bank and withdrew $191 of his newly acquired pension for services in the Revolutionary War. He sent $150 of this money with McNemar for the community and took the balance as spending money. While at South Union and Pleasant Hill, he spent freely, among other things buying tea for the sisters for a "love feast." On his way back to Watervliet, he withdrew another $47 from the bank, stating he was "determined to get all the money I could from the United States while I live." This behavior reached the ears of the New Lebanon Ministry, igniting another controversy that engulfed McNemar.[21]

Bates returned to Watervliet on September 16, and McNemar noted, "His health [is] poor & his life is deemed pretty precarious."[22] Bates was severely taken to task by the New Lebanon Ministry, who were unaware that any of the western Shakers had applied for and received pension monies. They considered military pensions a reward for "death and destruction" and the "price of blood."[23] Although Bates had conducted his service in "nature's darkness"; that is, before conversion, as a Shaker pacifist and missionary they considered that he would "have been one of the last men on earth" to accept a pension. In a pointed rebuke, they put forth the example of Amos Buttrick, a Shirley, Massachusetts, Shaker who had lost an eye during his service and was awarded a life pension beginning shortly after the war. Buttrick had carefully saved the considerable money he received in a stocking until finally, in consultation with his elders, he returned it to the government as a conscientious objector. Bates felt severely chastened by the ministry and wrote them a lengthy justification of his action.[24]

McNemar was the agent of many western brethren in securing their pensions—some of the surviving narratives are written in his own hand. As he had throughout his life, McNemar took up his pen and composed a powerful memorial to the New Lebanon Ministry on behalf of the Revolutionary veterans at Union Village and Watervliet, Ohio. McNemar argued that they had fought to establish "liberty of conscience" and the "sacred rights of man." He adopted a sharper tone than usual when he reminded the ministry, "You are now mostly of the single class of men and women—you have happily avoided most of the calamities & sufferings of your predecessors.... They had souls just like yours; but they had to hear see & feel what you have scarcely been permitted to think of. Surrounded by fleets and armies on the south and East, and by hosts of prowling savages on the north and west; fighting had to be done:—and it was done to good purpose." McNemar also reminded the ministry of the thousands of dollars in fines paid by Shaker communities east and west for refusing to train with local militias. Surely, accepting pension funds as recompense was justified. In closing, the memorialists vowed to accept the decision of the ministry regarding the monies, even if they were instructed "to purchase a spot of ground separate from your church premises where our bones may be deposited out of your sight." McNemar signed (as Eleazar Wright) on behalf of Bates and eight other veterans. McNemar bordered on insubordination in this letter, and the defiant closing statement is unlike anything else he wrote to his eastern superiors.[25]

The New Lebanon Ministry responded through their counterparts at Union Village on February 3, 1834. They advised that communication regarding pensions be limited or avoided altogether—the issue had clearly not arisen yet in the East. It was judged best to leave things as they were, with western pensioners deemed acceptable. As for the despondent Bates, they told him to "cease from his tribulation, for he that hath wrought so great salvation shall not die, nor lose his union for what he has honestly and innocently done in accepting his pension."[26]

Despite Bates's absence for part of 1833 and the unifying effect the pension crisis seems to have had, the issue of spiritual authority at Watervliet, Ohio, was anything but settled. Bates was still hearing the confessions of those who felt he was their elder; McNemar, not wishing to "scrouge Elder I[ssachar] out of any gift or privilege," went along with this practice. Observing this situation, Elder Archibald Meacham had commented to McNemar, "As long as Elder Issachar remained on the ground the people would never be gathered to another." The sisters were particularly solicitous of Bates and concerned with his health. McNemar wrote that their "study & labor day and night is to make Elder Issachar comfortable," and they were anxious for him to be relieved of his responsibilities. Bates, however, suspiciously regarded the sisters' sentiments as "most cruel & ungrateful," considering them to be part of a conspiracy to remove him from his eldership. Caught between these factions, McNemar resolved to "utterly refuse to head either party." This stance perhaps afforded him a clear conscience, but it left matters at Watervliet highly unstable.[27]

THE EAGLE AND THE DAMAGE DONE

Since their conversions in 1805, Richard McNemar's nuclear family and some extended family had surrounded him at Union Village. In light of the requirement to eschew blood relations, they had for many years faded into the background of his Shaker life. However, beginning in the 1830s, dealings with his blood relatives played an increasingly prominent role in his life. Some aspects were positive, but as the decade wore on, many became overwhelmingly negative. The majority of McNemar's surviving children had been tapped for leadership roles. Nancy McNemar had served as second eldress in the Union Village Ministry since 1829, and her brother James was second elder in the community's Centre House Family from 1828 to 1829 until his health failed (his father temporarily succeeded him). In 1830, when James recovered his health, he was appointed second elder at the Brick House Family.[28] On June 16, 1833, his eldest daughter Vincy, thirty-five, was appointed to the important position of second eldress at the North Union, Ohio, community. Finally, his nephew Levi McNemar was a solid believer who worked in agriculture and the building trades.[29] His son and namesake, Richard McNemar Jr., however, remained out of the fold since his apostasy in 1828. In 1833, he initiated a correspondence with his father. The man who had to some degree fomented Richard Jr.'s apostasy, Aquila Massie Bolton, still resided at Union Village. McNemar referred to Aquila as the "eagle," a literal translation of his name from the Latin and one that McNemar thought captured his rapacious and predatory nature toward the souls of his fellow Believers. Bolton and McNemar had clashed in 1828 over Bolton's promotion of Swedenborgianism, although things had calmed down following the more insidious problems with Abijah Alley. In the intervening years, Bolton continued to circulate Swedenborg's writings, even though he had agreed to keep them under lock and key as a condition of his remaining a Shaker. McNemar published two tracts against Bolton, *A Series of Lectures on Orthodoxy and Heterodoxy* (1832) and *Western Expositor, No. 4* (undated). Bolton finally left Union Village on January 31, 1833, thus ending the controversy, but McNemar was left deeply wounded by his son's apostasy.[30]

Richard McNemar Jr. had settled in Urbana, Ohio, about sixty-five miles northeast of Union Village. There, the twenty-eight-year-old worshipped with a circle of Swedenborgians started by four families in 1816.[31] McNemar's letter to his father of September 16, 1833, was apparently their first contact since his apostasy in 1828. The letter is lost, unfortunately, although much of its content can be gleaned from lengthy quoted passages in McNemar Sr.'s reply of October 8. His passions were clearly roused, as the letter fills six dense manuscript pages. He began by quoting Samuel to Saul, "Why hast thou disquieted me?" McNemar found his son's letter full of "duplicity," manifested in "affection and disaffection" and "respect and disrespect." McNemar found his son's letter lacking the key elements of a "serious address to an acknowledged superior." Accordingly, he structured his "sober and serious reply" as an educational rebuke, comprising variously "invocation, accusation, defamation, lamentation, self-exaltation, and high expectation." McNemar Jr. addressed his letter to his "Esteemed & Venerated Father," which Sr. dismissed, writing, "Your claim to sonship cannot be based on the mere circumstance of my being the reputed means of your animal existence." Sr. reminded Jr. that in 1820, Jr., in committing fully to Shakerism, had asked his father to "crucify all natural attachment." As a result, Sr. averred that Jr. must regard him only as a "teacher, care-taker or head of family." To prove his point, Sr. quoted Jr.'s letter, in which he wrote, "The relation which you have borne toward me has ever seemed not that of a Father, an affectionate & kind father, but rather that of a fear giving master." Sr. was appalled that his son used the very same words as apostate Henry Baily in Abram Van Vleet's 1818 anti-Shaker publication. Sr. railed at these accusations from "one who drew his first breath under my paternal care and every other breath for 21 years under my special providence!" and declared, "No chance of getting near me for a sociable chat!!"[32]

Echoing another charge commonly leveled by apostates and anti-Shakers, McNemar Jr. accused his father of neglecting his education. He wrote, "I was brought up in ignorance.... I was not instructed in any thing but the doctrines you inculcate." Sr. refuted this entirely, reminding Jr. of his thorough instruction in English, arts, and sciences, querying, "How many branches of manual labor were you instructed in?" Jr. complained that he was not allowed to visit with his Shaker friends at Union Village without a witness present, a circumstance Sr. credited to Jr.'s "bad character." Jr. also claimed he was denied liberty of conscience and that the Shakers withheld "books to learn the theories, doctrines & practices of others." Sr. fired back, "We prohibited Aristotles Masterpiece [a spurious obstetrics manual], Mary Dyer [a noted Shaker apostate], Paine, Hume & Voltaire, in short, every book that we considered corrupting to the minds of youth." Sr. reminded Jr. that he had "Websters spelling book... the New Testament, the Testamony, Manifesto & many other book, both religious and scientific." Jr. complained that he was not allowed to interact with those who believed in other doctrines. Sr. blasted back, "Were you debarred from intercourse with A. H. Bolton who had alternately been a Quaker, a lawyer, a merchant, a Swedenborgian an Owenite a Deist, an avowed Atheist, & at the time, capable of Believing and teaching any thing but the truth?" Revealing the depth of his fanatic devotion to Shakerism, Sr. cruelly unloaded on his son, "Poor fellow! What a sad fix you were in! A mind capable of boundless improvement, but pent up in the iron grasp of a 'fear-giving master.' No book! No teacher! no liberty of conscience to extend a thought beyond the narrow limits of our barren doctrine of virtue, innocence, and devotion to God in doing good!! What a stoic I must be not to drop a tear over the detail of your unparralelled sufferings!" Sr. forcefully asserted that he had raised Jr. to "confess Christ crucified" but had never compelled him to live as a Shaker.[33]

For McNemar Sr., the proof of Jr.'s liberty of conscience was found in his apostasy. Sr. could not acknowledge the validity of Jr.'s assertion that he had a "right which I had the liberty of any moment exercising with all its paralyzing consequences"—referring to his apostasy. Sr. asserted that Jr. exercised his civic and legal right to leave the community. Before that, however, Jr. had to abrogate his conscience as exercised when he signed the covenant. Sr., therefore, distinguished between liberty of conscience and rights of conscience; to leave the Shakers "was not included in the bill of Rights pertaining to the gospel, but to the bill of wrongs." Jr. begged Sr. not to hold him in a bad light. In response, Sr. callously declared to Jr. that he "let go my hold of you when you rejected my authority and claimed the liberty of independently choosing for yourself." As proof, he reminded Jr. that he had not contacted him since the day he "hoisted his umbrella & took up the line of march for Lebanon."[34]

Richard McNemar Sr. had no sympathy for Jr.'s lament that when he left the Shakers, he "was like a child thrown helpless among men, a forlorn cast off child." In reply, Sr. wrote, "I went to shift for myself when almost seven years younger than you were & with rather an inferior outfit." Despite being initially adrift, Jr. settled in Urbana and studied the law, telling his father he expected to succeed in the profession. Sr. dismissed Jr.'s "*High Expectations* of success in your profession [as] exclusively your own." Jr. threatened to cease the correspondence, provoking Sr. to state that his reply was his "first & last [letter], I submit it without apology or comment." Sr. closed by describing Jr. as someone who would "dirk my character, my faith & my only hope of future felicity." He asked that Jr. not impose his "weak & contemptible" letters on the church any longer. Thus ended the correspondence, although troubles in the extended McNemar family, as well as Richard Jr.'s genuine concern for his father, triggered subsequent communications during the crisis surrounding the end of Sr.'s life.[35]

The year 1833 had been a particularly difficult one for Richard McNemar, who was at odds with Issachar Bates, one of his spiritual mentors, as well as with his own son and namesake. A kind letter from Elder Rufus Bishop—second in the New Lebanon Ministry—surely lifted his spirits. Bishop's letter was in reply to one of McNemar's from nearly a year before. After apologizing for the delay, he passed along personal expressions of love from each member of the ministry. Bishop flattered McNemar and congratulated him on his faithful travel in the gospel.

> Beloved Friend, when we take a retrospective view of the different courses which have been pursued by the principal leaders in the Kentucky Revival, and consider that all must be rewarded according to their works, and how different the rewards must be at the final settlement, between such as devoted their all to build up the kingdom of God and those who have exerted their noble faculties in trying to destroy it, and in leading astray the souls of men, we feel a peculiar glow of love and blessing which flows freely to you, and

your honest hearted companions who opened your hearts and houses to the messengers of peace from Zion. Sometimes we say among ourselves, "What could our brethren have done towards opining [i.e., opening] the gospel in the West, if Eleazar, Malcham John Dunlavy, and some other who might be mentioned, had withstood the testimony like Barton Stone, Thompson & Marshall &c.["] These considerations serve to increas our love to you, and other who have been like minded; and surely there is no law against love.

Bishop assured McNemar that faithful Shakers "may rest assured that they have inlisted under a Captain who will in no wise cheat them out of their full reward for all their toils and sufferings in his cause, provided they continue true and faithful unto the end." Sadly, in time, he found the opposite to be true.[36]

For now, McNemar continued his efforts to implement the covenant at Watervliet. Elder Solomon King informed the New Lebanon Ministry that he awaited their guidance on the matter but added that the "anxiety in the west to prosecute the thing, has been & principally appears to be in brother Eleazar." McNemar informed Bishop that he had let the issue rest for the better part of the year following the signing of the articles of acquittance. Speaking in metaphorical language, he confided to Bishop:

> You know that your herdsman must first pen up his wild stock in the yard before he can get them into the stable, & each one's neck into its own bow. The stable door looks pokerish and more so the cramp stalls within the secret recesses, the snorting bullock flounces at any attempt to force him in; to drag or drive is preposterous, he must learn by gradual approaches to venture in of his own accord ... for if they perceive any design of taking any advantage to get them in where they can never get out, catch them if you can. So difficult it is to save a lost creature and get him into the yoke of Christ.

Intentionally or otherwise, McNemar's language vindicates the fears of Watervliet Shakers regarding signing the covenant! While dealing with such weighty matters, the sixty-three-year-old McNemar still found ample time for hand labor and worked at "pulling corn, cutting wood mending chairs & old wheels, setting types & binding books." He dismissed these efforts humorously, telling Bishop, "You know that Jack of all trades is good at nothing."[37]

McNemar's epistolary relationship with Bishop and Wells strengthened during these years, perhaps giving him an inflated sense of his place within the Shaker hierarchy. Doubtless, he was the most influential Shaker among the western communities. He had been at the center of all major events in the West since the beginning, and his value was such that he had been deliberately instructed not to sign the covenant to preserve his status as an independent, financially disinterested defender and advocate of Shakerism. McNemar received encouraging words from "Church Scribe" Wells, telling him on Bishop's behalf that "the freedom & openness of your communications have greatly increased his love to the writer," although in another letter, Wells referenced McNemar's "unguarded manner of communication."[38]

Receiving mixed signals, McNemar seems aware that he sometimes went too far in expressing his opinions frankly and openly. Wells assured him, however, that McNemar "must not feel any burden of that kind on my account, about any of your communications to me—Your freedom has always afforded me much satisfaction." In truth, the correspondence between Wells and McNemar betrays the large egos possessed by both men, although Wells was better at employing the rote language of Shaker humility. McNemar, alternatively, employed self-deprecating humor. Despite communicating primarily with his pseudonym Eleazar Wright, he now also adopted the persona of "me poor fellow," based on a Native American beggar he had seen on a Cincinnati-bound canal boat. McNemar assumed this identity whenever he sensed his letters devolving into special pleading on an issue. In one letter to Wells, he admitted, "With all the caution that I am master of I have doubtless many times extended my views, my tongue & my pen far beyond the bounds prescribed."[39] Indeed, he regularly bypassed the authority of his own immediate superior, Elder Solomon King at Union Village. McNemar touted his "divisibility" to Wells, claiming that he could "serve two masters"; that is, the eastern and western Shaker leadership. McNemar claimed, "I have learned in a measure how to be made all things to all men, that by all means I may keep my union with some."[40] There is a whiff of hubris about this statement, and such mistaken beliefs returned to haunt McNemar.

Again testing the prescribed bounds, or perhaps charting them for himself, McNemar unilaterally printed the new covenants and other legal agreements executed in the western Shaker communities during the late 1820s and early 1830s. Shaker leaders in the East and the West were reluctant to make these texts public so as to prevent lawyers from devising strategies to defeat them in court. Elder Solomon King had even cautioned McNemar against printing the covenants for just this reason. McNemar justified his actions to Wells, stating that the Pleasant Hill covenant was publicly available in the recorder's office at Harrodsburg. Despite this, he acknowledged that the work was not sanctioned by the ministry, "I have to confess, that I formed in my own mind the design of recording, in the manner I have done, the several covenants old & new & other important documents connected therewith. I would not say that I have done it out of union, yet it has been upon my own responsibility,

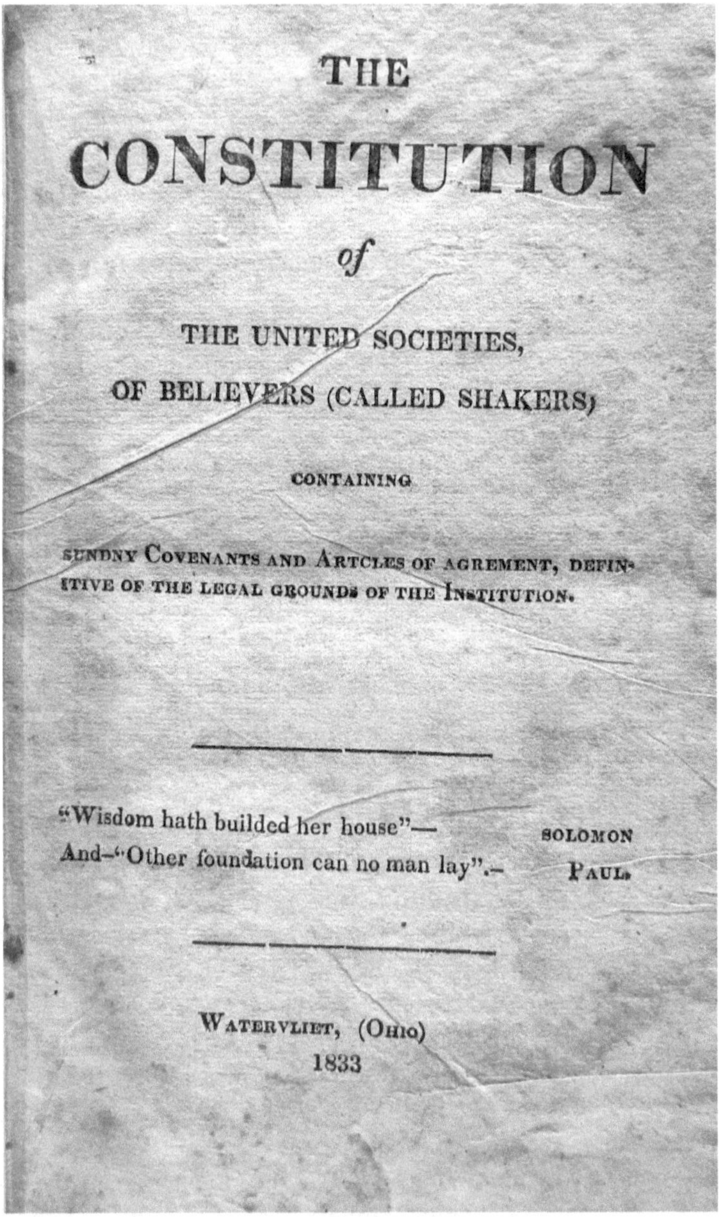

THE
CONSTITUTION
of

THE UNITED SOCIETIES,

OF BELIEVERS (CALLED SHAKERS)

CONTAINING

SUNDRY COVENANTS AND ARTCLES OF AGREMENT, DEFIN-
ITIVE OF THE LEGAL GROUNDS OF THE INSTITUTION.

"Wisdom hath builded her house"—   SOLOMON
And—"Other foundation can no man lay".—   PAUL.

WATERVLIET, (OHIO)
1833

Figure 20.1. *The Constitution of the United Societies, of Believers (Called Shakers)*, Richard McNemar's unauthorized printing of the covenants he had implemented at the western Shaker communities. Communal Societies Collection, Hamilton College.

and in as private secret a manner as circumstances would admit." He had only given copies to King and Benjamin Seth Youngs in the West and was reluctant to ship copies to the East, in case they were pilfered by dishonest postmasters. He assured Wells that he would send some with Shakers back East. The compilation was issued with a title page reading, *Constitution of the United Societies, of Believers (Called Shakers)* and was never circulated beyond Shaker communities, remaining a rare volume to this day. McNemar averred to Wells that the documents exhibited "a more perfect harmony than Matthew Mark Luke & John."[41]

As he aged, McNemar became more conscious of the nebulous position he occupied as an uncovenanted Shaker. He raised the issue in correspondence with Wells, who offered him friendly reassurance that the written covenant was but "an instrument of security ... to bind apostate rogues to their good behavior." Contrastingly, the "real Covenant," which Wells supposed both Bates and McNemar had signed, was the inward covenant written on the heart. He referred McNemar to Jeremiah 31:33 and Hebrews 8:10 for proof of this sentiment. McNemar confirmed that both he and Bates "were as much chh [church] members as if we had signed those written articles" and had indeed subscribed their names to the spiritual covenant, "the law put into the heart and written in the inward parts." He was confident that since he had sold his property to the New Lebanon trustees through the eastern missionaries nearly thirty years before, none of his heirs could make a demand on it. He had also legally partitioned his interest with his wife, Jennie, referred to in this letter to Wells as his "Kicksey-wicksey." This is one of the few references to Jennie found anywhere in the thousands of pages of his extant manuscript writing, and rather than name her, he employed a disdainful slang term for a wife. Despite his belief that he had satisfied any obligations to his wife or potential heirs, the constant lawsuits filed against the Shakers concerned him. He confided to Wells, "You need not think strange that my views & feelings should change to suit the times." McNemar worried that although he was firm in the spiritual covenant, the consecration of his property to the church was not safe, "where flesh and blood can get up any possible claim," without subscription to the Union Village covenant.[42]

The issue of McNemar and Bates's legal status regarding the covenant was being explored as New Lebanon Ministry Elder Rufus Bishop and Brother Isaac Newton Youngs were preparing for their journey to visit the western Shaker communities. Bishop carried a letter from Wells to McNemar that he delivered on his arrival. Wells had written that once McNemar and his companions met the visitors and felt the "influence of their rays, they will readily admit that they are stars from the east, and if not of the first magnitude, they are at least pure emanations from the atmosphere of New Lebanon."[43]

Wells also suggested a novel (and completely ineffectual) remedy for the legal insecurity felt by both McNemar and Bates. He stated that he had no doubt that they were "both honest men," but "lest Bates & McNemar should finally turn out to be rogues," his plan would "secure the rogue from future mischief." The two men were to "draw a good substantial & permanent bond," binding them in an everlasting covenant of union to the communities of Union Village and New Lebanon. This bond was to be executed in the presence of Elders Rufus Bishop and Solomon King, each representing the ministry of their communities, who would also hold copies for safekeeping. Wells hoped that his plan would "settle the matter at once & forever." It does not appear that it was ever executed, and the naivete of its conception, especially in light of the trouble McNemar shortly found himself in, evidences astonishing shortsightedness on the part of Seth Youngs Wells, the chief legal counsel of all Shaker societies.[44]

LOVING MESSENGERS FROM THE EAST

Richard McNemar's 1829 visit to the East was a tremendously affirming experience that left him yearning for the opportunity to see his eastern friends and spiritual mentors once more. In late 1833, his hopes seemed to be entirely dashed. In a letter to Wells, he wrote, "It was painful to learn ... that we were never to expect a visit from your Ministry. O center of Union! are we never to see a loving messenger, from your maternal bosom but forever to depend on the dead, dumb & unyielding letter."[45] Just when all hope seemed lost, the western communities received the joyous news that Elder Rufus Bishop, second elder of the New Lebanon Ministry and McNemar's correspondent, would visit them during the summer of 1834. Accompanying Bishop was Isaac Newton Youngs, the younger brother of Benjamin Seth Youngs, one of the original missionaries.

The forty-one-year-old Youngs was a brilliant man who served many roles in the New Lebanon community, including scribe and journalist.[46] In a letter to McNemar written on June 9, 1834, Wells did not address his concerns about the covenant but instead conveyed the "love of the whole Church to Br. Rufus & Br. Isaac." Further, McNemar was "authorized to hug and kiss them for us all."[47] Bishop and Youngs had left New Lebanon on June 2. They boarded a boat on the Erie Canal at Schenectady on June 5. On their way west, they visited Shaker communities at Watervliet and Sodus Bay, New York, and North Union, Ohio. They arrived at Union Village, Ohio, on June 29.[48] Bishop and Youngs stayed for ten days before departing for Watervliet, Ohio, on July 10. They arrived in the early afternoon. Youngs recorded the happy moment in his journal, "First met Elder Issachar—& pretty soon E. Eleazar. They were much pleased to see us, & hugged & kissed us; said they had orders to do so, right from Lebanon."[49] McNemar had followed Wells's instructions to the letter.

For the next seventeen days, McNemar basked in the presence of his eastern friends and spiritual mentors. At a public meeting on Sunday, July 13, Bates and Ashbel Kitchell preached in the presence of the easterners, after which McNemar demonstrated his poetic gifts by reciting a hymn from memory, a feat Youngs noted in his journal. The next day, Bishop and Youngs toured McNemar's printing office. There they saw some of the church records he had so carefully collected and preserved, including volumes of correspondence (which have been used in the writing of this biography). McNemar was gratified to read the men his manuscript, "history of the rise of progress of the society," at Watervliet, Ohio.[50]

Bishop and Youngs returned to Union Village on July 15. McNemar followed four days later and spoke at a public meeting on July 20 regarding "confession—Christ's suffering for sinners, & of the resurrection."[51] The eastern elders departed for White Water on July 24 and from there traveled to Pleasant Hill and South Union, Kentucky, staying through August and September, and returned to Union Village on September 17. While they itinerated through the western communities receiving love and welcome wherever they went, tensions at Watervliet, Ohio, were reaching crisis level. Despite all of the time Bishop and Youngs spent with the western leadership, it is unknown if the problems at Watervliet were ever broached.[52] It would not have been in Elder Solomon King's interest to bring them up, as the core issues evidenced his own weak and indecisive nature. McNemar and Bates probably shied away as well, not wanting to expose such base disunion to their eastern elders. Additionally, Bates was deeply suspicious that King harbored feelings of hostility and resentment toward him.

At Watervliet that August, McNemar and Bates continued to haggle over their respective statuses. McNemar suggested to Bates that Bates had been sent to the West as a minister to gather and establish the church, but he was not meant to serve as an elder in an established community. McNemar tempered that by assuring Bates that he "would forever be acknowledged & respected in his proper order & relation to us all & doubtless rewarded for all the good he had done." McNemar called Bates a "father" with regard to the Watervliet Shakers and asserted that their "mutual gift & calling had been as helps to the ministry." Bates agreed, recalling that Father David Darrow had often said,

"You & Eleazar are my ministers." Accordingly, following the collapse of West Union, Darrow had sent Bates as his agent to take charge of the Watervliet society; in the same vein, Elder Solomon King had sent McNemar there to implement the new covenant, a task as yet unaccomplished. The two men left matters there, although the underlying conflict of their hierarchical relationship to the flock at Watervliet remained unresolved. In his journal, McNemar reflected on the situation, "And what a pick[le] is it of a branch of the church in this latter day, and what is to be done to preserve the unity of the spirit in the [word missing] of peace?"[53]

By September 1, Bates, apparently emotionally unstable and deeply insecure about his role, had entirely changed his thinking. In his journal, McNemar recorded a lengthy conversation with his "aged friend." Bates recapitulated yet another retrospective analysis of the events that brought him to Watervliet, concluding that the "whole burden of every thing spiritual & temporal" had fallen primarily to him. Bates admitted that he found this mentally overwhelming and therefore welcomed McNemar's help to "lighten his load, but by no means to release from his original gift of care & bury him before he was actually dead." Bates made it clear that he still regarded himself as the leading male member of the society, irrespective of titles acknowledged or otherwise. If this was the case, McNemar and Bates agreed that it remained to be "settled by the higher authorities" whether or not Bates should be allowed to choose his successor. In leaving this question open, McNemar chose not to assert the fact that he had been sent to Watervliet as first elder in April 1832.[54]

Elder Solomon King invited McNemar, Bates, and others from Watervliet to Union Village to greet Bishop and Youngs on their return from Kentucky. On September 13, an angry and paranoid Bates found McNemar in his shop and expressed his unwillingness to go. Bates feared that King had "given his character to the visitants in the darkest colors, & it would go to the east that he was a poor old creature that never had any spiritual gift,—and never was qualified to lead a society." He asked McNemar to go on his behalf and defend his character to Bishop. Days later, Bates asserted that King "hated him & meant to take every advantage to afflict him" and that King treated him like the "meanest underling." In the end, he feared that despite all his "labors & suffering," which King "acknowledged were more than any one from the East had gone thro," he must at last come out "a mere cypher."—a zero.[55]

Despite his bitter dread, Bates accompanied McNemar and Eldresses Salome Dennis and Eunice Bedle to Union Village to take a final leave of Bishop and Youngs. Good feelings prevailed, as Bishop and Bates spontaneously joined McNemar and Eunice Bedle in singing and "a little spree at dancing" while touring the Square House and Grist Mill Families on September 25. Bates and McNemar likely attended the farewell meeting for Bishop and Youngs on Sunday, September 28. Bishop preached, telling the assembly that it was likely "the last time that we should all meet together." He admonished the Shakers that to prosper they "must be reconciled to the gift of God in their lead that is manifested for their protection & it must be by coming down into the valley of humiliation & being united with each other." Notably, he warned them not to have their faith "in persons but in the gift of God."[56]

Intentionally or not, Bishop indirectly highlighted the personality cults that had permeated western Shakerism, beginning with Father David Darrow and that were also manifested in former Pleasant Hill leader Father John Meacham and—destructively so—in apostate Abijah Alley, and that were still present with Issachar Bates. Assuming he was there, McNemar may not have counted himself among that number, but others were beginning to perceive that for all his dedication and zeal, his ego had long since left the valley of humiliation.[57] Bishop and Youngs departed for New Lebanon on October 1, 1834. Their tour had been edifying and a successful demonstration of the love borne to the West by the eastern Believers. It had also given Bishop a chance to assess for himself the state of affairs in the West, some aspects of which were cause for grave concern. Indeed, McNemar wrote Wells that while Bishop and Youngs were present, the western Shakers felt "as if the eye of God was upon us and that all our backwoods nastiness & disorder will speedily come to Judgment." His words proved prophetic.[58]

McNemar conveyed Bishop's sentiments regarding acquiescence to the gifts of the eastern ministry in a letter to Wells. He reported that Elder Solomon King asserted that the western Shakers had not yet even approached the order gained in the eastern communities and that they could do so only by sacrifice. McNemar asked rhetorically, regarding Watervliet, whether it was not time "to sacrifice a rogue whose work is finished, & make room for him whose right is to reign[?]"; specifically, to have "an Elder Br & Sister at the head of a family instead of a patriarchal skeleton." McNemar humorously and habitually referred to Bates and himself as "rogues" in letters to Wells, but it is hard to interpret "patriarchal skeleton" as referring to anyone else but Bates. Further, he asked whose example would be better for the community, Bates: "an image of the past standing in the temple of God," or himself: "a living man of God with xt[Christ] in him." McNemar's unkindness to Bates here is stunning, and he seems to have been aware of the fact, marking this letter to Wells as "confidentissimus" (highly confidential) and closing, "Doubtless my late communication & this with the rest will convince you that I am not as I ought to be."[59]

Perhaps not unreasonably, Bates's paranoia increased throughout the autumn of 1834. As his biographer Carol Medlicott points out, Bates may have been "regularly consuming raw spirits, albeit with medicinal intent, possibly along with opium preparations," practices that possibly contributed to his mental turmoil. On November 1, he engaged McNemar in a "long and serious talk" and expressed his "ardent wish for some testimony to be established that he had ministered the gospel & taught the orders of God in that place." McNemar demurred, saying he had not been present to witness such events and could find no written record of Bates's teachings. He agreed, however, to compile a "memorial of the genious & spirit of the gospel which we had received." The finished product, a series of pamphlets titled *The Western Review*, was issued from his press from November 1834 through January 1835. McNemar hoped it would "give a reviving pulse to church order which was passing off like the rays of the settling sun glimmering on the mountains brow."[60]

Although the printing is somewhat crude, the work's fifty-six pages present the clearest extant record of Father David Darrow's teachings, even delving into table manners. The work also contains a brief memorial of Mother Ruth Farrington and a chronological record of events and deaths. McNemar reported satisfaction with his efforts, although Bates is not featured prominently. As with the *Constitution*, McNemar had undertaken this project entirely on his own initiative. He sent a copy to Elder Solomon King, who warned him "that it contained some very good things but concluded that at the village it would not do to circulate it at present." McNemar also sent copies to Benjamin Seth Youngs and Rufus Bishop for their inspection, but the work was never circulated widely.[61]

BATES IS RECALLED TO THE EAST

The new year began with a troubling Sabbath night dream that McNemar wrote down, labeling it "confidential." On the night of January 4, 1835, McNemar dreamed that he was in a "great labor of mind" as to how to deal with the problems surrounding Bates. Father David Darrow appeared to McNemar, seated before him on a chair, "His countenance was beautiful as an angel and solemn as eternity his eyes were fixed on me with a penetrating look." Darrow's gaze communicated to McNemar the seriousness of the situation that confronted him. When Darrow understood that McNemar's eyes were open to the severity of the trouble, Darrow "looked pensive and pitiful at me, and the tears began to drop from his eyes, expressive of his heartfelt sorrow that his labors were in danger of being slighted, and the order he had established set at nought."[62]

A bitter confrontation ensued between Bates and McNemar on Tuesday, January 6. Bates, having come to Union Village, found McNemar in his shop and, as McNemar wrote, "proceeded to pour upon me such a sluice of accusations as had never before saluted my ears, of abuses & ill treatment sufficient to crush an angel." Bates accused McNemar of falsely informing mutual friends in the East that Bates was dead and stating that Bates had "never done any good" in the West. Bates said McNemar's treatment of him was "like the bite of a rattlesnake." According to his written account, McNemar remained perfectly composed and calmly refuted Bates's accusations. Bates's ire was quelled for the moment, but, unbeknownst to them, the two men had little time remaining to repair their friendship.[63]

The summons Issachar Bates had long dreaded arrived in the form of a letter from Elder Ebenezer Bishop, first in the New Lebanon Ministry. The seventy-seven-year-old Bates was commended for his labors in the service of the gospel, the last thirty years of which were carried out in the West. He was advised to return home, departing in "justification and union," thereby becoming "a bright zealous young man again!"[64] These words rang hollow to Bates, whom McNemar found "bathing his cheeks in tears." Writing retrospectively of this moment in a supplement to his "Autobiography," Bates recalled that he

> wandered up and down bewailing my fate, but all to no purpose; I must go and leave my people, that felt dearer to me than my natural life. For I could have died, and been buried on the ground that I had purchased with my life. I could have laid my old head down in peace. But perhaps the reader would say I am exposing myself, that it shows an unreconciled mind. Well what of all that, I am writing my experience and I mean to be honest about it. Perhaps you may have the brains beat out of your soul, some day, and then you will know what heart rending sorrow is and not till then.[65]

As a loyal Shaker, however, he was determined to comply, although he called it an "unreasonable requisition."[66]

The letter had arrived on March 20, 1835. McNemar observed, "The destiny of this great man is settled by one confessedly greater than he." Matters between the two men, however, were not yet settled. Bates still harbored resentment at what he perceived as McNemar's attempt to supplant "him of his office and title" as elder—as Bates expressed it, "rooting him out." Bates had a dream that he shared with many others at Watervliet of a "great long snouted hog" which he killed. Bates made it clear that the hog represented McNemar. By sad coincidence, earlier that same day, the two men had earnestly tried to resolve the long-running controversy over clerical primacy. This was satisfactorily achieved in the presence of the coterie of sisters who watched over Bates. The arrival of Bishop's letter, however, threw everything into a tumult. Bates reverted to ranting against Elder Solomon King and declaring that he never asked to be released from his position at Watervliet. Of particular concern to Bates was the disposition of his pension money. McNemar remarked snidely in his journal of Bates, "One thing is certain that where his treasure is, there will his heart be also."[67]

The disorder that prevailed at Watervliet only grew worse. McNemar noted in his journal on March 31, "I moved my important papers to the garret, & put them under double locks for safety. This evening there was a striking trial of spirits [in?] meeting, which induced me to lodge in the garret for safety." The defection from the community on April 16 of Elder Robert Baxter, a Shaker of twenty years standing and part of the uneasy leadership triumvirate along with Bates and McNemar, only furthered the palpable sense of dread. In his journal, McNemar derided Baxter as "a most filthy creature brim full of a reprobate sense & fully ripe for a dissolution." Paranoia mounted within the divided body of Shakers at Watervliet. By April 20, McNemar was forced to publicly deny rumors that he was "instrumental" in Bates's removal. In the meantime, Bates had gone to Union Village to say his goodbyes and plan his route of travel back to New Lebanon.[68]

The two men met for the last time at Union Village on April 30, 1835. As Carol Medlicott notes, it was "close to the very spot where they had first met thirty years before, nearly to the day."[69] King had warned Bates against making any public parting harangues, but in his anguish, he could not restrain himself and showed particular resentment for his old friend Richard McNemar, who recorded the scene in his journal: "[Bates] poured out his complaints with the highest degree of animosity against the ruling authorities represented Eleazar under the figure of a great snake, a monstrous hog that was rooting him out, that there was no gift of God in his going to the East ... he was driven off—that there was no gift of god in it, & continued his lectures to the last ... till he had got into the carriage & then with streaming eyes they took a pitiful look at each other & bid a last farewell."[70]

As Carol Medlicott has noted, Bates's final words to McNemar were drawn from Luke 22:32 and effectively called his faith into question: "Fare well, and when thou art converted strengthen thy Brethren." Reflecting on this stunning end to their friendship—perhaps the most pivotal relationship in the establishment of Shakerism west of the Appalachians—McNemar reverted to his trust in the gift of the Shaker leadership. Parsing Bates's rant, he reasoned, "If there was no gift of God in his returning to the east, there is good reason to doubt any gift of God in his coming to the west for his movements in both cases were clearly directed by the same authority. The ministry in the east sent him & the same parental gift recalled him."[71]

McNemar memorialized Bates twice in his journal following this painful climax to their years of cooperation, rent by the strife at Watervliet and Bates's declining health and mental well-being. In a passage that is as revealing about his perception of himself as it is about his friend Bates, McNemar epitomized their complementary working relationship:

> It was a fact never disputed by the Major that Richard has a gift beyond him for the learned and refined part of the religious word, as also on religious experience, disputed doctrines, church government, points of law, civil policy, arts and sciences, &c. so that in their mutual labors at home & abroad Richard was always most freely intrusted with the management of such subjects & sch characters. While Issaker under the vulgar name of Rough & Ready justly claimed superiority in managing everything else. Their respective places were clearly marked out by their respective educations, gifts and talents, but while they kept a mutual understanding neither of them claimed the highest seat in the synagogue unless occasionally as a help to the regular church ministry and eldership.[72]

His status as Bates's intellectual superior established, McNemar painted a striking word-portrait of his complex and colorful friend:

> He was manifestly a singular character an oddity in his creation and qualified to answer a special purpose, and that purpose he has answered to the full extent. He had formed the most intimate sociability with every class of mankind from the highest religious characters to the most vulgar, profane, & filthy beings in human shape, and could change his mind & manners in an instant to suit any company, and in every company and on every subject he scorned to be out done, but must be preement in all things even if it should be to act the most consummate blackguard. On the subject of religion he would seem to comprehend all worlds & the state of all the dead, to have all knowledge—to understand all mysteries—that is any thing was presented beyond his ken, he could waive it as nonsense, a thing not necessary to know.[73]

Bates's geniality and common touch had made him beloved by Shakers of all backgrounds. McNemar, in contrast, had long occupied a specialized role as a roving consultant on matters legal, governmental, theological, and practical, plying this trade for Shaker leadership east and west. The two men could not have been more different and were united more than anything by their love of poetry and music and their dedication to their faith.

Fittingly, McNemar rendered his closing thoughts about his friend in a poem:

> My much esteemed Brother Bates.
> When you came to the western states.
> 'Twas with a mutual feeling then
> we own'd each other mortal men.
>
> We each had got some precious light
> Which did our kindred souls unite
> But in our mutual free exchange
> were many things both new & strange.
>
> In point of order you agreed
> That Brother Richard had the lead
> And to the hall of social kin,
> He turn'd the key and let you in.
>
> As fellow servants we went on
> Subordinate to Elder John.
> And every thing I had to spare
> I gave you as my proper heir
>
> You freely gave me in return
> What made my haughty nature burn
> 'Twas yours to make the bright display
> And mine to steer the other way.
>
> You soon possessd a large estate
> And in your order waxed great
> Nor did I envy you that crown
> While I was laboring to get down
>
> When at West Union you were placed
> Where you were honor'd and caress'd
> My humble lot in Father's tribe
> I am not willing to describe.
>
> Now on the ancient centerplain
> Our lot has been to meet again exchange our gifts,
> But I leave you to tell the little story thro,
> W.V. 1835[74]

In his verses, McNemar rather immodestly juxtaposes his own efforts to mortify his soul against what he presents as Bates's self-aggrandizement. The poem also makes clear McNemar's ultimate perception that, with regard to the spread of Shakerism in the West, he was Bates's lead, and Bates was his heir. With that point settled, at least rhetorically, McNemar might have believed that Bates's departure from Watervliet would clear the way for his unrivaled eldership. Sadly, the disarray in the Shaker West had aroused the New Lebanon Ministry to intervene directly and unintentionally trigger McNemar's downfall.

TWENTY-ONE

UNREST IN THE WEST

ELDER SOLOMON KING, AGED SIXTY and often "lame in both his feet," did his best to balance astride the increasingly unstable Ohio Shaker communities.¹ King traveled to Watervliet for a ten-day sojourn on June 30. While there, he (once again) confirmed McNemar as first elder and appointed James Ball as his second and made similar appointments among the eldresses and trustees.² Despite his nominal exercise of power, King was reaching the height of his vulnerability. That same day, McNemar wrote to Seth Youngs Wells, quoting Psalm 61:2: "When my spirit is overwhelmed within me, lead me to the rock that is higher than I." McNemar clarified his sentiment, writing that he had no wish to leap to the highest rock; that is, the spiritual state of the New Lebanon leadership. However, in a remark cutting to King, he averred, "Perhaps you will suppose that it is jumping too far to pass my immediate lead in the west. Well, perhaps I will not have to fall back very far so I will venture."³

McNemar longed for good leadership and to live somewhere like Wells's "Jerusalem above, among the wise men of the east," rather than in his "mount Sinai in Arabia (Oribee the west)," as he called it. In light of Bates's departure and considering his own sixty-five years, the theme of McNemar's letter was "What becomes of the saints when their work is finished on earth." It still concerned him that he had not covenanted with a Shaker community where he could securely pass the rest of his days. In a previous letter to Wells, he speculated on where he might retire, quoting his own poetry and invoking the role of the ministry as "land office," "whether the New Lebanon, Union village W.U. Alfred or S. Unions plains be the beautiful spot or local lot where I am to gain the level of love I submit to the managers of the land office for I have neither made an explicit entry nor a permanent settlement & preemption."

Hinting that New Lebanon may have been a desired location, McNemar asked, "If parties are necessary to a legal bond, How would it do for Sy Wells or C. Green or some authorised character learned in the law to attach his signature to my indenture as obligor to hold McNamar to it in case he should attempt to strain the cord?"[4] Straining the cord, however, was the furthest thing from McNemar's mind in 1835.

The New Lebanon Ministry was dealing with far weightier matters than McNemar's future home. During their visit in the summer of 1834, Rufus Bishop and Isaac Newton Youngs were gradually made aware that the rank-and-file Shakers at Union Village and other Ohio communities lacked confidence in their own ministry: Elder Solomon King and Eldress Rachel Johnson. Many were reluctant to openly denounce them or explain their objections in detail, as Bishop sarcastically described, they seemed to expect "the Brethren would find them out by revelation." When the troubles in the West were revealed in full to the New Lebanon Ministry, it consumed them, so they spent their "days in tribulation, & our nights almost with out sleep, and no way to find relief." Accordingly, they dispatched a special group to the West to investigate matters and encourage Shakers there to be "free in opening their trials to Elder Solomon.... We consider it a gospel right & duty; and he ought to know wherein they are burdened & grieved."[5]

The team comprised Elder David Meacham Jr., fifty-nine, who presided over the Church Family at Lebanon. Meacham was the nephew of Father Joseph Meacham, who had gathered the Shakers into gospel order at New Lebanon. He was also the cousin of John Meacham, one of the original western missionaries. Assisting Meacham was thirty-five-year-old Luther Copley, formerly the bookkeeper for the New Lebanon Trustees' Office. His presence illustrates the ministry's concern with the state of accounting and finances in the West. Leading the female side was Eldress Betsy Hastings, formerly second eldress in the first order of the Church Family at Watervliet, New York, and lately an eldress at the North Family (or Gathering Order) at New Lebanon. Hastings was known to be very capable and was described as "wise & successful in dealing with intricate & difficult questions." She was being dispatched to replace Eldress Rachel Johnson of the Union Village Ministry. Joanna Kitchell, thirty-nine, accompanied Hastings. Born in southwestern Ohio, she was sent to New Lebanon in 1812 and had lived there in the First Order of the Church Family. Together, these four Shakers were tasked with exposing the root causes of the long-standing disorder in the West.[6]

Such disorder was reflected in Rufus Bishop's response to a letter from McNemar (now unlocated) that was personally delivered by Bates on his return journey. Using his direct channel to the ministry, McNemar had clearly unloaded all of his worries. Bishop assured him, "We think much of you and your companions in tribulation." He warned McNemar, however, to "borrow no trouble concerning what may be reported or imagined—troubles generally roll on fast enough without borrowing. If you faithfully discharge your duties in gathering, feeding and protecting the sheep and lambs, you will have the approbation of a good conscience, and will in no wise fail the blessing of God."[7] Bishop's reply was delivered by Meacham and company, whom Bishop styled as "faithful messengers in whom we have unshaken confidence."[8] The party arrived on August 19, 1835, and for many in the West, the end of their Shaker journey had commenced.[9]

The Union Village Ministry had deferentially relinquished their quarters in the meetinghouse for the visiting party. Meacham and company declined this offer, not wishing to be seen as usurpers, and lodged instead at the trustees' office.[10] After a few days of assessing the situation, they sent an apparently alarming letter to the New Lebanon Ministry. The contents of the letter (now unlocated) added to their "already overflowing crop of affliction." The ministry's first reaction was to "send for Elder Solomon to come back ... without any ifs or ands; and for you to appoint a new Ministry."[11] Additionally, the decision to recall Eldress Rachel Johnson, King's female counterpart in the ministry, which had been contemplated as early as McNemar's 1829 visit to New Lebanon, was now implemented.

After consideration, however, they decided that due to the recall of Issachar Bates and then Johnson, "If Elder Solomon was removed this fall, all the old believers in that country must be very soon, and who can foresee what a shock the building might experience by the removal of all the foundation pillars so suddenly." Rather, Meacham and company were to assess the other elders and eldresses and judge "their goodness, talents usefulness [and] which ... would gain the faith, confidence & love of the Society the most, in the Ministry, when Elder Solomon comes away or gets through." Matthew Houston and Richard McNemar, although "undoubtedly good men, & also gifted" were deemed "so far advanced in life that they could not stand in such trying place any great length of time." Meacham and party were given full license to assess the situation and make any changes in the leadership they felt necessary in the confidence that they had "gone in our behalf, and are fully authorized to act in the name & authority of the Ministry & Church"—to "strengthen the weak hands & to confirm the feeble knees."[12]

The visiting party and the Union Village Ministry left for White Water, Ohio, on September 3. Union Village trustee Nathan Sharp must have been unnerved by the arrival of accountant Luther Copley. On the morning of September 9, he abruptly and quietly absconded from the community, "taking with him a valuable horse, saddle, & saddle bags, a large trunk, with cash & property not yet known or estimated" and left the office "drawers nearly emptied of cash—not more than one hundred dollars left out of thousands that were supposed to be on hand." The ministry and Meacham's party returned to Union Village later the same day. This defalcation, the third such by a Union Village trustee, "gave a heavy shock to the Ministry & the company, at their return, and introduced a new scene of labors & sufferings throughout the body."[13] The incompetence of the western leadership had been further exposed.

At the Sabbath meeting on September 27, it was announced that Eldress Rachel Johnson, who had succeeded founding western eldress Mother Ruth Farrington in 1821, had been released from her position and would return to New Lebanon. Easterner Betsy Hastings would take her place in the ministry. The following Sunday, October 4, Elder Solomon King revealed at the meeting that he, too, would be returning to New Lebanon. The New Lebanon Ministry had encouraged his honest cooperation with Meacham and Hastings and had advised him, "If it be found that you cannot help the people any longer, we hope you will, like a man of God, honorably resign, and return to the bosom of your friends."[14] King framed his return to New Lebanon as a temporary visit and appointed Elder David Meacham as first elder in the ministry in his absence. It is likely, however, that many Union Village Shakers understood—and even hoped—that King would not return among them.

Matthew Houston wrote a private letter to New Lebanon Ministry elder Rufus Bishop declaring that no one among them had desired or sought to effect King's release from his office. He went on to say that if King had written the East for help sooner or even sought "the help of his own elders," it may have been the means of "cleansing the [Trustees'] office of those Devils which infested it—& which by the by has been the cause of the greatest part of the callamities we have been groaning under for years."[15] King and McNemar held lengthy private conversations before King's departure. McNemar's recapitulations of these show that King was especially worried that Issachar Bates had blackened his reputation back east and that such a turn might undermine everyone's confidence in the spiritual hierarchy and gifts that undergirded Shaker leadership and authority. McNemar reminded King that Bates's anger was primarily directed at McNemar at the point of his departure. McNemar said that if Bates ruined his—McNemar's—character, the consequences among the western Shaker communities would be far worse, "since the gospel was first received in the west measurably thro' my influence, and if in the end I should be proved out to be a deceiver and a grand rascal, it might strike a heavy blow on the feelings of many east and west." McNemar retired from the interview and was so affected by it that he took to his bed "and passed the afternoon under such deathly tribulation as has been common on such occasions."[16]

On October 13, King, Johnson, and Luther Copley embarked for New Lebanon. Following their departure, Nancy McNemar conducted Meacham and Hastings to the ministry's shop. Waiting there were the Centre House elders, Richard McNemar, Matthew Houston, and a company of singers. They marked the advent of Meacham's and Hastings's tenure in the ministry with songs and feeling testimony. Following this, they assisted in moving their things into the meetinghouse, a lodging they had initially declined but now were entitled to. Second elder Joshua Worley (Malcham's son) and second eldress Nancy McNemar had each survived the tumult and remained in their positions to assist Meacham and Hastings in the ministry. Although the leadership transition was complete, the matter of Nathan Sharp's apostasy and financial misdeeds remained unresolved for the beleaguered community.[17]

Meacham and Hastings wrote to the New Lebanon Ministry requesting that they send two reliable trustees to Union Village before winter to assist in unraveling the financial and legal mess, particularly regarding land titles, that was left in the wake of Sharp's apostasy.[18] News of the treacherous act was published throughout the nation. On finding out, the New Lebanon Ministry wrote in despair to Meacham. According to newspapers, they read that Sharp "had gone off with $60,000, and had taken with him the handsomest girl in Union Village. O shocking! O horid treachery!"[19] A committee of Shakers met with Sharp at a tavern in Lebanon, Ohio, on September 23. They proposed a settlement of $500 cash, provided Sharp returned everything else. Sharp utterly refused this and stormed out of the tavern. The Shakers opted not to go to the law, since they "would be able to secure nothing but his body, and that had been too long on our hands already." Finding themselves at an impasse, Shaker superiors once again tasked Richard McNemar with a daunting task—dealing with Sharp. He returned to Watervliet on October 26 prepared to take up the case.[20]

At Meacham's direction, McNemar wrote to Sharp on October 29, stating, "The Church & Society at Union Village [have] called upon me, as their former scribe & bookkeeper, to assist in examining the state of their temporal affairs and making out a bill of debts damages & other responsibilities preparatory to a fair & honorable settlement of accounts with thee." McNemar carefully enumerated the community's finances for Sharp since the beginning of 1835, which had been managed by Sharp, and found that $10,420 of the community's money was unaccounted for. Of greater concern, the deeds to the 1,300 acres comprising the core property of Union Village had not been secured. The ministries of New Lebanon and Union Village had been investigating the legality of the original deed transfers of these lands to eastern trustees by western converts in the period after 1805. It was found that many were vulnerable to legal challenge by non-Shaker relatives or heirs, since often no money was exchanged at the point of transfer, rendering a deed potentially invalid. McNemar's tone was cool and professional throughout; he had known Sharp since at least 1806 and probed for any sign of humanity in his longtime acquaintance. Advising Sharp of the "delicate feelings of the sisterhood," McNemar requested that he clarify his intentions regarding any personal claims he might make on property held in trust for the community. McNemar offered Sharp a settlement and urged him to accept it. The alternative was to expose both the community and Sharp to the "eagle eye of the civil authorities which are instituted for the punishment of evildoers & for the praise of them that do well."[21]

McNemar relied on Seth Youngs Wells for legal advice during his negotiations with Sharp. Of particular concern to McNemar were the titles to land at Union Village. Wells felt that the deeds were secure, but he advised McNemar that if it was deemed prudent to leave ultimate title with the New Lebanon trustees until the Sharp matter was resolved, that was fine. He wrote, "All we want is to have the Society at U.V. safe from the fangs of apostate tygers." Wells considered Sharp "far deeper in iniquity than old Judas was ... he was a natural man, and had never received the baptism of the Holy Ghost." Sharp, on the other hand, "has had far greater light than ever Judas had; and by giving way to sin, his light became darkness, even great darkness; and Satan entered into him." Wells opined that Sharp should return everything and then, like Judas, "go and hang himself," for if he didn't, he would "sink vastly below that old traitor." Wells's letter closed on an optimistic note, informing McNemar that the requested trustees, Daniel Hawkins (from New Lebanon) and Seth's natural brother Stephen Wells (from Watervliet, New York) had been dispatched. They arrived at Union Village on November 27 bearing a letter of introduction from the ministry, who cautioned that they were "not sent as great learned worldly wise men able to govern apostates and make the wicked do justly & love righteousness, but we can recommend them as plain honest dealing Brethren who have had many years experience in their respective families and have proved themselves faithful stewards and true to the cause of the gospel, and in whom we place confidence."[22] It was made clear that it was a burden for their respective families to loan these faithful trustees to the West but that their brethren and sisters had agreed to the sacrifice to assist "their western Brethren in affliction." They were, however, expected to return as soon as their work was done.[23]

In the meantime, McNemar had solicited the opinions of some of the greatest legal minds available to him regarding a lawsuit against Sharp. The Shakers first sought out Thomas Corwin of Lebanon, Ohio, a local prosecuting attorney who had previously represented them (and who later served as governor of Ohio and represented the state in Congress in both the House and the Senate). Unfortunately, Sharp had already engaged his services and felt he couldn't "change sides." McNemar wrote to Henry Clay next, but he wished to examine the covenant before giving an opinion. After Father David Darrow's death in 1825, Clay had in fact warned McNemar of the flimsy legal foundation on which his successors stood. Robert Wickliffe, the Shakers' Kentucky advocate, recommended making all covenanted Union Village Shakers plaintiffs and Sharp the defendant. Judge Francis Dunlavy (brother of deceased Shaker John Dunlavy) recommended suing Sharp and the previous apostate trustee John Wallace (who had left in 1818). The Shakers were extremely reluctant to settle the matter in court, since the suit would test the core principle of their covenant and communal order. McNemar dreaded the committed apostates and anti-Shakers "eagerly waiting for an attack expecting to blow up the church covenant as quick as it is touched with the sparks of legal testimony."[24]

McNemar confided his anxieties about the lack of experienced leaders in a letter to Wells. "We are unwilling to do any thing without special counsel—you have almost all our best counsellors there From Elder John [Meacham] the first to Elder Solomon & Elder Issachar the last, and what have we of the old stock left? I might exclaim like Micah of old you have taken away my gods and what have I more?" Trustees Hawkins and Wells were proving less helpful than the westerners hoped. McNemar wrote of the "two little simple deacons that you sent us: well, in fact they are so simple that they are waiting from day to day to be told what to do." McNemar proposed possible avenues for bringing a suit against Sharp that would not involve Union Village proper. One involved land titles from the now-defunct West Union, Indiana, community; another related to land owned by the Shakers in Illinois—Sharp was named among trustees for both. In the end, McNemar waited for eastern guidance before proceeding. He thanked Wells at the end of the lengthy and complex letter, writing, "You have always been very merciful & borne with all my eccentricities & in this trying day O forsake me not nor chastise me for any error that you may discover either in the matter or manner of this communication, for it is poorly written mostly with candlelight & a very mean pen."[25]

In November, the ministry visited Watervliet, Ohio, to put affairs in order at that community. Richard McNemar was released from his eldership (so recently contested) "to attend other necessary duties." He continued to lodge in the north garret of the meetinghouse, "where his bureau books and papers were deposited for safe keeping," as they had been since the tumult began in March. With the arrival of the eastern trustees, it was concluded that Elder David Meacham could return to New Lebanon. Elder Matthew Houston, McNemar's old colleague from the days of the Kentucky Revival, was given the privilege of accompanying him in what would be his first visit to the eastern communities. The party left Union Village on November 30, bringing an end to Meacham's brief tenure as first elder in the Union Village Ministry.[26]

Richard McNemar was happily relieved on two fronts during December 1835. It was decided that eastern trustee Daniel Hawkins would work with Daniel Boyd (who would be appointed Union Village trustee on January 27, 1836) "in bearing the burden and concern of prosecuting Nathan Sharp and affecting a settlement of his accounts." Finally, and most important, the ministry decided that McNemar should have "a steady home." He was informed of this development during a visit to Union Village, whereupon he was instructed to return to Watervliet and prepare for a final relocation. McNemar's decades of unceasing travel in service of the gospel were at an end; his anxieties about not having a permanent home were quelled. Unbeknownst to him, however, decisions being made at New Lebanon would nearly cost him that home and send him on one final Shaker journey—a journey of humiliation and repentance.[27]

TWENTY-TWO

FREEGIFT TO THE WEST

THE LEADERSHIP VOID AMONG THE western Shaker communities—whose center was located at Union Village—was made stunningly evident by the multiple failures, both spiritual and financial, endured throughout the late 1820s and 1830s. Elder (now Brother) Solomon King would not return to the West; he had publicly resigned his office at a church meeting in New Lebanon. The New Lebanon Ministry's original intent was to establish communities in the West under the guidance of eastern mentors. Once this was accomplished, they were to be recalled. Instead, however, a succession of eastern Shakers guided the Ohio and Kentucky communities well into the 1830s. The westerners, used to this hand-holding, lamented the absence of experienced outside help in their time of crisis. The fact was, the native talents that existed in the West were allowed to develop too slowly or were never given the chance to administer their own domains. By 1836, the first generation of converts was too old to assume top leadership positions, a fact recognized by the New Lebanon Ministry. Compounding this issue, the most senior among them, Richard McNemar, Matthew Houston, and Joshua Worley, were too loyal to seek out such roles for themselves. As a result, the New Lebanon Ministry fell back into familiar patterns and selected one of their own to journey to the West—thirty years after the initial mission—and once again right the gospel ship. The man selected was Freegift Wells.[1]

Wells had come to Watervliet, New York, from Long Island with his parents and seven siblings on May 17, 1802. They were converted by Seth Youngs Wells, who had joined the community in 1798. Freegift was his youngest natural brother and the nephew of Benjamin Seth Youngs and Isaac Newton Youngs. He was also the natural brother of trustee Stephen Wells, then at Union Village

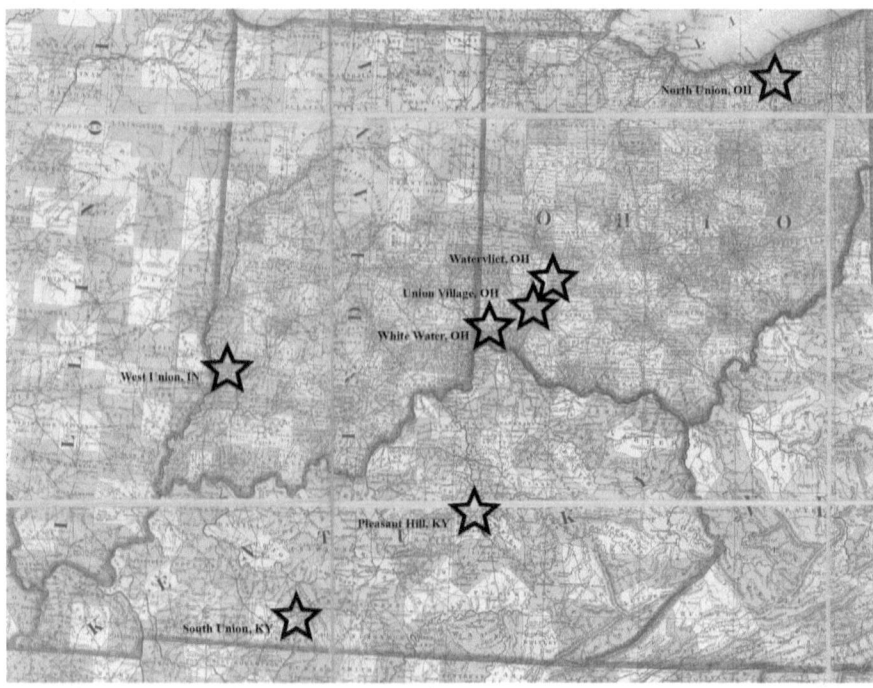

Figure 22.1. A map showing the locations of the western Shaker communities. The abandonment of West Union, Indiana, in 1827 solved some problems facing the western Shaker communities, but Elder Freegift Wells was confronted with many other festering issues when he arrived at Union Village in 1836.

helping to set financial and legal affairs in order. In describing Freegift, the New Lebanon Ministry noted, "He has travelled such a strait course that we think he has advanced considerably a head of some who started in the days of Mother Ann." Freegift Wells was certainly a dedicated Believer, serving throughout his career as a family and ministry elder, a schoolteacher, and a skilled mechanic and cabinetmaker. He made furniture and chairs and turned bowls, dipper handles, and thousands of pegs for the "pin rail," or pegboard, found in nearly every Shaker room. As scholars Jerry V. Grant and Douglas R. Allen note, Wells's commitment to severing the natural familial ties that Shakerism sought to negate was total. Toward the end of his life, he had the opportunity to join his three living Shaker siblings for a dinner. He declined, concerned that "such a dinner would be a bad example for other Shakers." Wells kept journals throughout most of his life, and they reveal him to be almost the ideal Shaker—truly simple, humble, faithful, hardworking, and dedicated. Wells continued to keep his journal while serving at Union Village, and it supplies many valuable details about the climactic events that took place there in the late 1830s.[2]

Ministry leaders Rufus Bishop and Ruth Landon rode to the Second Order in Watervliet, New York, to give Freegift Wells his new assignment on January 13, 1836. The New Lebanon Ministry explained their decision to the Union Village Ministry in a letter written on January 29. "We have come to the conclusion to lend you our true and worthy friend Freegift Wells, who has faithfully discharged the duties of an Elder in the church for the term of about 19 years without a blot or stain, that we know of. And we do not hesitate to recommend him as a good man, an offering without blemish, and an able counsellor in things both spiritual and temporal." The ministry sympathized with their fellow Shakers, who were "almost constantly wading in deep waters, and passing through strait places"; they assumed they longed for "any soul who would take the responsibility and tell you what to do." Accordingly, one was dispatched, but they must be aware that "a great sacrifice," even a "universal cross" must be taken up by the Believers there if there were any hope of salvaging the community.[3]

At the other Watervliet, in Ohio, Richard McNemar prepared to move once again, hopefully for the final time. He carefully filled his "big green box" with the "choicest books & papers" and loaded up a wagon for transport to Union Village. He took a break from packing to write Elder Rufus Bishop. He reflected that "for the last thirty years, I could say with the poet 'Nothing on earth I call my own.—A stranger in the world unknown—I calmly sojourn here.'" McNemar recalled his years as an assistant to the western ministry, "in protecting & feeding the chickens, and they set me to work at ridding up the old threshing floor and gathering out all the good grains of wheat that I could find among the straw and chaff of our old heaven & New-light systems, & putting this good grain into a situation to be preserved and to be useful." By the end of the lengthy, somewhat maudlin letter, McNemar expressed with some humor that Bishop might be concerned for him, writing, "Poor Eleazar what a fiz he is in." McNemar acknowledged the letter could give that impression, but he reminded Bishop of what he had lost over the previous few years: "Well, was not Sampson himself in a pretty curious fiz when the lord had departed from him? I can shake myself as he did. but I cannot go out as at other times, when I had Elder John, Father David, Elder Solomon, E Benjamin or Elder Issachar to inspire me with confidence; 'Poor old captain! (says R[ufus]) perhaps you'll be glad to see Elder Freegift & his escort.'" McNemar closed his letter hopefully. Alluding to a long-standing intestinal ailment, he indicated that being relieved of ministerial and legal duties had given much relief to his "pained bowels." He added, "Perhaps a few more discharges under the care of Br Freegift may restore my constitution to a degree of regularity."[4]

McNemar journeyed back and forth between Watervliet and Union Village throughout the late winter. On March 28, he arrived at Union Village along with a wagon carrying "part of his goods" and found himself "much at a loss for someplace to put them." By April 11, he was situated once again with his "office concerns" in an attic, "the old center house garret—a great accomodation."[5] His perambulations had come to an end. As he had done so often before, McNemar commemorated the moment in verse. In a poem titled "Validation," he marked his departure from Watervliet.

> Now for the 4 years that I've been in this place
> of strife or hard feelings I leave not a trace
> And this I can say for the people at least
> They've never attempted to worship the beast
> For any known duty that they could expect
> I have not been charg'd with a wilful neglect
> And such an important good visit I've had
> I can think of nothing that makes me feel mad ⎫
>   sad[6] ⎭

His inability to choose the right final word for the last line is telling. Although he claimed that nothing about his experience at Watervliet had triggered those negative emotions, the opposite was surely true.

At the eastern Watervliet, Freegift Wells gave a "farewell address" to his brethren and sisters on April 10. In his journal, Bishop noted, "The First & 2nd Orders assembled at the meetinghouse & took an affectionate farewell of Elder Freegift & Elder Matthew Houston. We sung 3 farewell Songs which were composed on the occasion, & also some others. In this meeting also there was many tears shed, & many expressed their good feelings concerning the faithfulness and good Example of their departing friend & Elder." They set out for the West the following Tuesday, traveling by way of New York City, Philadelphia, and Pittsburgh. On Wells's departure, the New Lebanon Ministry noted that "nothing but love and a real sense of duty could have induced us to part with a pillar so useful, so much esteemed and so much needed here."[7]

Wells arrived at Union Village on Wednesday, April 27, 1836, after a journey of sixteen days, accompanied by the returning Mathew Houston. They were received and fed at the trustees' office, then Wells was conducted to his new lodging in the meetinghouse. After recovering for a few days, Wells was introduced to the community on Sunday, May 1, at a special 8:30 a.m. meeting.

Figure 22.2. The meetinghouse of the Union Village, Ohio, Shaker community, where Elder Freegift Wells took up his lodging in April 1836. The steeple on the roof is a later addition made by subsequent owners. Courtesy of Canterbury Shaker Village, Canterbury, NH.

Houston addressed the assembly regarding his eastern visit, conveying the love of the Shakers there for their suffering western counterparts. Wells spoke next, merely "a few words,"[8] befitting the role he was assuming as a benevolent yet detached spiritual overseer.

Joshua Worley, Wells's second in the ministry, then read a lengthy letter from the New Lebanon Ministry to the Union Village Believers. The ministry confirmed Freegift Wells as a "minister and Elder commissioned by the Church." Acknowledging the "adverse scenes" that had afflicted them, the ministry urged all to let go of past events and wrongs; struggle daily to seek the "lowly valley of humiliation"; cultivate a "spirit of peace and harmony"; serve as an example to the non-Shaker world around them as the "people of God"; keep union with their ministry and follow the orders given "for your protection"; not enter into debt with non-Shakers; communicate freely with the ministry to stave off festering troubles; and finally, support one another, each in their own appointed station, to preserve the union of the whole body.[9]

The ministry emphasized that confession of sins—opening of minds—must be done according to church hierarchy and that to confess to someone other than the one appointed or to discuss the faults of others subverted the "order of God." The Union Village community had been put on notice, and their path to redemption was made clear. The burden was now on them collectively to live the principles of gospel union. In response, several brethren spoke their thanks for the aid of the "Mother chh. & the gift she had sent us." Momentously, the meeting closed with Richard McNemar's public surrender of "his title of Elder and all his official influence to Elder Freegift." It is unknown if the New Lebanon Ministry requested this or if the decision was made following Freegift's arrival in the West; regardless, it was dutifully carried out for all to see. McNemar was surely relieved to some degree, but the ceremony marked a pivotal transition in his life.[10]

In his journal, McNemar called May 1, 1836, "a day long to be remembered." In the afternoon, he conferred with Freegift Wells and his female counterpart Eldress Betsy Hastings. Despite the morning's proceedings, McNemar was instructed to gather the papers of Elder Solomon King for dispatch to New Lebanon. Wells and Hastings entrusted the task entirely to McNemar, waiving their right to inspect anything he sent east, a liberty they explicitly granted to him in all affairs. McNemar relished the opportunity to help absolve King of suspicions of incompetence or malfeasance, especially regarding the disastrous end of the West Union, Indiana, community.[11]

On May 3, the decision was made to create a new joint trusteeship made up of two brothers at Union Village and two at New Lebanon, thereby hopefully eliminating the chance for further abuse of the office. McNemar was appointed to draft the legal instrument effecting the change (although the idea was shelved by mid-1837). This development allowed eastern trustees Stephen Wells and Daniel Hawkins and eastern eldress Joanna Kitchell to depart for New Lebanon on May 9, thus ending their emergency services to the Union Village community. On May 13, McNemar moved his lodgings to yet another garret, this time rooming with Matthew Houston in the trustees' office. They were directed to take their meals "with the aged at the Brick house." Although McNemar had supposedly surrendered his "official influence," his continued importance in ongoing affairs was undeniable due to his institutional memory and deeply entrenched relationships.[12]

Seth Youngs Wells, in an unlocated letter, suspected that McNemar may have regretted his loss of prominence. McNemar addressed this honestly in his reply to Wells. After acknowledging that Elder David Meacham Jr. had been sent to the West to "govern [McNemar] and protect ME Poor Fellow," he expressed thanks for favorable reports regarding himself that Meacham had related to Wells on his return to New Lebanon. Nonetheless, McNemar realized that he now must find a new station among the community at Union Village. McNemar's ability and willingness to do so gave Meacham and Wells cause for concern. McNemar wrote,

> With regard to any particular lot or place in the body, it was very seasonable & well accepted for good Elder Br. to drop a hint on that point, we are so prone to aspire after distinction, and to seek honor of man, that I consider it a mark of true friendship, to put me on my guard in that thing for should I say that I am dead to all such feelings, Elder Br. would see at once that I was the most dangerous man on the ground, so the most I can say is that I mean to be obedient and cross my ugly nature & share the blessings that are sent to evry honest creature.

Indeed, that seems to have been McNemar's intention, and it certainly was his duty as a good Shaker.[13]

McNemar may have been in the minority regarding his willingness to accommodate to a new order. Freegift Wells wrote a lengthy report to the New Lebanon Ministry on July 2, 1836, having been at Union Village long enough to thoroughly assess the Shakers there. He was not happy with what he found and opined that there were "a large number who have strove for years to support themselves on the backs of others." There was a clear lack of gospel order and, more troubling, a lack of will to reclaim it. Wells knew he was facing a monumental task. His first job was to reorganize some of the communal families, appointing new elders and eldresses who "should be elders in fact." He found two worthy candidates among McNemar's children and appointed James McNemar as elder at the Second House. "Faithful and beloved" Nancy McNemar, already second eldress in the ministry, was moved from that position to minister to young women in the Centre House, a gathering order for potential new Shakers. Wells considered her the "best qualified under existing circumstances, to gather & protect . . . those females of her class, who have not as of yet come into the fold, so as to hear the voice of, & be led by the good Shepherd."[14]

More troubling was the state of affairs at Watervliet, where union was rent asunder by years of personality-driven conflict. Even before Wells's arrival, Elder Joshua Worley reported that some Shakers there had "fallen into some grievous bad habits such as drinking ardent spirits and taking opium, which seems to stupify all the life & spirit of the gospel that they might otherwise enjoy."[15] Wells traveled there in late May and was gratified to find that newly appointed elder James Ball "had purged out all the spirits & opium from the

Society." Eldress Eunice Bedle had also overcome her addictions and had not only "quit her opium, but tobacco also, of which she had been a great smoker." Additionally, Bedle had embraced a new diet, possibly the Graham diet, since Wells had brought a book on the system with him to the West.[16]

McNemar remained centrally involved in untangling the chain of trusteeship for deeds to Union Village lands. Seth Youngs Wells advised McNemar that the New Lebanon Ministry expected him to consult with Elder Freegift Wells before making any important decisions regarding nullifying and re-executing any deeds. Seth Youngs Wells also poignantly cautioned his sixty-five-year-old friend:

> You and I are rather too far advanced in age to take much upon us— our corporeal & mental powers are on the decline, and we cannot do as we once could—I am sensible I cannot; yet I am willing to be all the help I can when called upon, and I believe you are; but we ought not to carry our mental exertions beyond their elastic force power, or the cord may break & we shall lose our ability to do of doing the little good that we may yet be able to do if we are wise—We must be cautious of diving too deep in those turbid waters which require young & vigorous mental powers to cope with.

McNemar was, however, chosen to accompany Elder Freegift Wells on his second visit to the Watervliet community in late July.[17]

Another major figure departed the Shaker West that autumn. Elder Benjamin Seth Youngs, resident for twenty-six years as first in the South Union Ministry and virtually a law unto himself in the most southwestern Shaker community, informed Elder Freegift Wells that he wished to resign his office and return to his original home at New Lebanon. Youngs was the last of the original three missionaries of 1805 resident in the West, where he had lived for thirty-six years. He announced the news to his flock at South Union on September 22, 1836.

Youngs traveled home by way of Union Village, where he visited with McNemar for a final time. In a letter to Elder Rufus Bishop, McNemar described the events of October 16, his last worship meeting with Youngs. The occasion was "solemn & affecting & [there was] much freedom in recognizing and expressing the mercy & goodness of God mutually experienced since our early connection & relation in the gospel." In the meeting, following Youngs's farewell address, McNemar recapitulated the 1804 letter borne from New Lebanon by the original missionaries to the revivalists in the West. The feelings evoked sparked the idea that the western Shakers should compose a response to that letter for Youngs to take back to the East. McNemar sought "a clear correspondence between the Alpha & Omega of the work in this country." This letter was eventually drafted, although it may never have traveled beyond McNemar's own journal. McNemar described Benjamin Seth Youngs's exit to Bishop as "a sorrowful parting. But the Lord gave & the Lord taketh away & blessed be the name of the Lord." Youngs left Union Village for the last time on October 20. Although the two men had never corresponded much while both were in the West, they became ardent correspondents once Youngs returned east. Youngs was an important sounding board for McNemar during the eventful and dramatic final years of his life.[18]

Youngs carried a letter from McNemar to Rufus Bishop back to New Lebanon, the last paragraph of which was addressed to Issachar Bates. The two men had not communicated since Bates's bitter departure in April 1835, although Rufus Bishop had informed McNemar of Bates's resolution to cease "talking about past difficulties and trials." Bishop conveyed his sympathy to McNemar that Bates's "ready wit and lack of sound wisdom had subjected you to many trials." Bishop reasoned these trials were, in part, because western converts regarded Bates from the beginning as a Shaker of long standing and deep in wisdom. Bishop wrote that in 1805, Bates was a "a very young Believer" sent into the field to harvest souls "before there was much separation of the wheat and chaff in himself." These words must have soothed any guilt McNemar had over the conflict with a man he regarded as his gospel father.[19]

Sometime around October 10, when Youngs was at Union Village, McNemar had a "night vision," or dream, in which Bates paid him a "friendly visit." McNemar recounted the dream in his letter to Bishop, knowing the substance would be conveyed to Bates. In the dream, the two men conversed, and "after an agreeable interview [Bates] took his leave saying 'farewell my son' to which I responded 'Farewell Father' after which I awoke with comfortable feelings." This reaffirmation of the spiritual father-son relationship between the two men was the most powerful gesture of reconciliation McNemar could make. Additionally, McNemar apologized to Bates if he had ever "treated him with cold indifference or impertinence" and sent him his love.[20]

At New Lebanon, Rufus Bishop invited Bates to the ministry's shop and read him the letter, which moved him deeply. After hearing of McNemar's dream, Bates simply said, "Amen." Bates responded in writing on December 27, 1836, lamenting that "the time has felt long to me, to be shut out from any kind of communication with one, with whom I have spent thirty years with so much freedom, and friendship—one year and six months has passed away in lonely silence without one breath from Eleazar, either by word, by spirit, or by letter." Tellingly, Bates had dreamed of McNemar twice since receiving his communication, but in both instances, the dream ended before Bates could initiate a reconciliatory conversation. Due to this, he took up his pen. He apologized to McNemar for the final words he had said to him in the West, which had effectively questioned his faith; however, he unhesitatingly named what he perceived as McNemar's greatest shortcoming: "Nay I never scrupled your faith from the beginning, any more than Jesus Christ scrupled Peters faith but he saw where in he was lacking and had to be converted into it, and notwithstanding your eminent gifts and talents I could feel a lack in you of one of the most blessed gifts that is in heaven, or on earth—which is Mercy." Bates touched on the conflict that had poisoned their last years together and blamed it on jealousy—and a mutual lack of mercy. Wishing to put those things aside forever, he extended his final mercy to McNemar: "Brother Eleazer I love to feel Merciful to you—and if you feel Merciful to me I shall be thankful. . . . And now I shall close these few crooked lines By saluting you with the same love that I had for you from the begining."[21]

The separation from Youngs and the final settlement of affairs with Bates caused McNemar to fall into a deep depression. It began on October 20—the day Youngs left for the East—with a severe cold. For the following week, McNemar felt "uncommonly stupid." In a confessional letter to his new elder, Freegift Wells, he described that while ruminating on his life one afternoon, he

> began to inquire of myself whether there was any thing that I cared for, and it seemed for a while that there was nothing within the reach of my senses that I felt any care or concern about. I tried myself in relation to the love of my brethren, but my feelings answered nay. I care nothing about it. I then examined myself in relation to living, but I found that I cared nothing about it. My mind then turned to the subject of dying, but I cared nothing for that. I examined Myself concerning the increase of the gospel, but found that I cared nothing for it. I then began to exclaim within myself, If I die in this state I may not wake up for 500 years. Here I found Something that I cared for. I did not like to be left behind my brethren for so long a time.

McNemar was wracked by an awful cough that kept him awake at night. When he could no longer bear it, he got up and sat by the stove in his room, where he heard a voice command him to "Sing and Praise God." McNemar could barely breathe, but he willed himself to sing, after which he would cough, then sing again, and so on, repeating the process until he fell into a restful sleep for the remainder of the night.[22]

In this depressed state, McNemar confronted his own ego, realizing that as much as he had labored with "turnbacks"—Shakers who had fallen out of union—his own "high proud Sense hath ruined me, till I am a kind of turn-back." He candidly acknowledged to Wells that he "must be contented with my lot and calling and not murmur or think hard." In the following weeks, McNemar had an intense spiritual vision, communing alternately with Mother Ann Lee and another spirit that showed his soul to him. It was "the size of a small pea, it looked like a small round ball of light." On seeing it, McNemar realized how small he was yet how "vain I have acted in the presence of my brethren." The spirit taught him that for many years he had not been guided by his small soul but rather by the large and mighty "man of sin." Shocked, McNemar "saw this monster in myself" and exclaimed, "I could see nothing but an awful proud, haughty selfish nature that wanted all in heaven & earth to fall down and worship it." Even worse, the spirit conducted McNemar to a Shaker meeting at Union Village where he saw none other than the man of sin standing between the brethren and sisters, each one of whom secretly thought they had better right to the honor and material comforts of the community than any other. Viewing this, McNemar cried, "We have become a united body of selfishness." The spirit reassured him that all was not yet lost but that the progressive work of God must continue to ensure the spiritual repair of the Union Village.[23]

McNemar's letter to Wells then took a strange turn. Using a literary device he had employed many times in the past, he imagined a rhetorical dialogue between the spirit and the man of sin in order to illuminate current problems at Union Village. The man of sin began by acknowledging that he had received Christ "as a little child" thirty years before when he joined the Shakers. However, he was "not a little child now" and must "put away childish things." These included elements of eastern-style gospel regulations that Wells had begun to institute at Union Village, including such directives as "standing erect in meeting and locking our fingers with our right thumb & fingers uppermost" and all beginning the dance with the right foot. The man of sin had complied with some of these out of courtesy, but in his opinion, they were "no part of divine worship." The man of sin declared, "I have no opinion of any of your little useless orders, and I am not willing to be bound & cramped by them, as much as I have been." The man of sin also thought there were too many meetings in the evening and that if "a man has worked hard all day I believe he ought to be allowed to rest in peace" and not be required to ask to be excused from a meeting. Preaching, as well, had been essential when the community began, but the man of sin felt that for many years past, "it has done me no good. I have known all these things for years, I have no need of hearing them again." Finally, in an indictment of the whole communal system and his fellow Believers, he opined, "I cannot think it is right to give my hard earnings to poor drunken vagabonds

& lazy creatures, that will not work, the scripture says 'If any would not work, neither should he eat.' This feels to me like dealing justly with people."[24]

The dialogue at an end, the assemblage of Believers who witnessed it awakened from a torpor and declared, "This creature was a murderer, a robber a thief & a liar." Mother Ann Lee then appeared to them, showing them the contrasting example of an adorned soul; that is, God manifested in the soul, dressed with power, wisdom, and love. McNemar wrote, "The beauty, glory and shining brightness of this adorned soul I cannot describe, it was brighter than the sun." Having reached the end of his tormenting vision, McNemar realized that the spirit had been trying him "as it did Abraham of old." He confirmed to Wells that the vision was a gift of God and had changed his way of thinking. He promised, "I shall labor hard to come down so low that the increase of the gospel may come into my soul." Wells was surely glad to read these sentiments from McNemar, who was clearly reaching out in an attempt to reconcile himself as the new spiritual leader in the West. Sadly, McNemar ultimately failed to live according to the lessons taught to him by the spirit, thus setting the stage for a final crisis.[25]

The winter of 1836 was thankfully quiet for both Union Village and Richard McNemar. Further communal regulations were instituted by Wells, such as the ringing of the first bell for a rising time of 5:00 a.m., a general annual confession before Christmas, and stricter rules governing the interactions between brothers and sisters. There was a sense of optimism as the community experienced good leadership for the first time in years. McNemar preached at a public meeting occasionally and kept up his busy correspondence. Most important, in early December, a settlement was reached with former-trustee-turned-apostate Nathan Sharp. Sharp agreed to surrender and convey all of the titles to real estate at Union Village, Watervliet, White Water, and North Union, as well as canal stocks and other miscellaneous assets to the new joint trusteeship. In return, he retained $5,000 in bank stock at Life Insurance Company Bank in Cincinnati. The Union Village Shakers could finally put that nightmare behind them and move forward with renewed purpose and mutual dedication.[26]

McNemar's position in the society was still ambiguous. On January 6, 1837, he met with the elders at the Center Family, Stephen Spinning (brother of David Spinning, McNemar's colleague from Kentucky Revival days) and Andrew Houston. All agreed that it was an uncomfortable situation, as McNemar had been "ranked in the order of the ministry, at least as a help"[27] (as he described it). Spinning and Houston felt reluctant to ask McNemar to subject himself to their lead, but after a lengthy discussion, he agreed, reserving the right to appeal to the ministry at Union Village and New Lebanon should he be asked to do anything he felt he could not comply with. This was arguably an even more precarious situation to place himself in, but McNemar's career and status left everyone unsure about his proper place in the hierarchy.

One practical consideration to be resolved was where McNemar would stand in worship and sit at table. When the elders asked if he would accept a place they assigned him, he jokingly replied that he would happily take the place of Watch and Dragon, two dogs that had been killed a few days before. Apparently, in a deliberate humbling, he was tested by having to take his next fourteen meals in the family's dooryard, where the dogs had formerly eaten. When the fifteenth meal was served, however, "the kind, hospitable & attentive Elder, thought of me and of his promise to give me a place at his table & came personally & invited me to breakfast at the rear of the feast." This episode is reminiscent of the ritual humiliation McNemar suffered alongside Calvin Morrell very early in his Shaker journey. His religious enthusiasm undoubtedly tempered that experience, whereas, at this stage of his life, it was a long way down into the valley of humiliation.[28]

McNemar must have found some consolation in reconciling his differences with Issachar Bates, which was accomplished just in time. The venerable missionary died on March 17, 1837, at the age of eighty. Fortunately, a letter to him from McNemar (now unlocated) reached Bates in early February. Seth Youngs Wells reported to McNemar that Bates was "much pleased with his letter" and "sends his everlasting love & kindest thanks to Brother Eleazar." Before his death, he performed a last favor for McNemar, who had requested copies of Massachusetts statutes pertaining to religious societies and corporations. The spry Bates rode over Lebanon Mountain to the Shaker community at Hancock, Massachusetts, a distance of around five miles, and retrieved a law book containing the information. Wells transcribed the relevant statutes in a letter to McNemar and noted that Bates expressed "his thankfulness for the privilege of doing so small a favor for his western friends." It would be the last interaction between these men, who had labored so long and faithfully in shaping and protecting the Shaker world that they had helped to create.[29]

TWENTY-THREE

"THE NAME OR MEMORY OF MR. McNAMAR"

IN EARLY 1837, RICHARD MCNEMAR took the first concrete steps into the Shaker equivalent of retirement. His scribal and administrative responsibilities wound down until he was eventually released from them. On March 16, a committee comprising ministry second elder Joshua Worley, trustee Daniel Boyd, Abner Bedle, and incoming scribe Andrew C. Houston convened for "hearing and examining the church-records, as kept by Richard McNamar & Solomon King from April 6, 1831, to March 16, 1837." The accuracy of the records was confirmed, and that same day, "all the official and important papers in the care & safe keeping of Eleazar, were in good order delivered up to the Ministry such as Deeds, Declaration of trust &c. all the office books and papers having been previously examined & delivered to the office deacons." McNemar was told that Houston would assume the role of official scribe for the church journal. To his relief, McNemar was permitted to "retain his private papers and all other papers not belonging to that order." In his journal, Freegift Wells noted prosaically on March 30, "Eleazar has given up the Deeds." McNemar wrote approvingly of these events to Seth Youngs Wells, stating, "So you see that in this department there is so much order gained after ten years confusion." He was also glad to be released from the "stinking cell" of supervising the "prosecution against Sharp and other office concerns."[1]

McNemar's old friend and roommate Matthew Houston was sent to Watervliet, Ohio, in January 1837 by the ministry as "guardian, & counselor, & mediator."[2] The troubled community was still in recovery from years of disarray among the leadership and widespread substance abuse. Having lost his roommate, McNemar was moved once again within Union Village to the southwest room of the second floor of the Church (or Centre) Family's Brick House.

McNemar had always done hand labor, but in the absence of his scribal duties, he set a pace that suggests one trying to fill a void. He was given a space in the Church Family's "white shop," where, over several months, he made eighty chairs "big & little" and turned out enough chair parts to keep others busy for many years. Moving to the south end of the same building, he took up his original trade, weaving "145 yards of Linen and fine cotton cloth."[3]

Despite this vigor for handcraft, McNemar wrote Wells, rhetorically asking of himself in the third person, "Has he cast away his pen, abandoned his types and concluded to have no more concern with the dead letter?" In answer, he admitted that "all his zeal and devotedness to the labors of the lathe & the loom" could not entirely divert his mind from writing and printing projects devoted to the legacy of the founders of the Shakerism in the West. He told Wells that he had lately reviewed the 1804 *Apology* of the Springfield Presbytery. Rather disingenuously, he said he had done it "without any partial respect to the name or memory of Mr. McNamar or any other instrument in the work." He concluded (unsurprisingly) that the *Apology* and the *Kentucky Revival* "ought to be preserved to give an adequate understanding of the commencement of the work in this country," but he conceded that the final say on this matter lay with the ministry. He reassured Wells that he was not "sinking into the unhappy gulf of disappointed ambition into which some of our popular men have unhappily fallen"—doubtless referring to Issachar Bates, Solomon King, and Benjamin Seth Youngs, all of whom had been recently recalled to the East. McNemar still devoted some time to keeping a "general journal of events & a review of matters & things for the benefit of posterity." Additionally, the pace of his correspondence never slackened. In keeping with his eye toward the past, he playfully signed this letter "Eleazar Good Rich," a reference to Elizur Goodrich, the husband of Mother Ann's successor, Mother Lucy Wright. McNemar's pseudonym Eleazar Wright connected him referentially to Mother Lucy, and he played off that here in a rather circuitous and bizarre way.[4]

McNemar's letter to Wells also referred to the uptick in visionary spiritual activity at Union Village. Community journals mark February 5, 1837, as the beginning of a "Revival or a time of refreshing in this place." The next Sabbath was described as "the most Extraordinary of the kind that we ever witnessed in this place, attended with mortifying & humiliating gifts." McNemar, a veteran of such outpourings of the spirit, wrote coyly to Wells, "I must take care of my character as a phylosopher & not dip too deep into the subject of visions & revelations, but I could tell you some curious things which I cannot trust to paper." Freegift Wells had laboriously copied and transmitted a lengthy vision had by Brother James Smith to the New Lebanon Ministry. Smith's vision, received during a period of serious illness, spoke metaphorically to the healing of the western Shaker communities and their reconciliation to union with the East. McNemar called this "a special good work that is in progress this is honorable to your visible messengers," meaning Wells and the other easterners who had worked to save Union Village.[5]

McNemar, however, went even further, stating, "More have come to the help of the Lord than we are yet able or willing to name." Without wishing to be labeled an enthusiast, he suggested that "Father & Mother and others of the original stock are seen walking through the camp conversing with individuals showing them lacks & disorders & reminding them of their primary teaching."[6] This explicit and open interaction with the spirit world had waxed and waned in Shaker history, but the year 1837 marked the beginning of what the Shakers called the "New Era" and what scholars refer to as the "Era of Manifestations," or "Mother's Work." This was the return in spirit form through instruments (or mediums) of personages such as Mother Ann Lee. This development, although perceived initially by McNemar as a blessing, proved tragic for him and many other Shakers.[7]

McNemar's transition from his former station of extensive influence and relative freedom within the Shaker world was proving more difficult than he let on to his friend Seth Youngs Wells. In his journal entry for May 5, 1837, he wrote, "This is a time of uncommon bearing particularly from jealousies and misunderstandings as to my calling and duty. It being clearly understood, that in composing the body called the church I was reserved for the work or service of the ministry & not incorporated with the rest as a member."[8]

In a confidential letter (now unlocated) written on May 16, 1837, to the New Lebanon Ministry, Freegift Wells apparently expressed both his frustrations in dealing with McNemar and possibly also concern for his mental and emotional well-being. Wells noted in his journal that on June 21, "The Brethren in the Ministry & Elders Order have had an interview with Eleazar 4 1/2 hours long." The substance of this undoubtedly fraught meeting was not recorded.[9] The ministry did not answer Wells's entreaty until early August. Their response is an extremely illuminating document that confirms McNemar's crucial role within the Shaker world, displays their tremendous regard for him personally, and demonstrates their great sympathy for his situation. Due to its pivotal importance, it is reprinted here in full.

> Beloved Elder Freegift,
>
> Your confidential note of the 16th of May last, was read over and over with care & attention, and we felt very sorry that Brother Eleazer was on such

dangerous ground in his decline of life; and especially in such a trying time when every good gift & faculty is needed for the life, strength & growth of the body. However, as you informed us that he had humbled himself & sought his union we did not know as it was necessary for us to write any thing at that time, neither did we suppose you were lacking for an answer until we received your last communications; & after all this delay we are much straitened—we hardly know what to say or write.

It is painful to see great preachers who have been blest with excellent gifts & faculties, & have done much good, & suffered abundantly in defence of the work of God, and after all run aground & become cast-aways and be exposed to do as much hurt in the close of their days as they ever did good. These things ought not so to be; nevertheless, these sad effects will occur, more or less, except we find the causes & labor to put them away.

In the first place we will state according to our understanding some of the leading causes, & then propose means to remove them so that the effects may cease. It will no doubt be granted that the afore named characters generally possess very fruitful imaginations; they can see & understand, according to their own sense, almost every thing past, present & future much clearer than their Ministry or Elders who are of a different creation, and whose calling & labor keep them down under mortification & tribulation, while those are floating on the wings of imagination above their own travel and clear above the work of God; and we may even say they are exposed to rise above the attention of the heavenly orb, around which they are called to move. When souls get into this unsettled state, how can they help themselves until they are first gathered down by some friend who has kept his joining & relation to the body of Christ? And how can men of this description help getting a high sense, where it has been the common practice of their Ministry & Elders, as well as deacons, to call on them to officiate where they themselves felt incapable? Will they not in such cases be exposed to think they know the most? Hence the great necessity of laboring to keep such members with in the fold, or at least within the reach of those who are in it; and to be careful never to boost them so high that they cannot get down without falling, & then blame them for getting so high. We do not know as you are guilty in this particular, but you know others have been to their sorrow.

We are truly sorry to have Brother Eleazar feel dissatisfied or manifest any unreconciliation or bring any burden upon those in the Ministry or Eldership, as such a state of mind may prove a greater loss than he or the people are aware of. He is getting advanced into years, & has doubtless been through much greater labors of mind in times past to support & maintain his religion, both before & after he embraced the gospel than usually fall to the lot of any individual, and his mental powers begin to fail, and we have had our fears that in such an event he would not be able to rise above his constitutional weakness, and we should be very sorry to have him lose his senses and get into a state of derangement, lest it should be the means of bringing dishonor not only upon himself, but upon the whole Society.

From all the information we have been able to obtain, first and last, it appears pretty evident that among all that have received & maintained the gospel in the west, he has, in all times of trial from outward enemies, been one of its ablest, if not most able defender. If this is really so, ought he not in his now advanced age, and while he still remains in the body, to feel some reward for his past faithfulness & useful labors in the kindness of his younger brethren & sisters who were but children & unable to bear any part of the burden in those days when he, in the strength & vigor of his manhood, was exerting his best faculties to maintain the testimony against the powerful opposition that was constantly striving to overthrow the work of God in that country. If he is now getting into his dotage, and like some others that we have known in these parts, is more able to feel & sense the work of earlier days than to take hold of the present increase, he ought not to be dishonored nor exposed to dishonor himself on that account. We ought to respect the aged for the good they have done, that they may be able to bless us in our labors for a further increase. It appears that from the first of his faith his whole sense & the object of all his labors has been to support & build up the cause of God in that country—and it is evident that the disorders that have crept in since Father David's decease have caused him much tribulation for many years past—and it also appears that the help that has been sent there, and the change that has been effected by it, has been a great releasement to him—and doubtless he still feels desirous to do all the good he can, and probably feels himself able to do more than others think he can—and would it not be better to have him feel comfortable and rejoice in the fruits of his former labors, even at some sacrifice on the part of his brethren, than to feel as if he was set aside as a useless vessel, unfit for any further service?—We believe it to be the duty of the young among believers to honor and respect those who have borne the burden & heat of the day—They should be so dealt with as to feel that they are not only entitled to their penny, but have actually received it in full, and that no injustice has been done them—It would doubtless feel trying to any of us, after conscientiously doing the best we could to support & build up the gospel during the best of our days, to be at last left in circumstances that seemed to indicate to us that our zealous & interesting labors were held in no estimation. We feel it a matter of importance to us to have the blessings of the aged in our labors to support the gospel, even if they are not able to come up to our measure of sight & understanding. And if we can be wise enough to gain their blessing without any sacrifice of real duty, it will be our blessing; and our blessing will be theirs, & they will feel it & rejoice in it.

It is difficult to determine what allowance ought to be made for Brother Eleazar when we consider his peculiar creation, talents & education, and how he has been kept most of his time since he embraced the gospel, like a minute man, ready to go here or there, from Society to society & from family to family when needed; and to dip into all their concerns or troubles both spiritual & temporal, and frequently into the law. In one sense joined to almost every body & every thing, and in another hardly joined or gathered any where.

Sister Lucy Smith informed us some time since that he & Brother Matthew attended to the duties of the Ministry at Union Village when she was there last, ie, they were sent by the ministry from family to family to heal divisions, correct disorders & to restore peace order & union; and we well knew they were sent to Kentucky for the like purpose. Now can we think strange if Brother Eleazar feels a great change when the Ministry Elders & deacon[s] do their own work; unless you can find some kind of gift or employment for him which will take up his sense & be a steadiment to his mind in his declining years? We hope you will be blest with wisdom to do the thing that is right, & will be able to keep him comfortable and composed in the evening of his life, and if you err on either hand it had better be on the side of forbearance & charity. No more but our best love again. Farewell.

From the Ministry.
New Lebanon.[10]

This remarkable letter illustrates the extent to which the New Lebanon Ministry acknowledged that the difficult position Richard McNemar's found himself in was created, in part, by their reliance on him as their "minute man." Writing to their ministry colleague Freegift Wells, they candidly admitted their own failures, as well as those of their predecessors, to solve the problems festering in the western communities. Rather than acting decisively in these situations, they repeatedly dispatched McNemar *deus ex machina*, with the tacit sanction of the ministries, east and west. How could McNemar, a committed Shaker nonetheless, easily descend from such heights of power to assume a simple retirement of handcraft and humility? The New Lebanon Ministry phrased it best when they observed that McNemar was, by design, "in one sense joined to almost every body & every thing, and in another hardly joined or gathered any where."

In June of 1837, Elder Joshua Worley, the second in the Union Village Ministry (and son of McNemar's friend of nearly fifty years Malcham Worley), was tasked with persuading McNemar to hand over all books and manuscripts remaining in his possession, other than his private papers. These were to be transferred to Andrew Houston as "recorder & historian of the west." In a stunning act of defiance, McNemar refused to comply with Worley's request. Houston's appointment in McNemar's stead, when so much of his energy and intelligence had been devoted to preserving the history of Shakerism west of the Appalachians, must have been a staggering blow, and despite McNemar's Shaker training, he could not humble himself to the gift. McNemar solicited Worley's patience, claiming that the records were "too far scattered" to be collected at once. He also asserted that many of the most important facts were yet to be committed to paper at all, and what had been written was not in a codified and sanctioned form. McNemar cited the laborious process undertaken by Calvin Green and Seth Youngs Wells in the eastern communities during the 1810s to collect stories and testimonies about Mother Ann Lee from living witnesses. These were carefully edited and published in a book (*Testimonies of . . . Mother Ann Lee*, 1816), which McNemar had "never been permitted to see."[11]

McNemar viewed his role as *custos sacrorum* for western Shaker history as equivalent to that of Green and Wells. He advised Worley that "our young Brother" (Houston) could "get help from what has gone before him, to make a fair start and begin a permanent book in conformity to the records of the societies in the East." McNemar unwisely allowed his ego to show through to Worley, filling the remainder of his letter with concerns, such as who was to be acknowledged as the first to hospitably receive the Shaker missionaries in 1805, who was the first Shaker convert in the West, who first acclaimed David Darrow and Ruth Farrington as "father" and "mother," and settling the "clashing claim" regarding the superiority of Darrow or Issachar Bates (both deceased) as "Father" and "Patriarch," respectively. McNemar's overarching concerns to validate his own legacy and that of his peers led him to suggest in a most un-Shakerlike fashion that if agreement on these matters could not be achieved among those on the ground in the West, then the New Lebanon Ministry should be asked to settle the questions. Carefully, but with a distinct tang of disunion, he promised to "obligate my self to agree, provided it be not an obvious and palpable falsity."[12]

McNemar consulted his old friend Benjamin Seth Youngs regarding his decision to retain his papers, chiefly for fear that they would be destroyed. Youngs shared his concern, noting that he found himself in a similar position pertaining to papers in his care. Youngs confidentially wrote McNemar, "I consider with you that the waste or destruction of those valuable documents would be as great a fraud on our unknown successors as the alienation of houses & lands or the waste & destruction of any property whatever." Conversely, however,

Youngs urged McNemar to release himself from the obligation he felt to be a "faithful centinal," reiterating that Freegift Wells and Betsy Hastings had "assumed the whole responsibility" and, therefore, McNemar was "released from any and all concerns in these matters."[13] Despite this assistance from Youngs, Freegift Wells was still stymied. He asked the New Lebanon Ministry to reach out to one of McNemar's longtime associates in the West, Elder Archibald Meacham, at White Water. On a scrap of paper marked "Confidential," the ministry wrote,

> Elder Freegift thought you might have some influence over poor Brother Eleazar for his good, if anyone there can. If you can gather & help the poor man, prey do exert your best gift for his good, & his protection. Don't let him stray from the fold. Don't let him run distracted; and if possible keep him from coming to this country. His credit is very good in this country; But if he were to come here without union, it would be such a blot as he could not wash out in time. Therefore, for his good, for the good of others, & for the honor of the gospel do help him if possible; & we will love you & bless you forever for it.[14]

Surprisingly, while the ministry did their best to shepherd McNemar into his new place among the rank and file, they were still in direct correspondence with him. This situation was nearly unique for a Shaker who was not in a bishopric ministry or at least the elder or eldress of a family. The fact that McNemar could pick up his pen, bypass his elders at Union Village with their approval, and write directly to the New Lebanon Ministry was not conducive to submitting to his new lead. He wrote to Rufus Bishop—his "trusty and confidential friend"—on October 28, 1837. McNemar acknowledged the "unreserved freedom" in his letters but cited the license received for such expression from ministry scribe Seth Youngs Wells in 1834. McNemar reminded Bishop that Bishop had lovingly called McNemar his "attorney or agent," a powerful commission from the second elder in the New Lebanon Ministry. He informed Bishop that he had "cordially resigned & remitted my official concerns with law business and deacon business, and accepted a lot among the manufacturing class." He acknowledged the "well known vanity of human nature, in loving a degree of preeminence," but he reassured Bishop (disingenuously) that although "repeated exhibitions have been made of an unreconciled spirit, in many of our worthy patriarchs on occasion of their releasement," McNemar was "exceedingly thankful" for his new lot. Yet, he was not so devoted to "loom and turning lathe" as to neglect the "museum or book department." To justify this, he invoked Bishop's prior directive to

"KEEPING correct records." Perhaps McNemar thought Bishop was unaware that Freegift Wells had asked him to refrain from this activity and hand these duties to Houston, but this is unlikely given the regularity of letters between eastern and western ministries. McNemar admitted that his greatest concern was "among so many teachers & counsellors past and present, to render each their due, and acquit myself in the full discharge of duty to all." This, in fact, was what he had been asked to cease doing, so as to better leave the tumultuous events of the past behind.[15]

Bishop, in a now unlocated letter, apparently asked McNemar to stop his printing operation, which had been launched only five years before as the "Union Press." McNemar wrote to confirm that he had "strictly complied" with Bishop's injunction, leaving the printing equipment scattered between Union Village and Watervliet and taking on "as little concern about it as possible." McNemar worked his way around to addressing the "weightiest matter" on his mind: the New Lebanon Ministry's perception that he was undermining the authority of Freegift Wells. He alluded to the conflict that had arisen due to the arrival of Wells, in whom the ministry "placed unbounded confidence." Simultaneously, McNemar maintained his longtime role as "faithful centinel here, to observe how matters were going on." McNemar knew that his unguarded correspondence had "brought some burden on our Ministry," but he disavowed any "evil design" and wished to "humble myself in any degree that would give satisfaction, and as fast as possible back out of the whole concern." By the autumn of 1837, McNemar was acutely aware that his role needed to change, but thus far he had not accepted the new reality at Union Village. Unbeknownst to him, the consequences of this were about to be amplified by events out of his control.[16]

October brought another annoyance to McNemar in the form of his ne'er-do-well older brother Garner. Garner was seventy-one and had received his non-Shaker grandson Milton A. McNemar of Tennessee as a visitor during the summer of 1837. Although Garner was a covenanted member, Freegift Wells deemed him an "old hypocrite" and described him as "an intolerable burden to believers for near or quite 30 years." In late July, Milton confronted Trustee Daniel Boyd and demanded $100 as his inheritance from his aunt Nancy McNemar (Garner's daughter), who had died in 1815, at fourteen. Boyd rightly dismissed his demand and advised him to make for home. Unbeknownst to him, Garner had given Milton anti-Shaker manuscript writings of his own composition that libeled the sect and, specifically, three respected and longtime members at Union Village. Garner instructed Milton to publish these manuscripts after his death.[17]

Back home in Smith County, Tennessee, on September 22, Milton penned a fiendishly threatening letter to Trustee Boyd, demanding $100 as his inheritance:

Dear Sir

I will inform you something about what I said to you in July 24th when I was there and Mentioned something about sum money that was coming to me and you said that it was a lie that they was no money cumming that Garner did not have a nuff to keep him two years and never did give the Shakers nuthing sum old horses and waggon or sunthing so I will tell you I don't care what the Devil he gave they was 2 hundred acres of land and sumthen else and all of the children has to have 100 Dollars and you got all of it and one of them died before she was of age and now you sai the sh[e] was sick all the time she live their and her mother and all the family and had be a so and so and you sai that that is a place of union and when men cum their and spend their days and then you alter them and try to drive them off to the world by James Smith. what would the world think of this if they was to get hold of it. Why they would they would help to put such devils to death now I will tell you that I will be Dam if I dont have that money or satisfaction or money one and if they money is not sent by the 20th of october I will be on my way to yor village and if you send half the money the rest I will give yo the Balances and if you dont send me fifty dollars I will have the hundred or Revenge sum way or nuther—I will wish that you never heard of the name of M'Namar I will consum sum crime to words yor village By sum way or nuther if the money dont cum or answer to this by october tis to be understood I tell you that the Devil will turns his dogs now Nancy M'Namars part must cum.
Very respectfully
M. A. M'Namar[18]

Just as this crisis was peaking, another one superseded it for Richard McNemar. On Saturday, October 7, one of his roommates mentioned that the barn at the East House Family, McNemar's original property, was about to be relocated to the Second Family. The East House Family had been broken up on January 14, 1836, and its member dispersed to other families at Union Village. Since then, the buildings that formed McNemar's farmstead—his holy consecration to the church—had been given over to a variety of uses by non-Shaker tenants. His original double-pen log cabin was still in good condition and had lately been used to store sheared wool. McNemar strongly objected to the removal of the barn and complained to his elder, Stephen Spinning. He then went speedily to the East House Family, but by the time he "got there the teams & hands were all in motion starting out on the business." McNemar vented his frustrations to longtime friend Elder Ashbel Kitchell, quoting the Tenth Commandment: "Thou shalt not covet thy neighbors house." McNemar's citation of this verse indicates that he already perceived himself as somewhat separated from the body of Believers at Union Village.[19]

In the evening, he was summoned to a three-hour meeting "relative to [his] state and standing" with Spinning and Freegift Wells. All recognized that McNemar had been deliberately instructed not to sign the church covenant and that he was therefore "not an orderly member of the body." Instead, McNemar "had been reserved for ministerial services"—services no longer requested or necessary. Wells pointed out, in a vaguely threatening way, that as McNemar's services were no longer needed, he "was under no government nor protection." He had no official place or standing in the Shaker community at Union Village. McNemar defended himself, citing his diligent work at "chairmaking, weaving, bookbinding, printing &c.," but this was to no avail, as he had undertaken all of it by his own will—"no one had any authority to set [him] to work." Wells and Spinning let McNemar know that the other members might "be waked up to feel against me & hold me at a distance or out of union." This was more than McNemar's "high sense" could bear. In his journal, he recognized that although he "had been instrumental in doing much good," his position was "precarious & indeed very dangerous," and he was now "in danger of falling & losing my crown."[20]

The seemingly capricious way in which the new eastern leadership were moving, or dismantling, structures at Union Village was also unpopular with other members. McNemar noted that a number of members gathered in his room the next day to gripe about "destroying valuable buildings instead of repairing them." His brethren felt they had "labored in vain & spent our strength for naught." McNemar tried to distance himself from the talk but proffered that "property ought to be valued before it was removed in order to a final and fair settlement," which was in keeping with the covenant. In the privacy of his journal, he vented his full anger about the current state of his former home place, "A sacred building so long consecrated to chastity and again so long prostituted as a brothel to fleshmongers, a nurse shop for negroes; that such a filthy, stinking abomination should be set up within the palings of the most holy place is too abominable to think of. Such feelings are already beginning to wake up, & I know of at least one who would rather those buildings were burnt on the ground than to bring them into contact with other valuable buildings where the whole might be in danger of ruin." Despite his anger, McNemar realized he "must check my ken" (his opinion) and offer it only when he perceived it would be respected. Darkly, he considered the state of affairs in the community to be in "greater danger than under any circumstances heretofore." He believed that unless spiritual concerns overtook temporal ones, all could be lost.[21]

McNemar knew he was now being forced into defining his relationship to the body of Believers. In his journal, he explored his present position and his options, plainly evaluated the system he was being asked to embrace, and rendered a surprisingly stark verdict on the Shaker hierarchy and its divinely sanctioned leadership.

> Reflections—It is no doubt the wish of the ministry and Eldership that after so long a privilege and so much plain dealing I would make up my mind & inform them plainly whether it would be my choice to break every former band & obligation as to faith & morals & without reserve cast myself on the present lead exclusive of all other & with entire confidence in their wisdom submit to their counsel & commands in all things spiritual & temporal to be as a little child passive & obedient without will or choice of my own in any thing whatever, or whether I feel myself unprepared to enter sincerely into such a state & would count it a privilege to find my relation to a lower order of Believers.
>
> Now having as I believe clear view of the subject I am prepared to say, that I am unprepared to take on such obligation. I feel essentially lacking as to the degree of faith & confidence required, and waiving a thousand fruitless thoughts & imaginations, I offer to take the ground which Elder Issachar chose after his releasment from his ministerial charge, that is as one of the office boarders or hired servants, I feel willing to be excluded from every privilege to which my faith & works do not entitle me, & to be treated as a pensioner, to work for my living as far as I am able & wherein I fall short of clearing my way to depend on the charity of God & his people. I would really chuse to enter into a written article as the leading gift at New Lebanon proposed three years ago, but to sign an obligation to sacrifice & surrender, what I have neither faith feelings will nor power to surrender, I cannot, I dare not so act the hypocrite my faith must go foremost and according to the obedience of faith I expect to be justified with these considerations I submit my case to the leading authorities & shall patiently wait an answer.
>
> N.B. I hope there will be no misunderstandings or falsifications of my faith & feelings. It is not property or any liberty of the flesh that I am unwilling to sacrifice, and interest I ever had or expect to have is already consecrated to the use of the gospel, and any disposal of my personal concerns relative to a further step may & can be made in order & according to the common privilege of allowing every adult person, time to settle & adjust his temporal concerns.[22]

While Richard McNemar stewed about the culmination of his thirty-year commitment to the Shakers, his natural brother Garner's fate was about to be determined. Richard was sent off to White Water on the morning of October 12, surely glad to be away from his trials as well as the literal trial of Garner at Union Village. That day, a group of eighteen ministry, elders, and deacons (including James McNemar, son of Richard and nephew of Garner) convened at the Second Family to try the "first case ever prosecuted among Believers requiring a general council, since the United Society existed." Garner McNemar, who was not present, was accused of "writing scurrilous stuff about Believers, & conveying it to his grandson out in the world allowing him (as is said) to have it printed after his (Garners) death." Andrew C. Houston bitterly commented in the community's journal, "Such, it would seem, is the reward that we get for taking care of, & maintaining the Evil minded, aged infirm man."[23]

Freegift Wells presided over the trial, which opened with the reading of Milton McNemar's threatening letter to Trustee Daniel Boyd. Brother James Smith, who was named in Milton's letter, testified that he had seen Garner's scurrilous writings—and, damningly, so had Richard McNemar. The two men had read most of it, and Smith stated, "It contained some very hard things against individuals." Smith was accused of driving many members out of Union Village and attempting to drive Garner out on multiple occasions. Most alarmingly, Garner claimed in his writings that the Shakers had forced him to be castrated. This was a charge often leveled against the Shakers, especially in Ohio and Kentucky during the nineteenth century. Garner had in fact been castrated, but it was on the advice of two non-Shaker physicians to alleviate a condition known as hydrocele, a painless buildup of watery fluid around one or both testicles that causes the scrotum or groin area to swell.[24]

In light of all these offenses, it was decided that the community could no longer hold Garner McNemar in union; he was to be excommunicated. Although Garner had been "from the beginning a very trouble some member & a very great liar," after lengthy debate, Elder Ashbel Kitchell persuaded his brethren that the gospel demanded mercy for him. It was decided that his union could be maintained following an honest confession of his misdeeds, the attempt to recover his writings from his grandson Milton, and a written recantation of the charges he leveled against the sect if his anti-Shaker writings were ever published. Kitchell drafted this statement for Garner's signature.[25]

On Saturday, October 14, Garner was presented with Kitchell's statement, which served as Garner's admission that he had authored a narrative of his life from childhood through June 1837 (sadly, now unlocated) that contained false and negative descriptions of life among the Shakers. It stated that Garner wrote it "under the influence of a malicious spirit" and now entirely disowned it. Further, it stated that the Shakers "have been uniformly kind to me from the beginning, in sickness & in health." Finally, it addressed the issue of his castration, clarifying that he "was once afflicted with a disease called Hydrocele, which endangered my life; but by the counsel & advice of Doctors, Treon and Dubois, together with my own desire, I was castrated, in order to save my life, as that was the last, & only remedy. And I now fully, & freely aquit the Society, or any member thereof, from persuading, or counseling me on the subject." Garner was given the option of signing the statement and remaining with the Shakers or withdrawing from the society and going to his worldly relations. In the end, he chose neither and attempted to remain on the grounds without a resolution.[26]

Freegift Wells ordered that Garner be "shut out of union, & verbally prohibited from going to any other family." Shakers were ordered not to speak with him, and any communication had to be made through the elders in his family. Richard McNemar was even sent to reason with his brother, but it was to no avail. Finally, Union Village trustees contracted with a tenant named McCabe, who lived in the East House (Richard McNemar's old property), to board him. By February 1838, Wells was able to inform the New Lebanon Ministry that they had charitably provided Garner with "a good room, well furnished to live in, & since that time we have had no trouble with him." Audaciously, Garner wrote the Shakers once more, requesting a clock, "so that he could know when to get up in the morning." The Shakers responded that he could rise by the tolling of their community bell, the same as the McCabe family did. Thus ended the sad story of Garner McNemar's life as a Shaker.[27] Freegift Wells must have been shocked and dismayed at the multitude of troubles he was confronting related to the prominent McNemar family.

As Richard McNemar rode toward White Water, he contemplated his future course of actions. On his arrival, he took up his pen and recorded his thoughts. He realized that "for some time past it has been felt that my gift was out for the present at Union Village." A brother who was a visionary at Union Village had approached McNemar several times in the weeks before to inform him that an "immaterial messenger" appeared to him in broad daylight with news for McNemar, that he "would shortly be called away from that place & that he must notify me to settle my affairs as soon as possible and be in readiness." McNemar admitted he had paid little attention to these warnings until he "found that the feelings of the ministry & Elders were turned against me for no cause at all, or causes & reasons which I thought very unreasonable & unjust, & that things were required of me with which I could not possibly comply." The opportunity to travel to White Water conveniently presented itself at this time, providing McNemar with a temporary escape from the hard decisions and trials that awaited him at Union Village. He was gladly received there on October 12 by his old friend Archibald Meacham, who greeted McNemar with yet another nickname: "peregrinus," or pilgrim.[28]

McNemar's visit to White Water lifted him out of the "spirit of bondage" he had been under. He surrendered himself to Meacham's "fatherly care," opening his mind—or confessing to and confiding in him—in a way he could not bring himself to do with Freegift Wells. He was given a room of his own and the chance to "read, write or cypher or any thing that I chose." McNemar facetiously wrote that this was quite merciful behavior toward "<u>a hell deserving creature!!!!!</u>" He insisted on earning his keep, however, and assisted the community in gathering 111 barrels of winter apples.[29]

One night during his stay, he had what can only be described as a Shaker nightmare, but it was one quite indicative of the danger he felt himself in. He dreamed he was "turning a chairpost & by some obstruction of the gouge it flew off the point right at my head with such violence that it awoke me." This was very early on Sunday morning. He preached at a public meeting later that day "in a pretty pathetic manner" by his own estimation. One wonders how forcefully he could advocate for Shakerism given his circumstances. The most significant feeling one gets from reading his journal description of this visit is that McNemar felt free for the first time in quite a while. He noted that White Water's first elder Joseph Agnew was "not above conversing with me freely," indicating that perhaps Freegift Wells had sought to maintain the separation from the rank and file typically held by Shaker ministers. Additionally, McNemar appreciated that Agnew manifested "no jealousy or uneasiness to know what I am about in my times of retirement."[30]

Again, this indicates the suspicion McNemar felt he was under at Union Village since the arrival of Freegift Wells. What McNemar was doing in his free time was "revising, correcting & transcribing journals & filling out our principal book of records so as to surrender it in good order to the next in office when I am called off the stage of action." He was under no illusions about what awaited him on his return to Union Village. Perhaps though, he should have given more thought to the "immaterial messenger" that tried to warn him—a messenger that would be the first of many.[31]

TWENTY-FOUR

THE NEW ERA

RICHARD MCNEMAR RECEIVED STARTLING NEWS from his old friend Benjamin Seth Youngs in late November of 1837. Youngs had returned to the East the previous autumn, and this was the first letter he sent his "antient friend & fellow laborer." Youngs thanked his "beloved brother" for their more than thirty years of companionship and specifically for welcoming Youngs to Turtle Creek in 1805, and all the care and lodging provided to him when he was but a stranger. Youngs excitedly shared the news of a stunning upswell in spiritual activities at Watervliet and New Lebanon, New York. Public meetings were crowded with astonished visitors who came to listen to primarily young girls—"babes and sucklings," as Youngs called them—address them in "unknown tongues." Private meetings, as well, were filled with "extraordinary exercises:—Powerful shakings & quakings—testimonies, promises, threatenings, warnings, predictions, prophecies:—Trances, revelations, Visions, songs, and dances."[1]

The instruments for these spiritual gifts entered a trance state for up to seven hours at a time and often had to be carried, insensible, from the floors of the meetinghouse and meeting room. Pointedly, Youngs noted that of all the variety of gifts, the gift of repentance was "most earnestly taught and the most earnestly sought for—i.e. this is the leading characteristic of the times here." Youngs chided McNemar, revealing that he had heard that McNemar himself had "so far progressed towards the kingdom of heaven, as to have been "immersed unto John"! with the baptism of Repentance"!—This surely is new-news, and quite entertaining." While amusing to Youngs, who may not have realized the gravity of McNemar's personal situation and probably couldn't fathom McNemar having anything to repent of, the reality was deadly serious for McNemar. In closing, Youngs beseeched McNemar to send him news of his

Figure 24.1. Shaker worship during the New Era, or Era of Manifestations, as depicted in apostate David R. Lamson's book *Two Years' Experience Among the Shakers* (West Boylston, MA: Published by the Author, 1848). Communal Societies Collection, Hamilton College.

own visions once he had "re-emerged from (Jordan) the river of judgment." To McNemar and his former companions in the West, Youngs sent his "'first love,' that has never betrayed nor waxed cold."[2]

The onset of what the Shakers called the "New Era" or, simply, a "revival" and what scholars refer to as the "Era of Manifestations," or "Mother's Work," was the beginning of the most extended period of visionary spiritual activity among all the Shaker communities since the supernatural events that attended the work of Mother Ann Lee and her compatriots in the 1780s. Brother Isaac Newton Youngs was sent by the New Lebanon Ministry to investigate the onset of these marvelous proceedings at Watervliet's South Family in August 1837. Observing the young girls who were initial subjects of the manifestations both delighted and confounded him. He wrote, "The visionists were often taken by their guides to visit the spirits in their meetings, and their dwellings, at which times they would talk out what they saw and heard. They saw and discribed much that was delightful, & expressed unspeakable blessings for the faithful."³ These guides were often deceased members of the sect, sometimes personally known to the visionists, and other times figures from the Shaker past, such as Mother Ann Lee.

The New Lebanon Ministry welcomed this work, particularly as it was primarily among the young members. They hoped that it would be "a means of establishing many souls in the way of God beyond the possibility of a doubt." The ministry considered it propitious that the instruments were younger, rank-and-file members rather than ministry or elders. This mitigated the danger that "cavilers might ascribe some part of those gifts to priescraft." Instead, "eye & ear witnesses [who] knew the illiterate & bashful state of those youth & children, could no more ascribe those gifts to deception and fraud, than they could Balaam's Ass when she rebuked her master."⁴

As Benjamin Seth Youngs noted to McNemar, repentance and humiliation were the themes of the day. The ministry noted that "the unfaithful and disorderly (both male & female) were named out and put to shame" in meetings. Given the age of many of the visionists, the ministry knew it would require "some wisdom and caution to steer the young through those gifts without loss to themselves or dishonor to the cause. The gift of God is always good, but when fallen nature lays claim to the honor of it there is danger of great loss." This observation was more prescient than the ministry could ever know. The tumultuous events that unfolded well into the early 1850s fundamentally challenged the spiritual hierarchy of Shakerism, upended the lives and spiritual commitment of many individual members, and contributed to the decline of Shaker communities.⁵

Richard McNemar returned to Union Village from his brief respite at White Water on October 28, 1837.⁶ The day before, his eldest daughter, Vincy, was released from her position of eldress at the North Union, Ohio, Shaker community, and she returned to Union Village to live. Richard McNemar seems to have passed the autumn and winter uneventfully. Late in the year, he decided to abstain from meat, tea, coffee, and tobacco and wrote to his friend Benjamin Seth Youngs that he had experienced a "singular benefit both in [his] corporeal & mental powers."⁷ Although McNemar was tending to his physical health, he was mentally still consumed to an unhealthy degree with unraveling and accounting for the failures of western Shaker leaders since the death of Father David Darrow in 1825.⁸ McNemar had been dabbling in intrigue regarding these matters since shortly after Freegift Wells and Betsy Hastings arrived at Union Village. In December 1836, he wrote a letter to Hastings marked "confidential," in which he offered to give her controversial documents relating to the crisis surrounding Father David's succession from ten years before. He claimed, "I never aimed at being a dignitary in the church nor of men sought I honor"; nevertheless, he could not let go of the past, nor could he withdraw from the center of events.[9]

On March 18, 1838, McNemar wrote a rambling and bizarre letter to his friend Elder Richard W. Pelham of the North Union Ministry. Pelham was an intellectual like McNemar and a student of Greek and Hebrew. McNemar's letter was prompted by another letter (now unlocated) written by Elder David Spinning, apparently at the behest of Freegift Wells, who requested Spinning's views on the "radical causes of adversity & calamity to the church in the west." Wells was returning to New Lebanon on a visit that summer and was gathering documents to present to the ministry there. McNemar saw Spinning's letter and found his opinions to be differing "upon a pretty large scale." McNemar was concerned that Spinning had not touched on the twin crises triggered by Abijah Alley and Aquila Massie Bolton, both of whom McNemar viewed as pivotal to the degradation of younger membership in the western communities. Referring to records related to those notorious apostates, McNemar assured Pelham, "No one on earth has half the knowledge of what is contained in those papers documents and vouchers which I have hither to retained in my possession," indicating that he had still not handed many papers over to Andrew C. Houston. Further, McNemar implicated "more important characters" that "singly and directly I dare not approach even by way of suspicion." Instead, he confided in Pelham that he sought to prove the validity of his view of events in the Shaker West through the interpretation of words and names in "mystical Hebrew"—a possible reference to the arcane technique of gematria used in the cabala. Acknowledging Pelham's superior understanding of Hebrew and that his "gift extends into those mystical matters," McNemar asked him to investigate Hebrew names, such as Esau, Jacob, Judas, and Issachar, and "dig up those several roots give their derivations references & applications in such a manner as to shed light on those mysterious events that within the last three years have taken place at Union Village."[10]

Richard Pelham was so alarmed by the bizarre letter from McNemar that he wrote to Freegift Wells, saying he had received "a very ominous & mysterious letter from Eleazar." Pelham wrote that if it had been sent "in order," Wells would have seen it, but Pelham assumed that due to the contents he probably hadn't. Still puzzled as to the letter's import, Pelham confided to Wells that it contained "criticisms on certain Hebrew words &c. which [McNemar] seems to think of the utmost importance." Alarmed by the contents, Pelham offered Wells his candid assessment of McNemar: "I am induced to think as the scotchman said that he is 'cracked o' the skull.'" Pelham also informed Wells of McNemar's reference to "late occurrences under the influence of more important characters," an altogether damning statement that implicated McNemar in scheming and subversion completely contrary to the requirements of his new role at Union Village. Pelham asked Wells's counsel regarding a response to the troubling letter.[11] Wells's response, if he made one, is unlocated. Further, it is unknown if Wells subsequently discussed this letter with McNemar, but its subject matter would surely have given him further trepidation about McNemar's increasingly unhinged mental state.

Freegift Wells suffered from vertigo throughout January 1838 and was treated with doses of calomel and blistering on his legs in an attempt to draw the disease away from his head. By February, his condition had worsened, and he was nearly immobilized by large blisters. While coping with these difficulties, he was also preparing for a spring journey to New Lebanon. The party, which also included Elder Joshua Worley, William Davis, Eldress Betsey Hastings, and Sisters Sally Sharp and Nancy McNemar, planned to depart Union Village on May 14. Freegift Wells carried Spinning's letter and other documents assembled by McNemar, all of which would be turned over to the New Lebanon Ministry to attempt to finally determine the root causes of problems in the western Shaker communities.

On May 13, Richard McNemar wrote to Elder Rufus Bishop regarding the documents headed his way. McNemar was concerned, as ever, with proving the legitimacy of Solomon King's succession to Father David Darrow. He wrote, disingenuously, "As for the long argument to substantiate and prove the regular line of succession and the regularity of the first gift in Elder Solomon &c. let that stand for what it is worth." Firmly defending himself and his western counterparts, he wrote that he hoped the documents would not be "found disrespectful, ungenerous or unfair toward the east nor any thing vain arrogant neither mean nor degrading toward the West. Fair play on the both sides & the honor of the gospel is the impartial object." McNemar thanked Bishop for sending Wells and Hastings, and "especially for all the mortifications I have recd. under their administration." Finally, McNemar expressed regret that before he made his visit to New Lebanon in 1829, he was enjoined "not to trouble" the ministry there with news of any controversy in the West. In hindsight, he lamented that he "was so bound & straitened" that "so many important matters were passed unnoticed"—important matters later settled by "disorderly communications in writing."[12] McNemar, aware that patience with him had certainly worn thin in the West, must have been concerned about a similar trend among his old friends and admirers in the East.

Bishop's response of June 30 was addressed to "Beloved Brother Eleazar" and conveyed the "best love" of the ministry; it must have set McNemar's mind at ease. Further, Bishop assured him, "We all love you & feel interested in your prosperity." Bishop admitted that he hadn't had the time to examine the documents McNemar sent to the East due to the explosion in spiritual activities throughout eastern Shaker communities. Describing these to McNemar, he excitedly wrote, "Infidelity stands a poor chance in these days, for it has nothing to stand upon—It would do your soul good to hear a little ten year old boy deliver a message in great power & eloquence for nearly the space of two hours, or to see a five year old girl fall into a trance & after a while return with a tune, words and appropriate motions, & be able to minister heavenly sensations to all around."[13] These descriptions mirrored many such scenes witnessed by McNemar more than thirty years before, which he recounted in *The Kentucky Revival*.

While the Union Village Ministry were still in the East, Richard McNemar departed for White Water on July 23 with a load of pigs' leather and for a visit of indeterminate length.[14] Even in the ministry's absence, McNemar probably wished to escape the pressures he felt at Union Village. The ministry returned home on July 31, excited to share news of the spiritual manifestations they had witnessed at New Lebanon. One member of the party, however, was undoubtedly disturbed by what he experienced. When Joshua Worley, second elder in the ministry, initially met the visionists at Watervliet, New York, they had the same messages of Mother Ann's love and spiritual gifts for him as they did for his traveling companions. That changed when the party reached New Lebanon. Visionist Philemon Stewart, the leading spiritual instrument there, declared on behalf of "Jehovah" that Worley was "full of unbelief and had a reprobate spirit, and had not confessed [his] sins." Confounded by the conflicting messages, delivered within days of each other and only thirty miles apart, Worley was confined to his room and denied permission to go out or speak with anyone but his elders. In a sort of Shaker interrogation, he was visited up to four times daily by ministry elder Rufus Bishop, Freegift Wells, and Stewart. When they entered the room, Worley had to get on his knees and bow four times to Stewart and twice to the elders—kissing the floor each time. The ultimate resolution of this case is not recorded, but Worley returned to Ohio with Wells and was, at least for the time being, still second elder in the ministry. One wonders if he shared his dreadful experiences with his brethren on returning home.[15]

Despite a flurry of spiritual events at Union Village in 1838, the work had yet to begin there on anywhere near the scale then ongoing at South Union, Pleasant Hill, North Union, and in many eastern communities. Wells communicated this frustration to the New Lebanon Ministry in the first letter he wrote them after arriving home.

> When we compare our all, with the gifts, & superabundant manifestations of the power of God which we witnessed at N. Lebanon, the comparison seems quite as deficient, as that of a grass-hopper, among the Fowls of heaven. And altho we are somewhat disappointed as to the commencement of Mothers purging work at Union Village yet, we are by no means discouraged. The occasional shocks of the power of God above mentioned seems to strike a dread upon the most unbelieving. They almost seem to fear that something may come by, and by, that they will not be able to stand against. This little check to the progress of unbelief, is quite a comfort to us; & it is our prayer, and we believe it is the prayer of every honest sincere soul in this place, that we may be shaken, & purged, by gifts of mortification, & humiliation untill unbelief becomes extinct at U. Village.

Wells also reported that on a recent visit to Pleasant Hill, James McNemar "said he had seen shaking before, but had never seen any that would bear any comparison with what he saw there."[16] The gifts of mortification and humiliation were indeed nigh.

At the Sabbath meeting on August 5, the ministry conveyed love from the East and recounted the wonders they had witnessed there. Three days later, Brother William More was "powerfully operated on by a supernatural power" during the evening meeting at the Centre Family. Still more was needed, however, to fan this nascent spark into flames. Richard McNemar returned to Union Village on August 10, just as the manifestations were burgeoning. In another surprising twist, Joshua Worley (son of Malcham), second in the Union Village Ministry and recently returned from his humiliation at New Lebanon, was released from his position. This was yet another perceived blow to the founders of the western communities. The New Lebanon Ministry noted that Worley's removal was predicted by a visionist (or instrument) shortly after his departure. Worley had "despised" this visionist while there, perhaps indicating that he, like McNemar, was not in sympathy with the new manifestations.[17]

On Sunday, August 26, the Believers lined up in ranks, men and women facing each other. Freegift Wells addressed the meeting concerning the "marvellous work of God that was going on in other Societies of Believers." He told them with confidence that they would be "visited in like manner without doubt." A song was then started, and "shaking commenced, and it appeared almost like Electricity; the power of God seemed to shower upon the assembly, and to a number it appeared to be irresistible." On September 1, McNemar again departed the scene of these spiritual developments, decamping to Watervliet, Ohio. The next day, involuntary religious exercises, such as the jerks—a key component of worship during the Kentucky Revival—were again witnessed once at Union Village. Had he witnessed the sight, McNemar may have found them more threatening than something to be rejoiced at.[18]

McNemar returned to Union Village on September 11, resuming his place at the Centre Family. News of the manifestations continued to pour in from other communities, and a party of four Shakers from Union Village was dispatched to witness the "unspeakable supernatural work" at Pleasant Hill and South Union. The New Lebanon Ministry received news of the uptick in spiritual activity at Union Village and joyously responded, "We are thankful to hear from you; and to learn that Mother had begun her good work at Union Village, which we have the best reasons to believe will never close until all who profess to be her children are purified and made straight, or purged out from among the faithful; for she will not own one soul as her child who refuses subjection to her laws."[19] The gauntlet was clearly thrown; the faith of all would be tested and the impure purged out by the refining fire.

Matthew Houston wrote to Seth Youngs Wells on September 24, expressing concern about his old friend and ministerial colleague Richard McNemar. Houston was temporarily installed as first elder of the Watervliet, Ohio, community, which McNemar had just visited. Although Houston's letter is unlocated, Wells's reply reveals his anxieties. Marking his letter "confidential," Wells lamented, "Is it possible that after so long a privilege & so much instruction as E[leaza]r has had, that he can be so ignorant and so destitute of the true spirit of Mother's gospel as not to know that the work of God in this day . . . is under the direction & influence of their spirit?—And that it is truly the work of God & not of man?" Wells felt "heartily sorry" for McNemar and would have done anything "to satisfy his feelings & reconcile his mind to the present order of things at U.V. . . . If he would only suppress that spirit of unreconciliation in his own breast." He correctly identified that McNemar's "greatest difficulty" was himself, and if he continued to "indulge that darkening spirit," it would "cost him many sorrows" in the end.[20]

McNemar's biggest stumbling block was his unwillingness to accept the duly appointed ministry at Union Village. Wells reminded Houston that when McNemar was sounded out about the possibility of assuming a leadership role, he "desired that they would not put that burden on his shoulders, unless they meant to kill him." Wells asserted that McNemar, like older members at New Lebanon, must find contentment with his considerable past exertions for the gospel and reconcile himself to the divinely sanctioned gift of leadership at

Union Village. After all, the Union Village community had repeatedly beseeched New Lebanon for intervention, which was granted and not without sacrifice. Sending talented young Believers like Freegift Wells and Betsey Hastings to the West was "a tedious cross," not just for them personally but for the communities they left behind. Candidly and damningly, Wells admitted that neither Freegift Wells nor Hastings "would have gone to Ohio, if they could possibly have avoided it—Nor would our Ministry have sent them there, if they could have found any in Ohio that were able & willing to supply their places." Wells offered no solution to McNemar's problem, only hopeful sentiments that his eyes would eventually open to the "see the light breaking forth more bright and glorious than he has ever seen it." In closing, he told Houston he hoped "Mother's work" had begun at Union Village, as "it will soon make singeing work there & cause many stout hearts to fear & tremble."[21]

The same troubles were foremost in Freegift Wells's correspondence with the New Lebanon Ministry. They wrote to him on October 10, commiserating, "We have perused your last confidential writings over and over, and over again with great care and attention, and they have caused wearisome nights and days of tribulation and bearing. What can we do? What can we say? or what can we write to satisfy that people?" Even the saintly patience of Shakerism's spiritual leaders was wearing thin. Striking a directly personal tone unusual in Shaker letters, they wrote, "Beloved Elder Freegift, we feel very sorry for you, and for Elderess Betsey and sister Sally too; we know your trials are great. It seems that you need the wisdom of Solomon, the meekness of Moses & the patience of Job to support you under all your sore afflictions." They wished them wisdom to gather and protect the people, especially "such ones as are influential & able to do much good or hurt"—Richard McNemar among them. The ministry warned Wells, "No doubt but those who are the greatest trouble to your righteous souls are such as have had a long privilege in the gospel." Although McNemar had been a Shaker for thirty-three years, they averred that he had been "soaring far above the simple and mortifying work of God." Ominously, they prophesied, "But they must come down, or they will certainly fall, and great will be their fall!" Paraphrasing a Presbyterian hymn, they wrote, "What joys malignant shook the gates of hell, and Zion trembled when McNemar fell." It is sobering that McNemar's longtime friend and correspondent Elder Rufus Bishop was likely the primary author of this letter.[22]

The ministry knew that McNemar's mind would not rest and could lead him to dangerous places if not kept occupied. They recognized that he would be "improving his time and faculties about something; and if you do not imploy his literary talents in something favorable or useful, he will be very liable to do hurt with them, and make trouble for you." Accordingly, they recommended that he be allowed to "busy himself with his Hymns and printing press, even if you do not want his labor of that kind"—this despite Bishop's prior injunction. The ministry worried that McNemar, in combination with the disaffected members of the Worley family, might instigate long-feared legal challenges to the ownership of the land on which the Centre and East Families at Union Village were built—ironically, the very scenario McNemar had repeatedly warned them of throughout the 1830s. The ministry feared that if McNemar and Malcham and Joshua Worley were to "combine together and set up independence at the east house, or what would still be worse, at the center, you might have trouble upon trouble which would be hard to settle."[23] The situation was a powder keg ready to explode, and the sparks to ignite it came from the spirits.

McNemar received more news about the manifestations from Benjamin Seth Youngs in the East. Despite Youngs's glowing report of late 1837, his opinion of the phenomena had decidedly changed. Youngs noted that the visionists had repeatedly declared that Mother Ann Lee had made her second appearance and would "make thorough work in purging the church." Being the Shakers' foremost theologian, Youngs rightly questioned how many appearances of Christ there had been, and was not Mother Ann the culmination in the eighteenth century that led to the establishment of Christ's church in Shakerism? Furthermore, Mother's reappearance implied to Youngs that "the true power in the leadship has been lost"; in other words, the spiritual hierarchy of Shaker leadership had failed. For a system guided by divine revelation and a membership obeying a chain of inspired command, this was a devastating development. Youngs acknowledged that the manifestations had "stirred up fear and honesty particularly in the youth" and—for the moment—had stopped their "continual egress" from the Shakers. Additionally, the spirit in public and private meetings had been revived due to the sentiment that "there was something new something that seemed refreshing ahead." With regard to securing the "present and future state of the leadship," Youngs had not discovered a "particle" of good resulting from the tumultuous spiritual manifestations. This was an alarmingly frank assessment of events viewed by most as joyous and epochal.[24]

Youngs also informed McNemar of something even more disturbing. He had expressed a wish to return once more to the West, arguing that it was "indispensibly necessary" that he and McNemar should work together on final editions of *The Kentucky Revival* and the *Testimony of Christ's Second Appearing*, foundational texts of Shaker history and theology that they had authored in 1807 and 1808, respectively. Youngs's request was denied, and he was "shocked" to be told that Mother Ruth Farrington, the first Shaker eldress in the West (who died in 1821), had expressed the sentiment around 1813 that Richard McNemar and Malcham Worley were "dangerous men." Youngs warned McNemar that during the present difficulties, "this abominable idea has been gathered up and preserved among the filth and scrapings . . . & officially communicated to the ministry in writing." Wholly disgusted, Youngs reconfirmed his faith in and friendship with McNemar by reassuring him that "justice, candor & true friendship" required him to pass along that troubling news. The positive aspect was that it demonstrated Youngs's commitment to McNemar and the "scrupulous care [and] sacred conf[iden]ce I wish you to receive & to hold my communications." In the manuscript wherein McNemar transcribed their final correspondence, he wrote the following after his last known letter to Youngs: "I do love thee O my pretty father I do never want any other."[25]

Union Village was overwhelmed with sickness and death through the rest of September and into October. This may have hindered enthusiasm at meetings, as the next major spirit manifestation didn't occur until October 25. That evening, fifty-seven-year-old Brother Nathaniel Taylor "heard a trumpet sound & immediately heard very beautiful instrumental music." The next evening, Anna Middleton, Malcham Worley's fifty-eight-year-old former slave and the second Shaker convert west of the Appalachians, woke up "just before the clock struck 12 & directly heard very melodious instrumental music, which lasted about 10 minutes." The next night, Vincy McNemar, Richard's forty-one-year-old eldest daughter, heard the same music. Forty-five-year-old Asenath Edy had seen a light in her retiring room for two nights in a row. All of the aforementioned were adult long-term members of the community. Freegift Wells recorded these events carefully in his journal, noting "the above extraordinary exhibitions were no doubt performed by ministering spirits as a prelude to the great work which Mother has promised to perform among us, & in us. Altho we have been waiting, & earnestly looking for a long time without much visible manifestation of the commencement of this work, yet the above gifts seem to revive our spirits & makes us feel that the time is near at hand when Mother will notice us, as she has almost all other Societies of Believers."[26]

Richard McNemar is not mentioned as a participant in or subject of any of the manifestations up to this point. He solicited the opinion of Benjamin Seth Youngs (in a now unlocated letter) regarding the "present dispensation." McNemar feared that it might be "declared by inspiration" that he could not sign the church covenant and would not "be protected in the bounds of the church & in fact . . . not fit to live any where among the Shakers." Despite his own previously expressed reservations, Youngs responded with disbelief, "What in the name of common sense what among all the blind paradoxes on the Lords earth do you mean by all this? I do not understand you! Are you really gone mad, then I may whistle to know why you talk so. Are you in your right in your bright & sober senses?"[27] He was, however, aware of McNemar's precarious situation and subsequently advised him: "Hold on! Till the time original church grounds and church covenant are recovered & safe! The present strange & marvellous work among us is indeed full of paradoxes and many curious phenomenon. It is prudent there fore not to be too hasty in drawing conclusions nor too precipitate in following every various impulse of feeling, & caprice of the mind, till it may be distinctly known & understood what is what."[28] The decision to sign the covenant, however, was strictly in McNemar's hands.

On November 3, McNemar traveled to Watervliet, Ohio, to retrieve his printing press and move it to Union Village, as the New Lebanon Ministry had discreetly recommended. He helped Brother David Cory load it into his peddling wagon. McNemar seems to have maintained a degree of personal autonomy judging by his travels through the summer and fall of 1838. He may have felt shut out of community activities or may have consciously removed himself from events that were developing out of his control. Writing to Youngs, he expressed relief that his Kirjathsepher—as he referred to his printing office and archive—was being reestablished on the second-floor, southwest-corner room of the brick shop at Union Village's Centre Family. Here, McNemar eagerly anticipated carrying out a contracted job binding ninety law books for Robert Corwin, a lawyer in Lebanon, Ohio. Youngs had also sent a verbal message of reassurance to McNemar through his daughter Nancy, lately returned from her visit to the East. The sentiment of Youngs's message is not known, but its effect was to make McNemar "entirely patient." McNemar wrote to Youngs regarding the changing times, "We already know in a measure, 'what is what, and what is not what it once was.'" McNemar also shared that his correspondence with Seth Youngs Wells, who for fifteen years had been his spiritual and intellectual link to New Lebanon, had unceremoniously closed due to the long suspected and dreaded judgment that it was "disorderly."[29]

McNemar's two surviving daughters, Vincy and Nancy, each became instruments of the spirits during November. Vincy, who bore a great physical resemblance to her father, received a spirit message personally addressed to her from North Union, the community where she had served as eldress until October 1837, now a hotbed of spiritual activity. A message from visionist Nancy Lancaster of that community was read at a November 11 meeting. She described Union Village as being "in the most deplorable state, in the midst of all corruption, swallowed up in darkness, in the sin of covetousness, lust and pride and every obstacle to meet." As spiritual gifts, and tensions, mounted, physical

VINCY MCNEMAR
(Aged 80 years)

Figure 24.2. Vincy McNemar, pictured later in life, long after she served as the spiritual instrument for Mother Ann Lee. Historian John Patterson MacLean was told by elderly Union Village, Ohio, Shakers that "with the exception of her nose, Vincy resembled very much her father." This image was used as the frontispiece to MacLean's *Sketch of the Life and Labors of Richard McNemar*.

manifestations grew—Nancy McNemar was so wrought upon at the November 18 Sabbath meeting that she fell to the floor. Andrew Houston, the new church scribe, joyously recorded these events in the community's journal: "The Supernatural work of God, (called Mother's work) in its new increase, has now broken out into an open... the powerful bodily operations and heart-searching conviction that accompanies it, baffles all attempts at description."[30]

On Monday, November 19, Freegift Wells met personally with Richard McNemar and delivered a "general message" to him. This was probably Nancy Lancaster's warning of the sins of pride and covetousness at Union Village, something that Wells had been trying to impress on McNemar, particularly regarding his books, papers, and especially his unwillingness to sign the covenant. The fact that Wells had to meet with McNemar to convey the message to him indicates that he may not have been attending meetings by this time, a decidedly negative development. In the afternoon, Vincy McNemar—who had been "appointed by Mother Ann to labour with her father"—went to McNemar's shop to begin her efforts to penetrate his ego and pride and bring him to humility and submission. At the meeting that evening, Mother Ann made her first visit to the community—through Vincy—and gave "3 drops of Mothers love, which was distributed to all the family." Vincy labored with her father again throughout the next day, this time in Eldress Betsey Hastings's workshop, and again received three drops of Mother's love for her efforts at the meeting that Wednesday. As these dramatic events unfolded, Elder Freegift Wells busied himself with more mundane tasks, such as repairing a walkway that led from the ministry's shop to the kitchen. His journal records the whole spectrum of events that involved him each day and lacks any trace of judgment—positive or negative.[31]

Through the remainder of 1838, Vincy McNemar's position as the principal female visionist and voice of Mother Ann strengthened. She presided over meetings where "fierce war [was] waged against all evil & opposition to the work of God." Falling into a trance, she lay on the floor with her hands in motion before sounding forth with a multitude of new songs received from the spiritual world. Following one such episode, she was "taken to the office being stiff, & helpless," but she came to after singing one final song and returned to her retiring room in the dwelling. James McNemar, Richard's eldest surviving son, forty-three, joined his sister at the meeting, "thundering against Lust and pride." These activities, however, were far more prevalent among the families where young Believers lived. They had not yet widely occurred among the Centre Family, the home of the most seriously committed and spiritually experienced Shakers.[32]

At the November 26 meeting, Elizabeth Waits went into vision, dancing around the room, agitating her body and head. She announced that Mother had given her an eye glass with which to see. She walked between the ranks of brethren and sisters and announced, "All is not done yet." Then, shockingly, she revealed that Mother had armed her with a gun, a double-edged sword "to cut & whittle the flesh up & down," and a rod to thrash "the backs of the obstinate in Mother's name."[33] Community scribe Andrew C. Houston described the gun in a letter to New Lebanon sister Eliza Sharp.

> The gun was a strange instrument,—it went by turning a crank—she first thought it was a musical instrument, but the first she knew it went off in her hands & scared her—however, she soon learned to handle her gun very dexterously; she used it to shoot at monsters—said it gave a dreadful report when she shot, & no doubt it did, for it would stun, & jar, & cramp her thro the breast & shoulders most distressingly when she had in a heavy load: She would plead with Mother to load her gun light—"O Mother if you do put in one of your heavy bullets it would kill"[34]

Although the visionists had exhorted the community to mercilessly reprove and examine themselves for sin, gifts such as guns, swords, and rods marked a dark turn in the era of manifestations at Union Village. These were the first gifts to encourage external aggression, transforming a personal and inward work into an outwardly focused effort to purify the community through suspicion, coercion, and force.

Houston recorded further marvelous sights that occurred at public meetings, where visitors witnessed "the piercing conviction, self abasement the falling, shaking, bowing, dancing, and the many marvellous agitations of the subjects of this work." Offering his own opinion, he wrote, "The beholder is compelled to acknowledge the finger of divine agency in this work." Brother Daniel Miller saw enough of the power of God in the youth and children "to confound any infidel." The young were continuously undergoing spiritual operations, whether in meetings, at work, or even at the dining table. By the end of the year, Houston rejoiced that the exercises were "increasing and becoming more and more general." On December 23, at a windy and cold Sabbath meeting—mercury at zero—twenty-two-year-old Brother Oliver C. Hampton ominously announced that Mother had also given him a gun and that they all might "find a benefit with such weapons & enough to do."[35]

TWENTY-FIVE

WAR IN HEAVEN

BROTHER DANIEL MILLER WAS A faithful member of the Union Village community. Aged forty-three, he had converted to Shakerism in 1805. He worked primarily with animals in the community and was a skilled herdsman and butcher. Miller was appalled with the new tone that spiritual events had taken. In his journal for December 23, 1838, the day that Oliver Hampton wielded a spiritual gun in the meeting, Miller wrote, "Sabbath our coldest—about zero and windy in the bargain. Church meeting—too much spersing it brings death into our meetings. I can feel it just as sensible as I can heat or cold, the best way to help others is in my opinion to properly help our selves with a good example and do all the heart work in our own souls. If you hate evil in yourself you cannot love it in another."[1]

In January 1839, the Union Village community, although apparently in the throes of religious ecstasy with the return of Mother Ann Lee's spirit, was suffering inwardly and outwardly. Miller lamented that during the Sabbath public meeting, the meetinghouse had become so filthy from tobacco juice that it was a "real stinking place" and "during the exercising we inhale the noxious compound." Sickness had not abated. On New Year's Day, Freegift Wells noted in his journal, "Eleazer was taken quite sick last night." A week later, Richard McNemar was still "sorely afflicted" with the "cold plague or lung fever." McNemar was already in a low place psychologically, having been the subject of chastisement by the spirit of Mother Ann through his daughter Vincy. That same day, John Ross, a ten-year-old boy, entered a trance state that lasted thirty-seven and a half hours. Ross was just one of a number of little boys who left their bodies to cavort with departed friends in the spirit world, bringing back gifts of love and new songs.[2]

The tension between the *visible lead*—that is, the living ministry and the elders and eldresses—and the spirits was quickly coming to the fore as the manifestations grew more extreme and the agenda of the spirits more radical. Thus far, Union Village leadership seemed to have accepted the spiritual manifestations and messages as genuinely inspired, although some messages of a more pointed nature transmitted from the North Union, Ohio, community were cause for concern. Freegift Wells suspected that their visionists were "being led a part of the time by false spirits." He wrote to the New Lebanon Ministry seeking their guidance. They advised him that "doubtless there are hosts of disorderly spirits, wicked spirits, & lying spirits." However, they believed "the Visionists are yet sincere according to their present light and understanding, but if they do not turn about and change their sense they will most certainly fall. They must take care how they touch the lord's anointed."[3]

The New Lebanon Ministry had in fact warned North Union's elder David Spinning of the "danger that the Visionists were in, when left to themselves, of being led by false spirits, and how exposed they were to get exalted." This high, exalted sense was anathema to Shakerism, yet when assumed by a visionist under control of a spirit, it could be wielded as an incredibly powerful weapon. There was no doubt as to the beauty and power of the gifts they had received, but "if they lose their union and relation to those who stand nearer to God than they do, how can they partake of the sap and nourishment of the true vine?" The spirit of Mother Ann had informed the New Lebanon visionists that she would not "own any of their gifts that are out of union with their Elders" and reassured them that she would "never authorize any spirit to get between them and their Elders." As far as the New Lebanon Ministry were concerned, "this appears to be a safeguard against imposition from false spirits." They also acknowledged, however, that "Disobedient Visionists and prophets are as liable to fall and become tools in the service of the devil as any other characters."[4]

At a public meeting on Sunday, January 27, Freegift Wells read a letter from the New Lebanon Ministry confirming the doctrine of a "visible lead." With that formality in place, the shackles were loosened. The meeting was another high-energy affair and saw the emergence of a new visionist: Margaret McBrien. Shaker sister Susannah Cole Liddell, fifteen at the time, described McBrien's first visionary state: "It was in [a] society meeting that while we were in the march that this young Irish woman called Margaret (M'Brien) left her place in the circle and turning very swiftly mid the [a]isle. This broke up the exercise of the meeting and we took our seats around the wall of the room, watching the great turning swiftness of the wonderful opperation." McBrien, along with Mary Ann Ross and Sarah Cochran, was the first to go into vision at public meetings. All three sisters lived at the West Brick Family, a gathering order, or, a family for new Believers. At the close of the meeting, they were carried away from the meetinghouse, insensate, in wagons. In his private journal, Brother Daniel Miller wrote that the scene "bangs all things in creation." The various "exercises" and cries of "take care," "look out," and, more ominously, "look in" "echoed and reechoed" through the meeting room.[5]

Margaret McBrien emerged as the preeminent visionist at Union Village. Her origins are as mysterious as her sudden ascension to the pinnacle of spiritual power as the voice of Mother Ann Lee in January 1839. Shaker records indicate that she was born on January 17, 1817, presumably in Ireland, although no place is named. Her name is spelled variously as "McBrien," "McBryan," or "McBrian," with the first variant appearing most often in Shaker sources. She came to Union Village in 1837 accompanied by a baby boy named Emmet, born earlier that year on February 23. In the 1850 census, Emmet's place of birth is listed as the Atlantic Ocean, and in the 1860 census as "At Sea."[6] Evidently, Margaret McBrien was a pregnant twenty-year-old who emigrated from Ireland to the United States in 1837 and gave birth during the passage. She traveled with a male companion, possibly her husband or the father of her child.

McBrien first became acquainted with the Shakers at the Hancock, Massachusetts, community. She arrived at Union Village in the company of her "weakly husband who soon wandered away from the comforting prizes of heaven." At first appearance, she was described as "a very slight built round shouldered woman with an infant baby in her arms, she was nearly direct from Ireland and had the brogue in full." No account of her activities appears in Union Village records before her takeover of its spiritual life. She was housed at the West Brick Family. Her elders were Amos Parkhurst, thirty-eight, a member since 1815, and forty-seven-year-old Charles D. Hampton (father of visionist Oliver); her eldresses were Ann Parkinson, forty-nine, a member since 1817, and Jane Parkhurst, probably Amos's natural sister.[7]

McBrien and her visionary gifts had the immediate and unquestioning attention of Freegift Wells and the ministry. The text of only one of McBrien's spirit messages is known to survive, and it illustrates her uncanny ability to communicate to Wells *exactly* what he wanted to hear from Mother Ann Lee, while simultaneously downplaying McBrien's agency and exalting her humility and submissiveness to the ministry. In late January 1839, Wells had to deal with a particularly knotty issue concerning the visionists at North Union. Ministry elder David Spinning sought his advice in a desperate letter. Wells pondered his response, wrote it, and then asked the elders and eldresses at the West Brick Family to direct McBrien to "inquire of Mother, whether that which I had written was agreeable to her mind." McBrien was informed of the task by Ann Parkinson. Two hours later, McBrien entered vision and was met by her spirit guide Selinda, who told her that Mother wanted to see her. They found Mother Ann standing on the banks of a lake covered with doves and surrounded by a green plain. Mother told McBrien that she had the "precious privilege of being a little Errand girl for Elder Freegift; I hope you will know how to prize it as you ought." McBrien responded that she was "glad to run Mothers errands, & doubly glad to run one for Elder Freegift." Presciently, Mother warned her to "not get puff'd up by it." McBrien had not even posed Wells's question when Mother assured her that she approved of "every sentence" he had written to North Union and that she was present when he had written it. She also expressed her thankfulness that Wells and his ministry were in place to "do my work amongst my almost ruined children in Union Village." Further, the elders and eldresses were always to hear the counsel of their ministry as if the words came directly from Mother—since they did.[8]

McBrien asked Mother Ann to strengthen her faith. Shocked, she replied, "I cannot strengthen you, you must receive the strength you ask, from your Elders." Mother then gave her love to McBrien to carry back to the community. McBrien and Selinda departed but were met by the devil on the way. With "a sneering hell simper on his countenance," he said, "Ha! Running errands for the Ministry are you? I shall frighten you so you won't remember a word you were told to tell them." McBrien, however, defied the devil and eluded his grasp when he tried to snatch Mother's love from her hands. McBrien then awoke, safe at home, and delivered her message to Elder Charles Hampton, who wrote it down for Wells. In describing this incident to the North Union Ministry, an astonished Wells wrote, "Margaret received the foregoing message from Mother without communicating her errand at all!" Mother's message affirmed not only Wells's faith in her but also McBrien's gift and Wells's own mission to implement order throughout the "ruined children" of the Shaker West. McBrien's shrewdly constructed message cemented her place as Wells's chosen visionist.[9]

On Monday, January 28, Elders Parkhurst and Hampton brought another written vision from McBrien to the ministry's shop. In his journal, Wells described it as "marvelous, & full of instruction." Wells read two of her visions publicly at the next Sabbath meeting on February 3. How could McBrien avoid getting "puff'd up" under these circumstances? News of the incredible happenings at Union Village had spread, and the meeting was attended by a "great croud of young men." The spiritual instruments from the West Brick Family—McBrien, Cochran, and Ross—immediately went into vision. These young women, McBrien aged twenty, Cochran sixteen, and Ross (age unknown) unleashed power that would make "even devils believe and tremble." During the meeting, McBrien left her place in the dance, looking "bloodless pale, her eyes closed, at three times turning around she fell in the aisle." The dancing ceased, and McBrien "laid as one dead." Margaret then received "a heap of swords from Mother" and urged every Believer to arm themselves before the enemy could take the weapons. Thus, girded for battle, "terrible conflict ensued." In his journal, Wells wrote, "The thrusting, yelling, & barking, I will not attempt to discribe, but it seems it was sufficient to satisfy Mother, for that time. For she sent word a while before the meeting closed that there had been unbelief energy drove out to sink a nation. Soon after this, she sent her thanks to the Brethren & Sisters for using their swords so well." As had happened the week before, McBrien, Cochran, and Ross were loaded into a wagon and driven back to the West Brick Family. McBrien remained in a visionary state until three o'clock that afternoon, while the other two didn't regain their senses until that evening.[10]

Throughout February, the spirit of Mother Ann Lee—through Margaret McBrien—consolidated her hold on the community. Community scribe Andrew C. Houston described McBrien as "the most advanced visionist among us." In his journal, Daniel Miller noted, "Visions are now becoming an every day occurrence or nearly so."[11] Freegift Wells betrayed no doubt about the legitimacy of McBrien's gifts in his journal. In fact, the ministry and McBrien's West Brick Family elders asked "Margaret to go to Mother with 3 different errands which we felt anxious to know Mother's mind in relation too." Margaret disappeared after dinner, returning after an hour with answers to all three questions. An astonished Wells recorded, "Mother told her what she had come for, & answered each question without Margaret's asking a word about the matter!" McBrien also conducted parties of spiritual visitors through the West Brick Family. Their mission "was to point out the dirty, & confused state of their habitations, shops, out buildings, door yards." The spirit of John Dunlavy was among the company.[12]

Individual Shakers were now being held to account by the spirits. At the meeting on Monday, February 18, Andrew C. Houston read a "solemn and weighty" message from Mother Ann. Wells wrote that it caused "deep tribulation in many." Joshua Worley (son of Malcham), recently removed from the ministry, was invited to acknowledge "his failing" and ask "forgiveness of the Ministry for the troubles he had made them."[13] McBrien continued to assure everyone of Mother Ann's presence and poured forth new songs.[14] Wells admonished his flock "to attend to the still small voice and to let our words be few and seasoned with grace."[15] Energy in the meetings was directed against the spirit of unbelief. A message given through McBrien's elder Charles Hampton delivered on Sunday, February 24, admonished all that "unbelief [was] our greatest obstacle confess it & put it away & be subject in little things."[16] At the same meeting, Wells warned Believers against standing with their hands behind them "in meeting or else where. To beware sitting on the judgment seat."[17] Shakers typically worshipped with their hands before them in various gestures of supplication or gathering in / distributing love and blessings. To stand with hands behind one's back would have been a tacit gesture of nonparticipation. Indeed, the judgment seat loomed for those whose spirit of unbelief stood in the way of accepting and submitting to the marvelous gift of Mother Ann Lee, through her instrument Margaret McBrien.

Reception of these gifts was not forthcoming by long-term members such as Richard McNemar, Malcham Worley, and others of their founding generation. Very little evidence of their opinions from those tumultuous few months survives in writing. They may have been reluctant to note it down, or it may have subsequently been destroyed. McNemar wrote that he "was publicly pointedly interrogated on the subject of his faith and confidence." In response, he asserted that he had "honestly confessed all his sins & taken up his cross against all sin in his knowledge, & had kept his justification in the line of obedience to his teaching on to the present date." He stated that he had "never gratified his carnal nature once, in any shape or form" since taking up his cross in 1805. For this, he was called "self-righteous" by the visionists, a charge that laid the groundwork for his undoing.[18] Mother Ann Lee—through McBrien—warned the church (that is, the senior order of Shakers at Union Village) on Friday, March 1, that "she would not have much more business for the Visionists in the young Order, till the Church got started." Mother felt that the work had gone as far as was "profitable" in the young orders and that "when the Church is started, it will go on with rapidity." The next evening, Mother sent a message requesting that gathering orders attend a public meeting with the church the next morning.[19]

Freegift Wells described the Sabbath meeting of March 3 as "the most extraordinary meeting that I have hitherto witnessed." Twenty Shakers went into vision. Some brought messages for individual members from the spirit world. These messages expressed love and confidence and were accompanied by "many different motions, all of which displayed much simplicity, & thankfulness for Mothers notice." To complete the spectacle of the public meeting, many of the instruments remained entranced on the meetinghouse floor and were then carried home in wagons. The positive effects of these gifts in shoring up the faith of the young must have convinced Wells of their authenticity, despite the older members' reservations. If McNemar and Worley were seen as impediments to a process that could heal the broken Union Village community and were standing in opposition to their visible lead (Wells) and the spirits, then they were indeed on dangerous ground.[20]

Spiritual gifts soon took a novel turn. During the March 7 evening meeting, McBrien and Sarah Cochran received many messages for the membership. The next day, Mother instructed them to inform the ministry that these messages must be shared in a special meeting. That evening, McBrien, Cochran, their eldress Ann Parkinson, and Elder Charles Hampton manifested previously unseen spirits of various ethnicities and historical import. They opened with a song accompanied by shaking and bowing, then proceeded to deliver their messages, sent by "companies of French, Scotch, & Indians, & from a company of about 100 children from 2 to 5 years old" and Blacks, each party manifesting themselves with motions appropriate to their culture. The children sent their love by picking at the floor and eating what they found there, "then jumping up & clapping hands, & saying I tank pretty Muzza for her pretty love." Mother (McBrien) then called forth George Washington, the Marquis de Lafayette, Christopher Columbus, and Anthony Wayne. The assembled spirits sent their love through motions of "the flourish of the sword over the head & the cross made by the hands" and then knelt to pat the floor with their hands. Mother observed pointedly that this "was an example for great men to follow." McNemar and Worley would surely have gotten the intended message. The spirits of deceased Shakers John Dunlavy, John Houston, and William Morrison also gave sentiments of love. Mother ended with messages "to stimulate us to war, & fight unbelief, & every opposing spirit." Several bundles of swords were distributed at the meeting, and parties of brethren and sisters charged each other in battle.[21]

At this same meeting, Mother Ann requested that ministry eldress Betsy Hastings specifically "name those she wants to go into vision." A number were named, and they "soon fell & went into visionary struggle." Brother Andrew C. Houston described this scene as "a proof of faith" in a letter to a Shaker correspondent. The point was to demonstrate how Mother worked through her "visible order"; that is, the ministry. It remains a mystery whether such scenes were contrived spontaneously by the spirits or planned in collusion with the ministry, or whether they truly were miracles of God. Nevertheless, Houston noted, "These things are no doubt intended, (as they really do) to strengthen & encourage the faith & zeal of those here."[22] Sadly, this happy logic was not universally applicable.

The next Sunday, March 10, Richard McNemar received his first personal message from the spirits through instrument Oliver Hampton, an event noted by Freegift Wells in his journal. The contents of this or any other inspired messages received by Union Village visionists before 1840 have not survived. It is likely that they were deliberately destroyed; the reasons for this will emerge later in the narrative. McNemar himself, however, recorded the prevailing sentiment directed at him by Mother Ann Lee through Margaret McBrien: "the reputed crime of self-righteousness, repeatedly expressed by the visionists." Mother apparently said that McNemar was "covered over with such a thick coat of self-righteousness that there is no doing any thing with him." Ever the intellectual, McNemar parsed the phrase and examined its etymology in the safety of his journal. He noted that self-righteousness was not referred to in the Bible, which therefore removed it from the realm of sin. Further, in a theological turn, he compared the charge of self—or personal—righteousness with that of imputed righteousness, finding them to be opposite doctrines. McNemar declared, "A self-righteous person then is one who has no dependence on the good works of another for his justification." Doubling down on his resistance to Freegift Wells, he likened being called self-righteous to "reviving the old charge of Heresy so largely treated 37 years ago." At the end of his long Shaker career, McNemar, the Arminian epicenter of the Kentucky Revival, once again found himself deemed an outcast and a rebel.[23]

The same day, fifty-eight-year-old James Hodge also received two messages through Oliver Hampton. Hodge had joined the community in 1808 and had been McNemar's companion in early missionary work at North Union. The content of these messages is not known, but tellingly, by the following Friday, Hodge was "earnestly engaged in settling up matters," presumably having been warned out of the community (though he would return).[24] Aggressive gifts continued through the week. On the evening of the fourteenth, there was a gift to "mortify our pride and shame the devil, by hissing & barking separately." The brethren and sisters formed two rows, and one by one, each Shaker was required to walk the length of the aisle while hissing and barking. Two or three members did not unite with the gift. Although they are not named in the journals, McNemar was probably among them. Following the exercise, the remaining Believers were encircled by a spiritual golden chain given by Mother with a basket full of love for the ministry tied to its end. That evening, the love was shared out among the brethren and sisters, who ate it and were satisfied in their union with such "simple gifts."[25] After this pleasant interlude, a new "mortifying" gift was introduced on the next Sabbath, March 17, which was to be received, as Daniel Miller wrote, "by hammering ourselves."[26]

Astounding and disruptive spiritual gifts now occurred continuously. A village journal noted, "Extraordinary work has become so all pervading that

Figure 25.1. The meeting room of the meetinghouse at Union Village, Ohio, was the setting for spiritual tumult and tragedy in 1839. This photo was made immediately after the Shakers sold the building, circa 1913. Communal Societies Collection, Hamilton College.

it is exhibited almost at any time or place—even at the table, as was evinced this Evening." At the March 24 Sabbath meeting, six sisters, including McBrien, demanded that a general confession of sins be speedily made and warned that those who failed to do so before the next Sabbath would "be exposed, & sent right off to the world." The goal was "a separation between the faithful & unfaithful"; Mother demanded that all yield to the gospel requirements and that "each promised to be Mothers itty child." Joshua Worley could not yield and would make no such promise. Instead, he left the community that very day. In the privacy of his journal, Daniel Miller wrote, "Deep tribulation & sorrow abounds."[27] One day, Joshua Worley would return, seeking vengeance for his family.

On Tuesday, March 26, Elder Amos Parkhurst of the West Brick Family brought the ministry a message from Mother given through Margaret McBrien. On reading the message, Freegift Wells called a meeting of the church. When the group was assembled, the message was read. Effective immediately, Richard McNemar was stripped of his Shaker pseudonym Eleazar Wright, a name and accompanying persona that he had borne proudly for nearly twenty years. The annihilation of the name, with all its affirmative connections to Mother Lucy

Wright and its biblical allusion to the role of a loyal high priest, was a crushing blow for McNemar. It was surely designed to drive a stake into the heart of his pride, ego, and stubborn resistance to the new leadership at Union Village and the spiritual gifts abounding under their ministration. Daniel Miller called it "strong meat for the weak."[28]

The ministry was so completely under the spell of the visionists that when Mother—McBrien—summoned Freegift Wells to the West Brick to "attend to her call there for a season," he immediately complied. McBrien and Cochran went into vision and delivered messages to visionist Oliver Hampton, who was sick and lay before them. The sisters gave Wells a separate message that impressed him deeply. In his journal, he wrote that they "seemed to have a deep sense of the state of the church." There is no written evidence suggesting that Wells ever considered that this was because they were effectively in control of the community. The visionists warred throughout the next week against lust and the flesh. At the March 28 meeting, all the young people came forth to "shake, one at a time, as an Evidence of their hatred of the flesh." Daniel Miller was pleased, writing, "The Devil carried away much lust & never to return I pray."[29] This was but a prelude to the climactic weekend ahead.

On the morning of March 29, Elder Amos Parkhurst once again informed the ministry that Mother—through McBrien—had requested that visionists from the West Brick Family meet with the church that evening. One journal described the ensuing worship as "one of the greatest Church meetings ever known." Seventeen visionists lying on the floor delivered messages from Mother—"very pointed ones too against lust & every vice"—for nearly five hours to every individual present. Individual sins were named, and the guilty party was told to confess them the next morning "or put streight off from this ground." The aim of the messages was "the purging out of Evil." One anonymous Shaker regarded their "wonderful efficacy" as evidence of their divine origins.[30]

The purging of evil was focused directly on Richard McNemar on the morning of Saturday, March 30. Margaret McBrien went into vision and received a message from Mother Ann to have McNemar "confess his sins to-day, or put right off of the ground." Freegift Wells wrote in his journal that McNemar "resented it highly, & said he had no sins to confess." Mother then sent McNemar a final message of severance, "stating that he would administer poison, & unbelief to every one he conversed with, & that the brethren & sisters must have no union, or freedom with him at all, & that he should go, & should not stay on believers ground at all."[31]

There is no record of McNemar's immediate reaction. The ministry, elders, and visionists, however, proceeded to the meetinghouse, where each received instructions from Mother regarding their duties. Following this, the ministry and elders dispersed throughout the village to hear the confessions of the members. The rest of the day at Union Village was pure pandemonium. Freegift Wells called it a "work of unraveling." It commenced first among the sisters in the church, the most senior female members, and "was accompanied with loud screams." Wells rejoiced, "Surely Mother & the Angels of Heaven are at work for us." The chaos continued into the evening. Wells noted in his journal, "While I am now writing past 5 Oclock the screams of the sisters in the Kitchen rend the air." Supper was accompanied by "one continual roar of warring & screaming, & they marched back to the house with uplifted hands." Wells believed that Mother and her heavenly helpers were finally "extricating poor Union Village, or rather its inhabitants, from the doleful pit in which they have long been wallowing." The warring against lust, pride, and flesh continued until nearly ten o'clock. Toward the end of the meeting, the brethren and sisters were given the shocking news that Richard McNemar "had forfeited his union among Believers." In the privacy of his journal, Daniel Miller described the day as "mournful."[32]

The Sabbath meeting held in the wake of McNemar's expulsion was the most extravagant yet. Freegift Wells described it as "remarkable for the great freedom manifested in exposing flesh bands and in tormenting the beast, & the whore." The morning's public meeting featured the full array of spiritual manifestations, causing some spectators to behave "so unbecoming they were dismissed." A crush of visitors blocked the doors and prevented the easy removal of the disruptive guests. It was a while before order was restored and worship could resume. In his journal, Wells enthusiastically recounted the Shakers' private worship in the afternoon.

> Heavy warring began before all got into the M. House, and we had nothing to do but take off our coats & join the combat; the visionists were soon down on the floor. Blankets and pillows being prepared, were placed, or spread on the floor, & the visionists laid on them in two rows, nine Brethren in one row, & 9 or 10 Sisters in the other row. The two rows were placed with their heads towards each other, & about 6 feet apart. Soon after the visionists fell, & before all were down Mother began to send on Messages to individuals; this was continued together with some general messages, & many presents of Love, Swords, White Birds, Rasins, Sugar sticks, Candy, green Peas, Diamonds of Gold, Boxes of Flowers, & Gold boxes of Love and probably several other articles not now recollected. These, & such like gifts continued on without any intermission of consequence for the space of about 4 hours.

In this time there were a number who had their sins exposed, & promised that they would confess them.[33]

After the chaos of the morning's public meeting, the Shakers decided to close meetings to the public for a time. Notice of this closure was advertised in Lebanon, Ohio's *Western Star* newspaper. Trustee David Parkhurst and brother Philip F. Antes expressed their regret that the "well-bred genteel part of the community" would be unable to attend worship due to the "barbarian riotous spirit of a *certain class*," which had become intolerable. The Shakers' riotous spirit seems to have attracted its worldly counterpart in this case.[34]

In the aftermath of his expulsion, Richard McNemar confided his feelings in an April 1 journal entry, annotating a section written in October 1837, when his troubles were just beginning. At that time, he recognized that the ministry wished him to "submit to their counsel & commands in all things spiritual & temporal to be as a little child passive & obedient without will or choice of my own in any thing whatever." Eighteen months later, he had been unable to do this. Over the course of those months, he felt that the Union Village leadership had "gradually declind any attention to me whatever." The culmination of this was the "public sentence of excommunication." McNemar complained that this had been made "without naming the thing wherein I have refused subjection to the order nor has any cause of disunion been ever hinted to my knowledge—except that I continue as I was unprepared to enter into the aforesaid obligations."[35]

The ministry likely felt that McNemar had been asked enough times to sign the covenant, secure the deeds to his property to the church, and once again confess his sins, thereby submitting to his new lead, Freegift Wells. The fact that this last requirement was now being demanded of him by the spirit of Mother Ann Lee through McBrien seems to have hardened McNemar's resistance.[36] As McNemar was writing these words, McBrien was still at work among his former brethren and sisters, commanding a "gift for all to confess their sins publicly." A brother named Randolph West left the village that same day.[37] He would also meet a tragic end brought about by the chaos and spiritual despotism then prevalent at Union Village.

Richard McNemar's expulsion from the church added misery on top of misery. His health continued to decline. He copied treatments for pleurisy, diabetes, and inflammation of the kidneys into his journal on March 20, 1839. Unbeknownst to all but a few of his fellow Shakers, McNemar had been managing another crisis stemming from his nuclear family. Garner McNemar's effective exile from Union Village in early 1838 had not ended his grandson

Milton McNemar's attempt to extort money from the Shakers that he believed was owed him from his aunt Nancy McNemar's consecration to the church (Nancy died in 1815). After his initial aggressive letter of September 22, 1837, Milton apparently sent another—this time threatening to burn Union Village. Levi McNemar (Garner's son and Milton's uncle) was forced to reply on February 9, 1839, informing Milton that to burn the Shakers' property was to "burn my property and your grandfather's property also." Levi informed Milton that unless Garner's scurrilous anti-Shaker narrative was returned, there would be no end to his grandfather's "exilement until death puts an end to his sorrow."[38]

Milton A. McNemar was also corresponding with Richard McNemar Jr., who had apostatized from Union Village in 1828. Richard Jr. was an established lawyer and Swedenborgian living in Urbana, Ohio, about seventy miles north of Union Village. Milton wrote to Richard Jr. on February 19, after receiving the letter from Levi. The letter recounts Garner's expulsion, current living situation, and poor health with "dead palsey" (an archaic term for lockjaw). Milton sought Richard Jr.'s advice on suing the Shakers and his opinion on the chances of getting any money out of them. Milton planned to come north in April, promising to bring Garner's anti-Shaker manuscript with him and, if money could be obtained, to move Garner to live with relatives in Tennessee. He closed his barely literate letter, "I remain you affectionat friend until death."[39]

This intractable situation once again intruded on Richard McNemar Sr.'s life via a letter from Richard Jr. dated March 2, 1839—their first contact in six years. Richard Jr. informed his father of three letters he had received from Milton and asked if there was any validity to his claims for money from the community. Jr. was disinclined to favor Milton's side but said the golden rule must take precedence and justice be done. Jr. was also horrified to learn that his uncle Garner had been cast out of the village "in a feeble, sickly, and palsied state" by the influence of James Smith—son and namesake of McNemar's ancient nemesis James Smith Sr.[40]

Richard Jr. begged his father, for the honor of their shared blood and the name of the Shakers, to inform him if Garner "has not been thrown out upon this cold world to linger out the remainder of his days in pain, anguish, & sorrow, bereft of his earthly pittance and abandoned by those in whom he reposed confidence and who were the objects of his bounty." Jr.'s letter closes confidently, with news that his health was good and his law practice worth $800, "with a fair prospect of an increase in future." He acknowledged a deficiency in public speaking, acknowledging that he wished he "had the powers of eloquence & command of language which Father has." Addressing his estranged father as "My friend," he assured him that his friendship was faithful and wished him "the best of all that is allotted to man on earth; and of those treasures laid up for the righteous in heaven." Jr. expressed a desire to see his father and mother once again, "were it not that your strange unnatural forms and feelings forbid it." In closing, he declared lovingly, yet defiantly, "The affections of my heart I have not yet crucified."[41]

Richard McNemar Sr. received his son's letter the same day but handed it to village scribe Andrew C. Houston for a response, citing the "low ribaldry heretofore exhibited in the said Milton's letters to persons here, as well as the threats thrown out in them of private injury." Houston informed Richard McNemar Jr. that the Shakers considered Milton's claims invalid and that he was a "cheat or swindler." Further, Milton's father, John McNemar (possibly Garner's son), had received a share of Garner's consecration years before. Houston also assured Richard Jr. that Garner was very well cared for and now resided at the deconsecrated East House—Richard McNemar's former homestead—in a "good warm room in the Brick building." For this, the Shakers paid a caregiver eighty dollars annually strictly out of Christian forbearance, since Garner had "quarreled with every lead of the family where he lived, and in this James S[mith] has fared as others, only harder." Houston considered Smith the most patient man he had ever known, a man whose character was unquestioned other than in Garner's libelous manuscript. Pointedly, Houston hoped that Jr. would not give credence to malicious slanders leveled at his "former friends even tho' the un'crucified affections of your heart might prompt you to interference."[42]

Malevolent spiritual upheaval continued unabated at Union Village in early April under the direction of the visionists. By now, there were thirty visionists in the society: four brethren, eight boys, and the remainder sisters and girls. Small boys were made to confess their sins repeatedly by the zealously patient James Smith, who awakened them at three in the morning for a third round after Mother (McBrien) claimed their earlier confessions were incomplete. Mother and the spirit of Issachar Bates distributed spiritual guns and ammunition to the brethren and sisters and "set them to shooting, & counselled them to continue on, not only in meeting, but at the table, & about their work." Another village journal describes the commencement of "warring," effected by "the similitude of shooting,—or motions & noises representing shooting,—and much noise & shouting." Malcham Worley received a particularly disturbing message from the visionists at North Union, the contents of which are lost. Daniel Miller described the meetings of April 2 with one word: "severity."[43]

The next morning, Worley found himself under attack from his fellow Believers. The ringing of the morning bell served as a signal for shooting to commence. Worley was walking to the stairs of the Centre House when "a number of Sisters whose guns were well charged, soon collected & gave him several volleys which seemed to take effect, & he soon put back towards his hiding place." Along the path of his retreat through the garden, "James Hodge (his old, or former friend) gave him several running shot which caused him to wheel & emit portions of venom." That same day, sixty-eight-year-old Richard McNemar, recently recovered from five weeks of illness on top of the spiritual duress he had endured leading to his expulsion, "carried several loads of property, (such as he could carry himself) to the east house." Freegift Wells, who unsympathetically recorded the above details in his journal, speculated that McNemar was either placing the property under Garner's protection or he planned to move to the East House himself. The evening of April 3 saw more "powerful meetings ... with heavy shooting."[44]

Chaos and violence continued on April 4 as the "gifts of noise & war" continued, and "fire bangs are poured in from all quarters." An inspired message assured the community that the gifts were achieving their intended end: "to separate the Evil from the good." Worley raged at his fellow Shakers in the morning, crying "murder, murder," while McNemar continued "wheeling off plunder to the east house" (as Wells cruelly described). The ministry asked visionist Oliver Hampton for Mother's counsel. Regarding McNemar, Mother (McBrien) foresaw that he would leave the community the next Tuesday, April 9, if "he was not forced to go before that time." The verdict for Worley was more terrible. Mother said:

> E. Freegift must go to him & tell him he must put right of the ground, that he must be gone within 2 1/2 hours. And if E. Freegift cannot venture this on his own hook, he may say Mother says so. But E. Freegift must use his authority & he must be couragious, & prompt. Mother says the shooting among the Brethren & Sisters this morning is helping the matter on. Mother says Malcom is an old beast, yea a hound of hell. He is above me, & I can do nothing for him; he is entirely influenced by the old scarlet colored beast, & the Brethren & Sisters must take care, or they will get a tinge of the same.

Mother reassured the ministry, telling them they must feel "comfortable and be assured that her work would effect what it was intended to effect." She sent her love to Wells as encouragement.[45]

Girded by Mother's love, Wells delivered her message to Worley at ten o'clock in the morning "in a loud & strong voice," while Worley tried to drown it out by loud and continuous vociferations, but "hear it he must, & hear it he did." Worley refused to go and told Wells that Mother, not he, was "the old scarlet colored whore." While this ugly scene unfolded, McNemar continued moving personal possessions such as "baskets of papers, chairs & such like things to the east house by hand, or in his arms, [and] has now commenced moving heavier articles on a wheel barrow." He had moved three loads in this way. At five o'clock that evening, Trustee Daniel Boyd and Ithamar Johnson went to the East House and coldly gathered everything McNemar had brought there, returning it to the trustees' office in a horse cart. Wells closed his journal entry describing these events prosaically, writing "very fine weather, warm & smoky."[46]

Union Village was now more isolated than ever before. Public meetings were ended, and spiritual shooting continued day after day. Mother advised the community, "Keep up the noise." McNemar had completed his withdrawal to the East House by April 6. After administering gifts of humility and repentance through her visionists, Mother told the remaining body of Believers to receive these gifts through the visible order (i.e., the ministry). She warned that "no soul should Ever get around that order . . . tho' they should climb to the stars, yet she would place her order above them." In his private journal entry for April 11, Daniel Miller captured the madness of the times: "No sober days now half drunk and would go to god the other half was also drunk."[47]

From his quarters at the East House, Richard McNemar wrote to his son and namesake, safely removed from the chaos at Union Village and no longer a member of the Shakers. The date was April 12, Jr.'s thirty-fourth birthday. McNemar addressed his son as "my professed friend" and began, "This day it is 34 years since I first saw you—Doubtless you have many matters of reflection on your mind since that period—so have I." Chief among these was to know if Sr. had fulfilled every legal duty and obligation to his son with regard to his estate. "I am an aged man you are in your prime—A mortal disease of late brought me within a breath or two of eternity—The trembling spark rekindled and after five weeks close confinement I am again on the stage of action, but my once hardy constitution fast sinking under the dregs of disease and the infirmities of age. The presumption is that you will outlive me, of course our relation will shortly be that of predecessor and successor. You will be heir to my name and my nature, whatever become of my faith and morals."[48]

Sr. informed Jr. that in an effort to shore up the legal framework of the society, longtime members were required to have a signed receipt from non-Shaker heirs confirming that their portion of the member's consecrated assets had been received and that said member was free of further obligation. The complicating factor in McNemar's case was that he had never signed the covenant and had never officially consecrated his possessions in this way—all by the direction and design of the ministry, leaving him a disinterested party qualified to act on the Shakers' behalf at court and legislature. The long-term consequences of this decision were now immense, as McNemar was left homeless and without possessions, having been cast out of the society—a fact he withheld from his son.

McNemar stated that although he had kept his "faith unmarred & borne my cross against all sin in my knowledge since the day that I heard the testimony of Christs second appearing I am nevertheless an unprofitable servant, I have done that which was my duty to do and no more." He had no firm information regarding the legal status of his original farmstead, the East House property, even though he had sold it to Shaker trustees in August 1805. Despite his current circumstances, he was still resolved "that the property be secured to the uses and purposes originally intended." McNemar claimed he was content to sing with John Wesley: "Nothing on earth I call my own." His greatest wish was to be allowed to live out his days at New Lebanon under the protection of the "lovely old Believers." Regarding the controversy surrounding Milton and Garner McNemar, Richard advised his son not to hazard his reputation by becoming involved, although he left him free to do as he wished. Sr. considered Garner a "good firm Believer" despite everything and let Jr. know that he had done his best to mediate the crisis. Following Garner's excommunication, however, he had withdrawn, finding he was "in danger of getting myself into the same predicament"—the closest he came to divulging his current reality. McNemar closed his letter with a reminder that he needed his son's receipt "before I can be admitted into the innermost of the temple or gain the degree of saintship." Father offered son his "pretty respectable library of Latin Greek, Heb,. & English, some law, some gospel, Arts sciences," and he closed simply with "Farewell."[49]

On Sunday, April 14, Daniel Miller succinctly described Union Village as "Drunk."[50] The following Wednesday, a new male visionist, forty-year-old Philip F. Antes (who cosigned the newspaper proclamation that closed public meetings), delivered a message directly to Malcham Worley. In his journal, Freegift Wells described it as "the most powerful of any message that I ever heard delivered by a mortal being." Worley was given one last chance to humble himself and confess his sins. Worley remained silent in the face of these demands. Margaret McBrien, present at the scene, immediately went into vision, seeking instruction from Mother Ann. She decided that he "should leave the ground, he should not stay in that house another night, & he was accordingly carried out to the old office." Wells's description of these events belies no trace of complicity on his part. He seems to have had full faith in the visionists and their work of separation and described the evening meeting that day as "heavy." For his part, Daniel Miller described it as "deathly."[51]

Richard McNemar was summoned into the presence of Freegift Wells, Stephen Spinning, Andrew Houston, and Charles Hampton on the morning of Friday, April 19. Visionist Philip Antes had another message from Mother for McNemar. As Wells recorded, "This Message settled the bill with him." McNemar was told that "his time was out here, & he must leave the ground." Houston departed immediately for Urbana, Ohio, to meet with Richard McNemar Jr. to see if Sr. could go there to live at the Shakers' expense.[52]

The next day, Malcham Worley, along with his furniture and clothing, was taken to his new home ten miles from Union Village to board with one Joseph Keenan, also at the Shakers' expense. Worley insisted that he be carried to the carriage by Shaker deacons, and he selected Ithamar Johnson and John Baxter to do it. He was cheerful during the ride and noted how much the countryside had changed since he'd last seen it, having lived as a reclusive hermit at Union Village since Father David's death in 1825. On arriving at Keenan's, he told his host "he felt releas'd, & he believed that Providence had dictated in selecting that place for him &c. He cheerfully walked from the wagon to his room, & seemed well satisfied, & comfortable."[53]

Andrew Houston returned to Union Village on Sunday, August 21, having failed to locate Richard McNemar Jr. At the church meeting that day, described by Daniel Miller as a "real schorcher," Freegift Wells reinforced the rule that the community was "bound to support the visionists and they [the visionists] to be subject to a visible lead." In his journal, he wrote that "Mothers work was carried on with a strong arm." On Tuesday morning, Wells, the ministry, and visionists Charles Hampton and Philip Antes departed for North Union. The same day, John S. Houston, an old friend of the McNemar family, dispatched a hurried letter to Richard McNemar Jr. from a canal boat. He had just left Union Village and warned Jr. "that the Young order have gone crazy, visions, wild, hollowing, prevail in their meetings; they pretend to see Washington Columbus [and] Malcham & Eleazar denounce this as wild and foolish." Learning of Worley's expulsion, Houston inquired with Shaker George Legier about McNemar's fate. The seventy-eight-year-old Legier, who converted in 1805, replied callously, "If Eleazar don't repent he will have to go this is the last work of God." Houston advised Jr., "You may judge as you please, I just write to warn you of it." Houston suspected that apostate trustee John Wallace had hatched the whole thing as a plot to take control of Union Village lands. In closing, he declared, "If I was a son of Worley, or Eleazar I would waid through Hell to Expell him from there and all that damned clan of Young Shakers."[54]

On the next day, Wednesday, April 24, Richard McNemar was unceremoniously driven to Judge Francis Dunlavy's house in Lebanon, Ohio. Dunlavy was the brother of McNemar's longtime compatriot and brother-in-law John Dunlavy and a defender of the Shakers; he had known McNemar for nearly fifty years. What, if any, provision was made for McNemar's upkeep is unknown. Freegift Wells, absent at the time, made no mention of McNemar's fate in his journal. At Union Village that evening, the meeting was one of "unusual comfort & consolation." Mother gave messages of a "comforting & Encouraging character. Many little simple gifts were given, all tending to bring down a high sense." With the expulsion of Richard McNemar, the "highest sense" was indeed brought down. Following his departure, rumors circulated at Union Village that he had gone to his son Richard Jr. at Urbana and that they were preparing a legal battle to reclaim McNemar's original East House property. These rumors may have seemed plausible, as the Shakers had deconsecrated the land and buildings and leased them to tenants. The troublesome Garner McNemar was boarded there, having lost his union. There is no evidence to support these rumors, but they added to the growing cloud McNemar left in his wake.[55]

TWENTY-SIX

A WANDERING STAR

THE NEW LEBANON MINISTRY, UNAWARE of the expulsions of Richard McNemar and Malcham Worley, wrote to the Union Village Ministry on April 30, inquiring, "How is it with Richard, has he ever signed the Covenant? has he transferred his right to his real estate? has he given up or surrendered all the Books and papers which he formerly held as Clerk of the Church or Society?— And how is it with Malcom? will not he and his children lay claim to the land on which the church is built?" They hoped that Freegift Wells had managed these matters with wisdom, as the New Lebanon Ministry had serious fears "of what you may have to suffer from the tongues and pens of those two men."[1] Sadly, no personal concern for either man is expressed, a disturbing fact, considering that the letter was probably conceived and written by McNemar's longtime friends Rufus Bishop and Seth Youngs Wells. Unbeknownst to them, McNemar was already en route to New Lebanon, his faith in the leadership there unshaken.

McNemar's unilateral decision to travel to New Lebanon and appeal directly to the ministry was the ultimate act of defiance, evidencing his unyielding commitment to Shakerism, despite his expulsion. The previous year, Benjamin Seth Youngs had written McNemar, "Should circumstances render it necessary for you to make your appearance here, I for one shall not look upon you as a disembodied spirit, nor make any outcry about it! I will be happy to see you here or there, by day or by night."[2] At that time, Youngs yearned to return to the West and work with McNemar on the revision of key Shaker theological writings. Little did Youngs know that McNemar would return to the East under the worst imaginable circumstances. His exact route of travel is unknown, although when he arrived at Watervliet, New York, on May 29, he was accompanied by a man from Zoar, Ohio, which suggests that he took the Ohio and Erie Canal, a route he was very familiar with.

Arriving at Cleveland, he went to North Union, even though the visionists there had shown such hostility to him and Worley. When Freegift Wells was informed of this, he wrote the North Union Ministry that he "hardly believed [McNemar] would stop there. But inasmuch as he did stop, we were pleased that you got along with it as easy as you did." From there, McNemar likely took a Lake Erie steamboat to Buffalo, where he could take an Erie canalboat to complete the journey. Ministry Elder Rufus Bishop was in residence at Watervliet and recorded McNemar's arrival, "Richard does not pretend to have denied the faith, but has lost his union to the visible lead, of course he is like a wandering star." Bishop spent much of the following morning in conversation with "poor Richd. McNemer, who seems to feel much tribulation & seems to weep considerable. He is very feeble & looks almost like a corpse; I should think he was bordering on insanity." McNemar was sane enough, however, to write a letter on June 3 (now unlocated) to his son and namesake, Richard McNemar Jr., informing him of his journey and its purpose.[3]

Bishop's journal evidences no deeper contemplation of the events that led to McNemar's current state. The New Lebanon Ministry had warned the Union Village Ministry that during Mother's Work in the East, visionists had decreed that certain Shakers "must leave the ground immediately." In the East, however, such directives were not aimed at the actual person but at "that wicked spirit which dwelt within them that must be cast out." Additionally, the visionists were required to submit "all their gifts to the wisdom of their Ministry and Elders." Bishop advised Wells he need not think it strange, if "you find some tares and chaff among the wheat; and perhaps as much among the Visionists, in proportion to their number, as elsewhere." Most important, Bishop counseled of the danger visionists could be "if too much notice is taken of them, especially by their Ministry and Elders." With such attention, they were "exposed to get exalted, and to esteem themselves extraordinary vessels and as peculiar favorites of heaven, and of Mother and the good spirits, instead of considering themselves to be mere instruments or tools in the service of Mother and the good spirits."[4] One wonders if Freegift Wells had considered this possibility as he allowed Margaret McBrien and her cohorts to effectively take control of Union Village, usurping himself in the process.

The New Lebanon Ministry plodded home through deep mud on June 4. Richard McNemar traveled with them in a covered wagon. The next day, it rained steadily. As New Lebanon visionist Sister Semantha Fairbanks sat down to smoke her pipe, she found herself prevented by the spirit of Father David Darrow. Darrow announced he had accompanied McNemar from the West and now wished to speak to him through Fairbanks. Ministry elders Ebenezer Bishop and Rufus Bishop went to McNemar's room and informed him, "whereupon he manifested much joy and surprise." Fairbanks was led by the hand into McNemar's presence, her eyes closed, and "every gesture plainly indicated that she was inspired." One wonders if McNemar felt trepidation finding himself once again confronted by an inspired sister. Any angst he may have felt was quickly dispelled as Father David "acknowledged that he was one of the first who received and obeyed the gospel in the western country, and that he was one of its most able defenders." The spirit of Mother Lucy Wright, whose last name was bestowed on McNemar as Eleazar Wright, also manifested itself. Her words confirmed those of Father David and soothed McNemar. In his journal, Rufus Bishop wrote, "Richard seemed to receive the whole with great reverence and thankfulness, and was much affected, even to tears."[5]

Henceforth, McNemar became a focus of spiritual activities at New Lebanon. At the evening meeting on Saturday, June 8, visionist Philemon Stewart and some female instruments conveyed more encouragement to him from Father David and Mother Lucy. Harriet Goodwin, a thirteen-year-old visionist, perceived two tables within the circle of singers, with a large cake and two knives resting on each. The cake was to be cut into square pieces by the elders so all could have a share. Toward the end of the meeting, a visionist told Elder Ebenezer that there was one piece of cake remaining and requested him to place it on McNemar's head. Father David then told him he had come "to this country with him, & would never leave him while he labored to keep his relation to Mother's gospel.[6]

McNemar attended a "very solemn" Sabbath meeting on June 9 during which Philemon Stewart warned the assembled Believers to "put away all sin and uncleanness." Following the meeting, visionist Semantha Fairbanks roamed the hallways of the trustees' office singing a solemn song at Mother Ann's request. The song was directed at the "visitants" from Watervliet, a group likely including McNemar, who probably lodged at the office. Solemn songs were a particular genre of music among the Shakers. They dated to the beginning of the movement in the late eighteenth century and were usually slow, wordless (vocalized on syllables), and in a minor key. McNemar first heard solemn songs from the Shaker missionaries in 1805, but they had gone out of use shortly thereafter. The effect of hearing one of these doleful melodies probably moved him deeply, given his present circumstances. Visionists Stewart, Fairbanks, and Sarah Ann Standish then gave short, inspired messages to the visitants, which

Rufus Bishop thought "made them look & feel very sober," though he feared "the whole was more than they will make a good use of."[7]

McNemar's whereabouts for the next few days are unclear. He was likely among the visitants at New Lebanon's North Family on June 10. This party traveled to the Hancock, Massachusetts, Shaker community on June 12—just four miles east of New Lebanon—and lodged there overnight. By Friday, June 14, Bishop described McNemar as "much distressed with a Colic." McNemar had suffered chronic bowel complaints for many years; these had worsened with age and stress. New Lebanon's talented doctors and nurses administered medicine to McNemar, and he found relief by noon on Saturday. This was fortunate, as he would need all his strength to receive the spirit message awaiting him that evening.[8] The instrument was the venerable elder Calvin Green, whose pregnant mother had joined the Shakers in Mother Ann's day. Green had been cared for by the English Shaker founders as a boy and grew into a powerful public preacher, writer, theologian, missionary, and historian of the movement. Now fifty-nine, he was five feet and ten inches tall with a broad chest and shoulders. Green was heartened by the advent of Mother's Work, which had been foreshown to him. In his autobiography, Green wrote that he "fervently desired to be a full pertaker of elements & powers which might be brot forth by all its operations & Divine Gifts."[9]

On Saturday evening, June 15, Green delivered another communication from the spirit of Father David Darrow to Richard McNemar. The message acknowledged the trials recently endured by McNemar and his brethren and sisters in the West; it criticized, however, the lionlike nature manifested in both McNemar and his fellow Ohio Shakers. Recognizing the important role McNemar had filled for thirty-five years, Darrow stated that he had "moved, in his sphere, with the lion's life." But Darrow's spirit urged humility and submission and quoted Isaiah 11:6, saying that the lion must learn to eat straw like the ox, an ultimately come to a lamblike state.

> The trying scenes that Brother Eleazar has had to pass thro are such as are the necessary consequences of the state of human nature, from which man has to be redeemed, in order to be saved by the gospel. Similar trials always have been, and always will be, in a greater or less degree, wherever there is any body of people redeemed.
>
> 2. Such kind of trials come according to the peculiar state and sense of the people among whom they operate. And these trials must be borne, and therefore will fall on those who have moved in a sphere that renders them the necessary objects, upon whom such trials must fall, in the course of the needful changes of travail and order.

3. But if they endure them manfully and come down into that low and humble state in which they can overcome those trials by the spirit of the Lamb, then these peculiar trials will cease. If they do this, it will be the brightest diamond in their Crowns that they ever gained, or ever can gain, and will so appear in the world to come.

4. But it is the Lamb that overcometh. The Lion must "eat straw like the ox, and a little child shall lead them"; according to ancient prophecy. This work will finally be effected in the humbling operations of this gospel day. The strong and powerful principle in man is the Lion; but it is in its nature only a beast. And tho' it must be permitted to reign for a time among other Lions or powerful beasts; yet it [is] no more than a beast. And before the work of redemption can be affected this lion must be deprived of all means to support itself in its power, and "eat straw like the ox"; that is be merely serviceable, in obedience, as is the ox under the dominion of man. So this lion-like principle must be humbled, like all other principles of nature, that it may be led by the little child, formed in Christ, or it can have no final part in the work of redemption.

The people of Ohio had much of the Lion in their nature. Br. Eleazar has had much of it, and necessarily moved, in his sphere, with the lion's life. Hence the scene of trials he has now to pass thro' was unavoidable; he must pas thro' this scene, either in this world or in the other. And if he patiently passes thro' these trials in this world, until he comes into that lamb-like state, that he can be led by the little child in Christ, according to God's own appointment, it will be much more honorable to him, than if he should not do it untill he shall come into the spiritual world.

So Brother Eleazar be of good courage; stand fast, go thro' manfully, until you overcome by the Spirit of the Lamb, and it will be the brightest diamond in your crown that you have ever gained, or ever could gain in any other way; and in this my spirit shall ever help and bless you.[10]

McNemar embraced the loving advice of his spiritual mentor and steered his mind toward obedience. The next day, he attended the Sunday meeting with the First Order of the Church Family—the highest spiritual order at New Lebanon. Every Shaker received a "spiritual fiddle to serve God with" from the spirit of John Farrington, a convert from Mother Ann's day who had been first elder in the First Order and had died in 1833. McNemar likewise received a spiritual fiddle with a *double* bow from the spirit of another of his deceased mentors: Issachar Bates. Casting aside any reservations about participating in these gifts, McNemar played his fiddle with the rest. Bishop noted with approval, "The assembly looked very active, and simple."[11]

Gifts continued to flow in McNemar's direction. On the afternoon of Monday, June 17, visionary sister Eleanor Potter was picking strawberries when the spirit of Mother Ruth Farrington suddenly visited her. Mother Ruth was Father David's counterpart in the western Shaker communities and had died in 1821. She was the natural sister of John Farrington, whose spirit had gifted the fiddles. Mother Ruth informed Potter that she wished to have an interview with McNemar in the presence of the ministry. After dinner, Elder Rufus Bishop conducted McNemar to the ministry's shop, where Potter, under inspiration, was led into the room by First Order Eldress Betsey Bates (the daughter of Issachar Bates). Potter delivered "a most affecting message in the name of Mother Ruth," which was well received by McNemar. A portion of it survives:

> "Br Eleazar, you need not doubt the truth of this being me, who am now talking to you, tho it is communicated thro' a little child of New Lebanon, who knows nothing of your situation—It is from your kind Mother. If it was really the sincere intention of your heart in coming to this place to gather strength & support for your soul, you will be thankful to receive any thing, let it be ever so plain & crossing"—E[leazar] replied, "If I know my own feelings in sincerity, that was my object in coming." M. Ruth said, "You have come to the fountain head—Here is the door of hope—here is the door of mercy & charity—this is the first Ministry on earth."[12]

Potter declared that the spirits of Elder Peter Pease and Hortency Goodrich were also present. Pease was the first Shaker deacon in Ohio beginning in 1806 and a key associate of McNemar's as the western converts were gathered into order. Goodrich likewise was sent to Ohio in 1809 and was a beloved sister there until she succumbed to disease at forty-two in 1819. McNemar had written her memorial hymn. Spiritual visits from these long-lost friends surely comforted McNemar, mind, body, and soul.[13]

Support for McNemar's physical, mental, and spiritual recovery was steady through the week. Poignantly, Elder Rufus Bishop and other eastern Shakers whom McNemar revered still addressed him by his honorific "Eleazar," a display of respect he was stripped of in the West. Bishop noted in his journal, "These days I spend most of my time in copying Messages for the benefit of Eleazar." On the morning of Friday, June 21, visionist Philemon Stewart delivered another lengthy message to McNemar from Mother Ann Lee through the intercession of Father David Darrow.[14] Mother Ann acknowledged McNemar's peripatetic life spent in the promotion and defense of the gospel and the fact that he was never allowed to settle in one place. Now, however, at his advanced stage in life, he must end his resistance to the change of leadership in the West and assume his proper place under their protection and guidance. Mother Ann as manifested through Stewart was solicitous, kind, and comforting—a stark change from the terrible spirit manifested through Margaret McBrien at Union Village, where Mother Ann encouraged public humiliation and suffering, and distributed spiritual weapons to be used by Believers on each other. Stewart's message changed into a dialog wherein McNemar acknowledged his wrongs and affirmed his willingness to return to the West, submit to his lead, and find peace.

> Brother Eleazer, Mother Ann is here. She says she has come to cause a message to be communicated to you, thro' the cries and intercessions of your beloved Father David.—Father says that from the first of your faith, until his departure from this world, your calling had been to be in various places, Standing in defence of the rights of the people of God; preaching to an unbelieving world, and making labors with young believers; and he supported you in it, believing that your faculties could be best improved in that line. In consequence of this, you were deprived of the privilege of settling down in any particular family or order, for any length of time.
>
> 2. But your zeal and fortitude in doing your duty according to the instruction he gave you, was very great, and bro't you near to his soul: and while he remained in the body he was well satisfied with your labors.
>
> 3. Now Brother Eleazer Mother says she has not come to cast reflections, or bring reproofs upon you: but rather that you may find in her a spirit of loving kindness and Charity, now in your advanced stage of life; and to give you such instruction as will carry you safely thro' if you will strictly follow it.
>
> 4. Mother says, Souls that flourish and grow in the gospel will always fix the foundation of their faith, and place unshaken confidence in that anointing power, which is vested in the Lead that God has placed, and clothed with wisdom, to make all necessary changes, either in Ministry Elders, or Members, as may be found indispensable for the increase of his people.
>
> 5. And this anointing has been bro't forward, says Mother, and placed in such vessels as God himself hath chosen; and will continue so to be, so long as he hath a people on earth. And my children must love and bless, and labor to support this power, in yielding a willing obedience to whatever appointments or changes have heretofore been, or may hereafter be made thro' this anointing.
>
> 6. Whenever there is a change made in the leading influence of any society, the adversary of souls then strives hard to get the advantage and bring in darkness, thro' unreconciliation and a caviling spirit, that says "Justice has not been done:"—that "this has all come in consequence of intriguing members, and the appointments made by some whose judgments and abilities are no better than mine. I do not believe God had any thing to do with it."

7. Are you aware, Brother Eleazer, that this is true: "Yea, Mother I am," (said Eleazer)—Mother says "in this way the Devil seeks to distroy the soul; for no souls can prosper in this gospel, who do not feel their union and relation to that Lead which God has appointed for them."

8. "I have noticed" says Mother, your zeal and anxious labors in supporting the way of God, in times past, and that tender faith which you now have, and have ever maintained, notwithstanding you may have strayed from the true light in some instances. But so long as a soul cries to God for salvation, and desires to get hold of repentance and a broken heart, I can in no wise cast them off.

9. My spirit is at work to seperate between the good and the evil, and all these precious gifts of God, are given for this purpose. And where there is wisdom to direct these gifts aright, they will never injure the oil nor the wine. And by this shall my true spirit be known says Mother.

10. But when a soul is left unprotected by the wisdom of their Lead, to blend these precious gifts with their own carnal natures, they will do harm, and be liable to bring reproach. Every gift says Mother, must be tried upon the altar of Wisdom. And I cannot own them, that are not tried upon this altar.

11. Now Brother Eleazer can you return back to the west, if that should be the gift for you, and entertain no feelings of hardness against any creature, for what has been in times past, either to you or about you? Can you make such acknowledgments or confessions as will honor God, and the gospel, in healing the wounds that may have been made heretofore? (Yea, said Br. Eleazer, & not only do it willingly, but feel it absolutely necessary, that I may live in peace.)

12. If you will be faithful in this, Mother says you shall find rest and I will bless you. "The time has come now, Mother says for souls to work at home in their own hearts, and purge out all that is evil, by an honest confession. When this is done, and the soul is seeking after repentance, my spirit can find a dwelling place with them."

13. I have not come, says Mother, with vengeance, to crush and destroy; but to purge the soul, that it may bring forth more good fruit. If you will do this, and be faithful to obey your lead, in all things, you shall find a mansion of rest, and be honored when you come into the kingdom of God

14. "All souls are alike precious in my sight, and I can cry to God for any soul that sincerely hungers after good, whose labor is to be pure in body and in spirit; yea, says Mother, I can bless them with my love, and clothe them with my union.

15. "Mother says you may receive her kind love and blessing, together with Father David's: you may receive it with six low bows."[15]

Following this epochal message, McNemar remained at New Lebanon another eleven days. He was visited by Brother Comstock Betts, seventy-seven and living in Hancock. Betts was sent to the West in 1809 and worked closely with McNemar to establish Shaker communities in Ohio and Kentucky. On Tuesday, June 25, visionist Eleanor Potter had another message from Mother Ruth Farrington to McNemar, the contents of which are unknown.[16] All of these efforts served to gird McNemar for his return to Union Village. Elder Rufus Bishop prepared for McNemar's departure by writing a short letter to the Union Village Ministry concerning events at New Lebanon and giving instructions on how McNemar was to be received. Seth Youngs Wells entrusted this letter to McNemar, along with a large packet of other letters and inspired messages for Freegift Wells and company, a gesture demonstrating his faith and trust in his old friend. On Wednesday, July 3—a month after he arrived in the East—McNemar left New Lebanon for the final time. He was accompanied by his old friend Solomon King, whom he had loyally defended through the entirety of King's slow downfall as first elder of Union Village. Brother Luther Copley accompanied them by railroad as far as Philadelphia. King, probably realizing it would be the last time he saw McNemar, went with him a little farther to Harrisburg, where they surely had an emotional parting.[17]

TWENTY-SEVEN

LOOK HOMEWARD, ANGEL

MOTHER'S WORK HAD CONTINUED UNABATED at Union Village, Ohio, since Richard McNemar's expulsion on April 24. A village journal entry for May 2 reads, "The day of wonders & miraculous things, continues to move onward. The intercourse between the spiritual & natural worlds is no longer to be questioned even by skepticks, for it is of daily & hourly occurrence." On May 9, Pocahontas herself appeared at the evening family meeting and touched a sister on the head, who then began speaking in a Native American language. Despite these wonders, records of the meetings and their attendant gifts reveal a steady drumbeat of messages warning Believers to follow their visible lead; that is, their ministry and elders, and not to rely on the visionists for guidance and protection. Freegift Wells was pleased with the progress of the work. He wrote the South Union Ministry on June 1, 1839, that he was not alarmed about those who had been "purged out," even though some of them—this a clear reference to McNemar and Malcham Worley—were "eminent by profession, & so elevated by the voice of fame! Mother knows how to humble the high-minded, & bring into confusion, those who exalt themselves above the work of God, & trample on her orders."[1]

Reflecting on the past few months, Daniel Miller wrote the following in the privacy of his journal on June 2: "We have had a long & tedious storm to wether with much foul weather accompanied with gales of wind Lightning & thunder, a dull prospect by times for deliverance the captain proved good & resolute the crew submissive & the vessel sound, a few cast away & their lives lost, and we are now advancing under clear sky & fine weather, sail good & health in the bargain, hail the prospect."[2]

The storm was not yet over, however. On June 10, the body of Randolph West, who had been expelled by the visionists on April 1, was discovered in the woods near the residence of one Lewis Manning. West, seventy-two, was "found hanging by the neck to a rope which was fastened to a leaning sugar sapling with his feet within fourteen inches of the ground." The *Western Star* newspaper of Lebanon, Ohio, carried the dreadful news. An anonymous "Bystander" reported that West "had resided with the Shakers at Union Village for sixteen or seventeen years, and [he] was amongst those of that society who could not travel with their Brethren in the new light Revelation which they proposed to have received." Since leaving Union Village, West had told many with "tears in his eyes" that he had expected to end his days there. Finding himself homeless without family or friends, he ended his life instead. The news was reprinted throughout the country. At New Lebanon, New York, Benjamin Seth Youngs copied the story, as reprinted in the *New York Journal of Commerce*, onto a sheet among his private papers. The story was printed there the same day McNemar departed for Union Village—July 3. Youngs must have worried for his friend's future. Freegift Wells copied news of the suicide without additional comment in his private journal.[3]

Wells was not entirely unaffected by the tumult he had overseen at Union Village. On Friday, June 14, John Lot Eastwood left the community in a one-horse covered wagon carrying a bed, his clothing, provisions, and $50 in cash. The forty-nine-year-old veteran Shaker had left the community on April 15 under pressure from the visionists. He had made his financial settlement and was going to live with relatives in Indiana. Wells commented caustically that Eastwood "had quite too long a privilege among believers, considering the use he has made of it." As if thinking better of this harsh statement, he added, "It seems like a terrible thing to have to send people of to the world who have professed to be believers more than 30 years, but so it must be with those who have not, & will not bear their cross, for Mother has decreed that such shall not remain on the ground."[4]

The New Lebanon Ministry wrote to Freegift Wells informing him of McNemar's pending arrival. They let Wells know that McNemar carried with him "the most important Messages that have been dealt out to him since that time from the spiritual world." Bishop explained that even though the messages were initially delivered orally, the visionists were able to labor for a gift to write what had been spoken, "and they are again inspired, and will write the Message with an exactness which is truly astonishing." Regarding McNemar, Bishop described him as "feeble" and confided to Wells that he had "been very close mouthed about western matters among the people here, and he has opened but few trials to us." McNemar had, however, received "all the messages that have been to him in a respectful manner, and we hope he will benefit by them and find charity, forgiveness and union."⁵

McNemar's closest confidant among the Shakers (excepting possibly Benjamin Seth Youngs), proved less sympathetic to his old friend. Seth Youngs Wells wrote the North Union Ministry on July 12 regarding McNemar's time at New Lebanon. Wells declared that McNemar had "through lack of wisdom... strayed off the gospel track, and suffered the loss of his union to his established Lead." At New Lebanon, he was "faithfully taught the line of his duty—saw his error, and found that the charity & mercy of his spiritual parents had held him and saved him from greater loss." Describing McNemar's precarious physical state, Wells opined that he "probably will not continue long in this world"; therefore, it was crucial that McNemar regain his union. This was achieved through "a number of weighty messages from the spiritual world—from Father David, Mother Ruth, Elder Issachar, Mother Lucy, and one from Mother Ann sent to him by Mother Ruth." All these messages taught the same doctrine, submission to one's lead; and they all advised him to return to Union Village and seek reconciliation and peace. Happily, Wells reported that McNemar left New Lebanon "much strengthened in his faith relative to the true order of the gospel, and the importance of keeping in it."⁶

As letters about Richard McNemar's return sped westward, the man himself moved forward, albeit at a slower pace. When McNemar parted ways with Solomon King at Harrisburg, King had urged him to stop somewhere "a day or two & rest & recruit." Finding himself within twelve miles of the Harmonist settlement at Economy, Pennsylvania, McNemar stopped at a place where he "knew I would be kindly rec[eive]d and hospitably treated." McNemar arrived, "much exhausted, but exceeding thankful to get among a cross-bearing people." He asked to see Harmonist leader George Rapp, who had led his followers out of Württemberg to the United States in 1805. It was hay harvesting time, and McNemar was taken to a meadow where he found the eighty-three-year-old Rapp "fat and hearty and as pleasant as a boy." Rapp recognized McNemar from his visit many years before when the Harmonists lived at New Harmony, Indiana. McNemar wrote that Rapp "breathed friendship & confidence [and] inspired the people with good feelings toward the man from Union Village, so that I met with pleasant faces on all sides." McNemar toured the "virtuous & flourishing society," taking in their remarkable silk factory where he saw "various specimens of plain flowered striped & every species imaginable of silks & velvets." He stayed at the Harmonist's tavern, where the innkeeper Shriver told him with "deep sensations" the tragic tale of the recent schism involving the European prophet the Count de Leon, which had rent the Harmony Society. Two hundred Harmonists had left with Leon, taking with them a settlement of $120,000—a staggering sum. Despite this, the society seemed at peace. McNemar may have reflected on the troubles endured by Union Village and himself, which may have seemed light in comparison. McNemar stayed two nights at Economy, and Shriver nursed him, curing his stomach pains temporarily with oil of pennyroyal dropped into a lump of loaf sugar and washed down with brandy. McNemar still suffered from back problems.[7]

Taking his leave of Economy, McNemar traveled down the Ohio River to Pittsburgh. He wrote Bishop, "My entrance into the city the darkness of the place & the people spread a gloom over my feelings not easily described." He stopped at an expensive tavern but thought better of lodging there, realizing that he had already sent $41 on the trip and fearing he would not have enough if his "funeral expenses should have to come out of the remainder." He found cheaper accommodations and "quit the gentleman ranks." McNemar took deck passage from Pittsburgh on the steamer *Rochester*, landing at Cincinnati at 11:00 a.m. on July 15, 1839. He traversed the main street throughout the afternoon, hoping to meet some fellow Believers. By evening, he realized that he would have to take the passenger stagecoach to Union Village the next day. He wrote a final letter to Elder Rufus Bishop describing his journey and offering his thanks. McNemar told Bishop that he would reach the "field of action" the next day and asked of him, "Dear Br. Pray for me that my faith fail not." He signed it "Eleazar."[8]

Richard McNemar arrived at the Union Village trustees' office in the late afternoon on Friday, July 16. He was given lodging, as usual, in the south garret (attic) of the office. Freegift Wells visited him the next day and observed that he looked to be in a "very feeble state indeed, not being able to set up much." McNemar was most distressed, however, by something else. Before reaching Economy, he had entrusted the packet of letters and spiritual messages given to him by Rufus Bishop to an old friend named Guilford, who was going directly to Cincinnati. McNemar asked him to mail it immediately on his arrival so it would reach Freegift Wells without delay, as McNemar was planning to rest at Economy. Unfortunately, Guilford waited several days to mail the packet, and it had not reached Union Village when McNemar arrived. As Wells wrote Bishop, this circumstance "seemed to add considerably to the poor man's tribulation." Despite this, Wells was pleased to report that it was "easy to perceive that his sense was very much changed, & that he had got down where we never saw him before." McNemar told Wells that "he wanted to rectify his wrongs, & obtain forgivness, & that was all he wanted to live for." Wells agreed to let him recover his strength in order to undertake this reparative work. McNemar's condition worsened, however, and he was transferred to the nurse's room.[9]

Visionist Margaret McBrien, the terrible voice of Mother Ann Lee and counsel to the ministry, was "carried off" to Middletown, Ohio, on July 17—the day after McNemar's return—where she remained. The last mention of her in Wells's journal was on May 28. No clues survive as to the reasons for her swift downfall. Her eldress Ann Parkinson had come to the ministry on July 5, telling them "a long story about Margarets experience," but no more information is given. Perhaps the ministry finally saw that her gifts were undermining the constant warnings to cleave to the visible lead rather than to the destructive dictates of the visionists. McBrien's baby boy Emmet remained in the care of Believers. McNemar's reconciliation to his community would come much easier with McBrien's absence.[10]

Freegift Wells was also ailing, his condition no doubt exacerbated by the stress of McNemar's return. He was hobbled by rheumatism and was often confined to his bed in the meetinghouse "in a very helpless suffering condition." His right hand and knee were particularly afflicted, and he could walk only with the aid of crutches. He continued in this way into early August.[11] Andrew C. Houston reported to the New Lebanon Ministry that McNemar continued to be unwell. He suffered from internal hemorrhoids (also called blind piles), a disease that had afflicted him for years. Additionally, he was believed to have kidney problems. Despite these ailments, Houston was optimistic that he would recover. The ministry had interviewed him three times, and he had given "quite satisfactory proofs of his sincerity & repentance, & determination to seek his union on proper terms." As evidence of his sincerity, he had given the ministry "all his papers, messages, [and] journals." Wells's illness had arrested the reconciliation process, and Houston hoped McNemar would live long enough to complete it. Beyond that, Houston opined that McNemar had "enough to do to bear his suffering." Houston informed McNemar that he was writing the New Lebanon Ministry, and though he was too weak to write for himself, he requested Houston to say for him "that he had found matters and things at home much as you had encouraged him to look for,—that he felt satisfied with his reception." Against the backdrop of the suffering of both Wells and McNemar, "Mother's work" continued at Union Village, although, as Houston noted thankfully, "we have now the still small voice chiefly, in lieu of the fire winds & earthquakes.... The voice now proclaims order, obedience, simplicity, humility, & above all repentance."[12]

The breakthrough came on Sunday, August 4. After the Sabbath meeting, Freegift Wells and newly appointed Second Elder John Martin had a long talk with McNemar in which they "received considerable satisfaction." Wells and his ministry companions were due to visit Pleasant Hill, and, although the ministry were satisfied with McNemar's repentance, they wanted community members to "have some expression from him to that effect" so that all "would be able to feel that union & blessing for him." Wells asked McNemar if he was physically able to undertake this, and he said he was, provided Wells helped him and even spoke for him, to which Wells assented. The following Tuesday, August 6, a special evening meeting was convened at the meetinghouse for the purpose. Wells made introductory remarks, and then McNemar was helped forward by one of the brethren. In a feeble voice, he "spoke to the satisfaction of all," and although many could not hear him distinctly, his tone of voice and hand gestures implored "forgiveness, & charity." Wells reported that McNemar "did the work as thoroughly, & satisfactorily as could be expected in his weak state, & found forgiveness." Brother Daniel Miller concurred that McNemar "made fair and candid statements with full acknowledgements." To McNemar's great joy, expressions of forgiveness from the elders, eldresses, brethren, and sisters were unanimous. Wells then declared that there would be union in restoring the name "Eleazar" to Richard McNemar, and he was welcomed back into the Union Village Shaker community.[13]

Due to his increasingly poor health, McNemar was confined to his room for the month of August. The presumed peace he had found through reconciliation with his community may have been further enhanced by a letter from his son and namesake, Richard McNemar Jr., written on August 24, 1839. Jr. had received his father's letter from Watervliet on June 3 at the beginning of his eastern tenure. His response was delayed, as he did not know where his father could be reached. Hearing of his father's return and the dire state of health, Jr. assured him "how solicitous I am for your welfare and pleasant location, considering in what an unsettled state of body and mind I left you in May last." He planned to see him as soon as possible. By happy coincidence, Jr. had run into Joseph Worley, an ex-Shaker son and unnamed nephew of Malcham Worley. Sharing news about Malcham, his nephew said, "That good old man feels quite comfortable. He resigns himself to his lot, and passes his time as happily as circumstances will permit." Joseph reported that his father's health was "better now than it has been for many years past." And, in words that carried immense weight for McNemar, Joseph passed along that Malcham considered Richard to be "his best friend on earth, & he desired much to hear from you." Sadly, this communication never took place.[14]

Unable to write, McNemar asked community scribe Andrew C. Houston to reply to his son. Houston informed Richard McNemar Jr. that the cause of his father's bowel affliction was difficult to diagnose. McNemar believed it to be a form of pleuritic inflammation that had traveled from his thorax into his "lower viscera." The illness was described as "intractable and tedious," but Houston hoped for his recovery. Garner McNemar—still outcast from the community—was similarly afflicted with a bowel complaint. Despite the troubling news about his father's health, Jr. must have been overjoyed by these words: "Your Father authorizes me to say to you, for him,—that all the Embarrassments that he has heretofore labored under, are now removed, and that nothing now remains either moral or Religious literary or pecuniary to prevent the free operation of social union and gospel friendship among all his Br[ethe]n. & S[iste]rs.—Save these bodily infirmities:—and he wishes you not to feel disquieted about the sale of those things,—he feels in no haste about the matter."[15] Although father and son would never again meet, these words would have salved Jr.'s soul. He had never yet crucified his love for his flesh relations, and it appears that his father reached out as tenderly as his faith allowed to quiet the mind of his apostate son.

Richard McNemar died two weeks later on the rainy evening of September 15 at ten minutes past eight o'clock. Fittingly, it was a Sunday. About a week before, the spirit of his old friend Dr. Calvin Morrell had visited him "and showed him what it was to die." Morrell and McNemar had been ritually humiliated as the "doctor and the divine" in 1806, shortly after their conversion to Shakerism. Now Morrell, having died in 1833, came to help ease his friend's transition into the spirit world. Morrell told him he would pass in a week. McNemar took the warning seriously, putting his clothing and personal effects in order. The crisis, however, did not come until a few minutes before his death. He began to turn cold in his extremities. This was accompanied by "spasms of the principle nerves, which did not last but a short time, till he ended his existence." Those in attendance noted, "His mind appeared collected till nearly his last, and he spoke two or three times and asked if nothing could be done? This, however, was out of the question—his disease had extinguished his last spark of vitality, so that he seemed to go quite easy, and struggled but very little."[16] He was sixty-eight.

Early the next morning, twenty-three-year-old visionist Rachel Galloway suddenly found herself in the presence of Richard McNemar's spirit. Exercising his talent for music and verse from beyond the grave, he taught her the words to a new song to be sung at his funeral. The lyrics were quite poignant:

O holy Mother I do now repent
And place my confidence in the gift that's sent
For I know by coming down, I will gain the prize
A happy and contented and purified mind

With these words, McNemar's—Eleazar's—spirit assured those he'd left behind that he was truly at rest.[17]

McNemar's funeral was held at 8:30 on Tuesday morning, September 17. The rain hadn't stopped since Sunday. Union Village visionists had a steady stream of messages from his spirit, at the meeting the evening before the service and during the funeral. The message conveyed by his spirit was one of gratitude to his fellow Believers. The funeral was well attended, and the meetinghouse crowded, despite the rain. As the service progressed, a visionist interrupted, pointing through the window to the spirits Richard McNemar and John Dunlavy, each standing on a gatepost to the graveyard. The visionist also saw a long train of loaded chariots and mourners on foot proceeding to the graveyard—the spirits of Believers past. She tried to count them but gave up when she realized there were more spirits than there were living Believers in the meetinghouse. In his journal, Brother Daniel Miller remarked that there was "a general feeling of good will towards the deceased and double honor justly due." It was, he opined, "one of the best funerals I ever attended."[18]

Freegift Wells and the Union Village Ministry were absent at the time of McNemar's passing. He was, however, on their minds. At South Union, Kentucky, six days before McNemar's death on September 9, a merciful Mother Ann Lee manifested herself through visionist Zarilda Riley. Wells and his companions sought and received answers about how to proceed with McNemar and Malcham Worley. The substance of the conversation was not recorded, but Wells described it as "a truly a solemn scene, & one which had a powerful effect to increase the fear of God."[19]

Nearly a month after McNemar's death, news was still pouring in from visionists who had encountered him. The New Lebanon Ministry informed the Union Village Ministry that on July 23, one of their visionists had traveled spiritually to Union Village to see if McNemar "had returned, and whether he had found union."

> She never saw him in the body, but she told his state as well as you could, tho' his name was not mentioned to her, nor in her hearing. Mother Lucy went with her across Lake Erie, by North Union &c. It was very interesting indeed. She never mentioned his name, but said his hat was marked E.R. described

his person very particularly—did not know him, tried to get Mother to tell his name, but she would not—said there was a good spirit and an evil spirit with him—told what both said to him, which was very interesting, and no doubt true—said that brother would do well enough if the evil spirit could be driven off. When that was effected; she saw father David, Elder Freegift and Elder Issachar; then he gave up his Books, papers, &c.[20]

McNemar's spirit made a final appearance at Watervliet, New York, at the Sabbath meeting on November 3, 1839. Seventeen-year-old visionist Helen Smith received a letter from Mother Lucy Wright written by "Brother Eleazar." She presented the letter to Eleazar's old friend and confidant ministry elder Rufus Bishop. Mother Lucy had given McNemar permission to write and express his gratitude for the New Lebanon Ministry's "kindness in putting him into the right path when he was in danger of being entirely lost." Ever the itinerant, McNemar's spirit had wanted to deliver the message in person, but "Mother thought it was not best, so she gave him liberty to write." Perhaps Mother was right. Since McNemar had finally found a home, it was probably best that he remain safely ensconced with his heavenly parents.[21]

TWENTY-EIGHT

AFTERMATH AND LEGACY

FREEGIFT WELLS NEVER DIRECTLY COMMENTED on the tumultuous events that wracked Union Village during late 1838 and 1839 or on the hasty departure of Margaret McBrien from the community. There is evidence, however, that Wells intentionally obscured the manuscript record of those times after the fact. Texts of spiritual messages received by the visionists at Union Village, although meticulously ordered and extant beginning from December 1839, are conspicuously absent from the manuscript record before that date—and appear to have been purposefully excised from a key manuscript.[1] Additionally, Wells's successor as first elder in the Union Village Ministry explicitly stated that "Elder Freegift over halled Eleazar's papers after his death."[2]

Despite Wells's early cautions to the North Union Ministry regarding the influence of evil spirits and the devil on visionists, he seems not to have taken his own advice until at least 1840. In a March 29, 1841, letter to the New Lebanon Ministry, Wells finally discussed problematic aspects of the New Era. He described a visionist handing him a sheaf of spirit messages containing accusations of wrongdoing addressed to specific individuals in the community. Suitably alarmed, Wells approached one of the accused without divulging the reason and probed them for knowledge or evidence of the transgression. Finding none, Wells concluded that the messages were "dangerous to read" and "committed them to the fire."[3]

Although his faith in the underlying veracity and benefit of the majority of spirit communications never wavered, Wells ultimately decided that not all should be preserved. Candidly, he wrote the New Lebanon Ministry, "It is our judgment that it would be much better for a large portion of the communications which have been received in this country, from some source, or other (&

are still preserved in manuscript) to pass into oblivion than to be handed down to future generations; or even circulated among the present generation. Yet we have many which we esteem as very excellent, & valuable. But even among them, we occasionally find passages that, (according to an adage in this country) seems to taste of the barrel."[4]

In 1850, following his return to Watervliet, New York, Wells wrote an essay for the New Lebanon Ministry titled "A Series of Remarks Showing the Power of the Adversary in Leading Honest Souls Astray Through the Influence of Inspired Messages." Wells was protesting against the disuse of pork among the Shakers by direction of inspired messages. Attempting to undermine the visionists who had delivered the anti-swine messages, Wells addressed his experience in the West, where he had seen "many instances" of "innocently deceived" Believers accepting messages from the Lord that were, in fact, from the "father of Lies, or some wicked and deceiving spirit." Unfortunately, Wells chose to "pass over" any specifics of his western experience in the essay. Although his faith in "Inspiration from Heaven" was alive and well, Wells admitted:

> I once swallowed down without doubting, every thing that came in the shape of a Message from the heavens; & my eagerness for an increase of the same, was incessant. But after a while I got confounded by receiving a Message in the name of Mother Ann, which I knew was a positive lie! From that time I found it necessary to be more closely on my guard.
>
> However, I dare not for a long time doubt the genuineness of a Message, unless there was very positive evidence that it was not correct. But after a while I found that such evidences would occasionally appear in every Society in the West; & I found it necessary to be wide awake, so as to detect if possible, every counterfeit Message, but this could not be done.—For many Messages have been received, which passed well for a season, & sometimes for a lengthy season, but finally by some circumstance they would be proved to be spurious, and I am fully persuaded that one half of the Messages or more—that have been declared by the Instruments to be from our heavenly Parents, or good spirits, have been handed forth in disguise, by spirits of a very different character.[5]

Was Margaret McBrien—voice of Mother Ann—the bearer of the pivotal message that opened Wells's eyes? If so, Wells's awakening came too late, sadly, to save Richard McNemar.

The question remains, did Freegift Wells, confronted with a dysfunctional Shaker community in financial ruin and run largely by elderly personalities that had outgrown their required Shaker humility, engineer the expulsions of Richard McNemar and Malcham Worley in collusion with the visionists? In this author's opinion, he did not. No written evidence has survived that would support this idea, and Wells's own journals and letters confirm the New Lebanon Ministry's assessment of Wells: that he was a simple, honest Believer with full faith in the reality of divine revelation and spiritual guidance and communication. A belief system, it should be noted, that was fully shared by both Richard McNemar and Malcham Worley. McNemar himself wrote, "[I] have experienced many things & have had many precious gifts of God, I have had the gift of tongues & the interpretation of tongues, also the gift of healing the sick and of discerning spirits. I have also had the gift of visions & revelation and prophesying I have conversd in open vision with angels & departed spirits."[6]

Wells, McNemar, and Worley were each prepared by a lifetime's experience to embrace immediate revelations of the spirit. The manifestations of Union Village visionists followed patterns familiar to them. Their ages, McNemar's infirm health, and Worley's chosen status as an outsider since Father David Darrow's death made the two men especially vulnerable to the machinations of any visionist that may have borne them ill will.

Having said that, discerning any malevolent motivation for McBrien's part is challenging, mainly because she left hardly a trace in the manuscript record at Union Village. The strongest evidence that she was later viewed as a nefarious presence is in the fact that other female visionists, such as Mary Ann Jennings, not only remained with the community but were celebrated for their roles and remained active throughout the 1840s. McBrien's pivotal role in contrast was all but wiped from the record.

Sister Susanna Cole Liddell, aged fifteen in 1839, was an eyewitness to these events. Writing around 1903 for historian John Patterson MacLean, she retrospectively blamed Freegift Wells for overreliance on McBrien's gifts to shore up his ministry. Liddell described McBrien as "the greatest medium Union Village ever had in the introduction of Mother Ann Lee to her followers and people at Union Village." Liddell described McBrien stretching forth her hands from the clouds, "pushing aside the long dense curtain holding the view of the natural world from that of the heavenly realms and making a broad roadway in her descent to the earth for the people of earth to behold and their friends to return to come forth."[7] Such spiritual comfort must have been appealing to the many elderly Shakers at Union Village who had seen their community rent asunder by poor leadership and repeated financial scandal since 1825.

Liddell believed that McBrien's visionary mission was fulfilled after she reintroduced Mother Ann Lee to Union Village and "after some months time in this work Margaret's spiritual vision had left her as many could see." Sadly, Liddell felt McBrien was "fairly forced to keep up her spiritual medium ship gift." Liddell believed that if McBrien had been allowed to retire from her visionary role, much "sorrow would have been saved to herself and those to whom she brought messages of grief that were not true under the influence of fraudulent spirits."[8] If Liddell's assertions are true, then some of the blame for McNemar's downfall could rest on Freegift Wells for pushing McBrien into giving spiritual revelations that furthered his agenda. This argument, however, is belied by the frenzied intensity with which McBrien exercised her power over the other visionists and the community at large. With her newfound status, McBrien may have found herself caught in a trap of her own making, but, if so, she chose to fan the flames of persecution. The true circumstances surrounding these events will likely remain a mystery.

As the nineteenth century wore on, the Shakers became more cognizant of their own history. Richard McNemar assumed a place beside Issachar Bates as a colorful folk hero of the movement's western expansion. For late-nineteenth-century Shakers, McNemar and Bates embodied their sect's role in the American frontier, a place that had only recently passed from the national consciousness. McNemar's hymns and poems were regularly reprinted in Shaker publications. *The Kentucky Revival* was also reprinted in serialized form in the Shakers' monthly magazine *The Manifesto*, beginning in January 1891. McNemar's missionary adventures with Bates and others to the Shawnee Indians and across the frozen swamplands of southern Indiana became staples of Shaker folklore.

Richard McNemar's story was brought to the attention of the broader public by historian John Patterson MacLean. Following a series of articles about the Ohio Shaker communities published in *Ohio Archaeological and Historical Publications*, MacLean turned his attention to a book-length biography of the man central to Ohio Shaker history. MacLean had forged a good relationship with key remaining members of the Union Village community, especially Susannah Cole Liddell. Liddell's collected manuscripts, many of them bequeathed to her by Sister Abigail Clark, formed the basis for much of what MacLean wrote. Crucially, MacLean convinced Liddell to add her own reminiscences. In a 1903 letter to Trustee James H. Fennessy, who had joined the community in 1883, MacLean opined, "Sister Susan is the one connecting link between the first Believers and the present at Union Village. She remembers most of the old traditions, stories, etc. She remembers how the early pioneers looked." MacLean encouraged Fennessy to purchase a fountain pen, ink, and blank books for Liddell to write "every thing she knows about Union Village and its early characters.... She might exhaust about Richard McNemar, Bates, Youngs, Darrow, Houston, Spinning, Rollins, Dunlavy, King, Ruth Farrington."[9]

Liddell eagerly entered into this work, only instead of neat blank books, she used—in frugal Shaker fashion—hundreds of scraps of paper and the reverse of surplus advertising broadsides from Union Village medicinal products. Sadly, her writings are a chaotic mess with many iterations of the same stories and often lack any continuity from one sheet to the next (as they appear on microfilm). Nevertheless, her words appear nearly verbatim in MacLean's writings, particularly his biography of McNemar. Liddell had a great reverence for McNemar, viewing him through the prism of her childhood as a loving and wise man who was terribly wronged. In a note to herself dated September 25, 1903, she recorded that while she was copying materials from one of McNemar's scrapbooks, the spirit of her Shaker namesake, "Aunt" Susanna Liddell (died 1864), entered and said to her, "I am sent to say to you what you are doing (meaning my present writing) should be done and don't give back though you may suffer. There are wrongs that should be righted."[10] This spirit of writing wrongs carried through to some degree in Liddell's reverential compilations of information about the McNemar, Worley, and Houston families. Her fair treatment of Margaret McBrien, however, demonstrates that Liddell was reluctant to cast McBrien as the historical villain.

Liddell, however, was not MacLean's only informant at Union Village. A manuscript in MacLean's hand titled "Expulsion of Richard McNemar" is based on the testimony of an anonymous "aged sister" never named by MacLean. The narrative begins with "Freegift Wells was a weak, vain, jealous man" and continues in the same tone, leaving no doubt as to the sympathies of the aged sister.[11] Unfortunately, MacLean used much of this content for the sensationalized denouement of his biography. He described the circumstances under which the information came to him:

> The facts relating to the expulsion of Richard McNemar were not disclosed to me until on February 8, 1904.... On two previous occasions the aged sister commenced the story, but would suddenly stop and leave me. The third time several sisters and two of the brethren were present. I followed her very closely and wherever she would waver I pressed her with question after question until the whole was unravelled. At times her face bore the most fitful expression. Her lips would twist, and every indication appeared as though she would burst into tears. When her story ended I said to her: 'This is all knew new to me.' Looking at me reproachfully she said: 'If I had known that I would not have said a word to you about it,' and then fled to her room.[12]

> Just Published
>
> ## THE LIFE
>
> OF
>
> ## RICHARD McNEMAR
>
> BY J. P. MacLEAN
>
> Paper. 8vo. 65 Pages
>
> Edition Limited to ~~300~~ 250 Copies
>
> 210 Copies Sold Before Publication
>
> Net Price 50 Cents, Postage Prepaid
>
> Born and educated in Pennsylvania.
> Earliest preaching in Ohio and Kentucky.
> Leading spirit of the Great Kentucky Revival, 1799-1805.
> The greatest preacher of the Great Miami Valley, 1801-1805.
> The Leading Spirit in founding the Christian Church (New Light) 1803.
> Greatest of Shakers, 1805-1839.
> The father of Shaker Songs, Shaker Literature and Shaker Journalism.
>
> Address all orders, accompanied by cash to
>
> J. P. MacLEAN,
> Franklin, Ohio.

Figure 28.1. A publication announcement for John Patterson MacLean's *Sketch of the Life and Labors of Richard McNemar*. Communal Societies Collection, Hamilton College.

MacLean informed Trustee James S. Fennessy about this information. Although Fennessy had only lived at Union Village since 1883, he confirmed the sister's story and advised MacLean that "history should be written and not concealed." MacLean acknowledges in his recording of the sister's narrative that he "dressed up the matter with other facts" he had learned.[13] Intriguingly, based on the census of 1900, one of the few living sisters at Union Village who was present during the events of 1838 and 1839 was Margaret McBrien's fellow visionist Sarah E. Cochran, who didn't die until 1908. Nevertheless, it is unlikely that she or anyone else could ever be positively identified as MacLean's informant.

MacLean's *Sketch of the Life and Labors of Richard McNemar* was published in 1905. For the most part, it is a reliable patchwork of facts about McNemar's life gleaned from manuscripts and printed sources. The work takes a strange turn, however, in its discussion of the last years of McNemar's life. Following the lead of his anonymous informant, MacLean depicts Freegift Wells as a vindictive and malicious man bent on humiliating McNemar and Worley. MacLean stops short of accusing Wells of instructing McBrien as to the content of her spirit messages. Rather, he speculates that "Margaret read him closely, and worked upon his vanity." According to MacLean, the messages expelling McNemar and Worley were "sweet smelling balm in the nostrils of Freegift,— it was a potion sweeter than honey to his taste. His hated rivals were now to be disgraced and he should be freed from their presence." The biography ends with melodramatic scenes and quoted dialogue that appear to have been constructed of whole cloth. This senseless ending mars an otherwise decent biography based on sound facts and the extensive manuscript record made accessible to MacLean thanks to Liddell.[14]

MacLean's biography was not well received at Union Village. Brother Moore S. Mason, who was Fennessy's right-hand man and MacLean's regular correspondent, wrote MacLean on July 18, 1905, "Your Richard McNemar has made a terrible row." Brother Andrew Barrett was angered by the book, declaring, "It's not true." Worst of all, Susanna C. Liddell was left in tears, proclaiming, "She never said things about Richard McNemar or Freegift Wells she almost wild."[15] Liddell, despite her strong pro-McNemar bias, must have been crushed that all her carefully curated source material had been superseded by the account of one aged sister. She must have been equally disappointed that MacLean had not inquired with her about the story's veracity.

THE FATES OF MCNEMAR'S FAMILY, FRIENDS, AND ASSOCIATES

Richard McNemar's wife and children continued to live at Union Village following the traumatic events in 1839 that effectively ended his life. McNemar's widow, Jennie Luckey McNemar, died on March 16, 1843, aged seventy-seven. She was living in the First Order at the Center Family, a place worthy of her dedication to the gospel. Information about her life is very scarce. Susannah

C. Liddell recorded that she copied an account of Father David Darrow's death from Jennie McNemar's journal, as well as important letters carrying that news. We have those texts, thanks to Jennie McNemar, Abigail Clark, and Liddell. The whereabouts of Jennie McNemar's writings, other than her 1805 letter to New Lebanon, are unknown.[16]

Nancy McNemar, who had served in the ministry or as an eldress continually since her early adulthood, died on September 11, 1860, aged fifty-nine. In Brother Daniel Miller's opinion, she was "a sister clad with a goodly portion of wisdom, mild and persuading qualities." Her stout brother James McNemar, noted for his agricultural prowess, died on August 16, 1875, aged seventy-nine. Vincy McNemar, in whom many saw the resemblance to her father, was the last of Richard McNemar's children to die in the faith on August 12, 1878, aged eighty. A photograph of her survives and is the only known image of any of the McNemar family. Nancy, James, and Vincy had all lived their lives in the same family as their mother, the First Order of the Center House Family. In the Union Village cemetery, they joined their father; mother; and siblings Betsy (died 1812), Benjamin (died 1818), Elisha (died 1824); as well as Celia, or Seely, Anderson, the family's former slave who lived with them as a Shaker sister until her death in 1817.[17]

Richard McNemar's son and namesake, whose apostasy so shocked him, continued his successful career as a lawyer in Urbana and remained a member of the Swedenborgian Church (still an active congregation as of 2020). He married eighteen-year-old Tabitha Pearson on July 7, 1840. Their union produced at least one child, a son Richard (the third), born in 1843. Richard McNemar Jr. carried forth his father's love of print and polemics, serving as editor of the *Republic* newspaper of Springfield, Ohio. Sadly, he died of dysentery on August 24, 1852, aged forty-eight. His obituary, published in the *Republic*, notes that the legal bar associations of Urbana and Springfield turned out en masse to accompany his body to the cemetery, forming the longest line of carriages ever seen locally. McNemar Jr. had "won the respect of all who knew him" and was a good example of "how men can be religious without gloom, firm without austerity, and kind without weakness."[18] Richard McNemar the third sadly succumbed to tuberculosis and chronic diarrhea contracted while in the Union army. He returned home to die on May 27, 1863, aged twenty. Tabitha Pearson McNemar became the principal of the School for Girls in Urbana. She held this position until 1883 and died in Nashville, Tennessee, on October 28, 1887.

Garner McNemar died on July 5, 1841, aged seventy-five. He was still in the financial care of the Union Village Shakers. Despite his perfidy, he was given a Shaker funeral and was buried in the community's cemetery. His son Levi was described by Liddell as "a farmer, always the tallest man in the Union Village & one of the most useful... a fine man fully devoted, the last of his family." He died on November 11, 1866, aged seventy-three.[19] Following his threatening attempts to blackmail the Shakers, Levi's nephew Milton A. McNemar moved to Bloomington, Indiana, writing Richard McNemar Jr. several more letters of a much less vicious nature. Ultimately, he settled in Mississippi where he ran boardinghouses, including the Franklin House in Grand Gulf and the Magnolia House in Natchez. His uncle Garner's anti-Shaker manuscript has never come to light, and Milton never received a dime from the Shakers.[20] Richard's sister Cassie, who had married John Dunlavy, lived faithfully at Pleasant Hill until her death on May 6, 1856, aged eighty-eight.

Malcham Worley died on August 3, 1844, at the old trustees' office building at Union Village, aged eighty-two. Despite his expulsion, Worley never lamented his fate or seemed anything other than contented with his lot. His children, however, were another story. Joshua Worley, formerly second elder in the Union Village Ministry to Freegift Wells, never forgave his humiliating downfall at the hands of the visionists. Following the death of his father, he joined his apostate siblings Joseph and Rebecca in a lawsuit against the Shakers. Their goal was the one that the Shakers had long feared: the reclamation of the Worley farm, the core lands on which Union Village was founded. The premise of their suit was that their father was insane when he joined the Shakers in 1805 and deeded his land to them. The suit began in 1844 and was finally settled in 1848. The Worleys failed in court, and Union Village remained whole. That lawsuit effectively marked a cultural shift away from the first generation of Shaker life at Union Village.

Freegift Wells was called back to Watervliet, New York, and took his final leave of Union Village on July 13, 1843.[21] At his departure, Union Village had fewer members than when he arrived in 1836.[22] Following Wells's departure, the spirit of Richard McNemar was again invoked by Union Village visionists. At a meeting on February 24, 1844, a visionist manifesting the spirit of a relative of French king Louis Philippe revealed that McNemar had preached to the spirits of one thousand French, English, and Spanish spirits in the nearby spiritual French meetinghouse.[23] McNemar's missionary zeal, a core component of his personality, burned brightly beyond the grave.

The tumult unleashed by Mother's Work had taken a heavy toll on the community, which slowly declined over the remainder of the nineteenth century. Young people continued to drift away, including Emmet McBrien, who left on July 31, 1858, aged twenty-one.[24] Wells left some able leaders in his wake, including John Martin, Oliver C. Hampton, Amos Parkhurst, and the remaining

McNemars. Tragically, the most promising young Shaker at Union Village, scribe Andrew C. Houston, died after falling thirty-two feet from a scaffolding erected for the construction of the Center Family's new dwelling. Houston lived six hours after his fall. Gasping for breath, he addressed his physicians and the community's youth, telling them, "A justified conscience was a pretty thing in a time such as this."[25] Hopefully, Richard McNemar, Freegift Wells, and Margaret McBrien all felt the same way when their time came.

APPENDIX 1

Richard McNemar, "A general outline of the past Journal of my life"

Richard McNemar left only three reflective autobiographical writings. This brief text supplies more information about his early life than any other source. It offers more information than a very similar text found at the end of manuscript item 301 in the Shaker Collection at the Library of Congress, Manuscript Division.

Source: Richard McNemar, Diaries, Item 255, DLC-MSS.

Text:
A general outline of the past Journal of my life.

I was born in the Tuscarora Valley, Cumberland county state of Pena Nov. 20 1770—when five years old our family moved to a place called hearts log on the Juniata 5 miles above the standing stone now called Huntingdon, resided there about 4 years & thince moved about ten miles up Shavers creek where we lived about 3 years that is till I was about 12 years old. Thence about the close of the revolutionary war we moved south into the Kishacoquillis valley I think in the fall of the year 1783.

I continued with my parents in that place worked on the farm in summer & went to school in winter until I became master of the english language in its several branches including Arithmetic. In 1786, I was called to take charge of a school in the standing stone valley, & taught with acceptance for one year which commenced April 1, 1786, & terminated Apr. 1787. This summer I boarded at home & followed jobbing: In July I cut my foot badly & had to attend the warm springs in the fall I accompanied Garner to the redstone country & staid till the following March, Here I followed weaving & teaching a singing school March 1788 I returned to Kishacoquillis spent the summer about home, & in the fall took up a school for three months, & on that Christmas night I was cured of frolicking & thrown into a state of trouble from which no human power release me—In the spring of 1789, I again visited the backwoods: commenced a large school in Jacobs creek settlement, taught three days & then in a rambling fit slipped off took boating at the mouth of sewickly & landed at Limestone thence explored Kentucky as far as Lexington staid some time at McClellands station, wove several webs to get travling expences for my return in June I ascended the Ohio with a company of 15 as far as Mariatta, called there & had an interview with my brother John, thence by land to wheelen, & back to Jacobs creek where I harvested, then turned in to Journeyman weaving with Robt Newell, & hired a month with Saml Boyd to work on his farm, then to Ligonier Valley where I took up a school for one year commencing Jany. 1 1790—some time the next spring I visited Kishacoquillis, & got a remedy from [sh?] to the Epelipsy, gave him my horse & returned on foot continued my school till fall made another visit over the mountains & returned the Conomaugh road fell in with Mr McPherren & James Crow In July I had attended McPherrens ordination & got acquainted with him so on this occasion I was glad to see him & the matter was then hinted about my going to live with him, this was late in the fall of 1790, when near the close of my 20th year. I continued the school thro this winter, & very early in the spring of 1791, I went to Salem, & took up school there my first visit was with Elisha McCurdy toward the lattr part of Feb. 7, And I returned early in March.

March 13, 1791 was the first society meeting I ever attended, the meeting was at John Boyds & the power of God was manifested in a manner that no one present had ever before witnessed. I continued there about six months. In august Carey Allen visited us & invited me to go with him to virginia In September I attended the sacrament at Georges creek & agreed to go to Kentucky. The same month we descended the Ohio & landed at Limestone. 2 days after St. Clair's defeat.

This fall I took boarding at Jos Caldwells & began the study of Latin, with Malcom Worley, staid there till the spring of 1792. In March I visited Cincinnati Columbia, Round Bottom, &c. & returned in June took boarding in Malcham's schoolhouse & remained there till December. Then went to Cane ridge to live with R. Finley, spent the winter there & in April 1793 I went to live at John Luckies, and then in the spring of 1795 I moved to Paint lick & taught school a year moved back to Caneridge in the fall of 1796, and in December that year was licensed to preach 1797 I spent preaching in the vacancies & in the month of September moved to C. Creek.

Vincy was born at the upper place Oct 21, 1797 In the spring of 1798 I moved to the lower place and that year was ordained perhaps in augt In May 1799 I went to the general assembly, and returned about the last of June In sept Elisha was born 29, & in Octr I attended Pby at Orangedale. Trying time this winter. In 1800, I built a new house &c. raised corn attended the commission of synod emancipated Celia, & in Oct Nancy was born in the spring the revival broke out & in augt I set out for redbanks & returned late in the fall, then to Pby at Springfield then to Turtlecreek & in March 1802 moved thither.

APPENDIX 2

Richard McNemar, "Testimony of E[leazar] Wright"

Richard McNemar's other autobiographical reminiscence provides more information on his conversion to Shakerism and was written as an affirmative testimony to his faith.

Source: Richard McNemar, Diaries, Item 254, DLC-MSS.

Text:
Testimony of E Wright
June 1828

Being now in the 58th year of my age & having witnessed many scenes of an interesting nature, I feel under obligation at this time to give a brief narrative of the principal occurrences of my past life & particularly of the last 28 years which I have spent in the United Society among the people commonly called Shakers. The place of my nativity was the Tuscarora Valley in the county of Cumberland State of pennsylvania. ~~My birth was dated~~ I was born Nov. 20, 1770. My parents belonged to the church of England, & in that order I was baptized & taught the general doctrines of the Christian religion. being the youngest of the family & the more easily spared from manual labor I was early put to school & contracted a taste for learning, in which I made such proficiency that when 15 years of age I was employed as teacher of an English school. At twelve years old I began to think seriously about a future state, to reflect on my past life, to feel compunction for sin, to retire occasionally in secret & pray to God for pardon & forgiveness, from which period I was greatly protected from actual sin, as far as my light & knowledge extended, & was taken under the care of the Presbyterian church as a minor according to the general rules of which, I ever after felt conscientious to keep my justification.

In the 18th year of my age my troubles of mind increased to such a degree, that I took to travelling to see whether I could not get releasment & recover my early relish for the gay pleasures of the world. I visited kentucky which was then a new country & afforded many objects for amusement. But after spending about a year in that way to no purpose, & rather growing worse I returned to my occupation of school keeping in the western part of Pennsylvania, where a revival of religion broke out of which I became a subject. My conversion as it was called was deemed rather ~~of the extraordinary kind~~ singular; such as in that day was common among the Methodists ~~than the church to which I belonged~~. From that period I became what was called zealous in religion ~~conscientious in striving to know the will of~~ devoting all my leisure time to prayer meditation, reading, & pious conversation, from which I never after deviated, & having the confidence & respect of the church I was called & encouraged to engage in a course of [letters?] prepare for the Ministry, & having completed my education & preparatory trials was licensed in the 25th year of my age & the year following ordained pastor of a congregation in Mason county Kentucky. Where that memorable work called the Kentucky Revival broke out in the spring of the year 1801. In the early stage of that work I ~~early~~ received a renewed manifestation of the power of God similar to what I had felt in my first conversion, & altho I had never for one moment doubted the truth of revelation or the quality of my experience from the period of my first light yet I found to my great sorrow that as yet I remained far short of salvation which I now ~~engaged~~ set out to pursue at the risk of every thing dear on earth. During the KY Revival I persevered with unabating zeal partaking of all its most powerful operations & marvellous gifts, was among the number & first on the list of those branded with heresy & excommunicated from the church in the year 1804. still persevered in union with that separate body who styled themselves christians, in promoting what we then believed to be the best religion on earth.

In this work I was zealously engaged as hundreds can witness, when the Shakers first made their appearance in this country, The reception which they met from myself and others I have already detailed in a pamphlet called The Kentucky Revival, which it is unnecessary to repeat: a variety of matters in my experience & under my observation call more particularly for my present testimony, & especially what relates to the organization & economy of the society. & Church

1. All or many were admitted on trial who were willing to confess & forsake all known sin. The principal part of those who first set out were persons of good morals & zealous professors of religion; The motives which induced me to join the people was to get out of a dark, deceitful & wicked world & to get rid of the

wicked nature that I had in myself: I had by the light & revelation of God seen the heavens opened & the beauty & glory of the divine nature so attracted my soul that had I possessed all the wealth of this little globe I would have freely exchanged it for the meanest place in that region of divine light but my transports of this kind had been but transient scenes that still left me shrouded in a dark & hellish nature from which I knew not how to be extricated. The contract into which I entered with the Shakers was to barter the Devil that was in me for Christ. I very soon got to believe that Christ was in them, & I know that in me that is in my flesh the devil had a seat: To make this exchange had been my labor & study for many years & now forsooth I had a fair offer, but the terms were rather tighter than I had generally contemplated; but I determined however that I would advance the uttermost farthing that was demanded, & it was nothing short of giving to boot all my worldly honor wealth & pleasure. Now to be serious, I did believe & I still do believe that the gospel was & is a substantial reality: that Christ the power of God & the wisdom of God is not a phantom of the brain, but some thing of more intrinsic value in the estimation of an enlightened soul, than any material object in the universe, and believing as I did I most heartily complied with the terms of the gospel, in literally & lawfully conveying away my right title & personal claim to every thing that I possessed on this earth, without pocketing one cent, as a consideration: or even expecting a compensation or equivalent of this worlds goods to my self or my heirs forever. I had a title to a quarter section of land with some improvements a house & furniture a housekeeper, 7 children with all the aparatus for housekeeping, a servant the whole of which I surrendered, devoted & consecrated forever to the benefit of the poor, & cast myself singly on the charity of the church. This I absolutely did in the full exercise of my reason judgment & faith & with a head replete with languages arts & sciences: topped out with school divinity & a general knowledge of all the tenets systems & plans of salvation among the human race, Besides a mode[rate] acquaintance with politics, law, pharma[cy?] Freemasonry, & sundry other articles too tedious to Mention all these & every thing else that could be named of the kind, I did absolute bona fide barter exchange & dispose of for that single article called xt [Christ] or the gospel of his second appearing & to this day I feel perfectly well satisfied with the bargain. If any inquire of me whether my conveyance was merely a quit claim or a general warranty, I answer my contract was to warrant & defend, against myself my heirs executors administrators & assigns & all other persons claiming & to claim under me or by virtue of any right title or interest vested in me to the sd. premises forever: This transaction was in perfect accordance with my family who were more or less under the influence of the same spirit with myself. My personal property was distributed to the use of the different families in which we were respectively located & the price of the land was put into the hands of the deacon or trustee who had charge of the children's school & took the responsibility of all my temporal affairs and from that period to the present I have no personal interest whatever: Having food & raiment & other necessaries in common with others I am there with content, Nor have I ever seen the time since that I would exchange property with the richest man on earth that is I would not give up my claim to the blessings of the gospel & lose my relation to the [word missing in original] of people with whom I am united for all the riches of this globe and ten thousand more like it.

I have continued, for the most part, to preach to the world as occasion offered both at home & abroad but have never received a cent for any of my ministerial services; & probably upon an average my hand labor has more than cleared my expenses, altho gratitude obliges me to say that I have found the people exceeding kind in every respect so that I have lacked for nothing that was necessary to render me comfortable and notwithstanding it might be thought that my official standing entitled me to some singularities of treatment, it has even been my choice to take common fare & to content myself with being made equal with others.

I have had an opportunity of forming the most free & intimate acquaintance with all classes of the society, and witnessing the prinicpal in every department, for altho I never was legally initiated as a church member by signing the written articles called the church covenant, I never was debarred from any privilege as a witness & partaker of all that was common among the members, & having no interest in any one society more than another being totally divested of all claim to any personal property among the people I can with the greater confidence testify my certain knowledge of those facts which may be called in question, & first I will speak of their morals. When the chh was about to be instituted, The rule that was laid down & taught in the most forcible manner was to admit no one into that order who was known to be addicted to any vice or was chargable with any crime that was unrepented of. The jews on the occasion of the passover never searched their houses for leaven more carefully the people were searched for evil, to have it purged out, & to stand in a state of entire justification. It was looked upon as a most solemn transaction, of this I have the most certain knowledge having had the care of the largest family then in the society and hearing their particular opening relative to that business. It certainly was idea universally entertained, that the vows of God would be upon every one who enrolled himself as a church member to give up the world flesh & devil once for all & in future to live a life, holy, harmless undefiled & separate from sinners, after the example of christ. there is no manner of doubt can possibly exist as to the manifest intention of the people, & every thing in their after conversation & deportment proved the sincerity of the transaction. One thing I shall mention as a most convincing evidence that the people were in solid earnest.

All who had property whether much or little when they came into the society had taken an inventory of it, which they kept as an evidence of their just claim to the amount in case of their withdrawal, all these inventories were voluntarily destroyed by the individuals of which I was an eye witness, this was done professedly & purpos[efully?] that the property should never be called for, that the claim was forever relinquished, & at the time an acquittance was given by each individual for all past labor & service & every claim or demand whatever on the society or any member of it. Such were the steps taken to test the sincerity of each individual after which the covenant was signed & the church set in order.

APPENDIX 3

Richard McNemar, "My years on earth have been but few"

Richard McNemar wrote this autobiographical poem on November 20, 1832, to mark the occasion of his sixty-second birthday. He sent the text to the New Lebanon, New York, Ministry, commenting, "As the present date happens to be my birth day, and my morning meditations took an unusual glance over my past life, and my pen almost inadvertently, noted down some memorable waymarks on the interesting journey; in order to fill out the large blank on this page I venture to expose the out-line of my reflections to your charitable inspection, and momentary amusement."[1] Richard included a tune with the poem, which is presented here in a modern score. It was notated in standard music notation, as opposed to the Shakers' letteral notation.

In reply, Seth Youngs Wells wrote to McNemar on behalf of Ministry elder Rufus Bishop, saying that "your birthday poem, gave [Rufus] much satisfaction—He has given it a free circulation in these parts, & intends to extend it [to] the eastern Churches where the Ministry expect to visit this season."[2] Rufus Bishop was as good as his word.

A few years later, in a letter to Seth Youngs Wells, Richard included some more verses to his poem. These are also presented below to provide the fullest version of the poem.

Sources are provided in the endnotes.

Text:
POSTSCRIPT *to the answer of a letter from New Lebanon,—Nov. 20th, 1832. To the highly respected Ministry.*

As the present date happens to be my birthday, &
my morning meditations took an unusual glance over
my past life, and my pen, almost inadvertantly, noted
down some memorable way-marks; in order to fill out
the blank on this leaf, I shall venture to exhibit it to
your charitable inspection and momentary amusement.

MY years on earth have been but few,—
They just amount to sixty two:
But few and evil as they've been,
Some happy days I've surely seen.
Thro' ev'ry scene, at ev'ry date,
God's tender mercy has been great;
And by his providential care,
I have eluded many a snare.

2. I early learn'd to read and write,
And in book knowledge took delight,
That when at fifteen years of age,
In teaching school I did engage:
Through various changes I went on,
Till somewhere near my twenty-one,
I join'd the church, then went ahead,
And spent three years among the dead.

3. Dead languages I learned well,
And took a gen'ral rout through hell;
And there with science quite replete,

I fill'd an honorable seat.
Full twenty-six I did not reach,
Until they licens'd me to preach,
And put the Bible in my hand,
To make it speak thro' all the land.

4. At twenty-eight I was ordain'd,
And pastor of a church remain'd.
Till I arriv'd at thirty-one,
And then the pow'r of God came on.
As full of zeal and pure desire
As e'er a coal was full of fire,
I flash'd and blazed by day and night,
A burning and a shining light.

5. But should I say, it was Big I,
I'd surely tell a great big lie.
'Twas heaven's gift thro' mortal clay
That carri'd on the grand display.
Yea thanks to God that I have seen
Ten thousand sinnder on the green,
Where I a sinner with the rest,
With heavn'ly gifts was often blest.

6. Tho on the solemn camping ground,
Sin and uncleanness might be found,
In all that work, through all that time,
I kept my conscience free from crime.
Such was the power and such the light
That did compass us day and night,
That to feel lewd or lustful there,
I never did—I never dare.

7. For hope that anchor of the soul,
Did all my passions so control,
That in the work I kept alive,
Until I reach'd my thirty-five.
Now on reflection I could see,
A mighty work was wrought in me,
But after all I had to own,
I felt like Adam when alone. *not very good*

8. Here scenes commenc'd entirely new,
Which now with pleasure I review,
For thanks to God! I plainly see,
That hitherto he's helped me;
He gave me then a helper meet,
To help me out of all deceit,—
To help me to expose my loss,
And then set out to bear my cross.

9. Since I confess'd and was releas'd,
I've never gratifi'd the beast,
But kept alive that sacred fire,
That masters every base desire.
For since I've learned to unite
With those who travel in the light,
There's no necessity at all
For me to stumble or to fall.

10. I've always had a faithful guide,
In whom I safely could confide—
Good elders who in very deed,
Have help'd in ev'ry time of need
They've helped me up, & help'd me down
And help'd me thro', & help'd me round,
They'v help'd me forward helpd me back
And help'd me still to keep the track.

11. The faith that join'd me to a lead
Is of great consequence indeed,
For if my faith did not remain,
My helpers would help in vain.
Do any now interrogate,
And wish to know my present state,
Just take the answer, if you will,
That I compos'd at Pleasant Hill.
  in 183[blank in original]
I've lived to finish one year more
Which brings me up to 64,
and enter on my 65
With all my faculties alive,

When all the years rise in review
And all the scenes I've passed thro'
Tis like a vision or a trance
All comprehended at a glance

Pleasure at best is but a flash
honor & wealth but empty trash
And worldly wisdom it doth seem
Is nothing but a pleasant dream

The lawless scenes that men pursue
Are still more hateful to my view,
And nothing suits my trav'ling soul
But to reject & spurn the whole.

So with the poet I conclude
that there is no substantial good
In all thats felt and all that done
beneath the circuit of the sun.

This life's a dream an empty show
But the bright world to which we go
hath joys substantial & sincere
when shall I wake & find me there?[3]

APPENDIX 4

[Archibald McCorkle?], "A few mourning thoughts on McNemar's fall," and Richard McNemar, "An Answer to the Mourning Thoughts on McNemar's Fall"

The poems below were published by historian John Patterson MacLean in the *Western Star* newspaper of Lebanon, Ohio, on June 4, 1908. Brother Alonzo Hollister, a Shaker from New Lebanon, New York, loaned MacLean manuscripts containing a poem lamenting McNemar's conversion to Shakerism and a poem written by McNemar in response. MacLean made transcriptions of these poems and published them with a brief headnote in the article reprinted below. It is likely that (1) the original scribe misspelled or miscopied some words, (2) MacLean mistranscribed some words, or (3) the typesetter set them wrong. I have silently corrected a handful of typos, while more consequential editorial input is set in square brackets. "Camridge and Concord" most certainly refer to the Cane Ridge and Concord churches in Bourbon County, Kentucky, of which Barton W. Stone was minister and that were greatly threatened by the Shaker incursion. The author of the poem lamenting McNemar's conversion is identified at the end of the manuscript in "another hand" (someone else's writing) as "Mckorble." I have tentatively identified this as Archibald McCorkle, a Presbyterian who moved from South Carolina to Tennessee in 1806 and whose son Archibald McCorkle Jr. became a minister in the Cumberland Presbyterian Church.

Text:
SHAKER HISTORY. RICHARD McNEMAR SINKS INTO DEEP OBLIVION.
    Great Shaker Leader After Illustrious Career and Great Revivals Passes from Believers.

By J. P. McLean.

Among the Hollister papers I find the following, "Thoughts on McNemar's Fall." It gives a vivid exhibition of religious warfare a hundred years ago. The paper is the product of three different hands. Of McKorble [Archibald McCorkle] I know nothing. The probability is that his effort was never printed, but copies in script passed from hand to hand. It is probable the "Answer" was written by McNemar himself. In the text, "Dunlavy" is John, a brother of Judge Francis Dunlavy, "Houston" is Matthew, "Springfield" is now called Springdale, eleven miles north of Cincinnati, "Salem" was a church, west of Monroe, in Butler county, "Camridge [Cane Ridge] and Concord" are in Kentucky, noted for the great camp meetings held there during the Kentucky Revival. At Camridge [Cane Ridge] 20,000 people were present. Whenever McNemar was to preach at one of these camp meetings, great crowds were sure to be present. His very name aroused the multitude.

"A few mourning thoughts on McNemar's fall as they transpired from the author's heart."
What joys malignant shook the vault of hell
And Zion trembled when McNemar fell.

MCNEMAR WEEPS

My wife weeps—well let her weep.
The children too—well let them weep.
McNemar dropped a tear for them.
I'll join; tis ungenerous to refuse;
my rugged soul is melted with this female softness.
But must we weep alone—
Turtlecreek and Springfield surely will join us
and Salem won't refuse.
Camridge [Cane Ridge] and Concord,
you must share our common woes,
for you have often heard McNemar's voice in gospel sound.
Ye sister churches join our common grief,
yes all will mourn McNemar's fall, but Zion's foes.
Ah! ye Philistines rejoice not over us,
David's son and David's Lord is living in Israel;
is still upon his holy hill of Zion.
Your iron knee must bow to him
tho you have slain our holy Jonathan.
This day we're called to mourning; and mourn we will;
we'll freely vent the sorrows of our hearts, twill give us ease.

Make haste ye woman skillfull in lamentation,
bring your musick, raise your feeble voices to the highest key;
ye men of coarser mould sound loud the solemn base;
this day mourn a friend, a brother's fall.
An enemy has done it.
Sure some imp in deep disguise,
in angel form appeared before his eyes.
Some imp detached from the Tartarian band,
rose in the vizard of a mortal man;
hell lent its aid, and ever baneful gold,
Jesus, the Nazarene again is sold;
kind heaven and counter plot came on,
dashed tophets hopes and saved us from the dreadful storm.
He fell and with his horrid tail
drew many sparkling stars from heaven and cast them to the earth.
Their orbs are quite extinct they shine no more,
their place is found no more in heaven,
sisters and brothers once much loved,
farewell the separation day is come.
No more we join our hearts and voices in Emanuels praise,
we thought our friendship was eternal,
but alas you've gone, forever gone.
But 'tis not for to fix the dark damnation seal—
but sure the cloud you sit under is the impenitrable gloom.

SYMPATHETIC SORROW

Now ye mourning saints
ye drink deep the sweets of sympathetic sorrow;
and feel the mysteries of royal woe,
but stop ye skilful mourners,
hang up your harps,
or change the scene,
the horror drys our tears and chills our blood,
the mighty woe beats too heavy on our feeble strings.
Refresh your minds with days and seasons past
and tears will flow again,
think on those happy days
when McNemar's voice calmed our ears in gospel sound.
Arisen Saviour was his boast and joy;
we still hear or seem to hear that harmonious voice
pouring the consolations of the gospel into the wounded hearts

and with heavenly art pointing to the healing balm.
But the echo dies,
'tis heard no more;
Appollos' silver tongue is silent;
His ears are stopped,
his eyes are closed,
drunk deep with opiates,
not prepared with human art;
and cement of infernal kind,
forbid those eyes to see the light of heaven,
he sleeps or is he dead,
come near ye tender hearted saints,
surround the mournful hearse.
Is there no vital beatings near his heart,
no heaven-pulse,
or faintest symptom of returning life?
Brothers, sisters, there is none.
We'll let some strong-lunged saint
with trumpet voice sound loud McNemar's rise,
perhaps 'twill wake him from his antichristian.

MCNEMAR'S FALL

Awake, arise, McNemar,
or be forever fallen
'tis gone—no sign of life appears,
weep on ye saints,
we mourn a friend,
a brother slain.
McNemar fell and as he fell
he thrust a dagger deep into the heart of Zion,
see how she bleeds, she weeps,
weeps blood from every pore,
yes he grasped a pointed spear into that right hand of his
and plunged it deep into Nazarene
wider the wound and deeper too,
than woman's hand could do.
Our Jesus bleeds,
blame not the Jews,
McNemar gave the deadly state;
weep on fair Salem's daughters, weep.
Strangers behold our grief

and drop the sympathising tear;
our grief's too big for birth are strangled in our hearts.
Language fails, our sorrows swell too high stop your minstrel,
the mourning must be withdrawn,
we sink, dry up your tears,
surround the hearse no more.
There is other work prepared for us,
we're soldiers fighting for our God,
break up the mourning board.
Brethren farewell arise let us go hence.

Remark:—Thus sinks Mckorble [McCorkle] while McNemar's ghost, Is soaring up to join the heavenly host. By Another Hand.

An Answer to the Mourning Thoughts on McNemar's Fall

The work of God all Satan's art defies,
And Christians shout to see McNemar rise.
Rise from the doleful grave of death and sin,
While Zion's gate unfolds to let him in.

In Babel long by Antichrist confined,
Their systems dark, oppressed his laboring mind,
Till the last trump his slumbering spirit rewoke,
And light from heaven ye dire enchantment broke.

Predestination in its dark extreme,
He soon shakes off as a ficitious dream.
The boundless love of God to human souls,
Now from his tongue like heavenly music rolled.

What raptious joy of living truth imparts
And glows seraphic thro ten thousand hearts.
Behold ye vast assembly spread abroad,
Hang with attention on the word of God.

From East and West together, thousands ran.
And none to caution "Do not follow man."
Professors own of work to be divine,
But at ye doctrine murmur and repine
"A glorious work, but is true indeed,"
That poor McNemar's left his former creed.

There's danger friends, we fear this McNemar,
Will carry his new doctrine quite too far,
Hark what is this, we hear the artful knave
Begin to prove that sinner's can believe.

And what is worse he testifies forsooth,
That souls are born again just by the truth
Ye sinners come renounce the dire decree,
Believe the truth and that will make you free.

Next he enquires for what the Savior died
If he prepared a robe our sins to hide,
Now he denies that Jesus gave his blood
To satisfy or please an angry God.

His cruel hands tear off the wonderous cloak
And calls imputed merit all a joke
Justice O Justice art thou reconciled
To spare a rebel and destroy a child?

Is God atoned to sinners in this way
It must be sure by acting base as they
Jesus appeared to make an end of sin
And soon his righteous kingdom shall begin.

Now let the sinner all his sins forsake
Or take his portion in the burning lake
The day of Christ, the awful days at hand
When sin shall be consumed from the land.

The burning day in high prophetic strain
Is loud proclaimed o'er all the western plains
From thing to thing see how McNemar raved
To find out some new method to be saved.

Alarming work But what will be the crop
And where will these deluded creatures stop
They sing and pray with an alarming sound
While others fall and wallow on the ground.

Still they go on and say the work's advancing
And never stop until they get to dancing
Where will it end. Can any mortal tell?
McNemar's leading thousands on to hell
We'll stop in time—our fathers sure were right
And none but fools will follow this new light

Old Brethren you may tarry where you are,
But do not judge what's quite bevond your sphere
While covered o'er with Calvin's dark decree
Where the new lights are gone you cannot see.

Now what we know with confidence we speak
That alone is king at Turtlecreek
The Lord's annointed, there assumes his throne
And happy souls their rightful sovereign own.

Springfield and Salem, Cambridge [Cane Ridge] and Concord
Have waited for the coming of the Lord
But can it be that after so much prayer
They'll join to build a castle in the air.
Heaven forbid and give them shock on shock
Until they build on next the eternal rock.

What dismal spirit could obstruct their race
And stir up prejudice with lies so base
Some friend to Egypt flesh pots struck the damp
And quickly stopt the once harmonious camp

Will you go back to Egypt treacherous spy
Or in the wilderness consent to die,
Or keep the camp at an uncertain stand
Until they perish short of Canaan's land.

From Jordan's channel or the farther bank
Those who have marched along and kept their ranks;
Look back with pain on spirits once akin
Now wandering in the wilderness of sin.

We've found the path the blessed Jesus trod
And forward press to be alone with God
Our brethern all may follow if they choose
Or all that they have gained forever lose.

QUERIES

Are not saints holy people and if the holy people were scattered thro the reign of anti-Christ when or where were they gathered so as to form a Zion, a temple of God?

But parting friends will judge each other's state
The backward soul the forward light will hate
And judge the things they neither see nor feel
And almost fix the dark damnation seal.

Now some presume the work will still go on
Until the parties all unite in one.
Here the rejoicing Christians, hand in hand
Try hard with what they've got to make a stand.

The old denominations keep their ground
And guard their little parties all around
Drunk with the wine of the old scarlet shore
Against the new formed Zion loudly roar.

Others at work the stately building daub
But O poor Zion gets another stab
Dunlavy Houston and McNemar's fall
Has broke to pieces almost half the wall.

'Twas not the Shakers did McNemar ill
Before they came he made and signed his will
And died in peace and vanished out of view

E'er they had anything with him to do
They found him lying in his dusty bed
And came with power to raise him from the dead
He knew the camp of Israel was not saved
And died of choice just to make way for David.

If Zion is built up is she to sorrow anymore?—Is there not danger of mistaking the law when it conies forth out of Zion, for a delusion and those who proclaim it for imps of Tartory who can be more confident of their relation to God than the Jews who counted the blessed Jesus a deceiver and his power to be infernal?

Might not McNemar change his wood and hay
For a foundation God himself did lay
And in the stead of selling it for cash
Give up the things of time as worthless trash.

And might not Salem's daughters get to see
That they must die to sin as well as he
And that they may submit to such a death
McNemar means to pray while he has breath.

Turtlecreek Ohio cop. 3.2.4.6. 1806.

APPENDIX 5

The Expulsion of Richard McNemar

This narrative of the events surrounding the expulsion of Richard McNemar from Union Village in 1839 is of unknown authorship. It survives in the collection of the Western Reserve Historical Society in a manuscript copy that appears to be in the hand of John Patterson MacLean, the historian who worked closely with Shakers at Union Village, Ohio, in the early twentieth century to collect and preserve their materials. The text has some internal footnotes, indicated with asterisks, that are commentary by MacLean. This account, though highly romanticized, purports to be that of an eyewitness. MacLean clearly used it for the stirring finale of his biography *A Sketch of the Life and Labors of Richard McNemar*. While it is not to be relied on for the most part, it is included here as an appendix, since it presents the folklore surrounding those cataclysmic events as retold by an eyewitness more than sixty years later.

Source: VII:A-22, OClWHi.

Text:
Expulsion of Richard McNemar*[1]

Freegift Wells was a weak, vain, jealous man. Such power as was then invested in the first in the Ministry was fire in the hands of one so constituted as Elder Wells. He was raised to a position above many of his superiors, among whom was Richard McNemar, who, unquestionably was the brainest man that was ever connected with Shakerism in the West. In all things he had proved himself most faithful to its teachings and its genius. David Darrow had leaned upon him. If the Shakers, in any of the Western Societies were in tribulation or in lawsuits, Richard McNemar was dispatched to their assistance, and in every instance he proved himself a safe councilor and a wise friend. We people at Union Village looked up to him and Malcham Worley as children look up to a fond parent. If any one was in trouble, that person ~~restorted~~ resorted either to Richard or Malcolm. This was noticed by Elder Freegift, who thought his own importance was thereby slighted, and so ~~great~~ pronounced was his wounded pride that it was manifest to all. He refused both Richard and Malcham the freedom of the Office, where they could be more readily consulted.

In the midst of the revel of Spiritualism, in which Elder Freegift so much delighted, both Richard and Malcham were silent witnesses. What were their actual views no one knew; but they neither opposed nor sanctioned the progress of the new cult. This was a matter of great offence to Elder Freegift.

It is probable that Richard was studying and weighing the matter carefully. His composition rather inclined him to the supernatural, as may be instanced in his conversion to Shakerism. When the three missionaries—Issachar Bates, Benjamin Seth Youngs and John Meacham—visited what is now Union Village, they were anxious to convert Richard McNemar. Such a step would be a great stride in their direction.

Now, it so happened that Richard's son James was afflicted with screaming spells brought on by [fright?]. In those days it was a prevalent opinion that snakes had the power of charming. The mother missing her son started out in search of him. She found him in close proximity to a large blacksnake,—both gazing steadily at each other. The mother seized the child and fled with all possible speed to the house, believing the serpent was in persuit. Reaching the door, almost exhausted, she ~~rather~~ fell into the house, but retaining sufficient strength to close the door. In all probability it was the action of the mother that brought on the fits of the son. In time he learned to know when the spells were coming on, and there would speed away to his [word missing], reaching out for the one that was nearer. They too had learned that by holding him tightly in their arms his fit was less violent and would soon pass off. Whilst the missionaries were enjoined in their arguments with Richard, the boy rushed into his father's arms. Richard immediately turned to the missionaries and informed them that if they would cure his child of his malad he would accept their teachings. This was a blow to the trio. They did not claim supernatural powers. There was silence which became painful. Finally, Jennie, the wife, arose and said: "Let us kneel and pray." In the meantime the boy had slipped out of his father's arms, went out doors and engaged in play. The spasms never returned. A few days later, while Richard was walking alone, not far from his dwelling, he saw the naked arm of a woman reach out from heaven toward him. Looking intently upon it he said "I will follow thee." From that moment till the hour of his death Ann Lee never had a more faithful follower.

With the above circumstances before us it is not improbable that Richard looked favorably upon the phomena then operating among the Shakers. His son James was carried away with it; while as already noticed, his daughter Vincy was a sensitive.

For three years Elder Freegift suffered the rivalry of Richard and Malcham. The day of vengeance was at hand. Both were stumbling blocks and they must not remain where Freegift must be supreme. In the society was a recent convert, not long arrived from Ireland—one Margaret O'Brian. She was among the [artist?] sensitives, and her "gift was most beautiful," but her power was soon exhausted. But Freegift hounded her for more revelations. To please him she tried to continue in here art. Finally Mother Ann Lee took possession of her and revealed to the willing ears of Elder Freegift Wells that Malcham Worley, Richard McNemar and his brother Garner McNemar were stumbling blocks, and must at once be expelled from the society. The revelation was a sweet smelling balm in the nostrils of Freegift, and the potion was sweeter than honey to his taste. The edict at once went forth that these faithful aged brethren should no longer be numbered among the faithful, nor should they live among Believers. The Shakers were appalled at the [?]. All felt a great calamity had befallen them. There was sorrow, crying and dispair. Great hot tears rolled down the cheeks of Eldress Malinda Watts, and other sisters cried because the great strong pillars of Shakerism were to be removed. Freegift Wells stood undaunted, a proud victor in the fray. Ann Lee had spoken the word, and for authority there was the testimony of Margaret O'Brian. Had Margaret rendered any services to Shakerism during her short membership? Yea, verily she was the mouth piece of Mother Ann, and that should outweigh the 34 years of faithful service of Richard, Malcham and Garner. True the very land upon which Freegift stood had been donated of Malcham, yet that was nothing when he stood up in the way of Freegift. Had these brethren ever violated the covenant which they had so solemnly taken? Nay. They had never wavered. They were tried as by fire and were never found wanting. Would not the services of Richard's passing save [him?]? His son James was faithful, intelligent, and was active in the second coming of Mother Ann. In Vincy all might be found. Her life had been pure, she was devoted and intelligent. She had been one of the most affecting speakers, near the close of the great Kentucky Revival. Her father held her on his shoulder while she addressed the multitude, though she was but six years of age. She had become a prominent Shaker and was an Eldress. (Her picture is herewith given, taken after she was past 80. She was born in Madison County, Kentucky, and died at Union Village, August 12, 1878, aged 80 years. Her face, with the exception of the nose, resembled that of her father).

Amidst the triumph of Freegift Wells the souls of Richard and Garner McNemar and Malcham Worley were serene. They made no outcry, nor plotted treason. Richard was very long headed. He had not lost faith in Shakerism. He knew that Elder Freegift was about to violate the covenant. He knew the Laws of Ohio would protect him. He determined to rely on the principles of Shakerism to maintain his cause, and to those principles he looked for ~~justice~~ redress. The decree was now promulgated. Garner McNemar must leave at once and take up his board with one of the tenants. Malcham Worley must be sent to Berrien County, Ohio and boarded out, while Richard McNemar was to be dropped in the streets of Lebanon, Ohio. The edict was strictly carried out.*2 Freegift Wells was now without a rival. Richards and Malchams sympathy, words of encouragement and advice, were now no more. Those who desired consolation must ~~now~~ go to the head—Freegift Wells, who was the visible lead.

When the vehicle, bearing Richard McNemar, arrived in Lebanon he requested to be put down before the home of his brother-in-law, Judge Francis Dunlavy. He knocked at the door and requested admission until he could communicate with the Central Ministry at Mount Lebanon. His request was granted. Immediately he indited a complete recital of circumstances concerning his expulsion. He was summoned at once to New Lebanon, and without delay started on his long journey where he arrived during the month of June 1839, and there continued a period of ten days. The matter was ~~taken up~~ considered by the Ministry and Rufus Bishop, second in the Ministry lot took the ~~matter~~ question up. He called the most expert ~~medium~~ sensitive to his assistance and directed the medium to proceed in spirit at once to Union Village. The result was that a mandatory order was issued restoring the expelled brethren, and the placing of Margaret O'Brien to her proper station. This incensed her and she left the society.

Richard McNemar was received with great joy on his return from Mount Lebanon. So great was their feeling that the young men, on the following Sunday, carried him to the Meeing House in a chair. At the proper time a demand was made that he should speak. He was carried to the center of the church. Rising slowly and supporting himself by the chair, his eyes filled with tears, he ~~began~~ opened his mind. He recounted his labors, told them how he had always loved them, and labored on their behalf. As the orator proceeded all broke down in tears, and sobbing could be heard from every part of the house. Finally turning towards Freegift Wells, and stretching forth his arms he said, with moistened eyes and trembling voice: "I have always loved you. There never has been a moment when I entertained even the least ill-feeling towards you." What think you gentle reader? Freegift Wells did not allow the aged saint to finish his speech. Rushing upon him Freegift threw his arms around Richard, and declared that he had always loved him!!! I have no words of comment. Let others decide.

The journey to and from Mount Lebanon proved too much for the strength of Richard McNemar. It hastened his death. Soon after his return he passed into the great unknown. There is abundant proof that Elder Freegift used Spiritualism for his own personal aggrandizement. During the years 1838 and 1839, in the Center Family, there was a secrecy operation carried on by three members against the Ministry and some of the Elders. No clew, at that time, could be hit upon by Freegift, as to the conspirators. He resorted to Margaret O'Brian to disclose the secret through her spiritual powers. But in this she failed.

The high handed proceedings of Freegift Wells, in expelling the three brethren stamped him as utterly unfit for his position. But the Central Ministry did not remove him; and so far as now known, he was not ever censured. There must have been pressure brought to bear against him, for he resigned early in the year 1843. Let his soul rest in peace.

APPENDIX 6

[The Redemption of Richard McNemar]

This text is included for the same reasons as appendix 5. It is almost certainly by Susannah C. Liddell and is therefore an eyewitness account, albeit a highly romanticized and embellished one. It is hard to determine how much of it is reliable, and it is certain that some parts of it are not. Like appendix 5, however, it represents the folkloric evolution of the story of McNemar's fall and redemption. The account, like much of Liddell's manuscript corpus, is scattered and fragmentary. There are awkward transitions, indecipherable words, and an apparent loss of content that leads to an abrupt ending.

Source: Item 352c, DLC-MSS.

Eleazar McNemar had been lingering into a slow decline for several years, and for many months his place in the ranks of church had been filled by another, a sister (Lucy Miller) cooked his meals and carried them to his room and waited on him while he ate them, but one Sabbath morning while [text missing?] individual that entered, his head resting the while against the back of the great rocking chair, cushioned all over in which he was sitting, his arms were resting on the arms of his chair while his long pale fingers drooped over the curving over with him made worsted, pressed and glossy the chair he sat on, he had made himself, for he had made all the chairs that we used in those days, after we had formed in ranks and the first hymn was sung brother Andrew Houston went to elder Eleazar and asked him if he was ready to address his people, he answered nay that he was still feeling better, and that he desired to see once more in his world the saints of the household of faith go forth in the worship of God, and as we passed him in our marchings and dancings around the room his hands and feet keeping time with the songs, while his clear blue eyes swam in liquid depths of standing tears, but tears of joy and gladness were they, and his eyes glowed in their hopeful movings as thought lighted by luminary smiles through from behind them or as the morning sun's dawning approaches gladning through the dewy mists, we had an extra good meeting that day and the services were continued longer than usual, at the close of the marching and quick dancings, or circular dances as they are generally called, we assembled in our ranks again and a hymn was sung, then elder Eleazar spoke out and made known his feeling and desire to speak to the people once more, and requested to be borne on his feet to the foot of the aisle between the brethren and sisters, two young brethren asked the privilege, and their aid was accepted by the aged patriarch and one of the many great fathers in Israel, the two young brethren bore him along between them to the place selected by himself, when he commenced to speak the tears rolled down his face from his azure eyes. It is said that when father he was eating his breakfast he requested Lucy to go and ask the elder brethren (Stephen Spinning Davids brother and Andrew C Houston) to come over to his room, that he wanted to see them, his request was granted, and when the elder brethren had seated themselves before him, he informed them that he had been deeply impressed all the morning to go to church meeting that day and deliver his farewell address to all the brethren and sisters that he felt a little stronger than usual that morning, this short preface to the incident I am about to relate, I learned after it occurred, at this time elder Eleazar as we always called him, lived at the centre family, and I lived at the North House family, and I did not learn how he was conveyed to the meeting house, and now, I well remember the shock I felt, when entering the meeting house at the surprise of seeing the feeble, elder Eleazar, setting in a farther corner at the head of the house with his face toward the doors passing his large full calm eyes over each how changed was he that day, the poetical and variegated blendings of his mind in its matchless harmonious touches of description, charming as the rainbow in its arch over the evening sky, he still grew stronger and stronger as the inspiration of his discourse led him on, until he finally loosened himself from the support of the two young brethren and started up a song that thrilled me through and through with the strong melodious volume of his voice, he sung the song over and over—and the while timing it by dancing up and down the aisle between the brethren and sisters, his large white fore head reaching to the crown of his head his side head and back head fringed in silky silvered locks—his aquiline nose—periform face and straight thin cut lips diffused their new made, warm hearted glow, as the sunbeam measuring its warmth in at the door, his tall thin figure moved with elastic gracefulness, and his bearing was simple and trusting as a child, the song he sung and danced all himself was this,

> "My robe is new my crown is bright
> I'm happy blessed and free
> I feel as little as a mite as lively as a bee
> I sip the honey from the flower
> That blooms in Zion's vale
> I smell the odor from the bower
> That floats along the gale"

And when he had finished his exercises all the elders of the church, and all (I believe) of the brethren and sisters too expressed their intense happiness in beholding again the great father in Israel clothed with the living power of God, by this time, his strength failed him again, and the brethren bore him to a cushioned chair, when he requested the brethren and sisters to sing the following little anthem for his hearing (one of his own composing many years before) and this meeting was his last church meeting in this world.

James Whiticre I will here inclose a sketch of his life wept when he spoke as he often did when addressing the people in his day, that no heart was strong enough to withhold its tears, and so it seemed on this occasion when elder Eleazar was weeping while introducing the subject of his farewell address to his dearly beloved gospel kindred as he called his brethren and sisters, and while he was looking over them and speaking to them his voice grew stronger and stronger, his face grew brighter and brighter, and all the poetry of his nature arrayed itself in beauteous effusion, so it appeared to me, and my vision was, while he portrayed in dazzling brilliancy the victorious course of the true warrior on the side of God from step to step to the final results of, "he that overcometh shall inherit all things" [?], when they key of his voice changed all at once, it softend down, a moment of hushed silence ensued, the piercing sword in its glitter was sheathed, a deep sweet calm passed over his brow and in the transition from the present thought to its successor, his entire being seemed to transmit glows of satisfaction from its glimmerings of precious memories, like "shimmerings of sunshine" after a fertilizing shower, again he paused, as ne summons thought and takes in a fresh breath, after which he began illustrating the precious reward of the overcomer which stood up one by one in the range of my vision like jewels in a crown of glory (I fancied would look) nay it was even more than this, and I could command no imagination that was perfect enough to paint the picture of his goodness and talents combined, while telling the story of the heavenly estate. I was a youth then and had heard him preach many times, rolling out in shivering (to me) torrents of oratory "The flesh and spirit is not mixed there is a flaming sword betwixt" in substance for he was a mighty man of war on this subject, Eleazar was positive and stern in his natural make, But O [manuscript is fragmentary and content is missing from here]

NOTES

INTRODUCTION

1. Writings of Sister Susannah Liddell, Item 350f, Shaker Collection, DLC-MSS.
2. Ibid.
3. Ibid., Items 164c and 348b.
4. Ibid., Item 348a; John Patterson MacLean, *A Sketch of the Life and Labors of Richard McNemar* (Franklin, OH: Franklin *Chronicle*, 1905); John Patterson MacLean, *A Bibliography of Shaker Literature* (Columbus, OH: F. J. Heer, 1905), 4.
5. Further proof of McNemar's continuing impact on the Ohio River Valley came on July 17, 2021, at the Warren County Historical Society in Lebanon, Ohio. The museum was restoring one of the original log cabins built by the Bedle family, who were early Shaker converts, in a cordoned-off area on the museum's grounds. A group of trespassers breached the perimeter and "walked around the cabin blowing a Rams Horn, sprinkling something on the ground and praying." When museum staff asked what they were doing, they replied, "We are working against the evil the Shakers brought to the United States because all the ills of the country are tied to them." Most disturbingly, the day before, a woman had entered the museum demanding to know where Richard McNemar was buried, for what malign purpose, she did not reveal. Mary Allen to Christian Goodwillie, email message, July 17, 2021.
6. Rufus Bishop, A Daily Journal of Passing Events; Begun January the 1st, 1830, By Rufus Bishop, in the 56th Year of His Age, Journal 1830 January 1–1839 May 18 1839, Item 1, Shaker Collection, NN.

1. YOUTH

1. Richard McNemar, Diaries, Item 254, Shaker Collection, DLC-MSS.
2. Ibid., Item 255.
3. Ohio historian and collector of Shaker books and manuscripts John Patterson MacLean states, "His mother was a Knox," in *A Sketch of the Life and Labors of Richard McNemar*, 5. I am unable to locate MacLean's source for this information.
4. Tax assessment listing for Dublin Township, 1773, accessed January 9, 2018, http://www.pa-roots.com/bedford/taxlists/tl1773dublin.html.

5. Richard McNemar, Diaries, Item 254, Shaker Collection, DLC-MSS.

6. Richard McNemar, A Discourse Delivered at Harvard Aug 2d 1829 by Eleazar Wright of Union Village Ohio, 41 M 23, MWiW. An intriguing note in the Draper Manuscripts Kentucky Papers, Series CC, Volume 12, 246, Wisconsin Historical Society, states that "Dick Sommerville, near Lexington ... sd. he knew Rd. McNemar's fr., Morris McN. in Pa.—that he was a papist." Frontier conceptions of which religious affiliation and principles made one a papist were probably unclear, and this may be a reference to Church of England membership rather than Catholicism, but a definitive answer is elusive.

7. MacLean, Sketch, 4–5.

8. Patrick Hanks, ed., *A Dictionary of American Family Names*, vol. 2 (Oxford: Oxford University Press, 2003), 560; https://en.wikipedia.org/wiki/MacNamara.

9. Richard McNemar to Lucy Wright, September 13, 1807, ASC 1048, DeWint-M.

10. I thank Natasha Sumner, professor of Celtic languages and literature, Harvard University, for her valuable input on this question. In a December 17, 2020, email, Professor Sumner wrote that she would "lean toward Mac-Nuh-Mar." Carol Medlicott, professor of geography at Northern Kentucky University, also gave this question considerable thought. Based on poetic evidence, as well as communications with present-day McNemars in the Ohio Valley region, she is an advocate of the "Mic-Nee-Mer" pronunciation.

11. See William T. Swaim, "The Evolution of Ten Pre-1745 Presbyterian Societies in the Cumberland Valley," *Cumberland County History* 2, no. 1 (Summer 1985): 3–30.

12. See, for example, the hymn "Gospel Liberty" in Seth Youngs Wells, comp., *Millennial Praises* (Hancock, MA: Josiah Tallcott Jr., 1813), 272–74.

13. John B. Frantz and William Pencak, *Beyond Philadelphia: The American Revolution in the Pennsylvania Hinterland* (University Park: Pennsylvania State University Press, 1998), 118.

14. J. Simpson Africa, *History of Huntingdon and Blair Counties, Pennsylvania* (Philadelphia: Louis H. Everts, 1883), 408; McNemar give the date of 1775 in [Union Village, OH] Church Records [rear pastedown], Item 301, Shaker Collection, DLC-MSS.

15. Frantz and Pencak, *Beyond Philadelphia*, 153.

16. Africa, *History of Huntingdon*, 409.

17. Historical Committee of Huntingdon (Pa.), *Historic Huntingdon, 1767–1909: Being a Brief Account of the History of Huntingdon from Its Earliest Settlements to the Present Day* (Huntingdon, PA: Committee, 1909), 52.

18. Africa, *History of Huntingdon*, 309.

19. McNemar, Diaries, Item 254.

20. Ibid.

21. Richard McNemar to Richard McNemar Jr., October 8, 1833. Vault MSS 270, Special Collections, UPB.

22. McNemar, Diaries, Item 255.

23. George Dallas Albert, *The Frontier Forts of Western Pennsylvania* (n.p.: Clarence M. Busch, State Printer of Pennsylvania, 1896), 382.

24. The *Carlisle Gazette* carried advertisements for a singing school conducted by Ishmael Spicer (October 13, 1790) and a subsequent advertisement for a tunebook compiled by Andrew Adgate and Spicer that would be sold in town (April 20, 1791). The *Uranian Harmony* by D. Russ was also advertised in the newspapers on August 10, 1791. Karl Kroeger reports that singing master, composer, and tunebook compiler Asahel Benham taught a singing

school in Carlisle in 1790. Karl Kroeger, ed., *Two Connecticut Composers: The Collected Works of Asahel Benham and Merit Woodruff* (New York: Garland, 1995), xxi.

25. McNemar, Diaries, Item 255.

26. Ibid., Item 254.

27. John McNemar appears on the 1790 Federal Census as a resident of Washington County, Ohio. He is listed as "John McNemarre."

28. Information on Robert Newell was located on ancestry.com: accessed April 21, 2020, https://www.ancestry.com/family-tree/person/tree/161077080/person/162105058392/facts?_phsrc=PXD6&_phstart=successSource; also *History of the County of Westmoreland, Pennsylvania* (Philadelphia: L. H. Everts, 1882), 537.

29. McNemar, Diaries, Item 254.

30. "Morris McNamar" appears on the 1789 assessment roll for Armagh Township, as published in *History of That Part of the Susquehanna and Juniata Valleys, Embraced in the Counties of Mifflin, Juniata, Perry, Union and Snyder, in the Commonwealth of Pennsylvania* (Philadelphia: Everts, Peck & Richards, 1886), 522. He is listed on the 1790 Federal Census for Mifflin County, Pennsylvania, as the head of a family with one free white male and one free white female. In 1791, he is included (as "Morris McNamara") on the assessment roll for Union Township (formed from the western end of Armagh Township, Mifflin County) as the owner of one hundred acres, as published in *History . . . of the Susquehanna and Juniata Valleys*, 617. This is the last reference I have located to Morris McNemar.

31. Benjamin Seth Youngs, Diary, 1805, ASC 859, DeWint-M.

32. John C. Otto, *An Inaugural Essay on Epilepsy* (Philadelphia: Lang & Ustick, 1796), 5.

33. McNemar states that he attended McPherrin's ordination in July 1790. However, according to a brief biography of McPherrin in Joseph Smith, *Old Redstone, or, Historical Sketches of Western Presbyterianism* (Philadelphia: Lippincott, Grambo, 1854), 367, McPherrin was ordained on September 22, 1791, and made pastor of Salem and Unity Congregations in Westmoreland County, Pennsylvania.

34. McNemar, Diaries, Item 255.

35. Smith, *Old Redstone*, 125.

36. David Elliott, *The Life of the Rev. Elisha Macurdy* (Allegheny, PA: Kennedy & Brother, 1848), 21.

37. Elliott, *Life of the Rev. Elisha Macurdy*, 254. McNemar, Diaries, Item 255. In his diary (Item 253) and in a letter to Rufus Bishop dated March 10, 1836 (IV:A-84, OClWHi), McNemar gives the date of this event as March 13, 1790, but according to his diary (Item 255), 1791 appears to be the correct year: "In the spring of 1791, I went to Salem, & took up school there my first visit was with Elisha McCurdy toward the lattr part of Feb. 7."

38. George P. Hutchinson, *The History behind the Reformed Presbyterian Church, Evangelical Synod* (Cherry Hill, NJ: Mack, 1974), 40.

39. McNemar, Diaries, Items 254 and 255.

40. Ibid., Item 254.

41. Richard McNemar to Rufus Bishop, March 10, 1836. IV:A-84, Shaker Collection, OClWHi.

42. John H. Wigger, "Taking Heaven by Storm: Enthusiasm and Early American Methodism, 1770–1820," *Journal of the Early Republic* 14, no. 2 (Summer 1994): 167–94.

43. Robert Davidson, *History of the Presbyterian Church in the State of Kentucky* (New York: Robert Carter, 1847), 109.

44. McNemar, Diaries, Item 255.

2. WESTWARD MIGRATION AND EDUCATION

1. Frazer Ells Wilson, "St. Clair's Defeat," *American Monthly Magazine* 21, no. 1 (July 1902): 7–19.

2. Richard McNemar, Diaries, Item 255, Shaker Collection, DLC-MSS. In McNemar, Diaries, Item 253, he gives November 8, 1790, as the date of his arrival.

3. James Kendall Hosmer, *A Short History of the Mississippi Valley* (Boston and New York: Houghton Mifflin, 1901), 96.

4. James B. Finley and W. P. Strickland, eds., *Autobiography of Rev. James B. Finley; or, Pioneer Life in the West* (Cincinnati: Methodist Book Concern, 1853), 23–26. Finley erroneously dates this journey to the autumn of 1788. In fact, it seems to have taken place in late 1791, as McNemar states. The Transylvania Presbytery received Robert W. Finley for the first time at their February 28, 1792, meeting at Cane Run Church. See Transylvania Presbytery, Minutes, vol. 1, 60, Louisville Presbyterian Theological Seminary, E. M. White Library. Additionally, according to Robert Davidson, *History of the Presbyterian Church in the State of Kentucky* (New York: Robert Carter, 1847), Marshall did not enter Kentucky as a missionary until 1791 (p. 106), and Allen not until 1792 (p. 108). So, it appears that Finley has muddled his dates somewhat, which is understandable, since he made the trip as a ten-year-old and wrote about it for the first time at the age of sixty-five in 1846, and published this narrative in 1853.

5. James B. Finley, "Reminiscences of Early Life," *Ladies Repository* 6, no. 6 (June 1846): 165.

6. Craig Thompson Friend, *Along the Maysville Road: The Early American Republic in the Trans-Appalachian West* (Knoxville: University of Tennessee Press, 2005), xvi–2. Information on the 1790 Census in Kentucky located at this site: accessed March 10, 2012, www.kykinfolk.com/carroll/1790census.htm. This census was conceived when Kentucky was still a part of Virginia, but was conducted shortly after its separation into a territory.

7. McNemar, Diaries, Item 255. Caldwell appears as a resident of North Huntington, Pennsylvania, in the 1790 Federal Census. In Transylvania Presbytery, Minutes, vol. 1, 114, at their April 24, 1794, meeting, Caldwell was appointed as a collector of funds for the Cane Ridge congregation to support the education of serious students.

8. Joseph Smith, *Old Redstone, or, Historical Sketches of Western Presbyterianism* (Philadelphia: Lippincott, Grambo, 1854), 456.

9. See Christian Goodwillie, "First in the West: The Shaker Experience of Visionary Malcham Worley and his Family," *American Communal Societies Quarterly* 16, no. 2 (April 2022): 84–141, for a biography of Worley and his family. Shaker and non-Shaker manuscript records spell Malcham Worley's first name in a variety of ways, including the standard "Malcolm" with a second *l*, "Malcom" with no second *l*, and "Malcham." He seems to have preferred "Malcham."

10. H. Clark Dean, "Caleb Worley (Say 1730–circa 1790) of Virginia and Kentucky, Grandson of Francis Worley of Pennsylvania," *American Genealogist* 70, no. 2 (April 1995): 75–81. Dean lists thirteen children of Caleb and Rebecca Worley as given in Rebecca's will, whereas Malcolm Worley told Richard McNemar in 1838 that there were fifteen children, two having died in infancy; see Union Village, Ohio, Church Records [Conversation with Malcolm Worley, March 4, 1838], Item 301, Shaker Collection, DLC-MSS.

11. See Levi Purviance, *The Biography of Elder David Purviance* (Dayton, OH: Published for the Author, 1848), 287, for details on Worley's family. See *Catalogue of the Officers and Alumni of Washington and Lee University, Lexington, Virginia: 1749–1888* (Baltimore: John

Murphy, 1888), 52, for Worley's graduation record. A biography of Joseph H. Daviess in William B. Allen, *A History of Kentucky* (Louisville, KY: Bradley & Gilbert, 1872), 251, notes that Daviess was born on March 4, 1774, moved to Kentucky in 1779, and "at the age of eleven years Joseph was sent to a grammar school taught by a Mr. Worley, where he continued about two years, making considerable progress in the English and the Latin languages." Worley is first listed as an elder in the Transylvania Presbytery, Minutes, vol. 1, 63, at their April 24, 1792, meeting. Worley was present at the same capacity at the presbytery's meeting on July 24, 1793, see Transylvania Presbytery, Minutes, vol. 1, 91; April 22, 1794, see Transylvania Presbytery, Minutes, vol. 1, 108; October 7, 1794, see Transylvania Presbytery, Minutes, vol. 1, 129.

12. McNemar, Diaries, Item 255; McNemar, Diaries, Item 253. McNemar gives March 31, 1791, as the date of his visit to Cincinnati.

13. Benjamin Seth Youngs, Diary, ASC 859, DeWint-M.

14. McNemar, Diaries, Item 255.

15. Ibid. Not much is known of John Luckey, but an amusing anecdote survives in the collection of early Kentucky historian Rev. John D. Shane's notes, as published in Lucien Beckner, ed., "Reverend John D. Shane's Notes on Interviews, in 1844, with Mrs. Hinds and Patrick Scott of Bourbon County," *Filson Club History Quarterly* 10, no. 3 (July 1936): 174. Luckey and Col. James Smith were trying to gather a congregation and, being short of possible members, were considering adding a former follower of seceding Presbyterian Adam Rankin. Smith said to Luckey: "'Well, Brother John, what do you think of him?' Luckey replied, 'Well I reckon if we canna get hewn stone, we must tak donics.'" A search of a number of dictionaries of old Scots language hasn't yielded a definitive meaning for "donics," but a possible explanation is the word "doon," which can mean the fine chaff or dust left after meal is ground.

16. *Record of Marriages in Bourbon County Kentucky, for the Period of Years 1785 to 1851, Inclusive*, 33, Kentucky Department of Libraries and Archives, Frankfort, KY. McNemar's original marriage license is preserved in the Bourbon County Clerk's Office, Paris, Kentucky.

17. John Luckey family tree can be found on ancestry.com: accessed May 14, 2020, https://www.ancestry.com/family-tree/person/tree/31313464/person/180196042200/facts.

18. John Luckey is listed as an elder as early as the October 5, 1790, Transylvania Presbytery meeting at Walnut Hill Church. Transylvania Presbytery, Minutes, vol. 1, 42.

19. Bourbon County, Will Book G, Kentucky Department of Libraries and Archives, Frankfort, KY, 179. Seely's, or Celia's (later surnamed Anderson), birthdate is given in Union Village, Ohio, Membership List Compiled from Various Sources by Oliver C. Hampton, 1805–1898, III:B-33, OClWHi.

20. Index of Names, microfilm reel 123, Shaker Collection, OClWHi.

21. Finley and Strickland, *Autobiography of Rev. James B. Finley*, 113–14.

22. "Memoir of Judge Trimble," *American Jurist and Law Magazine* 1, January and April 1829, 151. Identification of this institution as Finley's is further cemented by the statement in this memoir that the Bourbon Academy began to decline in 1796 due to the loss of its principal. This was the same year Finley was finally disgraced for habitual public drunkenness.

23. Stephen Aron, *How the West Was Lost: The Transformation of Kentucky from Daniel Boone to Henry Clay* (Baltimore: Johns Hopkins University Press, 1996), 172.

24. Davidson, *History of the Presbyterian Church*, 83.

25. Transylvania Presbytery, Minutes, vol. 1, 119–21.

26. James Smith and Joseph Darlinton, eds., *An Account of the Remarkable Occurrences in the Life and Travels of Col. James Smith* (Cincinnati: Robert Clarke, 1870), viii.

27. Smith and Darlinton, *Account of the Remarkable Occurrences*, v. See Patrick Spero, *Frontier Rebels: The Fight for Independence in the American West, 1765–1776* (New York: W. W. Norton, 2018), for the best recent treatment of James Smith's experiences as a captive of Native Americans and his rebellion against British authority.

28. John B. Frantz and William Pencak, *Beyond Philadelphia: The American Revolution in the Pennsylvania Hinterland* (University Park: Pennsylvania State University Press, 1998), 112–13.

29. Smith and Darlinton, *Account of the Remarkable Occurrences*, 131–38.

30. Transylvania Presbytery, Minutes, vol. 1, 138.

31. Ibid., 147–48.

32. McNemar, Diaries, Item 255.

33. Davidson, *History of the Presbyterian Church*, 110.

34. E. Rankin Huston, *History of the Huston Families and Their Descendants, 1450–1912* (Mechanicsburg, PA: Carlisle, 1912), 195–96. Peter Houston lived a remarkably long life, from 1764 to 1854. In 1842, he wrote down his reminiscences of Daniel Boone and the conflict attending the settlement of Kentucky. This manuscript has since been published as Peter Houston and Ted Belue, eds., *A Sketch of the Life and Character of Daniel Boone* (Mechanicsburg, PA: Stackpole, 1997).

35. Transylvania Presbytery, Minutes, vol. 1, 169–75.

36. Ibid., 183–87, 194–98.

37. Ibid., 189. A letter addressed to "Dear Matty," apparently a relative of John Dunlavy's, written by an unknown Shaker before 1875 (based on internal evidence) contains this physical description of John Dunlavy, Item 355l, Shaker Collection, DLC-MSS; Gwendolyn Dunlevy Kelley, *A Genealogical History of the Dunlevy Family* (Columbus, OH: Issued for Private Distribution, 1901), 220, 233, 247 (p. 233 notes that the names "Francis" and "John" do not appear in Canonsburg Academy records. Only the name "James Dunlevy" appears in 1791; this may have been John, as there was no James Dunlevy in the family); https://en.wikipedia.org/wiki/History_of_Washington_%26_Jefferson_College; https://en.wikipedia.org/wiki/John_McMillan%27s_Log_School. It is possible that the Dunlavy brothers instead attended the nearby academy of Presbyterian minister Thaddeus Dod, according to this source: Richard Beard, *Brief Biographical Sketches of Some of the Early Ministers of the Cumberland Presbyterian Church, Second Series* (Nashville, TN: Cumberland Presbyterian Board of Education, 1874), 48. This school also became part of Washington & Jefferson College.

38. Transylvania Presbytery, Minutes, vol. 1, 203–204, 206–207.

39. "Trial of Robert Finley, 1795," #92 1123, PPPrHi. See also ibid., 208.

40. MS F 49, Acc. no. 76385, PPPrHi.

41. Transylvania Presbytery, Minutes, vol. 1, 208–209.

42. Ibid., vol. 2, 68, 74, 82–83. John Dunlavy's assigned scripture was Acts 4:8–12.

43. Index of Names, microfilm reel 123.

44. Transylvania Presbytery, Minutes, vol. 2, 103.

45. See *Catalogue of the Officers and Alumni*, 52, for Houston's graduation record.

46. Transylvania Presbytery, Minutes, vol. 2, 109–10, 114, 124.

47. McNemar, Diaries, Item 255.

48. Transylvania Presbytery, Minutes, vol. 2, 127–33.

49. Ibid., 134.
50. Ibid., 143, 145–46.
51. Ibid., 159.
52. Ibid., 209–13.
53. Ibid., 176–77.
54. McNemar, Diaries, Item 255.
55. W. H. Perrin et al., *Kentucky: A History of the State* (Louisville, KY: F. A. Battey, 1887), 609.
56. Cabin Creek Presbyterian Church Records, 1805–1839, M-789, KyU, 4.
57. McNemar, Diaries, Item 255.
58. Transylvania Presbytery, Minutes, vol. 2, 181.
59. Ibid., 201.

3. ORDINATION

1. Transylvania Presbytery, Minutes, vol. 2, Louisville Presbyterian Theological Seminary, E. M. White Library, 203–204.
2. Although these questions are not recorded verbatim in the minutes of the presbytery (they never are, being formulaic), they are found printed in *The Constitution of the Presbyterian Church in the United States of America* (Philadelphia: Robert Aitken, 1797), 408–409.
3. Transylvania Presbytery, Minutes, vol. 2, 202–206. John Dunlavy served as clerk for this meeting of the presbytery, and, accordingly, he personally recorded the record of events in the manuscript minutes.
4. Cabin Creek Presbyterian Church Records, 1805–1839, 5–8, M-789, KyU. For a discussion of the concept of "experimental religion" in Presbyterianism, see Sherman Isbell, "Recovering Experimental Religion": accessed March 11, 2012, www.the-highway.com/Recovering-Experimental-Religion_Isbell.html.
5. Transylvania Presbytery, Minutes, vol. 2, 214–16, 218–19.
6. Barton W. Stone, *The Biography of Elder Barton Warren Stone, Written by Himself* (Cincinnati: J. A. James and U. P. James, 1847), 29–30.
7. Cabin Creek Presbyterian Church Records, 9–10.
8. Transylvania Presbytery, Minutes, vol. 2, 228–30.
9. Washington, First Presbytery (Pres. Ch. in the U.S.A.), Minutes and Records, 1799–1810, 1–6, Vault BX 8958.W199 A3 v. 1, PPPrHi. The location of Johnston's Fork was established by a reference in Fortescue Cuming, *Sketches of a Tour to the Western Country* (Pittsburgh: Cramer, Spear, and Eichbaum, 1810), 153.
10. *Acts and Proceedings of the General Assembly of the Presbyterian Church . . . May 16, 1799* (Philadelphia: William W. Woodward, 1799), 13.
11. Ibid., 19.
12. Richard McNemar, Diaries, Item 255, Shaker Collection, DLC-MSS.
13. Washington, First Presbytery, Minutes and Records, 7–10.
14. For the location of Orangedale, see R. C. Galbraith, *The History of the Chillicothe Presbytery* (Chillicothe, OH: Scioto Gazette, 1889), 26. Washington, First Presbytery, Minutes and Records, 11–12; Union Village, Ohio, Church Records, 52, Item 301, DLC-MSS.
15. McNemar, Diaries, Item 255. A search for deeds to land owned by McNemar in Mason County, Kentucky, yielded no results.

16. See Andrew Lee Feight, "James Blythe and the Slavery Controversy in the Presbyterian Churches of Kentucky, 1791–1802," *Register of the Kentucky Historical Society* 102, no. 1 (Winter 2004): 13–38, for an excellent discussion of Presbyterians and the issue of slavery.

17. Notes by Union Village Sister Susannah Cole Liddell circa 1903 state, "Feb 28 (1817) Celia Anderson (colored) died today, aged 27. Hester thinks she was raised in John Dunlavy's family her mother John Dunlavy's slave her given name Cloe, or else Cloe was R McNemar's slave I have often hear Vincy talk about a Cloe a colored woman of her acquaintance," Liddell, Writings, Item 250, DLC-MSS.

18. Washington, First Presbytery, Minutes and Records, 13–17.

19. Index of Names, microfilm reel 123, Shaker Collection, OClWHi.

20. Washington, First Presbytery, Minutes and Records, 18–30.

21. Ibid.

22. Cabin Creek Presbyterian Church Records, 10–11.

23. W. W. Woodward, *Increase of Piety, or the Revival of Religion in the United States of America* (Philadelphia: W. W. Woodward, 1802), 97–98. The letter is also reprinted in W. W. Woodward, *Increase of Piety, or the Revival of Religion in the United States of America* (Newburyport, MA: Angier March, 1802), 104–105. I thank David D. Newell for bringing this reference to my attention.

24. Richard McNemar, *The Kentucky Revival, or, A Short History of the Late Extraordinary Out-Pouring of the Spirit of God, in the Western States of America* (Albany, NY: E. and E. Hosford, 1808), 71.

25. "Chambersburg (Pen.) Nov. 13," *Hartford Courant* (Hartford, CT), December 28, 1801. This article features McNemar (spelled "M'Namaar") and Barton W. Stone.

26. Washington, First Presbytery, Minutes and Records, 31–34; Gwendolyn Dunleavy Kelley, *A Genealogical History of the Dunlevy Family* (Columbus, OH: Issued for Private Distribution, 1901), 247.

27. Robert Davidson, *History of the Presbyterian Church in the State of Kentucky* (New York: Robert Carter, 1847), 221–22.

28. Washington, First Presbytery, Minutes and Records, 34–44.

29. Ibid.

4. REVIVAL

1. James McGready, "A Short Narrative of the Revival of Religion in Logan County," *Western Missionary Magazine*, February 1, 1803, 27.

2. John B. Boles, *The Great Revival: Beginnings of the Bible Belt* (Lexington: University Press of Kentucky, 1996), 47–58.

3. John Rankin Sr., "Autobiography," in Record Book A, South Union, Kentucky, KyBgW-K.

4. Richard McNemar, *The Kentucky Revival, or, A Short History of the Late Extraordinary Out-Pouring of the Spirit of God, in the Western States of America* (Albany, NY: E. and E. Hosford, 1808), 21.

5. Ibid., 29.

6. Barton Warren Stone, *The Biography of Elder Barton Warren Stone, Written by Himself* (Cincinnati): J. A. James and U. P. James, 1847), 45.

7. McNemar, *Kentucky Revival*, 21–23.

8. *Acts and Proceedings of the General Assembly of the Presbyterian Church ... in the Year 1801* (Philadelphia: R. Aitken, 1801), 8–9.

9. McNemar, *Kentucky Revival*, 23–25.

10. John Lyle, Diary (typed transcript), 8–9, KyHi.

11. Washington, First Presbytery, Minutes and Records, 41, PPPrHi.

12. Stone, *Biography of Elder Barton Warren Stone*, 37, 39–42. Douglas Winiarski has conducted extensive research documenting the outbreak of physical manifestations such as the jerks; see Douglas L. Winiarski, "Shakers & Jerkers: Letters from the 'Long Walk,' 1805, Part 1," *Journal of East Tennessee History* 89 (2017): 90–110; Douglas L. Winiarski, "Shakers & Jerkers: Letters from the 'Long Walk,' 1805, Part 2," *Journal of East Tennessee History* 90 (2018): 84–105; and Douglas L. Winiarski, "Seized by the Jerks: Shakers, Spirit Possession, and the Great Revival on the Trans-Appalachian Frontier," *William and Mary Quarterly*, 3d ser., 76 (2019).

13. Lyle, Diary, 10.

14. Stone, *Biography of Elder Barton Warren Stone*, 45.

15. Lyle, Diary, 10–11.

16. Richard McNemar, Diaries, Item 254, Shaker Collection, DLC-MSS.

17. Washington, First Presbytery, Minutes and Records, 45.

18. Lyle, Diary, 16–17.

19. Sam Haselby, "Sovereignty and Salvation on the Frontier of the Early American Republic," *Past and Present*, no. 215 (May 2012): 166.

20. McNemar, *Kentucky Revival*, 34–35, 39.

21. McNemar, Diaries, Item 255.

22. McNemar, *Kentucky Revival*, 20.

23. Washington, First Presbytery, Minutes and Records, 46–8, 51.

24. David Spinning, A Short Sketch of the Life of David Spinning, Comprising His Dietetic, His Moral & Religious Experience, MS 119, Box 2, Item 13, OHi.

25. Spinning, Short Sketch of the Life of David Spinning.

26. Cabin Creek Presbyterian Church Records, 1805–1839, M-789, 12–13, KyU.

27. Ibid., 14–16.

28. Ibid., 21–23.

29. Presbytery of Springfield, *An Apology for Renouncing the Jurisdiction of the Synod of Kentucky* (Lexington, KY: Joseph Charless, 1804), 4–7.

30. Washington, First Presbytery, Minutes and Records, 53–54.

31. Presbytery of Springfield, *Apology*, 4–7.

32. Ibid., 7–8.

33. Washington, First Presbytery, Minutes and Records, 54–55.

34. Presbytery of Springfield, *Apology*, 9–10. There is a misprint in the original 1804 Lexington imprint, where McNemar is acknowledging the truth of the first allegation against him. Printed is "Rom. 10, 4," but the scripture cited is Romans 10:14.

35. Cabin Creek Presbyterian Church Records, 24–26.

36. Presbytery of Springfield, *Apology*, 11. In the *Apology*, it is stated that McNemar went to Turtle Creek in March. McNemar makes the same statement in his Diaries, Item 255.

37. Union Village, Ohio, Church Records, 53, Item 301, Shaker Collection, DLC-MSS.

38. Henry Howe, *Historical Collections of Ohio, Vol. II, Ohio Centennial Edition* (Norwalk, OH: Laning, 1896), 743.

39. Ibid., 740.

40. Transylvania Presbytery, Minutes, vol. 2, Louisville Presbyterian Theological Seminary, E. M. White Library, 159.

41. See John Zimkus, "Beedle's Station and the Shakers: A Struggle of Tears," Warren County History Center, Lebanon, OH, ca. 2005, for more information on the early settlement of Bedle's Station.

42. Josiah Morrow, "Richard McNemar: Remarkable Story of an Eloquent Pioneer Preacher," *Western Star* (Lebanon, OH), November 28, 1907. Anthony Howard Dunlevy was born in 1793 and would have been nine when McNemar was appointed to Turtle Creek. He died on December 1, 1881.

43. Presbytery of Springfield, *Apology*, 12–13.

44. Washington, First Presbytery, Minutes and Records, 66.

45. Cabin Creek Presbyterian Church Records, 26–34.

46. Presbytery of Springfield, *Apology*, 11–13. Here it is noted that an unnamed elder of Kemper's congregation accused McNemar. The Washington Presbytery Minutes, p. 65, name the elders present as Joseph Reeder, Robert Gill, Stephen Wheeler, and Moses Miller. In "Historical Sketch of the First Presbyterian Church, Cincinnati," *Presbyterian Magazine*, June 1852, 2, 265, Reeder and Miller are named as ruling elders in Kemper's congregation.

47. Presbytery of Springfield, *Apology*, 13–16.

48. Washington, First Presbytery, Minutes and Records, 65–73.

49. Kentucky Synod, Minutes, 1802–1883, Louisville Presbyterian Theological Seminary, E. M. White Library.

50. Washington, First Presbytery, Minutes and Records, 74–83; Presbytery of Springfield, *Apology*, 20.

51. Ibid.; ibid., 17.

52. C. A. Weslager, *The Log Cabin in America* (New Brunswick, NJ: Rutgers University Press, 1969), 72–74. See also "The Log Architecture of Ohio," *Ohio History* 80, nos. 3/4 (Summer/Autumn 1971, special issue), entirely devoted to this topic. Double-pen structures are discussed on pp. 242–43.

53. David Rice, *A Sermon on the Present Revival of Religion in This Country* (Lexington, KY: Joseph Charless, 1803), 9–10.

54. Kentucky Synod, Minutes.

55. Ibid.

56. Ibid.

57. Ibid.

58. Ibid.

59. Ibid.; Stone, *Biography of Elder Barton Warren Stone*, 47.

60. Presbytery of Springfield, *Apology*, 32–34.

5. REBELLION

1. Kentucky Synod, Minutes, Louisville Presbyterian Theological Seminary, E. M. White Library; for information on David Rice, see R. A. Johnstone, *Historical Sketch of the Presbytery of Transylvania, Kentucky* (Louisville, KY: Printed by Bradley & Gilbert, 1876), 12.

2. Robert Davidson, *History of the Presbyterian Church in the State of Kentucky* (New York: Robert Carter, 1847), 202–3.

3. Barton F. Stone, *The Biography of Elder Barton Warren Stone, Written by Himself* (Cincinnati, OH: Published for the author by J. A. James and U. P. James, 1847), 47.

4. Kentucky Synod, Minutes.

5. Presbytery of Springfield, *An Apology for Renouncing the Jurisdiction of the Synod of Kentucky* (Lexington, KY: Printed by Joseph Charless, 1804), 37–39.

6. Ibid., 40–41.

7. Kentucky Synod, Minutes.

8. Synod of Kentucky, *A Circular Letter from the Synod of Kentucky, to the Churches under their Care* (Lexington, KY: Joseph Charless, 1803), 3–4, 15–16, 18, 21–23, 28.

9. Richard McNemar, *The Kentucky Revival, or, A Short History of the Late Extraordinary Out-Pouring of the Spirit of God, in the Western States of America* (Albany, NY: Reprinted by E. and E. Hosford, 1808), 42–44.

10. Worley's land was located in section twenty-four of the fourth township of the third (or military) range. The deed is in the Land Record No. 1, Warren County, Edna L. Bowyer Records Center and Archives, 42–43. Davidson, *History of the Presbyterian Church*, 337, notes with derision Worley's involvement in antislavery measures with the Presbyterian Church as early as 1795.

11. See front matter map "A plan of the section of land on which the Believers live in the state of Ohio, Nov. 7th, 1807." G4084.O825 1807 .P6, Library of Congress Geography and Map Division Washington, DC.

12. David Darrow and John Meacham to David Meacham, March 19, 1806, IV:A-66. OClWHi.

13. Josiah Morrow, "The First Shaker Convert: West of Alleghany Mountains was Malcham Worley at Turtlecreek, March 1805," *Western Star* (Lebanon, OH), January 25, 1912. Anthony Howard Dunlevy was born in 1793 and would have been twelve in 1805 when Worley converted. Dunlevy died on December 1, 1881.

14. Levi Purviance, *The Biography of Elder David Purviance* (Dayton, OH: Published for the author, 1848), 287.

15. David Spinning, A Short Sketch of the Life of David Spinning, comprising his Dietetic, his Moral & Religious Experience, MS 119, box 2, item 13, OHi.

16. Stone, *Biography*, 147.

17. Presbytery of Springfield, *Apology*, 62, 93, 108–9, 113, 122, 124.

18. I. A., *Two Letters Written by a Gentleman to His Friend in Kentucky* (Lexington, KY: Printed by Joseph Charless, 1804), 44–45. Although Worley and Purviance are not named, it is clear from other sources such as McNemar's *Kentucky Revival* and Purviance's *Biography of Elder David Purviance* that Worley and Purviance must have been the men I. A. was commenting on, since they were the only quasi-official appointments of the Springfield Presbytery before they disbanded. *Two Letters* is especially harsh toward Robert Marshall, who is referred to as "Mr. M" throughout.

19. McNemar, *Kentucky Revival*, 53–54. Barton W. Stone, *Atonement: The Substance of Two Letters Written to a Friend* (Lexington, KY: Printed by Joseph Charless, 1805). According to Robert Marshall and John Thompson, Stone wrote this in the winter of 1804, and it is also from them that we know the letters were written to Matthew Houston; see Robert Marshall and John Thompson, *A Brief Historical Account of Sundry Things in the Doctrines and State of the Christian, or as It Is Commonly Called, the Newlight Church* (Cincinnati, OH: Published by J. Carpenter, 1811), 7.

20. Stone, *Atonement*, 24.

21. McNemar, *Kentucky Revival*, 53–54.

22. Marshall and Thompson, *Brief Historical Account*, 6.

23. McNemar, *Kentucky Revival*, 46–48.
24. Ibid., 49–53.
25. Marshall and Thompson, *Brief Historical Account*, 4.
26. Rice Haggard, *An Address to the Different Religious Societies on the Sacred Import of the Christian Name* (Lexington, KY: Printed by Joseph Charless, 1804). John B. Boles, *The Great Revival: Beginnings of the Bible Belt* (Lexington: University Press of Kentucky, 1996), 154–55.
27. McNemar, *Kentucky Revival*, 21–22.
28. Marshall and Thompson, *Brief Historical Account*, 3–5, 22.
29. McNemar, *Kentucky Revival*, 56–57.
30. Ibid., 58–60.
31. Ibid., 61–63.
32. Ibid., 61–63.
33. Ibid., 60.

6. REBIRTH

1. Barton Warren Stone, *The Biography of Elder Barton Warren Stone, Written by Himself* (Cincinnati: J. A. James and U. P. James, 1847), 62.
2. Benjamin Seth Youngs, Diary, 1805, ASC 859, DeWint-M.
3. See Carol Medlicott, *Issachar Bates: A Shaker's Journey* (Hanover, NH: University Press of New England, 2013), for an excellent biography of Bates, a detailed account of the 1805 missionary journey, and a thorough analysis of the western expansion of Shakerism. See Douglas L. Winiarski, "Shakers and Jerkers: Letters from the 'Long Walk,' 1805, Part 1," *Journal of East Tennessee History* 89 (2017), for a wonderful illustrated account of the Shaker missionaries' journey, with much contextual information.
4. Benjamin Seth Youngs to Ebenezer Cooley, March 20, 1806, IV:A-66, OClWHi. John Meacham to Ministry, New Lebanon, New York, January 31, 1805, IV:A-66, OClWHi.
5. Youngs, Diary.
6. John Meacham to Ministry, New Lebanon, New York; Youngs, Diary, 22–23.
7. Youngs, Diary.
8. Ibid.
9. Ibid.
10. Ebenezer Cooley, Stephen Markham, David Meacham, and Amos Hammond, in behalf of the Church, December 26, 1804, IV:A-31, OClWHi.
11. Youngs, Diary.
12. Ibid.
13. Transylvania Presbytery, Minutes, vol. 3, Louisville Presbyterian Theological Seminary, E. M. White Library, 107–108.
14. Youngs, Diary.
15. Stone, *Biography of Elder Barton Warren Stone*, 62.
16. Youngs, Diary.
17. Ibid. The exact magazine article used by the missionaries remains a mystery. Youngs's diary cites "a N.Y. Magazine." Searches of relevant New York magazines for that time period fail to yield any article about the Shakers. The most likely candidate for the article seems to be "A Short Account of the People Known by the Name of Shakers, or Shaking Quakers," *Theological Magazine* 1, no. 1 (September/October 1795): 81–88. This text was later reprinted

as an appendage to Rowland Hill, *Village Dialogues: Between Farmer Littleworth and Thomas Newman, Rev. Mr. Lovegood, Parson Dolittle and Others* (Danville, KY: s.n., 1805). The only known copy, held by Hamilton College, is incomplete, with all after p. 2 missing.

18. Youngs, Diary.
19. Ibid.
20. Richard McNemar, *The Kentucky Revival, or, A Short History of the Late Extraordinary Out-Pouring of the Spirit of God, in the Western States of America* (Albany, NY: E. and E. Hosford, 1808), 75.
21. Youngs, Diary.
22. Ibid.
23. Ibid. For McNemar's reaction to Worley's conversion, see McNemar, *Kentucky Revival*, 81.
24. Presbytery of Springfield, *Observations on Church Government* (Albany, NY: E. and E. Hosford, 1808), 3–4.
25. Youngs, Diary.
26. Ibid.
27. McNemar, *Kentucky Revival*, 78–79.
28. Youngs, Diary. See McNemar, *Kentucky Revival*, 82, for an encapsulation of God/Christ speaking in the Shakers.
29. Youngs, Diary.
30. Ibid.
31. Ibid.
32. Ibid.
33. Ibid.
34. Ibid.
35. Ibid.
36. Ibid.
37. Ibid.
38. Ibid.

7. THE NEW AND LIVING WAY

1. John Meacham to Ministry, New Lebanon, New York, April 27, 1805, IV:A-66, OClWHi.
2. Benjamin Seth Youngs, Diary, 1805, ASC 859, DeWint-M.
3. Ibid.
4. Ibid.
5. Ibid.
6. Ibid. Dunlavy's letter is not known to survive in the original; it is transcribed in Susannah C. Liddell to John Patterson MacLean, April 19, 1903, IV:A-75, OClWHi. Liddell gives the date of Dunlavy's letter as 1804, thus, John Dunlavy to Richard McNemar, 1804, IV:A-75, OClWHi.
7. Youngs, Diary, 109–11; John Meacham to Ministry, New Lebanon, New York, June 1, 1805, IV:A-66, OClWHi.
8. John Meacham to Ministry, New Lebanon, New York, June 1, 1805.
9. Youngs, Diary.
10. Ibid.

11. Ibid.
12. Ibid.
13. Ibid.
14. John Meacham to Ministry, New Lebanon, New York, June 1, 1805.
15. Youngs, Diary, 128–29.
16. John Meacham to Ministry, New Lebanon, New York, June 1, 1805.
17. Reuben Rathbone, *Reasons Offered for Leaving the Shakers* (Pittsfield, MA: Chester Smith, 1800). For more information on the Rathbun family and annotated copies of their anti-Shaker writings, see Christian Goodwillie, ed., *Writings of Shaker Apostates and Anti-Shakers, 1782–1850*, vol. 1 (London: Pickering and Chatto, 2013).
18. "A Short Account of the People Known by the Name of Shakers, or Shaking Quakers," *Theological Magazine* 1, no. 1 (September/October 1795): 81–88; republished as an appendix to Rowland Hill, *Village Dialogues: Between Farmer Littleworth and Thomas Newman, Rev. Mr. Lovegood, Parson Dolittle and Others* (Danville, KY: s.n., 1805).
19. Benjamin Seth Youngs, *Testimony of Christ's Second Appearing* (Lebanon, OH: John M'Clean, 1808), 5.
20. Youngs, Diary.
21. Richard McNemar to Lucy Wright, September 13, 1807, ASC 1048, DeWint-M.
22. Youngs, Diary. The *Observations on Church Government* was first published in 1807 as an appendix to Richard McNemar, *The Kentucky Revival, or, A Short History of the Late Extraordinary Out-Pouring of the Spirit of God, in the Western States of America* (Albany, NY: E. and E. Hosford, 1808).
23. Youngs, Diary.
24. Ibid.
25. Ibid.
26. Ibid. Esther Knox was Esther Luckey, Jennie's sister. She married John Knox. He and his brother William became Shakers, as did Esther and John's children; see Hattie S. Goodman, *The Knox Family: A Genealogical and Biographical Sketch of the Descendants of John Knox of Rowan County, North Carolina* (Richmond, VA: Whittet and Shepperson, 1905), 39–40. John Dunlavy's slave Lucy eventually opened her mind to the missionaries, converting on October 14, 1805.
27. Ministry at New Lebanon to "the Brethren at Ohio," June 19, 1805, IV:A-31, OClWHi.
28. Youngs, Diary.
29. Ibid.
30. David Darrow et al. at Union Village, Ohio, to New Lebanon, New York, December 19, 1805, Shaker Library, Box 25, Sabbathday Lake, ME.
31. Youngs, Diary; Darrow et al. at Union Village, Ohio to New Lebanon, New York.
32. Ibid.
33. Youngs, Diary.
34. Ibid.
35. John Meacham to Ministry, New Lebanon, New York, June 1, 1805.
36. For more information on the King family, see Christian Goodwillie, "The Shakers in Eighteenth-Century Newspapers. Part Three: 'Calvin' versus 'A Lover of Truth,' Abusing Caleb Rathbun, the Death of Joseph Meacham and the Tale of His Sister," *American Communal Societies Quarterly* 6, no. 1 (January 2012): 39–63; New Lebanon, NY, Daniel Miller, Domestic journal of important occurrences kept for the elder sisters at New Lebanon, 1780–1862, V:B-60, OClWHi.
37. Youngs, Diary.

38. Ibid.
39. Ibid.
40. Ibid.
41. David Darrow to Ministry, New Lebanon, New York, July 20 [must be July 30], 1805, IV:A-66, OClWHi.
42. Youngs, Diary.
43. Ibid.
44. Richard M'Nemar, *The Kentucky Revival, or, A Short History of the Late Extraordinary Out-Pouring of the Spirit of God, in the Western States of America* (Cincinnati, OH: John W. Browne, 1807), 93.
45. Youngs, Diary; Richard M'Nemar, *The Kentucky Revival, or, A Short History of the Late Extraordinary Out-Pouring of the Spirit of God, in the Western States of America* (Cincinnati: John W. Browne, 1807), 92–93.
46. Youngs, Diary.
47. Ibid.

8. COMMUNITY FOUNDATIONS

1. The Shakers separately purchased an additional 160 acres directly from Dayton, closing with him in Cincinnati on September 6, 1805. David Darrow et al. to David Meacham, New Lebanon, September 25, 1805, WRHS IV:A-66; Susannah Cole Liddell assessed the quality of McNemar's "table land" in a manuscript written for John Patterson MacLean around 1900, Item 348a, Shaker Collection, DLC-MSS.
2. Benjamin Seth Youngs, Diary, 1805, ASC 859, DeWint-M.
3. Ibid.
4. Richard McNemar to Ministry, New Lebanon, September 25, 1805, IV:A-66, OClWHi.
5. Jennie McNemar to Ministry, New Lebanon, September 25, 1805, ASC 1048, DeWint-M.
6. David Darrow et al. to David Meacham, New Lebanon.
7. Youngs, Diary; David Darrow et al. at Union Village, Ohio, to New Lebanon, New York, December 19, 180, MePosS.
8. Youngs, Diary.
9. Ibid.
10. David Meacham at New Lebanon to David Darrow et al., October 26, 1805, IV:A-31, OClWHi.
11. Youngs, Diary. For additional details on this incident, see David Darrow et al. to Ministry at New Lebanon, December 19, 1805, IV:A-66, OClWHi.
12. Youngs, Diary, 258–62. Daniel Rathbun, *A Letter, from Daniel Rathbun, of Richmond, in the County of Berkshire to James Whittacor, Chief Elder of the Church, Called Shakers* (Springfield, MA: Printing Office near the Great Ferry, 1785). Barton Warren Stone, *A Reply to John P. Campbell's Strictures on Atonement* (Lexington, KY: Joseph Charless, 1805), 67–68. The last letter in Stone's pamphlet is dated September 4, 1805, so it could not have been published before that date.
13. Union Village Shaker leadership to Lucy Wright, January 13, 1807, IV:A-67, OClWHi.
14. Youngs, Diary.
15. Ibid. For the full text, tune, and commentary on "Typical Dancing," see Seth Youngs Wells, comp., *Millennial Praises, Containing a Collection of Gospel Hymns, in Four Parts; Adapted to the Day of Christ's Second Appearing. Composed for the Use of His People* (Hancock,

MA: Josiah Tallcott Jr., 1813), and Christian Goodwillie and Jane Crosthwaite, *Millennial Praises: A Shaker Hymnal* (Amherst: University of Massachusetts Press, 2009), 65–66.

16. Youngs, Diary.

17. Ibid. For additional details on this incident, see David Darrow et al. to Ministry at New Lebanon.

18. Youngs, Diary.

19. Ibid.

20. Ibid. David Darrow et al. to Ministry at New Lebanon. Benjamin Seth Youngs to Ebenezer Cooley, December 25, 1805, IV:A-66, OClWHi.

21. Youngs, Diary.

22. Union Village Shaker leadership to Ministry, New Lebanon, March 18, 1806, ASC 1048, Winterthur, DE.

23. Record Book A, South Union, KY, KyBgW-K; Gwendolyn Dunlevy Kelley, *Genealogical History of the Dunlevy Family* (Columbus, OH: Issued for Private Distribution, 1901), 220.

24. Record Book A.

25. Ibid.

26. Ibid.

27. Ministry at New Lebanon to David Darrow et al., February 1, 1806, IV:A-31, OClWHi; David Meacham at New Lebanon to Beloved Elders, Ohio, et al., February 4, 1806, IV:A-31, OClWHi.

28. Benjamin Seth Youngs to Ebenezer Cooley.

29. Ibid.

30. David Darrow and John Meacham to David Meacham, March 19, 1806, IV:A-66, OClWHi.

31. Ministry, New Lebanon to "Beloved Brethren" at New Lebanon, April 18, 1806, IV:A-31, OClWHi.

32. Ebenezer Cooley to Benjamin Seth Youngs, May 31, 1806, IV:A-66, OClWHi.

33. Ministry, New Lebanon, to David Darrow and John Meacham, April 18, 1806, IV:A-31, OClWHi.

34. Record Book A.

35. Matthew Houston was similarly humbled by Anne Bruner at Turtle Creek on November 22, 1805. See Record Book A.

36. Record Book A. The party included Samuel Turner, Constant Moseley, Peter Pease, Ruth Farrington, Martha Sanford, Lucy Smith, Prudence Farrington, Molly Goodrich, and Ruth Darrow. John Wright accompanied them but later returned east with John Meacham on August 19, 1806.

37. David Darrow and John Meacham to "Beloved Elders" at New Lebanon, June 5, 1806, IV:A-66, OClWHi.

38. David Darrow and John Meacham to "Beloved Elders"; Record Book A; Journal of Elder Peter Pease, 1806–1815, Item 232, Shaker Collection, DLC-MSS.

39. David Darrow et al. to "Beloved Mother" at New Lebanon, August 13, 1806, IV:A-66, OClWHi.

40. Union Village Shaker leadership to Ministry, New Lebanon, August 13, 1806.

41. This manuscript is likely the "Religious Exposition Written at Turtle Creek by John Meacham [or David Darrow]," VII:B-239, OClWHi.

42. Record Book A.

43. David Darrow et al. to Ministry at New Lebanon, August 16, 1806, IV:A-66, OClWHi.
44. John Dunlavy to Ebenezer Cooley, August 17, 1806, IV:A-66, OClWHi.
45. David Meacham to David Darrow, September 23, 1806, IV:A-31, OClWHi.
46. Ministry, New Lebanon to "Beloved Brethren," Turtle Creek, October 9, 1806, IV:A-31, OClWHi.
47. Lucy Wright to David Darrow, October 9, 1806, IV:A-31, OClWHi.
48. Peter Pease to David Meacham, September 3, 1806, IV:A-66, OClWHi.
49. David Darrow to David Meacham, November 2, 1806, Item 245, Shaker Collection, DLC-MSS.
50. John Meacham to "Beloved Deacon," David Meacham, November 25, 1806, IV:A-66, OClWHi.
51. Union Village Shaker leadership to Lucy Wright.
52. Benjamin Seth Youngs, Pamphlet Journal of Union Village, 1806–1807, #10,130, NOcaS.
53. Ibid.
54. For the full text and tunes for "The Day of Redemption," see Goodwillie and Crosthwaite, *Millennial Praises*, 125–26.
55. Youngs, Pamphlet Journal.
56. David Darrow to Lucy Wright, January 12, 1807, IV:A-67, OClWHi; Union Village Shaker leadership to Lucy Wright; Youngs, Pamphlet Journal.
57. David Darrow to Lucy Wright; Union Village Shaker leadership to Lucy Wright.
58. David Darrow and John Meacham to Lucy Wright, May 15, 1807, IV:A-67, OClWHi.
59. Union Village Shaker leadership to Lucy Wright; Youngs, Pamphlet Journal.
60. David Darrow to Lucy Wright.
61. David Darrow to David Meacham, January 15, 1807, IV:A-67, OClWHi.
62. Youngs, Pamphlet Journal.
63. Ibid.

9. SHAKERS AND THE SHAWNEE PROPHET

1. Benjamin Seth Youngs, Pamphlet Journal of Union Village, 1806–1807, #10, 130, NOcaS; David Darrow to Lucy Wright, September 10, 1807, IV:A-67, OClWHi. The standard biography of Tenskwatawa is R. David Edmunds, *The Shawnee Prophet* (Lincoln: University of Nebraska Press, 1985).
2. Richard M'Nemar, *The Kentucky Revival, or, A Short History of the Late Extraordinary Out-Pouring of the Spirit of God, in the Western States of America* (Cincinnati: John W. Browne, 1807), 112.
3. M'Nemar, *Kentucky Revival*, 113.
4. Ibid., 113–17; Journal of Elder Peter Pease, Item 232, DLC-MSS.
5. Youngs, Pamphlet Journal; David Darrow and John Meacham to Lucy Wright, May 15, 1807, IV:A-67, OClWHi.
6. David Darrow and John Meacham to Lucy Wright; Youngs, Pamphlet Journal.
7. Youngs, Pamphlet Journal.
8. David Darrow and John Meacham to Lucy Wright. For the full text, tune, and commentary on this hymn, see Carol Medlicott and Christian Goodwillie, *Richard McNemar, Music, and the Western Shaker Communities: Branches of One Living Tree* (Kent, OH: Kent State University Press, 2013), 187.

9. Youngs, Pamphlet Journal.
10. Ibid.; Journal of Elder Peter Pease.
11. Youngs, Pamphlet Journal.
12. Ibid.
13. Ibid.; Peter Pease to David Meacham, July 17, 1807, IV:A-67, OClWHi.
14. Youngs, Pamphlet Journal; Journal of Elder Peter Pease.
15. Youngs, Pamphlet Journal.
16. David Darrow, Benjamin Seth Youngs, and Richard McNemar to Lallu'a tsee kah [Tenskwatawa], June 6, 1807, IV:A-67, OClWHi.
17. Lucy Wright to David Darrow, July 11, 1807, IV:A-31, OClWHi.
18. Ministry, New Lebanon to David Darrow, July 11, 1807, IV:A-31, OClWHi.
19. Youngs, Pamphlet Journal.
20. Vincy McNemar, Hymnbook and Notes, Item 349d, Shaker Collection, DLC-MSS.
21. Journal of Elder Peter Pease; Daily Record of Events of the Church Family, Union Village, OH, V:B-230, OClWHi.
22. M'Nemar, *Kentucky Revival*, 118.
23. Benjamin Seth Youngs, Issachar Bates, and Richard McNemar to Lal-lu-e-tsee-kah [Tenskwatawa], September 1, 1807, IV:A-67, OClWHi; Daily Record.
24. M'Nemar, *Kentucky Revival*, 119.

10. SHAKER PUBLICATIONS AND THE EXPANSION OF MISSIONARY EFFORTS

1. Joseph Meacham, *A Concise Statement of the Principles of the Only True Church, according According to the Gospel of the Present Appearance of Christ, as Held to and Practised upon by the True Followers of the Living Saviour, at New-Labanon, &c. By James Whittaker, Minister of the Gospel in this Day of Christ's Second Appearance. Dated October the 9th, 1785* (N.p., n.d.); Joseph Meacham, *A Concise Statement of the Principles of the Only True Church, according to the Gospel of the Present Appearance of Christ. As Held to and Practiced upon by the True Followers of the Living Saviour, at Newlebanon, &c. Together with a Letter from James Whittaker, Minister of the Gospel in This Day of Christ's Second Appearing—to His Natural Relations in England. Dated October 9th 1785* (Bennington, VT: Haswell & Russell, 1790). There are two editions of *A Concise Statement*. The 1790 edition published at Bennington, Vermont, carries clear publication information, while the other edition bears no date or place of publication. It may have been published in 1785 at Worcester, Massachusetts, but there is no definitive evidence of that.
2. Benjamin Seth Youngs, Pamphlet Journal of Union Village, 1806–1807, #10, 132, NOcaS; McNemar also traveled to Cincinnati on June 15, Journal of Elder Peter Pease, 1806–1815, Item 232, DLC-MSS.
3. Peter Pease to David Meacham, July 17, 1807, IV:A-67, OClWHi. This letter reports the cost as $150, while Deacon Peter Pease's (probably more accurate) letter of January 1, 1809, to Deacon Richard Spier states that it was $154, Item 245, Shaker Collection, DLC-MSS. The date for completion of printing is surmised by McNemar recording the Shawnee visit of August 29, 1807, in Richard McNemar, *The Kentucky Revival, or, A Short History of the Late Extraordinary Out-Pouring of the Spirit of God, in the Western States of America* (Albany, NY: E. and E. Hosford, 1808), 118.

4. Richard McNemar to Lucy Wright, September 13, 1807, ASC 1048, DeWint-M. Rufus Bishop's 1836 copy of this letter, along with two other transcripts, can found in IV:A-67, OClWHi.

5. Ibid.
6. Ibid.
7. Ibid.
8. Ministry, New Lebanon to Malcham, Worley, October 22, 1807, IV:A-31, OClWHi.
9. Journal of Elder Peter Pease; Daily Record of Events of the Church Family, Union Village, Ohio, V:B-230, OClWHi.
10. David Darrow to Ministry at New Lebanon, December 12, 1807, ASC 1048, DeWint-M.
11. Record Book A, South Union, KY, KyBgW.
12. M'Nemar, *Kentucky Revival*, 26.
13. M'Nemar, *Kentucky Revival*, 26–27.
14. David Darrow to Ministry at New Lebanon.
15. Ibid.
16. David Darrow to Nathaniel Deming, December 12, 1807, ASC 1048, DeWint-M.
17. David Darrow to Ministry at New Lebanon.
18. Peter Pease to Richard Spier, December 12, 1807, IV:A-67, OClWHi.
19. Samuel Turner to Calvin Green, February 28, 1808, IV:A-67, OClWHi.
20. Christian Goodwillie and Jane Crosthwaite, *Millennial Praises: A Shaker Hymnal* (Amherst: University of Massachusetts Press, 2009), 239.
21. https://en.wikipedia.org/wiki/Black_Joke. I thank Carol Medlicott for this information.
22. Record Book A; Union Village Leadership to New Lebanon Ministry, July 31, 1808, ASC 1048, DeWint-M.
23. Daily Record. Journal of Elder Peter Pease states that on December 23, 1807, "John McLean Recd Money to Prepare for Printing Ben Book."
24. Benjamin Seth Youngs, *Testimony of Christ's Second Appearing* (Lebanon, OH: John M'Clean, 1808), 602–603; for the text, tune, and commentary on this hymn, see Goodwillie and Crosthwaite, *Millennial Praises*, 49–51.
25. Journal of Elder Peter Pease; Record Book A.
26. McNemar, *Kentucky Revival*; Ministry, New Lebanon to David Darrow, April 28, 1808, WRHS IV:A-31, OClWHi. Another edition of *Kentucky Revival* was published by Phinehas Allen in Pittsfield, Massachusetts, in 1808. It is not known if the Shakers were involved in this publication, and few copies survive.
27. Record Book A.
28. Daily Record.
29. Record Book A.
30. Peter Pease to Richard Spier, January 1, 1809, Item 245, Shaker Collection, DLC-MSS.
31. Record Book A.
32. Union Village Shaker leadership to Lucy Wright, December 28, 1808, IV:A-67, OClWHi.
33. Union Village Leadership to New Lebanon Ministry.
34. At a meeting on Sunday, October 29, a "poetic epistle composed by Richard McNemar was read to the Believers inviting all hands to come forward tomorrow to finish the lower part of the new meetinghouse." Record Book A. The meetinghouse was completely finished on December 24, 1809, Daily Record.

35. Union Village Leadership to New Lebanon Ministry, July 31, 1808, IV:A-67, OClWHi; Early Records of Pleasant Hill, Kentucky, 1806–1836, Item 00006, Archives, SVPH.

36. See Carol Medlicott, *Issachar: A Shaker's Journey* (Hanover, NH: University Press of New England, 2013), 133–36, for an account of this journey, and Peter Cartwright's anti-Shaker efforts.

37. Record Book A.

38. Ibid.; Joseph Allen to Nathaniel Deming, April 10, 1809, IV:A-67, OClWHi.

39. Record Book A.

40. Record Book A; Joseph Allen to Nathaniel Deming.

41. The details of Slover's life can be found in *Narratives of a Late Expedition against the Indians: With an Account of the Barbarous Execution of Col. Crawford; and the Wonderful Escape of Dr. Knight and John Slover from Captivity, in 1782* (Philadelphia: Francis Bailey, 1783). Slover misremembers Lord Dunmore's War as happening in 1773 in his narrative.

42. Richard McNemar to Lawrence Roelesson, March 3, 1809, Communal Societies Collection, Hamilton College. For the full text of this letter and a lengthy introduction, see Christian Goodwillie, "Letter from Richard McNemar," *American Communal Societies Quarterly* 3, no. 3 (July 2009): 146–55.

43. Record Book A.

44. Ministry, New Lebanon to Union Village Leadership, February 23, 1809, IV:A-31, OClWHi.

45. David Darrow and Benjamin Seth Youngs to Ministry, New Lebanon, April 20, 1809, IV:A-67, OClWHi.

46. Record Book A gives April 12 as the date of departure; Pease's journal (n. 44) is an earlier source; David Darrow and Benjamin Seth Youngs to Ministry, New Lebanon; Journal of Elder Peter Pease.

47. David Darrow and Ruth Farrington to Ministry, New Lebanon, July 10, 1809, IV:A-67, OClWHi.

48. Journal of Elder Peter Pease.

49. Union Village Leadership to Ministry, New Lebanon, July 4, 1809, IV:A-67, OClWHi.

50. David Darrow and Ruth Farrington to Ministry, New Lebanon.

51. David Darrow to Lucy Wright, July 15, 1809, IV:A-67, OClWHi.

52. Journal of Elder Peter Pease; Record Book A.

53. Record Book A; Susan Liddell named Jethro Dennis as the chair thrower many years after the event in Susannah Liddell, Writings, Items 164c, 250, 348a, 348b, 348d, 348d, 349d, 350c, 350d, 350f, 352b, 352c, 355j, DLC-MSS, Item 355j. See Richard McNemar [Philos Harmoniae, pseud.], *A Selection of Hymns and Poems for the Use of Believers* (Watervliet, OH: 1833), 171–72, for the text of "Robbery." See Carol Medlicott and Christian Goodwillie, *Richard McNemar, Music, and the Western Shaker Communities: Branches of One Living Tree* (Kent, OH: Kent State University Press, 2013), 294, for more information about this poem, as well as the robbery.

54. McNemar [Philos Harmoniae, pseud.], *A Selection of Hymns and Poems for the Use of Believers* (Watervliet, OH: 1833), 171–72.

55. Some of the thieves were apprehended in Xenia, Ohio, on August 19, 1809, Record Book A.

56. Journal of Elder Peter Pease.

57. Polly Smith and her sister Peggy left Union Village with the brother of James Smith Jr. on February 24, 1810. Record Book A.

58. Smith arrived on October 24, 1809. Daily Record.

11. GOSPEL ORDER IN THE WEST, JAMES SMITH, AND THE OHIO MOB

1. David Darrow and Ruth Farrington to Ministry, New Lebanon, March 6, 1810, IV:A-68, OClWHi.
2. Ibid.
3. McNemar and Youngs left Turtle Creek for Mad River on January 3 and returned on the tenth. McNemar went again at an unknown date and returned to Turtle Creek on March 8, 1810. Journal of Elder Peter Pease, Item 232, DLC-MSS.
4. Daily Record of Events of the Church Family, Union Village, Ohio, V:B-230, OClWHi.
5. David Darrow and Ruth Farrington to Ministry, New Lebanon, March 6, 1810, IV:A-68, OClWHi.
6. David Darrow and Ruth Farrington to Ministry, New Lebanon, November 27, 1809, IV:A-67, OClWHi.
7. Bates and McNemar had set out from Turtle Creek for Busro on December 5 but had to turn back due to high waters. They returned to Turtle Creek on December 10, 1809; Journal of Elder Peter Pease, Item 232; Daily Record.
8. Daily Record.
9. Calvin Green and Seth Youngs Wells, *Testimonies of the Life, Character, Revelations and Doctrines, of Our Ever Blessed Mother Ann Lee* (Hancock, MA: 1816), 37.
10. William Deming, Journal of William's travel to the state of Ohio, 1810, ASC 818, DeWint-M.
11. "The Little Quail" was published in *Shaker and Shakeress* 3, no. 1 (January 1873): 8.
12. Ibid.
13. Record Book A, South Union, KY, KyBgW.
14. Ibid.
15. James Smith, *Shakerism Detected: Their Erroneous and Treasonous Proceedings, and False Publications Contained in Different News-papers, Exposed to Public View by the Depositions of Ten Different Persons Living in Various Parts of the States of Kentucky and Ohio: Accompanied with Remarks* (Paris, KY: Joel R. Lyle, 1810), 17–18.
16. James Smith, "An Attempt to Develope Shakerism," *Supporter* (Chillicothe, OH), July 10, 1810, 2. This printing of the "Attempt" states that it is reprinted "From the Western Citizen, A paper printed at Paris, Kentucky." This may have been the first printing.
17. Ibid.
18. James Smith, *Remarkable Occurrences, Lately Discovered among the People Called Shakers: Of a Treasonous and Barbarous Nature, or Shakerism Developed* (Paris, KY: Joel R. Lyle, 1810). At least three other editions of this pamphlet were published in 1810 and 1811.
19. Smith, *Remarkable Occurrences*, 15, 21, 23.
20. Anonymous, "Who Are the Shakers?" *American Commercial Daily Advertiser* (Baltimore), August 15, 1810.
21. Record Book A.
22. Deming, Journal, ASC 818, DeWint-M. For Smith and children in the debtor's cell, see entry for August 29, 1810.
23. Benjamin Seth Youngs, *Transactions of the Ohio Mob, Called in the Public Papers "An Expedition against the Shakers"* [New York?, 1847], 2–3.
24. Ibid., 2.
25. Ibid., 3–4.

26. Ibid., 4–6.
27. Ibid., 6–7.
28. Ibid., 7–9.
29. Ibid., 9.
30. See, for instance, Anonymous, "Mobbing the Shakers at Union Village, Ohio," *Supporter* (Chillicothe, OH), September 8, 1810.
31. McNemar's poem can be found appended to some copies of Youngs, *Transactions of the Ohio Mob*, 11–12.
32. An extract taken from a letter to the Elder Brother Jethro, David Darrow to Jethro Turner, January 21, 1811, IV:A-68, OClWHi.
33. McNemar and Smith's newspaper debate can be reconstructed from surviving issues of the *Western Star*, *Ohio Centinel*, and *Liberty Hall Gazette*.
34. The printed copyright date on the surviving copy of *Shakerism Detected* at the Library of Congress is obscured, but it appears to read "21st day of November."
35. Richard McNemar, *"Shakerism Detected &c." Examined & Refuted, in Five Propositions* (Lexington, KY: Thomas Smith, 1811), 2.
36. For 1810, only the September 29 and October 13 issues survive. Both of those contain anti-Shaker writings, but not McNemar's address to Smith.
37. Smith, *Shakerism Detected*, 4, 24.
38. Ibid., 28.
39. McNemar, *"Shakerism Detected &c,"* 5.
40. Smith, *Shakerism Detected*, 5.
41. Ibid., 9.
42. *Reporter* (Lexington, KY), September 12, 1812, p. 2.
43. Ibid., May 8, 1813, p. 3.
44. Reuben Rathbone, *Reasons Offered for Leaving the Shakers* (Pittsfield, MA: Chester Smith, 1800).
45. Richard McNemar to Proctor Sampson, March 5, 1811, IV:A-68, OClWHi; Benjamin Seth Youngs to William Deming, January 22, 1811, IV:A-68, OClWHi.
46. Proctor Sampson, "Reasons for Joining the Shakers," VII:B-50, OClWHi.
47. Ibid.
48. Richard McNemar to Proctor Sampson.
49. *Journal of the Senate of the State of Ohio, Being the First Session of the Ninth General Assembly, Begun and Held at the Town of Zanesville, in the County of Muskingum, Monday, December Third, 1810. And in the Ninth Year of the Said State. Vol. IX* (Chillicothe, OH: Joseph S. Collins, 1810), 70–71.
50. Joseph R. Swan, *Statutes of the State of Ohio of a General Nature in Force August, 1854: With References to Prior Repealed Laws* (Cincinnati: H. W. Derby, 1854), 870–72.
51. An extract taken from a letter to the Elder Brother Jethro.
52. Only two installments of this are known to have survived: Thomas Freeman, "Retrospective View of Shakerism, No IV" (fragmentary), *Western Star* (Lebanon, OH), September 29, 1810; "Retrospective View of Shakerism, No. V," *Western Star* (Lebanon, OH), October 13, 1810.
53. David Darrow to Richard Spier, January 1812, IV:A-68, OClWHi.
54. Peter Pease to Richard Spier, March 10, 1811, Item 245, Shaker Collection, DLC-MSS; Daily Record.
55. Record Book A.

56. Journal of Elder Peter Pease, Item 232; Record Book A.

57. "To the General Assembly of the State of Ohio from the Society Called Shakers a Declaration," September 24, 1811, in "Mixed or Unidentified Communities, Copies of Letters from Different Communities, 1811–1841," IV:B-36, OClWHi. I thank Thomas L. Sakmyster for bringing the declaration to my attention and generously sharing his transcription of it with me.

58. The text of this remonstrance is not known to have survived.

59. David Darrow to Richard Spier.

60. Daniel Moseley to Richard Spier, February 19, 1812, IV:A-68, OClWHi. For the full text and tunes for "The Earthquake," see Christian Goodwillie and Jane Crosthwaite, *Millennial Praises: A Shaker Hymnal* (Amherst: University of Massachusetts Press, 2009), 199–201.

61. Solomon King to Rufus Bishop, April 27, 1812, IV:A-68, OClWHi.

62. Letters written by David Darrow in the Shaker Collection at the Western Reserve Historical Society name Turtle Creek as the location in the dateline until November 1811, when it changes to Union Village.

63. David Darrow to Richard Spier.

64. Benjamin Seth Youngs to Richard McNemar, "Packet of May 1838," contained in Union Village, Ohio, Church Records, Item 301, Shaker Collection, DLC-MSS; David Darrow and Ruth Farrington to Ministry, New Lebanon, March 6, 1810, IV:A-68, OClWHi. See also McNemar's letter to Rufus Bishop, November 28, 1833, in which he wrote, "My standing in this country as a witness to the Covt debarred me from signing it, or claiming any interest in the temporalities of the institution, in this view my standing was that of a minor under the sole care of the Ministry" and "As a qualified witness in Lebanon court I lately affirmed that I had divested myself of all my personal interest at U.V. [Union Village] that I had never signed the chh. covenant,—that I had no claims on the interest at U.V. as a member not even for my support," IV:A-84, OClWHi.

65. Eleazar Wright [pseud. Richard McNemar], A Review of the Most Important Events Relating to the Rise and Progress of the United Society of Believers in the West (Union Village, OH: 1831), 22–23.

12. WAR COMES TO THE WABASH

1. Archibald Meacham's letter, dated April 20, 1812, is quoted at length in David Darrow to Daniel Moseley and Peter Pease, May 11, 1812, IV:A-68, OClWHi.

2. Richard McNemar to Robert Gill [and Busro Shakers generally], May 12, 1812, IV:A-68, OClWHi.

3. Richard McNemar to Archibald Meacham, May 14, 1812, IV:A-68, OClWHi.

4. Ibid.

5. Dates of the trips are as follows: McNemar and Houston to Preble County, February 4, returned February 7; McNemar and Houston to Beaver Creek, February 10, returned February 15; McNemar and Rankin to Beaver Creek, June 22, and again on June 28, 1812 (no return dates given); Journal of Elder Peter Pease, Item 232, DLC-MSS.

6. David Darrow and Ruth Farrington to Ministry, New Lebanon, November 28, 1812, IV:A-68, OClWHi; David Darrow to Richard Spier, November 28, 1812, Item 245, Shaker Collection, DLC-MSS; Daily Record of Events of the Church Family, Union Village, Ohio, V:B-230, OClWHi. For a detailed account of the evacuation of West Union, see Peter Pease to Richard Spier, January 12, 1813, IV:A-68, OClWHi.

7. Union Village, Ohio, Records, I:A-19, OClWHi.
8. Ibid.
9. Ibid; Journal of Elder Peter Pease, Item 232.
10. David Darrow to Richard Spier, November 28, 1812, Item 245. For the case of Robert Wilson vs. David Darrow, see Trial Record A, no. 2, p. 113, State Supreme Court Records, Ohio.
11. David Darrow to Richard Spier, February 22, 1813, IV:A-68, OClWHi.
12. David Darrow and Ruth Farrington to Ministry at New Lebanon, April 20, 1813, IV:A-68, OClWHi.
13. Ibid.
14. Daily Record; Richard McNemar, *Western Review* no. 2 (Watervliet, OH: 1834): 26–27.
15. David Darrow to Richard Spier, November 2, 1813, IV:A-68, OClWHi, and David Darrow to Richard Spier, December 4, 1813, IV:A-68, give the fullest accounts of the events surrounding the drafting of the seven brethren: Samuel Rollins, David Spinning, Samuel McClelland, Robert Baxter, William Davis, Rufus Davis, and Adam Gallaher.
16. "Instructions, to all whom it may concern," October 1, 1813, IV:A-68, OClWHi. The seven men were marched to Xenia and ultimately Sandusky on the shore of Lake Erie. It was feared that they would be in the service for six months, but they returned to Union Village on November 24, 25, and 28, 1813. Daily Record.
17. Journal of Elder Peter Pease, Item 232; Daily Record.
18. Jethro Turner and Seth Youngs Wells to Ministry, New Lebanon, New York, August 6, 1811, IV:A-77, OClWHi.
19. See Christian Goodwillie and Jane Crosthwaite, *Millennial Praises: A Shaker Hymnal* (Amherst: University of Massachusetts Press, 2009), for a full account of the compilation and printing of the hymnal and a comprehensive edition of texts, tunes, and commentary, for all 140 hymns.
20. Ministry, New Lebanon, New York, to David Darrow, November 21, 1811, IV:A-32, OClWHi.
21. David Darrow and Ruth Farrington to Ministry, New Lebanon, New York, January 27, 1812, IV:A-68, OClWHi.
22. Daniel Moseley to Richard Spier, February 19, 1812, IV:A-68, OClWHi.
23. Journal of Elder Peter Pease, Item 232; Daily Record.
24. Solomon King to Archibald Meacham, October 4, 1814, IV:A-68, OClWHi; Daily Record.
25. Union Village, Ohio, Financial Accounts, Item 153, Shaker Collection, DLC-MSS.
26. Abigail Clark, "Journal and Other Writings, 1805–1900," Item 164c, Shaker Collection, DLC-MSS.
27. Ministry, Union Village, Ohio, to Ministry, New Lebanon, New York, March 25, 1815.
28. Ministry, New Lebanon, New York, to Ministry, Union Village, Ohio, February 22, 1815, IV:A-32.
29. Ibid.
30. Ministry, Union Village, Ohio, to Ministry, New Lebanon, New York.
31. Daniel Drake, *Natural and Statistical View, or Picture of Cincinnati and the Miami Country* (Cincinnati: Looker and Wallace, 1815), 40–41.
32. Ministry, Union Village, Ohio, to Ministry, New Lebanon, New York.
33. "To the Public," *Western Star* (Lebanon, OH), [March 3?], 1815.
34. David Darrow to Richard Spier, October 23, 1815, IV:A-69, OClWHi.

35. Ministry, Union Village, to Ebenezer Bishop and Calvin Reed, October 23, 1815, IV:A-69, OClWHi; Ministry, Union Village, to Archibald Meacham and Issachar Bates, December 1, 1815, IV:A-69, OClWHi; Richard McNemar, *Western Review* no. 2 (Watervliet, OH: 1834), 27; Item 350d, Shaker Collection, DLC-MSS.

36. Malcham Worley, Richard McNemar, Francis Beedle, Joseph Stout, Calvin Morrel, Samuel Rollins, and Ashbel Kitchell to Mother Lucy Wright, April 14, 1816. Three copies of this letter can be found in IV:A-69, OClWHi.

37. David Darrow and Ruth Farrington to Mother Lucy Wright, April 15, 1816, IV:A-69, OClWHi.

38. Malcham Worley . . . to Mother Lucy Wright.

39. Ibid.

40. Daily journal of current events and activities by John Wallace and Nathan Sharp, V:B-236, OClWHi; Richard McNemar, Diaries, Item 253, Shaker Collection, DLC-MSS. Historical records copied by Susan Liddell late in the nineteenth century contain the following reference: "Feb 28 (1817) Celia Anderson (colored) died today, aged 27. Hester thinks she was raised in John Dunlavy's family her mother John Dunlavy's slave her given name Cloe, or else Cloe was R McNemar's slave I have often hear Vincy talk about a Cloe a colored woman of her acquaintance," Item 250, DLC-MSS. I thank Carol Medlicott for these references.

41. Richard McNemar to John Davis, March 2, 1832, in McNemar, Diaries, Item 255.

42. John Zimkus, "Beedle's Station and the Shakers: A Struggle of Tears," Warren County History Center, Lebanon, Ohio, ca. 2005. There are many references to the Davis families in Benjamin Seth Youngs, Diary, ASC 859, DeWint-M.

43. Eunice Chapman et al., *An Account of the Conduct of the Shakers, in the Case of Eunice Chapman & Her Children, Written by Herself; A Refutation of the Shakers Remonstrance to the Proceedings of the Legislature of New-York, in 1817, by Thomas Brown; The Deposition of Mary Dyer, Who Petitioned the Legislature of the State of New-Hampshire, for Relief in a Similar Case; Also Depositions of Others Who Have Been Members of the Shaker Society; Also, the Proceedings of the Legislature of the State of New-York, in the Case of Eunice Chapman* (Lebanon, OH: Van Vleet & Camron, 1818), 85–92; Daily Record; Benjamin Seth Youngs, *Transactions of the Ohio Mob, Called in the Public Papers "An Expedition against the Shakers"* (Albany, NY: C. Van Benthuysen?, 1847). 1.

44. Zimkus, "Beedle's Station."

45. Jonathan Davis, "Affidavit of Jonathan Davis," *Western Star* (Lebanon, OH), September 24, 1817.

46. David Darrow to Richard Spier, September 21, 1816, IV:A-69, OClWHi.

47. Daily journal . . . by John Wallace and Nathan Sharp.

48. David Darrow to Richard Spier, October 20, 1817, IV:A-69, OClWHi.

49. Richard McNemar, *The Other Side of the Question* (Cincinnati: Looker, Reynolds, 1819), 116–17, 149–51.

50. David Darrow to Richard Spier, October 20, 1817; McNemar, *Other Side*, 117; Daily journal . . . by John Wallace and Nathan Sharp.

51. Daily Record.

52. The State of Ohio vs. Samuel Rollins and Richard McNemar, Court Records, August Term, 1818, 255–58. Warren County Records Center and Archives, Lebanon, Ohio.

53. McNemar, *Other Side*, 118, 122; Davis, "Affidavit of Jonathan Davis."

54. Eunice Chapman, *An Account of the Conduct of the People Called Shakers: In the Case of Eunice Chapman and Her Children, Since Her Husband Became Acquainted with That People, and Joined Their Society* (Albany, NY: Printed for the Authoress, 1817). Ilyon Woo has written

the definitive account of the Chapman controversy: *The Great Divorce: A Nineteenth-Century Mother's Extraordinary Fight against Her Husband, the Shakers, and Her Times* (New York: Atlantic Monthly Press, 2010).

55. David Darrow to Ministry, New Lebanon, New York, March 2, 1819, IV:A-69, OClWHi.

56. McNemar, *Other Side of the Question*, 130–32.

57. Daily Record.

58. [Ministry, Union Village, Ohio?], to [Ministry, New Lebanon, New York?], March 2, 1818, IV:A-69, OClWHi.

59. Richard McNemar to Matthew Houston, December 29, 1817, IV:A-69, OClWHi. McNemar and Morrell's "Remonstrance" was printed in the *Columbus Gazette*, December 11, 1817. A letter from the Ministry, New Lebanon, New York, to the Ministry, Union Village, Ohio, January 23, 1818, mentions, "While writing this letter we were fortunately favoured with you Remonstrance, signed by 123 Brethren. It was in the *Columbus Gazette* printed in Ohio December 11th. Our Enfield Brethren procured it of a Printer in hartford (Connecticut)," IV:A-33, OClWHi. The memorial was printed in early 1818 as *An Address to the State of Ohio, Protesting against a Certain Clause of the Militia Law, Enacted by the Legislature, at their Last Session; and Shewing the Inconsistency of Military Power Interfering with Persons or Property Consecrated to the Pious and Benevolent Purposes of the Gospel by Order of the United Society Called Shakers* (Lebanon, OH: Office of the Farmer, by George Smith, March 1818).

60. Thomas Brown, *An Account of the People Called Shakers* (Troy, NY: Parker and Bliss, 1812), 323.

61. Richard McNemar to Matthew Houston.

62. Ibid.

63. Daily Record.

64. Richard McNemar to Richard McNemar Jr., October 8, 1833, Vault MSS 270, Special Collections, Lee Library, UPB.

65. In his biography *A Sketch of the Life and Labors of Richard McNemar*, 33, John Patterson MacLean supplies the apocryphal story that Mother Lucy Wright personally met with McNemar and gave him the name Eleazar Right because he "understands Mother's gospel right." McNemar asked to add a "W" to make his name the same as Wright's. This meeting never occurred, as McNemar never traveled to the eastern Shaker communities until 1829—eight years after Wright's death. MacLean learned this story from Sister Susannah Cole Liddell, a Union Village Shaker who was fifteen when McNemar died. Her version can be found in Item 352c, Shaker Collection, DLC-MSS.

13. PERFIDY, PILGRIMS, PROSECUTION, PROGRESS, AND PESTILENCE

1. Benjamin Seth Youngs, Diary, 1805, ASC 859, DeWint-M.

2. Daily Record, Union Village, Ohio, V:B-230, OClWHi.

3. David Darrow to Richard Spier and Stephen Munson, October 12, 1818, IV:A-69, OClWHi.

4. Daily Record.

5. "Modern Pilgrims," *New York Telescope*, May 6, 1826, 195. Ascot as a place of residence is mentioned in Zadock Thompson, *History of Vermont, Natural, Civil, and Statistical* (Burlington, VT: Chauncey Goodrich, 1842), 203.

6. For a detailed account of Bullard and the Pilgrims, see Christian Goodwillie, "Mummy Jum: The Shaker Pilgrim Encounter of 1817–1818," *Communal Societies* 34, no. 1 (2014).

7. New Lebanon, New York, Records Kept by Order of the Church, 1780–1855, New Lebanon, New York, Shaker Manuscript Collection, Item 7, NN. The account is dated August 25, 1817, but it was clearly written retrospectively, as evidenced by the following addendum to the account: "When they left us they bent their course to the South, and, as we were afterwards informed, pursued their journey to the western states, where their prophet and some of his followers died, and the rest were scattered abroad, and one family of them by the name of Ball, who went from Vermont, afterwards joined the Society of our people at Union Village, in the state of Ohio."

8. Daily Record; Union Village, Ohio, Daily journal of current events and activities by John Wallace and Nathan Sharp, V:B-236, OClWHi.

9. Testimony of "Sarah Lucas of Union Village, Oh.," VII:B-110, OClWHi.

10. Daily journal of current events . . . John Wallace and Nathan Sharp.

11. *Western Spy* (Cincinnati), April 15, 1818, p. 3.

12. See Goodwillie, "Mummy Jum," for details on what became of the survivors.

13. Peter Pease to New Lebanon, New York, November 1, 1819, IV:A-69, OClWHi.

14. The State of Ohio vs. Samuel Rollins and Richard McNemar, Court Records, August Term, 1818, Warren County Records Center and Archives, Lebanon, Ohio, 255–58.

15. Daily Record.

16. Seth Youngs Wells to Issachar Bates, July 26, 1817, IV:A-77, OClWHi.

17. Ministry, Union Village, Ohio, to Ministry, New Lebanon, New York, October 20, 1817, IV:A-69, OClWHi. Karl J. R. Arndt's *Documentary History of the Indiana Decade of the Harmony Society, 1814–1824*, 2 vols. (Indianapolis: Indiana Historical Society, 1975), contains extensive records of interactions between the Harmony Society and the Shaker communities in Indiana and Kentucky.

18. Daily journal of current events . . . John Wallace and Nathan Sharp.

19. Ibid.

20. David Darrow to Richard Spier and Stephen Munson.

21. Issachar Bates to Ministry, New Lebanon, New York, January 29, 1819, IV:A-69, OClWHi.

22. Although the title page bears the date of 1818, and the preface is dated "November, 1818," a postscript in a letter from Darrow to the New Lebanon, New York, Ministry dated March 2, 1819 (IV:A-69, OClWHi) states, "After we had folded our letters ready for sealing word came to use that Eunice Chapman's libel was reprinted in Lebanon & began to circulate—that was the first we had heard of her pamphlets since last sumer." It is possible that due to the size of the work it took many months to print, and that the first signature with title page and preface was printed in November 1818, and the full work was finished later.

23. Union Village Ministry to New Lebanon Ministry, August 30, 1819, IV:A-69, OClWHi.

24. Eunice Chapman et al., *An Account of the Conduct of the Shakers, in the Case of Eunice Chapman & Her Children, Written by Herself; A Refutation of the Shakers Remonstrance to the Proceedings of the Legislature of New-York, in 1817, by Thomas Brown; The Deposition of Mary Dyer, Who Petitioned the Legislature of the State of New-Hampshire, for Relief in a Similar Case; Also Depositions of Others Who Have Been Members of the Shaker Society; Also, the Proceedings of the Legislature of the State of New-York, in the Case of Eunice Chapman* (Lebanon, OH: Van Vleet & Camron, 1818), ii.

25. Ibid., 94–95.

26. Daily journal of current events . . . John Wallace and Nathan Sharp.

27. Richard McNemar, *The Other Side of the Question* (Cincinnati: Looker, Reynolds, 1819), 125–27; Union Village Ministry to New Lebanon Ministry; Daily Record; Peter Pease to New Lebanon, New York.

28. Ministry, Union Village, Ohio, to Ministry, New Lebanon, New York, August 30, 1819, IV:A-69, OClWHi.

29. David Darrow to Richard Spier and Stephen Munson.

30. McNemar, *Other Side*, 149; supplement, i, vi–vii.

31. *History and Biographical Encyclopaedia of Butler County, Ohio, with Illustrations and Sketches of Its Representative Men and Pioneers* (Cincinnati: Western Biographical, 1882), 39.

32. For biographical information on Daniel Doty and his family, see J. Littell, *Family Records or Genealogies of the First Settlers of Passaic Valley (and Vicinity) above Chatham (New Jersey)* (Feltville, NJ: Stationers' Hall, 1851–1852), 142–43. For a more colorful account, see H. Simms, *Middletown in Black and White* (Middletown, OH: Journal Printing, 1908), 2–4.

33. *Belief of the Rational Brethren of the West* (Cincinnati: Printed for the Society, 1819), 119–20.

34. See McNemar, *Other Side*, 160–64.

35. Daniel Doty and William Ludlow, *An Address to the People at Union Village, and a Solemn Warning to the Whole Human Family against Shakerism and Delusion; also, An Address to Calvin Morrel and Richard M'Nemar, on the Appendix to the Other Side of the Question* (Lebanon, OH: Van Vleet, February 19, 1820), 9.

36. Ibid., 24.

37. Ibid., 11.

38. Ibid., 21.

39. Ibid., 18.

40. Ibid., 40.

41. Ibid., 59.

42. Simms, Middletown in Black and White, 4.

14. THE END OF THE BEGINNING

1. Ministry, New Lebanon, New York, to David Darrow, November 27, 1820, IV:A-34, OClWHi.

2. David Darrow to Ministry, New Lebanon, New York, February 12, 1821, IV:A-70, OClWHi.

3. E. W. Humphreys, *Memoirs of Deceased Christian Ministers; or, Brief Sketches of the Lives and Labors of 975 Ministers, Who Died between 1793 and 1880* (Dayton, OH: Christian Publishing Association, 1880), 4, 123–25; Martha Boice, Dale Covington, and Richard Spence, *Maps of the Shaker West: A Journey of Discovery* (Dayton, OH: Knot Garden, 1997), 77–84; J. P. MacLean, *Shakers of Ohio* (Columbus: F. J. Heer, 1907), 229–33.

4. Humphreys, *Memoirs*, 4, 123–25; Boice, Covington, and Spence, *Maps of the Shaker West*, 77–84; MacLean, *Shakers of Ohio*, 229–33.

5. Henry Howe, *Historical Collections of Ohio* (Cincinnati: State of Ohio, 1902), 716.

6. MacLean, *Shakers of Ohio*, 230.

7. Daily journal of current events and activities by John Wallace and Nathan Sharp, V:B-236, OClWHi.

8. Solomon King to Richard Spier and Peter Pease, February 10, 1821, IV:A-70, OClWHi.

9. Ministry, New Lebanon, New York, to Ministry, Union Village, Ohio, February 14, 1821, IV:A-34, OClWHi.

10. Richard McNemar, Diaries, Item 253, Shaker Collection, DLC-MSS; Ministry, Union Village, Ohio, to Ministry, New Lebanon, New York, October 31, 1821, IV:A-70, OClWHi; Folder 350d, Shaker Collection, DLC-MSS.

11. "June 16 [1820] Matthew Houston & Richard Pelham return home from Portage," Daily Record of Events of the Church Family, Union Village, Ohio, V:B-230, OClWHi. Stow, Ohio, was originally in Portage County, although today it is in Summit County, which was created in 1840.

12. Cathie Winans, "From the Russells to the Pilots: The Beginning and End of North Union," *American Communal Societies Quarterly* 2, no. 3 (July 2008): 135–47.

13. James Prescott, The History of North Union, 1880, VII:B-221, OClWHi.

14. Daily Record; McNemar, Diaries, Item 253; Ministry, Union Village, Ohio, to Ministry, New Lebanon, New York, June 7, 1824, IV:A-70, OClWHi; Brief Record of the Rise and Progress of the Society of Believers at North Union, Ohio, V:B-176, OClWHi; Records of the Church at North Union Containing the Rise and Progress of the Church, North Union, Ohio, V:B-177, OClWHi.

15. Ministry, Union Village, Ohio, to Ministry, New Lebanon, New York, December 8, 1821, IV:A-70, OClWHi.

16. "We feel in union with your reprinting Christs second Appearing. Mother had considerable feeling about its being reprinted here. She thought there ought to be come more in it concerning the life &c. of Mother Ann. We rec'd your letter the evening before we came to Watervliet, so we have requested Br. Seth to write & note some amendments which he & we think proper to make if you feel union therewith—what he has written will be enclosed with this. He is now preparing a book for the press, but he will inform you about it. He is a useful man in such labours." Ministry, New Lebanon, New York, to David Darrow, January 1, 1822, IV:A-78, OClWHi.

17. "Concerning the amendments to Christ's second appearing, I have consulted the Ministry, & they feel fully satisfied to have the amendments as few & as short as possible, and have left it with me to state the manner of those we have proposed, which I will do on a separate piece of paper & inclose it in this letter." Seth Youngs Wells to Ministry, Union Village, Ohio, April 25, 1822, IV:A-78, OClWHi.

18. Richard McNemar to Seth Youngs Wells, October 27, 1823, IV:A-70, OClWHi.

19. Biographical Account of Solomon King, written by Richard McNemar, c. 1835, VI:A-10, OClWHi.

20. Matthew Houston to Solomon King [undated, ca. 1822 or 1823], Item 347c, Shaker Collection, DLC-MSS.

21. Ibid.

22. Daily Record.

23. Richard McNemar to Seth Youngs Wells, October 27, 1823. In fact, the Union Village Ministry wrote to the New Lebanon Ministry on July 1, 1823, requesting, "Please to tell Brother Seth that we have not received he amendments to the testimony yet—and the printing is now going on fast—we began it rather sooner then what we expected." Ministry, Union Village, Ohio, to Ministry, New Lebanon, July 1, 1823, IV:A-70, OClWHi; Richard McNemar to Proctor Sampson, July 4, 1824, Item 245, Shaker Collection, DLC-MSS; Richard McNemar to Seth Youngs Wells, March 22, 1824, IV:A-70, OClWHi.

24. Stephen J. Paterwic, *Historical Dictionary of the Shakers* (Lanham, MD: Scarecrow, 2008), 234–35. Well's mother was Abigail Youngs Wells,

25. Seth Youngs Wells to Richard McNemar, February 10, 1824, Item 246, Shaker Collection, DLC-MSS.

26. Daily Record; Richard McNemar to Seth Youngs Wells, March 22, 1824. Sargent and the Halcyon sect are woefully understudied. See *The Winchester Centennial, 1803–1903: Historical Sketch of the Universalist Profession of Belief* (Boston and Chicago: Universalist, 1903), 121–22, for a basic outline of Sargent's career and some of his publications.

27. Richard McNemar to Seth Youngs Wells, March 22, 1824.

28. Daily Record. See Stephen J. Paterwic, *The Shakers of Enfield, Connecticut: 1780–1868* (Clinton, NY: Richard W. Couper, 2020), 245–48, for more information on people who converted to Shakerism from western Rhode Island and eastern Connecticut, including the Farnumites and later converts that joined the Enfield, Connecticut, community.

29. Richard McNemar to Seth Youngs Wells, March 22, 1824.

30. Seth Youngs Wells to Richard McNemar, May 31, 1824, Item 246, Shaker Collection, DLC-MSS.

31. Richard McNemar to Proctor Sampson.

32. Daily Record.

33. Garner McNemar, Union Village, Warren Co., Ohio, to David Thomson, December 7, 1824, in Laura J. Yeater and Elvira Hunley, *General David Thomson* [place of publication not identified; publisher not identified], [1922?], 27–29.

34. David Thomson, Scott County, Kentucky, to Garner McNemar, November 15, 1825, in Laura J. Yeater and Elvira Hunley, *General David Thomson* [place of publication not identified; publisher not identified], [1922?], 27–29.

35. Ministry, Union Village, Ohio, to Ministry, New Lebanon, New York, July 4, 1825, IV:A-70, OClWHi; Richard McNemar to John Dunlavy, June 29, 1825, Item 356, Shaker Collection, DLC-MSS.

36. Matthew Houston to John Dunlavy, Item 347c, Shaker Collection, DLC-MSS.

37. See Carol Medlicott, *Issachar Bates: A Shaker's Journey* (Hanover, NH: University Press of New England, 2013), 215–16.

38. McNemar, Diaries [Father David's Last Address], Item 253.

39. Ministry, Union Village, Ohio, to Ministry, New Lebanon, New York. Richard McNemar provides a very detailed physical and medical description of Father David Darrow's decline and death in Richard McNemar to John Dunlavy, June 29, 1825, Item 356.

40. Ministry, Union Village, Ohio, to Ministry, New Lebanon, New York.

41. Documents on Father David Darrow's Funeral, Item 245, Shaker Collection, DLC-MSS.

42. Ibid.

43. Ibid.; Ministry, Union Village, Ohio, to Ministry, New Lebanon, New York.

44. Remarks on the Church Covenant of the United Society Called Shakers, New Lebanon, July 12, 1829, Item 347a, Shaker Collection, DLC-MSS; McNemar, Diaries, Item 253.

15. THERE'S SOMETHING DEAD UPON THIS GROUND, OR, THE BUZZARDS AND THE FLESH

1. Ministry, New Lebanon, New York, to Archibald Meacham, July 30, 1825, IV:A-35, OClWHi.

2. Documents on Father David Darrow's Funeral, Item 245, Shaker Collection, DLC-MSS. McNemar's reflections on this time were written in January 1832.

3. Ibid.

4. Richard McNemar, Biographical Account of Solomon King, written by Richard McNemar, c.1835, VI:A-10, OClWHi.

5. Documents on Father David Darrow's Funeral, Item 245; Carol Medlicott, *Issachar Bates: A Shaker's Journey* (Hanover, NH: University Press of New England, 2013), 216–17; Ministry, Union Village, Ohio, to Ministry, New Lebanon, New York, October 24, 1825, IV:A-70, OClWHi.

6. Ministry, Union Village, Ohio, to Ministry, New Lebanon, New York, October 24, 1825; Daniel Miller, Journal of Passing Events, Union Village, Ohio, V:B-237, OClWHi.

7. Miller, Journal; Union Village, Ohio, Church Record of the Appointments to the Office of the Ministry, Elders, and Trustees, of Union Village, III:B-34, OClWHi, 32.

8. Ministry, Union Village, Ohio, to Ministry, New Lebanon, New York, July 3, 1826.

9. Ministry, Union Village, Ohio, to Ministry, New Lebanon, New York, July 4, 1826.

10. Medlicott, *Issachar Bates*, 172–73, 218; see also Carol Medlicott, "Conflict and Tribulation on the Frontier: The West Union Shakers and Their Retreat," *American Communal Societies Quarterly* 3, no. 3 (July 2009): 111–37.

11. Ministry, Union Village, Ohio, to Ministry, New Lebanon, New York, July 4, 1826.

12. Daily Record, Union Village, Ohio, V:B-230, OClWHi; "Journal of Samuel Swan McClelland," in Cheryl Bauer, ed., *Shakers of Indiana: A West Union Reader* (Milford, OH: Little Miami, 2008), 167.

13. Remarks on the Church Covenant of the United Society Called Shakers, New Lebanon, July 12, 1829, Item 347a, Shaker Collection, DLC-MSS; Richard McNemar, Diaries, Item 253, Shaker Collection, DLC-MSS.

14. Archibald Meacham to Ministry, New Lebanon, New York, October 11, 1826, IV:A-70, OClWHi.

15. Ministry, Union Village, Ohio, to Ministry, New Lebanon, New York, December 11, 1826.

16. "Journal of McClelland," 169–70; Archibald Meacham to Ministry, New Lebanon, New York, May 8, 1827.

17. "Journal of McClelland," 170.

18. "Journal of McClelland," 172; Samuel Turner to Calvin Green, April 26, 1827, Item 245, Shaker Collection, DLC-MSS. McNemar, Diaries, Item 254, contains many poems written during, and about, the final months of the West Union community.

19. "Journal of McClelland," 175–76.

20. Archibald Meacham to Ministry, New Lebanon, New York, May 8, 1827.

21. Philos Harmoniae [Richard McNemar, pseud.], *A Selection of Hymns and Poems for the Use of Believers* (Watervliet, OH: 1833), 198. The hymn is attributed to "W. R."—possibly William Reynolds, in McNemar, Diaries, Item 254.

22. Benjamin Seth Youngs to Nathaniel Deming, September 8, 1828, Box 12, f. 1, MePoSS.

23. Ministry, Union Village, Ohio, to Ministry, New Lebanon, New York, April 18, 1825.

24. Miller, Journal.

25. Robert Owen, *New View of Society: Or, Essays on the Principle of the Formation of the Human Character, and the Application of the Principle to Practice* (London: Cadell and Davies, 1813).

26. Donald E. Pitzer, "The New Moral World of Robert Owen and New Harmony," in Donald E. Pitzer, ed., *America's Communal Utopias* (Chapel Hill: University of North Carolina Press, 1997), 88–134.

27. Benjamin Seth Youngs to Nathaniel Deming.

28. John Whitbey, *Beauties of Priestcraft, or, A Short Account of Shakerism* (New Harmony, IN: Office of the *New-Harmony Gazette*, 1826).

29. Ibid., 4.

30. Ibid., 17, 27, 36, 39–40.

31. Benjamin Seth Youngs to Nathaniel Deming.

32. Ibid., 44–46.

33. Ministry, Pleasant Hill, Kentucky, to Ministry, South Union, Kentucky, August 1, 1825, IV:A-53, OClWHi. Richard McNemar, under the pseudonym "Peregrinus," later printed a pamphlet about these events: *A Record Relating to the Cogar Mob and Boon Suit* [n.p., 1831]. The only known surviving copy is at the Western Reserve Historical Society, Cleveland, Ohio.

34. Whitbey, *Beauties of Priestcraft*, 53, 63, 69.

35. Benjamin Seth Youngs to Nathaniel Deming.

36. Daily Record.

37. Ministry, New Lebanon, New York, to Ministry, Union Village, Ohio, June 23, 1827, IV:B-7, OClWHi; McNemar, Diaries, Item 254.

38. Benjamin Seth Youngs to Nathaniel Deming; Daily Record.

39. McNemar was in Harrodsburg on June 23, 1827. McNemar, Diaries, Item 254.

40. "An Account of the Sickness of Eldress Lucy Smith," April 20, 1817, IV:A-60, OClWHi.

41. McNemar, Diaries, Item 254.

42. Remarks on the Church Covenant.

43. McNemar, Diaries, Item 254.

44. Ibid.

45. Ibid.

46. Ibid.

47. Ibid.

48. Ministry, New Lebanon, New York, to Ministry, Union Village, Ohio, August 18, 1827.

49. Ibid.

50. Richard McNemar, *Investigator; or A Defence of the Order, Government & Economy of the United Society Called Shakers, against Sundry Charges and Legislative Proceedings; Addressed to the Political World; by the Society of Believers at Pleasant Hill, KY* (Lexington, KY: Smith & Palmer, 1828), iii.

51. Richard McNemar to [Seth Youngs Wells?], April 25, 1827, IV:A-53, OClWHi; Richard McNemar, ed., evidence that this letter was directed to Wells can be found in Richard McNemar to Seth Youngs Wells, May 12, 1827, IV:A-84, OClWHi, which contained the enclosure "R. McNemar on authority of Trusteeship in Church Covenant"; "The Church Covenant, Executed at Pleasant-Hill June 2d, 1814," in *Constitution of the United Societies of Believers (Called Shakers), Containing Sundny [sic] Covenants and Articles of Agrement [sic], Definitive of the Legal Grounds of the Institution* (Watervliet, OH: 1833), 85.

52. McNemar, *Investigator*, v–viii.

53. Richard McNemar to Seth Youngs Wells, September 15, 1830, Item 245, Shaker Collection, DLC-MSS.

54. "An Act to Regulate Civil Proceedings against Certain Communities Having Property in Common," in *Acts Passed at the First Session of the Thirty-Sixth General Assembly for the Commonwealth of Kentucky, Begun and Held in the Town of Frankfort, on Monday, the Third Day of December, in the Year Eighteen Hundred and Twenty-Seven, and of the Commonwealth the Thirty-Sixth* (Frankfort, KY: Jacob H. Holman, 1828), 137–39.

55. McNemar, *Investigator*, iv; McNemar, Diaries, Item 254.
56. McNemar, *Investigator*, iii–iv, 12.
57. Ibid., 13–14, 18.
58. Ibid., 23, 27–28, 43.
59. McNemar, Diaries, Item 254.

16. THE STRUGGLE WITH ABIJAH ALLEY AND AQUILA BOLTON

1. A Church Record, III:B-34, OClWHi, 202.
2. Richard McNemar, Diaries, Item 256, Shaker Collection, DLC-MSS.
3. Church Record, 148–49.
4. Much of the material in this chapter is condensed from Nancy Gray Schoonmaker and Christian Goodwillie, "Abijah Alley of Long Hollow: Preacher, Shaker Apostate, and Backwoods Prophet of the American South," *American Communal Societies Quarterly* 11, no. 3 (July 2017).
5. Item 164c, Shaker Collection, DLC-MSS.
6. Church Record, 138.
7. McNemar, Diaries, Item 256.
8. Hymns, correspondence, and other papers . . . mostly concerning the Shaker communities at Pleasant Hill and South Union, Kentucky, and Union Village, Ohio, 1818–1838, 1851, Item 349c, Shaker Collection, DLC-MSS.
9. McNemar, Diaries, Item 256.
10. Ibid.
11. Ibid.
12. Ibid.
13. Ibid.
14. Ibid. Different sections of this source document refer to Alley being removed as elder of the North Lot or of the East House. Regarding the various families at Union Village during this period, especially when the family names and geographic locations are often confusingly substituted for one another in manuscript sources, it is difficult to state with certainty which family Alley had been leading when he was removed, although it seems to have been the newly constituted East Family gathered in the wake of the "great move."
15. Names of those who left were taken from Diary, Union Village, Ohio, 1826–1860, Item 167, Shaker Collection, DLC-MSS. They are as follows: 1828, September 2 Archabald Houston, Sept. 6 John Watts, Sept. 15 Solomon Smith, Sept. 25 Patience Spining, Dexter Ball, October 7 Martha Kimble, Oct. 9 Mildon Kitchell, Amos Holloway, Oct. 12 Luther Babbit, Oct. 13 James Blue, Oct. 22 Rachel Baxter, Oct. 25 Thomas Millikin, Oct. 27 Samuel Anderson, Richard McNemar Jr. (from Brick House), Oct. 30 Irene Watts, November 3 Phebe Johnson, Nov. 18 Lovisa Milligen, Nov. 25 Samuel Smith, December 19 John Galloway; 1829, January 1 James Wallace, February 10 Jonathan Gandy, Feb. 11 Joseph Watt, March 26 Molly Sering, March 27 Margery Mackeen, April 2; "Abijah Alley abscon[d]ed this morning from the office."
16. Richard McNemar to Richard McNemar Jr., April 22, 1828, in McNemar, Diaries, Item 255; Sandra A. Soule, *Independency of the Mind: Aquila Massie Bolton, Poetry, Shakerism and Controversy* (Clinton, NY: Couper, 2010).

17. Aquila Massie Bolton, *The Whore of Babylon Unmasked; or, A Cure for Orthodoxy; Being a Letter Addressed to Richard Mott, of New York* (Philadelphia: n.p., 1827).

18. Soule, *Independency*, 7–11.

19. Richard McNemar to Richard McNemar Jr., April 22, 1828, Item 25.

20. Soule, *Independency*, 31–32.

21. "Hewitt" is spelled in a variety of ways, including "Huet" and "Hewet." For this paper, it is standardized as "Hewitt" according to his own handwriting on his statement in Hymns, correspondence, and other papers, Item 349c.

22. McNemar, Diaries, Item 256.

23. Ibid.

24. Ibid.

25. Hymns, correspondence, and other papers, Item 349c. The date of this statement is ascertained from the transcription of it given in McNemar, Diaries, Item 256.

26. Ibid.

27. Ibid. For a fuller discussion of Scales's life and relations with the Shakers and the text of his publication, see David D. Newell, "William Scales' 1789 'Mystery of the People Called Shakers,'" *American Communal Societies Quarterly* preview issue (September 2006): 6–20.

28. McNemar, Diaries, Item 256.

29. Ibid.

30. Ibid.

31. Hymns, correspondence, and other papers, Item 349c.

32. McNemar, Diaries, Item 256.

33. Ibid.

34. Ibid.

35. Ibid.

36. Ibid.

37. Ibid.

38. Ibid.

39. Ibid. Pages 81–87 of McNemar, Diaries, Item 256, appear to contain Hewitt's confession. The item is untitled, unsigned, and unattributed, but its content and placement in McNemar's journal suggest that it is Hewitt's confession to McNemar.

40. Ibid.

41. Ibid.

42. Ibid.

43. Ibid. "S. M." is identified as Samuel C. Manning on pages 173–79.

44. Ibid.

45. Ibid.

46. Ibid.

47. This hymn can be found in Philos Harmoniae [Richard McNemar, pseud.], *A Selection of Hymns and Poems* (Watervliet, OH: 1833), 103.

48. McNemar, Diaries, Item 256.

49. Ibid.

50. Ministry, Union Village, Ohio, to Ministry, New Lebanon, New York, May 15, 1829, IV:A-70, OClWHi; Richard McNemar to Calvin Green and Seth Youngs Wells, June 29, 1828, IV:A-53, OClWHi; McNemar, Diaries, Item 254.

17. ELEAZAR GOES EAST

1. Richard McNemar, Diaries, Item 253, Shaker Collection, DLC-MSS.
2. Richard McNemar, Diaries, Item 253, Shaker Collection, DLC-MSS; Carol Medlicott, *Issachar Bates: A Shaker's Journey* (Hanover, NH: University Press of New England, 2013), 209–10.
3. Daily Record, Union Village, Ohio, V:B-230, OClWHi; Ministry, Union Village, Ohio, to Ministry, New Lebanon, New York, May 15, 1829, IV:A-70, OClWHi.
4. Freegift Wells, Memorandum of Events, V:B-291, OClWHi; New Lebanon, New York, Records, Book No. 2, kept [in part] by Rufus Bishop, Item 6, Shaker Collection, NN.
5. Richard McNemar to Calvin Green and Seth Youngs Wells, June 29, 1828, IV:A-53, OClWHi.
6. Calvin Green and Seth Youngs Wells to Richard McNemar, August 16, 1827, Item 245, Shaker Collection, DLC-MSS.
7. McNemar, Diaries, Item 254.
8. Rufus Bishop, Day Book kept by Rufus Bishop as a record of the Ministry, V:B-85, OClWHi.
9. Richard McNemar, Remarks on the Church Covenant of the United Society Called Shakers, Item 347a, Shaker Collection, DLC-MSS.
10. Records, Book No. 2, Item 6.
11. McNemar, Diaries, Item 254.
12. Ministry, Canterbury, New Hampshire, to Ministry, New Lebanon, New York, July 24, 1829, IV:A-3, OClWHi.
13. McNemar, Diaries, Item 253.
14. Canterbury, New Hampshire, Current Record of Events from 1792 to 1885, Shaker Collection, NCH.
15. Ministry, Canterbury, New Hampshire, to Ministry, New Lebanon, New York.
16. Shirley, Massachusetts, Journal of an Unknown Resident, V:B-199, OClWHi; Shirley, Massachusetts, Journal of the North Family, V:B-190, OClWHi; Joseph Hammond, Day Book, Shirley, Massachusetts, V:B-203, OClWHi.
17. Harvard, Massachusetts, Church Family Journal, HVD 2, 3112, MaShaTR; Hammond, Day Book.
18. Richard McNemar, "A Discourse Delivered at Harvard Aug 2d 1829 by Eleazar Wright of Union Village Ohio," Shaker Collection, 41 M 23, MWiW.
19. Ibid.
20. Ibid.
21. Church Family Journal; Ministry, Harvard, Massachusetts, to Ministry, New Lebanon, New York, August 2, 1829, IV:A-2, OClWHi.
22. Bishop, Day Book; Sodus Bay, New York, A Record of the Commencement and Progress of the Believers at Sodus and Port Bay, V:B-21, OClWHi; Sodus Bay, New York, Journal, V:B-22, OClWHi; Richard McNemar to Seth Youngs Wells, September 20, 1829, IV:A-51, OClWHi.
23. Richard McNemar to Matthew Houston, September 9, 1829. McNemar, Diaries, Item 255.
24. Richard McNemar to Seth Youngs Wells.
25. Ibid.
26. Ibid.; Richard McNemar to Ebenezer Bishop, October 21, 1829, IV:A-70, OClWHi.

18. ELEAZAR AND THE COVENANT

1. Daily Record, Union Village, Ohio, V:B-230, OClWHi; Church Record, 32, III:B-34, OClWHi.
2. Richard McNemar, Diaries, Item 253, Shaker Collection, DLC-MSS.
3. Ibid.
4. Ibid.
5. Ibid.
6. Daily Record; Church Record, 32; McNemar, Diaries, Item 255.
7. Daily Record.
8. McNemar, Diaries, Item 253. These remarks were made at Union Village, Ohio, at a church meeting to reconfirm the covenant on September 16, 1832.
9. Ibid.; Documents copied from Shaker Communities at Union Village and Watervliet, Ohio, Item 262, Shaker Collection, DLC-MSS; Richard McNemar to Seth Youngs Wells, March 25, 1830, Item 245, Shaker Collection, DLC-MSS; Daily Record.
10. Daily Record; Covenant, Union Village, Ohio, 1829, I:B-70, OClWHi; Documents copied from Shaker Communities, Item 262; Richard McNemar to Seth Youngs Wells, March 25, 1830, Item 245.
11. Documents copied from Shaker Communities, Item 262; Daily Record; Richard McNemar to Seth Youngs Wells, March 25, 1830, Item 245; McNemar, Diaries, Item 253; the vegetable wagon anecdote was recorded by Sister Susannah Cole Liddell circa 1900 and can be found in Item 350d, Shaker Collection, DLC-MSS.
12. Daily Record.
13. Ibid.
14. Samuel Turner to Rufus Bishop, August 16, 1830, IV:A-54, OClWHi.
15. McNemar, Diaries, Item 255.
16. Ibid.
17. Ibid.
18. Ibid.; Seth Youngs Wells to Richard McNemar [April 28, 1830?], IV:A-79, OClWHi. This letter survives only in an undated, unfinished fragmentary draft. The date I have assigned it is based off of McNemar's reply, which references Wells's letter of April 28, 1830, which fits their correspondence chronologically.
19. *A Revision and Confirmation of the Social Compact of the United Society Called Shakers, at Pleasant Hill, Kentucky* (Harrodsburg, KY: Randall and Jones, 1830).
20. McNemar, Diaries, Item 255; Richard McNemar to Seth Youngs Wells, June 14, 1830.
21. Church Record Book A, Pleasant Hill, Kentucky, Archives, SVPH.
22. McNemar, Diaries, Item 255.
23. Ibid.
24. Richard McNemar to Nathaniel Deming, August 17, 1830, SA 1216.13, DeWint-M.
25. Journal A, South Union, Kentucky, KyBgW-K; Richard McNemar to Nathaniel Deming, August 17, 1830, SA 1216.13, DeWint-M.
26. Daily Record; Journal A.
27. Journal A.
28. Richard McNemar to Seth Youngs Wells, November 20, 1830, Item 245, Shaker Collection, DLC-MSS.
29. Covenant, South Union, Kentucky, I:B-63, OClWHi.
30. McNemar, Diaries, Item 255; *A Memorial Remonstrating against a Certain Act of the Legislature of Kentucky* (Harrodsburg, KY: Union Office, 1830), 1–2.

31. Andrea S. Ramage, "Love and Honor: The Wickliffe Family of Antebellum Kentucky," *Register of the Kentucky Historical Society* 94, no. 2 (Spring 1996): 115–33; Richard McNemar to Seth Youngs Wells, April 5, 1831, Item 245. Robert Wickliffe, *Speech of Robert Wickliffe, in the Senate of Kentucky, on a Bill to Repeal an Act of the General Assembly of the State of Kentucky, Entitle [sic] "An Act to Regulate Civil Proceedings against Certain Communities Having Property in Common"* (Lebanon, OH: Star Office, 1831), and *The Shakers. Speech of Robert Wickliffe. In the Senate of Kentucky—Jan. 1831. On a Bill to Repeal an Act of the General Assembly of the State of Kentucky, Entitled, "An Act to Regulate Civil Proceedings against Certain Communities Having Property in Common"* (Frankfort, KY: A. G. Hodges, 1832). McNemar also included copies of the speech in some bindings of his compilation *The Constitution of the United Societies, of Believers (called Shakers) Containing Sundny [sic] Covenants and Artcles [sic] of Agrement [sic], Definitive of the Legal Grounds of the Institution* (Watervliet, OH: 1833).

32. McNemar, Diaries, Items 253 and 255; Daily Record; Richard McNemar to Seth Youngs Wells, April 5, 1831, Item 245.

33. Daniel Miller, Journal of Passing Events, Union Village, Ohio, V:B-237, OClWHi; Richard McNemar to Seth Youngs Wells, April 5, 1831, Item 245.

34. McNemar, Diaries, Item 253.

35. Mario S. De Pillis first wrote about the Shakers at North Union, Ohio, and the Mormons in "The Development of Mormon Communitarianism, 1826–1846" (PhD diss., Yale, 1960). See also Robert F. W. Meader, "The Shakers and the Mormons," *Shaker Quarterly* 2, no. 3 (Fall 1962): 83–96, and Lawrence R. Flake, "A Shaker View of a Mormon Mission," *BYU Studies* 20, no. 1 (Fall 1979): 94–99.

36. McNemar, Diaries, Item 253.

37. Ibid.

38. Ibid.; Richard McNemar to Seth Youngs Wells, May 10, 1831, Item 245.

39. Richard McNemar writings in: Miscellaneous documents primarily concerning communities in New Lebanon, New York, and Whitewater and Union Village, Ohio, circa 1817–1904, Item 347a, Shaker Collection, DLC-MSS; McNemar, Diaries, Item 253. John Lin Carson is simply referred to as "JLC" in McNemar's diary. I have established his identity by consulting James R. Innis Jr., *Footprints at White Water Shaker Village: A Directory of Shakers, Visitors, Business Associates and Thieves 1823–1916* (Harrison, OH: n.p., 2015).

40. McNemar, Diaries, Item 253.

41. Ibid.

42. Richard McNemar writings in: Miscellaneous documents, Item 347a; McNemar, Diaries, Item 253.

43. McNemar, Diaries, Item 253. Thomas Sakmyster and James R. Innis Jr. give an excellent recapitulation of these tumultuous times in their essay "History," in Innis and Sakmyster, eds., *The Shakers of White Water, Ohio, 1823–1916* (Clinton, NY: Richard W. Couper, 2014), 24–25.

44. Richard McNemar to Seth Youngs Wells, May 10, 1831, Item 245.

45. Richard McNemar writings in: Miscellaneous documents, Item 347a; McNemar, Diaries, Item 253.

46. Richard McNemar to Seth Youngs Wells, May 10, 1831, Item 245; Daily Record; the complete poem "Contented at Home" can be found in a folder of Richard McNemar imprints, BX 9786.S5343 1830z no. 8, in the Rare Book Room of the Library of Congress, Washington, DC; Richard McNemar to Seth Youngs Wells, August 17, 1831, Item 245.

47. Richard McNemar to Seth Youngs Wells, August 17, 1831, Item 245.

48. Richard McNemar to Nathan Sharp, December 8, 1831, also Sharp's reply and McNemar's "Remarks on Sharp's Letter," Item 246, Shaker Collection, DLC-MSS. An additional manuscript source for this can be found in Item 347a, Shaker Collection, DLC-MSS.

49. Richard McNemar to Solomon King, January 5, 1832, IV:A-71, OClWHi.

50. Richard McNemar to Seth Youngs Wells, January 7, 1832, Item 245.

51. Samuel Turner to Richard McNemar, October 1831, Item 347c, Shaker Collection, DLC-MSS.

52. Ministry, New Lebanon, New York, to Ministry, Union Village, Ohio, December 30, 1831, IV:B-7, OClWHi.

53. Richard McNemar to Seth Youngs Wells, January 7, 1832, Item 245.

54. Richard McNemar to Solomon King, January 5, 1832.

55. Daily Record.

56. McNemar, Diaries, Item 255.

57. Ibid.

58. Carol Medlicott, *Issachar Bates: A Shaker's Journey* (Hanover, NH: University Press of New England, 2013), 231.

59. McNemar, Diaries, Item 255.

60. McNemar, Diaries, Items 256 and 253.

19. CUSTOS SACRORUM

1. Ministry, Canterbury, New Hampshire, to Ministry, New Lebanon, New York, July 24, 1829, IV:A-3, OClWHi.

2. Richard McNemar to Rufus Bishop, March 10, 1836, IV:A-84, OClWHi.

3. Richard McNemar, Diaries, Item 253, Shaker Collection, DLC-MSS.

4. Richard McNemar, Diaries, Item 253, Shaker Collection, DLC-MSS; *A Memorial Remonstrating against a Certain Act of the Legislature of Kentucky* (Harrodsburg, KY: Union Office, 1830). No copy has been located of the South Union printing of the *Memorial*.

5. McNemar, Diaries, Item 253; Calvin Green and Seth Youngs Wells, *A Brief Exposition of the Established Principles and Regulations of the United Society Called Shakers* (Albany, NY: Packard and Van Benthuysen, 1830).

6. McNemar, Diaries, Item 253.

7. Ibid.

8. Richard McNemar to Seth Youngs Wells, April 6, 1832, Item 245, Shaker Collection, DLC-MSS.

9. Seth Youngs Wells to Richard McNemar, April 17, 1832, IV:A-36, OClWHi.

10. Richard McNemar to Seth Youngs Wells, July 2, 1832, Item 245; Richard McNemar to Seth Youngs Wells, July 17, 1832, Item 245.

11. Seth Youngs Wells, *Testimonies concerning the Character and Ministry of Mother Ann Lee and the First Witnesses of the Gospel of Christ's Second Appearing* (Albany, NY: Packard & Van Benthuysen, 1827); Richard McNemar to Seth Youngs Wells, July 17, 1832, Item 245.

12. McNemar, Diaries, Item 256.

13. Richard McNemar, *Epistle Dedicatory of the Union Press* (Watervliet, OH: 1832), 4.

14. McNemar, Diaries, Item 256.

15. Richard McNemar to Rufus Bishop.

16. Ibid.

17. Richard McNemar to Seth Youngs Wells, October 2, 1833.

18. Richard McNemar, Watervliet, Ohio, to Seth Youngs Wells, New Lebanon, New York, July 17, 1832, Item 246, Shaker Collection, DLC-MSS.

19. See Carol Medlicott and Christian Goodwillie, *Richard McNemar, Music, and the Western Shaker Communities: Branches of One Living Tree* (Kent, OH: Kent State University Press, 2013), for a critical edition of this hymnal that reunites the texts with their Shaker tunes.

20. See Christian Goodwillie and Jane Crosthwaite, *Millennial Praises: A Shaker Hymnal* (Amherst: University of Massachusetts Press), 2009.

21. Richard McNemar, *Selection of Hymns and Poems; for the Use of Believers. Collected from Sundry Authors, by Philos Harmoniae* [pseud.] (Watetvliet [sic], OH: 1833), 3.

22. McNemar, *Epistle Dedicatory*.

23. Ibid.

24. McNemar, *Selection of Hymns and Poems*, [errata note].

25. Seth Youngs Wells to Richard McNemar, April 6, 1833, Item 246, Shaker Collection, DLC-MSS.

26. Richard McNemar to Seth Youngs Wells, July 28, 1834.

27. McNemar, Diaries, Item 256.

28. 347 b, DLC-MSS.

29. McNemar, Diaries, Item 256.

30. Seth Youngs Wells, New Lebanon, New York, to Richard McNemar, Watervliet, Ohio, December 1, 1834, IV:A-36, OClWHi.

31. Seth Youngs Wells to Richard McNemar, December 1, 1834, Item 246.

32. Richard McNemar to Seth Youngs Wells, December 22, 1834.

33. McNemar, Selection of Hymns and Poems, 3.

20. THE GREAT SNAKE AND THE PATRIARCHAL SKELETON

1. Richard McNemar, Diaries, Item 255, Shaker Collection, DLC-MSS.

2. Richard McNemar to Seth Youngs Wells, July 17, 1832, Item 245, Shaker Collection, DLC-MSS.

3. Richard McNemar to Seth Youngs Wells, July 2, 1832, Item 245.

4. Ibid.

5. Richard McNemar to Seth Youngs Wells, July 17, 1832, Item 245.

6. Ibid.

7. Seth Youngs Wells to Richard McNemar, October 24, 1833, IV:A-36, OClWHi.

8. "Deposition of R McNemar," in McNemar, Diaries, Item 255; Patricia L. Goitein, "Strangers along the Trail: Peoria's Shaker Apostates Enter the World," *American Communal Societies Quarterly* 4, no. 1 (January 2010), 3–19.

9. Philanthropos [Seth Youngs Wells, pseud.], *A Brief Illustration of War and Peace, Showing the Ruinous Policy of the Former, and the Superior Efficacy of the Latter, for National Protection and Defence* (Albany, NY: Packard and Van Benthuysen, 1831); McNemar, Diaries, Item 255. See Christian Goodwillie, "'The Price of Blood': "Shaker Revolutionary War Veterans," special issue, *American Communal Societies Quarterly* 14, nos. 3/4 (July and October 2020), for a detailed examination of the Shakers' handling of the military pension issue, as well as the pension narratives of many Shakers who served in the Revolutionary War.

10. Carol Medlicott, *Issachar Bates: A Shaker's Journey* (Hanover, NH: University Press of New England, 2013), 234.

11. McNemar, Diaries, Item 255.

12. Ibid.

13. Ibid.

14. Watervliet, Ohio, General Rules of the United Society . . . Watervliet, Ohio, Jan. 1833, Item 303, Shaker Collection, DLC-MSS. This was also printed as part of Richard McNemar, *Constitution of the United Societies of Believers (Called Shakers), Containing Sundny [sic] Covenants and Articles of Agrement [sic], Definitive of the Legal Grounds of the Institution* (Watervliet, OH: 1833).

15. Richard McNemar to Seth Youngs Wells, February 13, 1833, Item 245.

16. The Union Village covenant of 1810 can be found in McNemar, *Constitution of the United Societies*, 1–2. Richard McNemar to Seth Youngs Wells, February 13, 1833, Item 245. See also Medlicott, *Issachar Bates*, 128.

17. Seth Youngs Wells to Richard McNemar, April 6, 1833, Items 246 and 347c, Shaker Collection, DLC-MSS. The confidential postscript is found in 347c.

18. Richard McNemar to Seth Youngs Wells, October 2, 1833, IV:A-84, OClWHi.

19. Seth Youngs Wells to Richard McNemar, April 6, 1833, Items 246 and 347c. The confidential postscript is found in 347c.

20. Church Records, Union Village, 69–70, Item 301, DLC-MSS.

21. Church Records, Union Village, 71, Item 301; Daily Record, Union Village, Ohio, V:B-230, OClWHi.

22. Church Records, Union Village, 71, Item 301; Richard McNemar to Seth Youngs Wells, October 2, 1833.

23. For a full examination of the pension issue, see Goodwillie, "'The Price of Blood'": 142–96.

24. Issachar Bates to Calvin Wells, November 30, 1833, in Church Records, Union Village, 71–74, Item 301.

25. Church Records, Union Village, 80–82, Item 301. See Medlicott, *Issachar Bates*, 238–40, 248–49, for more on the pension controversy.

26. Ministry, New Lebanon, New York, to Ministry, Union Village, Ohio, February 3, 1834, in Church Records, Union Village, 76–77, Item 301.

27. McNemar, Diaries, Item 253.

28. Church Record, Union Village, Ohio, 4, 34–35, III:B-34, OClWHi.

29. Daily Record.

30. Daily Record; Sandra A. Soule, *Independency of the Mind: Aquila Massie Bolton, Poetry, Shakerism and Controversy* (Clinton, NY: Couper, 2010), 31–33; Richard McNemar, *A Series of Lectures on Orthodoxy and Heterodoxy, in Allusion to the Testimony of Christ's Second Appearing. Introduced by a Reply to Sundry Defamatory Letters Written by A. M. Bolton, Late, a Catechumen in the United Society at Union Village. Designed for the Edification of Young Believers* (Dayton, OH: 1832); *Western Expositor. No. 4. A Brief Exposition of Rev. 12,—Ezek. 17, &c. Communicated to a Friend* [Watervliet, OH?: 1833?].

31. Accessed November 4, 2019, urbanaswedenborgianchurch.org/local-history.

32. Richard McNemar to Richard McNemar Jr., October 8, 1833, Vault MSS 270, UPB; Eunice Chapman et al., *An Account of the Conduct of the Shakers, in the Case of Eunice Chapman & Her Children, Written by Herself; A Refutation of the Shakers Remonstrance to the Proceedings of the Legislature of New-York, in 1817, by Thomas Brown; the Deposition of Mary*

Dyer, Who Petitioned the Legislature of the State of New-Hampshire, for Relief in a Similar Case; Also Depositions of Others Who Have Been Members of the Shaker Society; Also, the Proceedings of the Legislature of the State of New-York, in the Case of Eunice Chapman (Lebanon, OH: Van Vleet & Camron, 1818), 94–95.

33. Richard McNemar to Richard McNemar Jr. In fact, McNemar lamented privately to Seth Youngs Wells about the lack of proper schoolteachers in the western Shaker communities: "In furnish[ing] the grand mission of laborers to the west, why is it that we have never had a school-master afforded us from the Mother church not even a visitor to inspect our literary institutions? Why has every spot on our consecrated premises been blessed with the special influence of unity & uniformity the school house excepted. It is with pain that I reflect on this subject which to me has ever been one of much importance, to recollect the fatal advantages which the enemy has had by reason of the want of a regular jointing & bonding & knitting together of our children youth & I may say adults, as respects that kind of teaching which properly originates in school order ... We have had Parents and Elders trustees & deacons. Have you none of a lower class that you could spare to teach the young Idea how to shoot[?]," Richard McNemar to Seth Youngs Wells, December 22, 1834.

34. Richard McNemar to Richard McNemar Jr.

35. Ibid.

36. Rufus Bishop to Richard McNemar, November 2, 1833, IV:B-8, OClWHi.

37. Ministry, Union Village, Ohio, to Ministry, New Lebanon, New York, January 2, 1834, IV:A-71, OClWHi; Richard McNemar to Rufus Bishop, November 20, 1833, IV:A-84, OClWHi.

38. Seth Youngs Wells to Richard McNemar, January 7, 1834, Item 347c.

39. Seth Youngs Wells to Richard McNemar, January 7, 1834, Item 347c; Richard McNemar to Seth Youngs Wells, March 5, 1834; the Native-American "me poor fellow" is described in Richard McNemar to Rufus Bishop; Seth Youngs Wells to Richard McNemar, April 1834.

40. Richard McNemar to Seth Youngs Wells, May 3, 1834.

41. Ibid.; Richard McNemar to Seth Youngs Wells, May 3, 1834; McNemar, *Constitution of the United Societies*, is a bibliographic conundrum. Numerous copies exist comprising variant gatherings of pamphlets bound by McNemar with the standard title page.

42. Richard McNemar to Seth Youngs Wells, May 3, 1834.

43. Seth Youngs Wells to Richard McNemar, May 31, 1834.

44. Ibid.

45. Richard McNemar to Seth Youngs Wells, October 2, 1833.

46. For the definitive treatment of Youngs, see Glendyne R. Wergland, *One Shaker Life: Isaac Newton Youngs, 1793–1865* (Amherst: University of Massachusetts Press, 2006).

47. Seth Youngs Wells to Richard McNemar, June 9, 1834, Item 246.

48. Carol Medlicott, ed., "Br. Isaac Youngs' Journal, Tour with Br. Rufus Bishop, through the States of Ohio and Kentucky, in the Summer of 1834," in *Journals of New Lebanon Shaker Elder Rufus Bishop*, ed. Peter H. Van Demark, vol. 1 (Clinton, NY: Richard W. Couper, 2018), 197–217.

49. Ibid., 223.

50. Ibid., 224–25. McNemar's manuscript history of the Watervliet, Ohio, Shaker community is contained in Union Village, Ohio, "Documents copied from church records at Watervliet, Ohio," Item 263, Shaker Collection, DLC-MSS.

51. Medlicott, "Br. Isaac Youngs' Journal," 228.

52. There is no evidence that the troubles between Bates and McNemar were discussed in Isaac Newton Youngs's journal, nor is there evidence of extant correspondence between Bishop and his colleagues at New Lebanon.

53. 347. b, DLC-MSS.

54. McNemar, Diaries, Item 253.

55. 347. b, DLC-MSS; Ibid.

56. Medlicott, "Br. Isaac Youngs' Journal," 276.

57. Medlicott, "Br. Isaac Youngs' Journal," 274–76; Documents copied from Shaker Communities at Union Village and Watervliet, Ohio, Item 262, Shaker Collection, DLC-MSS.

58. Richard McNemar to Seth Youngs Wells, July 28, 1834.

59. Ibid.

60. Medlicott, *Issachar Bates*, 275–276; Richard McNemar, "Memorandum," November 1, 1834. Bound into BX9759 A2 (sammelband) begins with *Last Will and Testament of the Springfield Presbytery* (Albany, 1808), bound in after *Improved Edition of the Church Covenant* (R 925), before R 965 *Western Review*, OClWHi; Richard McNemar, ed., *The Western Review, or A Memorial of the Labors of Our Parents and Ministers, in Founding the Church in the West* (Watervliet, OH: 1834).

61. Ibid.

62. Church Records, Union Village, 88, Item 301.

63. Church Records, Union Village, 87, Item 301.

64. Medlicott, *Issachar Bates*, 253, 397.

65. Issachar Bates, Sketch of the Life and Experiences of Issachar Bates, Special Collections, KyBgW-K.

66. McNemar, Diaries, Item 253.

67. Richard McNemar to Solomon King, March 24, 1835, in ibid., Item 255; Church Records, Union Village, 88–89, Item 301; ibid.; the remark on Bates's love of money was made on September 1, 1834.

68. McNemar, Diaries, Item 253.

69. Medlicott, *Issachar Bates*, 255.

70. McNemar, Diaries, Item 253.

71. Ibid., 279; McNemar, Diaries, Item 253; Issachar Bates to Richard McNemar, December 27, 1836, Item 246, Shaker Collection, DLC-MSS.

72. Church Records, Union Village, 95, Item 301.

73. McNemar, Diaries, Item 253.

74. McNemar, Diaries, Item 255.

21. UNREST IN THE WEST

1. Hymns, correspondence, and other papers ... mostly concerning the Shaker communities at Pleasant Hill and South Union, Kentucky, and Union Village, Ohio, 1818–1838, 1851, Item 349c, Shaker Collection, DLC-MSS.

2. Daily Record, Union Village, Ohio, V:B-230, OClWHi.

3. Richard McNemar to Seth Youngs Wells, June 30, 1835, in Richard McNemar, Diaries, Item 255, Shaker Collection, DLC-MSS.

4. Ibid.; Richard McNemar to Seth Youngs Wells, July 28, 1834, IV:A-84, OClWHi. McNemar here quotes the hymn "The New Purchase," published in Richard McNemar,

Selection of Hymns and Poems; for the Use of Believers. Collected from Sundry Authors, by Philos Harmoniae [pseud.] (Watetvliet [sic], OH: 1833), 55.

5. Ministry, New Lebanon, New York, to David Meacham et al., September 14, 1835, in Mt. Lebanon, New York: copies of letters sent by the ministry to various communities, 1833–1839, IV:B-8, OClWHi, 80–81.

6. Isaac Newton Youngs, Domestic Journal of Daily Occurances (1834–46) New Lebanon, New York State Library, Albany, New York, Manuscripts and Special Collections, Shaker Collection, 1784–1992 (SC20330) Box 19, Folder 1 (microfilm reel 10); Mt. Lebanon, New York: various lists and notes bearing names, births, and deaths of Shakers, III:A-8, OClWHi.

7. Rufus Bishop to Richard McNemar, August 5, 1835, IV:B-8, OClWHi, 80–81.

8. Ibid.

9. Documents copied from Shaker Communities at Union Village and Watervliet, Ohio, Item 262, Shaker Collection, DLC-MSS.

10. David Meacham and Betsy Hastings to Ministry, New Lebanon, New York, August 21, 1835, IV:A-71, OClWHi.

11. Ministry, New Lebanon, New York, to David Meacham et al.

12. Ibid.

13. Documents copied from Shaker Communities.

14. Ministry, New Lebanon, New York, to Solomon King, September 14, 1835, IV:B-8, OClWHi, 93–95.

15. Mathew Houston to Rufus Bishop, December 11, 1835, IV:A-71, Shaker Collection, OClWHi.

16. Documents copied from Shaker Communities.

17. Daily Record; Ministry, Union Village, Ohio, to Ministry, New Lebanon, New York, October 25, 1835, IV:A-71, OClWHi; Church Record, Union Village, Ohio, III:B-34, OClWHi, 3.

18. Ministry, Union Village, Ohio, to Ministry, New Lebanon, New York.

19. Ministry, New Lebanon, New York, to Ministry, Union Village, Ohio, October 14, 1835, IV:B-8, OClWHi, 98–99.

20. Documents copied from Shaker Communities.

21. Richard McNemar to Nathan Sharp, October 29, 1835, IV:A-84, OClWHi.

22. Ministry, New Lebanon, New York, to Ministry, Union Village, Ohio, November 15, 1835, Item 347c, Shaker Collection, DLC-MSS.

23. Seth Youngs Wells to Richard McNemar, November 10, 1835, Item 246, Shaker Collection, DLC-MSS; Daily Record.

24. Documents copied from Shaker Communities; Richard McNemar to Seth Youngs Wells, December 2, 1835, IV:A-71, OClWHi.

25. Richard McNemar to Seth Youngs Wells.

26. Documents copied from Shaker Communities.

27. Ibid.; Church Record, Union Village, 158.

22. FREEGIFT TO THE WEST

1. Ministry, New Lebanon, New York, to Ministry, Union Village, Ohio, January 29, 1836, 109–113, IV:B-8, OClWHi.

2. Ministry, New Lebanon, New York, to Ministry, Pleasant Hill, Kentucky, February 13, 1836, 120–124, IV:B-8, OClWHi; Stephen J. Paterwic, *Historical Dictionary of the Shakers*

(Lanham, MD: Scarecrow, 2008), 234–35; Jerry V. Grant and Douglas R. Allen, *Shaker Furniture Makers* (Hanover, NH: University Press of New England, 1989), 22–33.

3. Peter H. Van Demark, ed., *Journals of New Lebanon Shaker Elder Rufus Bishop*, vol. 1 (Clinton, NY: Richard W. Couper, 2018), 328; Ministry, New Lebanon, New York, to Ministry, Union Village, Ohio, January 29, 1836, 109–13.

4. Richard McNemar to Rufus Bishop, March 10, 1836, IV:A-84, OClWHi.

5. Documents copied from Shaker Communities at Union Village and Watervliet, Ohio, Item 262, Shaker Collection, DLC-MSS.

6. Richard McNemar to Rufus Bishop, March 10, 1836.

7. Van Demark, ed., *Journals of New Lebanon Shaker*, 335–36; Ministry, New Lebanon, New York, to Jeremiah Tallcott, April 9, 1836, IV:A-79, OClWHi.

8. Documents copied from Shaker Communities; Ministry, New Lebanon, New York, to the community at Union Village, Ohio, April 9, 1836, IV:B-8, OClWHi, 124–30.

9. Ibid.

10. Ibid.

11. Richard McNemar, Diaries, Item 256, Shaker Collection, DLC-MSS; In Richard McNemar to Rufus Bishop, October 19, 1836, McNemar wrote, "It is possible that I may have committed a great error in your esteem in taking such liberties in the absence of the Ministry to send so much loose matter to Br Seth & others & not even consult the Elders on the subject or forward any of my communications with their approbation—Well, as an apology I can inform you that E. Freegift soon after his arrival gave me this liberty & he has never taken it back, so you are the person to whom I have to answer for these kind of freedoms & I shall wait your instructions as to the limits & endeavor to square my self accordingly."

12. Documents copied from Shaker Communities; Freegift Wells, Journal, V:B-294, OClWHi; for the abandonment of the joint trusteeship idea, see Richard McNemar to Seth Youngs Wells, May 1, 1837, Item 347a, Shaker Collection, DLC-MSS.

13. Richard McNemar to Seth Youngs Wells, May 2, 1836, IV:A-71, OClWHi.

14. Ministry, Union Village, Ohio, to Ministry, New Lebanon, New York, July 2, 1836, IV:A-71, OClWHi.

15. Ministry, Union Village, Ohio, to Ministry, New Lebanon, New York, February 16, 1836.

16. Ministry, Union Village, Ohio, to Ministry, New Lebanon, New York, July 2, 1836. The reference to the Graham diet is found in Richard McNemar to Seth Youngs Wells, May 2, 1836, where he wrote, "I had forgot the book handed me by Elder Freegift on the Graham system of Diet. I have not yet had time to read it thro but as far as I have read I like it much I thank you kindly for it."

17. Seth Youngs Wells to Richard McNemar, September 12, 1836, Item 246, Shaker Collection, DLC-MSS; Wells, Journal.

18. Wells, Journal; Richard McNemar to Rufus Bishop, October 16, 1836; Richard McNemar to Rufus Bishop, October 19, 1836; Documents copied from Shaker Communities. The reply to the 1804 missionary letter can be found in Church Records, Union Village, Ohio, Item 301, DLC-MSS.

19. Rufus Bishop quoted in Rufus Bishop to Richard McNemar, November 14, 1835, 93–94, Item 301, Shaker Collection, DLC-MSS. This is only an extract of Bishop's letter, the complete form of which is unlocated.

20. Richard McNemar to Rufus Bishop, October 19, 1836.

21. For much more on this exchange, as well as the full text of Bates's letter to McNemar, see Carol Medlicott, *Issachar Bates: A Shaker's Journey* (Hanover, NH: University Press of New England, 2013), 276–80.

22. Richard McNemar to Freegift Wells, November 16, 1836, Item 355d, Shaker Collection, DLC-MSS.

23. Ibid.

24. Ibid.

25. Ibid.

26. Documents copied from Shaker Communities.

27. Church Records, Item 301.

28. Ibid.

29. Seth Youngs Wells to Richard McNemar, February 16, 1837, Item 246.

23. "THE NAME OR MEMORY OF MR. MCNAMAR"

1. Richard McNemar to Seth Youngs Wells, May 17, 1837, IV:A-71, OClWHi; Freegift Wells, Journal, V:B-294, OClWHi; the signed attestation of the veracity of McNemar's recordkeeping can be found in Item 355m, Shaker Collection, DLC-MSS.

2. Freegift Wells to Ministry, New Lebanon, New York, January 31, 1837, IV:A-71, OClWHi.

3. Richard McNemar to Seth Youngs Wells.

4. Ibid.

5. Ibid.

6. Ibid.

7. Ibid.

8. Church Records, Union Village, Ohio, Item 301, DLC-MSS.

9. Freegift Wells, Journal.

10. Ministry, New Lebanon, New York, to Freegift Wells, August 7, 1837, IV:B-8, OClWHi.

11. Richard McNemar to Joshua Worley, June 13, 1837, Item 347b, Shaker Collection, DLC-MSS. Calvin Green and Seth Youngs Wells, *Testimonies of the Life, Character, Revelations and Doctrines of Our Ever Blessed Mother Ann Lee* (Hancock, MA: J. Tallcott & J. Deming, 1816).

12. Richard McNemar to Joshua Worley, June 13, 1837, Item 347b.

13. Richard McNemar quoted in Benjamin Seth Youngs to Richard McNemar, March 17, 1838, Church Records, Item 301.

14. Ministry, New Lebanon, New York, to Archibald Meacham, n.d., IV:A-30, OClWHi. The beginning of this letter to Meacham indicates the ministry's desire that he remain in the West for the time being, allaying some of his fears that he was also to be recalled to the East. This issue was also discussed in Ministry, New Lebanon, New York, to Freegift Wells, May 17, 1837. Since the ministry replied to Wells regarding McNemar in August 1837, I believe that this "Confidential" note to Meacham can be safely dated to sometime between May and August 1837. It appears to be in the hand of Rufus Bishop.

15. Richard McNemar to Rufus Bishop, October 28, 1837, IV:A-71, OClWHi.

16. Ibid.

17. Ministry, Union Village, Ohio, to Ministry, New Lebanon, New York, March 5, 1838, IV:A-71, OClWHi.

18. Milton A. McNemar to Daniel Boyd, September 22, 1837, Item 349c, Shaker Collection, DLC-MSS.

19. Church Record, Union Village, Ohio, Item 140, III:B-34, OClWHi; Miscellaneous documents primarily concerning communities in New Lebanon, New York, and Whitewater and Union Village, Ohio, circa 1817–1904, Item 347a, Shaker Collection, DLC-MSS; the information concerning McNemar's log house was recorded by Susannah Cole Liddell circa 1900, Item 352b, Shaker Collection, DLC-MSS.

20. Miscellaneous documents, Item 347a.

21. Ibid.

22. Wells, Journal; Miscellaneous documents, Item 347a.

23. Wells, Journal; Daily Record, Union Village, Ohio, V:B-230, OClWHi.

24. Wells, Journal; Miscellaneous documents, Item 347a.

25. Miscellaneous documents, Item 347a.

26. Wells, Journal.

27. Ministry, Union Village, Ohio, to Ministry, New Lebanon, New York, March 5, 1838, IV:A-71, OClWHi; Wells, Journal.

28. Richard McNemar, Journal, 1837, Item 348h, Shaker Collection, DLC-MSS.

29. Ibid.

30. Ibid.

31. Ibid.

24. THE NEW ERA

1. Benjamin Seth Youngs to Richard McNemar, November 22, 1837, Item 246, Shaker Collection, DLC-MSS.

2. Ibid.

3. Isaac Newton Youngs, A Concise View of the Church of God and of Christ, on Earth, ASC861b, DeWint, 104.

4. Ministry, New Lebanon, New York, to Ministry, New Hampshire Bishopric, November 8, 1837, 216–19, IV:B-8, OClWHi. The term "revival" is used to describe the onset of this period in Ministry, New Lebanon, New York, to Ministry, Pleasant Hill, Kentucky, December 4, 1837, 221–29, IV:B-8, OClWHi. In this letter, the New Lebanon Ministry state, "This Revival began here early last June." The term "New Era" is used by Isaac Newton Youngs in his A Concise View, and also by the New Lebanon Ministry in their letter to the elders at Sodus Bay, New York, December 19, 1837, IV:B-8, OClWHi, 231–34.

5. Ministry, New Lebanon, New York, to Ministry, New Hampshire Bishopric. For a discussion of the negative aspects of the New Era, see Glendyne R. Wergland, "The Abuse of Spirit Messages during the Shaker Era of Manifestations: 'A Hard Time of It in This Hurrycane of Gifts, to Know What Is Revelation and What Is Not,'" *American Communal Societies Quarterly* 3, no. 1 (January 2009): 27–38.

6. Freegift Wells, Journal, V:B-294, OClWHi.

7. Richard McNemar quoted in Benjamin Seth Youngs to Richard McNemar, March 17, 1838, Church Records, Union Village, Ohio, Item 301, DLC-MSS.

8. Daily Record, Union Village, Ohio, V:B-230, OClWHi.

9. Richard McNemar to Betsey Hastings, December 6, 1836, 347b, Shaker Collection, DLC-MSS.

10. MacLean, *Shakers of Ohio*, 170; Richard McNemar to Richard W. Pelham, March 18, 1838, 347b, DLC-MSS.
11. Richard W. Pelham to Freegift Wells, April 2, 1838, IV:A-51, OClWHi.
12. Richard McNemar to Rufus Bishop, May 13, 1838, IV:A-71, OClWHi.
13. Rufus Bishop to Richard McNemar, June 30, 1838, LoC 246, also in IV:B-8, OClWHi.
14. Daniel Miller, Journal of Passing Events, Union Village, Ohio, V:B-237, OClWHi.
15. Joshua Worley, Letter, Joshua Worley to Mrs. Hollaway, "Corruptions of Shakerism," *Voice of Truth and Glad Tidings of the Kingdom at Hand* 14, no. 7 (May 12, 1847): 56; Ministry, Union Village, Ohio, to Ministry, New Lebanon, New York, September 10, 1838, IV:A-71, OClWHi.
16. Ministry, Union Village, Ohio, to Ministry, New Lebanon, New York.
17. Daily Record; Miller, Journal; Ministry, New Lebanon, New York, to Ministry, Union Village, Ohio, October 10, 1838, IV:B-8, OClWHi.
18. Daily Record; Miller, Journal.
19. Daily Record; Miller, Journal; Wells, Journal; Ministry, New Lebanon, New York, to Ministry, Union Village, Ohio, October 9, 1838, 264–65.
20. Seth Youngs Wells to Matthew Houston, October 9, 1838, IV:A-37, OClWHi.
21. Ibid.
22. Ministry, New Lebanon, New York, to Ministry, Union Village, Ohio, October 10, 1838.
23. Ibid.
24. Benjamin Seth Youngs to Richard McNemar, March 17, 1838, Item 301. This letter is contained in a volume of transcriptions made by McNemar, and it survives in McNemar's hand. The date assigned is based on the date of the first letter from Youngs in that section of McNemar's manuscript. The content quoted in this passage, however, likely dates from later in the year 1838. The terminal date for the section in McNemar's manuscript is December 15, 1838, which may be the date he transcribed the text but may also relate to the content of Youngs's letter.
25. Benjamin Seth Youngs to Richard McNemar, March 17, 1838, Item 301; Richard McNemar to Benjamin Seth Youngs, November 4, 1838, Church Records, Union Village, Ohio, Item 301, DLC-MSS.
26. Daily Record; Miller, Journal; Wells, Journal.
27. Benjamin Seth Youngs to Richard McNemar, March 17, 1838, Item 301.
28. Benjamin Seth Youngs to Richard McNemar, October 13, 1838, Item 301.
29. Richard McNemar to Benjamin Seth Youngs, November 4, 1838, Item 301; Daily Record; Miller, Journal; Wells, Journal. McNemar made an entry in one of his personal manuscripts on May 26, 1838, which indicates he was restarting his Union Press printing operation at that time. It is unknown if this was undertaken in consultation with the ministry, or if it was—as seems more likely—wishful thinking on his part: "U.V. Saturday May 26. 1838. Whereas it appears from various considerations that the time is come for making some use of our types and press, for the benefit of the children or use of the school in furnishing sundry articles requested by the ministry: and also for reprinting some small tracts here to fore deemd profitable to distribute among young believers and for the information of inquirers.—& whereas by an original agreement of Ministers Elders & others the said types and press were procured expressly for the general use & benefit of the gospel & to be stationed at the center of union for that purpose, & from sundry causes has been for some years past dispersed about in different places and of little or no use or benefit. We the undersigned being consulted on the subject agree that Brother Eleazar who has the principal charge of said

property be permitted and encouraged to collect the same to some suitable place within the bounds of this society where it may be thought the least offensive & the most accommodating to those concerned and that he be countenanced & encouraged in putting the said printing concern in suitable order for executing such jobs as have been agreed upon or may hereafter be agreed upon in union & conformity to the chh. and society at New Lebanon," Item 355d, Shaker Collection, DLC-MSS. The list of books that McNemar bound for Robert Corwin can be found in Item 355d, Shaker Collection, DLC-MSS; incredibly, he completed the job in just over a month!

30. John Patterson MacLean, *A Sketch of the Life and Labors of Richard McNemar* (Franklin, OH: Franklin *Chronicle*, 1905), 25; Richard McNemar to Benjamin Seth Youngs, November 4, 1838, Item, 301; Daily Record; Miller, Journal; Wells, Journal.

31. Daily Record; Miller, Journal; Daniel Miller Daybook, Union Village, Ohio, Item 165, DLC-MSS; Wells, Journal.

32. Daily Record; Wells, Journal; Miller, Journal.

33. Andrew C. Houston to Eliza Sharp, December 22, 1838, as quoted by Benjamin Seth Youngs in a manuscript compilation of extracts from correspondence, Shaker Collection, Box 45: 99 v.3 #51, MWiW.

34. Ibid.

35. Daily Record; Miller, Journal.

25. WAR IN HEAVEN

1. Daniel Miller, Daybook, Union Village, Ohio, Item 165, Shaker Collection, DLC-MSS.

2. Freegift Wells, Journal, V:B-294, OClWHi; Miller, Daybook, Item 165; Daily Record, Union Village, Ohio, V:B-230.

3. Ministry, New Lebanon, New York, to Ministry, Union Village, Ohio, January 9, 1839, IV:B-8, OClWHi.

4. Ministry, New Lebanon, New York, to Ministry, Union Village, Ohio, January 9, 1839, IV:B-8, OClWHi; Ministry, New Lebanon, New York, to Ministry, Union Village, Ohio, February 23, 1839, Item 309, IV:B-8, OClWHi.

5. Daniel Miller, Journal of Passing Events, Union Village, Ohio, V:B-237, OClWHi; Wells, Journal; Miller, Daybook, Item 165; Susannah Cole Liddell, Notes, Item 355j, Shaker Collection, DLC-MSS. Sarah Cochran's name is also spelled "Coughran" in Shaker sources.

6. United States Census for 1860.

7. Liddell, Notes, Items 348d and 355j; Andrew C. Houston supplies one of the few contemporary accounts of Margaret McBrien's origins and arrival at Union Village in Andrew C. Houston to David A. Buckingham, March 21, 1839, ASC 1048, DeWint. This letter survives in two versions: the Winterthur one and a shorter copy found in IV:A-71, OClWHi. The Winterthur version contains a lengthy postscript dealing with McBrien not found in the Western Reserve Historical Society's copy.

8. Freegift Wells to Ministry, North Union, Ohio, February 2, 1839, IV:B-24, OClWHi. The substance of another of McBrien's spirit messages and one quoted line can be found in Andrew C. Houston to David A. Buckingham, March 21, 1839, ASC 1048, DeWint.

9. Freegift Wells to Ministry, North Union, Ohio.

10. Ibid.; Daily Record; Wells, Journal; Miller, Journal; Liddell, Notes, Item 348d. Liddell's description of McBrien at the meeting was written many years later, circa 1903. Since

Liddell was describing McBrien's first visionary episode in public, I have assumed that it was the meeting on February 3, 1839.

11. Miller, Daybook, entry for February 10, 1839.
12. Andrew C. Houston to David A. Buckingham, March 21, 1839, ASC 1048, DeWint; Wells, Journal, February 5, 12, 1839.
13. Miller, Journal; Wells, Journal.
14. Wells, Journal, entry for February 21, 1839.
15. Miller, Journal.
16. Miller, Daybook, Item 165.
17. Miller, Journal.
18. Church Records, entry for April 18, 1839, Union Village, Ohio, Item 301, DLC-MSS.
19. Wells, Journal, March 1, 1839.
20. Ibid.; Daily Record.
21. Wells, Journal; Andrew C. Houston to David A. Buckingham, March 21, 1839, IV:A-71, OClWHi.
22. Andrew C. Houston to David A. Buckingham, March 21, 1839, IV:A-71, OClWHi.
23. Church Record, entry for April 18, 1839.
24. Wells, Journal.
25. Wells, Journal; Miller, Journal.
26. Miller, Journal.
27. Daily Record, March 23–24, 1839; Miller, Journal; Miller, Daybook, Item 165; Wells, Journal, entry for March 24, 1839.
28. Wells, Journal; Miller, Daybook, Item 165.
29. Wells, Journal, March 27, 1839; Miller, Daybook, entry for March 28, 1839; Daily Record, entry for March 28, 1839.
30. Miller, Daybook, Item 165; Daily Record; Wells, Journal.
31. Wells, Journal.
32. Wells, Journal; Miller, Daybook, Item 165.
33. Wells, Journal.
34. Daily Record; "To the Public," *Western Star* (Lebanon, OH.), April 5, 1839.
35. Miscellaneous, Item 347a, DLC-MSS.
36. Ibid.
37. Miller, Daybook, Item 165.
38. McNemar copied the treatments from "Gunn's domestic medicine" on March 20, 1839, Item 355a, Shaker Collection, DLC-MSS; Levi McNemar to Milton A. McNemar, February 9, 1839; Church Records, Item 301.
39. Milton A. McNemar to Richard McNemar Jr., February 19, 1839. John H. James Family Papers, Walter Havighurst Special Collections, OOxM. I thank Etta Madden for bringing this letter to my attention.
40. Richard McNemar Jr. to Richard McNemar Sr., March 2, 1839, Item 347b, Shaker Collection, DLC-MSS.
41. Ibid.
42. Andrew C. Houston to Richard McNemar Jr., March 2, 1839, John H. James Family Papers.
43. Wells, Journal; Miller, Daybook, Item 165; Daily Record. The number of visionists and more information about them can be found in Freegift Wells to Ministry, Pleasant Hill, Kentucky, March 20, 1839, IV:B-24, OClWHi.

44. Wells, Journal.
45. Daily Record, Union Village; Wells, Journal.
46. Wells, Journal.
47. Miller, Daybook, Item 165; Wells, Journal; Daily Record.
48. Richard McNemar to Richard McNemar Jr., April 12, 1839, in Church Records, Item 301.
49. Ibid.
50. Miller, Daybook, Item 165.
51. Wells, Journal; Miller, Daybook Item 165.
52. Wells, Journal.
53. Ibid.
54. Ibid.; Miller, Journal; Miller, Daybook, Item 165; Daily Record; John S. Houston to Richard McNemar Jr., April 23, 1839, John H. James Family Papers.
55. Miller, Journal; Daily Record. The journal reference in Daniel Miller's Journal of Passing and Important Events states that McNemar was taken to "Dunlavey's" in Lebanon. I have assumed that this refers to Judge Francis Dunlavy's house, as he is referenced in Richard McNemar Jr. to Richard McNemar, August 24, 1839, Item 348c; Peter Boyd, Journal, 1833–1840, Item 57, Shaker Collection, DLC-MSS.

26. A WANDERING STAR

1. Ministry, New Lebanon, New York, to Ministry, Union Village, Ohio, April 30, 1839, IV:B-8, OClWHi, 321–25.
2. Benjamin Seth Youngs to Richard McNemar, March 17, 1838, Church Records, Union Village, Ohio, Item 301, DLC-MSS.
3. Ministry, Union Village, Ohio, to Ministry, North Union, Ohio, July 12, 1839, IV:B-24, OClWHi; Rufus Bishop, A Daily Journal of Passing Events; Begun January the 1st, 1830, By Rufus Bishop, in the 56th Year of his Age, Journal 1830 January 1–1839 May 18 1839, Item 1, Shaker Collection, NN; the reference to McNemar's letter is found in Richard McNemar Jr. to Richard McNemar, August 24, 1839, Item 348c, Shaker Collection, DLC-MSS.
4. Ministry, New Lebanon, New York, to Ministry, Union Village, Ohio, April 30, 1839, IV:B-8, OClWHi, 321–25.
5. Bishop, Daily Journal, Item 1.
6. Ibid.
7. Account of Meetings, New Lebanon, New York, 1838–1842, WRHS V:B-132, OClWHi; Bishop, Daily Journal, Item 1.
8. Bishop, Daily Journal, Item 1. On June 10, the New Lebanon Ministry received a now-unlocated letter written by Freegift Wells from Union Village on May 31, 1839. No extant paper trail between the Ministries of New Lebanon and Union Village exists to evidence the development of a coordinated approach to dealing with McNemar.
9. Stephen J. Paterwic, *Historical Dictionary of the Shakers* (Lanham, MD: Scarecrow, 2008), 136–38; Calvin Green, "Biographic Memoir of the Life and Experience of Calvin Green," in Glendyne R. Wergland and Christian Goodwillie, *Shaker Autobiographies, Biographies and Testimonies, 1806–1907*, vol. 3 (London: Pickering & Chatto, 2014), 46, 147.
10. "A Communication from Father David Darrow. Made on Saturday Evening, June 15th; 1839 to Eleazar Wright (formerly called Richard McNemar.)," in Daniel Miller, A True

Record of Sacred Communications; Written by Divine Inspiration, By the Mortal Hand of Chosen Instruments; in the Church at New Lebanon, 1838–1841, Chapter XLIV, 176, VIII:B-116, OClWHi. This spirit message was recorded in the manuscript compilation April 2, 1841, and credited to "Inst. C.G.," i.e., instrument Calvin Green. The same text is also included on pages 173–75, VIII:B-127, OClWHi.

11. Bishop, Daily Journal, Item 1.

12. The exact text of Mother Ruth Farrington's message to Richard McNemar is unlocated. A recapitulation is found in Seth Youngs Wells to Ministry, North Union, Ohio, July 12, 1839, IV:A-37, OClWHi.

13. Bishop, Daily Journal, Item 1; Goodrich's funeral hymn can be found in Richard McNemar, *Selection of Hymns and Poems; for the Use of Believers. Collected from Sundry Authors, by Philos Harmoniae* [pseud.] (Watetvliet [sic], OH: 1833), 90–92.

14. Bishop, Daily Journal, Item 1.

15. "A Message from Mother Ann to Brother Eleazer Wright, Delivered to Him thro' the Intercession of Father David Darrow, New Lebanon June 21st 1839," in Miller, True Record of Sacred Communications, 179. This spirit message was recorded in the manuscript compilation April 2, 1841, and credited to "Instrument Philemon S." The scribe noted that the message was "written mostly in the words of the Instrument, as inspired by Mother." The same text is also included on pages 176–80, VIII:B-127, OClWHi.

16. Bishop, Daily Journal, Item 1. Betts "came over the mountain" on Monday, June 24.

17. Ibid.; Records, 6, NN.

27. LOOK HOMEWARD, ANGEL

1. Daily Record, entry for April 27, 1839, Union Village, Ohio, V:B-230; Daniel Miller, Journal of Passing Events, entry for May 5, 1839, Union Village, Ohio, V:B-237, OClWHi; Freegift Wells to Ministry, South Union, Kentucky, June 1, 1839, IV:B-24, OClWHi.

2. Daniel Miller, Daybook, Union Village, Ohio, Item 165, DLC-MSS.

3. Ibid.; "Suicide," *Western Star* (Lebanon, OH), June 14, 1839; Benjamin Seth Youngs, handwritten copy of article "Suicide," IV:A-71, OClWHi; Freegift Wells, Journal, V:B-294, OClWHi. MacLean in his biography *A Sketch of the Life and Labors of Richard McNemar* (Franklin, OH: Franklin *Chronicle*, 1905), 56, asserts that Randolph West had learned to imitate McNemar's handwriting and forged "scurrilous scraps" that he left around the village to enrage Freegift Wells. Accordingly, Wells believed that McNemar was undermining him and persecuted McNemar. West supposedly later confessed his deeds, left the village, and hung himself two years later. This chronology of events does not jibe with the known trajectory of West's apostasy and death. Also, no mention of any scenario like this is to be found anywhere in the manuscript record, either contemporary to the late 1830s or in Liddell's later historical reminiscences. So, it does not seem plausible. There is, however, evidence that the practice of leaving scraps of controversial writing around Union Village did happen; for example, see Richard McNemar's "Confidential" letter to Betsy Hastings, December 6, 1836, Item 347b, Shaker Collection, DLC-MSS.

4. Wells, Journal.

5. Ministry, New Lebanon, New York, to Ministry, Union Village, Ohio, July 2, 1839, 1–3, IV:B-9, OClWHi.

6. Seth Youngs Wells to Ministry, North Union, Ohio, July 12, 1839, IV:A-37, OClWHi.

7. Richard McNemar to Rufus Bishop, July 15, 1839, IV:A-71, OClWHi.

8. Ibid.

9. Freegift Wells to Ministry, New Lebanon, New York, August 19, 1839, IV:A-54, OClWHi.

10. Wells, Journal; Miller, Journal.

11. Ministry, New Lebanon, New York, to Ministry, South Union, Kentucky, August 12, 1839, 6; Wells, Journal, entries for July 20, 26.

12. Andrew C. Houston to Ministry, New Lebanon, New York, July 28, 1839, IV:A-71, OClWHi; Freegift Wells to Ministry, New Lebanon, New York.

13. Wells, Journal; Freegift Wells to Ministry, New Lebanon, New York; Miller, Daybook. A lengthy and seemingly romanticized account of this pivotal meeting was written by Susannah Cole Liddell circa 1903 and can be found in Item352c, Shaker Collection, DLC-MSS. Liddell was an eyewitness to these events, and her account provides tantalizing details, but it varies so much from the few contemporary descriptions that I have opted not to include information from it into the main body of this biography. The full text can be found in an appendix to this volume.

14. Richard McNemar Jr. to Richard McNemar, August 24, 1839, Item 348c, Shaker Collection, DLC-MSS.

15. Andrew C. Houston to Richard McNemar Jr., August 31, 1839. John H. James Family Papers, Walter Havighurst Special Collections, OOxM. I thank Etta Madden for bringing this letter to my attention.

16. Elders, First Order, Union Village to Ministry, Union Village, Ohio (while visiting at Pleasant Hill, Kentucky), September 23, 1839, IV:A-71, OClWHi. Benjamin Seth Youngs's partial transcription of this letter can be found in his manuscript compilation of extracts from correspondence, Shaker Collection, Box 45: 99 v.3 #51, MWiW; Miller, Daybook, Item 165.

17. Elders, First Order, Union Village, to Ministry, Union Village, Ohio.

18. Ibid.; Miller, Daybook, Item 165.

19. Wells, Journal.

20. Ministry, New Lebanon, New York, to Ministry, Union Village, Ohio, October 5, 1839.

21. Rufus Bishop, A Daily Journal of Passing Events; Begun January the 1st, 1830. By Rufus Bishop, in the 56th Year of His Age, Journal 1830 January 1–1839 May 18 1839, Item 1, Shaker Collection. NN.

28. AFTERMATH AND LEGACY

1. At least the first eight leaves of A Compilation of Inspired Messages and Communications, 1839–1840, VII:B-229, OClWHi, appear to have been excised. The first extant spirit message in that manuscript is from December 1839. The other four volumes of Union Village spirit messages (VII:B-224 through 228) also lack messages from before that date. Tellingly, these were transcribed by Freegift Wells between 1841 and 1843.

2. Ministry, Union Village, Ohio, to Ministry, New Lebanon, New York, September 4, 1846, IV:A-72, OClWHi. Indeed, McNemar's manuscripts in the collection of the Library of Congress Manuscript Division bear extensive physical evidence of disbinding and rearrangement.

3. Freegift Wells to Ministry, New Lebanon, New York, March 29, 1841, IV:A-72, OClWHi. I thank Thomas L. Sakmyster for providing me with this reference.

4. Ibid.

5. Freegift Wells, A Series of Remarks Showing the Power of the Adversary in Leading Honest Souls Astray through the Influence of Inspired Messages, or a Lamentation Because the Beauty of Zion Hath Faded, and Her Light Become Dim, 8, 16–17, VII:B-266, OClWHi.

6. Richard McNemar writings, Item 355d, Shaker Collection, DLC-MSS.

7. Susannah Cole Liddell, Notes, Item 348d, Shaker Collection, DLC-MSS.

8. Ibid.

9. John Patterson MacLean to James H. Fennessy, August 21, 1903, Item 354c, Shaker Collection, DLC-MSS.

10. Susannah Cole Liddell, Notes, Item 349d, Shaker Collection, DLC-MSS.

11. John Patterson MacLean, Expulsion of Richard McNemar, VII:A-22, OClWHi. The full text can be found in an appendix to this volume.

12. Ibid.

13. Ibid.

14. John Patterson MacLean, *A Sketch of the Life and Labors of Richard McNemar* (Franklin, OH: Franklin *Chronicle*, 1905), 59.

15. Moore S. Mason to John Patterson MacLean, July 16, 1905, IV:A-66, OClWHi. I thank Carol Medlicott for bringing this letter to my attention.

16. Susannah Cole Liddell, Notes, Items 348b and 350c, Shaker Collection, DLC-MSS.

17. Liddell, Notes, Item 348a.

18. "Death of Richard R. McNemar," *Republic* (Springfield, OH), September 3, 1852.

19. Liddell, Notes, Items 348d and 350d.

20. Milton A. McNemar's last letters to Richard McNemar Jr. can be found in the John H. James Family Papers, Walter Havighurst Special Collections, OOxM. Advertisements for Milton A. McNemar's hotels are found in *Mississippi Free Trader* (Natchez, MS), December 7, 1848, and Natchez *Daily Courier* (Natchez, MS), May 4, 1852.

21. Church Record of the Appointments to the Office of the Ministry, Elders, and Trustees of Union Village, III:B-34, OClWHi.

22. Stephen J. Paterwic, *Historical Dictionary of the Shakers* (Lanham, MD: Scarecrow, 2008), 319.

23. Notes and copies of spiritual communications of David Darrow, Ruth Farrington, Ann Lee, William Lee, Mother Wisdom, Lucy Wright, and others, circa 1807–1905, 351d, DLC-MSS. I thank Thomas L. Sakmyster for bringing this reference to my attention.

24. Emmet McBrien's ultimate fate is unknown. He appears in the 1860 census at Turtle Creek, Ohio, and is listed as a painter. It is not clear, however, if he was still a Shaker or just lived in the surrounding community. His mother's post-Shaker life has proven as nebulous as her pre-Shaker life. A woman named Margaret McBrien, born in Ireland circa 1817, died in Patterson, New Jersey, on April 9, 1897, aged eighty. She was listed as single. This may be the same Margaret McBrien, but it cannot be proven definitively.

25. Ministry, Union Village, Ohio, to Ministry, New Lebanon, New York, October 10, 1844.

APPENDIX 3

1. Richard McNemar, Watervliet, Ohio, to Rufus Bishop, New Lebanon, New York, November 20, 1832, OCWR, IV A:79.

2. Seth Youngs Wells, New Lebanon, New York, to Richard McNemar, Watervliet, Ohio, April 6, 1833, WLCMs, Shaker Collection, Item 347c.

3. Richard McNemar, Watervliet, Ohio, to Seth Youngs Wells, New Lebanon, New York, December 22, 1834, OCWR, Shaker Collection, Item IV A:84.

APPENDIX 5

1. *The facts relating to the expulsion of Richard McNemar were ~~not~~ disclosed to me ~~until~~ on February 8, 1904—or over a year after this paper had been placed in the hands of the editor. On two previous occasions the aged sister commenced the story, but would suddenly stop and leave me. The third time several sisters and two of the brethren were present. I followed her very closely and wherever she would waver I pressed her with question after question until the whole was unravelled. At times her face bore the most fitful expression. Her lips would twist, and every indication appeared as though she would burst into tears. When her story ended I said to her: "This is all ~~knew~~ new to me." Looking at me reproachfully she said: "If I had known that I would not have said a word to you about it," and then fled to her room. I have not represented her words nor ideas, but dressed the matter up with other facts I have learned. I submitted the matter to Mr. Fennessy, for his approval. He said these things were all known to him, and that he had advised several that nothing should be hidden from me; that history should be written and not concealed.

2. *From my valued correspondent, Sister Aurelia G. Mace, principal leader of the Sabbathday Lake, Maine, Society, I learn that during the same period the mediums at Alfred, Maine, began to make trouble, and declared they were inspired by Mother Ann that such and such persons should be removed. Elder Elisha Pote, then first in the Ministry, said "Those revelations must be stopped." The mediums answered, "It is Mother's voice." Springing upon the floor Elder Elisha exclaimed, "It is the voice of the Mother of Harlots." He then proceeded to instruct the people that the Covenant was the basis upon which he should stand; that no revelation received by the mediums could superceed that. At another time an urgent measure was about to be executed in the Alfred Society. The brethren called a meeting by themselves and protested, and gave out word that they would close the Meeting House; that they would have no Ministry if the proposition was effected. Immediately the matter was adjusted.

Another valued correspondent, Alonzo G. Hollister, writes me that at Mount Lebanon the mediums were not allowed to transcend the authority of the Elders where they resided, although great latitude was allowed them. All the messages were of no account unless approved by the Elders or the Ministry. "It is a fundamental principle of the system that the lead for the direction of the visible body is in our visible leaders; and no gift or direction from the spirit world has any force without their approbation. That was one test for dealing with disorderly spirits!" But Freegift was first in the Ministry and approved of the expulsions.

BIBLIOGRAPHY

MANUSCRIPT COLLECTIONS, INSTITUTIONAL MARC ORGANIZATION CODES

DeWint-M	Henry Frances DuPont Winterthur Museum, Joseph Downs Manuscript and Microfilm Collection, Winterthur, DE
DLC-MSS	Manuscript Division, Library of Congress, Washington, DC
KyBgW-K	Western Kentucky University, Kentucky Library
KyHi	Kentucky Historical Society, Frankfort
KyU	University of Kentucky, Special Collections
MaShaTR	The Trustees of Reservations, Archives and Research Center, Sharon, MA
MePosS	United Society of Shakers, Shaker Library, Sabbathday Lake, ME
MWiW	Williams College, Williamstown, MA
N	New York State Library, Albany
NCH	Burke Library, Hamilton College, Clinton, NY
NN	New York Public Library, New York
NOcaS	Shaker Museum | Mount Lebanon, Chatham, NY
OClWHi	Western Reserve Historical Society, Cleveland, OH
OHi	Ohio History Connection, Columbus
OOxM	Miami University, Oxford, OH
PPPrHi	Presbyterian Historical Society, Philadelphia
SVPH	Shaker Village of Pleasant Hill, Harrodsburg, KY
UPB	Brigham Young University, Harold B. Lee Library, Provo, UT

PRIMARY SOURCES

Manuscript Sources

Note: Individual items of correspondence are cited in the endnotes. They have been drawn from the following collections: DeWint-M, DLC-MSS (245, 246,

347a, 347b, 347c, 348c, 349c, 354c, 355a, 355d, 355l), MePosS, MWiW, and OClWHi (IV:A and IV:B).

"An Account of the Sickness of Eldress Lucy Smith," April 20, 1817. IV:A-60. OClWHi.

Bates, Issachar. Sketch of the Life and Experiences of Issachar Bates, Special Collections. KyBgW-K.

Bishop, Rufus. A Daily Journal of Passing Events; Begun January the 1st, 1830. By Rufus Bishop, in the 56th Year of His Age, Journal 1830 January 1–1839 May 18 1839, Item 1. Shaker Collection. NN.

———. Day Book kept by Rufus Bishop as a record of the ministry. V:B-85. OClWHi.

Cabin Creek Presbyterian Church Records, 1805–1839. M-789. KyU.

Canterbury, New Hampshire. Current Record of Events from 1792 to 1885. Shaker Collection. NCH.

Clark, Abigail. "Journal and Other Writings, 1805–1900," Item 164c. Shaker Collection. DLC-MSS.

Deming, William. Journal of William's travel to the state of Ohio, 1810. ASC 818. DeWint-M.

Documents on Father David Darrow's funeral, Item 245. Shaker Collection. DLC-MSS.

Documents copied from Shaker communities at Union Village and Watervliet, Ohio, Item 262. Shaker Collection. DLC-MSS.

Hammond, Joseph. Day Book, Shirley, MA. V:B-203. OClWHi.

Harvard, Massachusetts. Church Family Journal, HVD 2. 3112. MaShaTR.

Hymns, correspondence, and other papers . . . mostly concerning the Shaker communities at Pleasant Hill and South Union, Kentucky, and Union Village, Ohio, 1818–1838, 1851, Item 349c. Shaker Collection. DLC-MSS.

Kentucky Synod. Minutes, 1802–1883. Louisville Presbyterian Theological Seminary, E. M. White Library.

Liddell, Susannah. Writings, Items 164c, 250, 348a, 348b, 348c, 348d, 349d, 350c, 350d, 350f, 352b, 352c, 355j. DLC-MSS.

Lucas, Sarah. Testimony. VII:B-110. OClWHi.

Lyle, John. Diary (typed transcript). KyHi.

MacLean, John Patterson. Expulsion of Richard McNemar. VII:A-22. OClWHi.

McNemar, Richard. Biographical Account of Solomon King, written by Richard McNemar, c.1835. VI:A-10. OClWHi.

———. A Discourse Delivered at Harvard Aug 2d 1829 by Eleazar Wright of Union Village, Ohio. Shaker Collection. 41 M 23. MWiW.

———. Diaries, Items 253, 254, 255, 256. Shaker Collection. DLC-MSS.

———. Journal, 1837, Item 348h. Shaker Collection. DLC-MSS.

———. Papers, Item 349. DLC-MSS.

———. Richard McNemar to Richard McNemar Jr., October 8, 1833. Vault MSS 270. Special Collections, Lee Library. UPB.

———. Richard McNemar writings in: Miscellaneous documents primarily concerning communities in New Lebanon, New York, and Whitewater and Union Village, Ohio, circa 1817–1904, Item 347a. Shaker Collection. DLC-MSS.
McNemar, Vincy. Hymnbook and Notes, Item 349d. Shaker Collection. DLC-MSS.
Miller, Daniel. Daybook, Union Village, Ohio, Item 165. Shaker Collection. DLC-MSS
———. Journal of Passing Events, Union Village, Ohio. V:B-237. OClWHi.
New Lebanon, New York. Account of Meetings, 1838–1842. WRHS V:B-132. OClWHi.
———. Domestic Journal of important occurrences kept for the elder sisters at New Lebanon, 1780–1862. V:B-60. OClWHi.
———. Records. Book No. 2. Kept [in part] by Rufus Bishop, Item 6. Shaker Collection, NN.
———. Records Kept by Order of the Church, 1780–1855, New Lebanon, New York. Shaker Manuscript Collection, Item 7. NN.
———. A True Record of Sacred Communications; Written by Divine Inspiration, By the Mortal Hand of Chosen Instruments; in the Church at New Lebanon, 1838–1841. VIII:B-116. OClWHi.
———. Various Lists and Notes Bearing Names, Births, and Deaths of Shakers. III:A-8. OClWHi.
North Union, Ohio. Brief Record of the Rise and Progress of the Society of Believers at North Union, Ohio. V:B-176. OClWHi.
———. Records of the Church at North Union Containing the Rise and Progress of the Church, North Union, Ohio. V:B-177. OClWHi.
Pease, Peter. Journal, 1806–1815, Item 232. DLC-MSS.
Pleasant Hill, Kentucky. Church Record Book A. SVPH.
———. Early Records of Pleasant Hill, Kentucky, 1806–1836, Item 00006. SVPH.
Prescott, James. The History of North Union, 1880. VII:B-221. OClWHi.
Rankin Sr., John. "Autobiography." Record Book A. South Union, Kentucky. KyBgW-K.
Remarks on the Church Covenant of the United Society Called Shakers, New Lebanon, July 12, 1829, Item 347a. Shaker Collection. DLC-MSS.
Shirley, Massachussets. Journal of the North Family. V:B-190. OClWHi.
———. Journal of an Unknown Resident. V:B-199. OClWHi.
Sodus Bay, New York. Journal. V:B-22. OClWHi.
———. A Record of the Commencement and Progress of the Believers at Sodus and Port Bay. V:B-21. OClWHi
South Union, Kentucky. Covenant. I:B-63. OClWHi.
———. Record Book A. KyBgW-K.

Spinning, David. A Short Sketch of the Life of David Spinning, Comprising His Dietetic, His Moral & Religious Experience, MS 119, Box 2, Item 13. OHi.

The State of Ohio vs. Samuel Rollins and Richard McNemar, Court Records, August Term, 1818. Warren County Records Center and Archives, Lebanon, Ohio, 255–58.

Transylvania Presbytery. Minutes. Louisville Presbyterian Theological Seminary, E. M. White Library.

"Trial of Robert Finley, 1795," #92 1123. PPPrHi.

Union Village, Ohio. Church Records, Item 301. Shaker Collection. DLC-MSS.

———. Church Record of the Appointments to the Office of the Ministry, Elders, and Trustees of Union Village. III:B-34, OClWHi.

———. Covenant, Union Village, Ohio, 1829. I:B-70. OClWHi.

———. Daily journal of current events and activities by John Wallace and Nathan Sharp. V:B-236. OClWHi.

———. Daily Record of Events of the Church Family, Union Village, Ohio. V:B-230. OClWHi.

———. Diary, Union Village, Ohio, 1826–1860, Item 167. Shaker Collection. DLC-MSS.

———. Documents copied from church records at Watervliet, Ohio, Item 263. Shaker Collection, DLC-MSS.

———. Financial Accounts, Item 153. Shaker Collection. DLC-MSS.

———. Membership List Compiled from Various Sources by Oliver C. Hampton, 1805–1898, III:B-33. OClWHi.

———. Notes and copies of spiritual communications of David Darrow, Ruth Farrington, Ann Lee, William Lee, Mother Wisdom, Lucy Wright, and others, circa 1807–1905, 351d. DLC-MSS.

———. Records. I:A-19. OClWHi.

———. "To the General Assembly of the State of Ohio from the Society Called Shakers a Declaration," September 24, 1811. IV:B-36. OClWHi.

Washington, First Presbytery. Minutes and Records, 1799-1810, 1–6, Vault BX 8958. W199 A3. PPPrHi.

Watervliet, Ohio. General Rules of the United Society ... Jan. 1833, Item 303. Shaker Collection. DLC-MSS.

Wells, Freegift. Journal. V:B-294. OClWHi.

———. Memorandum of Events. V:B-291. OClWHi.

———. A Series of Remarks Showing the Power of the Adversary in Leading Honest Souls Astray through the Influence of Inspired Messages, or a Lamentation Because the Beauty of Zion Hath Faded, and Her Light Become Dim. VII:B-266. OClWHi.

Youngs, Benjamin Seth. Diary, 1805. ASC 859. DeWint-M.

———. Pamphlet Journal of Union Village, 1806–1807, #10, 130. NOcaS.

Youngs, Isaac Newton. A Concise View of the Church of God and of Christ, on Earth, ASC861b. DeWint.

———. Domestic Journal of Daily Occurances (1834–46) New Lebanon. Shaker Collection, Box 19, Folder 1. N.

PUBLISHED SOURCES

Articles

D., A. H. (Anthony H. Dunlevy). "The Great Kentucky Revival of 1800 and the Late Richard McNemar, of Union Village, O." *Western Star* (Lebanon, OH), April 30, 1874.
Davis, Jonathan. "Affidavit of Jonathan Davis." *Western Star* (Lebanon, OH), September 24, 1817.
"Death of Richard R. McNemar." *Republic* (Springfield, OH), September 3, 1852.
Finley, James B. "Reminiscences of Early Life." *Ladies Repository* 6, no. 6 (June 1846): 165–67.
Freeman, Thomas. "Retrospective View of Shakerism, No IV" (fragmentary). *Western Star* (Lebanon, OH), September 29, 1810.
———. "Retrospective View of Shakerism, No. V." *Western Star* (Lebanon, OH), October 13, 1810.
"Historical Sketch of the First Presbyterian Church, Cincinnati." *Presbyterian Magazine*, June 1852, 2, 265.
"Lebanon Temperance Society." *Western Star* (Lebanon, OH), October 19, 1832.
MacLean, John Patterson. "Shaker History. Richard McNemar Sinks into Deep Oblivion." *Western Star* (Lebanon, OH), June 4, 1908.
McGready, James. "A Short Narrative of the Revival of Religion in Logan County." *Western Missionary Magazine*, February 1, 1803.
McNemar, Richard, and Calvin Morrell. "Remonstrance." *Columbus Gazette* (Columbus, OH), December 11, 1817.
"Memoir of Judge Trimble." *American Jurist and Law Magazine* 1, January and April 1829, 149–57.
"Mobbing the Shakers at Union Village, Ohio." *Supporter* (Chillicothe, OH), September 8, 1810.
"Modern Pilgrims." *New York Telescope*, May 6, 1826.
Morrow, Josiah. "A Miami Valley Reformer." *Western Star* (Lebanon, OH), January 27, 1916.
———. "The Turtlecreek Church." *Western Star* (Lebanon, OH), November 30, 1911.
"A Short Account of the People Known by the Name of Shakers, or Shaking Quakers." *Theological Magazine* 1, no. 1 (September/October 1795): 81–88.
Smith, James. "An Attempt to Develope Shakerism." *Supporter* (Chillicothe, OH), July 10, 1810, 2.
"Suicide." *Western Star* (Lebanon, OH), June 14, 1839.
"To the Public." *Western Star* (Lebanon, OH), [March 3?], 1815.

"To the Public." *Western Star* (Lebanon, OH), April 5, 1839.
Western Spy (Cincinnati), April 15, 1818, 3.
"Who Are the Shakers?" *American Commercial Daily Advertiser* (Baltimore), August 15, 1810.
Worley, Joshua. Letter, Joshua Worley to Mrs. Hollaway, "Corruptions of Shakerism." *Voice of Truth and Glad Tidings of the Kingdom at Hand* 14, no. 7 (May 12, 1847): 56.

Books

A., I. *Two Letters Written by a Gentleman to His Friend in Kentucky*. Lexington, KY: Joseph Charless, 1804.
Acts and Proceedings of the General Assembly of the Presbyterian Church . . . in the Year 1801. Philadelphia: R. Aitken, 1801.
Acts and Proceedings of the General Assembly of the Presbyterian Church . . . May 16, 1799. Philadelphia: William W. Woodward, 1799.
An Address to the State of Ohio, Protesting against a Certain Clause of the Militia Law, Enacted by the Legislature, at Their Last Session; and Shewing the Inconsistency of Military Power Interfering with Persons or Property Consecrated to the Pious and Benevolent Purposes of the Gospel by Order of the United Society Called Shakers. Lebanon, OH: Office of the Farmer, by George Smith, March 1818.
Bauer, Cheryl, ed. *Shakers of Indiana: A West Union Reader*. Milford, OH: Little Miami, 2008.
Belief of the Rational Brethren of the West. Cincinnati: Printed for the Society, 1819.
Bolton, Aquila Massie. *The Whore of Babylon Unmasked; or, A Cure for Orthodoxy; Being a Letter Addressed to Richard Mott, of New York*. Philadelphia: n.p., 1827.
Brown, Thomas. *An Account of the People Called Shakers*. Troy, NY: Parker and Bliss, 1812.
Chapman, Eunice. *An Account of the Conduct of the People Called Shakers: In the Case of Eunice Chapman and Her Children, Since Her Husband Became Acquainted with That People, and Joined Their Society*. Albany, NY: Printed for the Authoress, 1817.
Chapman, Eunice, et al. *An Account of the Conduct of the Shakers, in the Case of Eunice Chapman & Her Children, Written by Herself; A Refutation of the Shakers Remonstrance to the Proceedings of the Legislature of New-York, in 1817, by Thomas Brown; the Deposition of Mary Dyer, Who Petitioned the Legislature of the State of New-Hampshire, for Relief in a Similar Case; Also Depositions of Others Who Have Been Members of the Shaker Society; Also, the Proceedings of the Legislature of the State of New-York, in the Case of Eunice Chapman*. Lebanon, OH: Van Vleet & Camron, 1818.
The Constitution of the Presbyterian Church in the United States of America. Philadelphia: Robert Aitken, 1797.
Cuming, Fortescue. *Sketches of a Tour to the Western Country*. Pittsburgh: Cramer, Spear, and Eichbaum, 1810.

Doty, Daniel, and William Ludlow. *An Address to the People at Union Village, and a Solemn Warning to the Whole Human Family against Shakerism and Delusion; Also, an Address to Calvin Morrel and Richard M'Nemar, on the Appendix to the Other Side of the Question*. Lebanon, OH: Van Vleet, February 19, 1820.

Drake, Daniel. *Natural and Statistical View, or Picture of Cincinnati and the Miami Country*. Cincinnati: Looker and Wallace, 1815.

Finley, James B., and W. P. Strickland, eds. *Autobiography of Rev. James B. Finley; or, Pioneer Life in the West*. Cincinnati: Methodist Book Concern, 1853.

Galbraith, R. C. *The History of the Chillicothe Presbytery*. Chillicothe, OH: Scioto Gazette, 1889.

Goodwillie, Christian, ed. *Writings of Shaker Apostates and Anti-Shakers, 1782–1850*. London: Pickering and Chatto, 2013.

Green, Calvin, and Seth Youngs Wells. *A Brief Exposition of the Established Principles and Regulations of the United Society Called Shakers*. Albany, NY: Packard and Van Benthuysen, 1830.

———, eds. *Testimonies of the Life, Character, Revelations and Doctrines of Our Ever Blessed Mother Ann Lee, and the Elders with Her; through Whom the Word of Eternal Life Was Opened in This Day of Christ's Second Appearing: Collected from Living Witnesses, by Order of the Ministry in Union with the Church*. . . . Hancock, MA: J. Tallcott & J. Deming, Junrs., 1816.

Haggard, Rice. *An Address to the Different Religious Societies on the Sacred Import of the Christian Name*. Lexington, KY: Joseph Charless, 1804.

Hill, Rowland. *Village Dialogues: Between Farmer Littleworth and Thomas Newman, Rev. Mr. Lovegood, Parson Dolittle and Others*. Danville, KY: s.n., 1805.

Howe, Henry. *Historical Collections of Ohio, Vol. II, Ohio Centennial Edition*. Norwalk, OH: Laning, 1896.

Kentucky. *Acts Passed at the First Session of the Thirty-Sixth General Assembly for the Commonwealth of Kentucky, Begun and Held in the Town of Frankfort, on Monday, the Third Day of December, in the Year Eighteen Hundred and Twenty-Seven, and of the Commonwealth the Thirty-Sixth*. Frankfort, KY: Jacob H. Holman, 1828.

Marshall, Robert, and John Thompson. *A Brief Historical Account of Sundry Things in the Doctrines and State of the Christian, or as It Is Commonly Called, the Newlight Church*. Cincinnati: J. Carpenter, 1811.

A Memorial Remonstrating against a Certain Act of the Legislature of Kentucky. Harrodsburg, KY: Union Office, 1830.

McNemar, Richard. *Constitution of the United Societies of Believers (Called Shakers), Containing Sundny [sic] Covenants and Articles of Agrement [sic], Definitive of the Legal Grounds of the Institution*. Watervliet, OH: 1833.

———. *Epistle Dedicatory of the Union Press*. Watervliet, OH: 1832.

———. *Investigator; or A Defence of the Order, Government & Economy of the United Society Called Shakers, against Sundry Charges and Legislative Proceedings; Addressed to the Political World; by the Society of Believers at Pleasant Hill, KY.* Lexington, KY: Smith & Palmer, 1828.

———. *The Kentucky Revival, or, A Short History of the Late Extraordinary Out-Pouring of the Spirit of God, in the Western States of America.* Albany, NY: E. and E. Hosford, 1808.

———. *The Other Side of the Question.* Cincinnati: Looker, Reynolds, 1819.

———. *A Record Relating to the Cogar Mob and Boon Suit.* N.p., 1831.

——— [Eleazar Wright, pseud.]. *A Review of the Most Important Events Relating to the Rise and Progress of the United Society of Believers in the West.* Union Village, OH: 1831.

———. *A Selection of Hymns and Poems; for the Use of Believers. Collected from Sundry Authors, by Philos Harmoniae* [pseud.]. Watetvliet [sic], OH, 1833.

———. *A Series of Lectures on Orthodoxy and Heterodoxy, in Allusion to the Testimony of Christ's Second Appearing. Introduced by a Reply to Sundry Defamatory Letters Written by A. M. Bolton, Late, a Catechumen in the United Society at Union Village. Designed for the Edification of Young Believers.* Dayton, OH: 1832.

———. *"Shakerism Detected &c." Examined & Refuted, in Five Propositions.* Lexington, KY: Thomas Smith, 1811.

———. *Western Expositor. No. 4. A Brief Exposition of Rev. 12,—Ezek. 17, &c. Communicated to a Friend.* [Watervliet, OH?: 1833?].

———. *The Western Review, or A Memorial of the Labors of Our Parents and Ministers, in Founding the Church in the West.* Watervliet, OH: 1834.

———. *Western Review no. 2.* Watervliet, OH: 1834.

M'Nemar, Richard. *The Kentucky Revival, or, A Short History of the Late Extraordinary Out-Pouring of the Spirit of God, in the Western States of America.* Cincinnati: John W. Browne, 1807.

Narratives of a Late Expedition against the Indians: With an Account of the Barbarous Execution of Col. Crawford; and the Wonderful Escape of Dr. Knight and John Slover from Captivity, in 1782. Philadelphia: Francis Bailey, 1783.

Ohio. *Journal of the Senate of the State of Ohio, Being the First Session of the Ninth General Assembly, Begun and Held at the Town of Zanesville, in the County of Muskingum, Monday, December Third, 1810. And in the Ninth Year of the Said State. Vol. IX.* Chillicothe, OH: Joseph S. Collins, 1810.

Otto, John C. *An Inaugural Essay on Epilepsy.* Philadelphia: Lang & Ustick, 1796.

Owen, Robert. *New View of Society: Or, Essays on the Principle of the Formation of the Human Character, and the Application of the Principle to Practice.* London: Cadell and Davies, 1813.

Presbytery of Springfield. *An Apology for Renouncing the Jurisdiction of the Synod of Kentucky.* Lexington, KY: Joseph Charless, 1804.

———. *Observations on Church Government*. Albany, NY: E. and E. Hosford, 1808.
Purviance, Levi. *The Biography of Elder David Purviance*. Dayton, OH: Published for the Author, 1848.
Rathbone, Reuben. *Reasons Offered for Leaving the Shakers*. Pittsfield, MA: Chester Smith, 1800.
Rathbun, Daniel. *A Letter, from Daniel Rathbun, of Richmond, in the County of Berkshire to James Whittacor, Chief Elder of the Church, Called Shakers*. Springfield, MA: Printing Office near the Great Ferry, 1785.
A Revision and Confirmation of the Social Compact of the United Society Called Shakers, at Pleasant Hill, Kentucky. Harrodsburg, KY: Randall and Jones, 1830.
Rice, David. *A Sermon on the Present Revival of Religion in this Country*. Lexington, KY: Joseph Charless, 1803.
Smith, James. *Remarkable Occurrences, Lately Discovered among the People Called Shakers: Of a Treasonous and Barbarous Nature, or Shakerism Developed*. Paris, KY: Joel R. Lyle, 1810.
———. *Shakerism Detected: Their Erroneous and Treasonous Proceedings, and False Publications Contained in Different News-papers, Exposed to Public View by the Depositions of Ten Different Persons Living in Various Parts of the States of Kentucky and Ohio: Accompanied with Remarks*. Paris, KY: Joel R. Lyle, 1810.
Smith, James, and Joseph Darlinton, eds. *An Account of the Remarkable Occurrences in the Life and Travels of Col. James Smith*. Cincinnati: Robert Clarke, 1870.
Stone, Barton Warren. *Atonement: The Substance of Two Letters Written to a Friend*. Lexington, KY: Joseph Charless, 1805.
———. *The Biography of Elder Barton Warren Stone, Written by Himself*. Cincinnati: J. A. James and U. P. James, 1847.
———. *A Reply to John P. Campbell's Strictures on Atonement*. Lexington, KY: Joseph Charless, 1805.
Swan, Joseph R. *Statutes of the State of Ohio of a General Nature in Force August, 1854: With References to Prior Repealed Laws*. Cincinnati: H. W. Derby, 1854.
Synod of Kentucky. *A Circular Letter from the Synod of Kentucky, to the Churches under Their Care*. Lexington, KY: Joseph Charless, 1803.
Thompson, Zadock. *History of Vermont, Natural, Civil, and Statistical*. Burlington, VT: Chauncey Goodrich, 1842.
Van Demark, Peter H., ed. *Journals of New Lebanon Shaker Elder Rufus Bishop*. Clinton, NY: Richard W. Couper, 2018.
Wells, Seth Youngs, comp. *Millennial Praises, Containing a Collection of Gospel Hymns, in Four Parts; Adapted to the Day of Christ's Second Appearing. Composed for the Use of His People*. Hancock, MA: Josiah Tallcott Jr., 1813.
Wergland, Glendyne R., and Christian Goodwillie. *Shaker Autobiographies, Biographies and Testimonies, 1806–1907*. London: Pickering & Chatto, 2014.
Whitbey, John. *Beauties of Priestcraft, or, A Short Account of Shakerism*. New Harmony, IN: Office of the *New-Harmony Gazette*, 1826.

Wickliffe, Robert. *The Shakers. Speech of Robert Wickliffe. In the Senate of Kentucky—Jan. 1831. On a Bill to Repeal an Act of the General Assembly of the State of Kentucky, Entitled, "An Act to Regulate Civil Proceedings against Certain Communities Having Property in Common."* Frankfort, KY: A. G. Hodges, 1832.

———. *Speech of Robert Wickliffe, in the Senate of Kentucky, on a Bill to Repeal an Act of the General Assembly of the State of Kentucky, Entitle [sic] "An Act to Regulate Civil Proceedings against Certain Communities Having Property in Common."* Lebanon, OH: Star Office, 1831.

Woodward, W. W. *Increase of Piety, or the Revival of Religion in the United States of America.* Philadelphia: W. W. Woodward, 1802.

Youngs, Benjamin Seth. *Testimony of Christ's Second Appearing.* Lebanon, OH: John M'Clean, 1808.

———. *Transactions of the Ohio Mob, Called in the Public Papers "An Expedition against the Shakers."* [New York, 1847?].

SECONDARY SOURCES

Articles

Beckner, Lucien, ed. "Reverend John D. Shane's Notes on Interviews, in 1844, with Mrs. Hinds and Patrick Scott of Bourbon County." *Filson Club History Quarterly* 10, no. 3 (July 1936): 164–77.

Dean, H. Clark. "Caleb Worley (Say 1730–circa 1790) of Virginia and Kentucky, Grandson of Francis Worley of Pennsylvania." *American Genealogist* 70, no. 2 (April 1995): 75–81.

Feight, Andrew Lee. "James Blythe and the Slavery Controversy in the Presbyterian Churches of Kentucky, 1791–1802." *Register of the Kentucky Historical Society* 102, no. 1 (Winter 2004).

Goitein, Patricia L. "Strangers along the Trail: Peoria's Shaker Apostates Enter the World." *American Communal Societies Quarterly* 4, no. 1 (January 2010): 3–19.

Goodwillie, Christian. "First in the West: The Shaker Experience of Visionary Malcham Worley and his Family." *American Communal Societies Quarterly* 16, no. 2 (April 2022): 84–141.

———. "Letter from Richard McNemar." *American Communal Societies Quarterly* 3, no. 3 (July 2009): 146–55.

———. "Mummy Jum: The Shaker Pilgrim Encounter of 1817–1818." *Communal Societies* 34, no. 1 (2014).

———. "'The Price of Blood:' Shaker Revolutionary War Veterans and Military Pensions." *American Communal Societies Quarterly* 14, nos. 3/4 (July and October 2020): 142–96.

———. "The Shakers in Eighteenth-Century Newspapers. Part Three: 'Calvin' versus 'A Lover of Truth,' Abusing Caleb Rathbun, the Death of Joseph

Meacham and the Tale of His Sister." *American Communal Societies Quarterly* 6, no. 1 (January 2012): 39–63.

Haselby, Sam. "Sovereignty and Salvation on the Frontier of the Early American Republic." *Past and Present*, no. 215 (May 2012): 165–94.

"The Log Architecture of Ohio." *Ohio History* 80, nos. 3/4 (Summer/Autumn 1971, special issue).

Medlicott, Carol. "Conflict and Tribulation on the Frontier: The West Union Shakers and Their Retreat." *American Communal Societies Quarterly* 3, no. 3 (July 2009): 111–37.

Morrow, Josiah. "The First Shaker Convert: West of Alleghany Mountains Was Malcham Worley at Turtlecreek, March 1805." *Western Star* (Lebanon, OH), January 25, 1912.

———. "Richard McNemar: Remarkable Story of an Eloquent Pioneer Preacher." *Western Star* (Lebanon, OH), November 28, 1907.

Ramage, Andrea S. "Love and Honor: The Wickliffe Family of Antebellum Kentucky." *Register of the Kentucky Historical Society* 94, no. 2 (Spring 1996): 115–33.

Schoonmaker, Nancy Gray, and Christian Goodwillie. "Abijah Alley of Long Hollow: Preacher, Shaker Apostate, and Backwoods Prophet of the American South." *American Communal Societies Quarterly* 11, no. 3 (July 2017).

Swaim, William T. "The Evolution of Ten Pre-1745 Presbyterian Societies in the Cumberland Valley." *Cumberland County History* 2, no. 1 (Summer 1985): 3–30.

Wergland, Glendyne R. "The Abuse of Spirit Messages during the Shaker Era of Manifestations: 'A Hard Time of It in This Hurrycane of Gifts, to Know What Is Revelation and What Is Not.'" *American Communal Societies Quarterly* 3, no. 1 (January 2009): 27–38.

Wigger, John H. "Taking Heaven by Storm: Enthusiasm and Early American Methodism, 1770–1820." *Journal of the Early Republic* 14, no. 2 (Summer 1994): 167–94.

Wilson, Frazer Ells. "St. Clair's Defeat." *American Monthly Magazine* 21, no. 1 (July 1902): 7–19.

Winans, Cathie. "From the Russells to the Pilots: The Beginning and End of North Union." *American Communal Societies Quarterly* 2, no. 3 (July 2008): 135–47.

Winiarski, Douglas L. "Seized by the Jerks: Shakers, Spirit Possession, and the Great Revival on the Trans-Appalachian Frontier." *William and Mary Quarterly*, 3d ser., 76 (2019).

———. "Shakers & Jerkers: Letters from the 'Long Walk,' 1805, Part 1." *Journal of East Tennessee History* 89 (2017).

———. "Shakers & Jerkers: Letters from the 'Long Walk,' 1805, Part 2." *Journal of East Tennessee History* 90 (2018): 84–105.

Zimkus, John. "Beedle's Station and the Shakers: A Struggle of Tears." Warren County History Center, Lebanon, OH, ca. 2005.

Books

Africa, J. Simpson. *History of Huntingdon and Blair Counties, Pennsylvania.* Philadelphia: Louis H. Everts, 1883.

Albert, George Dallas. *The Frontier Forts of Western Pennsylvania.* N.p.: Clarence M. Busch, 1896.

Allen, William B. *A History of Kentucky.* Louisville, KY: Bradley & Gilbert, 1872.

Aron, Stephen. *How the West Was Lost: The Transformation of Kentucky from Daniel Boone to Henry Clay.* Baltimore: Johns Hopkins University Press, 1996.

Beard, Richard. *Brief Biographical Sketches of Some of the Early Ministers of the Cumberland Presbyterian Church, Second Series.* Nashville, TN: Cumberland Presbyterian Board of Education, 1874.

Boice, Martha, Dale Covington, and Richard Spence. *Maps of the Shaker West: A Journey of Discovery.* Dayton, OH: Knot Garden, 1997.

Boles, John B. *The Great Revival: Beginnings of the Bible Belt.* Lexington: University Press of Kentucky, 1996.

Catalogue of the Officers and Alumni of Washington and Lee University, Lexington, Virginia: 1749–1888. Baltimore: John Murphy, 1888.

Davidson, Robert. *History of the Presbyterian Church in the State of Kentucky.* New York: Robert Carter, 1847.

Edmunds, R. David. *The Shawnee Prophet.* Lincoln: University of Nebraska Press, 1985.

Elliott, David. *The Life of the Rev. Elisha Macurdy.* Allegheny, PA: Kennedy & Brother, 1848.

Frantz, John B., and William Pencak. *Beyond Philadelphia: The American Revolution in the Pennsylvania Hinterland.* University Park: Pennsylvania State University Press, 1998.

Friend, Craig Thompson. *Along the Maysville Road: The Early American Republic in the Trans-Appalachian West.* Knoxville: University of Tennessee Press, 2005.

Goodman, Hattie S. *The Knox Family: A Genealogical and Biographical Sketch of the Descendants of John Knox of Rowan County, North Carolina.* Richmond, VA: Whittet and Shepperson, 1905.

Goodwillie, Christian, and Jane Crosthwaite. *Millennial Praises: A Shaker Hymnal.* Amherst: University of Massachusetts Press, 2009.

Grant, Jerry V., and Douglas R. Allen. *Shaker Furniture Makers.* Hanover, NH: University Press of New England, 1989.

Hanks, Patrick, ed. *A Dictionary of American Family Names.* Oxford: Oxford University Press, 2003.

Historical Committee of Huntingdon (Pa.). *Historic Huntingdon, 1767–1909: Being a Brief Account of the History of Huntingdon from Its Earliest Settlements to the Present Day.* Huntingdon, PA: Committee, 1909.

History and Biographical Encyclopaedia of Butler County, Ohio, with Illustrations and Sketches of Its Representative Men and Pioneers. Cincinnati: Western Biographical, 1882.

History of That Part of the Susquehanna and Juniata Valleys, Embraced in the Counties of Mifflin, Juniata, Perry, Union and Snyder, in the Commonwealth of Pennsylvania. Philadelphia: Everts, Peck & Richards, 1886.

History of the County of Westmoreland, Pennsylvania. Philadelphia: L. H. Everts, 1882.

Hosmer, James Kendall. *A Short History of the Mississippi Valley.* Boston and New York: Houghton Mifflin, 1901.

Howe, Henry. *Historical Collections of Ohio.* Cincinnati: State of Ohio, 1902.

Humphreys, E. W. *Memoirs of Deceased Christian Ministers; or, Brief Sketches of the Lives and Labors of 975 Ministers, Who Died between 1793 and 1880.* Dayton, OH: Christian Publishing Association, 1880.

Huston, E. Rankin. *History of the Huston Families and Their Descendants, 1450–1912.* Mechanicsburg, PA: Carlisle, 1912.

Hutchinson, George P. *The History behind the Reformed Presbyterian Church, Evangelical Synod.* Cherry Hill, NJ: Mack, 1974.

Innis Jr., James R. *Footprints at White Water Shaker Village: A Directory of Shakers, Visitors, Business Associates and Thieves 1823–1916.* Harrison, OH: n.p., 2015.

Innis Jr., James R., and Thomas Sakmyster, eds. *The Shakers of White Water, Ohio, 1823–1916.* Clinton, NY: Richard W. Couper, 2014.

Johnstone, R. A. *Historical Sketch of the Presbytery of Transylvania, Kentucky.* Louisville, KY: Bradley & Gilbert, 1876.

Kelley, Gwendolyn Dunlevy. *A Genealogical History of the Dunlevy Family.* Columbus, OH: Issued for Private Distribution, 1901.

Littell, J. *Family Records or Genealogies of the First Settlers of Passaic Valley (and Vicinity) above Chatham (New Jersey).* Feltville, NJ: Stationers' Hall, 1851–1852.

MacLean, John Patterson. *A Bibliography of Shaker Literature.* Columbus, OH: F. J. Heer, 1905.

———. *Shakers of Ohio.* Columbus, OH: F. J. Heer, 1907.

———. *A Sketch of the Life and Labors of Richard McNemar.* Franklin, OH: Franklin Chronicle, 1905.

Medlicott, Carol. *Issachar Bates: A Shaker's Journey.* Hanover, NH: University Press of New England, 2013.

Medlicott, Carol, and Christian Goodwillie. *Richard McNemar, Music, and the Western Shaker Communities: Branches of One Living Tree.* Kent, OH: Kent State University Press, 2013.

Paterwic, Stephen J. *Historical Dictionary of the Shakers.* Lanham, MD: Scarecrow, 2008.

———. *The Shakers of Enfield, Connecticut: 1780–1868.* Clinton, NY: Richard W. Couper, 2020.

Perrin, W. H., et al. *Kentucky: A History of the State.* Louisville, KY: F. A. Battey, 1887.

Pitzer, Donald E., ed. *America's Communal Utopias.* Chapel Hill: University of North Carolina Press, 1997.

Record of Marriages in Bourbon County Kentucky, for the Period of Years 1785 to 1851, Inclusive, 33. Kentucky Department of Libraries and Archives, Frankfort, KY.

Simms, H. *Middletown in Black and White.* Middletown, OH: Journal Printing, 1908.

Smith, Joseph. *Old Redstone, or, Historical Sketches of Western Presbyterianism.* Philadelphia: Lippincott, Grambo, 1854.

Soule, Sandra A. *Independency of the Mind: Aquila Massie Bolton, Poetry, Shakerism and Controversy.* Clinton, NY: Couper, 2010.

Spero, Patrick. *Frontier Rebels: The Fight for Independence in the American West, 1765–1776.* New York: W. W. Norton, 2018.

Wergland, Glendyne R. *One Shaker Life: Isaac Newton Youngs, 1793–1865.* Amherst: University of Massachusetts Press, 2006.

Weslager, C. A. *The Log Cabin in America.* New Brunswick, NJ: Rutgers University Press, 1969.

The Winchester Centennial, 1803–1903: Historical Sketch of the Universalist Profession of Belief. Boston and Chicago: Universalist, 1903.

Yeater, Laura J., and Elvira Hunley. *General David Thomson* [place of publication not identified; publisher not identified], [1922?].

INDEX

Account of the Conduct of the Shakers, in the Case of Eunice Chapman and Her Children, An, 172, 181
Account of the Remarkable Occurrences in the Life and Travels of Col. James Smith, An, 144
"Act providing relief and support of women who may be abandoned by their husbands," (Ohio, 1811), 154, 155–156, 167
"Act to regulate civil proceedings against certain communities having property in common," (Kentucky, 1828), 219–221, 253, 255–256, 257, 269
Address to the Different Religious Societies on the Sacred Import of the Christian Name, An, 66
Address to the People at Union Village, and a Solemn Warning to the Whole Human Family against Shakerism and Delusion, 184–185
Agnew, Brant, 198
Agnew, Joseph, 340
alcohol (abuse), 299, 319
Allen, Carey, 15, 17, 22, 404
Allen, Douglas R., 314
Allen, Joseph, 132
Alley, Abijah, 222–236, 288, 298, 344
Anderson, Celia (Seely), 19–20, 26, 32, 55, 87, 92, 132, 169, 400, 405

Anderson's Fort, Pennsylvania, 11
"Answer to the Mourning Thoughts on McNemar's Fall, An," 417, 421–424
Antes, Philip F., 367, 372, 373
Anti-Shakers, 86, 87, 88, 91, 93, 95, 97, 98, 101, 105, 106, 108–109, 113, 116, 117, 123, 132, 136, 138, 139, 141, 142–143, 143–153, 154, 156, 159, 165, 167, 170–173, 181–185, 212, 213, 218–219, 229, 230, 234, 251, 253–254, 311, 344
Apollonius, 85
Apology for Renouncing the Jurisdiction of the Synod of Kentucky, An, 61, 63, 66, 327
Apostates. *See* Anti-Shakers
Aron, Stephen, 20–21
articles of acquittance (Shaker, Union Village and Watervliet, Ohio), 250, 291
Arminianism (theological doctrine), 3, 52–53, 54, 57, 60, 363
Arminius, Jacobus, 53
Asbury, Francis, 44
atonement, 52–53, 64–65
"Attempt to Develope Shakerism," 145, 151

Bacon, Lucy, 126
Baily, Henry, 182
Ball, Fanny, 178–179
Ball, James, 305, 319

Ball, Peter, 178–179
Ballance, Charles, 251, 253–254
Banta, Samuel, 106, 213, 218, 253, 282
Banta family, 99, 111
Baptists, 42
Barrens (region), Kentucky, xiii, 131–132
Barrett, Andrew, 399
Bates, Betsey, 380
Bates, Issachar, 71, 72, 77, 78–79, 83, 86, 87, 88, 89, 90, 91, 92, 96, 97, 98, 100, 101, 105, 106, 108, 109, 110, 111, 114, 115, 117, 118, 119, 123, 126, 131, 132, 140, 148, 162, 169, 179, 181, 189, 191, 193, 194–196, 198, 200, 201, 204, 206, 214, 250, 257, 258, 265, 266, 267, 270, 276, 279, 285, 287, 294, 296, 305, 308, 321–322, 325, 327, 332, 337, 369, 379, 386, 391, 396, 397, 426; conflict with Richard McNemar, 280–281, 283–284, 285–287, 290, 296–304, 306, 311, 315; death of, 325; mission to Kentucky and Ohio, 71–76; mission to Pickaway, 137, 139; mission to Wabash, 134–137
Battle of the Wabash, 16
Battle of Tippecanoe, 159
Baxter, John, 373
Baxter, Robert, 280, 285, 301
Beauties of Priestcraft, or, A Short Account of Shakerism, 211, 212, 220
Beaver Creek, Ohio, 112, 115, 137, 139, 161, 163. *See also* Watervliet, Ohio
Beaver Creek Church (Beulah), 68, 90, 94, 163
Bedford, Pennsylvania, 21
Bedle (Beedle), William, 50, 62, 170
Bedle, Abner, 326
Bedle, Esther, 50
Bedle, Eunice, 277, 285, 297, 320
Bedle, Francis, 45, 51, 62, 78, 168, 283
Bedle, James, 50, 92, 93, 109, 165
Bedle, Lydia. *See* Davis (Bedle), Lydia
Bedle, Mary. *See* Hole (Bedle), Mary
Bedle, Phebe, 50
Bedle, Polly, 45
Bedle, Susanna. *See* Davis (Bedle), Susanna

Bedle family, 50, 78, 143
Bedle's (Beedle's) Station, 50
Belief of the Rational Brethren of the West, 184
Bethany Church, 32, 43, 44, 49
Betts, Comstock, 138, 383
Bishop, Ebenezer, 239, 300, 377
Bishop, Job, 241
Bishop, Rufus, 156, 239, 268, 273, 277, 278, 281, 290–291, 305, 306–307, 308, 315, 316, 320–321, 333–334, 345–346, 349, 375, 376, 377, 378, 379, 380, 383, 385–386, 387, 392, 413, 428; visit to western Shaker communities, 294–298
"Black Joke, The" 132–133, 150
Blacks, 362
Blue Jacket, 16, 124
Blue Jacket, George, 121, 124
Blythe, James, 28,
Boles, John B., 66
Bolton, Aquila Massie, 225–226, 232, 288, 344
Bonnel, Abner, 283
Book of Mormon, 257
Boon, John, 254–255
Boone, Daniel, 17, 22, 106
Boon Lawsuit, 254–255
Bourbon Academy, 20
Bovel, Stephen, 51, 54
Boyd, Anna, 189
Boyd, Daniel, 312, 326, 334–335, 338, 371
Boyd, John, 14, 404
Boyd, Samuel, 13, 404
Brannon, A., 98
Breathitt, John, 255
Brief Exposition of the Established Principles and Regulations of the United Society Called Shakers, A, 269, 281
Brief Historical Account of . . . the Newlight Church, A, 67
Brief Illustration of the Principles of War and Peace, A, 282
Brown, John W., 32–33, 127
Brown, Samuel J., 270
Brown, Thomas, 181, 183
Bryant, James, 212
Bryant, John R, 255

Bryant, Lucy, 212
Bryant, Rufus, 215, 256, 268, 270
Buchanan, Peggy, 112
Bullard, Isaac, 176–179, 187
Burlingame, Nathan, 187, 198
Burnett, Andrew, 192–193
Burr, Aaron, 147
Busro, Indiana, fig. 12.1, 135, 136, 140, 141, 147, 155, 159–162, 170, 171. *See also* West Union, Indiana
Buttrick, Amos, 286
"Buzzards and the flesh. W.U. 1827, The," 209
Buzzell, John, 152

Cabala, 344
Cabin Creek, Kentucky, xiii, 26, 32, 40, 48, 111, 134, 404
Cabin Creek Church, 26, 27–28, 29, 30, 33, 35, 39, 45–49, 51–52, 54, 68, 93, 109
Caldwell, Joseph, 18, 404
Campbell, Cornelius, 123
Campbell, John P., 27, 30, 32, 33, 36, 39, 46, 56, 64, 107
camp meeting, 37, 39, 40, 41
Camron, William A., 181
Cane Ridge, Kentucky, 17, 19, 20, 21, 22, 24, 25, 41, 44, 65, 66, 75, 96, 105, 106, 107, 111, 199, 404
Cane Ridge Church, 26, 28, 40, 68, 78–79, 93, 131, 139, 417, 418, 423
Cane Run Church, 24
Canonsburg, Pennsylvania, 23
Canonsburg Academy, 23
Canterbury, New Hampshire, Richard McNemar visits, 240–241
Carlisle, Pennsylvania, 10
Carson, John Lin, 259
Cartwright, Peter, 135
castration, 95, 138, 185, 338–339
celibacy, 27, 76, 77, 79–80, 81–82, 83–84, 93, 104, 105, 140, 179–180, 257
Chapman, Eunice, 172, 181, 183, 193
Chapman, James, 172
children (among the Shakers), 145, 148, 149, 156, 172, 181–182, 183
Christian Connexion, 186

Church of Christ unto a People in Kentucky & the Adjacent States, The, (missionary letter, 1804), 74, 75, 77, 82, 92, 320–321
Church of England, 9, 407
Cincinnati, Ohio, 18, 178, 263, 270, 271, 285, 387, 404
Circular Letter from the Synod of Kentucky, 61, 63
Clark, Abigail, 2, 396, 400
Clark, Asenath, 239
Clay, Henry, 311
Cleveland, Ohio, 237, 244–245
Cobb, Elias, 187
Cochran, Sarah, 357, 359, 360, 362, 365, 399
Cole, Susanna (Anna), 126, 134, 254
Columbia, Ohio, 18, 404
Columbus, Christopher, 362, 373
Columbus, Ohio, 172–174
Columbus Gazette (Columbus, Ohio), 173
communalism, 67, 88, 95, 111, 118, 133, 140, 169, 170, 218, 410–411
Concise Statement of the Principles of the Only True Church, A, 127
Concord Church, 26, 40, 68, 98, 99, 101, 417, 418, 423
Confession of Faith (Presbyterian). *See* Westminster Confession
Constitution of the United Societies of Believers, The, fig. 20.1, 291–294, 299
"Contented at Home," fig. 18.2, 261–263
Cooley, Ebenezer, 110, 112, 113
Coon, Peter, 124–125
Copley, Luther, 306, 308–309, 383
Corwin, Ichabod, 152
Corwin, Robert, 352
Corwin, Thomas, 263, 311
Cory, David, 88, 114, 352
Count de Leon, 387
covenant (Shaker), 218–220, 234, 239–240, 246, 281; Pleasant Hill, Kentucky, 213, 218, 219, 251–254, 292; South Union, Kentucky, 254; Union Village, Ohio, 4, 157, 168, 180, 249–250, 264; Watervliet, Ohio, 257–259, 280, 284–285, 291; White Water, Ohio, 251, 259–260
Coventry, Rhode Island, 187
Cowdery, Oliver, 257

Cox, Benjamin, 283
Crane, Elizabeth. *See* Doty (Crane), Elizabeth
Creek Tribe, 136
Crosthwaite, Jane, 132
Cumberland Gap, xiii, 25, 73
Cumberland Presbytery, 26, 417
Curtis, Hopewell, 138

dancing, 67, 68, 87–88, 89, 91, 92, 109, 111
dancing stand at Turtle Creek, 94–95, 97–98, 100, 105, 124, 138
Danville, Kentucky, 22, 91
Darby Plains, Ohio, 186–188, 189, 194, 198, 259, 260, 261
Darlinton, Joseph, 28, 35, 46, 48
Darrow, "Father" David, 95–96, 97, 100, 101, 105, 108, 109, 110, 112, 113, 115, 116, 117, 118–119, 127, 132, 134, 135, 138, 139, 141, 151, 155, 156, 157, 158, 159, 161, 162, 163, 164, 165, 166, 167, 168, 169, 171, 172, 176, 177, 180–181, 186, 189, 198, 210, 224, 226, 227, 230, 231, 235, 239, 240, 248, 296, 298, 299, 311, 315, 330, 332, 343, 345, 373, 378–379, 380–382, 386, 391, 395, 397, 425; death of, 200–204; mission to Shawnee, 120, 123–126; and *Testimony of Christ's Second Appearing* (1823), 190–193; visit to Harmony Society, 180
Darrow, James, 189
Darrow, Ruth, 112, 141
Davidson, Robert, 21, 35, 59
Davis (Bedle), Lydia, 50, 170–171
Davis (Bedle), Susanna, 50, 170, 172
Davis (Sering), Elizabeth, 138, 170
Davis, Daniel, 170
Davis, Elijah, 109, 170–171
Davis, Hulda, 171
Davis, John, 138, 170–171, 174, 179
Davis, Jonathan, 80, 138, 170–172
Davis, Jonathan (son of Elijah), 171
Davis, William, 115, 170–172, 345
"Day of Redemption," 117
"Day of Retribution," 165
Dayton, Jonathan, 55, 100, 119
Dayton, Ohio, 123, 161

Deism, 20, 60, 99, 225, 289
Delaware (Lenape) Tribe, 11, 136
Deming, John, 141
Deming, Nathaniel, 239
Deming, William, 141, 239
Dennis, Jethro, 139, 163
Dennis, Salome, 276, 285, 297
disease, 121–122, 141, 161–162, 163, 181, 351
Doty (Crane), Elizabeth, 183
Doty, Daniel, 80, 183–185
Drake, Daniel, 166–167
Dualism, 132
Duncan, Nancy, 123
Dunlavy (McNemar), Cassie (Cassia), 12, 35, 93, 95, 97, 99, 105, 401
Dunlavy, Anthony, 111
Dunlavy, Betsy, 189
Dunlavy, Francis, 22, 44, 49, 101, 147, 148, 263, 311, 373–374, 418, 428
Dunlavy, John, 20, 23, 24, 25, 26, 30, 31, 32, 33, 35, 36, 39, 40, 42, 46, 47, 49, 56, 58, 59, 60, 61, 66, 87, 93, 95, 96, 97, 99, 100–101, 105–106, 107, 110, 111, 116, 118, 119, 122, 134, 200, 207, 211, 212, 235, 261, 291, 360, 362, 391, 397, 401, 418
Dunlevy, Anthony H., 50, 62
Dunn, Nancy, 162
Dyer, Mary, 181, 193, 289

Eades, Charles, 132
Eades, Sally, 255
Eagle Creek, Ohio, 30, 32, 44, 95, 99, 110, 111, 115, 118, 123, 133, 134, 155
Eagle Creek Church, 40, 68, 95, 97, 107, 109
E. and E. Hosford, 133
earthquake (New Madrid, 1811–1812), 156
Eastwood, John Lot, 385
Economy, Pennsylvania. *See* Harmony Society
education (among Shakers), 138, 149, 163
Edy, Asenath, 351
Embargo Act, 133
Enfield, Connecticut, Richard McNemar visits, 244
Enfield, New Hampshire, 240, 268

Epicurus, 220
epilepsy, 13–14, 18, 38, 89, 91,
Epistle Dedicatory of the Union Press, 272–273, 276
Era of Manifestations. *See* New Era
Erie Canal, 238, 244, 295, 376
Ewing, James, 56
"Expulsion of Richard McNemar," 397–399, 425–429

Fairbanks, Semantha, 377–378
Faith, Lucy, 247
"False Prophet," 235
"Farewell loving sister," 122
Farnum, Douglas, 186–188
Farnumites, 186–188, 189–190, 260
Farrington, John, 379–380
Farrington, "Mother" Ruth, 112, 114, 118, 132, 157, 158, 161, 165, 166, 168, 169, 180, 189, 200, 248, 299, 308, 332, 350, 380, 383, 386, 397
Farrington, Prudence, 118, 122–123
Fennessy, James H., 396, 398
"Few mourning thoughts on McNemar's Fall, A," 417–421
Filson, John, xiii
Finley, James, B., 16, 20
Finley, John E., 30,
Finley, Robert E., 48
Finley, Robert W., 16, 19, 20, 22, 23, 24, 26, 404
Fisher, Brownlow, 193
Fithian, Philip, 11
Fort Hartslog (Lytle's Fort), Pennsylvania, 11
Fort Houston, Kentucky, 22
Fort Loudon, Pennsylvania, 21
Fort Washington, Ohio, 18
Fox, George, 132
Frankfort, Kentucky, 219, 255, 256, 268
Freeheart, Eunice, 132
Freeman, Thomas, 155, 162, 179
Freemasonry, 173–174, 409
Freewill Baptists, 152
French and Indian War, 145
French Prophets, 132
Fruit, Eli, 175

Galloway, Rachel, 390
Gasper, Kentucky, xiii, 131, 134, 155, 162. *See also* South Union, Kentucky
Gasper River Church, 25, 37, 131–132, 136
Gass, James, 253, 282
Gematria, 344
General Assembly of the Presbyterian Church, (1801) Philadelphia, Pennsylvania, 39; (1799) Winchester, Virginia, 30–31
"General outline of the past Journal of my life, A," 403–405
general rules (Shaker, Watervliet, Ohio), 284–285
George's Creek (New Geneva), Pennsylvania, 15
Georgetown, Kentucky, 13
Gill, Robert, 136, 147
Goodrich, Daniel, 113
Goodrich, Elizur, 175, 327
Goodrich, Hortence (Hortency), 138, 180, 380
Goodrich, Molly, 112, 118, 122
Goodwin, Harriet, 377
Graham diet, 320
Grant, Charles, 21
Grant, Jerry V., 314
Gray, Robert, 123
Great Miami River, 18
Great Scioto River, 17
Green, Calvin, 132, 238, 268, 281, 305, 332, 378
Green, William, 108
Greenville, Ohio, 123, 124, 125, 126, 133, 150
guns (spiritual), 355, 369–370, 371

Haggard, Rice, 66, 67
Halcyon sect, 194
Hammond, Charles, 263
Hammond, Joseph, 242
Hampton, Charles, 189, 194, 358, 359, 361, 362, 373
Hampton, Oliver C., 355, 362, 363, 365, 370, 401
Hancock, Massachusetts, 91, 141, 358; Richard McNemar visits, 239, 244, 378

Harmony Society, 179–180, 220, 386–387
Harris, Edward, 31
Harrisburg, Pennsylvania, 383, 386
Harrison, William Henry, 159, 188
Harrodsburg, Kentucky, 24, 106, 213, 253, 255, 268, 282, 292
Hart, John, 10
Hart's Log (Alexandria), Pennsylvania, 10
Harvard, Massachusetts, Richard McNemar visits, 241–242
Harvard Ministry, 244
Haselby, Sam, 44
Hastings, Betsy, 306, 308–309, 318, 333, 343–344, 345, 349, 354, 362
Hawkins, Daniel, 310–312, 318
Hawkins, David, 238
Hebrew, 344
Henderson, Andrew, 28, 45
Hewitt, William, 226–233
hierarchy (Shaker), 113–114, 118, 119, 145–146, 158, 164, 203–206, 211, 217, 224, 227, 231, 234, 247, 260, 337
Hill, David, 89, 109
Hill, Samuel, 182
Hodge, James, 189, 363, 370
Hole (Bedle), Mary, 50, 170
Hollister, Alonzo, 417, 488
Houston (Luckey), Sarah Jane, 22, 96, 106
Houston, Andrew, 193, 206, 207, 324, 326, 332, 334, 338, 344, 354, 355, 360, 362, 369, 373, 388, 390, 402, 431, 432
Houston, Archibald, 225, 251
Houston, John, 22, 23, 283, 362
Houston, John S., 373
Houston, Matthew, 24, 25, 26, 41, 43, 53, 54, 56, 57, 59, 60, 61, 64, 71, 74, 75, 78, 79, 96, 98, 111, 114, 116, 117, 127, 131, 133, 134, 147, 148, 155, 161, 163, 165, 166, 174, 189, 191, 192, 200, 225, 227, 228, 229, 231, 233–234, 244, 248, 250, 257, 263, 265, 266, 274, 307, 308, 309, 311, 313, 316–317, 318, 326, 331, 348, 349, 397, 418
Houston, Peter, 22, 23, 96, 99, 105–106, 107
Houston, Robert, 137
Howard, Benjamin, 283

Howe, Henry, 50
Hume, David, 289
Hunt, Thomas, 172

Illinois, 311
Increase of Piety, or the Revival of Religion in the United States of America, 34
Indian Creek, Kentucky, 118
Investigator; or A Defence of the Order, Government & Economy of the United Society called Shakers, 217, 219–221
Ireland, 19, 358; County Clare, 10
Irvin, Wiliam, 151
Irwin, James, 182

Jacob's Creek, Pennsylvania, 13, 404
James River, 18
Jaycock, William, 178
Jefferson, Thomas, 133, 170
Jennings, Mary Ann, 395
jerks, 14, 42, 67–68, 72, 76, 77, 91, 92, 348
Johns, Urban, 254
Johnson, David, xiv, 183
Johnson, Ithamar, 264, 371, 373
Johnson, Phoebe, 182–183
Johnson, Rachel, 126, 204, 237, 239, 241, 244–245, 247, 249, 306, 307–309
Johnston's Fork Meetinghouse, 30
"John the Baptist" (hymn), 34
Jones, Abner, 186
Juniata River, 10

Keenan, Joseph, 373
Kemper, James, 32, 50, 52, 53, 54, 56, 60, 61
Kenton, Simon, 17
Kentucky, 117; Bourbon County, 19, 21, 22, 98, 111, 417; Cumberland County, 132; Fayette County, 18; General Assembly, 219–220; House of Representatives, 255; Logan County, 25, 37, 39, 44, 131–132, 255; map, xiii; legislature, 21, 22, 219–220; Senate, 1; Warren County, 132, 255
Kentucky Revival, 3, 14, 37–45, 56, 62, 72, 127–129, 131, 184, 242–243, 290–291, 348, 363, 405, 408, 427

Kentucky Revival, fig. 10.1, 65, 66, 126, 127–129, 131, 133, 152, 270, 327, 346, 350, 396, 408
Kentucky River, 208, 256
Kentucky Synod, 53, 54, 56, 58, 59–61, 63, 64, 65, 66, 99
Kimball, Hiram, 237
Kimball, Polly, 89, 92, 109, 123
King, Gideon, 96
King, Solomon, 96, 97, 109, 118, 133, 156, 163, 180, 188, 191, 192, 200, 201, 204–205, 227, 228, 229, 231, 241, 247, 248–249, 257, 264, 280, 284, 285, 291, 292, 295, 296, 297, 298, 299, 301, 305–309, 311, 313, 315, 318, 326, 327, 345, 383, 386, 397
Kirjathsepher, 273, 352
Kirkham, Samuel, 274
Kitchell, Ashbel, 156, 168, 178, 195, 245, 263, 270, 296, 336, 338
Kitchell, Joanna, 306, 318
Kitchell, John, 32
Knox (Luckey), Esther, 90, 93, 98
Knox, John, 93, 95, 107, 110

Lafayette, Marquis de, 362
Lake Erie, 238, 245, 376, 391
Lamanites, 257
Lamme, William, 54
Lamme's Petition, 54, 56, 57, 58, 59, 61
Lancaster, Nancy, 352, 354
Lancaster, Pennsylvania, 19
Landon, Ruth, 239, 315
Last Will and Testament of the Springfield Presbytery, 66, 67, 78
Laughery [Locry] Creek, Indiana, 135
Lebanon, Ohio, 49, 124, 133, 139, 141, 174, 177, 229, 230, 263, 309, 311, 352, 367, 385, 428
Lee, "Father" William, 201
Lee, "Mother" Ann, 4, 66, 74, 100, 116, 117–118, 119, 131, 141, 183, 185, 188, 190, 200, 201, 226, 231, 234, 236, 238, 240, 243, 244, 247, 249–250, 314, 323, 324, 327, 328, 342, 343, 346, 350, 354, 356, 357, 358, 359, 360, 361, 362, 363, 364, 366, 367, 369, 372, 374, 376, 377, 378, 380–382, 386, 388, 391, 392, 394, 395, 427

Legier, George, 373
Letter, from Daniel Rathbun, of Richmond, in the County of Berkshire to James Whittacor, Chief Elder of the Church, Called Shakers, A, 107
Lexington, Kentucky, 13, 17, 29, 40, 53, 404
Lexington, Virginia, 18, 24
Lexington Presbytery, 24
Liberty Hall Academy, 18, 24, 127
Licking River, 18, 26, 30
Liddell, "Aunt" Susanna, 397
Liddell, Susannah Cole, 1–3, 357, 395–399, 400, 401, 431
Life & Experience of Issachar Bates, The, 280–281
Limestone, Kentucky. *See* Maysville, Kentucky
Limited Atonement (doctrine of), 38
Little Miami River, 18, 49, 105
"Little Quail," 142
Little Turtle, 16
Lockwood, John, 162
log house, 55, 108
Lord Dunmore's War, 136
Louis Philippe, 401
Luckey (Patterson), Mary "Anna," 19
Luckey, George, 31
Luckey, John, 19, 24, 404
Luckey, Joseph, 99
Luckey, Robert, 19
Ludlow, William, 184–185
Lyle, John, 41, 42, 43, 56

MacLean, John Patterson, 3, 9, 180, 395–399, 417, 425
Macurdy, Elisha, 14, 404
Mad River, 137, 141
Manifesto (serial), 396
Manifesto, 261, 289
Manning, Lewis, 385
Manning, Samuel C., 234
Map, Kentucky, xiii; Turtle Creek, Ohio, xiv, xv; Union Village, Ohio, [xvi–xvii]; Watervliet, Ohio, fig. 19.1; West Union, Indiana, fig. 12.1
Marietta, Ohio, 13

Marshall, Margaret, 143
Marshall, Robert, 17, 28, 56, 57, 58, 59, 60, 61, 63, 66, 67, 78, 87, 94, 98, 291
Martin, John, 258, 389, 401
Mason, Moore S., 399
Maysville, Kentucky, xiii, 13, 16, 17, 26, 30, 404
Maysville Road, 17–18
McBrien, Emmet, 358, 388, 401
McBrien, Margaret, 357–367, 368, 370, 372, 376, 381, 388, 393, 394–397, 399, 402, 427–428
McCarver, Betsy, 211, 254
McClelland's Station, Kentucky, 13, 404
McCorkle (McKorble?), Archibald, 417
McCorkle, Archibald, Jr., 417
McDonald, Chloe, 92
McGee, John, 37,
McGee, William, 25, 37
McGready, James, 25, 37, 136
McLean, Eli, 255
McLelland, Samuel Swan, 208
McMillan, John, 23
McNemar (Luckey), Jane (Jennie), 19, 26, 76, 80, 83, 89, 92, 95, 104–105, 118, 149, 157, 198, 250, 265, 266, 294, 399–400
McNemar (Pearson), Tabitha, 400
McNemar, Benjamin, 20, 87, 180, 400
McNemar, Betsy (daughter of Richard), 55, 87, 161, 400
McNemar, Betsy (sister of Richard), 12
McNemar, Betsy (wife of Garner), 111, 155, 168
McNemar, Elisha, 31, 87, 400, 405
McNemar, Garner, 12, 95, 111, 155, 168, 189, 198–199, 250, 334–335, 338–339, 367–369, 370, 372, 374, 390, 400–401, 403, 427–428
McNemar, Hugh, 250
McNemar, James, 24, 87, 157, 198–199, 247, 250, 251, 319, 338, 347, 354, 400, 426
McNemar, John, (brother of Richard), 12, 404
McNemar, John, (father of Milton), 369
McNemar, Levi, 198, 250, 288, 368, 400–401
McNemar, Martha, 189

McNemar, Milton A., 334–335, 338, 367–369, 372
McNemar, Morris, 9, 13
McNemar, Nancy, 32, 87, 183, 247, 249, 287, 309, 319, 345, 352, 354, 400, 405
McNemar, Nancy (daughter of Garner), 168, 334, 368
McNemar, Richard: and Abijah Alley, 224–236; "Answer to the Mourning Thoughts on McNemar's Fall, An," 417, 421–424; and *Book of Mormon*, 257; "Buzzards and the flesh. W.U. 1827, The," 209; and Cabin Creek Church, 27–29, 33–34, 35, 39, 45–49; and Canterbury, New Hampshire, (travels to), 240–241; and child abuse (accusations), 182; childhood of, 9; Church of England affiliation of, 9; *Constitution of the United Societies of Believers, The*, fig. 20.1, 291–294, 299; "Contented at Home," fig. 18.2, 261–263; conversion experiences of, 11, 15, 81, 83, 85, 91; and covenant (Shaker), 157–158, 239–240, 249–250, 259–260, 280, 284, 285, 294–295, 305, 324–325, 328, 336, 351–352, 354, 371–372, 375; "Day of Retribution," 165; death of, 390, 429; dreams of, 86, 265–266, 299, 321, 323, 340; education of, 12, 18, 20, 403, 404, 407; ego of, 322–323, 327, 329, 332, 334, 336, 337, 345, 348, 354, 363, 365, 378–379, 380; elder at West Brick Family, Union Village, 205–206; and Enfield, Connecticut, (travel to), 244; epilepsy of, 13, 91; *Epistle Dedicatory of the Union Press*, 272–273, 276; expulsion of, 366, 367, 373–374; "Expulsion of Richard McNemar," 397–399, 425–429; "False Prophet," 235; "Farewell loving sister," 122; and Farnumites, 188, 189–190; finances of, 90, 100; and Freegift Wells, 316, 318, 328–331, 334, 336, 344–345, 349, 354, 356, 364, 384, 387–388, 389, 394; and Freemasonry, 173–174, 409; funeral of, 391; and General Assembly in Winchester, Virginia in 1799, 30–31; "General outline of the past Journal of my life, A," 403–405;

and Halcyon sect, 194; and Hancock, Massachusetts, (travels to), 239, 244, 378; hand labor of, 166, 219, 251, 252, 253, 291, 327, 336, 340, 352, 403, 404, 405, 410; Harmony Society, 179–180, 386–387; and Harvard, Massachusetts, (travels to), 241–244; health of, 263, 284, 315, 322, 343, 344–345, 356, 367, 371, 376, 378, 385, 386, 387, 388, 389, 390, 403, 431; heresy, 47–48, 52–53, 54, 57–58; home of, 105, 108, 109, 111–112, 114, 117, 405; humbling of, 114, 325, 354; humor of, 291, 292, 315, 318, 325, 327; hymns of, 107–108, 122–123, 129–130, 132, 133, 139, 141, 142, 164–165, 274–276, 380, 390–391, 396; *Investigator; or A Defence of the Order, Government & Economy of the United Society called Shakers*, 217, 219–221; and Issachar Bates (conflict), 280–281, 283–284, 285–287, 296–304, 321–322; Kentucky, immigration to, 16–17, 404, 408 first visit to, 13; *Kentucky Revival*, fig. 10.1, 65, 66, 126, 127–129, 131, 133, 152, 270, 327, 346, 350, 396; *Last Will and Testament of the Springfield Presbytery*, 66, 67, 78; legal troubles, 162–163, 179; letter to New Lebanon Ministry (first), 101–104, 106; "Little Quail," 142; marriage of, 19; *Memorial Remonstrating against a Certain Act of the Legislature of Kentucky, A*, 255–256, 269; and *Millennial* Praises, 164–165; mission to Gasper, Kentucky, 131–132; mission to Shawnee Tribe, 120–121, 124, 126; mission to Wabash, 134–137; "Moles little path ways," 129–130; "My years on earth have been but few," 413–416; and Nathan Sharp, 309–312; and New Era, 351–354, 361, 362–363, 365–366 370–392; and New Lebanon, New York, (travels to), 238–240, 244, 375–383, 386, 428–429; *Observations on Church Government*, 78; Ohio, immigration to, 49, 55; ordination of, 27–28; *Other Side of the Question, The*, 183–184; papers of, 237, 245, 251, 273, 315, 326, 331–332, 340, 344, 354, 375, 388, 392, 393; parents of, 9, 13, 91–92;

and Pleasant Hill, Kentucky, 213–221, 251–254, 256, 416; preaching of, 3, 42, 43, 46, 51, 79–82, 84, 86, 89, 108, 110, 141, 166, 201, 214–215, 235, 238, 241, 242–243, 244, 256, 266, 340; Presbyterian affiliation and ministry of, 11, 23–25, 27–28, 407; and printing, fig. 19.2, fig. 20.1, 268–279, 292–294, 296, 299, 327, 334, 349–350, 352; property of (East House Family), 90, 100, 119, 133, 140, 165, 294, 335–337, 339, 350, 369, 370–372, 374, 375, 409–410; pseudonyms of, custos sacrorum, 273, 332, Eleazar Wright, 174–175, 238, 327, 364–365, 377, 380, 389, 391, 392, Philos Harmoniae, 274, peregrinus, 340; remonstrance to Ohio Legislature (1817), 172–173; and revivalism, 15, 33–34, 43–44; and Richard McNemar Jr., 80, 87, 225, 236, 249, 288–290, 368–369, 371–372, 373, 374, 376; "Robbery, The," 139; "Seasons, The," 132; *Selection of Hymns and Poems for the Use of Believers, A*, fig. 19.3, 209, 274–279; *Series of Lectures on Orthodoxy and Heterodoxy, A*, 288; and sexuality, 18–19, 81; and Seth Youngs Wells, 193–197, 219, 238, 245, 250, 252, 255–256, 261–263, 270–271, 273–274, 277–279, 280–282, 284–285, 291–296, 298, 305, 310, 311, 318–319, 320, 322–324, 327–328, 348–349, 352, 386, 413; "*Shakerism Detected &c.*" *Examined & Refuted*, 150; and Shaker missionaries, 76–84, 91; and Shirley, Massachusetts, (travels to), 241–242; singing of, 3, 12, 90, 97, 98, 241, 322; and slavery, 169–170; and Sodus Bay, New York, (travels to), 244; and South Union, Kentucky, 253–255; spirit of, 1–2, 390–392, 401; Springfield Presbytery, 60–61; and Stone, Barton, 79; surname origins, pronunciation, and meaning, 10, 130–131; and Swedenborgianism, 225–226; as teacher, 12, 13, 14, 22, 403, 404, 407; and *Testimony of Christ's Second Appearing* (1823), 191–193; "Testimony of E[leazar] Wright," 407–411; "Testimony of Eternal Truth," 133, 276; theology of, 38, 44,

McNemar, Richard (*Cont.*)
  45–48, 52–53, 64–66, 67, 165, 216, 243, 409;
  travels to the eastern Shaker communities
  (1829), 237–246, 268; trial of Robert W.
  Finley, 22–23; "Typical Dancing," 108;
  and Tyringham, Massachusetts, (travels
  to), 244; Union Press, 272–276, 277, 279,
  281, 334; "Validation," 316; as weaver, 12,
  13; and Watervliet, New York, (travels
  to), 238, 244, 375–376; and Watervliet,
  Ohio, 257–259, 270, 283–287, 296–304,
  305, 309, 311–312, 315–316, 348, 352; *Western
  Expositor, No. 4*, 288; *Western Review*, 299;
  and West Union, Indiana, (Busro), 159–162,
  206, 208; and White Water, Ohio, 259–261,
  266–267, 338–340, 346; writing of, 119, 152
McNemar, Richard, III, 400
McNemar, Richard, Jr., 80, 87, 225, 236, 249,
  288–290, 368–369, 371–372, 373, 374, 376,
  389, 400
McNemar, Richard G., 198, 250
McNemar, Vincy, fig. 24.2, 26, 87, 157, 183,
  247, 250, 288, 343, 351, 352, 354, 356, 400,
  405, 427
McPherrin, John, 14, 404
Meacham, Archibald, 126, 133, 141, 159, 181,
  203, 204, 206–207, 208, 259, 260–261, 287,
  333, 340
Meacham, David, 100, 106, 112, 113, 117
Meacham, David, Jr., 306–309, 312, 318
Meacham, "Father" Joseph, 96, 116–117, 188,
  200, 204, 283, 306
Meacham, John, 71, 72, 77, 78, 85, 86, 88, 89,
  91, 106–108, 113, 115–116, 117, 118, 121, 123,
  134, 141, 148, 204, 209, 214, 215, 216, 298,
  306, 311, 315, 426; mission to Kentucky and
  Ohio, 71–76
Meacham, Ruth, 96, 204
medical practice, (of Shakers), 122
Medlicott, Carol, 135, 187–188, 195, 200, 204,
  206, 267, 283, 301
Meigs, Jr., Return, 161
*Memorial Remonstrating against a Certain
  Act of the Legislature of Kentucky, A*,
  255–256, 269

"Messenger Dove," 119
Methodism, 15, 42, 71, 111, 135, 173, 174, 211,
  408
Miami Tribe, 136
Middleton, Anna, 78, 351
Middletown, Ohio, 184–185, 388
military pensions, 282–283, 285–287
militia service (of Shakers), 163–164, 173, 188,
  206
Miller, Daniel, 355, 356, 358, 360, 363, 364,
  365, 366, 369, 371, 372, 373, 384, 389, 391,
  400
Miller, Henry, 258
Miller, James, 90
Miller, Lucy, 431
Miller, Moses, 52
Millennial Praises, 133, 164–165, 193, 274
Millennium, 68
Ministry (Shaker). *See* New Hampshire
  Ministry; New Lebanon Ministry;
  Pleasant Hill Ministry; Union Village
  Ministry
Mississippi River, 178
M'Lean, John, 133
mob, (Pleasant Hill, 1825), 212; (Union
  Village, 1810), 147–150, (Union Village,
  1813), 165; (Union Village, 1817), 171, 174;
  (Union Village, 1819), 182–183
"Moles little path ways," 129–130
Monongahela River, 12, 16
More, William, 347
Morehead, James Turner, 255–256
Morrell, Calvin, xiv, 80, 82, 88, 89, 91, 114,
  117, 155, 168, 172–174, 176, 177, 180, 181,
  183, 184, 185, 188, 189, 198, 237, 259–261, 325,
  390
Morrell, Prudence, 237
Morrell, Rhoda, 185
Morris, Reuben, 174, 283
Morrison, William, 362
Moseley, Constant, 134, 137
Moseley, Daniel, 96, 97, 105, 109, 156, 165, 240,
  241, 244
Mother's Work. *See* New Era
Muddy Creek, Kentucky, xiii

Muddy River Church, 25, 37, 136
Munson, Stephen, 180
Muscatatuck River, 135
"My robe is new my crown is bright," 433
"My years on earth have been but few," 413–416

Native Americans, 11, 17, 21, 26, 50, 86, 123, 135, 159, 257, 292, 362, 384; conversion of to Shakerism, 120, 125–126, 150–151; ruins of settlement, 108. *See also* Shawnee Tribe
Naylor, John, 162
Naylor, Sarah (Magy), 162
Newell, Robert, 13, 404
New Era (Shaker), 4, 328, 342–343, 346–397
New Hampshire Ministry, 240–241, 268
New Harmony, Indiana (Owenite period), 184, 208, 210, 212
New Harmony, Indiana. *See* Harmony Society
New Harmony Gazette, 211
New Lanark, Scotland, 210
New Lebanon, New York, 3, 71, 73, 82, 85, 90, 96, 106, 110, 113, 117, 134, 138, 175, 236, 238, 253, 263, 305, 306, 312, 318, 372, 386, 428; East Family, 239; New Era at, 341, 343, 346; Pilgrims at, 177; Richard McNemar visits, 238–240, 244
New Lebanon Ministry, 93, 95, 97, 112, 119, 125–126, 127, 133, 137, 138, 139, 164, 177, 183, 186, 190, 193, 201, 203, 205, 206, 207, 208, 210, 212, 213, 214, 215, 216, 232, 236, 239, 241, 244, 246, 249, 251, 252, 257, 263, 265, 268, 276, 278, 283, 286, 287, 291, 300, 304, 305, 306, 307, 308, 309, 310, 313, 315, 316, 317–318, 319, 320, 324, 327, 328–331, 332, 333, 337, 339, 343, 346–347, 348, 349, 352, 357, 375, 376, 383, 385, 388, 391–392, 393, 394, 395, 428
New Lights, 65; Cabin Creek, 51–52
New Orleans, Louisiana, 254
Newton, Isaac, 111, 132
New View of Society, 210, 211
New York Journal of Commerce, 385

North Carolina, 20, 22, 25, 85, 131; Rowan County, 19
North Union, Ohio, 189, 192, 198, 237, 238, 257, 263, 278, 288, 295, 324, 343, 344, 363, 376, 391; New Era at, 346, 352, 357, 358, 359, 369, 373; Richard McNemar visits, 245, 376. *See also* Warrensville, Ohio
North Union Ministry, 344, 358–359, 376, 386, 393

Observations on Church Government, 78, 91, 127
Ohio, General Assembly, 154, 155–156, 188; Butler County, 172; Legislature, 154, 163, 172–173; Preble County, 161; Warren County, 162, 172
Ohio Archaeological and Historical Publications, 396
Ohio Canal, 237
Ohio River, 17, 18, 117, 178, 208, 256
opium (abuse), 319
Orangedale, Ohio, 32, 35, 53, 54, 68, 80, 82, 405
Other Side of the Question, The, 183–184
Owen, Robert, 210–212, 220, 255
Owen, William, 210
Owenism, 225, 289

Paine, Thomas, 289
Paint Lick, Kentucky, xiii, 22, 75, 111, 114, 126, 404
Paint Lick Church, 25, 68, 74
Pangburn, Hampton, 95
Paris, Kentucky, 18, 22, 24, 25, 43, 99
Parkhurst, Amos, 358, 359, 364, 365, 401
Parkhurst, David, 367
Parkhurst, Jane, 358
Parkhurst, Samuel, 222, 228, 229, 231
Parkinson, Ann, 358, 359, 362, 388
Patterson, John, 123,
Pearson, Tabitha. *See* McNemar (Pearson), Tabitha
Pease, Peter, 112, 113, 115, 117, 124, 132, 134, 148, 165, 179, 263, 264, 380
Pegg, Caleb, 195

Pelham, Abijah, 283
Pelham, Richard, 189, 192, 344–345
Penn, John, 21
Pennsylvania: Cumberland County, 9–10, 403, 407; Franklin County, 10, 21; Huntingdon County, 11, 403; Juniata Valley, 11, 403; Kishacoquillas Valley, 11, 12, 13, 14, 403; Ligonier Valley, 13, 14, 404; Mifflin County, 13; Redstone Country, 12, 403; Redstone Creek, 12; Scotch-Irish migration to, 9–10; Standing Stone Creek, 12, 403; Tuscarora Valley, 9, 403, 407; Westmoreland County, 14, 18, 21
pensions (military), 282–283, 285–287
Peter Cornstalk, 123, 124
Pickaway, Ohio, 137, 139
Pickett, Mercy, 138
Pilgrims (sect), 176–179, 187
Pisgah Church, 24
Pittsburgh, Pennsylvania, 226, 387
Pleasant Hill, Kentucky, 134, 155, 181, 192, 204, 207, 208, 237, 256, 264, 266, 268, 278, 284, 286, 296, 416; covenant (1830), 251–254, 292; leadership crisis, 209–221, 236, 240; mob, (1825), 212; New Era at, 346, 348. *See also* Shawnee Run, Kentucky
Pleasant Hill Ministry, 209, 213–216, 251
Pocahontas, 384
Potter, Eleanor, 379–380, 383
Presbyterian Church, 3, 10, 11, 18; education of clergy, 20–21; General Assembly (Winchester, Virginia, 1799), 30–31
Price, Harry, 136
Providence Presbytery, 26
publishing (Shaker), 116–117, 127, 128–129, 133, 134, 150, 183, 190–193, 219–221, 252–253, 255–256, 261, 268–279, 292–294, 299, 350
Purviance, David, 56, 57, 62, 63, 66, 96, 97, 98, 151, 154, 155, 156

Quakerism, 225, 289

Rand, John, 187
Randall, Benjamin, 152
Rankin, James, 211
Rankin, John, 37, 131, 132, 134, 161
Rannels, Samuel, 43, 60, 61
Rapp, "Father" George, 180, 210, 386
Rathbone (Rathbun), Reuben, 91, 152
Rathbun, Daniel, 107
Rathbun, Valentine, 91
Rational Brethren of the West, 183–184
Reasons Offered for Leaving the Shakers, 91
Red Banks (Henderson), Kentucky, 44, 134, 136–137, 141, 162, 405
"Redemption of Richard McNemar, The," 431–434
Red River Church, 25, 37, 136
Redstone Old Fort, Pennsylvania, 12
Redstone Presbytery, 14
Reeder, Joseph, 52, 54
Remarkable Occurrences, Lately Discovered among the People Called SHAKERS, 145
Reply to John P. Campbell's Strictures on Atonement, 107
Republic (Springfield, Ohio), 400
"Retrospective View of Shakerism, A," 155
Revision and Confirmation of the Social Compact of the United Society Called Shakers, at Pleasant Hill, Kentucky, A, 252–253
revival (among the Shakers), 166, 327–328
Revolutionary War, 18, 145, 282–283, 285–287, 403
Rice, David, 56, 59, 60
Rice, Samuel, Sr., 187, 260
Riley, Zarilda, 391
Robb, Robert, 28, 29, 33, 45, 46, 48, 51, 54
"Robbery, The," 139
Robertson, William, 57
Robinson, John, 147
Robinson, Robert, 28, 46, 48
Robinson, William, 27, 61, 149
Rocky Hill, New Jersey, 21
Roelosson, Lawrence, 136–137
Rollins, Samuel, xiv, 80, 100, 114, 134, 161, 168, 171, 179, 397
Ross, John, 356
Ross, Mary Ann, 357, 359, 360
Round Bottom, Ohio, 18, 404

Ruddle, Stephen, 150–151
Runyon, George, 211
Runyon, William, 237
Russell, Ralph, 189
Russellville, Kentucky, 254

Salem, Pennsylvania, 14
Salem Church, 87, 418, 423
Sampson, Proctor, 152–153, 154, 197–198
Sandy River, 18
Sargent, Abel Morgan, 194
Sasseen, Francis, 253
Scales, William 228
Schismatics, 61, 62, 63, 64, 65, 66, 67, 68, 130, 184
Scotch-Irish, 9, 10, 11
Scotland, 19
"Seasons, The," 132
Separatists at Zoar, Ohio, 237
Series of Lectures on Orthodoxy and Heterodoxy, A, 288
"Series of Remarks Showing the Power of the Adversary in Leading Honest Souls Astray Through the Influence of Inspired Messages, A" 394
Sering, Elizabeth. *See* Davis (Sering), Elizabeth
Sering, Eunice, 204
Sering, Samuel, 62, 91, 198
Sering, Sarah. *See* Wallace (Sering), Sarah
Sewickley, Pennsylvania, 13, 404
sex, 223, 228, 233, 234, 243
Shakerism Detected, 150–151
"*Shakerism Detected &c.*" *Examined & Refuted*, 150
Shakers, mission to Kentucky and Ohio, 71–76
Shannon, Samuel, 21
Sharp, Elizabeth, 162, 355
Sharp, Nathan, 163, 167, 172, 208, 263–264, 307–312, 324
Sharp, Sally, 345, 349
Shaver's Creek, Pennsylvania, 11, 403
Shawnee Prophet. *See* Tenskwatawa

Shawnee Run, Kentucky, 99, 111, 126, 134, 155. *See also* Pleasant Hill, Kentucky
Shawnee Run Church, 68
Shawnee Tribe, 11, 16, 120–121, 123–126, 133, 136, 150, 396
Sherman, Ezra, Sr., 259–260
Shirley, Massachusetts, Richard McNemar visits, 241–242
Shrofe, Sebastian, 48
Sketch of the Life and Labors of Richard McNemar, A, 398–399, 425
slavery, 19–20, 22, 32, 169–170
Slover, John, 136, 141
Smith, Colonel James, Sr., 21–22, 96, 99, 143–153, 182, 211; and Black Boys, 21, 150
Smith, Elias, 186
Smith, Helen, 392
Smith, James, Jr., 96, 98, 99, 106, 107, 111, 139, 143, 223, 274, 327–328, 335, 338, 368, 369
Smith, "Mother" Lucy, 134, 209, 213–217, 236, 237, 331
Smith, Polly, 139, 143, 147, 149, 151
Smith, Uriah, 187
Smith, William Henry, 187
Sodus Bay, New York, 238, 257, 295; Richard McNemar visits, 244
Soule, Sandra, 225
South Union, Kentucky, 131, 181, 207, 208, 209, 253–255, 268, 278, 286, 296, 320; New Era at, 346, 348, 391. *See also* Gasper, Kentucky
South Union Ministry, 320, 384
Spier, Richard, 134, 157, 162–163, 165, 167–168, 171, 180
Spinning, David, 44, 63, 80, 90, 92, 95, 96, 109, 133, 162, 185, 222, 224, 225, 231, 250, 281, 324, 344, 345, 357, 358, 397, 432
Spinning, Matthias, 62
Spinning, Patience, 225
Spinning, Stephen, 335–336, 373, 432
Springfield (Springdale), Ohio, 30, 46, 54, 400
Springfield Church, 32, 35, 44, 61, 68, 86, 418, 423
Springfield Presbytery, 3, 60–62, 63, 64, 65, 66, 67, 84, 87, 96, 151, 207, 405

Squahghkewelenoh, 124
Square House, Harvard, Massachusetts, 242, 243–244
Standish, Sarah Ann, 377
St. Clair, Arthur, 16, 404
Steele, Archibald, 20, 32, 36
Stewart, John, 123
Stewart, Philemon, 346, 377, 381
Stewart, William, 90, 94
Stockwell, John, 98
Stone, Barton W., 3, 25, 26, 28, 39, 40, 41, 42, 54, 56, 57, 58, 59, 60, 61, 62, 63, 64, 66, 75, 78–79, 95, 96, 98, 106–107, 111, 139, 291, 417; letter to Richard McNemar, 79, 87
Stone, William Leete, 183
Stout, Joseph, xiv, 80, 168, 283
Stow, Ohio, 189
Straight Creek (Georgetown), Ohio, 194
Stuart, Robert, 56
Sturr, Charles, 188
suicide, 138, 385
Summary View of the Millennial Church, A, 193
Swedenborgianism, 221, 225–226, 288, 368, 400
swords (spiritual), 355, 360, 362
Symmes, John Cleves, 55

Tate, Robert, 72
Taylor, Henry, 49
Taylor, Nathaniel, 351
Tecumseh, 120, 124, 126, 152, 159
Tennessee, 72, 86, 112, 334, 335, 368
Tenskwatawa, 4, 120–121, 123–126, 151–152, 159
Terry, Josiah, 183
Testimonies Concerning the Character and Ministry of Mother Ann Lee, 193, 270–271
Testimonies of the Life, Character, Revelations and Doctrines of Our Ever Blessed Mother Ann Lee, 332
Testimony of Christ's Second Appearing 221, 289, 350; (1808), 91, 116–117, 133, 134, 137, 190; (1810), 190, 197; (1823), 190–193, 194, 197, 199
"Testimony of E[leazar] Wright," 407–411
"Testimony of Eternal Truth," 133, 276

Thomas, Cornelius, 149
Thompson, John, 14, 20, 35, 43, 44, 47, 53, 54, 56, 58, 59, 60, 61, 63, 64, 66, 67, 68, 76, 82–83, 86, 87–88, 94, 98, 291
Thomson, David, 199
Tichner, Jonathan, 32, 51, 52, 54
tobacco, 320, 356
Total Depravity (doctrine of), 38
Transylvania Presbytery (first), 21, 22, 23, 24, 25, 26, 27, 29, 50
Transylvania Presbytery (second), 30, 49, 53, 56, 75
Trimble, Robert, 20
Trousdale, Samuel, 126
trustee, duties of (among Shakers), 217–218, 219, 250, 258, 259, 261, 263–264, 294, 306, 308–312, 318, 320
Tullis, Aaron, 62
Turner, Jethro, 164
Turner, Samuel, 113, 122, 132, 134, 210, 213–217, 256, 264–265
Turtle Creek, Ohio, xiv, xv, 3, 49, 85, 97, 99, 100, 105, 106, 108, 109, 110, 111, 112, 114, 115, 117, 118, 119, 121, 124, 125, 126, 134, 137, 138, 139, 141, 143, 155, 159, 341, 405, 424; mob at (1810), 147–150. *See also* Union Village, Ohio
Turtle Creek Church, 26, 32, 44, 45, 49, 50–51, 53, 54–55, 61, 62, 67, 68, 77, 79, 86, 88, 91, 93, 176, 283, 423
Tuttle (Tuthill), Samuel, 178–179
Two Letters Written by a Gentleman to His Friend in Kentucky, 63
"Typical Dancing," 108
Tyringham, Massachusetts, Richard McNemar visits, 244

Unconditional Election (doctrine of), 38, 45, 63
Union Presbytery, 26
Union Village, Ohio, 1, 4, 50, 166–167, 207–209, 221, 236, 239, 259, 260, 261, 266, 267, 278, 282, 285, 295, 301, 310, 316, 318, 343, 351–352, 386, 389, 396–399, 426; buildings at, 335–336, dwellings, 111, 113,

117, 140, 149, 166, 402, garden house, 180, meetinghouses, fig. 22.2, fig. 25.1, 101, 133, 134, 180; Centre Family, 204, 205, 247, 251, 256, 287, 319, 320, 323, 326, 347, 348, 352, 354, 432; East House Family, 133, 140, 165, 222, 223, 226, 229, 230, 335–336, 339, 350, 369, 370–372, 374; Grist Mill Families, 297; meetinghouse, fig. 22.2; mobs at (1810), 147–150, (1813) 165, (1817) 171, 174, (1819), 182–183; New Era at, 346–374; North Lot Family, 222, 224, 230, 257; Pilgrims at, 177–179; property at, 167–168, 203, 256–257, 261, 263–264, 309–310, 320, 324, 350, 401; revival at, 327–328; South Family, 222, 233; Square House Family, 244, 297; West Branch, 222; West Brick Family, 205, 232, 358, 359, 360, 364; West Lot Family, 222, 224. *See also* Turtle Creek, Ohio

Union Village Ministry, 138, 169, 190, 192, 200, 201, 203, 204–206, 207, 210, 215, 216, 236, 249, 259, 264, 265, 267, 276, 282–283, 284, 305–309, 311–312, 315, 324, 331, 337, 347, 348, 349–350, 357, 367, 370, 376, 383, 391, 400

Universalism, 194

Urbana, Ohio, 288, 290, 368, 373, 374, 400

Valentine, Amos, 133, 149
Valentine, Henry, 264
"Validation," 316
Van Vleet, Abram, 172–173, 181–185
Versailles, Kentucky, 24
Vincennes, Indiana, 135
Virginia, Botetourt County, 18
Virginia Synod, 26, 29–30, 49
Voltaire, 220, 289
Voris, Francis, 208

Wait, Lewis, 172
Waits, Elizabeth, 355
Wallace (Sering), Sarah, 176
Wallace, John, 122, 143, 156, 162, 167, 171, 176, 180, 263, 311, 373
Wallace, Matthew, 52, 54, 56, 147–149

Walsh, James, 17
War of 1812, 152, 159, 163
Warrensville, Ohio, 189. *See also* North Union, Ohio
Washington, George, 170, 249, 362, 373
Washington, Pennsylvania, 13
Washington Presbytery, 30, 31, 32, 35, 39, 41, 43, 44, 46, 49, 51, 52, 53, 54, 55, 56, 57, 58, 61, 63, 148
Watervliet, New York, 164, 188, 193, 295, 306, 315, 316, 377, 389, 394; New Era at, 341, 342–343, 346; Richard McNemar visits, 238, 244, 376, 392
Watervliet, Ohio, fig. 19.1, 90, 188, 198, 204, 207, 209, 245, 250, 257, 265, 266, 267, 270, 276, 278, 283–304, 305, 309, 311–312, 316, 319–320, 324, 326, 348, 352. *See also* Beaver Creek, Ohio
Watts, Malinda, 138, 165, 223, 224, 427
Wayne, Anthony, 18, 362
weaving, 12
Wells, Freegift, 193, 238, 313–320, 322, 326–334, 336, 338–340, 343, 344, 346–347, 349, 351, 354, 356, 357, 358, 359, 360, 361, 362–363, 364, 365, 366, 370, 372–374, 375, 376, 383, 384, 385, 387–388, 389, 391, 392, 393–395, 396, 397, 399, 401, 402, 425–429; "Series of Remarks Showing the Power of the Adversary in Leading Honest Souls Astray Through the Influence of Inspired Messages, A," 394
Wells, Seth Young, 164, 179, 190–191, 193–194, 196–197, 219, 238, 245, 250, 252, 255, 256, 261, 263, 264, 268, 270–271, 273, 274, 277, 278, 280, 281–282, 284–285, 291–292, 294–295, 298, 305, 310, 311, 313, 318–319, 320, 322–324, 327–328, 332, 333, 348–349, 352, 375, 383, 386, 413
Wells, Stephen, 310, 311, 313, 318
Welsh, James, 57, 59
Wesley, John, 372
West, Randolph, 367, 385
Western Expositor, No. 4, 288
Western Review, 299
Western Spy (Cincinnati, Ohio), 178

Western Star (Lebanon, Ohio), 133, 141, 149–150, 155, 167, 172, 367, 385, 417
West Lexington Presbytery, 30, 35, 49, 53, 56
Westminster Confession of Faith, 28, 38–39, 46, 48, 51, 58, 60, 61, 63, 64, 66
West Union, Indiana, fig. 12.1, 159, 163, 165, 180, 181, 203, 204, 206–209, 210, 212–213, 230, 231, 235, 240, 252, 259, 260, 261, 296–297, 311, 318. *See also* Busro, Indiana
Wheeler, Stephen, 54
Whitbey, John, 210–212, 219–220, 222, 235, 255
Whitbey, Richardson, 212, 255
White River, 135–136
White Water, Ohio, 135, 180, 194, 198, 207, 208, 209, 251, 256, 278, 285, 296, 307, 324, 338–340, 343, 346
Whittaker, "Father" James, 188, 201, 242, 433
"Who are the Shakers?," 147
Whore of Babylon Unmasked, 225
Whyte, Frances, 132, 254
Wickliffe, Robert, fig. 18.1, 1, 256, 311
Williams, Enos, 162
Williams, Thomas, 258
Wilson, John, 26, 27, 29, 149, 155
Wilson, Robert, 149, 155, 162
Winchester, Virginia, 30–31
Woodruff, Polly, 166
Woods, John, 138, 224, 228
Woodstock, Vermont, 176
Woodward, William W., 34
Worley (Allen), Rebecca, (mother of Malcham), 18
Worley (Montfort/Monfort), Miriam "Peggy," 76, 77, 78, 95, 118
Worley, Caleb, 18
Worley, Joseph, 223, 389, 401
Worley, Joshua, 193, 247, 249, 309, 313, 317, 319, 326, 331–332, 345–347, 350, 360, 364, 401
Worley, Malcham, xiv, 18, 19, 22, 23, 24, 41, 53, 56, 57, 62, 63, 64, 65, 76, 77, 90, 94, 97, 98, 99, 108, 109, 111, 113, 114, 116, 118, 127, 133, 134, 168, 191, 195–196, 204, 205, 206, 231, 247, 291, 350, 351, 389, 404; conversion to Shakerism, 78; expulsion of, 370–371, 372, 373, 375, 384, 395, 401, 426–428; and New Era, 361–362, 369–371, 372, 373, 375, 376, 391; property of, 90, 350, 375; as teacher, 138
Worley, Nathan, 18, 94, 98
Worley, Rebecca, (daughter of Malcham), 78, 401
Worley family, 350, 375, 401
Wright, Eleazar. *See* McNemar, Richard: pseudonyms
Wright, "Mother" Lucy, 92, 107, 116–117, 118, 120, 123, 125, 130–131, 134, 135, 140, 158, 168–169, 175, 183, 188, 190, 200, 201, 250, 327, 364, 377, 386, 392
Wyandot Tribe, 124

Xenia, Ohio, 176, 177

Yellow Springs, Ohio, 225
Youghiogheny River, 13
Youngs, Benjamin Seth, 13, 71, 72, 77, 78, 82, 83, 86, 87, 88, 89, 90, 91, 92, 94, 95, 96, 97, 98, 99, 106–110, 111, 112, 113, 117, 118, 127, 134, 140, 141, 155, 193, 210–211, 212, 214, 253–254, 256, 267, 268, 283, 285, 294, 313, 315, 325, 327, 332–333, 341–342, 343, 350–351, 375, 385, 386, 397, 426; arrival in Ohio, 76; 79–80, 93; mission to Kentucky and Ohio, 71–76; mission to Shawnee, 120, 123, 124–125, 126; mission to Wabash, 134–137; moves to Gasper (South Union), Kentucky, 155; and Ohio mob (1810), 147–148; preaching of, 73–76; and *Testimony of Christ's Second Appearing*, 116, 119, 133, 138; returns to New Lebanon, New York, 320–321
Youngs, Isaac Newton, 177, 193, 277, 278, 279; visit to western Shaker communities, 294–298, 305, 313, 342

Zoar, Ohio, 237, 376

CHRISTIAN GOODWILLIE is Director and Curator of Special Collections at the Burke Library of Hamilton College in Clinton, New York. He was Curator of Collections at Hancock Shaker Village in Pittsfield, Massachusetts, from 2001 to 2009. He has served as President of the Communal Studies Association and was recognized with their Distinguished Scholar Award in 2021. He has authored, coauthored, or edited eleven books and has written numerous articles on the Shakers and other intentional communities, early American history, Freemasonry, and other topics.

www.ingramcontent.com/pod-product-compliance
Lightning Source LLC
Chambersburg PA
CBHW021414300426
44114CB00010B/485